GOD's WAR

Why Christians Should Rule the World!

The case for Christian involvement in every sphere of life on the planet Earth

SCHEIDBACH

The author, Dr. Jerry Scheidbach, pastors the Lighthouse Baptist Church in Santa Maria, California. He is the executive editor for *The Intercessor* magazine, and hosts *The Brain Massage®* radio/podcast. To contact Pastor Scheidbach write to Lighthouse Baptist Church, PO Box 2803, Santa Maria, CA 93457, or call (805) 714-7731. To contact him by email use the email address *DistinctivelyBaptistPub@gmail.com*. To purchase *God's War*, or other titles by Dr. Scheidbach, go to *www.santamarialighthouse.org* or www.booksatdbp.com. To engage with his radio/podcast show, go to *www. brainmassage.net.*

To Order More Copies

Go to *www.booksatdbp.com or call 805.714.7731*

(Over 30 color illustrations)

$41.99 retail; $48.00 Canada

(Special pricing available for schools and churches, or bulk orders: call 805.714.7731 or go to www.booksatdbp.com)

~ Distinctively Baptist Publications ~
4876 Bethany Lane • Santa Maria, CA • 93455
DBP
2 0 1 9

~*Dedication*~
To the Lord Jesus Christ

Special thanks to my dear and very patient wife and son. My church family also. All who had to put up with my distracted, absorbed, compulsive, and obsessed devotion to this project for what has been a six year journey, I trust you will be rewarded for your sacrifice. Special thanks to all who encouraged me to continue with this book when I felt overwhelmed by the intense spiritual warfare I had to endure while writing it. To my dear friends Dr. Beckum, and Lloyd Campbell who encouraged me to finish this book, and Jim Kaufmann who financed this publication—

Thank you!

~ Table of Contents ~

i

~ Table of Contents ~

~ Table of Contents ~

~ Table of Contents ~

~ Table of Contents ~

Dear Reader:

My humble apologies, in advance, for the annoyance of all the typo gremlins that got past all our efforts to find and dispatch them. Beyond that, please allow me to explain some of our technical style decisions.

We capitalize *Church* only when referring to the institution as a whole. We capitalize *Antichrist* even when we are not referring to that individual directly. We capitalize *Sword* in *Sword of the Lord*, and *Word* in *Word of God*. We used GOD and God, LORD and Lord, in the manner these are used in the KJV (GOD and LORD refer specifically to the name *Jehovah*). We capitalize *Gospel*. We use semicolons and em dashes according to the older rules. When quoting Scripture we followed the forms used in the text. Sometimes we used the singular *body* when we might have used the plural *bodies*. It's technical, but at least you know we did it on purpose. As for any other annoying anomalies, please bring them to our attention. If we cannot justify it, we'll include your suggestion in a revision, should we be so blessed to have need to reprint *God's War!* Thank you! — *the author.*

"The blessing and protection of Heaven are at all times necessary but especially so in times of public distress and danger. The General hopes and trusts that every officer and man will endeavor to live and act as becomes a Christian soldier, defending the dearest rights and liberties of his country."

~ George Washington

(George Washington, *The Writings of George Washington,* John C. Fitzpatrick, editor (Washington: Government Printing Office, 1932), Vol. 5, p. 245, July 9, 1776 Order.)

Dr. Benny Beckum
Founder/President, The Intercessor Ministries, Inc.

I

N THIS, HIS LATEST BOOK, *GOD'S WAR*, Dr. Jerry Scheidbach expounds on a complex subject with remarkable clarity. It is an encyclopedia of information on the Sovereignty of God, the Priesthood of the believer, and the spiritual war we are engaged in each day.

Starting with Chapter One, <u>Jesus Is The King, And All Men Are His Subjects</u>, we understand that a war raging, the king of darkness versus the King of light. This Great War is fought here on earth and we are Christ's soldiers. We soon learn that our part in this war is critical.

Dr. Scheidbach stresses the importance of using the Word of God to reach the lost world for Christ. To do this, we must be able to withstand the attacks of Satan. To overcome the methods, trickery, and devices of the wicked one, we must put on the whole armor of God (Ephesians 6:11). And we must advance the cause of Christ by submitting to God and resisting the Devil to make him give up the territory in this world that he has taken.

This war that the author is speaking of is not against flesh and blood, but against principalities, against powers, against the rulers of the darkness of this world, against spiritual wickedness in high places (Ephesians 6:12).

Dr. Scheidbach, in a very scholarly manner, unfolds the history of God's War with Satan, and explains our part in that war. Anyone who fails to see the reality that there is a war raging is in error. Indeed, Satan's most effective ruse is to convince Christians there is no spiritual war and that they have no part to play in world affairs today. This book proves that is a lie.

The greatest blessing will come to the reader of this book who follows the teacher as he leads his students through the Word of God. There are hundreds of Bible verses used by Dr. Scheidbach explaining his subject. Every chapter is engaging and enlightening.

The portions of this book that I found to be particularly interesting are those in which Dr. Scheidbach lays out the history of God's War! The insight presented here is clarifying. It puts everything we are seeing happen in America today into context. The Spirit of Jesus Christ is warring through the saints against the spirit of Antichrist that is warring through the sinners. The assumption is that the world belongs to Satan and his followers. The Scripture says it belongs to Christ. The secularist says Christians have no part in world affairs. The Scripture says differently. The war is on!

We know that in the end we will win! The kingdom will be given to the Saints. However, as in any war, there are many battles to be fought, and the outcome of our battles is not guaranteed. We are losing our battles in America! And those losses have real consequences. Learn about it in this book, and learn how to win!

One last thought! Dr. Scheidbach is not a compiler of the writings of other men. Here is a fresh, stimulating study on a much misunderstood subject. I pray you, the reader, will receive much profit and pleasure from it.

Dr. Benny L. Beckum
Founder/President
Intercessor Ministries

"You do well to wish to learn our arts and ways of life, and above all, the religion of Jesus Christ. These will make you a greater and happier people than you are."

~ George Washington

Advice given by George Washington to the Indians that it would be well for every American to heed today!

(George Washington, *The Writings of Washington,* John C. Fitzpatrick, editor (Washington: Government Printing Office, 1932), Vol. XI, pp. 342-343, General Orders of May 2, 1778.)

"I conceive we cannot better express ourselves than by humbly supplicating the Supreme Ruler of the world . . . that . . . the kingdoms of our Lord and Savior Jesus Christ may be everywhere established, and the people willingly bow to the scepter of Him who is the Prince of Peace."

~ Samuel Adams

In other words, *Jesus is the King, and all mankind are His subjects!*

(From a Fast Day Proclamation issued by Governor Samuel Adams, Massachusetts, March 20, 1797, in our possession; see also Samuel Adams, The Writings of Samuel Adams, Harry Alonzo Cushing, editor (New York: G. P. Putnam's Sons, 1908), Vol. IV, p. 407, from his proclamation of March 20, 1797.)

Chapter One

Jesus Is The King, And All Men Are His Subjects!

Pilate asked, "Art thou a king, then?" Jesus answered, "Thou sayest that I am a king."

JESUS WAS DEAD—AND BURIED. Pilate, the Roman governor of Judea who confessed he could find no fault in Jesus, relented to the demands of the rulers of the Jews and crucified Him. The Jewish leaders and the Roman soldiers were in such a hurry to carry out His execution that they forgot an important detail: Jesus had not been formally charged with a crime. Roman law required that the accusation be nailed to the cross from which the criminal hung. Pilate, apprised of this oversight, to spite the Jews, and to mock the rumor that Jesus was their King, had the following posted to Christ's Cross: "Jesus of Nazareth, the king of the Jews."

Did Pilate know the prophecy?

"Jesus of Nazareth!" Nazareth was in Galilee. Seven hundred years earlier, a Jewish prophet named Isaiah said a Jewish ruler would come from Galilee to be a light to lead the Gentiles out of ignorance.[1] Another Jewish prophet said this ruler would be called The Branch[2]—which many believe is from the Hebrew word used for the name of the

---

[1] Isaiah 9:1-2
[2] Zechariah 6:12

city called Nazareth.[3] The prophet Isaiah also declared this promised king would rule the world from the throne of David—"the king of the Jews."[4]

It does not seem likely that Pilate knew the prophecy! But his accusation unwittingly declared Jesus to be Isaiah's promised ruler, nonetheless.

Rather than accuse Jesus of any crime, Pilate's inscription accused those who crowned the promised king with thorns and snuffed the promised light instead.

These things might have become footnotes in someone's history book, except that three days later, Jesus was seen alive!

And that changed everything.

The Secret of Galilee Revealed!

Before His crucifixion, Jesus told His disciples He would be crucified and rise from the dead the third day.[5] And He instructed them to gather in Galilee at a particular mountain, where He would meet with them after He arose.[6] On the morning of His resurrection, some of His followers came to visit His tomb. An angel commanded them to alert all the disciples that Jesus had risen and also to remind them that they should go to Galilee where they would see Him.[7] Later that same morning, Jesus appeared to them personally and commanded them to gather the disciples to Galilee.[8] The risen Lord had an important announcement to make, and He was particular about where on Earth He would make it.[9]

To Galilee, they trekked. Perhaps during their walk along

---

[3] Matthew 2:23
[4] Isaiah 9:6-7
[5] Luke 24:7; Matthew 12:40
[6] Matthew 26:32
[7] Mark 16:7; Matthew 28:7
[8] Matthew 28:10
[9] Matthew 28:16-20

the dusty trails into upper Galilee or while they hiked up into the appointed mountain,[10] Peter, James, and John decided it was time to reveal the secret of Galilee that Jesus told them to keep until He had risen from the dead.[11]

About a year earlier in Upper Galilee, Jesus took Peter, James, and John onto a special mountain where they saw Jesus' clothing and countenance radiate in glistening glory.[12] Elijah and Moses appeared and communed with their Lord. God, the Father, spoke aloud. Peter recognized this was a manifestation of Jesus as the promised King of kings—the Lord of glory.[13] Returning from the heavenly scene, Jesus instructed His disciples to keep the revelation a secret until after He had risen from the dead.[14] This extraordinary manifestation of Christ had particular relevance to the time following His resurrection. Jesus appointed this same mountain to be the place where He would reveal Himself to His disciples after He had risen—the Mount of Transfiguration:[15] Mount Hermon, in Galilee.[16]

Standing before His disciples on this mountain where earlier He had secretly manifested Himself as the King of Earth, Jesus made His much-anticipated announcement: "All power is given unto me in heaven and in earth."[17]

A stunning declaration!

---

[10] Matthew 28:16

[11] Matthew 17:9

[12] Luke 9:29; see Daniel 10:5-9

[13] Matthew 17:1-13

[14] Matthew 17:9

[15] Matthew 17

[16] Jesus was in Caesarea Philippi, in upper Galilee, when he took Peter, James, and John up onto a "high mountain" and was "transfigured before them" (Matthew 16:13, 17:1-2). This city is located in the foothills of Hermon, the highest mountain peak in Israel. The only "high mountain" near them would have been the famous Mt. Hermon.

[17] Matthew 28:18

When Jesus said He received all power, He used the same word for *power* that Paul used when he revealed that God ordains all principality "and power."[18] The word means *the right to rule* or *authority*. Paul was talking about the authority of governments. Jesus declared that God had given Him the right to rule Heaven and Earth.

More than 500 years before in Babylon, Daniel declared, "The most High ruleth in the kingdom of men, and giveth it to whomsoever he will."[19] Jesus said God had given it to Him. The word *it* refers to the kingdom of men. The kingdom of men is mankind. God gave Jesus the right to rule the earth.

A kingdom is a domain governed by a king. God gave to Adam and his descendants (mankind) dominion over the earth to rule and subdue it—*the dominion*. The dominion is the kingdom of man. Initially, this kingdom (mankind and his domain) was under GOD as its only King.

In time, mankind defied their GOD-King and, stirred by Satan, set about to establish separate kingdoms independent of His rule. God began picking and choosing to which kingdom He would give the dominion under God. At one time, He gave it to Israel. She held it for about 843 years until Satan seduced her into rebellion, so it was taken from her and given to Babylon. Satan corrupted Babylon provoking God to take it from Babylon and give it to Persia, and then it passed to Greece. By the time of Christ, Satan succeeded to receive from God all power over all the kingdoms of the world.[20] But after Jesus' resurrection, He declared all authority to rule over Heaven and Earth was His. This

---

[18] Romans 13:1-6
[19] Daniel 4:17, 25, 32
[20] Matthew 4:8-9; Luke 4:5-7

meant the dominion God originally gave to Adam had been taken from Satan and given to Him. By this fantastic announcement, Jesus declared Himself the King of the world—and all mankind became His subjects.

All believers and devils know Jesus will rule the world when He comes to set up His throne on the earth. But the Messiah was expected to make His announcement on Mount Olivet. His Jewish disciples might have wondered why Jesus made this declaration in Galilee and not in Jerusalem. After all, didn't Zechariah prophecy the King of the Jews would appear on Olivet?[21] If Jesus intended to declare Himself the king promised by the prophets, why did He choose to make this declaration on a mountain in Galilee? His disciples had much to learn about the kingdom, and Jesus would spend forty days teaching them the things pertaining to the kingdom of God.[22]

The Bible does not reveal what Jesus taught His disciples about the kingdom of God during that forty days' conference on the subject. But we do know that Isaiah said a prophet from Galilee would be a light to the Gentiles. He said this prophet would be born of a virgin, grow to manhood, heave the government up onto one shoulder, and finally rule the world from the throne of David.[23] This promised king is none other than Jesus, the Son of God.

Isaiah also spoke of another day called the day of the Lord.[24] Zechariah prophesied that on the day of the Lord, Christ would descend upon Mount Olivet to execute His judgment upon the nations.[25]

---

[21] Zechariah 14:4

[22] Acts 1:3

[23] Isaiah 9:6-9

[24] Isaiah 13:9

[25] Matthew 24-25; see Zephaniah 1:15 and Revelation 6:17

Jesus insisted on making His regal declaration, that all power in Heaven and Earth were now His, on Mount Hermon of Galilee. The reason was that He was fulfilling the prophecy concerning Mount Hermon[26] and Galilee,[27] not the prophecy concerning Mount Olivet and Jerusalem.[28]

There are two comings!

First, He came that the world might be saved[29] through His Gospel.[30]

Second, He will judge the nations and rule with a rod of iron when He returns.[31]

He is presently the King in absentia, ruling from the heavens by His Spirit on the earth.[32] In His second coming, He will be physically present, sitting upon the throne of David and ruling the world from Jerusalem.

At His first coming, Jesus took the kingdom of man from Satan and repeatedly offered to restore Jerusalem to her status before she lost it to Babylon. Jerusalem would have had the honor of carrying the light of the Gospel to the world,[33] but she refused, so the privilege was given to the Gentiles.[34]

Jesus had foreseen this! Isaiah predicted that partial spiritual blindness would come upon Israel because of their unbelief.[35] Based on this prophecy, Jesus declared that the

---

[26] Psalm 133:3

[27] Isaiah 9:1

[28] Zechariah 14:4

[29] John 3:17

[30] The word *gospel* means good news, and it identifies the message that when preached, if believed, effects the salvation of a man's soul. All who receive Christ Jesus as Lord and Savior are saved from the wrath of God. That's *the good news.*

[31] Matthew 25:31-46; Revelation 19:15

[32] Luke 19:12-27; John 16:7-13

[33] Matthew 23:37; Luke 13:34; Acts 1-27

[34] Acts 28:28; Matthew 21:43

[35] Isaiah 6:9-13; Luke 21:23; Matthew 13:13; see Deuteronomy 29:4; Isaiah 6:9-13; Romans 11:25

kingdom He had offered to them would be taken from them and given to the nation that delivers the required fruit.[36] The fruit God looks for is repentance toward God, and faith in the Lord Jesus Christ.[37] Any nation that will have the dominion must acknowledge God's righteousness and His Son's Lordship. The fruit (evidence) of that acknowledgment will be righteousness in judgment and justice.

Doubly fitting, then, that Jesus would reveal Himself as the possessor of Heaven and Earth from this mountain in Galilee of the nations![38]

In Galilee, Jesus declared, "All power is given unto me in heaven and in earth," and upon that declaration He commanded us to "Go ye therefore and teach all nations, baptizing them in the name of the Father, and of the Son, and of the Holy Ghost, teaching them to observe all things whatsoever I have commanded you."[39] The message we are commanded to teach and preach is the Gospel.[40] The word *gospel* means good news. The good news is Christ died on the cross for our sins, was buried, and then rose from the dead. So that now, all who repent and believe in Him will be saved from the wrath to come.[41] And His commandments may be summarized in this: that we are to love one another as He has loved us.[42]

---

[36] Matthew 21:43

[37] Acts 20:21

[38] The word *nations* in the expression *Galilee of the nations* translates the Hebrew word הַגּוֹיִם (*ha-gowy-eem*) (Strong No. 1471 גּוֹי "gowy, *go'-ee;* . . . apparently from the same root as 1465 (in the sense of massing); a foreign nation; hence, . . . a Gentile") The ה at the beginning of the word is the article *the,* and the ם at the end of the word makes it plural. It is translated *nation(s)* 265 times, *people* 11 times, *heathen* 143 times, and *Gentile(s)* 30 times. It is the only Hebrew word that is translated *Gentile.* (Isaiah 9:1 concludes Isaiah 8 in the Hebrew Bible.)

[39] Matthew 28:18-20

[40] Mark 16:15-16

[41] I Corinthians 15:1-3; Acts 17:30

[42] I John 3:23

Christ's disciples are authorized to go into all nations with the Gospel by the highest authority in Heaven and on Earth—Jesus the Christ.[43]

Jesus said all power, both in Heaven and on Earth, is His now.

The Secret of Galilee is that Jesus Christ, the Son of God, the heir of the Kingdom and "the prince of the kings of the earth"[44] has come into the world—and "all power is given unto [Him] in heaven and in earth."[45]

All earthly rulers are put on notice to lay their scepters at Jesus' feet[46]—and bow to Him as Lord of all.

All that refuse will "drink of the wine of the wrath of God, which is poured out without mixture into the cup of His indignation." All such will be "tormented with fire and brimstone in the presence of the holy angels, and in the presence of the Lamb."[47]

If any obey the Gospel command to repent[48] and believe on Him,[49] that is, "confess with [their] mouth the Lord Jesus, and believe in [their] heart that God hath raised Him from the dead,"[50] they will be saved from the wrath to come.[51]

---

[43] Mark 16:15; Matthew 16:16

[44] Revelation 1:5-6

[45] Matthew 2:2; Matthew 28:18

[46] Samuel Adams and John Hancock, signers of the Declaration, each made official proclamations acknowledging a present reign of Christ in the earth with a prayer that "all nations may bow to the scepter of our Lord and Saviour Jesus Christ." Samuel Adams, see *Fast Day Proclamation,* issued by Governor Samuel Adams, MA, Mar. 20, 1797, and *The Writings of Samuel Adams,* Harry Alonzo Cushing, editor (New York: G.P. Putnam's Sons, 1908), Vol. IV, p. 385, Oct. 14, 1793. John Hancock, see *A Proclamation for a Day of Public Thanksgiving,* Oct. 28, 1784; Oct. 29, 1788 and 1791.

[47] Revelation 14:10

[48] Acts 17:30

[49] Acts 20:21

[50] Romans 10:9

[51] I Thessalonians 1:10

Meanwhile, God has extended to all Gentile nations the promise of His blessing upon the nation that acknowledges Him.[52] And Jesus promised He would give the kingdom He originally offered to Israel to any nation that brings forth the fruit of repentance and faith in Christ.[53]

Jesus described His current rule over the earth as being the king in absentia, with His servants occupying His kingdom on His behalf. He described Himself as having gone on a "long journey" to receive "a kingdom."[54] He predicted that while He was gone, His citizens would rebel and refuse His Lordship.[55] And He promised that when He returned, He would judge the earth.[56]

The implications of this great truth will be sorted out in the following pages: Jesus is King, and all mankind are His subjects. When Christ came, He brought the power (authority) of the kingdom of God upon this world.

A great war rages: the king of darkness versus the King of Light, the children of disobedience versus the children of obedience, the Spirit of Jesus Christ versus the spirit of Antichrist. It involves the rise and fall of nations, the advances, and retreats of two armies at war—God's great army in battle against His great enemy—and the epic conflict between the forces of evil and the forces of good in this world.

Earth is the battleground, and Christ's disciples are His soldiers. Their commission is to be salt and light in this world, to charge the gates of hell in full armor, to swing the Spirit's sword, which is the Word of truth. Their enemy

---

[52] Psalm 33:12
[53] Matthew 21:43
[54] The eternal Kingdom that He will establish at His Second Coming.
[55] Luke 19:14
[56] Luke 19:12-27

is Satan and his lies, and their arsenal is the truth. In every realm and sphere of life, the battle rages. Christians are Heaven sent, and divinely empowered to engage the enemies of truth, justice, and righteousness. We offer the terms of surrender for peace with God: the command of God to all men everywhere to repent and to surrender to Jesus' claim to be Lord of Heaven and Earth. The stakes are high: control over the resources of the planet, freedom to preach the Gospel to every nation, and—at the end of this life and this world—eternal life or eternal damnation. The prize is the souls of men. This is God's War!

~

Chapter Two

The Mystery of Iniquity Revealed
(Part One)

The Spirit of Jesus Christ Versus the Spirit of Antichrist

PARADOXICAL! JESUS IS LORD over Heaven and Earth, having all power in His hands and ruling the earth from the Throne of His Father in Heaven. It appears, however, that Satan is running the world and wreaking havoc at will. Some might think King Jesus is not doing a very good job governing His kingdom.

A riddle! King Jesus' final instructions to His followers were to take His Gospel message to every nation. Yet most of Earth's nations have made laws barring the Gospel from being preached freely. Is Jesus too weak a leader to overcome the powers that have risen in the world that directly challenge His authority?

A certainty! Before His resurrection, Jesus proclaimed He would cast Satan out.[57] After His resurrection, His Apostles affirmed that Christ had made good on His promise. About 2,000 years ago, Paul declared Christ had "spoiled all principality and power."[58] The ancient Scriptures testify that God has made Christ "head of all principality and power."[59] They exalt Christ "Far above all principality, and power, and might, and dominion, and every name that is named,

---

[57] John 12:31
[58] Colossians 2:15
[59] Colossians 2:10

not only in this world, but also in the world to come."[60]
Yes!—both in this world right now and in that which is
to come.

A contradiction? Although Jesus has cast out Satan, the
Devil continues to work his mischief in the world.[61]

The answer! Paul explained, "The mystery of iniquity
doth already work."[62]

What Is the Mystery of Iniquity?

Considering the truth that Jesus Christ is King of Heaven
and Earth, the seemingly unchecked iniquity rampant
around the globe would seem a mystery indeed. But the
mystery of iniquity is far more sinister—and mysterious.

A *mystery* is something hidden, secret, and difficult to
understand or explain. *Iniquity* refers to acts of lawlessness,
violations of God's laws, and unrighteousness.

Paul said the mystery of iniquity doth "already work."
As if it were something long expected, but not so soon as
it arrived. After all, Jesus had cast out Satan; how did he
reinsert himself into Earth's affairs?

Daniel spoke of a mysterious, future world ruler
described as little horn, who will rise to power in four stages.
First, he will begin with promises of peace through disarmament. Second, but after obtaining extraordinary military
might, little horn will take peace from the earth. In the third
stage, he will gain control over the world's economies.
Finally, he will use his amassed power to destroy one-fourth
of the planet's population. Daniel's mysterious future
world ruler will extend his remarkable powers into the

---

[60] Ephesians 1:21
[61] I Peter 5:8; I Thessalonians 2:18; II Corinthians 2:11; 4:4; Ephesians 6:11
[62] II Thessalonians 2:7

spiritual realm and cast angels to the ground, defy the God of the Bible, and claim the title for himself.[63] When he calls himself God, he will have committed the abomination of desolation that Jesus warned us would trigger great tribulation on the earth—the outpouring of the wrath of God.[64]

This future world ruler is called by many names: the "man of sin,"[65] the "son of perdition,"[66] and "the beast"[67]; but he is popularly called the Antichrist. His objective is to unite the world under his absolute power.

The spiritual force pushing the world toward a one-world government ruled by the "man of sin" is what John called the "spirit of Antichrist, whereof ye have heard that it should come; and even now already is it in the world."[68]

Satan is a spirit,[69] and he is Antichrist. He desires to raise the man of sin, the Antichrist, to preside over a one-world government. This man will rule by Satan's power—*one kingdom under Satan.*

The entrance of the spirit of Antichrist into the world is the mystery of iniquity. And it's at work!

Only about four years before Jesus declared Himself possessor of all power in Heaven and Earth,[70] Lucifer (also known as Satan, the Devil, and the Serpent) could boast that all the kingdoms of the world and their glory was his.[71] In other words, Satan held *the dominion.*

---

[63] Daniel 11:36-37; II Thessalonians 2:4
[64] Matthew 24:15
[65] II Thessalonians 2:3
[66] Ibid.
[67] Revelation 20:10
[68] I John 4:3
[69] Hebrews 1:13-14; Ezekiel 28:16; see Isaiah 14:12-17
[70] Matthew 28:18; John 13:3
[71] Luke 4:5-6; Isaiah 14:12

Lucifer moved God to give him power over the dominion by tempting men out from under God, and into sin. Because God established the wages of sin is death, by tempting men into sin, Satan gained the power of death over humanity.[72] Through seduction into sin (transgression of God's laws), Satan finally moved God to deliver all mankind and all the dominion over which He ruled to the power of Satan.[73]

When Christ appeared in the flesh, Satan knew He was the heir of the dominion and the kingdom that would hold it. To keep the dominion in his power, Lucifer offered to put all the kingdoms under Jesus' authority if Jesus would bow down and worship him.[74]

Why Doesn't Satan Simply Rule the earth Directly?

Remember, the dominion was given to Adam and through him to his posterity—that is, to mankind.[75] It was a Divine grant of power over the earth and its resources, and man was to rule it under God. As pointed out above, Satan succeeded in turning mankind out from under God and into his power. However, because the Creator put the dominion under the rule of man, Satan required a man through whom he could rule the earth. Once Satan succeeded at moving God[76] to deliver the glory of the kingdoms of men to his

---

[72] Genesis 2:17; Romans 6:23; Hebrews 2:14

[73] I John 3:4

[74] Luke 4:5-8

[75] Genesis 1:26-28

[76] See Job 2:3. The story of Job is in some ways a microcosm of the great story of God's war. In Job 2:3, God says to Satan, "thou movedst me against him [Job], to destroy him." Satan gains power over man by moving God against him. He generally does this by tempting men to sin against God. In Job's case, however, God said Satan had moved Him against Job "to destroy him without cause" (Job 2:3). This is *mysterious* indeed. In this instance, God used Job to illustrate the glorious plan by which GOD would deliver mankind from the power of Satan. At the end of the book, God declared to Job's friends, who self-righteously accused Job of sin, that He would accept an offering from Job on their behalf—the guiltless who suffered as a sinner and who's offering was accepted to cover the guilty. It is a picture of God's

power, he began searching for the man he would appoint to rule it under him.[77] But God interfered with Satan's plan and sent His own Son into the world as a man,[78] to save the world from Satan's power.[79]

The Devil tried to recruit Jesus by offering to give Him power over all the kingdoms of the earth if Jesus would bow down and worship him.[80] In other words, Jesus had to acknowledge Satan as the god of this world[81] and agree to rule it under Satan.

Jesus refused Satan's offer! He took up His Cross instead, and by His sacrificial death He paid the wages of sin.[82] Because Jesus never sinned, Satan had no claim on Him, and so Christ was able to take up His life again—He arose from the dead.[83] By His resurrection He was "declared to be the Son of God with power."[84] Jesus broke Satan's power over the kingdom of man, and all power over Heaven and Earth became His. So the Father reclaimed all the kingdoms of the world from Satan and turned them over to His only begotten Son. Because the Son of God is also the Son of man, He can rule the earth directly as God-King.

And so it is that *Jesus is the King and all mankind His subjects.*[85]

---

own Son, the guiltless, suffering as a substitute for sinners and Who's offering would be accepted by God to cover the sins of mankind (John 3:16; II Corinthians 5:21; I John 3:5; 2:1-2).

[77] We will be exploring this in great detail later. The important thing to keep in mind here is that God had given the dominion to man, and so only a *man* could rule it.

[78] I Timothy 3:16; John 1:1, 14

[79] Acts 26:18

[80] Matthew 4:8-9; Luke 4:5-8

[81] II Corinthians 4:4

[82] Romans 6:23; 5:8; I John 2:1-2

[83] John 10:18

[84] Romans 1:4

[85] Matthew 16:13, 16; John 1:1, 14; I Timothy 3:16

But we are back to our original dilemma: how has Satan succeeded at reasserting himself into the affairs of men so that it would appear he has reclaimed his status as the possessor of all the kingdoms of this world?

Ask anyone! They will tell you, "Satan rules the world." Satan's PR campaign has been so effective, even God's children believe it. Anyway, most of them do.

Sinners Rebel Against Christ's Right to Rule, and the Saints Facilitate Their Rebellion.[86]

Jesus promised to return and destroy the wicked and establish His Sovereign rule over all the earth physically in the "day of vengeance of our God."[87]

But God has postponed the coming "day of vengeance of our God"[88] to allow Jesus' subjects an opportunity to be saved from the wrath to come.[89] Remember, all mankind are His subjects.[90] He loves them all!

---

[86] This parable reveals that Jesus regards all men on the earth as either His "servants" or His "citizens" (Luke 19:14). The "citizens" reject Him as their ruler (Luke 19:14, 27). These citizens will be destroyed at His return (Luke 19:15, 27). Those who have been "delivered . . . from the power of darkness, and . . . translated . . . into the kingdom of His dear Son" (Colossians 1:13), are redeemed by His blood, forgiven, and assured a place with Him in Heaven (Colossians 1:14; John 14:1-3; I John 5:13). In other words, the "citizens" Jesus is talking about in Luke 19:14, 27, are not *citizens* of the kingdom He went away to receive. They are *citizens* of His present kingdom, His present rule over the earth. But they reject His rule. So when He returns, He will destroy them. (Luke 19:12-27; Psalm 2; Ephesians 4:27)

[87] Isaiah 61:1

[88] After Jesus was tempted in the wilderness, He came in the power of the Holy Ghost into Nazareth and went into the synagogue (Luke 4:14-16). He opened the Scriptures to Isaiah 61 and read up to the phrase, "*to preach the acceptable year of the Lord,*" then closed the book. Many have noticed that Jesus stopped reading mid-sentence and that He obviously purposely stopped reading before the phrase, "*and day of vengeance of our God.*" When Jesus declared to the Jews in the Synagogue that day that this Scripture was being fulfilled before their eyes, He intentionally left off the part about the vengeance of God since that was not to be fulfilled until later.

[89] II Peter 3:9; I Timothy 2:4

[90] I John 2:1-2; see I Timothy 2:4

After securing His right to rule the present kingdoms of this world, Jesus ascended into heaven to receive another kingdom,[91] the one He will establish when He returns to the earth. He waits for the Father's signal to return to judge the nations, at the time of "THE END," and then He shall "have delivered up the Kingdom to God, even the Father," and will accomplish His mission to "put down all rule and all authority and all power."[92]

Is that the answer? Are we merely waiting until Jesus returns to deliver on His promise to "put down all rule and all authority and power"? That is what Satan would like for you to believe. The deceiver wants you to think the world belongs to him, at least for now. So, you might as well sit helplessly on the sidelines and watch what he does with it while you wait for your King to return. The Devil wants to keep you ignorant of your spiritual power to influence the affairs of the earth right now. He does not want you to know you can pull down the strongholds protecting his territory. He wants you to feel helpless to resist him and make him flee, to bring the authority of Christ upon nations and their rulers—now, in this life, today!

The Spirit of Jesus Christ Wars Against the Spirit of Antichrist in the World Today.

Jesus sent His Holy Spirit into the world to reprove it

---

[91] Luke 19:12; Daniel 7:14, 22, 27; Revelation 5:1-14

[92] The drama of the kingdom of men unfolds as follows: The Almighty rules in the kingdom of men and gives it to whomsoever He will (Daniel 4:17). Over time, Satan succeeded to tempt man into sins so offensive to God that He turned the kingdom of men over to the power of Satan (Matthew 4:8,9; see Acts 26:18). Jesus, the Son of God, came into the world to destroy the work of Satan (I John 3:8) and break the power of Satan to hold the kingdoms of the world (Hebrews 2:14); and because of His perfect righteousness and victory over Satan, God gave to Him all power in Heaven and in Earth (Matthew 28:18). When He completes this work, Jesus will then return it to God, the Father (I Corinthians 15:24). (Isaiah 61:1) (I Corinthians 15:24)

of sin, righteousness, and judgment.[93] By His Spirit, Christ empowers believers to declare that He is Lord[94] and to command all men everywhere to repent[95] and flee the wrath to come.[96] All who obey the Gospel command to repent and believe on the Lord Jesus Christ receive the Holy Ghost as His gift.[97] The Spirit of Jesus Christ dwells in their hearts,[98] and Jesus said His Spirit moves into the world through their belly.[99] The Spirit delivers His reproof upon the consciences of mankind in this world and draws them to Jesus when believers preach the Gospel "with the Holy Ghost sent down from heaven."[100] (What it means for the Spirit to flow through the belly of a believer will be explained later.)

The Spirit of Christ takes the body of the believer as His Temple.[101] When the body (Temple of the Holy Ghost) is dedicated and presented to Him holy, He fills it and moves into the world through it, exerting the authority of the Kingdom of God among men.[102]

Jesus manifests in this world through the flesh of His disciples.[103] Furthermore, by His Spirit, He sometimes defies human authorities and asserts His Divine right—that is, His authority (power) over principalities and powers.

For example, God allowed Herod to behead James,[104] but

---

[93] John 16:7-13
[94] I Corinthians 12:3
[95] Acts 17:30
[96] Luke 3:7; II Thessalonians 1:8
[97] Ephesians 1:13-14; Acts 2:38; Romans 6:17; II Thessalonians 1:8; I Peter 4:17
[98] Galatians 4:6
[99] That the Holy Spirit would flow from our belly is one of the strangest things Jesus taught us. Nevertheless, this is what Jesus said would happen. I offer a very thorough examination of this later. Be patient. (John 20:22; 7:38-39)
[100] I Peter 1:12
[101] I Corinthians 6:19-20
[102] Romans 12:1-2; John 7:38-39
[103] II Corinthians 4:11
[104] Acts 12:1-2

when that wicked king placed Peter in jail, God intervened and delivered Peter from Herod's authority.[105] Christ did a jailbreak—walked Peter right out of his cell to freedom.

Of course, the immediate question is why did Christ (the King) allow James to be beheaded but intervened so dramatically on Peter's behalf? It was not because James had offended, or because Peter was exceptionally significant, and James was not. Acts 12:5 reveals the reason—the church prayed without ceasing for Peter. A praying church made the difference.

Many Christians do not understand their part in God's War. They wonder why Jesus is not doing something when the problem is He is waiting for them to do their part. God does His work with us: we are "laborers together with God."[106]

Jesus gave the "keys of the kingdom"[107] to His church. These keys are used when the Gospel is preached, allowing entry into Christ's kingdom to all who believe.[108] These keys also confer upon the churches spiritual authority to act in the kingdom of men on Christ's behalf, with implications affecting this present, evil world.

The Spirit purposely brings to our attention the fact that the church prayed without ceasing for Peter.[109] That is the reason Peter received the supernatural intervention. The church has spiritual authority in this world to bring Christ's influence into the affairs of men.

Conclusion

That's what this book is about: how believers can engage

---

[105] Acts 12:3-19
[106] I Corinthians 3:9
[107] Matthew 16:19; 18:18-20; see Colossians 1:4
[108] Colossians 1:13
[109] Acts 12:5

in spiritual warfare, bringing Christ's authority to bear upon the affairs of this world. When believers express the power of God in their communities, they may say as Jesus did, "The kingdom of God is come upon you."[110]

Jesus Christ sent His Spirit into the world, and Satan was cast out and now operates as the spirit and power of the air.[111] As Christians grieve and quench the Holy Spirit in their personal lives, they give place to the devil in this world.[112] By the time the last Apostle wrote his letters, the believers had already retreated significantly, allowing the spirit of Antichrist to enter and set up a headquarters for Satan on Earth.[113]

Jesus did indeed cast out Satan as the "prince of this world."[114] Nevertheless, the Devil continues his rebellion as the "prince of the power of the air."[115] He opposes the claim of Jesus Christ to be Lord over the kingdoms of the earth. From his banished position, Satan has reasserted his influence in the world through the children of disobedience. Satan's activity in the world through the children of disobedience is the spirit of Antichrist that John said was "already in the world."[116]

How Satan got the Antichrist spirit into the world, and how he has been able to gain so much influence in it, is the topic of chapter three.

∼

---

[110] Luke 11:20
[111] Ephesians 2:2
[112] Ephesians 4:27, 30-31; I Thessalonians 5:19
[113] Revelation 2:13
[114] John 12:31
[115] Ephesians 2:2
[116] I John 4:3

Chapter Three

The Mystery of Iniquity Revealed
(Part Two)

How Did the Spirit of Antichrist Enter the World and Give Satan So Much Influence in It?

S ATAN IS A FALLEN ANGEL, a spirit. Jesus referred to him as the "prince of this world" and said he would be cast out. Jesus fulfilled this promise when He died on the cross and rose from the dead, thereby breaking the power of Satan over mankind. As He promised, Jesus sent His Spirit into the world to reprove it of sin, righteousness, and judgment. Satan became the "prince of the power of the air." We established in the last chapter that Satan has reasserted himself in the earth. In this chapter, we will explain how he was able to do this. The answer will shock you!

Satan is the spirit of Antichrist; he denies that Jesus Christ (Messiah—Prince of God, the rightful heir of the dominion) has come in the flesh.[117] He works tirelessly to oppose Christ's rule in the earth today.

The Devil deploys a limited but large host of "seducing spirits" into the world and, by them, plies the minds of men with "doctrines of devils."[118] Every doctrine (teaching, philosophy, belief) that these devils espouse serves one way or another to incite spite in the hearts of men against the rule of Christ. Those he can deceive he controls, using

[117] I John 4:3
[118] I Timothy 4:1-4

them to work his will in the world. They are called the "children of disobedience."[119]

Satan is "a liar, and the father of it,"[120] and he uses wily deceit to blind men in the darkness of these devilish doctrines.[121] He tells them that Jesus is not the Lord of the earth. He seduces them to join him in his rebellion, to rage against the right of Christ to rule the earth today. Satan turns the hearts of Christ's subjects against Him to despise His Word, His Church, His people, and His laws. These children of disobedience are stirred against Christ to cry, "We will not have this man to reign over us."[122]

The "Light" of the world was sent from Galilee to lead men out of this darkness.[123] However, Jesus explained that some men love darkness rather than light because their deeds are evil.[124] Satan uses these darkness-loving evil-deed-doers as his agents—to war against Christ's Lordship in the earth. His primary targets are Christ's servants. His success depends entirely upon his ability to neutralize the servants of Christ.

It's an old war! At the beginning of Satan's rebellion,[125] one-third of God's angels followed him.[126] These fallen angels are spirit agents of the Devil, and so they are called devils. As the "prince of the power of the air," Satan uses his devils as "seducing spirits" to teach doctrines of devils.[127]

[119] I John 4:3; Ephesians 2:2
[120] John 8:44
[121] II Corinthians 4:4; Ephesians 6:11
[122] Luke 19:14 — Hopefully you are beginning to "get it." This explains the irrational hatred against biblical Christianity that we see manifested all over the world and beginning to manifest in American with increasing power.
[123] Isaiah 9:1-2; II Corinthians 4:6; I Peter 2:9
[124] John 3:17-21
[125] Isaiah 14:12; see Ezekiel 28:14-19; Luke 10:18
[126] Revelation 12:4; see Revelation 1:20
[127] II Timothy 4:1-4

Devilish philosophy and vain deceit[128] today encourage people to vainly imagine they can overthrow the Lordship of Jesus Christ in the earth.[129] The Antichrist spirit inspires rulers to reject the claims of Jesus Christ, to break away from the authority of God and His Anointed, to conspire together to overthrow His rule. The objective is to provoke God to allow Satan to set up a one-world government, over which he will place his son, the "son of perdition," the "man of sin."[130] He can only succeed if he can deceive Christ's servants to cooperate with him.

The flipside of this conflict is the Spirit of Jesus Christ moving through the children of obedience to restrain the spirit of Antichrist that works in the children of disobedience, frustrating their purposes.[131] So long as God's Spirit is present in the earth,[132] He withholds the spirit of Antichrist from fulfilling Satan's mission.[133]

Jesus left us with clear instructions to occupy until He returned.[134] He displaced the Devil and broke his power.[135] We have been instructed to give no place to the Devil.[136] Like an occupying force, Christ's soldiers [137]are called upon

---

[128] Colossians 2:8

[129] Psalm 2:1-7

[130] II Thessalonians 2:3

[131] II Thessalonians 2:7-8

[132] John 16:7-13

[133] *Let* translates κατέχων (*kat-'ekh-on*, from Strong No. 2722, κατέχω "*kat-'ekh-o* to hold down (fast), in various applications (literally or figuratively):—have, hold (fast), keep (in memory), let, x make toward, possess, retain, seize on, stay, take, withhold." See also Strong Nos. 2596 and 2192. The entry *Let* in Webster's 1828, 1913, offers the following: "*Let* (lĕt), *v. t.* [OE. *letten*, AS. *lettan* to delay, to hinder, fr. *laet* slow; akin to D. *letten* to hinder, G. *verletzen* to hurt, Icel. *letja* to hold back, Goth. *latjan*. See Late.] To retard; to hinder; to impede; to oppose. [Archaic]." Curious that the word has taken the opposite meaning today.

[134] Luke 19:13

[135] John 12:31

[136] Ephesians 4:27

[137] II Timothy 2:3

to hold the territory that Jesus took. Christ's Spirit in us is greater than the spirit that is in this world.[138] Satan could never have reentered the world unless Christians let him in.

Satan uses the same devices he employed to compromise the congregation of Israel. He wars against us through the lusts of our flesh.[139] As soldiers, we "wrestle . . . against powers, against the rulers of the darkness of this world, against spiritual wickedness in high places."[140] The Spirit of Christ manifests Jesus in us, and He works through us in this world.[141] But Satan seduces believers to indulge their fleshly lusts and thereby grieve the Holy Ghost [142] and to "quench the Spirit."[143] This removes the only influence in the world that can overcome Satan.

Agents of darkness seduce men into the Devil's snares,[144] blind minds to the light of the Gospel,[145] and do all in their power to hinder our work.[146] However, Jesus has empowered the children of obedience[147] as kings and priests unto God[148] who, by the Holy Ghost,[149] do battle against the unholy spirit of Antichrist.[150] The Bible promises, "Greater is He that is in you than he that is in the world."[151] My purpose is to show how to use the greater power that is in us to overcome these agents of evil in the world.

---

[138] I John 4:4
[139] I Peter 2:11
[140] Ephesians 6:12
[141] Colossians 1:27; John 7:38-39; II Corinthians 4:11
[142] Ephesians 4:30-31
[143] I Thessalonians 5:19
[144] I Timothy 4:1-4; II Timothy 2:26
[145] II Corinthians 4:4
[146] I Thessalonians 2:18
[147] I Thessalonians 1:8
[148] Revelation 1:5-6
[149] Acts 1:8
[150] I John 4:3
[151] I John 4:4

The conflict between the Spirit of Jesus Christ and the spirit of Antichrist is what we call spiritual warfare. It is acted out in the great conflict in the world between the children of obedience, ostensibly controlled by the Spirit of Jesus Christ,[152] and the children of disobedience under the control of Satan.[153]

The Conflict Arises Over Who Is King—Jesus Christ or Antichrist.

Jesus sent us to proclaim He is Lord, to command all men everywhere to repent,[154] and to announce His readiness to save from the wrath to come all who will believe.[155] But the spirit of Antichrist works to keep us from fulfilling this mission.[156] This book aims to help believers understand how to fulfill their role as soldiers in God's War.[157]

Our Lord Jesus summarized all this in His parables.

In the famous Parable of the Sower, Jesus told us He bought the field and, as He later explained, the field represented the entire world[158]—so it all belongs to Him. We are commissioned to go into the world (the field), sowing the seed (the Gospel) into the soil (the hearts of men). Considered together with His declaration that to Him is given authority over Heaven and Earth,[159] we understand that no man has the right to bar us from this work. Upon His authority, we are to teach all nations, baptize all who believe, and teach them to observe all things whatsoever

---

[152] Ephesians 5:18-21
[153] Ephesians 2:2
[154] Acts 17:30
[155] Hebrews 7:25
[156] I Thessalonians 2:16
[157] II Timothy 2:3-4
[158] Matthew 13:44; see Matthew 13:36-38
[159] Matthew 28:18

He has commanded. Therefore, Jesus is King of the earth, all humanity is subject to Him, and we are commanded to preach the Gospel to everyone, everywhere, under His authority.

The world belongs to Christ; it does not belong to Satan. No man on this Earth has the power (right, authority) to forbid us from preaching the Gospel of Jesus Christ. But Satan stirs them up to oppose us.

Satan can hinder Christians from preaching the Gospel today because they have so little power with God. The reason for this is troubling: God commands all who name the name of Christ to depart from iniquity. But many who name the name of Christ are precisely the opposite; they are workers of iniquity. Essentially, the reason so many Christians have little or no power against Satan is that they have unwittingly joined the rebellion.

In the Parable of the Nobleman,[160] Jesus represents Himself as King of the kingdom of men, ruling in absentia, Who will return to judge His servants and His citizens. His servants are His disciples, and the earth's inhabitants are His citizens.[161] While He is in Heaven, Jesus explained, "his citizens hated him, and sent a message after him, saying, We will not have this man to reign over us."[162] With this parable, Jesus warned He would return and judge His servants for their faithfulness, or lack thereof, and then He will say, "But those mine enemies, which would not that I should reign over them, bring hither, and slay them before me."[163]

---

[160] Luke 19:12-27
[161] Luke 19:12-14
[162] Luke 19:14
[163] Luke 19:27

The world Christ purchased is scheduled for destruction.[164] Meanwhile, Jesus has departed to a "far country" to receive another kingdom.[165] The kingdom He has gone to receive is the one He will set up when He returns to judge the earth.[166]

In the Parable of the Nobleman mentioned above, Jesus said the nobleman gave provision to His servants and instructed them to "occupy" until He returned.[167] The word *occupy* means to be busy, to tend to one's business. We use it to speak of holding territory gained in battle. In this context, it means His servants are charged to carry out the instructions of the King as an occupying presence.

In another parable, called the Parable of the Talents, Jesus tells of a Master "travelling into a far country, Who called his own servants, and delivered unto them his goods."[168] In this parable Jesus mentions the significant fact that the Master "delivered unto them his goods." The goods Christ gave His disciples include the spoils of His war against Satan for the kingdom.

Sadly, some of Christ's servants have sold out to evil, saying in their heart, "My lord delayeth His coming," smiting their fellow servants, and eating and drinking with the drunken.[169] These traitors have joined the rebellion of the *citizens* who reject Jesus' right to rule in the earth.

David spoke of the time that all who reject the true God would cry against the Messiah's right to rule, saying, "We will not have this man to reign over us."[170] He put it this

---

[164] See Daniel 7:9-14, 27-28; 8:17; 12:1-4; II Thessalonians 1:8; Revelation 19-20
[165] Luke 19:12
[166] Luke 19:15-27; Revelation 19-20
[167] Luke 19:13
[168] Matthew 25:14
[169] Matthew 24:49
[170] Luke 19:14

way: "Why do the heathen rage, and the people imagine a vain thing? The kings of the earth set themselves, and the rulers take counsel together, against the LORD, and against His anointed (a.k.a., Christ Jesus) saying, Let us break [His servant's] bands asunder, and cast away their cords from us."[171] This is the spirit of Antichrist that rages against the rule of Christ Jesus in the earth.

Christ's Sovereign authority over the earth is challenged.

Perhaps you have noticed that many today become nearly insane when a Christian takes a position of power in government. Now you understand why. The citizens of this present evil world[172] reject Christ Jesus as the rightful ruler of the world, and seducing spirits know they can't get genuine Christians to deny Him. So, they whisper into the minds of Christians the lie that Jesus has no authority right now. They convince Christians that Satan rules the world today and that Christians have no say in the affairs of this world.

Thusly is the battle set in array on battleground Earth. Christ's servants are charged to hold what belongs to Him and to be faithful stewards. Their primary mission is to preach the Gospel, commanding all men everywhere to repent and believe on Jesus Christ to be saved from the wrath to come. These are the children of obedience. Opposing them, the children of disobedience defy Christ and reject His rule now or ever, and work to resist the Gospel that delivers men from the power of Satan. They labor night and day to rid the earth of the Spirit of Christ and desire the spirit of Antichrist to prevail over the hearts of men. These are the children of disobedience.

---

[171] Psalm 2:1-3
[172] Galatians 1:4

Conclusion

Our Lord has warned His servants to give no place to the Devil in this world.[173] We have failed to heed that warning, and today powerful devils hold so much territory in our land that we are about to lose our place in it.[174]

The message is urgent. As Satan gains more place in the world, Christians are increasingly displaced. Consequently, greater and stronger barriers to the Gospel are erected and fortified in defiance of Christ's command to preach the Gospel to every nation. Unless believers learn the truth about spiritual warfare and discover how to resist the Devil so that he is compelled to flee, we will fail our Lord. Hence, the title, *God's War—Why Christians Should Rule the World. (The right and responsibility of Christians to engage in every sphere of life on Earth)*. The purpose of *God's War* is to provide the guidance and direction necessary to win. In the pages that follow, you will learn how to reclaim territory given over to Satan in our nation, our states, our cities, our churches, our families, and the lives of our children. The goal is to pull down every stronghold hindering the Lord's churches until the Gospel is preached to all nations—and then shall the end come.[175]

---

[173] Ephesians 4:27

[174] In Romans 11, the Spirit, by the Apostle Paul, explains that unbelieving Israel has been cut off from the "good olive tree" that represents Abraham and God's promise to give the kingdom/dominion to his seed. He also explains that believing Gentiles have been grafted into that tree, allowing them to have inheritance in the promise of Abraham. Paul warns that if God cut off unbelieving Israel from the tree, He will not hesitate to cut off unbelieving Gentiles also. Consider: "For if God spared not the natural branches, take heed lest He also spare not thee. Behold therefore the goodness and severity of God: on them which fell, severity; but toward thee, goodness, if thou continue in His goodness: otherwise thou also shalt be cut off" (Romans 11:21-22).

[175] Matthew 24:14. Paul said, "Their sound went into all the earth, and their words unto the ends of the world" (Romans 10:18). In the days of Paul, the unbelieving felt the impact of the Gospel and declared: "These that have turned the world up-

Next, we will deepen our understanding of Christ's rule in the earth over the kingdoms of men and how He works through nations to advance His purposes. Also, we will gain greater knowledge of how Satan stirs up nations to oppose Christ. Finally, we will gain critical insight into the role of Christ's Church in this conflict.

∼

---

side down are come hither also" (Acts 17:6). The faith of the Christians in Rome was spoken of "throughout the whole world" (Romans 1:8). So it might be argued that the Gospel has already been preached to all nations and that Jesus' prophecy given in Matthew 24:14 has been fulfilled. It is possible Jesus had this in view when He proclaimed the prophecy recorded in Matthew 24. However, He placed this statement in a place in his Olivet Discourse that connects it with events He said would occur toward the end of this world, when "iniquity shall abound" and "the love of many shall wax cold," descriptions similar to those Paul gives regarding the end-time generation in II Timothy 3:1-7. Notice also the proximity of this particular part of the prophecy to the events given in Daniel that signal the end of the world: the abomination of desolation and outpouring of God's wrath upon the world (Matthew 24:14-31). I think Jesus is telling us that His Gospel will be preached throughout the entire world in the rapture generation; that is, in the generation of those who will be "alive and remain" when the dead in Christ are raised, and who will be "caught up together with them in the air" (I Thessalonians 4:13-17).

Chapter Four

The Origins Of God's War
And the Beginning of Kingdoms

GOD'S WAR is not a "Game of Thrones"; it's for real! The message of the prophet Daniel is that God rules in the kingdom of men and gives it to whomever He will.[176] Daniel's prophecy promises that God will finally give it to the "saints."[177] Good. They lose; we win. Now let's watch TV—how about a little Game of Thrones?[178] Not so fast!

The fact that we will win the war does not guarantee we win every battle. Nor does it mean our losses are not real. The believer who relaxes in the knowledge that we will win in the end is foolish. We are responsible for the battles confronting our generation, and our failures have eternal consequences for which we are accountable.

Spiritual warfare involves the ongoing battle over control of the dominion, but the primary target is the souls of men. In this chapter, I'll offer insight into the backdrop to this cosmic war. The major players in this drama are as follows: first, God; second, Satan; and then men.

---

[176] Daniel 4:25
[177] Daniel 7:18
[178] https://en.wikipedia.org/wiki/Game_of_Thrones: "*Game of Thrones* is an American fantasy drama television series created by David Benioff and D. B. Weiss for HBO. . . . "

The Origins of the War!

God created all things.[179] Of course, this includes the angels, who are God's ministering spirits.[180] Satan was one of them.

Angels were present when God created the Heaven and the earth.[181] Satan sang with them, exulting in the glory of God's power displayed when God created the Heaven and the earth.[182]

Satan was the greatest in power, beauty, and wisdom of all the angels God had created. When the prophet Ezekiel described the king of Tyrus he was addressing the spiritual power that stood behind that human king.[183] Similarly to how Jesus once rebuked Peter saying to the power behind him, "Get thee behind me Satan."[184]

Two simple observations prove that Ezekiel was describing Satan in his prophecy. First, Ezekiel identified this king of Tyrus as the "covering cherub,"[185] and according to Ezekiel, a cherub is an angelic creature, like the cherubim he described surrounding the Throne of God.[186] Second, Ezekiel wrote more than 3,400 years after God banished Adam and Eve from Eden, and yet Ezekiel said to the king of Tyrus, "Thou hast been in Eden the garden of God."[187] Ezekiel describes Satan as the most powerful of all God's angels.

Here is the prophecy concerning the "covering cherub":

---

[179] Ephesians 3:9; Colossians 1:16
[180] Hebrews 1:14
[181] Job 38:7
[182] Genesis 1:1
[183] Ezekiel 28:12
[184] Matthew 16:23
[185] Ezekiel 28:11-17
[186] Ezekiel 10:1-20
[187] Ezekiel 28:13

Moreover the word of the LORD came unto me, saying,

Son of man, take up a lamentation upon the king of Tyrus, and say unto him, Thus saith the Lord GOD; Thou sealest up the sum, full of wisdom, and perfect in beauty.

Thou hast been in Eden the garden of God; every precious stone was thy covering, the sardius, topaz, and the diamond, the beryl, the onyx, and the jasper, the sapphire, the emerald, and the carbuncle, and gold: the workmanship of thy tabrets and of thy pipes was prepared in thee in the day that thou wast created.

Thou art the anointed cherub that covereth; and I have set thee so: thou wast upon the holy mountain of God; thou hast walked up and down in the midst of the stones of fire.

Thou wast perfect in thy ways from the day that thou wast created, till iniquity was found in thee.

By the multitude of thy merchandise they have filled the midst of thee with violence, and thou hast sinned: therefore I will cast thee as profane out of the mountain of God: and I will destroy thee, O covering cherub, from the midst of the stones of fire.

Thine heart was lifted up because of thy beauty, thou hast corrupted thy wisdom by reason of thy brightness: I will cast thee to the ground, I will lay thee before kings, that they may behold thee.

Thou hast defiled thy sanctuaries by the multitude of thine iniquities, by the iniquity of thy traffick; therefore will I bring forth a fire from the midst of thee, it shall devour thee, and I will bring thee to ashes upon the earth in the sight of all them that behold thee.

All they that know thee among the people shall be astonished at thee: thou shalt be a terror, and never shalt thou be any more. —Ezekiel 28:11-19

The iniquity found in this covering cherub is described

in Isaiah's prophecy concerning *Lucifer*,[188] the proper name given to Satan after his fall. This prophecy is found in Isaiah 14:12-20, and once again, the Spirit is addressing the spiritual power behind a human ruler:

> How art thou fallen from heaven, O Lucifer, son of the morning! how art thou cut down to the ground, which didst weaken the nations!
>
> For thou hast said in thine heart, I will ascend into heaven, I will exalt my throne above the stars of God: I will sit also upon the mount of the congregation, in the sides of the north:
>
> I will ascend above the heights of the clouds; I will be like the most High.
>
> Yet thou shalt be brought down to hell, to the sides of the pit.
>
> They that see thee shall narrowly look upon thee, and consider thee, saying, Is this the man that made the earth to tremble, that did shake kingdoms;
>
> That made the world as a wilderness, and destroyed the cities thereof; that opened not the house of his prisoners. —Isaiah 14:12-20

In Satan's declaration of rebellion against God, he boasted that he would be "like the most High" and "set [his] throne

---

[188] Many believe the Hebrew word translated *Lucifer* in Isaiah 14:12 means *shining one*. This is taken from the fact that *Lucifer* is the Latin word used to translate the Hebrew word used here. The Latin word is rooted in *lucere* which means to shine, be clear, become light—hence *shining one*. It became commonly understood as the proper name of Satan. However, the Hebrew word here is הֵילֵל (*Biblia Hebraica Stuttgartensia*, Isaiah 14:12, p. 696). It is found only once, in Isaiah 14:12, and it is not found in any other Hebrew literature. In English we call it a gerund, a verb used as a noun. This unique noun is constructed from a Hebrew verb meaning *to howl*, and in Isaiah it is used as a proper noun for Satan (See Strong No. 3213). It sounds like *halel*, which means *to praise* (הָלַל— *halal*), but the word used in Isaiah 14:12 is actually pronounced *hillel*, which means *to howl*. Notice that the yod ׳ is not used in the word that means *to praise*. But it is used in the word translated *Lucifer*. This means the first letter signals the article *the*, followed by the verb, *yalal*, and literally means *the howling one*.

above the stars of God."[189] GOD, Who resists the proud,[190] repudiated his boast; and Jesus watched "Satan as lightning fall from heaven."[191]

It is reasonable to believe Satan was master of the earth when every precious stone was his covering (house).[192] And that God destroyed the planet in rebuke against his wicked boast.[193] Then He formed it to be inhabited[194] by a new creature He called man.[195]

---

[189] Isaiah 14:12-17

[190] James 4:6

[191] Luke 10:18

[192] The word *covering* (in Ezekiel 28:13) translates מְסֻכָתֶךָ, *mes-ook-kaw-ha-ka* (from Strong No. 4540), from סָכַךְ, *saw-kak,* or שָׂכַךְ, *sakak* (Strong No. 5526). The word refers to a construction that provides cover. It describes Satan's *house,* as it were.

[193] Genesis 1:1 declares God created the Heaven and the earth. This is past tense. Many believe the next verse describes the condition of the earth brought about by an event that made it *without form and void* (Genesis 1:2). I believe that event was the fall of Satan. The arguments supporting this view are summarized here. Isaiah by the Spirit declared the earth was not *created in vain* (Isaiah 45:18). The word *vain* translates תֹּהוּ (*tohu*—Strong No. 8414), which is the same word translated *without form* in Genesis 1:2. God did not originally *create* the earth in this condition. Furthermore, we notice that only the earth is described as *without form and void.* If Genesis 1:2-31 describes original creation, why does it not say the Heaven and the earth were without form and void? Add to this that the word translated *create* is not used for the earth; instead, the Spirit uses the word *made* (וַיַּעַשׂ— from עָשָׂה. *aw-saw, Biblia Hebraica Stuttgartensia (BHS)* Genesis 1:7, p. 1, see Strong No. 6213) in Genesis 1:7, 16, 25, 31, and 2:1-4. And yet, the Spirit does use the word that is translated *create* in Genesis 1:1 (בָּרָא—*bara,* BHS, p. 1) when He speaks of the creation of the *great whales* and the living creatures of the sea (Genesis 1:21), and of *man* (Genesis 1:26-27). And it is appropriate to suggest *creation* was involved in the *making* of the living creatures that walk on the earth. However, it is interesting that in each case when God speaks of the heavenly bodies, or the earth itself, He does not use the word that is translated *create* in verse 1, but He does use this word when He speaks of the living creatures and of man. Finally, Ezekiel 28 speaks of an angelic creature called the "covering cherub" and describes him as having a dwelling place on the earth: Ezekiel 28:11-20. Some dispute this view, and while the evidence supporting the conclusion is strong and I am of the opinion that it is correct, I do not encourage anyone to encourage a spirit of divisiveness over disagreements about it.

[194] Isaiah 45:18

[195] Genesis 1:26-27

Satan claimed he would be "like the most high," and as if to reprove the prideful spirit, God took dust from the earth and formed man, and to this lowly creature, He gave His image and His likeness.[196] And with that image and likeness, He gave to man *the dominion*, which is the right to rule Earth under God.

Satan set out to usurp God's place in the earth over man, to bring mankind under the power (authority) of darkness,[197] which is the kingdom of Satan.[198]

The Beginning of Kingdoms

There are three kingdoms: the Kingdom of God, the kingdom of men, and the kingdom of darkness. The kingdom of men was created to be under God. The kingdom of darkness began when Satan rebelled against GOD. Satan attempts to usurp God's place over mankind by bringing the kingdom of men under the power of darkness.

Ultimately there is one King and one Kingdom. In what follows, I will explain what it means when the King grants the dominion to a man or a nation under God.

One King and One Kingdom:

The word *kingdom* is constructed from the word *king*, which denotes a ruler, with the suffix *dom*, which means domain. A domain refers to territory under the authority of a ruler, also called a realm. Hence, a kingdom is a ruler's domain. The kingdom of men refers to a domain under the rule of men.

God has placed the earth, and every creature in it, under the dominion of men.[199] This is *the dominion*. God

---

[196] Genesis 1:26-27
[197] Colossians 1:13
[198] Matthew 12:26; Luke 11:18
[199] Genesis 1:26-27; Psalm 8:6-8

is its King. Devils and men contest God's right to rule it. But despite every effort to break out from under God's Sovereignty, as the prophet Daniel declared, it continues to be subject to His Sovereign Rule. He initially gave it to mankind. But because of the rebellion of Satan and man, God exercises His prerogative as Sovereign over the earth to give the dominion to the man or nation He chooses that will acknowledge Him as the one, true GOD-King.[200]

Spiritual warfare refers to the unseen spiritual powers that work through physical agents in this contest between God and Satan. They contend for the right to rule the kingdom of men. Sinful men rebel against the true King of the earth and attempt to make for themselves kingdoms independent of God's Sovereign rule. Satan seduces men into this vanity to bring them under the power of darkness, that is, the kingdom of Satan. He does not care what form the governments of men take; his objective is served if he can get men to rebel against the authority of the Kingdom of God. Remember, King David's second Psalm predicted the rebellion.

> Why do the heathen rage, and the people imagine a vain thing?
>
> The kings of the earth set themselves, and the rulers

---

[200] Daniel 4:17; see Psalm 47:2-7 — God is the King: Psalm 5:2; 44:4; 68:24; 84:3; 95:3; 145:1—*over the entire Earth* (Psalm 47:2-7); *an everlasting king* (Jeremiah 10:10); *working salvation in the midst of the earth* (Psalm 74:12). The New Testament also bears testimony to this truth: I Timothy 1:17, Revelation 15:3. Of particular interest is the testimony that Jesus is the "King of Israel" (John 1:49). (Cross-reference this to the testimony of the Old Testament prophet Isaiah, that the LORD (Jehovah) is the "King of Israel" (Isaiah 44:6).) Zechariah testified that the LORD God would be "king over all the earth" in a day when there will be "one LORD, and His name one" (Zechariah 14:9). According to the testimony of Daniel (Daniel 4:3,17), God has never ceased to be the "everlasting king" (Jeremiah 10:10), "possessor of heaven and earth" (Genesis 14:22). However, Satan has moved men to usurp this role in the earth, and the prophet, Zechariah, is declaring the day this usurpation will be put down and the earth will be united under the true King.

take counsel together, against the LORD, and against
his anointed, saying,
Let us break their bands asunder, and cast away their
cords from us.
He that sitteth in the heavens shall laugh: the Lord
shall have them in derision.
Then shall he speak unto them in his wrath, and vex
them in his sore displeasure.
Yet have I set my king upon my holy hill of Zion.
I will declare the decree: the LORD hath said unto me,
Thou art my Son; this day have I begotten thee.
Ask of me, and I shall give thee the heathen for thine
inheritance, and the uttermost parts of the earth for
thy possession.
Thou shalt break them with a rod of iron; thou shalt
dash them in pieces like a potter's vessel.
Be wise now therefore, O ye kings: be instructed, ye
judges of the earth.
Serve the LORD with fear, and rejoice with trembling.
Kiss the Son, lest he be angry, and ye perish from the
way, when his wrath is kindled but a little. Blessed are
all they that put their trust in him. —Psalm 2

All efforts of devils and men to the contrary, the dominion remains in the Kingdom of God. God made man in His image and likeness and placed His Kingdom authority in man when He gave to him "the dominion." (This is what Jesus was alluding to when he explained, "the kingdom of God is within you.")[201] Remember, Satan boasted that he would set his throne above the stars of God and be "like the most High."[202] Envious that man holds the Imago Dei

---

[201] Luke 17:21 — Many stumble over this verse into a wide variety of errors. This is because the Kingdom of God is misunderstood on a fundamental level. The truth is, there is only one Kingdom. All other kingdoms are formed in rebellion against the one true Kingdom. This will be resolved when Jesus brings all kingdoms under Him, into one kingdom, and then delivers it up to God (I Corinthians 15:20-28).
[202] Isaiah 14:12-17

(image of God) and resentful that God gave mankind the dominion, Satan desires to usurp God's place over it and bring man under his power.

Ultimately, there is only one Kingdom, and God is the only legitimate King. Lucifer rebelled against God's rule and set about to establish an independent kingdom, laboring to seduce men to align themselves under him against God. Satan tempts men to imagine themselves independent of the Sovereign Rule of the Creator.

Perhaps you ask why God allowed Israel to have kings? When His chosen people, Israel, demanded to have a king like the other nations, God said to Samuel, "They have not rejected thee, but they have rejected me, that I should not reign over them."[203] God allowed Israel to appoint a king over them, but He did not condone it.[204]

God insists there is but one King, and all of Heaven and Earth are under His authority.

God has not abdicated His Sovereign rule of the earth. As Daniel declared, God rules in the kingdom of men, and He appoints over it whomever He will.[205]

What Does It Mean for GOD to Give "The Kingdom" to a Nation?

It means God has given to that nation the dominion. We have already established that when God gives the dominion to a ruler, it means He has given that ruler power over the earth and control of its resources.[206]

---

[203] I Samuel 8:7
[204] It is possible God intended to raise up David and establish his seed as stewards of the throne until Christ would come. But the people were rebellious and demanded Samuel "make [them] a king to judge [them] like all the nations" (I Samuel 8:5).
[205] Daniel 4:17
[206] Genesis 1:26-28, see Daniel 2:38; and compare to Psalm 8:6-8

It also means God has given to that nation His sword.[207] The nation that has the dominion is empowered to serve as God's executor of wrath upon evildoers.[208]

It does not mean every nation is obliged to live under the direct rule of the government that possesses the dominion. Nor does it mean that every government will necessarily acknowledge the preeminence of the nation to which God has given the dominion. The rule of the kingdom that has the dominion will not likely be felt in every corner of the earth. What it does mean is that God has favored that nation with great prosperity and increased it above all the nations of the earth, empowering it to be His sword of punishment upon those nations He has appointed for judgment.

Behind every war is the ambition of some despot who wants to rule the kingdom of men. The coveted prize is control over the natural resources of the earth, such as oil, gold, food, and people. Such rulers desire to enslave men to their will, to gain power over them through control of the earth's natural resources.

Conclusion

The hand of God moves unseen in the affairs of men. Nevertheless, every war fought in the world has been decided by God's Divine intervention, sometimes correcting a rebellious nation, and sometimes removing the dominion from one and giving it to another of His choosing. The Bible provides a historical record of man's rebellion against

---

[207] Ezekiel 30:25; Romans 13:1-6

[208] The point is illustrated in each of the following verses: Romans 13:1-6; see Judges 7:18-20; I Chronicles 21:12; Jeremiah 12:12; 47:6; and see Deuteronomy 32:42; Isaiah 34:5; Ezekiel 21:3-5; see especially Ezekiel 30:25 with Jeremiah 51:20. Clearly, God executes His judgment upon the wicked nations by placing a "sword" in the hand of the nation He has chosen to execute that judgment. (Ezekiel 30:25; see Romans 13:1-6)

God's authority over the earth and His direct intervention into the affairs of men; He asserts His Divine Right as Sovereign Lord over all the earth—giving and then taking away the dominion from this or that nation according to His will.

In the next chapter, I will address the governing principles of God's rule over the kingdom of men.

~

"[May] the peaceful and glorious reign of our Divine Redeemer . . . be known and enjoyed throughout the whole family of mankind.

~ Samuel Adams

(Samuel Adams, A Proclamation For a Day of Public Fasting, Humiliation and Prayer, given as the Governor of the Commonwealth of Massachusetts, from an original broadside in our possession; see also, Samuel Adams, The Writings of Samuel Adams, Harry Alonzo Cushing, editor (New York: G. P. Putnam's Sons, 1908), Vol. IV, p. 385, October 14, 1795.)

Chapter Five

The Governing Principles of God's Rule

G OD RULES in the kingdoms of men and gives the dominion of the earth to whomever He chooses. The dominion includes power over the resources of our planet, including all the creatures that inhabit it.[209] God intended to be the King, the Sovereign of this kingdom, with man serving under Him as stewards over the dominion.[210] The kingdom of man was to be under God. That is the first principle: the nation that will hold the dominion must acknowledge God's Sovereign rule over the kingdoms of men.

The First Principle: The Nation That Holds the Kingdom Must Be Under God.

Israel was one nation under God. So long as she remembered that GOD ruled in the kingdoms of men, she prospered. But when Israel finally repudiated the rule of GOD, the dominion was taken from Israel and given to the Gentiles.

Although GOD had removed the dominion from His chosen people, He did not abdicate His Sovereign right to rule the kingdoms of men. This is the essential message of

---

[209] Genesis 1:26; see Daniel 2:38
[210] Psalm 47:2; Malachi 1:14

the first six chapters in the prophecy of Daniel. At the time the dominion was transferred to the Gentiles, God expressly declared that He favors only those nations that acknowledge His rule from the heavens.[211] God releases every nation to the power of hell that forgets this essential truth.[212]

The first Gentile king to receive the dominion was Nebuchadnezzar, king of Babylon. He was called God's servant.[213] It was known throughout Babylon: God took the kingdom from Israel and gave it to Nebuchadnezzar because Israel had forsaken the Lord. The captain over Nebuchadnezzar's guard said to Jeremiah:

> And the captain of the guard took Jeremiah, and said unto him, The LORD thy God hath pronounced this evil upon this place. Now the LORD hath brought it, and done according as He hath said: because ye have sinned against the LORD, and have not obeyed His voice, therefore this thing is come upon you. And now, behold, I loose thee this day from the chains which were upon thine hand. If it seem good unto thee to come with me into Babylon, come; and I will look well unto thee: but if it seem ill unto thee to come with me into Babylon, forbear: behold, all the land is before thee: whither it seemeth good and convenient for thee to go, thither go. —Jeremiah 40:1-4

For as long as Nebuchadnezzar acknowledged God as supreme, he prospered. When he turned from this essential first principle of the dominion, God chastened him.

God went to great lengths to establish the first principle of the dominion at the beginning of the times the Gentiles would have it.[214]

---

[211] Daniel 4:26
[212] Psalm 9:17
[213] Jeremiah 25:9
[214] This period is called "the times of the Gentiles" (Luke 21:24).

For example, He gave Nebuchadnezzar a dream that forecast the passing of the dominion from one Gentile nation to the next until the time that Christ would come to the earth to restore the kingdom to Israel.[215] He caused Nebuchadnezzar to remember that he had a significant and troubling dream, but took the memory of it from him. Meanwhile, God prepared the Jewish prophet, Daniel, to remind Nebuchadnezzar of the vision and to interpret it for him. We will look more closely at this dream later, but there is one thing we must understand. Even though God took the dominion from His chosen people and gave it to the Gentiles, He continued to reign as Sovereign Lord over all the kingdoms of the world.

Repeatedly, in the course of the reign of Nebuchadnezzar, God intervened to demonstrate His Sovereign rule over the kingdoms of men.

Once, Nebuchadnezzar became arrogant and ordered the construction of an image made of gold that was 90 feet tall. He demanded everyone in his kingdom to bow down to the statue at his command. When three Jewish officials of his kingdom—Shadrach, Meshach, and Abednego—refused to bow to the king's image, Nebuchadnezzar became furious. He commanded them to bow to his statue or burn in his furnace. They declined, and into the furnace they went. God revoked the king's commandment: Nebuchadnezzar blustered in astonishment that he saw four men in the fire and that the fourth was like the Son of God.[216] The king called the men to come out of the furnace, and all could see the fire did not hurt them. Nebuchadnezzar confessed before all in attendance that the GOD of Shadrach, Meshach,

---

[215] Daniel 2
[216] Daniel 3:1-25

and Abednego had "changed the king's word, and yielded their bodies, that they might not serve nor worship any god except their own God." He then made the following proclamation:

> Therefore I make a decree, That every people, nation, and language, which speak any thing amiss against the God of Shadrach, Meshach, and Abednego, shall be cut in pieces, and their houses shall be made a dunghill: because there is no other God that can deliver after this sort. — Daniel 3:29-30

Nebuchadnezzar had another dream he needed Daniel to interpret. He dreamed of a great tree that grew till it reached into Heaven and filled the earth. A *watcher* cried against it:

> Hew down the tree and cut off his branches, and scatter his fruit: let the beasts get away from under it, and the fowls from his branches: Nevertheless leave the stump of his roots in the earth, even with a band of iron and brass, in the tender grass of the field; and let it be wet with the dew of heaven, and let his portion be with the beasts in the grass of the earth: let his heart be changed from man's, and let a beast's heart be given unto him; and let seven times pass over him. This matter is by the decree of the watchers, and the demand by the word of the holy ones: to the intent that the living may know that the most High ruleth in the kingdom of men, and giveth it to whomsoever He will, and setteth up over it the basest of men.
> — Daniel 4:10-17

Daniel interpreted the dream to mean Nebuchadnezzar (the tree in his dream) would exalt himself pridefully and so be cut down. He would lose his power of reason, be removed from his kingdom, and exiled, left to pasture like a beast, where he would stay for seven years. Daniel explained he would be returned to his throne "after that thou shalt have known that the heavens do rule."[217] Then Daniel advised Nebuchadnezzar to delay the judgment by humbling himself to God.

Twelve months later, Nebuchadnezzar's heart swelled with pride over all his glory and accomplishments, and the judgment fell swiftly upon him. At the end of the seven-year curse, when the king lifted his eyes toward heaven, he praised the GOD of Heaven:

> Mine understanding returned unto me, and I blessed the most High, and I praised and honoured Him that liveth for ever, whose dominion is an everlasting dominion, and his kingdom is from generation to generation: and all the inhabitants of the earth are as nothing: and he doeth according to his will in the army of heaven, and among the inhabitants of the earth: and none can stay His hand, or say unto Him, What doest thou?[218] — Daniel 4:34-35

Through Nebuchadnezzar, God showed all nations, that first principle of the dominion did not change: the nation that would have the dominion must be under God.

The Second Principle: The Nation Holding the Kingdom Is Not Sinless.

The second principle recognizes the truth that the nation to which God gives the dominion is not a perfect people. God did not choose Israel because of her righteousness. Moses was very explicit on this point:

> Understand therefore this day, that the LORD thy God is he which goeth over before thee; as a consuming fire he shall destroy them, and he shall bring them

---

[217] Daniel 4:16

[218] During the succeeding kingdom, Persia, when Darius the Mede was king over Babylon, another dramatic intervention by God occurred in which He demonstrated His Sovereign rule over the kingdoms of the earth. It is recorded in Daniel 6, and it is the famous story of Daniel in the Lion's Den.

down before thy face: so shalt thou drive them out, and destroy them quickly, as the LORD hath said unto thee.

Speak not thou in thine heart, after that the LORD thy God hath cast them out from before thee, saying, For my righteousness the LORD hath brought me in to possess this land: but for the wickedness of these nations the LORD doth drive them out from before thee.

Not for thy righteousness, or for the uprightness of thine heart, dost thou go to possess their land: but for the wickedness of these nations the LORD thy God doth drive them out from before thee, and that he may perform the word which the LORD sware unto thy fathers, Abraham, Isaac, and Jacob.

Understand therefore, that the LORD thy God giveth thee not this good land to possess it for thy righteousness; for thou art a stiffnecked people."

—Deuteronomy 9:3-6

The nation to whom God gives the dominion must acknowledge Him, but God does not expect it to be especially righteous. It does appear, however, that she must be at least more so than the nation God uses it to judge.

The Third Principle: The Nation Holding the Kingdom Will Serve as God's Sword of Divine Judgment.

God used Nebuchadnezzar to illustrate another primary principle of the Kingdom: the nation that holds the dominion is God's sword to execute Divine wrath upon those marked for judgment.

At the time God removed the dominion from Israel and gave it to Nebuchadnezzar, there lived a king in Tyre, Lebanon, called the "king of Tyrus."[219] He was wiser than Daniel,[220] and by his wisdom and understanding, he amassed great wealth.[221] When he saw that God had destroyed

---

[219] Ezekiel 28:1-2
[220] Ezekiel 28:3)
[221] Ezekiel 28:4-5

Jerusalem, he rejoiced, saying, "Aha, she is broken that was the gates of the people: she is turned unto me: I shall be replenished, now she is laid waste."[222] The heart of this king puffed up!

The heart of Tyrus filled with pride as he thought on his great wisdom and riches. In his proud boast against God's people, Tyrus declared himself to be a God. So God sent His prophet to rebuke him: "Say unto the prince of Tyrus, Thus saith the Lord God; Because thine heart is lifted up, and thou hast said, I am a God, I sit in the seat of God, in the midst of the seas; yet thou art a man, and not God, though thou set thine heart as the heart of God."[223]

Earlier, I showed that the power behind this king of Tyrus was none other than the "covering cherub"—Satan himself.[224] Think about this. Satan corrupted Israel and Judah to the point God took the dominion from His chosen people and destroyed His city, even His own House. And at that moment, Satan had a king under his power that was calling himself God.

But God rebuked Tyrus and used His servant, even Nebuchadnezzar, to punish him.[225] God said to Nebuchadnezzar through His prophet Ezekiel:

> Son of man, Nebuchadrezzar[226] king of Babylon caused his army to serve a great service against Tyrus: . . . yet had he no wages, nor his army, for Tyrus, for the service that he had served against it: Therefore thus saith the Lord GOD; Behold, I will give the land

---

[222] Ezekiel 26:1-2
[223] Ezekiel 28:2 — The passage, carefully read, shows that the *prince* is the spiritual power behind the *king.*
[224] Ezekiel 28:11-19; see Chapter Four: The Origin of the War
[225] Ezekiel 26:7-14
[226] *Nebuchadrezzar* is believed to be the Aramaic spelling of the Hebrew name *Nebuchadnezzar.*

> of Egypt unto Nebuchadnezzar king of Babylon; and
> he shall take her multitude, and take her spoil, and
> take her prey; and it shall be the wages for his army.
> I have given him the land of Egypt for his labour
> wherewith he served against it, because they wrought
> for me, saith the Lord GOD. — Ezekiel 29:18-20

God rules in the kingdoms of men and sets over it whomever He will. He does not choose a nation because it is particularly righteous, or even good. He selects a nation that will acknowledge Him and humble itself under His rule and serve as His sword of vengeance. He uses the king and the kingdom to which He gives the dominion to execute His judgments upon the nations, and He rewards them for their service.

As we have seen thus far, at the beginning of the times of the Gentiles (the period during which Gentile nations would have the dominion), God established all the core principles of the dominion. We have seen three: 1) the nation must formally acknowledge God, 2) it may have imperfections, and 3) it must faithfully steward the Sword of the Lord. However, there is a subtle insight in this last principle I want to highlight.

God went out of His way to make the point that Nebuchadnezzar served Him by defeating a king that was under the power of Satan, who proudly proclaimed himself to be God. This underscores the truth that God's War is about the conflict between God and Satan over who will be God of mankind and who will hold the dominion.

When God was removing the dominion from Israel, Satan was ready with a "God-King" of his own in the wings, as they say. But God used Nebuchadnezzar to chastise this arrogant usurper, and then rewarded him for his service.

God uses the nation under Himself to chastise Satan's efforts to bring the world under the power of darkness.

We come now to the fourth principle.

The Fourth Principle: The Nation That Holds the Dominion Does So as God's Steward and Not as Earth's Owner.

Nebuchadnezzar was given the dominion as God originally described it when He created man and gave it to him. Compare the following descriptions of the dominion.

> And God said, Let us make man in our image, after our likeness: and let them have dominion over the fish of the sea, and over the fowl of the air, and over the cattle, and over all the earth, and over every creeping thing that creepeth upon the earth.
>
> So God created man in his own image, in the image of God created he him; male and female created he them.
> — Genesis 1:26-27

Now read the description of the kingdom God gave to Nebuchadnezzar:

> Thou, O king, art a king of kings: for the God of heaven hath given thee a kingdom, power, and strength, and glory.
>
> And wheresoever the children of men dwell, the beasts of the field and the fowls of the heaven hath he given into thine hand, and hath made thee ruler over them all. Thou art this head of gold. — Daniel 2:37-38

Daniel described the kingdom that God removed from Israel and gave to Nebuchadnezzar in the same language God used to describe the dominion He gave to man through Adam. Because men rebelled and presumed to usurp the dominion over all mankind, God intervened and, as Daniel repeatedly declared in his prophecy:

> The most High ruleth in the kingdom of men, and giveth it to whomsoever he will, and setteth up over it the basest of men. —Daniel 4:17

And again . . .

> The most High ruleth in the kingdom of men, and giveth it to whomsoever he will. —Daniel 4:25

And again . . .

> The most High ruleth in the kingdom of men, and giveth it to whomsoever he will. —Daniel 4:32

And at the end of the Babylonian Empire, Daniel reminded Belshazzar what his grandfather, Nebuchadnezzar, understood:

> The most high God ruled in the kingdom of men, and that he appointeth over it whomsoever he will.
> —Daniel 5:21

Earthly kings and their kingdoms hold the dominion as a steward under God. They are responsible to God for how they exercise their rights under Him over the dominion. For example, God gave all the beasts of the field and the fowl of heaven to Nebuchadnezzar, but that did not mean individuals could not own property, or hunt on their lands. It is certain that God's grant of the dominion to Nebuchadnezzar did not give him the right to usurp the property rights of his subjects. God made Nebuchadnezzar His steward over the dominion, but it would be a violation of that stewardship for Nebuchadnezzar to use his power to oppress the people. God hates oppression!

Three times God reveals to Nebuchadnezzar that God gives *the kingdom* (aka, the dominion, the right to rule the world under God) to whomever He chooses. At the end of the Babylonian Empire, Daniel reminded Belshazzar what God so dramatically taught his grandfather, Nebuchadnezzar.[227]

---
[227] Daniel 5:21

Nebuchadnezzar ruled in peace till his death in c.562 B.C. after he finally learned the first principle of the dominion: acknowledge God. The kingdom suffered much confusion in the transition years that followed, but finally, one of his generals, the husband of his daughter, Kassaya, prevailed to take the throne of Babylon. His name was Nabonidus. They had a son, grandson to Nebuchadnezzar, named Belshazzar. This brings us to the end of the Babylonian Empire, and to the last principle: thou shalt not blaspheme God or repudiate His rule. Of course, this is an extension of the first principle.

The Fifth Principle: Thou Shalt Not Blaspheme God.

In Daniel 5, we read the remarkable and famous account of the "handwriting on the wall."[228] While Nabonidus, his father, was in the East fighting the king of Persia, Belshazzar ruled in Babylon as the second ruler of the dominion. He gave a great feast, invited all the nobles of the empire, and brought out of storage the Temple treasures his grandfather had taken from the Temple in Jerusalem. Belshazzar defied the God of Heaven and profaned the Temple treasures. That's when the hand appeared that wrote the famous writing on the wall that none in Belshazzar's kingdom could decipher, except Daniel, the prophet, who served the king's grandfather, Nebuchadnezzar. Daniel was an older man with little patience for the arrogant descendant of that once great king.

Daniel was summoned. First, he reminded Belshazzar of a story renowned in the kingdom. His grandfather, Nebuchadnezzar, had lost his mind and was driven into the fields to eat grass with the oxen for seven years. His sanity returned when he looked toward heaven and "knew

---

[228] Daniel 5:5

that the most high God ruled in the kingdom of men and that He appointeth over it whosoever He will." Then the old prophet rebuked Belshazzar:

> And thou his son, O Belshazzar, hast not humbled thine heart, though thou knewest all this; but hast lifted up thyself against the Lord of heaven and defiled the vessels of God's House using them to praise the false gods of Babylon, and "the God in whose hand thy breath is, and whose are all thy ways, hast thou not glorified. — Daniel 5:22-23

Daniel interpreted the writing: "Thou art weighed in the balances, and art found wanting. Thy kingdom is divided, and given to the Medes and the Persians."[229]

Babylon fell. Belshazzar was killed. Darius, king of the Medes, entered the city and overtood Nebuchadnezzar's once impenetrable fortress.[230] At the same time, Belshazzar's father, Nabonidus, was defeated by Cyrus, king of Persia.

Conclusion

There are five governing principles of the dominion under God. First, the king and the kingdom that will hold the dominion must acknowledge GOD rules in the realm of men and gives it to whomsoever He will—a point made with emphasis. Second, the nation holding the dominion is not expected to be perfect, or sinless. (Regarding this second principle, remember God said He would "wink at"[231] their foolish worship of idols, so long as they acknowledged that GOD is above all gods.) Third, the kingdom under God wields His sword of vengeance, to execute wrath upon those who do evil, especially against those nations under the power of Satan that attempt to usurp God's place in the

---

[229] Daniel 5:27-28
[230] Daniel 5:30-31
[231] Acts 17:30

world. Fourth, the nation holding the dominion does so as God's steward and not as the owner of all Earth's resources, and so must not exercise its prerogatives oppressively. Fifth, the holder of the dominion must not defile God's House, blaspheme, or mistreat His people. Else God will judge them and ultimately remove the dominion from their hands to give to another.

The next chapter begins an overview of the history of God's War in the kingdom of men. The insights are fascinating, but more importantly, they are essential to rightly understand the role of God's children in God's War.

~

"[That] we may with one heart and voice humbly implore His gracious and free pardon through Jesus Christ, supplicating His Divine aid . . . [and] above all to cause the religion of Jesus Christ, in its true spirit, to spread far and wide till the whole earth shall be filled with His glory." ~ Samuel Adams

(Samuel Adams, Proclamation for a Day of Fasting and Prayer, March 10, 1793.)

Chapter Six

The History of God's War
(Part One)
The Transfer of the Kingdom From Nimrod to Abraham and then to Nebuchadnezzar

GOD RULES in the kingdoms of men and gives the dominion of the earth to whomever He chooses. Mankind has rebelled against the right of God to rule and is in constant war against God's will. This rebellion began in the Garden of Eden when man presumed to act in defiance to God's will. Jesus summarized the essence of the conflict in the words of the model prayer He gave us to use when learning how to pray: "Our Father, which art in heaven, hallowed be thy name. Thy kingdom come. Thy will be done, as in heaven, so in earth."[232] This chapter begins an overview of this struggle: the history of God's War!

The kingdom of men refers to the dominion over the earth that God gave to mankind. It includes power over the resources of the planet, including all the creatures that inhabit it.[233] God intended to be the King, the Sovereign of this kingdom, with mankind serving under Him as stewards over the dominion.[234] The realm of man was to be under God. But man rebelled! The history of God's War begins with the fall of man.

---

[232] Luke 11:2
[233] Genesis 1:26; see Daniel 2:38
[234] Psalm 47:2; Malachi 1:14

From the Fall to the Flood

Man sinned, rebelling against God's authority, thus bringing great evil into the world. This evil increased until, at one point, God decided to destroy the entire population of the planet by a worldwide flood.[235] Noah found grace (Divine favor) in the eyes of the Lord, so humanity would continue through Noah's family.[236]

From the Flood to Abraham

Men began forming kingdoms out from under God soon after the flood.

Nimrod was the first. He founded Babel (which became Babylon in the land of the Chaldees) and began usurping God's authority in the earth over men.[237] God commanded humankind to spread out over all the globe and replenish it,[238] but Nimrod led them in direct disobedience against God's Word. He attempted to establish a government over the world, with him as the King. God destroyed his efforts and scattered the people, dividing them into language groups. These groups became separate nations that followed the pattern set by Nimrod—setting up kings over their respective kingdoms out from under God. However, being divided, no single ruler could bring the entire world under his control without great difficulty. Meanwhile, God would grant the dominion to the kingdom of His choosing.

God chose Abraham and his seed,[239] from whom He would form one nation under God.

From Abraham to Nebuchadnezzar

---

[235] Genesis 6:7; see Genesis 6-9
[236] Genesis 6:8
[237] Genesis 10-11
[238] Genesis 9:1-17
[239] Genesis 12:1-4; 15:2-21; 17:7-10; 18:19

God promised to give the dominion to a people to whom He would reveal Himself, a people called after His name—which would form a nation under God. Ironically, God called Abraham out of Ur of the Chaldees,[240] Nimrod's old stomping grounds, to be the progenitor of that people.[241]

Abraham had the dominion, and God's power was with him. Whoever blessed Abraham would be blessed, and whoever cursed him would be cursed.[242]

The "sword of the Lord" was with Abraham. It goes with the dominion. When his nephew, Lot, was taken captive by the armies of five kings, Abraham armed his servants, defeated all their armies, and rescued his nephew.[243] Remarkable! The servants of a herdsman defeated the armies of four powerful kings!

At that time, the Amorites held Divine right and title to the land God promised to give to Abraham's seed, the area we call the *Promised Land.*

An Amorite king named Melchizedek was called the priest of the Most High God in the days of Abraham.[244] After Abraham defeated the four kings of the East with his band of armed servants, God organized a meeting between Abraham and this king to receive the king's blessing.[245] Melchizedek reigned over Salem—which is Jerusalem. God had a king of righteousness (the meaning of *Melchizedek*) ruling in Jerusalem in the days of Abraham? Wow! God brought them together so Abraham could receive the blessing of the man who held Divine right to the Promised Land at that time: Melchizedek.

---

[240] Genesis 11:28-31; Nehemiah 9:7
[241] Genesis 12:1-3
[242] Genesis 12:1-4
[243] Genesis 14
[244] Genesis 14:18-20
[245] Genesis 14:18-20

Shortly after his meeting with Melchizedek, God told Abraham He would not transfer the Promised Land to his seed until the iniquity of the Amorites had come to the full.[246]

God gave what we might call favored-nation-status to the nation that blessed Abraham and his seed. Melchizedek enjoyed this favor during his lifetime.

Under Joseph, the Pharaoh of Egypt honored God's people, and the blessing of Abraham, through Joseph, came upon the king of Egypt and his nation.[247] However, when a Pharaoh that knew not Joseph rose to the throne and turned against Jacob's seed,[248] God sent Moses and destroyed Egypt by great plagues.

It was at about this time that the iniquity of the Amorites had come to the full. God moved to establish His nation under God in the hands of Abraham's seed, Israel. He used Moses to establish Israel under His Law as a nation under God.

Moses did not instruct Israel to follow the example of the nations (Gentiles) by setting up a king, for God would be their King.[249] But Moses prophesied they would opt for a king like the nations around them. So, he provided the law of kings in Deuteronomy 17:14-20.

The office of king in Israel was different from that of heathen nations. For example, Israel's king was under the Law of God; Gentile kings were a law unto themselves. Also, in Israel, there was a strictly maintained separation of powers between the Law, the king, and the priesthood. (God's Law covered the legislature, the king was the executive, and the priests, who applied and taught the Law,

---

[246] Genesis 15:16
[247] Genesis 39-50
[248] Israel—Exodus 1
[249] I Samuel 12:12-19

served as the judiciary.) In heathen nations, the king was the head of their religion and often acknowledged as an incarnation of their god.

Israel became a nation under God with the dominion, and with it came the Sword of the LORD to execute wrath upon him that doeth evil.[250] Israel was used by God to execute Divine wrath upon the kings of Canaan.[251] The LORD finally established His people over the land that came to be called the land of Israel.

As Moses predicted, Israel came to desire a king like the nations around them.[252] It was her first step out from under God. Nonetheless, Israel kept the dominion for almost 500 more years.[253] Saul was their first king and began his reign in c.1095 B.C. The last king of an independent Judah, Josiah, died in 608 B.C., the year Jeremiah declared God had transferred the dominion to Nebuchadnezzar.[254]

However, Jerusalem, the city of the ancient king Melchizedek, c.1895 B.C.,[255] did not become the capital of Israel until David took Zion in the eighth year of his reign, c.1047 B.C.[256] Most would agree that the kingdom was not formally settled until the reign of David, with whom God entered into a special covenant[257] and by whom God measured all succeeding kings.[258]

---

[250] Romans 13:4

[251] See the book of Joshua.

[252] I Samuel 8:5-20; 12:12-19; Deuteronomy 17:14

[253] If we accept the idea that God gave Abraham "the dominion" at the time of his call (Genesis 12:1-4) c.1921 B.C., we may say Abraham and his seed held the dominion for over 1,300 years. If we take the Exodus as the beginning of Israel's possession of the dominion, they held it for 883 years.

[254] Jeremiah 26:1-7; 27:1-11; see II Chronicles 35:25-36:1-8

[255] Genesis 14:18—*Salem* is *Jerusalem*

[256] II Samuel 5:7; see II Samuel 2:11

[257] II Samuel 7:12-17

[258] I Kings 3:14; 11:4, 33; 15:3; 22:2; II Chronicles 17:3; 21:12; 34:2

The third king of the kingdom, Solomon, introduced the ways of the heathen (Gentile nations) into the kingdom of Israel.[259] Because of this, God divided the congregation of the children of Israel into two factions: one He called Israel (ten tribes); the other He called Judah (two tribes).[260]

Jeroboam was the first king of the ten tribes of Israel, and he immediately established the sins in Israel that brought them to destruction.[261]

The degeneration of Judah took longer, but at last, Manasseh established the sins in Judah that brought it to destruction.[262]

Because Judah, like her sister, Israel, forgot God, God removed the stewardship of the dominion (a.k.a., the kingdom) from His chosen people and gave it to the Gentiles.

Intriguing! The first Gentile nation to receive the stewardship of the dominion after Judah lost it was Babylon—the city founded by Nimrod, in the vicinity of the birthplace of Abraham, Ur of the Chaldees.

---

[259] I Kings 11:3-4; see Deuteronomy 17:17
[260] I Kings 11:31
[261] Jeroboam had made two golden calves and hired vain men to serve as priests to offer sacrifices to these golden calves (II Kings 10:29). Of course, we know Jeroboam had spent a significant amount of time in Egypt, hiding from Solomon (I Kings 11:28-40). His "golden calves" hail back to the days of the children of Israel in Egypt: remember when Moses was long in the mountain, they grew weary of waiting for him, turned to the idols of Egypt, and built for themselves a golden calf to worship (Exodus 32:1-8). Satan is called "the cherub that covereth" in Ezekiel 28:14. Ezekiel speaks of the four cherubim that are posted at the four corners of the Throne of God (Ezekiel 10:1-20). Later, the prophet John described these throne cherubim as four beasts that surround the Throne, with the face of a lion, of a calf, of a man, and of an eagle (Revelation 4:7). Perhaps this explains why Satan inspires his followers to worship him in the form of a calf. The children of Israel were seduced into worshiping Satan in the form of the golden calf (I Kings 14:16).
[262] II Kings 24:3

From Nebuchadnezzar to Christ (Overview)

At the time GOD assigned the dominion to the Gentiles, He went to great lengths to establish His Sovereignty. It bears repeating that although He had removed the dominion from His chosen people, He did not abdicate His Sovereign rule over the territories of men. God expressly declared through His prophet Daniel that He favors only those nations that acknowledge His rule from the heavens.[263] Those nations that forget this essential truth are turned into hell.[264]

God declared the transfer of the dominion to Nebuchadnezzar, king of Babylon, by Jeremiah the prophet in 608 B.C.[265] A short time after this transfer, Daniel received revelations from God forecasting the events that would lead to the restoration of the dominion to Israel.

Nebuchadnezzar had a dream.[266] He saw an image. The head was gold, the upper torso was silver, the belly and thighs were brass, the legs were iron, and the feet and ten toes were iron mixed with miry clay.[267] Daniel interpreted the dream to mean the LORD would transfer the dominion from Babylon to Persia, from Persia to Greece, and from Greece to "the fourth kingdom."[268] Then the end would come upon all kingdoms of the earth, which was depicted by a stone that would come from heaven, fall upon the feet

---

[263] Daniel 4:26
[264] Psalm 9:17
[265] Jeremiah 27:4-8; Daniel 2:37-38; see Genesis 1:26-28
[266] Daniel 2
[267] Daniel 2:31-38, 42-44
[268] Most students identify the fourth kingdom with Rome for the obvious reason that the Roman Empire succeeded Greece, which Daniel identified as the third kingdom represented in Nebuchadnezzar's dream image. However, as we shall show, there is a good reason God did not name Rome as the fourth kingdom. You can get my book *The Visions Of Daniel* if you want a thorough study of Daniel's prophecies.

of the image, and break all the kingdoms it represented to "chaff of the summer threshingfloors," which "the wind [would carry] . . . away." At this time, "the stone that smote the image [will become] a great mountain [Kingdom]," that will fill "the whole earth."[269]

Conclusion

The prophecy given to Nebuchadnezzar is being fulfilled. Much of it is already history. The history of God's War will continue in the next chapter: from Nebuchadnezzar to Cyrus and then to Alexander the Great.

~

---

[269] Daniel 2:35

Chapter Seven

The History of God's War
(Part Two)

The Transfer of the Kingdom From Nebuchadnezzar to Cyrus and then to Alexander

God TOOK THE DOMINION (kingdom) away from His people, Israel, and gave it to the Gentiles. The first Gentile king to receive it was Nebuchadnezzar, whom God called "My servant."[270] He visited the king of Babylon with a prophetic dream. In the dream, Nebuchadnezzar saw an image. Its head was gold, its upper torso was silver, its belly and thighs were brass, its legs were iron, and its feet and toes were iron mixed with miry clay.[271] Daniel interpreted the dream to be a prophecy of how the dominion would move from one nation to the next until Christ, the Messiah, the King appointed by God, would come to rule on the earth.

Daniel explained to Nebuchadnezzar that the head of gold was Babylon.[272] As for the succeeding sections of the dream image, he said they represented empires that would follow Babylon and would be inferior to the *head of gold*.

Daniel identified the kingdoms represented by the silver upper torso and the belly and thighs of brass after Nebuchadnezzar died, when his grandson sat upon his throne.

[270] Jeremiah 27:6
[271] Daniel 2:31-33, 41-43
[272] Daniel 2:37-38

Persia Receives the Kingdom

The kingdom to succeed Babylon was to begin as a combined kingdom consisting of Media and Persia,[273] which would become the Persian Empire. The image of a ram that had two horns was used to represent this kingdom to Daniel. The horn that came up last grew higher and dominated the kingdom. These are the two kings of the Empire who received the dominion after Babylon lost it: Darius the Mede, the king of Media; and Cyrus, the king of Persia. Darius came up first, and he was the elder of the two.[274] He was uncle to Cyrus. Cyrus became the larger of the two horns and ruled the Empire called Persia.

Darius the Mede was "made king over the realm of the Chaldeans,"[275] but Cyrus was the ruler of the Empire.[276] God's preference for Cyrus is remarkable. Isaiah spoke of him more than 100 years before:

> That saith of Cyrus, He is my shepherd, and shall perform all my pleasure: even saying to Jerusalem, Thou shalt be built; and to the Temple, Thy foundation shall be laid.
>
> Thus saith the LORD to his anointed, to Cyrus, whose right hand I have holden, to subdue nations before him; and I will loose the loins of kings, to open before him the two leaved gates; and the gates shall not be shut;
>
> I will go before thee, and make the crooked places straight: I will break in pieces the gates of brass, and cut in sunder the bars of iron:
>
> And I will give thee the treasures of darkness, and hidden riches of secret places, that thou mayest know that I, the LORD, which call thee by thy name, am the God of Israel.

---

[273] Daniel 8:20
[274] Daniel 5:31
[275] Daniel 9:1
[276] Daniel 1:21; 6:28; 10:1

> For Jacob my servant's sake, and Israel mine elect, I
> have even called thee by thy name: I have surnamed thee,
> though thou hast not known me. —Isaiah 44:28; 45:1-4

Isaiah prophesied that Cyrus would decree Jerusalem to be rebuilt and the foundation of the Temple to be laid and Cyrus did exactly that.[277]

God called Cyrus "My shepherd." He had called Nebuchadnezzar "My servant." When God took the dominion from Babylon, He gave it to His shepherd, Cyrus. Thus far, God has had someone connected directly to Him to whom to give the dominion. Like Nebuchadnezzar, Cyrus extolled the mighty God.[278] Consider his statement below:

> Now in the first year of Cyrus king of Persia, that the
> word of the LORD by the mouth of Jeremiah might be
> fulfilled, the LORD stirred up the spirit of Cyrus king
> of Persia, that he made a proclamation throughout all
> his kingdom, and put it also in writing, saying,
>
> Thus saith Cyrus king of Persia, The LORD God of
> heaven hath given me all the kingdoms of the earth;
> and he hath charged me to build him an house at
> Jerusalem, which is in Judah.
>
> Who is there among you of all his people? his God be
> with him, and let him go up to Jerusalem, which is in
> Judah, and build the house of the LORD God of Israel,
> (he is the God,) which is in Jerusalem.
>
> And whosoever remaineth in any place where he
> sojourneth, let the men of his place help him with
> silver, and with gold, and with goods, and with beasts,
> beside the freewill offering for the house of God that
> is in Jerusalem. —Ezra 1:1-4

Cyrus declared God had given him the kingdoms of the earth. In homage, he ordered the rebuilding of Jerusalem and the Temple.

---

[277] Ezra 1:1; 3:10
[278] Ezra 1:1-4

Persia held the dominion through several successive kings: Cyrus, Cambyses, Smerdis, Darius I, Xerxes, Artaxerxes, Xerxes II, Darius II, Tissaphernes, Artaxerxes II, Mausolus, Artaxerxes III, and then Darius III. Most of these were evil men. Remember that many of Judah's kings also did evil, and yet God gave considerable latitude to these rulers until their "sins . . . reached unto heaven."[279]

God names only three of the first six Persian rulers: Cyrus, Darius, and Artaxerxes. Cyrus initiated the return of the Jews to their homeland, and each of the other two recognized by God is noteworthy for having furthered the decree of Cyrus to build and restore Jerusalem.[280]

The Empire degenerated until God moved to take the dominion away from Persia and pass it off to another king, and another kingdom.

Greece Receives the Kingdom

Daniel identified the name of the third kingdom represented in Nebuchadnezzar's dream but did not acknowledge the name of its founding king, a significant departure from the pattern set before.

He named Babylon and its founding ruler, Nebuchadnezzar. He called Nebuchadnezzar "My servant." He named the succeeding kingdoms, Media and Persia, and their respective founding rulers, Darius and Cyrus. He identified Cyrus as "My shepherd." He identified Greece as the kingdom to succeed Persia.[281] But He did not name its first ruler, nor call him His servant or shepherd.

Daniel describes the first ruler of the third kingdom so that no one can mistake him for any other than Alexander

[279] Revelation 18:5
[280] Ezra 6:14
[281] Daniel 8:21

the Great.[282] Nonetheless, the fact that the prophet neither names this ruler nor refers to him as God's servant signifies an important change in the status of the dominion.

Alexander did not acknowledge the God of Israel as both Nebuchadnezzar and Cyrus had done before him. Those men, both servants of the Most High God, extolled the God of heaven with profuse praise.

Josephus relates the legend of Alexander's dream. The renowned conqueror saw a priest, adorned in the fashion used by Jewish High Priests at that time, who said to Alexander that he would give him "dominion over the Persians."[283]

According to Josephus, Alexander commanded Jaddua, who was the High Priest in Jerusalem at that time, to break his alliance with Darius the Persian and align under him. Jaddua refused! Alexander was furious and sent word that he intended to come to Jerusalem and deal with him. The High Priest, fearful for himself, his family, and his people, sought the LORD. In a dream, God instructed him to present himself to Alexander in his priestly regalia, with all others in the company dressed in white. They obeyed. When Alexander recognized the attire of the High Priest from his dream, he accepted it as a sign his dream would be fulfilled; Persia would fall under his power.

As the story goes, Alexander entered Jerusalem and

---

[282] See Daniel's description given in Daniel 8:5-8, 21-22. First, Daniel tells us the ram represents Media-Persia, and the he-goat represents Greece (Daniel 8:20-21). The great horn of the he-goat is the first king of Greece, as a world Empire, and that is Alexander. The horn is broken, and four horns rise up in its place, which Daniel said means the first ruler will be cut off and his kingdom will be divided into four parts. This is exactly what happened with Alexander and his kingdom.

[283] Josephus, Flavius, *The New Complete Works Of Josephus,* translated by William Whiston, with commentary by Paul L. Maier, Grand Rapids, MI, Kregel Publications, 1999, pp. 382-386, see specifically 11.8.5 (Book 11, chapter 8, paragraph 5).

sacrificed at the Temple. The prophecy concerning him from the book of Daniel was read to him, which pleased him well, and he treated the Jews with favor. Soon after Alexander left Jerusalem, he engaged and decisively defeated the full army of Darius the Persian. From there, Alexander went on to conquer the world.

We see the principles mentioned above at work here, but with some changes that make a difference. When Alexander met the person of his dream, he thought it proper to "adore . . . that God who . . . honored him with his high priesthood."[284] But Alexander identified himself as the son of Zeus. Zeus was the Egyptian sun god, Ammon (a.k.a., Ammon-Ra), made famous in Macedonia by a poet named Pindar.[285] Called Zeus-Ammon, he was regarded by virtually all pagans as the supreme God of the world. Christians identify him with the god of this world,[286] that is, Satan.

True! After Alexander's encounter with the Jews in Jerusalem, he did homage to their God. But only a few years later he went into Egypt, visited the "oracle of Ammon," and was officially declared to be the son of Zeus-Ammon—the Master of the Universe.[287] Alexander never extolled the GOD of Heaven as the absolute Sovereign over all kingdoms of the world.

When Alexander took into his power every known kingdom of the world, he decided to establish his throne in

---

[284] Josephus, p. 386; 11.8.5 (333).

[285] Livius, *Livius.org*, Alexander 2.8, https://www.livius.org/articles/person/alexander-the-great/alexander-2.8/.

[286] II Corinthians 4:4

[287] Ancient History Encyclopedia, *Alexander the Great Timeline,* https://www.ancient.eu/timeline/Alexander_the_Great/. (The dates used in this timeline are a matter of dispute between historians. But what it does show is the correct order of the key events in the life of Alexander. He visited Egypt after he conquered the Persians.)

Babylon, where he died. There are several accounts of his death, the most recent suggesting that he died of typhoid fever, which, it is believed, was common in Babylon then. Daniel's prophecy foretold the death of Alexander:

> Therefore the he goat waxed very great: and when he was strong, the great horn was broken; and for it came up four notable ones toward the four winds of heaven.
> —Daniel 8:8

The sense is that when the *notable horn* (the symbol for Alexander in Daniel's vision) became great, at the zenith of his strength, God destroyed him.

Nebuchadnezzar and Cyrus could be called servants of the Most High God, recognized by each as the God of Israel. But Alexander was a servant of the Egyptian sun god, Ammon-Ra, that is, Satan. Alexander's token reverence for the God of Israel when he sacrificed on the altar in Jerusalem notwithstanding, in the end, he chose instead to be a god.

By this time in history, God did not have a servant or a shepherd under Him to whom He would give the dominion. The entire world came under the power of a man who called himself the son of Zeus—the son of Satan. Satan finally succeeded at taking into his power all the kingdoms of the earth.

Conclusion

Alexander died. As Daniel put it, the great horn was broken, and four horns arose in its place.[288] After a struggle between his generals over succession, the empire was divided into four kingdoms. Daniel's prophecy focuses on two: the northern and the southern kingdoms. The southern kingdom, Egypt, was called the Ptolemaic. Assyria was the

---

[288] Daniel 8:8

northern kingdom ruled by the Seleucids. Egypt and Assyria were the dominant warring factions of the divided empire until the ascendancy of Rome. Most historians reckon the Roman Empire began when Augustus Caesar was declared Emperor in 27 B.C., about 300 years after the death of Alexander.

This brings us to the beginning of the fourth kingdom, represented by the legs of iron and the feet and toes of iron mixed with miry clay in Nebuchadnezzar's dream.[289]

~

---

[289] Daniel 2:32-33, 41-43

Chapter Eight

The History of God's War
(Part Three)

The Transfer of the Kingdom From Alexander to Christ — Is Rome the Fourth Kingdom?

N EBUCHADNEZZAR, GOD'S SERVANT, was the first Gentile king to receive the dominion after God removed it from Israel. God gave Nebuchadnezzar a dream, and in the dream, the king saw an image. Its head was gold, its upper torso was silver, its belly and thighs were brass, its legs were iron, and its feet and toes were iron mixed with miry clay.[290] At the end of the dream, Nebuchadnezzar saw a stone fall from Heaven upon the feet of the image, crush it all to powder, then grow to become a mighty mountain. Daniel explained that the dream depicted the transfer of the dominion in a succession of world empires to the coming of the everlasting Kingdom.

We have considered the first three of these successions of the dominion: from Israel to Babylon, from Babylon to Persia, and then from Persia to Greece. Now we will consider the mysterious way the dominion passes from the third to the fourth kingdom.

The Fourth Kingdom

Naturally, most recognize Rome as Daniel's fourth kingdom. But it's not that simple. Indeed, the fourth transfer of the dominion is very mysterious and a proper

---

[290] Daniel 2:32-34, 37-45

understanding of how this transfer takes place brings us to the main point of this book.

As I said, Daniel's prophecy of the fourth kingdom is very different from the first three; indeed, it is very mysterious. Let's begin by examining what we learn about this fourth kingdom from Daniel's interpretation of the fourth section of the dream image.

Insights into the Nature of the Fourth Kingdom from Nebuchadnezzar's Dream Image—Daniel 2

First, as depicted in the dream of Nebuchadnezzar, the fourth kingdom continues to the end, when the "stone cut without hands" falls upon the feet, destroys all the kingdoms of the earth, and grows into a world-wide empire ruled by Messiah. The realm we identify with the fourth section of the dream image continues to the end.

The Roman Empire began in 27 B.C. when Octavian was called Augustus Caesar and declared to be Emperor, according to consensus. It ended in c.AD 476 when the Germanic prince, Odovacar, conquered Rome and was named the king of Italy.[291] But the fourth kingdom of Daniel's prophecy has not ended, proving the Roman Empire cannot be the fourth kingdom.

Second, the fourth kingdom passes through three distinct phases of development: the iron legs, the feet of iron mixed with miry clay, and then the ten toes. In the first stage (iron legs), it is strong. In the second (feet), it is divided and weakened by the presence of the "miry clay" mixed with the iron, and so it is partly strong and partly weak. In the

---

[291] Some theorize the continuation of the rule of Rome through the "Holy Roman Catholic Church" in the phase during which it is partly strong and partly weak. There is some merit to this theory, but I shall show that while this is Satan's effort to keep the kingdoms under his power, it is not "the kingdom" of God on Earth today.

third and final stage (the ten toes), it continues in its divided and weakened condition ruled by a coalition of ten kings.

The king that is the subject of Daniel's prophecies, identified as little horn (a.k.a., the Antichrist), does not appear until the end of the fourth kingdom. The first king is identified clearly in each of the preceding kingdoms. But with the fourth kingdom, the attention is focused on the last king of the kingdom. And the last king of the fourth kingdom is the infamous Antichrist—the much-anticipated end time world ruler Christians have been talking about for two millennia.

Third, Daniel gives far more attention to the fourth kingdom of Nebuchadnezzar's dream than to the first three, insinuating its unusual character in his interpretation. For example, Daniel identifies the ten toes as ten kings that rule the fourth kingdom at the time of its end. Also, he speaks of a very mysterious effort on the part of these kings to "mingle themselves with the seed of men."[292] At this time the LORD of glory comes and destroys all the kingdoms represented in Nebuchadnezzar's dream.[293]

Further insight into the mysterious nature of the fourth kingdom is given in Daniel's visions recorded in Daniel 7-11. One insight of special interest to us is that we are now living in the fourth kingdom.

Insights into the Nature of the Fourth Kingdom from Daniel's Visions of the Four Beasts—Daniel 7

Daniel's Four Beasts Represent the Four Kingdoms of Nebuchadnezzar's Dream Image.[294]

---

[292] Daniel 2:43
[293] Daniel 2:44-45
[294] Daniel 7

Daniel depicts the four kingdoms of Nebuchadnezzar's dream image as they will appear when little horn (the Antichrist) rises to power. Little horn rises to power at the end of the fourth kingdom.[295] The four beasts, therefore, represent the four kingdoms as they will appear at the time of the end.

Daniel tells us the fourth beast will be destroyed, and when that happens, he said the other three would have "their dominion taken away: yet their lives [would be] prolonged." That tells us all four of these kingdoms are contemporary with one another."[296] He says the four beasts are "four kings, which shall arise out of the earth" and will be present together on the earth at the arrival of the Antichrist.[297]

The first three beasts represent national powers corresponding to the first three sections of Nebuchadnezzar's dream image, but Daniel does not call them kingdoms. He uses the word *kingdom* only for the fourth beast: "the fourth beast shall be the fourth kingdom upon earth." In other words, the fourth beast is the fourth kingdom to receive the dominion in succession from Babylon, which identifies the fourth beast as the fourth section of Nebuchadnezzar's dream image. And it helps us understand that the first three correspond to the first three sections of that prophetic dream image.

Daniel uses earthly creatures to describe the first three beasts in his visions but does not use any worldly creature to portray the fourth.

The combination of a lion and the wings of an eagle is

---

[295] Daniel 7:1-8, 10-14
[296] Daniel 7:11-12
[297] Daniel 7:17; 20-22

used to describe the first beast. Pretty weird! The second beast, a bear, raised on one side with three talking ribs in its mouth, is the most natural of these bizarre beasts. Consider the third, for example, a leopard with four heads and four wings of a fowl.[298] But strange as these creatures are, apparently no earthly creature or combination of creatures exist that could represent the fourth kingdom. That's because the fourth kingdom is unique, different—otherworldly.

Daniel describes the fourth beast in a manner that sets it apart from the first three.

Daniel describes the fourth beast as "dreadful and terrible, and strong exceedingly," with "great iron teeth," with "ten horns,"[299] "diverse from all the others," with "nails of brass," that "devoured and brake[300] in pieces, and stamped the residue with his feet."[301]

Daniel says that while each of these beasts is "diverse from one another,"[302] the fourth beast is "diverse from all the beasts that were before it; and it had ten horns."[303]

The fourth beast corresponds to the end of the fourth section of Nebuchadnezzar's dream image, not the beginning.

The ten horns correspond to the ten toes of Nebuchadnezzar's dream image, which means the fourth beast coincides with the end of this present world.[304] Daniel

---

[298] Daniel 7:1-8

[299] Daniel 7:7

[300] *Brake* is an archaic form of *break*. Webster's American Dictionary of the English Language, — Brake, indicates it is the participle passive of *break,* and that in 1828 it was already obsolete. The 1913 edition of Webster's indicates it as the imperative of *break.*

[301] Daniel 7:19

[302] Daniel 7:3

[303] Daniel 7:19, see also Daniel 7:7

[304] Daniel 7:22

said the fourth beast represents both a kingdom that rises out of the sea[305] and a king that shall arise out of the earth.[306] The king that is represented by the fourth beast does not appear at the beginning of the fourth kingdom, which starts with the iron legs of Nebuchadnezzar's dream image. Nor does this king rise at the time of the feet. The fourth beast-king appears at the time of the ten toes—at the very end of the prophecy, which adds to the mysterious nature of this fourth kingdom.

<u>The fourth beast with ten horns marks the time little horn will appear on the earth to begin his prophesied career.</u>

Daniel's focus was on a ruler that appeared in his visions as a *little horn* that subdued three horns of the ten-horned beast:[307]

> Then I would know the truth of the fourth beast, which was diverse from all the others, exceeding dreadful, whose teeth were of iron, and his nails of brass; which devoured, brake in pieces, and stamped the residue with his feet;
> And of the ten horns that were in his head, and of the other which came up, and before whom three fell; even of that horn that had eyes, and a mouth that spake very great things, whose look was more stout than his fellows.
> I beheld, and the same horn made war with the saints, and prevailed against them;
> Until the Ancient of days came, and judgment was given to the saints of the most High; and the time came that the saints possessed the kingdom.
> —Daniel 7:19-22

Let's contemplate what the above insights contribute to our understanding of the mystery of the fourth kingdom.

The Mystery of the Fourth Kingdom

---

[305] Daniel 7:3
[306] Daniel 7:17
[307] Daniel 7:7-14

The Spirit of prophecy[308] revealed to Daniel the order of God's transfer of the dominion (a.k.a. *the kingdom*) from Israel to four successive kingdoms until the coming of Christ to the earth. The first three transfers are very straightforward. It was taken from Israel and given to Babylon, then from Babylon to Persia, and from Persia to Greece. Daniel identifies the first king of these three kingdoms, and the name of each kingdom is stated expressly: Nebuchadnezzar's Babylon, Cyrus' Persia, and Alexander's Greece.

Something strange happened at the time Greece received the dominion. The Spirit of prophecy identified Nebuchadnezzar as the first king of the first kingdom and called him "My servant." He identified the first king of the second kingdom by name, Cyrus, and called him "My shepherd." He did not name the first king of the third kingdom—that's the first anomaly. And although He described him so that his identity is unmistakable—Alexander the Great—He does not refer to Alexander either as "My servant," or "My shepherd." As pointed out above, Alexander self-identified as the "son of Zeus-Ammon"— the son of Satan. And that's the second anomaly of the third kingdom.

Then we come to the fourth kingdom. Of course, it begins after the third kingdom ends. But the Bible does not provide any clear historical event by which we can identify when the third kingdom ends, and the fourth one begins. It is a challenge to figure out precisely when the third kingdom ended, and the fourth began.

Is Rome the Fourth Kingdom?

---

[308] See Revelation 19:10

Most Bible students identify Rome as the fourth kingdom and historically speaking, Rome is the fourth world Empire to rise upon the earth after Babylon. But there are four good reasons to challenge this assumption. First, God does not call it Rome. Second, the prophets do not provide any way to identify the first king of this fourth kingdom. Third, all the attention of prophecy is on the last king of the fourth kingdom, which, as was pointed out above, is a clear break from the pattern set for the first three. And then, fourth, historians disagree over when the Roman Empire began.[309]

The city of Rome was founded in c.753 B.C., about 200 years before Daniel received this prophecy. Daniel could have identified the fourth kingdom with Rome. But he didn't. Perhaps the reason Daniel did not identify the fourth kingdom as Rome is because it is not Rome.

Let's examine the theory that Rome is the fourth kingdom. What you are going to learn will astound you. The fact is, Jesus is the only rightful King of the fourth kingdom. Intrigued? Good! Read on!

The New Testament Perspective

The most agreed to date for the beginning of the Roman Empire is 27 B.C., when Octavian came to power under the title Augustus Caesar. And yet well over fifty years later, the perception of the early Church was that the world was Jew and Greek. At least four times in the New Testament, the Apostle Paul, a Roman citizen, speaks of the world as made up of Jews and Greeks—the word *Greek* had by that time become a metonym for Gentile. Not Jews and Rome, or Jews and Romans, but Jew and Greek. Greece continued to figure dominantly in the world view of early Christians.

---

[309] For a brief study on dating the beginning of the fourth kingdom, see Appendix: Dating The Beginning of Rome.

From the Perspective of Prophecy

From a prophetic perspective, the fourth kingdom appears to begin with the fourth beast. Daniel identifies the fourth kingdom with the fourth beast that rises at the time the Antichrist comes to power, and we know that does not occur until the time leading to the end of the world.

And yet, according to Daniel's interpretation of the dream image of Nebuchadnezzar, the fourth kingdom begins with the legs of iron, not with the feet and ten toes.

The observations offered above are by no means definitive proofs against the theory that Rome is the fourth kingdom. But they do show that the fourth kingdom is difficult to ascertain. It's mysterious! Now, how about some proof?

Proof that Rome is not the fourth kingdom

There is no doubt that the Roman Empire was the fourth world empire, beginning with Babylon, followed by Persia, Greece, and then Rome. However, there are three mysterious things about the fourth kingdom that convince me it is not Rome.

First, the fourth kingdom continues to the end of the world. The end has not yet come, but the Roman Empire ended over 1,500 years ago. Those who believe Rome is the prophesied fourth kingdom get around this problem by saying the Roman Empire continued in a mystery form as the Roman Catholic Church. The idea is that there will be a revival of the Roman Empire.

The fourth kingdom is certainly mysterious. And there is merit to the expectation that Rome will ascend to a position of global dominance. However, while John received a prophecy about Rome recorded in Revelation 17, which supports this expectation, the same prophecy proves Rome is not the fourth kingdom of Daniel's visions.

We know the fourth beast is the fourth kingdom.[310] We know the blasphemy of little horn[311] initiates the end of the fourth kingdom.[312] We know that when this happens, the other three kings represented by Daniel's first three beasts lose their dominion, but their lives are prolonged.[313] According to Revelation, this will be followed by the rise of the scarlet-colored beast from the bottomless pit. A woman rides the beast.[314] She has a name written on her forehead: "Mystery, Babylon the Great, the mother of harlots and abominations of the earth."[315] However, the woman that rides the beast is not the beast. And it is the woman that is identified as Rome, not the beast.[316] The beast she rides is only partially and then tenuously connected with that city.[317] The fact is, the ten horns (kings) on this beast will turn on her, that is, on Rome, and destroy her.[318]

Rome certainly factors into the prophecies concerning the end of the world, but Rome is not the fourth kingdom.

Second, add to the above the fact that Daniel named each of the first three kingdoms but did not name the fourth. Daniel did not so much as identify it with the Latin people in Daniel's day that would become Rome.

This is an important observation. From the perspective of faith in the inspiration of the Scripture, we must wonder

---

[310] Daniel 7:23
[311] Daniel 7:11
[312] Daniel 7:26
[313] Daniel 7:12
[314] Revelation 17:1-6
[315] Revelation 17:5
[316] Revelation 17:18
[317] Revelation 17:9-10
[318] Revelation 17:12, 16-18

why God did not name the fourth kingdom. I'll give you the answer to that question now, and we will elaborate on it later.

During the first two phases of the fourth kingdom, King Jesus moves *the dominion* from one nation to another. He stipulated the criteria He would use when He rebuked the Jews who had rejected His offer for them to receive it.[319] He said it would be given to the nation that brings forth the fruit of the kingdom.[320] The fruit Christ seeks is repentance toward God and faith in Him. The evidence of this fruit is acknowledgment that Christ is Lord and surrender to His righteousness in the exercise of judgment, and justice. Jesus said *the dominion* would move from one nation to the next depending on what nation brought forth the fruit of it. Because it moves around, no single nation could be named as the *fourth kingdom.*

Third, finally, other world powers have risen since the fall of Rome that would qualify as possessing the kingdom. Usually, these powers are argued to be extensions of Rome. Great Britain is one example. But Britain had an uncomfortable relationship with Rome—on again, off again, and mostly, in the end, off. Indeed, the tenuous relationship between Great Britain and Rome supports the idea that Britain was at one time identifiable with the fourth kingdom, but not with Rome.

The effort to connect America to Rome is popular, but in truth, the effort proves more problematic than connecting Rome with Britain. In the early days of America, Rome was anathema to most of the population. Before Kennedy, America would never accept a Catholic president. Moses'

---

[319] Matthew 23:37
[320] Matthew 21:43

Law and Christ's Gospel had more to do with the founding of America than did any memory of the Roman Republic.

This is not to say there are no Roman influences discernible in our laws or traditions. But those who say America is an extension of the Roman Republic cannot be taken seriously, at least not if the history of our founding is rightly understood. This nation was founded on the Bible, and not on Cicero.[321]

Conclusion

In the next chapter, I shall continue our discussion of the mystery of the fourth kingdom by clarifying the intriguing role played by angels and devils in God's War!

~

---

[321] Morris, Benjamin, F., *The Christian Life and Character of the Civil Institutions of the United States,* American Vision, Powder Springs, GA, 2008. www.AmericanVision.org. This is an excellent, thoroughly documented resource showing the Christian roots of America's founding. Another very helpful resource is *What Hath God Wrought: A Biblical Interpretation of American History,* by Dr. William P. Grady, Grady Publications, Inc. Schererville, IN, 1996.

Chapter Nine

The History of God's War
(Part Four)

The Transfer of the Kingdom to Christ & the
Mystery of the Fourth Kingdom—Angels & Devils

ONCE YOU KNOW the role of angels in the affairs of men, you will be prepared to understand the mystery of the fourth kingdom. Daniel provides a window into the spirit realm in his prophecy at chapter 10. You are going to be amazed!

Daniel Opens a Window Into the Spiritual Dimension of God's War.

The word *dimension* is misused today, I think.[322] I'm using it here to signify the space in the physical universe that is occupied by spiritual entities. That these entities exist is well attested, although our senses do not generally perceive them. Spiritual entities are incorporeal, that is,

---

[322] Alternate realities are figures of imagination that do not exist in the *real* world; and by *real,* I mean what has existence in God's creation. Notions such as multiple realities, or parallel universes, are playful fancies that, when taken seriously, distort perception. Take, for example, the mystical view of time and space that is the basis for so many fantasies today: time travel being the most popular. Time is an abstract arising from the existence of matter and motion. We notice that there is no mention of God "creating" time, or space, in the creation account (Genesis 1-2). That is because time and space are aspects of physical reality that came into being with the creation of matter and the movement of matter. They are measurements of matter and motion, and have no existence independent to these *things*. Space is a finite feature of the physical universe, created by the existence of any *thing* that has dimensional qualities—any measurable extent such as length, breadth, or height. Time is the measurement of the movement of a thing relative to other things, or any sequence of events.

they are without a physical body, at least in their natural state. What is vital to our present discussion is this: angels are powerful spiritual beings that exist in the same physical universe with us. They carry out their duties in this world, and sometimes they manifest and engage with us as corporeal beings.[323] The Bible tells us God has appointed His angels to be ministering spirits "sent forth to minister for them who shall be heirs of salvation."[324] He also warns us about fallen angels, called devils, and seducing spirits, which work against the heirs of salvation.[325] These angels are very active in God's War.

Daniel recorded the visits he received from the angel named Gabriel.[326] During one of those visits, Gabriel[327] explained that a devil called the "prince of Persia" interfered with his efforts to answer Daniel's questions that troubled him earlier. Daniel 10 provides an astounding glimpse into the activity of angels:

> And, behold, an hand touched me, which set me upon my knees and upon the palms of my hands.
> And he said unto me, O Daniel, a man greatly beloved, understand the words that I speak unto thee, and stand upright: for unto thee am I now sent. And when he had spoken this word unto me, I stood trembling.
> Then said he unto me, Fear not, Daniel: for from the first day that thou didst set thine heart to understand, and to chasten thyself before thy God, thy words were heard, and I am come for thy words.
> But the prince of the kingdom of Persia withstood me

---

[323] Hebrews 13:2

[324] Hebrews 1:14

[325] I Peter 5:8; I Timothy 4:1; I John 4:1

[326] Daniel 8:16; 9:21

[327] Daniel does not expressly identify the angel that gave him the prophecy of Daniel 10-12, but for many good reasons we assume it is the same angel that God used to explain the first two visions (Daniel 8:16; and 9:21).

one and twenty days: but, lo, Michael, one of the chief princes, came to help me; and I remained there with the kings of Persia.

Now I am come to make thee understand what shall befall thy people in the latter days: for yet the vision is for many days.

And when he had spoken such words unto me, I set my face toward the ground, and I became dumb.

And, behold, one like the similitude of the sons of men touched my lips: then I opened my mouth, and spake, and said unto him that stood before me, O my lord, by the vision my sorrows are turned upon me, and I have retained no strength.

For how can the servant of this my lord talk with this my lord? for as for me, straightway there remained no strength in me, neither is there breath left in me.

Then there came again and touched me one like the appearance of a man, and he strengthened me,

And said, O man greatly beloved, fear not: peace be unto thee, be strong, yea, be strong. And when he had spoken unto me, I was strengthened, and said, Let my lord speak; for thou hast strengthened me.

Then said he, Knowest thou wherefore I come unto thee? and now will I return to fight with the prince of Persia: and when I am gone forth, lo, the prince of Grecia shall come.

But I will shew thee that which is noted in the scripture of truth: and there is none that holdeth with me in these things, but Michael your prince."
—Daniel 10:10-21

Gabriel mentioned three other angelic entities. The first two are "the prince of the kingdom of Persia"[328] and "Michael, one of the chief princes."[329] Later he speaks of another

---

[328] Daniel 10:13, 20
[329] Daniel 10:13, 21; 12:1; see Jude 9, and Revelation 12:7-8

prince called "the prince of Grecia."[330] (The word *prince*[331] is used here to speak of one who holds a principality, that is, a personality with power and authority in a kingdom.)

We can learn a lot about these princes from the above passage quoted from Daniel and from what the Bible reveals to us elsewhere concerning Michael.

Three Chief Princes Head the Three Companies of the Angelic Host.

Michael is called "one of the chief princes," which tells us there are other chief princes. We know of three angelic princes: Michael, Gabriel, and Lucifer. Lucifer has many names: the great dragon, that old serpent, the Devil, Satan,[332] Beelzebub,[333] and Leviathan.[334]

Speaking to Daniel, Gabriel referred to Michael as "Michael your prince."[335] Later, Gabriel refers to Michael as "the great prince which standeth for the children of thy people."[336] Michael watches over the Jewish people, the children of Abraham. If Michael stands for the children of Israel, for whom does Gabriel stand? Does Satan stand for any group?

The Bible divides the people of the earth into two major families: the Jews and the Gentiles.[337] Michael is the chief

---

[330] Daniel 10:20

[331] *Prince* translates שַׂר (*sar,* from Strong No. 8269, שׂר *sar:* "A head person (of any rank or class):—captain (that had rule), chief (captain), general, governor, keeper, lord, ((-task-)) master, prince(-ipal), ruler, steward." A *principality* is מַרְאָשָׁה, *mar-aw-shaw* (Strong No. 4761, "headship, i.e. (plural for collective) dominion:—principality."

[332] Revelation 12:9

[333] Matthew 10:25

[334] Isaiah 27:1; Psalm 74:13; 104:26; see Job 41

[335] Daniel 10:21

[336] Daniel 12:1

[337] John 7:35; Acts 14:5; Romans 2:9-10; 3:9; etc.

prince that stands for the Jews. Gabriel seems to be particularly active in the affairs of the Gentiles. For example, Gabriel is the angel sent to Daniel after God moved the dominion to the Gentile kings, and he interprets the prophecies related to the times of the Gentiles. Gabriel is the angel that announced the first coming of Christ when His mission was to bring light to the Gentiles.[338] Therefore, we may assume he is the chief prince of the Gentiles.

Jesus called Lucifer (Satan) the prince of this world,[339] the father of the lie,[340] king over all the children of pride,[341] and the father of all children of disobedience.[342] We know Lucifer was first in rank over all the angels at one time and has immense power. For example, when a dispute arose between Michael and Lucifer, Michael dared not bring a railing accusation against him, but instead declared: "The LORD rebuke thee."[343] The prince of the kingdom of Persia and the prince of Grecia are enemies of Gabriel and Michael, powerful devils that serve under the auspices of Satan at war with God's mighty angels.

Michael and Gabriel Are at War With Lucifer.

Daniel fasted 21 days.[344] When Gabriel finally appeared, he explained what took him so long:

> Then said he unto me, Fear not, Daniel: for from the first day that thou didst set thine heart to understand, and to chasten thyself before thy God, thy words were heard, and I am come for thy words.

---

[338] Isaiah 49:6; 60:3; see Luke 2:32
[339] John 12:31; 14:30; see 16:11
[340] John 8:44
[341] Job 41:34
[342] Ephesians 2:1-2; I John 3:10; Acts 13:10
[343] Jude 9; see Zechariah 3:2, where GOD establishes that His is the only power greater than Satan.
[344] Daniel 10:2-3

> But the prince of the kingdom of Persia withstood me
> one and twenty days: but, lo, Michael, one of the chief
> princes, came to help me; and I remained there with
> the kings of Persia.
>
> Now I am come to make thee understand what shall
> befall thy people in the latter days: for yet the vision
> is for many days. —Daniel 10:12-14

The prince of the kingdom of Persia must be a mighty devil if it took two of God's "chief" princes to overcome him. Is the prince of Persia Satan? Could be! But then we must wonder why he is called the prince of Grecia next? It's possible the prince of this world, Satan, takes the title that identifies him with each successive kingdom that possesses the dominion. So he is the prince of the kingdom of Persia so long as the Persians hold "the kingdom," and then he takes the title *prince of Grecia* when the dominion is moved to Greece. However, it seems more natural to understand the passage as identifying the two chief princes of God juxtaposed to the two chief princes of Satan.

Scripture warrants Satan is extraordinarily powerful, and it should not be surprising to discover his princes are too. We know that Satan took one-third of the angelic host with him into his rebellion.[345] These fallen angels operate in the world as devils, agents of the Devil, who oppose GOD

---

[345] Revelation 12:3-4 describes Satan as "another wonder in heaven . . . a great red dragon, having seven heads and ten horns, and seven crowns upon his heads." These ten horns correspond to the ten rulers that coalesce in the fourth kingdom, represented in Daniel 7 by the ten horns of the fourth beast (Daniel 7:7), thus signifying that the power of Satan takes full control of that kingdom after Little Horn rises to power. We are told the tail of this dragon "drew the third part of the stars of heaven, and did cast them to the earth" (Revelation 12:4). The *star* is used in the Revelation to symbolize angels: "The seven stars are the angels of the seven churches" (Revelation 1:20). Satan drew one-third of the angels away from God and cast them to the earth to serve him as his *devils* (Leviticus 17:7; Deuteronomy 32:17; Psalm 106:37; see Matthew 8:16, 28, 31, and etc., or *seducing spirits* (I Timothy 4:1).

and His holy angels. And they are strong. I'll explain what gives these angels and devils their power over men as we proceed.

Angels and Devils at War for Control of the Kingdom

An extraordinary insight emerges from Daniel's revelation about what goes on in the spiritual realm of this world: angels and devils war over control of the dominion.

God had taken the dominion from Babylon and given it to His shepherd, Cyrus, king of Persia. About three years into the reign of Cyrus, Gabriel came to Daniel with a message, a prophecy from the Creator that declared the end of Satan's rule on the earth. Satan did not want Daniel to receive that message. So he dispatched one of his most potent devils at that time, identified by Daniel as the prince of the kingdom of Persia, to intercept Gabriel and hinder him from getting to Daniel. This prince was able to overcome Gabriel for twenty-one days and would have continued to resist him if Michael had not come to his aid.

Gabriel explained he would continue his war against the prince of Persia, and then he would have to fight the prince of Grecia.[346]

Three years earlier, Gabriel explained, he had "stood to confirm and to strengthen" Darius the Mede. That would have been 539 B.C., the year Babylon fell to the combined powers of Darius, king of the Medes, and Cyrus, king of the Persians.[347]

Do you see it? Remember Nebuchadnezzar's dream image revealed the dominion would pass from Babylon to Persia and then to Greece. Gabriel "stood to confirm" Darius when the dominion passed from Babylon to the Medes and

---

[346] Daniel 10:20-21
[347] Daniel 11:1; see 5:30-31

the Persians. The prince of Persia was fighting against Gabriel during the kingdom of the Persians. Gabriel explained to Daniel that he would have to continue that fight, and then he would be busy warring with the prince of Grecia. We may assume angels and devils were also active during the transfer of the dominion from Israel to Babylon.[348]

Angels are commissioned by God to defend the nation that holds the dominion, the nation that is under God.[349] He also uses them to punish the nation under God when necessary.[350] We see this acted out repeatedly in the history of Israel during the time she held the dominion.

However, God had no servant, like Nebuchadnezzar, or shepherd, like Cyrus, available to Him when He was ready to move the dominion from Persia to Greece. It ended up in the hands of Alexander, a servant of Satan who styled himself the "son of Zeus." Keep this in mind—in the desert of Christ's temptation, Satan could rightly boast all the kingdoms of the world, and all the glory of them were in his power.[351] At the transfer of the dominion from Persia, God turned all the kingdoms of the world over to Satan. There was no nation *under God*.

Satan finally succeeded in getting the dominion under his power.

Conclusion

Satan seduced Israel into sin through her leaders until she lost the dominion to God's servant, Nebuchadnezzar, king of Babylon.[352] Then Satan and his devils corrupted Babylon until God took the dominion from Babylon and

---

[348] For an example, see Zechariah 3:1
[349] Judges 2:1-4; 5:23; 6:11-22; and many more
[350] II Samuel 24
[351] Luke 4:5-6
[352] Jeremiah 9:12-19; 16:10-14; 22:8-9; 40:1-4

gave it to God's shepherd, Cyrus, the king of Persia.[353] Then Satan succeeded to corrupt the kingdom of Persia through ungodly kings until God was ready to take the dominion from Persia and give it to Greece. However, by this time in history, there was no *servant* or *shepherd* to whom He would give the dominion.

For the first time in the history of God's War, there was no nation under God. The Devil had all the kingdoms of the world, and the glory of them, delivered into his hands.[354] This included the power to give the kingdoms and the glory of them to whomever he would choose. Think about this: Daniel had repeatedly declared this power belonged exclusively to GOD. Now Satan could boast that GOD had turned this power over to him.

Satan understood the portent of the prophecy of Daniel, even if he did not fully comprehend every aspect of it. He knew God had foreseen the man of sin would reign supreme over the entire Earth by Satan's power. He knew his time would come when he could freely impose his evil will over all the earth.[355] Satan had Alexander the Great entirely in his power—the self-styled "son of Zeus-Ammon," the son of Satan. But Alexander was the first ruler of the third kingdom. The prophecy spoke of a Satanically empowered ruler who would rise in the fourth kingdom, not the third. Satan was ahead of schedule. God exercised His prerogative as Sovereign and cut off Alexander suddenly, dividing his kingdom and retarding Satan's effort to unite the world into one kingdom under Satan.

Satan knew the prophecy—Antichrist would rise in

---

[353] Daniel 5:1-31; 10:1; see Isaiah 45:1-2
[354] Luke 4:5-6
[355] Daniel 11:38; 8:24-25; 12:7

the fourth kingdom—so he bided his time, holding the kingdoms of the world in his power and working to prepare for the prophesied little horn to arrive, by whom he would unite the world into one kingdom under Satan. But God was preparing the world for the arrival of another King!

When the time came to transfer the dominion from Greece to the fourth kingdom, Satan got the surprise of his life—and that takes us to the revelation of the mystery of the fourth kingdom.

~

Chapter Ten

The History of God's War
(Part Five)

The Mystery of the Fourth Kingdom—
The Arrival of the King

B EYOND THE STRANGENESS already brought forward regarding the fourth kingdom is the fact that at the time it was to appear Jesus Christ entered the world—to the shock of devils and a king of theirs named Herod!

According to consensus, the Roman Empire began in 27 B.C. when Octavian received the title Augustus Caesar, Emperor of Rome. Jesus was born in 5 B.C.

The newly formed Roman Empire barely had time to finish celebrating before their new Emperor became ill (23 B.C.). Although Octavian continued to reign until A.D. 14, by 6 B.C., he was compelled to adopt his heir apparent, Tiberius, whose full name was Tiberius Claudius Nero.[356] One year later, the promised King of kings was born into the world.

Tiberius became Emperor upon the death of his adoptive father, Augustus, in A.D. 14, when Jesus was about nineteen. Caesar Tiberius occupied the Roman throne the day Rome crucified Jesus. On that day, the rulers of the Jews chose Tiberius over Jesus, and rejected their promised Messiah.[357]

---

[356] This is not the infamous Nero who ruled from A.D. 54 to his death in A.D. 68.
[357] John 19:12

When Gabriel appeared in the humble home of Mary to declare the coming birth of Christ, did Satan take notice? Gabriel—so famous an angel, one of the chief princes of God's host—must have gotten his attention. Perhaps, Satan gave it little notice. Having defeated Gabriel and Michael, and the kingdoms of the world now securely in his power, maybe the appearance of Gabriel did no more than pique his curiosity. But you can bet the Serpent was keenly interested when the heavenly host massed over a shepherd's field near Bethlehem. And surely that interest morphed into concern when he heard them shouting, "Glory to God in the highest, on Earth peace, good will toward men." No doubt, Satan's concerns were heightened when the angel instructed the amazed shepherds to see where the child lay. Then, seeing a host of God's most formidable angels surrounding the babe, his concern grew into consternation and alarm.[358]

Devils recognized Jesus! One possessed with a devil cried out, "I know thee who thou art, the Holy One of God."[359] On another occasion, a particularly fierce devil cried: "What have we to do with thee, Jesus, thou Son of God? art thou come hither to torment us before the time?"[360] *Before the time?* Lucifer and his devils anticipated the coming of Messiah, but the Devil's own man of sin was expected first. Christ was not supposed to come until after the time of the ten toes, at the end of Nebuchadnezzar's dream—at the end of the world. From the Devil's point of view, Christ appeared *before His time.*

Devils knew Who Jesus was: the Son of God. And they knew He was prophesied one day to come and execute

---

[358] I Peter 1:12
[359] Mark 1:24
[360] Matthew 8:29

God's wrath upon them. But ironically, the devils missed the same part of the prophecy of Christ's coming that the Jews missed,[361] that even Christ's disciples missed.[362] Christ's first coming and His mission to die on the cross for the sins of mankind[363] caught them all off guard.[364] Not even the angels of God understood it, with the possible exceptions of Michael and Gabriel.[365]

I imagine the devils swirling frantic and confused, and Satan demanding the book of Daniel be brought and reexamined carefully, wondering what he had missed. Then plotting his response!

Unforeseen by Satan and his devils, it was not, however, altogether unexpected.

While Daniel served Babylon as Master of the Magi, he received a prophecy that predicted the arrival of Christ down to the year.[366] Certain Magi of the East, purported to have been alumni from the legendary school of Daniel,[367] antici-pated His birth. A star appeared in their sky at about the time the promised King was to be born. This star guided these wise men to Jerusalem, and there it inexplicably disap-peared. Assuming Herod would know about the prophecy and could direct them to the promised child, the magi sought and gained an audience with the Jewish king. The wise men asked king Herod: "Where is he that is born King of the

---

[361] Luke 19:42

[362] Luke 19:11, the disciples were included in the number of those whose mistaken notions about when the kingdom should appear was corrected by Christ's parable; and they continued to have questions about this all the way until Jesus was received up into Heaven (Acts 1:6-8).

[363] I John 2:1-2

[364] I Peter 1:12; see Psalm 22; Isaiah 53

[365] Daniel 10:21

[366] Daniel 9:24-26. For a detailed study of this amazing prophecy, get my book *The Visions of Daniel.* www.booksatdbp.com.

[367] Daniel 4:9

Jews?" And they explained, "For we have seen his star in the east and are come to worship him."[368] Unintentionally, they perturbed the dark mind of that black-hearted king with the news that a rival for his throne had been born.

Herod demanded the chief priests and scribes tell him where the prophets said the Messiah would be born. They informed the king that a prophecy in the ancient book of Micah foretold the child would be born in Bethlehem.[369] Herod called the Magi into a private conference and asked how long ago the star appeared. Learning the star first appeared about two years before, he sent them to Bethlehem, where they could hope to find the newborn King of the Jews. The Magi departed with Herod's blessing. He instructed them to send word back to him when they found the child so he too could pay Him proper homage.

Surprised that the star reappeared when they departed the palace, the Magi happily followed it to the place where Jesus, then about two-years-of-age, toddled about the feet of his mother and father. They presented their famous gifts, and went to sleep, intending the next day to inform Herod of their success. However, the Magi were warned of God in a dream to return to their home another way. They obeyed.

When Herod discovered that the Magi fled Jerusalem without informing him where he could find the child, he was furious! If there was any sincerity in Herod's expressed intention to visit the promised King, it was gone. Perhaps it occurred to him to present the scepter of David's throne, for which he was then the steward, at the feet of this promised child. A fitting complement to the gifts the other kings presented. But any such notions were throttled by

[368] Matthew 2:1-2
[369] Micah 5:2

suspicion, envy, fear, and murder. Herod was too shrewd a politician not to realize the implications of a story like this one getting out. He sent troops into Bethlehem to murder every child up to two years old.[370]

The angel of the LORD had warned Joseph to move the Child from Bethlehem to Egypt for safekeeping until God told them it was safe to return.[371]

Herod died shortly after; it would be left to Herod's successor and namesake to continue the resistance! Meanwhile, Joseph moved back into Israel and settled in Nazareth.

John the Baptist began to preach: "Repent ye: for the kingdom of Heaven is at hand."[372] John's announcement of the arrival of the "Lamb of God, which taketh away the sin of the world,"[373] might have puzzled Satan. But he understood well the implications that the Son of God, King of the Kingdom of Heaven, and heir to the kingdom of men had arrived. The Baptist's message sent shock waves throughout the kingdom of darkness.

Satan immediately went on the offensive. Vigorously defending his hold on the kingdoms of this world, he attacked the kingdom of Heaven. God's War escalated! The conflict between God's angels and Satan's devils intensified. The angels of God, with the Son of God, invaded Satan's domain and challenged his authority in the earth. Jesus said John's announcement began, "The kingdom of Heaven [suffering] violence, and the violent [taking] it by force."[374]

---

[370] Matthew 2:16-18
[371] Matthew 2
[372] Matthew 3:1-6
[373] John 1:29
[374] Matthew 11:12

Christ threatened Lucifer's power, and the Devil needed a new strategy!

As a man, Jesus was "a little lower than the angels,"[375] and vulnerable to Satan. Protected by the Holy Ghost, and heavily guarded by the mightiest of God's angels, Satan could not get to Him. So, when the Holy Ghost drove Jesus into the wilderness to be tempted by the Devil and withdrew the Heavenly guard, Satan seized his opportunity.[376]

Failing to seduce Jesus into acting independently of the Father, Satan twice offered to give Jesus all the kingdoms of the world, if only He would bow down and worship him.[377] Perhaps Satan could not kill Jesus, but maybe he could recruit him. Jesus refused the offer, and counter-offered. Satan could take his place behind the LORD where he belonged: "Get thee behind me Satan."[378] Rejecting Christ's command to get behind Him, and insulting the Son of God by repeating his vile offer, Satan was abruptly dismissed: the Son of God demanded, "Get thee hence, Satan."[379]

Did Satan know that failure on his part would bind him under Christ's power, and bar him from direct access to the Creator's Son? Jesus understood He must "bind the strong man" of the house before He could spoil it.[380] And He taught us that devils are brought under our power by prayer and fasting.[381] By prayer and fasting, Jesus bound Satan and then went on to spoil his house.

---

[375] Psalm 8:5

[376] Job was shielded by a hedge barring Satan from troubling him until God removed that hedge and allowed Satan to tempt him (Job 1:6-12; 2:1-13).

[377] There are two accounts of the temptation in the desert. One is found in Matthew 4:1-11. The other is in Luke 4:1-14. They are not parallel accounts. For insight into the significance of this, see Appendix — *The Temptation of The Christ.*

[378] Luke 4:8

[379] Matthew 4:10

[380] Matthew 12:29

[381] Matthew 17:21

Although Satan gave up attacking Jesus directly, he attempted to thwart His plan indirectly. Once, when Jesus was explaining to His disciples that He would be crucified, and be buried, and rise the third day, Satan took hold of Peter's proud heart and, through Peter, attempted to rebuke Jesus: "Be it far from thee, Lord," Peter said, "this shall not be unto thee." Looking at Peter and immediately recognizing the source of this opposition to His message, Jesus said, "Get thee behind Me, Satan."[382]

Jesus began His assault on the kingdom of darkness in this world: casting out devils and delivering men from the bondage of Satan.

When Jesus cast out devils, He declared it was nothing more than the move of God's finger. That such a small gesture from God in Heaven would command devils in the world below is power indeed. Jesus said that His demonstration of power over devils indicated that the Kingdom of God had come upon them.[383]

Jesus found a woman who had been bound by Satan for eighteen years.[384] Not all sickness was the direct consequence of Satan's activity, but much of it was and is.[385] Jesus demonstrated that the authority of the kingdom of God was present in the earth when He broke Satan's power over those he had bound. He said to the woman bound by

---

[382] Matthew 16:23
[383] The *finger* of God was evident in the powerful miracles demonstrating God's authority over Egypt to deliver His people from their oppression (Exodus 8:19). In Exodus 31:18 and Deuteronomy 9:10, we read testimony that the Law of God was written by "the finger of God," which, again, indicates the authority of the Kingdom of God among men expressed in the Law of God. The *finger of God* is an expression that communicates that the thing done is done by the authority of God. (Luke 11:20; see Exodus 8:19; 31:18; and Deuteronomy 9:10)
[384] Luke 13:16
[385] John 9:2-3

Satan, "Woman, thou art loosed from thine infirmity." And when He laid his hands on her, she was healed.

Jesus gave this power to His disciples, and they cast out devils everywhere they went and healed all manner of sickness in His name.[386]

Our Lord's open assault on Satan's *house* continued while the power of darkness was bound. But when it was time for Christ Jesus to die on the Cross to fulfill His mission, the "power of darkness"[387] was released.

Jesus directed His disciples to prepare for Passover.[388] Satan, now loosed, found easy entry into Judas, and set his mind to betray Jesus to the rulers of the Jews.[389] During the famous Last Supper, Jesus exposed Judas as the betrayer and dispatched him to work out his evil purpose.[390]

While Satan (through Judas) set the trap, Jesus led His disciples to the Mount of Olives, to a garden He often used for prayer.[391] They gathered at a familiar clearing, and the disciples began settling down. Peter, James, and John were called to follow, and they walked with Jesus some distance from the others.

Suddenly, the Father withdrew His Son's angelic guard. Satan, having returned from his evil errand, and seeing Jesus now vulnerable, swiftly leaped on Him and began clawing deep into His emotions. Christ exclaimed, "My soul is exceeding sorrowful, even unto death." Jesus bid His companions, "Watch with Me,"[392] then, looking deeply

---

[386] Luke 9:1; Matthew 10:1, 8
[387] Luke 22:53
[388] Matthew 26:17-20
[389] Matthew 26:14-16; John 12:31
[390] Matthew 26:22-24
[391] Luke 22:39
[392] Matthew 26:37-38

into the cup His Father had given Him to drink, and being deeply troubled by what He saw, He staggered off from them alone.

In the cup that shook in His trembling hand, the poisoned potion that would complete the transformation danced mockingly. It bid Him Who left the form of God to take the form of lowly man[393] to now go down from the fashion of man to the worm, the dust-eating creature of darkness.[394] This final step in the transformation of the Son of God meant He would be made "to be sin for us, who knew no sin."[395]

For the Holy One, disgust and loathing was the only appropriate response to what stirred fully fermented in that cup. He knew one day He would be called upon to drink it,[396] but now it was time to take it to His lips and, for the first time in His eternal existence, taste of sin—worse, become it!

Alone, He fell to His face, prostrate before God, and cried: "O my Father, if it be possible, let this cup pass from Me: nevertheless not as I will, but as thou wilt."[397] Silence!

His prayer became more urgent: "Abba, Father, all things are possible unto thee; take away this cup from me: nevertheless not what I will, but what thou wilt."[398] The angels that had been charged to protect the Son from so much as a stone bruise, now forbidden to attend Him, stood helpless, puzzled, chagrined, Michael and Gabriel were flummoxed—for the Father was silent.

---

[393] Philippians 2:5-7

[394] See Psalm 22:6; Isaiah 41:14; see Mark 9:44, 46, 48; Jacob is said to be a *worm* (Isaiah 41:14). Jesus spoke of those that go to hell as being where "the worm dieth not." The fallen soul of man is represented as a *worm*.

[395] II Corinthians 5:21

[396] Matthew 20:22

[397] Matthew 26:39

[398] Mark 14:36

The intensity increased yet more as Jesus strove against sin.[399] Writhing in agony, so intense sweat like great drops of blood fell from His face to the ground,[400] He cried: "Father, if thou be willing, remove this cup from Me: nevertheless not my will, but thine be done."[401]

The Father would not remove the cup. However, we know God agreed to send more than twelve legions of angels to deliver Christ if He decided not to drink from it. Later that night, when Peter drew his sword and attacked the leader of the Temple guard, Jesus said to Peter, "Thinkest thou that I cannot now pray to My Father, and He shall presently give me more than twelve legions of angels?"[402] This agreement must have been secured during his prayer vigil in the garden.

Doubtless, Jesus, and Satan too, watched as Michael and Gabriel marshaled their angelic bands. Prepared to descend on the scene, to engage all Satan's devils and deliver God's Son, the mighty angelic princes watched breathlessly for the Creator's signal to charge.

Jesus struggled to His feet and returned to where He left Peter, James, and John and found them sleeping. He reproved them: "What, could ye not watch with Me one hour?" and commanded them: "Watch and pray, that ye enter not into temptation."[403] And He warned them: "The spirit indeed is willing, but the flesh is weak."[404] Returning to where His blood had mingled with the garden dirt, He knelt, and, with resignation, He accepted the Father's terms: "O my Father, if this cup may not pass away from me, except I drink it, thy will be done."[405]

---

[399] Hebrews 12:4
[400] Luke 22:44
[401] Luke 22:42
[402] Matthew 26:53
[403] Matthew 26:40-41
[404] Matthew 26:41
[405] Matthew 26:42

Satan could see he was losing, again! Beelzebub lashed his devils into a more frenzied attack and sunk his teeth ever more deeply into Jesus' mind and heart. And with his sulfurous breath, the fiend blew the loathsome stench of the tainted cup into Jesus' face. Grappling against all this, Jesus battled to His feet and returned to His friends and caught them sleeping, again.

He felt their weakness in His own flesh and pitied them. Alone, He returned to His prayer closet, knelt, and prayed the same words again: "O my Father, if this cup may not pass away from me, except I drink it, thy will be done."[406]

At Jesus' final resolve lightning flashed in the Throne Room and a single angel was instantly dispatched and appeared at Jesus' side, restoring His strength.[407] Satan and his horde were scattered, but they regrouped! With a peace that passes understanding, Jesus returned to His sleeping friends. He understood! "Sleep on," He said, "Behold, the hour is at hand, and the Son of man is betrayed into the hands of sinners."[408]

Satan's effort to provoke Jesus to drop the cup failed. Jesus was resolved to go through with it. The Devil would alter his devilish strategy. If he could not get the cup out of Jesus' hands, he would provoke Jesus to call for the angels to attack. This would bring the world of men to an end and consign all the souls of men, including God's elect, to endure the eternal flames with him. The power of death would be his forever.

Gabriel and Michael, swords drawn, their mighty hosts in rank behind them, all stood ready. The two angelic princes kept one eye fixed on the Creator's Hand, watching for the

---

[406] Matthew 26:44
[407] Luke 22:43
[408] Matthew 26:45

signal to begin the charge, the other eye watched Satan and his devils. Anxiously, Gabriel cast a glance at Michael who looked back with fire in his eyes. The mighty host watched from the battlements of Heaven while devils lept from one to another of Christ's enemies. Desperately, they cajoled Jesus to pray the prayer that would initiate the last great battle—the torrid clash that would destroy the earth and all mankind—the Apocalypse!

It does not serve the immediate purpose of this book to detail the torture devils inflicted upon Jesus in their effort to provoke Him to initiate the ending of mankind. I will not describe the beating He endured at the hands of the High Priest and his court of Christ haters. Nor will I speak of the spittle they blew into His face or the slapping and punching inflicted upon Him. I will spare you my sketch of His trial before Pilate, who turned Him over to those ruthless Roman soldiers, experts at the scourge. My reader's distaste for violence is safe, for I will not sketch the bloody lashing laid upon Jesus by the Roman soldiers with the infamous cat-of-nine tails: nine leather straps embedded with metal to pummel and bruise, and sheep's bone to claw and rip the flesh. I'll spare your sensibilities the spectacle of Christ being given a mock crown made of thorns, and a reed to mock a scepter, or the mocking of the soldiers who knelt before this king of Jews, then took the reed and hammered the thorns into his brow.[409] Nor will I scribe upon your mind the awful sound of those children of Abraham crying, "Crucify Him, Crucify Him," on the day they chose Caesar over the promised Seed—Christ. Finally, for pity's

---

[409] We must not imagine this *reed* was limp, like a thin switch. A *reed* was used to lift a sponge full of vinegar to Jesus' lips (Mark 15:36). Although, as a scepter it would be considered ridiculous, this reed could inflict a serious wound upon the head and could have drive the thorns into the flesh of His brow.

sake, I will not etch the image of Jesus on Calvary upon the fleshly table of your heart, nailed to a cross made from a tree. Jesus was crucified. The manifold sufferings of crucifixion, by all accounts, make it by far the most disgraceful and cruel way for any human to die. So, I will offer only a few observations essential to our purpose.

First, all the humiliation and torture inflicted upon Jesus was inspired by Satan working in the hearts of the envious Jews in league with the profane and wicked Romans— murderers all. The only real hope Satan had to keep the kingdoms of the world in his power was to stop Christ, the Lamb of God, from drinking the cup. Once Jesus drank the cup, and cried from the Cross, "It is finished" . . . Satan was finished. The grave could not hold Jesus because He had never sinned. And God accepted Christ's death as payment in full against the "wages of sin."[410] Breaking the power of death, Jesus released all mankind from the power of Satan, and all who will do so may call on Jesus' name and be saved from the wrath to come.

And so, we have completed the first full lap in our story, and we are back where we began. Jesus arose from the grave and declared: "All power is given unto me in heaven and in earth." God officially transferred to Jesus all the kingdoms of the world and the glory of them. Jesus is the King, and all men are His subjects.

Rather than set up His throne on the earth, He left His goods to the care of His servants. He went into Heaven to receive another kingdom—the eternal kingdom that will commence when He returns. These things will be explored in the pages to follow.

---

[410] Romans 6:23

Conclusion

What is the *mystery* (secret, puzzle, enigma) of the fourth kingdom? At the end of the third kingdom, when the fourth kingdom was expected to begin, God intervened and put Daniel's prophecy on hold. The Satan empowered end-time world ruler whose evil would precipitate the destruction of all the kingdoms of the world was expected to follow the end of the third kingdom. However, to the Devil's chagrin and the surprise of his devils, God sent His Son to deliver the kingdom of man from the power of Satan.

Jesus is King of Heaven and Earth. And all mankind, including kings and all in authority, are commanded to repent and believe on Him. Believing on Him involves confessing that Jesus Christ is Lord—that is, Jesus is the King and all mankind are His subjects.

In the next chapter, I'll conclude my overview of the history of God's War. I'll explain our current warfare over the kingdom of God, and this will include a peek into the future of God's War.

~

Chapter Eleven

The History of God's War
(Part Six)
Conclusion—The Present Status and Future of God's War

THE CURRENT STATUS and the future of God's War are briefly overviewed in this chapter. It serves as a preface for our in-depth examination of the critical part Christians play in national and international politics, in the shaping of culture and world events.

The Present Status of God's War

As explained in chapter two (<u>The Mystery of Iniquity</u>), Jesus conquered Satan, cast him out and took the dominion back into His power. He left His churches in the world guided by His Holy Spirit to occupy until He returned. As Ambassadors of Christ, we are sent into the world to declare the terms of surrender to the conquering King. The terms of surrender demand all men repent, confess with their mouth the LORD JESUS, and believe in their heart that God has raised Him from the dead, "and thou shalt be saved."[411]

However, Satan managed to reintroduce his influence into the affairs of this world through the children of disobedience.[412] These are the *citizens* Jesus prophesied would send word after Him while He is away in Heaven, saying, "We will not have this man to reign over us."[413] This is

---

[411] Romans 10:9-13
[412] Ephesians 2:1-2
[413] Luke 19:14, 27; see Psalm 2

going on right now in God's War—in America, and all over the world.

Satan attempts to neutralize Christ's authority in the earth so he can regain the kingdoms under his power. At this point in God's War, Satan has lost his power in the world—a major setback for the kingdom of darkness. Satan is back where he was before the third kingdom, working to corrupt God's people and trying to get the dominion back under his control. However, his strategy is a little different.

When Israel had the kingdom, the Tabernacle of Moses was God's House. He dwelt with His people in the Holy Place of the Temple, upon the Mercy Seat, behind the great veil.[414]

Today, the House of God is the Church of the living God, which is the pillar and ground of the truth.[415] The body of the believer is the Temple in God's *House*;[416] and the heart is the Holy of Holies.[417] The priesthood of Aaron has given way to the greater priesthood of Christ, which is after the order of Melchizedek.[418] Today, like Melchizedek, every believer is a priest and a king unto God.[419] Jesus' strategy today is for His Spirit to move into the world through His priests. This is what He had in mind when He talked about His Spirit moving through our belly like rivers of living water.[420] In this way, Jesus extends His kingdom's authority into the earth, working the will of God among men.

---

[414] I Samuel 4:4; 6:2; II Kings 19:15; I Chronicles 13:6; Psalm 80:1; 99:1; Isaiah 37:16

[415] I Timothy 3:15

[416] I Corinthians 6:19-20

[417] Ephesians 3:17; Colossians 3:16

[418] To whom Abraham paid tithes (Genesis 14:20); the significance of which is touched on in Hebrews 7:4: it means the priesthood of Melchizedek is greater than that of Levi. Note that Melchizedek was both a priest and a king.

[419] Revelation 1:6; I Peter 2:5

[420] John 7:38-39

Jesus went to Heaven and entrusted His Church to carry out His work on Earth in His absence. He sent His Holy Spirit to empower the churches for their work. Therefore, Satan specifically targets Christ's priests and His churches. He attempts to destroy them from within by corrupting their hearts, and from without by opposition from unbelievers.

From within, Satan attacks through false teachers who lead Christians astray.[421] Satan attempts to get Christians to believe the world is still his, that Satan is the one in control right now, that Jesus Christ, King of the world, has not yet come. It's a devious seduction: *Jesus will come; He will rule someday, but not today.* Christians who adopt this belief are effectively denying that Christ has come in the flesh. According to the Bible, this doctrine comes from the spirit of Antichrist.

The denial that Jesus Christ has come in the flesh can take on various manifestations. But the bottom line is Satan wants men to believe he is in control of the earth, not Jesus. To the extent he has convinced Christians of this, he has brought them under the influence of the spirit of Antichrist.

From without, Satan attacks through the children of disobedience. He raises leaders in nations who will favor laws that prohibit the preaching of the Gospel. He attempts to interfere with any declaration of the truths of Scripture. Satan is behind the current trend to categorize—and criminalize—what the Bible says as hate speech. Everywhere Satan is given place, he uses it to turn the coercive power of government against God and His Son, Jesus Christ. This is the work of the spirit of Antichrist.

The idea that the world belongs to Satan and that we Christians need only to bide our time, waiting for the LORD

---

[421] II Peter 2:1

to return, plays directly into Satan's hands. Of course, we look for the return of our Lord. However, the truth is our Lord is now King of the earth, and all mankind are His subjects. We are sent by Him to declare the terms of surrender to the conquering King, lest they face the wrath of God when Christ returns.

The fact is, no nation, no ruler, no government, has any legitimate power to deny any Christian the right to preach the Gospel or declare the truth.

All governments are under Christ—whether they submit to Him is another matter. Jesus Christ has sent His Spirit into the world, and the Spirit of Jesus Christ is greater than the spirit of Antichrist. If Christians will obey Christ's instructions, they can pull down every stronghold established by Satan in this world. They can scatter the power of the Antichrist spirit, remove the children of disobedience from controlling the governments in this present evil world, and hold the kingdom (a.k.a. *the dominion*) as stewards of Christ until He returns. This is because Jesus gave the keys of the kingdom to His Church. Furthermore, any nation that brings forth the fruit of repentance and faith in Jesus Christ will be given the dominion (a.k.a. *the kingdom*) to hold until He returns, so long as they abide faithful.[422]

Satan resists Christ! He works to stop our LORD from exerting His authority in the world through the children of obedience. He mobilizes his devils, and the children of disobedience under their power, to fight against the children of obedience. The children of disobedience, under the influence of the spirit of Antichrist, marginalize Christians and try to bar them from influencing culture, whether in education, in politics, or science.

---

[422] Matthew 21:43

The spirit of Antichrist is rising. We have witnessed a disturbing increase in satanic power and influence in America, especially in California. Feinstein attempted to disqualify Justice Kavanaugh from sitting on the Supreme Court because of his faith. Christians have suffered passive persecution for many decades in America, but lately, it's occurring with increasing frequency and hostility.

We are at war! Our part in this war is the focus of the rest of the book. I will conclude my overview of the history of God's War with an outline of how the future of this war will progress.

The Future of God's War

Presently, the Spirit of Jesus Christ is active in the world through the children of obedience. The children of obedience, remember, are those who have obeyed the Gospel command to repent and believe in Jesus Christ. They have submitted to His terms and confessed He is Lord. Every Christian has at least a basic understanding of the Gospel. But many don't understand the implications of its message.

Yes, He died for our sins and rose from the dead according to the Scriptures. But few consider that Jesus Christ was declared to be the Son of God with power (*exousia*—right to rule, authority), according to the Spirit of holiness "by the resurrection from the dead."[423] Furthermore, the Spirit of Christ is given to every priest-king, and His Spirit actively restrains the spirit of Antichrist in this world. This is huge! It means the Spirit in believers is holding back the beginning of Daniel's prophecy regarding little horn, the prophesied king of the fourth kingdom. Remember, Daniel's little horn is none other than the long-anticipated Antichrist.

---

[423] Romans 1:6

The Antichrist cannot be revealed until the Lord Jesus calls His own out of the earth in an event described in the Bible as "our gathering together unto Him."[424] Most Evangelical Christians call it *the rapture.* Because the Spirit of Jesus Christ dwells in the believer's heart, this will virtually mean the withdrawal of the Holy Ghost from the earth.[425]

When the Spirit's restraining influence is withdrawn, all impediments against the rise of Antichrist are removed.[426] Daniel's prophecies will begin their fulfillment: the man of sin shall rise to power in the earth—the Antichrist.

Daniel disclosed to us what marks the beginning of the career of little horn. In his vision of the fourth beast, which he called the fourth kingdom, he saw ten horns which represented ten kings.[427] During this phase of the fourth kingdom, the dominion will be held by a ten-king confederacy. Daniel described this fourth beast as having near-total authority and power, trampling upon all the other kingdoms of the earth. (I covered this at length in chapter eight.)[428] The other nations will come to resent being "bullied." This is where I believe little horn comes in. Daniel revealed that little horn begins his career by

---

[424] II Thessalonians 2:1; see I Corinthians 15:51-58

[425] The omnipresence of GOD is greatly misunderstood. True, there is no place outside of the reach of GOD's presence, as David testified: "If I make my bed in hell, behold, thou art there" (Psalm 139:8). And yet, the Bible says God's Spirit dwelt between the cherubim that stretched out their wings over the Mercy Seat of the Ark in the Holy of Holies of God's Temple. When the Ark was removed, and lost to the Philistines, it was said that *the glory was departed;* and this meant God was no longer *with* His people. Jesus described the Spirit as the wind, and while air is everywhere, wind blows here and there. The idea is that the activity of the Spirit withholding the spirit of Antichrist will be removed, allowing the spirit of Antichrist to raise up the man of sin.

[426] II Thessalonians 2:7

[427] Daniel 7:23

[428] For an extensive study of this fourth beast, please see my book, *The Visions Of Daniel.* www.booksatdbp.com.

subduing three of these ten horns, taking power over the fourth beast. This will give him control over the dominion. Because this marks the beginning of the prophecy of little-horn, I believe it is what Paul called the revelation of the *man of sin*.[429] It's the event that will unveil him as the ruler that fulfills Daniel's prophecy. *Little horn* will rise to power in four stages, as depicted by the famous four horsemen of the Apocalypse.[430]

At first, he will preach disarmament and peace.[431] Public sentiment will be ready for his call to "Beat your swords into plowshares and your spears into pruninghooks." Coupled with the promise that "Nation shall not lift up sword against nation, neither shall they learn war anymore,"[432] Antichrist will sway a war-weary world. A false prophet will arise, working amazing miracles and declaring this newly risen world ruler to be the saviour of the world. Many—vainly believing they have entered the promised millennial reign of Christ—will hail the man-of-sin as the coming of Messiah. The Spirit warns they will say, "Peace, peace, when there is no peace." By this, the Antichrist will gain political power over the dominion. This is the white horse of John's Revelation, with a rider that has a bow, but no arrows.[433]

The peace will be short-lived. A great sword will be put into the hands of *little horn*, ostensibly to enforce the peace. With his great sword, he will have power over the military might of the kingdoms. He will use his sword to "take peace from the earth."[434] This is the red horse of the Apocalypse.[435]

---

[429] II Thessalonians 2:3,8 (Italics added for emphasis.)
[430] Revelation 6:1-8
[431] Daniel 11:21
[432] Isaiah 2:4; see Micah 4:3-5
[433] Revelation 6:1-2
[434] Revelation 6:3-4
[435] Ibid.

After that, he will receive power over all the world's economies by taking control of the oil, the wine, and the world's food supply. This is the black horse of the Apocalypse.[436]

Having acquired political, military, and economic power over the kingdoms of the earth, the fourth horse of John's prophecy will begin its run. The man of sin will be exposed as Death, with Hell following him. This is the pale horse of the Apocalypse.[437] He will have power over the earth to kill with the sword (military power), with hunger (economic power), and with pestilence: indeed, the beasts of the earth will be under his power.

Remember, the dominion includes authority over the resources of the earth, including the creatures that inhabit it. At this point in little horn's career, he has the management of the world politically, militarily, and economically he will control the oil, the wine, and the world supply of food. Little horn will have taken the dominion into his hands by force. Once he has the dominion, he will turn his combined powers toward the destruction of humankind, and he will succeed to kill one-fourth of the planet's population.

Seeing the coming of this future holocaust, many of the scornful rulers of the Jews will reach out to the man of sin to make their "covenant with death."[438] This covenant will mark the beginning of what the Bible calls the *Seventieth Week*,[439] a period of seven years, commonly called "The Tribulation."[440] As noted above, Antichrist will proceed with his rampage destroying one-fourth of the earth's population, which today would be over two billion people.

---

[436] Revelation 6:5-6
[437] Revelation 6:7-8
[438] Isaiah 28:15-18
[439] Daniel 9:27
[440] Matthew 24:31 — taken from Jesus' warning of great tribulation.

Three-and-one-half years into the Tribulation, Antichrist will commit the abomination of desolation.

The Jews will have constructed their third Temple and resumed their daily sacrifices.[441] But Antichrist will interrupt their daily sacrifices and place himself in the holy of holies where he will proclaim himself to be God. This is the abomination of desolation spoken of by Jesus and Daniel. But when Antichrist establishes his palace on Mount Zion (the Temple Mount), he will be struck down and wounded to his death.[442]

At the time Antichrist is slain, God's War between angels and devils will have reached into Heaven itself. Michael, prevailing over Satan, will cast him down to Earth.[443] Satan will fall to Earth full of fury, knowing he has only a short time.[444] Mysteriously, Satan will mock the resurrection, and take up the body of the man-of-sin—his deadly wound will be healed. All the kingdoms of the world will be pulled together under Satan. For the remaining three and one-half years of Israel's Seventieth Week (The Tribulation), he will "scatter the power of the holy people."[445] It is during this time that God will pour out His wrath in the seven last plagues.[446]

Satan will try to destroy every human being remaining on Earth, and he would succeed—except Jesus promised that for the elect's sake, "those days [will] be shortened."[447]

---

[441] Isaiah 2 and Micah 5 reveal that the Jewish Temple will be rebuilt and daily sacrifices will resume during a time when Israel and the entire middle east will follow a policy of freedom of religion, allowing all faiths to "coexist" in Jerusalem.
[442] Daniel 11:45; see Isaiah 31:8
[443] Revelation 12:7
[444] Revelation 12:12
[445] Daniel 12:7
[446] Revelation 15-16
[447] Matthew 24:22

Jesus—King of kings and Lord of lords—will return with all His saints.[448] The fiery maw of the burning Lake will swallow the Beast and the false prophet, but the great red dragon will be confined to the Bottomless Pit. There he will be banished for 1,000 years.[449] During the 1,000 years (called the Millennial) of Satan's banishment, Jesus will rule on the earth with His saints, free from the interference of Satan.

Christ will rule Earth with a "rod of iron," and all nations will be under His direct command from Jerusalem. Jesus will demand all the nations to gather before Him. After the goats and sheep are separated, Christ will instruct His servants to set before Him all who said, "We will not have this man to reign over us."[450] Then He will command His servants to slay them in His presence.

After the Millennial, Satan will be loosed for a short time. He will be allowed to go about deceiving the world again, and he will succeed to bring the nations to rise against Christ.[451] When this rebellion forms into an armed attack on Jerusalem, God will intervene in one final, dramatic gesture. He will destroy the earth entirely, melting the elements with fervent heat.[452] When this rebellion forms into an armed attack on Jerusalem, God will intervene in one final, dramatic gesture. He will destroy the earth entirely, melting the elements with fervent heat. All yet remaining in their graves will be called to gather before His Great White Throne for judgment. He will reward them according to their works, which He recorded in His books. All whose

---

[448] Revelation 19
[449] Revelation 20:1-5
[450] Luke 19:27
[451] Revelation 20:6-10
[452] II Peter 3:10

names are not found written in the Lamb's Book of Life will be cast into the Lake of Fire with Satan and all his devils.[453] God's War ends!

Conclusion

Now we turn our attention to the present conflict, the spiritual war in which you and I are engaged. And this is important because although God wins His War, His servants do not win every battle in it. While the consequences of lost battles are severe, the reward of victory is spectacular.

We will continue as follows: first, you will be given a clearer understanding of the Kingdom of God and the Kingdom of Heaven, then I'll explain how the kingdom of Heaven suffers violence today and what that means to God's War and our part in that conflict. After that, we'll learn more about the role of Christ's churches in God's War. Finally, you'll be ready to learn about your place in God's War: first as God's king and then as God's priest. This part of the book goes into matters of the spiritual realm that you will find astonishing, intriguing, and crucial to our purpose—equipping the saints to engage the spiritual forces of darkness as God's soldiers in God's War!

I will conclude with a chapter on the role of prayer and fasting in spiritual warfare and a challenge for you to step into the battle and do your part to claim victory for the Kingdom of Christ.

~

---

[453] Revelation 20:11-15

"[May we] with true contrition of heart to confess [our] sins to God and implore forgiveness through the merits and mediation of Jesus Christ our Savior.   ~ Samuel Adams

(Samuel Adams, Proclamation for a Day of Fasting and Prayer, March 15, 1796.)

Chapter Twelve

God's War & the
Kingdom of God and of Heaven

W HAT IS THE KINGDOM OF GOD? Is it different from the Kingdom of Heaven? Jesus said the kingdom of Heaven suffereth violence and the violent take it by force.[454] How is that possible in the place where God's will is always done?[455] He told us, "every man presseth into"[456] the Kingdom of God. This word *presseth* comes from the same root as the word rendered *violence* in Matthew 11:12. How can a man *force* his way into the Kingdom of God? We will sort all of this out in this chapter, for only when these things are rightly understood will we correctly understand the Kingdom of God and spiritual warfare.

What Is the Kingdom of God?

The answer seems obvious—the domain over which God is King. However, there is confusion over the relationship between the kingdom of God and the kingdom of Heaven, and over the relationship of these to the kingdom of men.

The Bible uses the expressions *kingdom of God* and *kingdom of Heaven* interchangeably.

---

[454] Matthew 11:12
[455] Matthew 6:10
[456] Luke 16:16

Mark 1:15 is what we call a parallel passage with Matthew 4:17. Both offer an account of what Jesus began to preach after Herod cast John into prison.[457]

According to Mark, after John went to prison, Jesus began "preaching the kingdom of God," saying, "The time is fulfilled, and the kingdom of God is at hand: repent ye, and believe the Gospel."[458]

According to Matthew, after John was cast into prison, "Jesus began to preach, and to say, Repent: for the kingdom of Heaven is at hand."[459]

When John was cast into prison, Jesus began preaching the same message John had been preaching in the wilderness of Judaea: "Repent ye: for the kingdom of Heaven is at hand."[460]

By comparing Scripture with Scripture, we notice that Jesus used two expressions to identify this kingdom. He called it *the kingdom of God*; also, He called it *the kingdom of Heaven*. He used the phrases interchangeably.

For example, Jesus used the expressions *kingdom of God* and *kingdom of Heaven* interchangeably in His Parable of the Sower. In Matthew 13:11, Jesus referred to His Parable of the Sower as describing the kingdom of Heaven. However, in Mark 4:11, Jesus described the same parable as depicting the kingdom of God.[461]

---

[457] Mark 1:14; Matthew 4:12
[458] Mark 1:14-15
[459] Matthew 4:17
[460] Matthew 3:2
[461] I am aware that many believe Jesus did not use the expressions *kingdom of Heaven* and *kingdom of God* interchangeably. Furthermore, I recognize the Spirit intended that we understand distinct truths about the kingdom from each of these expressions. Nevertheless, Jesus did use them interchangeably in reference to the same *kingdom*. For a complete study of this question, see the appendix titled *The Kingdom of Heaven and the Kingdom of God*.

When the Spirit uses different words to speak of the same thing, it is because He is bringing our attention to different aspects of that same thing. In the case before us, the *kingdom of God* describes the domain inclusive of all Creation, in which God exerts His power and manifests His glory. The *kingdom of Heaven* identifies the specific realm of creation from which God rules over His domain.[462] Therefore, the *kingdom of Heaven* is the seat of God's Sovereign Rule, from which He extends His power throughout the *kingdom of God*. Hence, when Jesus exerted His Father's authority over the activity of devils on the earth, He said it meant that the kingdom of God has come into the world.[463]

Jesus described *the kingdom of Heaven* in the parables He called *the mysteries of the kingdom*.[464] He also used the expression, *kingdom of God,* in these parables.[465] We call these *the parables of the kingdom*. In the parables of the kingdom, Jesus describes how the kingdom of God would operate in the kingdom of men from His first coming to His second coming.[466]

Matthew and Mark each describe the kingdom of Heaven in language that we wouldn't expect to be used when speaking of the place where invariably the will of God is done.[467]

If we think of the *kingdom of Heaven* as being Heaven, then the mysteries of the kingdom that Jesus taught us are mysterious indeed. Jesus said a sower went forth to sow, and He described different sorts of soil into which the seed

---

[462] See Psalm 14:2, 53:2, 57:3, 33:13, 80:14, Romans 1:18, I Thessalonians 4:16, II Thessalonians 1:7, and the hundreds of verses that show God speaking, acting, and ruling from heaven. (Daniel 4:26)
[463] Matthew 12:28
[464] Matthew 13
[465] Mark 4
[466] Daniel 4:26
[467] Matthew 6:10

was sown. He explained that the seed was the Word of God, and these different types of soil represent different types, or conditions, of the human heart.[468] Clearly, this does not describe Heaven. It does describe God's rule from Heaven over the earth, however. It describes something God is doing in the earth presently.

But that's not all. Jesus said the kingdom of Heaven is likened to a man who sowed good seed in his field, but an enemy came behind him and sowed tares among the wheat.[469] He told us that the field in which the wheat and tares were sown was the world.[470] He explained that in the end He would gather the tares "out of his kingdom."[471] What? How is it that tares could be sown among the wheat in the kingdom of Heaven? Is Jesus telling us the *world* is His kingdom? Yes! Remember, Jesus is the King, and all men are His subjects!

These kingdom parables describe the kingdom of God in the earth under the present rule of King Jesus. Anyone who sets the realm of man outside of the kingdom of God has, perhaps unknowingly, fallen into the snare of the Devil and accepted Satan's lie regarding Christ. He effectively denies that Christ the King has come in the flesh.[472]

Conclusion

All things in the realm of Creation are under the rule of the Kingdom of God. When a Roman legion expressed the demands of Rome anywhere in the Empire, it was said that the power of Rome had come upon them. Likewise, when Jesus demonstrated the power of God openly, He often

---

[468] Matthew 13:18-23
[469] Matthew 13:24-30, 37-43
[470] Matthew 13:24, 38
[471] Matthew 13:40-41
[472] I John 4:2-3

declared this meant the kingdom of God had come upon them.[473] Today, when we exercise the authority of Christ in the earth, the kingdom of God has come upon them.

Confusion arises when we juxtapose the future and the present rule of Christ. We pray for His coming rule: *Thy kingdom come.* And we recognize His current rule when we confess He is Lord, and acknowledge He presently has all power in Heaven and on Earth. The kingdom *present* and the kingdom *to come* are separate manifestations of the kingdom of God. They are different dispensations of the kingdom of God, but the same King presides over each.

To answer the question of this chapter, the kingdom of God and the kingdom of Heaven are Christ's rule in Heaven and on Earth today!

Understanding that the kingdom of God is present in Earth via Christ's current reign over the realm of man from Heaven helps us understand this mystery: how can the kingdom of God suffer violence, and how can the violent take it by force? That is the topic of Chapter Thirteen.

~

---

[473] Matthew 12:28; Luke 10:9-11, 20

"Sensible of the importance of Christian piety and virtue to the order and happiness of a state, I cannot but earnestly commend to you every measure for their support and encouragement."

~ *John Hancock*

(John Hancock, A Proclamation For a Day of Public Thanksgiving 1791, given as Governor of the Commonwealth of Massachusetts, from an original broadside in our possession.)

Chapter Thirteen

How Can the Violent Take the Kingdom of Heaven by Force?

ESUS SAID, "From the days of John the Baptist until now, the kingdom of Heaven suffereth[474] violence, and the violent take it by force."[475] When did this start, and why? Jesus informed us that, "The law and the prophets were until John: since that time the kingdom of God is preached, and every man presseth into it."[476] The kingdom of Heaven has suffered violence, with the violent taking it by force, ever since John the Baptist began preaching "repent ye: for the kingdom of Heaven is at hand."[477]

Satan Assaults the Kingdom of Heaven

Presseth in Luke 16:16 translates the same word rendered *suffereth violence* in Matthew 11:12.[478] Something about John's message triggered a violent assault on the kingdom of Heaven, with every man clamoring to take it by force. The mystery is resolved when we understand that the kingdom of Heaven and the kingdom of God refers to Christ's present rule over the kingdom of man. John declared the kingdom of God was at hand. That threatened

[474] Webster, 1828 "SUFFERABLE, a. That may be tolerated, or permitted; allowable."
[475] Matthew 11:12-13
[476] Luke 16:16
[477] Matthew 3:2)
[478] Matthew 11:12, *suffereth violence* (βιάζεται from βιάζω — *biadzo* (Strong No. 971)) and Luke 16:16, *presseth* (βιάζεται from βιάζω — *biadzo* (Strong No. 971)).

the kingdom of darkness. But it also threatened man's hold on the dominion.

Remember, the descendants of Adam received the dominion by Divine Decree.[479] Only a man could hold it. But the sons of Adam sold themselves to Satan and finally yielded control of the kingdoms of the world to God's enemy. That was unacceptable. Jesus came as God manifest in the flesh,[480] the last Adam.[481] As GOD, He could rule Heaven. As man, He could rule Earth.

Jesus was a threat to the sinners of Adam's race, and Satan's usurped place. For Christ as a man could take the dominion from Adam's fallen race, and as God, He could cast Satan out of his place in the earth.

The heir has come, and Adam's sons refuse to yield the dominion to Him. Satan moves his human agents to reject Christ's rule. By their violence, they take the rule that belongs to Christ Jesus, forcing themselves into the kingdom that belongs to God—to take the dominion by force. But the dominion is destined for the saints. The sinners of Adam's race who are made saints by the sacrifice of the last Adam—who become the sons of God by His Spirit when they receive God's Son.[482] These receive *the kingdom* that holds *the dominion*.

Earlier, we received testimony from Daniel that spiritual warfare had been going on in the first heaven long before John the Baptist came preaching.[483] It would seem, therefore,

---

[479] Genesis 1:26-27

[480] I Timothy 3:16

[481] I Corinthians 15:45

[482] John 1:9-11; 3:1-6; Galatians 3:6

[483] Daniel 10:10-21—Jesus said He saw Satan as lightening fall from heaven (Luke 10:18). He must have fallen from the third or the second heaven since he is operating now in the first heaven—exerting his influence in the earth through the children of disobedience (Ephesians 2:2). We know he will lose his place as "prince of the

that the kingdom of Heaven suffering violence was nothing new. But at that time, the kingdom of men operated as a kingdom distinct from the kingdom of Heaven. The kingdom of men was a dominion granted to Adam's race, whereas the kingdom of Heaven was not. They were distinct. But when God Who made man became man that He made, He was of both realms.[484]

As I pointed out above, this meant that as the Son of man, He could rule the dominion directly; and as the Son of God, He could rule Heaven, too. But it also meant that Jesus combined the kingdoms. The kingdom of men was brought into and made part of the kingdom of GOD. This confounded the Devil and all his devils, for God now had a man that was God Who could join the domains and rule Heaven and Earth directly.

When Christ, the God-Man, defeated Satan and took the kingdom of man out from under his power, the kingdom of man was made one with the kingdom of Heaven within the kingdom of God. *Today*, the kingdom of Heaven is Christ's rule over *Heaven* and *Earth* (emphasis added to highlight this essential fact).

Now you understand how the kingdom of Heaven can suffer violence and how the violent can take it by force. The

---

power of the air" (the first heaven) when Michael stands against him and casts him into the earth (Daniel 12:1-2; Revelation 12:7-9). It appears that the second heaven is the domain of the angels: first, the stars are the primary feature of heaven, and stars are representative of angels (Revelation 1:20); second, since God gave man a dominion, it seems reasonable that He would have given one to angels, and that their dominion would be the second heaven; third, the scene that develops in the mind when reading Daniel 10 and 12 suggests that God's angels engage Satan's angels in the first heaven over matters related directly to God's rule in the earth; and fourth, since God's angels are greater in number and in power, it is reasonable to suppose they would not allow Satan to have place in their domain after his rebellion.

[484] John 1:1, 14; I Timothy 3:16; Philippians 2:5-6

kingdom of Heaven includes the dominion God gave to mankind and all the kingdoms of men within it. For Satan to reclaim supremacy over all the kingdoms of the world, he must overcome Christ Jesus' rule in the earth over the dominion. To take any territory in the world under his power, he must overcome the kingdom of God—the power of God in the world today by the Spirit of Jesus Christ. Any territory Satan holds he gained by violence against the kingdom of Heaven.

How Does Satan Work His Will in the World Today?

Men do not have Divine authority to rule over the kingdom of men unless they receive that power from Christ Jesus, the Lord over Heaven and Earth. Otherwise, to get it, they must take it by force.

Remember, when Nebuchadnezzar acknowledged that God rules in the kingdom of men he was allowed to hold the kingdom. When he refused to yield to that truth he was overruled, or he temporarily lost the kingdom.[485] We must understand that it's the same today. Except, the Lord Jesus, God's Son, holds the rights and prerogatives of rule over men, and His churches have the keys of His kingdom and the words and commandments of His law. Men are under the authority (power) of Christ, whether or not they acknowledge it.

The Holy One limits the spirit of Antichrist. How does Satan get Jesus to withdraw and yield territory to his control in the earth today? Saints limit the Holy One by unbelief.[486]

Satan's power is vast, to be sure. When God cast Satan from Heaven, he took with him one-third of the "stars of

---

[485] Daniel 3-4
[486] Psalm 78:41

heaven."[487] One-third of the angels of heaven followed him in his rebellion against God. The Scripture testifies to Satan's great wisdom and strength—there is no creature in all creation so wise, beautiful, and powerful. However, that power is under the rule of GOD. Satan is limited.

Satan is God's enemy, and yet he is constrained under God's will.[488] He can work no mischief unless he gains a license from God.[489] Therefore, while Satan opposes the rule of God on Earth, usurping the role of "god of this world,"[490] he must operate within limits imposed on him by the Sovereign rule of Christ Jesus from His Heavenly Throne. So, the question remains: how is Christ maneuvered to cede place to the Devil?

As you know, God had given the dominion of the earth to Adam and his descendants. The only way Satan could gain control of the planet was to entice men to come out from under the rule of God's kingdom through disobedience to His will. But today, the sinners of Adam's race have lost the dominion. It has been given to the *last Adam,* Jesus Christ, and His descendants—Christians. The Spirit of Christ is in them, and through them, Christ exerts His authority into the world. The only way Satan can gain power in the earth today is to neutralize the saints. Therefore, Satan concentrates on manipulating Christians to quench the Spirit of God. Only then can he keep Christ's Spirit from moving into the world through them and disrupting his designs. The only power on Earth that can withstand the Devil is the Holy Spirit of God working in and through the believer.

Satan uses the stratagem the prophet Balaam taught king

---

[487] Revelation 12:4
[488] Isaiah 54:16
[489] Job 1-2; Luke 22:31-32; see I Kings 22:22-23
[490] II Corinthians 4:4

Balak.[491] A king named Balak hired the prophet Balaam to curse God's people. But it was impossible! Every time Balaam opened his mouth, all that came from GOD through him was a blessing upon Israel. Frustrated, Balak threatened to withhold Balaam's wages. Balaam presented an alternative plan. The false prophet instructed Balak how to prevail over God's people: entice them into a compromise with the world.[492] Balaam instructed Balak to put before the men of Israel lewd women who would seduce them into intermarriages, assuring him this would provoke God to curse His people. It worked! And it's the same with us.

Christ will never leave us nor forsake us. God's Word is on our part; God's Word declares Christ Jesus is King, and we are kings and priests unto God. The Word of God speaks of our power in Christ to resist the Devil, who sets temptations before us that draw our hearts away from Christ must flee before the weakest Christian submitted to God.[493] Satan will never succeed to turn Christ against us. However, what he can do is turn us away from Christ. Satan sets temptations before us that draw our hearts away from Christ. He snares us with appeals to the lust of the flesh, the lust of the eyes, and the pride of life.[494] When we succumb to his temptations, we grieve[495] and finally quench[496] This gives Satan an opening. The spirit of Antichrist can move in, take territory, establish a stronghold, and work the Devil's will in the earth.

Remember, Satan has been cast out and is now the "prince of the power of the air, the spirit that now worketh in the

---

[491] Numbers 22
[492] I John 2:15-16
[493] James 4:7
[494] I John 2:15-16
[495] Ephesians 4:30-31
[496] I Thessalonians 5:19

children of disobedience."[497] His sole objective is to steal, kill, and destroy.[498] To accomplish this, he needs to gain territory in this world. He can only get *place* if Christians yield it to him.[499] He uses his fallen angels, called devils, to seduce men into believing "doctrines of devils."[500] One of the most effective doctrines devils use to keep Christians out of Satan's way is to trick them into denying that Jesus Christ has come in the flesh.[501] But how can any Christian deny that Christ has come in the flesh? Beware Satan's wiles!

Lucifer need only convince believers that all the kingdoms of the world rightfully belong to him, *for now.* This effectively denies that Christ has received all power (authority to rule) in Heaven and Earth, *now.* Believing his lie, God's king-priests willingly give up to Satan control over the dominion and expose the kingdom of Heaven to violent takeover.

What Is the Same and What Is Different in God's War Today?

In many respects, the tactics employed by God have not changed. God continues to use His angels as agents, executing His will in the kingdom of Heaven into the realm of men.[502] Their main job is to minister to those who will believe on the Son of God and be saved. In performing this responsibility, they often engage in the affairs of this world in a manner very similar to how God used angels in the time of the Old Testament. Please note the relationship between prayer and the activity of angels.

---

[497] Ephesians 2:2
[498] John 10:10
[499] Ephesians 4:23
[500] I Timothy 4:1-4
[501] I John 4:2-3
[502] Hebrews 1:13-14

For example, GOD sent His Angel to lead the children of Israel through the wilderness.[503] He did this after He heard their cry.[504] Well, GOD sent the angel of the Lord to break Peter out of Herod's prison,[505] after "prayer was made without ceasing of the church unto God for him."[506] Also, the angel of the Lord led Philip to the steward of Ethiopia's Queen, whose heart prayed for someone to guide him in understanding the Scriptures.[507] And an angel appeared to Cornelius in response to his prayers[508] and instructed him to call for Peter, who was praying when the invitation reached him.[509] God continues to use His angels.

God's holy angels engage rulers of the earth. Toward the end of David's reign, he saw a mighty angel standing over the threshing floor of Ornan, with his sword drawn and stretched out over Jerusalem.[510] David's sacrifice and prayer averted the destruction of his beloved Zion. During the reign of Hezekiah, king of Judah, God sent an angel to destroy the army of Sennacherib, who threatened Judah and cursed God. One hundred eighty-five thousand (185,000) enemy troops were decimated in one evening's work by one mighty angel.[511] This angel was sent after Hezekiah prayed.[512] God's angels were also involved in confirming and strengthening Gentile rulers.[513] And there was a praying saint then, too. His name was Daniel.[514]

[503] Exodus 23:23; 32:34
[504] Exodus 2:23
[505] Acts 12:5-19
[506] Acts 12:5
[507] Acts 8:26
[508] Acts 10:3-7, 30
[509] Acts 10:9
[510] I Chronicles 21:15-16
[511] II Chronicles 32:1-23
[512] II Kings 19:14-19
[513] Daniel 11:1, see Daniel 10:10-11:1
[514] Daniel 9

When king Herod received worship from the foolish men of Tyre, the *angel of the Lord* smote that king, and worms feasted on his flesh while his worshipers watched.[515] By this the Spirit announced He is present to restrain the spirit of Antichrist that encourages the worship of kings. I am sure this judgment upon Herod was secured during the prayer meeting that precipitated Peter's miraculous jailbreak from Herod's prison mentioned above. Indeed, Paul encouraged the believers to pray for deliverance from unreasonable and wicked men.[516]

In spiritual warfare today, God sends forth His angels into the earth to minister "for them who shall be heirs of salvation";[517] and we sometimes unknowingly entertain these angels.[518] Angels minister in the earth on our behalf, executing the will of Christ and defending us from the attack of devils. They also attack devils, challenging them for usurped territory. Still, in all these events, God has connected the prayers of saints to the movement of angels.

Angels and devils war in high (heavenly) places,[519] while the children of obedience on God's part[520] and the children of disobedience on Satan's part[521] engage in this war on the earth.

The wickedness in high places (*the heavenly places*)[522] is undoubtedly a reference to the activity of Satan as the "prince of the power of the air."[523] Believers decide each battle. Will they exercise their authority in the kingdom

---

[515] Acts 12:20-25
[516] II Thessalonians 3:1-2
[517] Hebrews 1:14
[518] Hebrews 13:2
[519] Ephesians 6:12
[520] Romans 6:17
[521] Ephesians 2:2
[522] Ephesians 6:12
[523] Ephesians 2:2

of heaven over the realm of men, or will they yield the kingdoms of men to the children of Satan. Most believers today are yielding to Satan by default.

This battle between angels and devils has been going on throughout God's War. But there is something different today. The Holy Spirit is present in the hearts of the saints, and He guides them to "all truth."[524] Satan cannot long deceive those who hear the Shepherd's voice and follow Him.[525] That's why Satan and his devils must work to seduce God's people into sin. He must, at all costs, stop the Holy Ghost from moving into this world through Christ's disciples.[526]

Satan's Strategy Is Always the Same.

Satan used Jezebel to corrupt Israel. Earlier, we recounted the history of Israel's corruption by Satan (see Chapter Six: From Abraham to Nebuchadnezzar), which began with Solomon's idolatry.[527] Ten of the twelve tribes were taken from the house of David and given to Jeroboam, and it was called Israel. David, of the tribe of Judah, kept only Benjamin. Jeroboam led Israel to worship at the altar of his golden calves. Worshiping idols diverts worship from God and to devils. Devil worship opened the door for the future daughter of a pagan king of Sidon to marry a king of Israel named Ahab—her name was Jezebel.

This wicked queen planted the seeds of Baalism in Israel.[528] Worshiping devils corrupted Israel to such evils GOD was moved to destroy and scatter her all over the world.[529] Through the compromise of an otherwise good

---

[524] John 16:13
[525] John 10:27
[526] John 7:38-39
[527] I Kings 11:1-13
[528] I Kings 16:31; see I Kings 18
[529] I Kings 14:15, the sins of Ahab provoked God to declare the prophecy Israel

king named Jehoshaphat, his son, Jehoram, married the daughter of Jezebel, Athaliah, who planted the seeds of Baalism in Judah.[530] This wicked seed finally fully saturated Judah in the days of her most wicked king, Manasseh.[531] When God took the kingdom from Judah and gave it to Nebuchadnezzar, He referred to the sins of Manasseh as the cause of Judah's downfall.

Satan used the strategy by which he corrupted and destroyed Israel to spoil the churches too. After Christ ascended and sent His Spirit into the world to empower and guide His churches, Satan planted a Jezebel namesake in one of them. Before the last Apostle died, the church in Thyatira embraced the teachings of their *Jezebel*. She taught God's people to commit fornication and to eat foods sacrificed to idols.[532] By these sins, the infamous namesake of wicked Jezebel led the unfaithful into "the depths of Satan."[533]

Summary Status of God's War Today

Jesus is the King, and all men are His subjects. He prophesied that His "citizens" (subjects)[534] would rebel against Him while He was gone and that many of His servants would become lax and unfaithful.[535]

King Jesus gave the keys of the kingdom to His

---

would be scattered, and its fulfillment is recorded in II Kings 17:1-23.

[530] II Kings 8:26; II Chronicles 24:7

[531] II Kings 21:11

[532] Revelation 2:20-22

[533] Revelation 2:24

[534] The word translated *citizens* is πολῖται from πολίτης *pol-ee'-tace*. See Strong No. 4177, "a townsman: — citizen." It is rooted in πόλις, *polis*, Strong No. 4172, which, according to Strong, is "probably the same as 4171 (πόλεμος, *polemos*, "warfare (literally or figuratively; a single encounter or a series): — battle, fight, war." Or else it is related to πολύς meaning *many, plenteous* (see Strong No. 4183).

[535] Luke 19:11-27

churches, establishing their authority in the world under Him. He commissioned them to announce He has risen from the dead, and by His resurrection is declared to be the Son of God with power. Having broken the power of Satan over the earth and humankind, He sent us into the world to command all men to repent and believe in Him to be saved from the wrath to come. Those nations that receive the Gospel—and acknowledge Christ as the Son of God and Lord of Heaven and Earth—will be blessed and given "the kingdom."[536] However!

The seeds of Jezebel's error have grown into the Roman Catholic Church, which will finally become the Whore of Babylon.[537] Today, the spirit of Jezebel has spread far and wide among the churches. Sexual perversion is commonly named among God's people. In some churches, it is open; in most, it is hidden. But the churches have plunged deeper into the depths of Satan. Believers commit adultery against Christ: "Ye adulterers and adulteresses, know ye not that the friendship of the world is enmity with God? whosoever therefore will be a friend of the world is the enemy of God."[538] Remember, the Spirit of God was sent into the world to "reprove the world of sin, righteousness, and judgment."[539] Many believers today want to reprove the holy and applaud the profane.

Lucifer seduces believers into sin by the lusts of the flesh

---

[536] Matthew 21:43; Psalm 33:12

[537] Revelation 17 presents the great Harlot riding the "scarlet colored beast," which represents the kingdom of men in the time of the end. What John saw was the institutional "Church," corrupted by Baalism, until it became the great Whore holding the golden cup in her hand (Revelation 17:4). Jezebel planted the seeds in the church at Thyatira that grew into the religious system of Rome that in the end of the world will ride on the back of the *kingdom of men* as if a Queen, and will hold in her hand the "golden cup" of Babylon. (Revelation 17)

[538] James 4:4

[539] John 16:7

to defile the "Temple of God"[540] (the believer's body). This is a key stratagem, for he knows that his enemy, the Holy Ghost, moves into the world through the belly of the believer.[541] The Devil heard Jesus call His disciples the salt of the earth, and warn them if they lose their savor, they would be cast into the street and trampled under the foot of men.[542] Satan labors to compromise believers until they are good-for-nothing so that God will throw them into the street to be trampled under the feet of his children of disobedience.

Satan is the prince of the power of the air, the spirit that now works in the children of disobedience.[543] He takes them captive at will.[544] And he uses them to frustrate and hinder the work of Christ in the world.[545]

One day, the Lord will remove His saints from the earth. The presence of the Holy Ghost in the saints is the only force on Earth withholding the rise of Antichrist. So the removal of the saints will allow Satan's son of perdition to make one last violent assault to take the dominion into his power once again. But God will defeat him.

So long as the saints are on the earth, they have the power to thwart Satan's plans. The saints can overcome! For they are kings and priests unto God, endowed with power from on high. Fellow saints, we need only stir ourselves in this war, in God's War, and we may be confident of victory.

Conclusion

Spiritual warfare refers to the ongoing struggle between the Spirit of Jesus Christ through the believer and the spirit

---

[540] I Corinthians 3:17; I Peter 2:11; see Galatians 5:16-21
[541] John 7:38-39
[542] Matthew 5:13; Luke 14:33-35
[543] Ephesians 2:1-2
[544] II Timothy 2:26
[545] Acts 12; 13:10

of Antichrist through the unbeliever. The core issue in the conflict is that Jesus, Who is both God and man, received all power in Heaven and Earth. All the kingdoms of the world (the dominion) are under Jesus' authority in the kingdom of Heaven. Satan is the spirit that works in the children of disobedience, and through them, he claims the dominion rightly belongs to the sinners of Adam's race. Together, they usurp the kingdom by violence and howl against Jesus' right to rule the world.

Hence, the Lordship of Jesus Christ and His claim that all power is given to Him in Heaven and Earth is at the heart of this conflict. At this juncture of God's War, the saints call all sinners to surrender to Christ. The terms of surrender are as follows: "That if thou shalt confess with thy mouth the Lord Jesus, and believe in thine heart that God hath raised Him from the dead, thou shalt be saved."[546]

Christ's Spirit exerts the authority of the Kingdom of God into the world through the children of obedience. Our primary mission is to preach the Gospel to every creature in the world, heralding the command of God to repent and believe in Jesus Christ. In no other way can sinners of Adam's race be saved from the wrath to come—the wrath of the Lamb.

The spirit of Antichrist, meanwhile, operates in the children of disobedience to resist the preaching of the Gospel. Seducing spirits teach doctrines of devils deceiving the children of disobedience, and they use these deceptions to commandeer principalities and powers (Antichrist governments) to block the preaching of the Gospel of Jesus Christ.

Why does it seem like we are losing? Greater is He that is in us than he that is in the world. How Satan has succeeded in manipulating entire countries to blockade the Gospel

---

[546] Romans 10:9

of Jesus Christ? And how does he keep our loved ones in bondage to darkness?

You are well on your way to understanding Satan's deceptions and learning what you can do to break the hold of Satan on the minds and hearts of men and nations.

~

"Pray . . . that universal happiness may be established in the world [and] that all may bow to the scepter of our Lord Jesus Christ, and the whole earth be filled with His glory."

~ John Hancock

(John Hancock, A Proclamation For a Day of Public Thanksgiving 1791, given as Governor of the Commonwealth of Massachusetts, from an original broadside in our possession.)

Chapter Fourteen

The Role of the Church in God's War

WARS ARE FOUGHT to take or to protect. Spiritual warfare is no different: Satan wars to take the kingdom by violence; Christ wars to protect what is His, and to deliver men from the power of darkness. God's War is a contest over who has the right to rule the earth and the kingdoms of men. Our role in this war is to preach the Gospel to the ends of the earth. The Gospel declares Jesus is Lord and all humanity are His subjects, and so it commands all men to repent and believe in Jesus Christ. To this end, He has sent His Holy Spirit into the world to empower and guide His churches to complete this mission.[547]

However, the Devil, called the prince of the power of the air,[548] opposes Christ's rule in the earth. Satan is the spirit that works in the children of disobedience to hinder the preaching of Christ's Gospel.[549] The children of disobedience use various tactics. Today, it is fashionable to legislate immorality, making it a crime for Christians to speak against sin. Or they turn the minds of men away from truth through social peer pressure, imposing what today we call political correctness—a direct opposition to the truth and the

---

[547] Acts 1:5-8; John 16:7-13; John 7:38-39
[548] Ephesians 2:2
[549] I Thessalonians 2:18; II Corinthians 4:4

preaching of the Gospel. But when Christians, filled with the Spirit, stand up to these servants of the spirit of Antichrist, the power of God's kingdom manifests with amazing results. There are many illustrations of this: consider Acts 13:8; II Timothy 4:14-15; and I Timothy 1:20 as examples.

When Paul preached the Gospel to a deputy of the Roman government named Sergius, who had expressed a desire to "hear the word of God," Elymas, the sorcerer, attempted to interrupt them and "turn away the deputy from the faith."[550] The Apostle Paul looked straight at Elymas and said, "O full of all subtlety and all mischief, thou child of the devil, thou enemy of all righteousness, wilt thou not cease to pervert the right ways of the Lord?"[551] The typical, pathetic, adulterous Christian would never dare do such a thing today. But Paul did not stop there; he went on, "And now, behold the hand of the Lord is upon thee, and thou shalt be blind, not seeing the sun for a season."[552] Immediately, God struck Elymas with dimness of sight so that he required someone to lead him by the hand.[553]

You can quickly ascertain what spirit you are of by how you react to the account above. If you are under the control of seducing spirits, you will likely see this as Paul being mean spirited and unkind. If you see this as an illustration of God's kingdom power working to overcome an effort by the spirit of Antichrist to stop the Gospel from being preached, you are of the same Spirit that wrote the Bible.

Here is another example, but keep in mind that there are many. II Timothy 4:14-15—a man named Alexander, who was a coppersmith, did much evil against Paul and attempted

---

[550] Acts 13:7-8
[551] Acts 13:10
[552] Acts 13:11
[553] Acts 13:11

to hinder his Gospel ministry. Paul warned Timothy about this man and prayed, "The Lord reward him according to his works."[554] I already mentioned the two heretics Paul cursed and turned over to Satan that they might learn not to blaspheme.[555]

Satan is the spirit of Antichrist that works against the Holy Spirit of Jesus Christ in this world.[556]

Paul said our body is the Temple of the Holy Ghost.[557] The word *ghost* refers to a manifestation or appearance of a spirit, in this case, of the Spirit of God. Jesus said His Holy Spirit would flow into the world through the *belly* of those that believe on Him.[558] The *belly* represents that part of us that intersects with the physical world around us. (You'll learn a lot more about this later.) Jesus moves through the Temple of God, which is the body of the believer. The door of this Temple to the world around us is our *belly*.[559]

The Antichrist spirit operates in the world through unbelievers and opposes Christ's rule. This spirit especially resists Jesus' command that His Gospel is to be preached to all nations in every generation.

As you might imagine, the conflict between the children of disobedience and the children of obedience can become personal. For this reason, we must remember that the "weapons of our warfare are not carnal";[560] that is, they are not physical. It's a spiritual war that rages between the

---

[554] II Timothy 4:14
[555] I Timothy 1:20
[556] I John 2:18, 4:3; II John 7
[557] I Corinthians 6:19
[558] John 7:38-39
[559] Probably the most often asked question of me on this subject is what exactly did Jesus mean when He said His Spirit would flow through our belly. An entire chapter is devoted to answering that question.(See pp. 251-280)
[560] II Corinthians 10:4

two archenemies: Satan and his devils versus Jesus Christ and His holy angels. And we must understand our part in this conflict.

Spiritual Warfare and the Church in the Kingdom of Jesus Christ

The Catholics and Protestants think that the Lord's Church is the Kingdom of God on Earth. In a limited sense, this is correct.

King Jesus gave the keys of the kingdom to His Church.[561] Additionally, Christ's Church is made up of kings and priests[562] under Christ, the King of kings and High Priest of our souls, to Whom all power is given "in heaven and in earth."[563] When the Spirit of God manifests Christ's kingdom power and glory in the earth, the kingdom of God has come upon them.[564]

Nevertheless, Christians are charged to obey magistrates and to recognize the Divine appointment of human governments.[565] The ordained authority of civil government comes under the jurisdiction of Christ, possessor of all power in heaven and Earth. Although the Church has the keys of the kingdom, it doesn't have the scepter of earthly government. Its mission is different. It proclaims the Gospel to the nations, instructing them in the commandments of the Lord; and it wields the Sword of the Spirit, the Word of God—but not the sword of civil authority.

---

[561] When I use the word *Church* in this way, I am speaking of it in a generic way. Technically, Jesus has organized His Church into churches (Revelation 1:19-20). In other words, I do not subscribe to the doctrine called the universal, invisible church. (Matthew 16:18-19)
[562] Revelation 1:5-6
[563] Matthew 28:18
[564] Matthew 12:28
[565] Romans 13:1-6; Titus 3:1

Jesus promised, however, that the nation that brings forth the fruit of the kingdom would be given stewardship of the dominion until He comes.[566] Hence, the Church has the keys, but Christ holds the scepter of His kingdom, and as His Father did before Him, He gives the dominion to whomever He chooses.

When Jesus came, He declared that He had been sent exclusively to the "house of Israel"[567] with His message to repent that they might receive the kingdom.[568] He announced, "The time is fulfilled, and the kingdom of God is at hand: repent ye, and believe the gospel."[569] Israel rejected His call to repent. Toward the end of His ministry, Jesus wept over Jerusalem, because Israel missed their opportunity to be restored as God's steward of the kingdom that held the dominion.[570] He grieved over the wrath that would come upon them.[571] He said the kingdom would be withdrawn and given to a nation that would bring forth the fruit of the kingdom[572]—which is repentance toward God and faith in the Lord Jesus Christ.[573]

---

[566] Matthew 21:43

[567] As the "Lamb of God," He would die for the sins of the world (John 1:29, 36; 3:16; I John 2:1-2), but as *Messiah,* or *Shiloh,* He came particularly to those to whom the *kingdom* was promised—to Israel.

[568] Matthew 10:6; 15:24—Peter declared the "times of refreshing" were available after Pentecost (Acts 3:19; see Isaiah 28:12). The gift of tongues was a sign to Jews that their "times of refreshing" had come (I Corinthians 14:20-21; Isaiah 28:11-12). God did not withdraw His offer of the kingdom to Israel until Paul declared the fulfillment of Isaiah's prophecy concerning the partial blindness of Israel for their unbelief (Isaiah 6:9-13; Acts 28:25-29), thus fulfilling the prophecy of Jesus.

[569] The context of the prophecy is the "last days" (Genesis 49:1). When *Shiloh* comes, "unto Him shall the gathering of the people be" (Genesis 49:10). This "gathering" precludes a "scattering." From the end of the Babylonian captivity, God has been willing to gather His people back to their land. Shiloh (*Messiah, Jesus*) offered to "gather them," but "they would not!" Nevertheless, they will be gathered to their land in the last days, and Judah will hold the "scepter" until Shiloh comes—again. (Mark 1:15; see Genesis 49:1, 10)

[570] Luke 19:41-42

[571] Luke 19:43-46; 21:5-24

[572] Matthew 21:43

[573] Acts 20:21-25

It is necessary to clarify something about the kingdom. Jesus was not, at His first coming, offering to Israel the kingdom in which He would rule and reign on the earth with a "rod of iron."[574] He clarified this in one of His parables when the disciples thought the kingdom would "immediately appear."[575] Jesus explained that He would be leaving His House in the care of stewards[576] while he went away on a "far journey"[577] to receive for Himself a kingdom and then to return.

Jesus made it clear He did not come to judge the world.[578] He spoke of judging the nations in connection with His promised return.[579] Therefore, the kingdom Jesus was offering to Israel was not the one to come, but the one described in His parables—with the King in absentia.[580]

Christ knew His Father would deliver the kingdom of men to Him.[581] And He knew that after a "long time,"[582] He would return to judge the servants who were left here as stewards of His house, holding the keys of the kingdom under His authority. If Israel had received their Messiah, they would have received the dominion under Christ until He returned to set up His "rod of iron"[583] rule on the earth. Because they rejected Him, Jesus declared the offer withdrawn and set aside for whatever nation would obey the Gospel and bring forth the fruit of the kingdom.[584]

---

[574] Revelation 20:1-15
[575] Luke 19:11
[576] Mark 13:34-35
[577] Luke 19:11-27; compare Matthew 25:14-30
[578] John 12:47; see Acts 17:31; I Corinthians 6:2; and Psalm 96:13
[579] Matthew 25:31-46
[580] Matthew 25:14-30; Luke 19:10-27; Mark 13:34-35 See also Matthew 13
[581] Matthew 28:18
[582] Matthew 25:19; Mark 13:33-35
[583] Psalm 2:9; Revelation 2:27; 12:5; 19:15
[584] Matthew 21:43; Acts 20:21-25

The Present Role of Believers in the Kingdom of Men

Daniel speaks of a stone cut without hands that would grow into an eternal kingdom in the earth.[585] Jesus is this *stone*. The *builders* (Israel) rejected the *stone*, but God has elevated it to be the chief cornerstone[586] of the foundation. Jesus said He would build His Church on this rock (for the stone is Christ).[587] He is building it to be a "habitation of God by the Spirit,"[588] the House of God, the "pillar and ground of the truth"[589] in the world today. Unbelievers are stumbling over this *stone*, but those who fall on it, presumably thereby broken and humbled, will be saved from the wrath to come.[590]

The Church of the Living God[591] is the House of God that Jesus established in the earth and left in the care of His stewards while He went away to "receive for himself a kingdom, and to return."[592]

Meanwhile, the believing Gentiles, who were not a people, are "now the people of God,"[593] and inheritors of the promise. Christ has delivered to us "His goods."[594] As His stewards, we hold the "keys of the kingdom," and we are required to "occupy" until He returns.[595] We are charged to abstain from fleshly lusts that war against the soul, and to have our conversation honest among the Gentiles (nations). He wants the unbelievers to behold our good works and glorify God in the day of visitation.[596]

---

[585] Daniel 2:45
[586] Matthew 21:42-43
[587] Matthew 16:18
[588] Ephesians 2:20-22
[589] I Timothy 3:15
[590] I Peter 2:6-8; Isaiah 8:14
[591] I Timothy 3:15; Matthew 16:16
[592] Luke 19:12; see Mark 13:34
[593] I Peter 2:10
[594] Matthew 25:14
[595] Matthew 16:19; Luke 19:13
[596] I Peter 2:10-12

Concerning earthly authorities, we are told to "submit (ourselves) to every ordinance of man for the Lord's sake."[597] We are charged with the command to preach the Gospel, calling on all men everywhere to repent and believe on the Lord Jesus Christ. Every nation that heeds our call will be exalted in the earth and will be given stewardship of the kingdom until Christ returns.[598]

Jesus commissioned His Church to minister to the nations. We are to "teach all nations, baptizing them in the name of the Father, and of the Son, and of the Holy Ghost, teaching them to observe all things whatsoever [Christ has] commanded [us]."[599] It is instructive that when Jesus directed us to evangelize the nations, He prefaced it by declaring, "All power is given unto me in heaven and in earth."[600]

Under His authority, we are to preach the Gospel and baptize converts. As ambassadors for Christ and kings and priests unto God in the kingdom of Heaven, we train His disciples to obey everything Christ the King has commanded.[601] In the course of our ministry to the nations, if they obey the Gospel and bring forth the fruit of the kingdom, that nation will be honored with stewardship of the dominion. Those nations that refuse will do so at their peril, for the King will return to judge them.[602]

Satan continues to assault the kingdom of Heaven and take it by force. As spiritual warfare rages in the heavens,[603] it manifests in open conflict between the children of obedience and the children of disobedience in the world.

The spirit of Antichrist is working in the children of disobedience, moving them to set up a global dictatorship

---

[597] I Peter 2:13
[598] Matthew 21:42-43
[599] Matthew 28:19-20
[600] Matthew 28:18
[601] II Corinthians 5:20
[602] Matthew 25:14-31; Luke 19:11-27; see especially Luke 19:14, 27
[603] Ephesians 2:2; 6:12-18

in the world in opposition to the kingdom of Christ. The Spirit of Jesus Christ is restraining the spirit of Antichrist.

Until the restraining influence of the Spirit of Christ is withdrawn from the world by the removal of God's Temple (the believer's body),[604] Satan's man of sin cannot be revealed. Meanwhile, God has commissioned all born again children of the kingdom as "kings and priests"[605] unto God in this world. Jesus is the King of kings and the Chief Priest over these priests. We represent His kingdom authority in the earth as ambassadors of the kingdom of God. We have the keys, although we do not, at present, hold the scepter. We serve Him by providing a place where He manifests the kingdom of God in the world by the Holy Ghost. This place is our physical body and the corporate body of the churches.

We are stewards of the House that Jesus left,[606] which is a habitation of God by the Spirit.[607] The churches are called "the body of Christ,"[608] and the Spirit of God comes upon the churches, empowering them to charge the gates of hell in every nation by preaching the Gospel with the Holy Ghost.[609] The churches provide a corporate presence of Christ in the kingdom of men.[610]

When the churches are revived (fully awake to the righteousness of God),[611] the discipline of the kingdom of God will be manifested in the church and in the community where it ministers. The church in Jerusalem demonstrated the power and authority of the kingdom of God in their communities. Consider the following examples of Christ's

[604] II Thessalonians 2:7; I Timothy 3:15
[605] Revelation 1:5-6
[606] Mark 13:34-35
[607] I Timothy 3:15-16
[608] I Corinthians 1:2; 12:27
[609] I Peter 1:12; Matthew 16:18; Acts 1:8; 2:1; 4:31-33
[610] I Corinthians 12-14; see especially I Corinthians 14:20-21
[611] I Corinthians 15:34

churches revealing the power of God openly in the communities where they minister.

Discipline was strong in the early churches. When two members of the church in Jerusalem, Ananias and Sapphira, attempted to lie to the Holy Ghost, they dropped dead in the church-house.[612]

God's power was also openly manifested outside the walls of the churches. King Herod imprisoned Peter, but the church prayed for him without ceasing.[613] The angel of the Lord gloriously delivered Peter from Herod's hand.[614] Later, Herod made an oration that inspired the fickle pagan community of Tyre to worship him. Because he "gave not God the glory,"[615] the angel of the Lord fed him to worms. This is a perfect example of the Spirit of Christ restraining the spirit of Antichrist.

When the church in Ephesus was in revival, many burned their books on sorcery and "curious arts."[616] So many turned

---

[612] Acts 5:1-11—Perhaps they were assembled in the Upper Room (Acts 1:13) or on Solomon's porch (Acts 5:12-13).

[613] Acts 12:5

[614] In Acts 12:1-19, a wicked political leader kills an Apostle and then his authority is virtually mocked by Christ. Remember Pilate had no power over Jesus that God did not give him. After the resurrection, all power in Heaven and in Earth was transferred to Jesus—Herod had no power over James that Jesus did not give him. Sometimes the Lord delivers His own into the power of His enemies as a chastisement for some error. More often, it is done to establish greater occasion of wrath against the enemies of Christ (Romans 2:5; II Peter 2:9; see Revelation 16:6).

[615] Acts 12:20-25—This story is a clear demonstration of the work of the Spirit of Jesus Christ resisting the spirit of Antichrist. As we have noted already, Satan (together with his minions) is the spirit that operates in the children of disobedience, moving the world toward a global dictatorship under the "son of perdition," the man of sin, who will call himself God (II Thessalonians 2:1-9). The Spirit of Jesus Christ resists the spirit of Antichrist. We are confident the man of sin will come from Lebanon, and particularly from Tyre (Ezekiel 28:2-19; 31:3; see Isaiah 23:8). When Herod presumed to receive the accolade of deity from men of Tyre, the angel of the Lord checked this spirit, indeed!

[616] Acts 19:19-20

from the vanity of idol worship that the idol merchants became alarmed about lost business.[617] Satan fought back through the children of disobedience and put some of Christ's servants into prison,[618] killed others,[619] raised violent mobs in protest against them,[620] and generally stirred up persecution against the churches.

Only when churches became corrupted through compromise in both doctrine and godly living could Satan stop their onslaught against his power of darkness in this world.[621] Remember, Satan was able to reestablish his throne in the earth, in the city with a compromised church, before the last Apostle passed.[622]

When the saints are in revival, believer-kings and priests bring the authority and power of the kingdom of God into the world of the kingdom of men.[623] However, as Jesus prophesied, His "citizens hated him, and sent a message after him, saying, We will not have this man to reign over us."[624] Therefore, when the King returns, He will first judge the stewards of His House,[625] then He will say, "Those mine enemies, which would not that I should reign over them, bring hither, and slay them before me."[626]

Today, the Spirit of GOD Works in the earth Through Two Bodies

One of the *bodies* that Christ uses to extend the reach of His kingdom authority into the world (the kingdom of men)

---

[617] Acts 19:21-27
[618] Revelation 2:10
[619] Acts 7:54-59; 12:2
[620] Acts 18-19
[621] Revelation 2-3; Matthew 16:16; Colossians 1:13
[622] Revelation 2:13
[623] Matthew 12:28
[624] Luke 19:14
[625] Luke 19:15-26
[626] Luke 19:27

is His Church.[627] The churches do not hold the scepter, but the keys of the kingdom—calling on all men everywhere to confess, "Jesus Christ is Lord." If a nation affirms Jesus' Lordship, they may receive the stewardship of the dominion that was intended for Israel, "until Shiloh come."[628]

Also, the body of the individual believer is used in spiritual warfare. God's power and authority is extended into the kingdom of men through our bodies by manifesting Christ's life in our mortal flesh.[629]

Jesus' life is displayed in our mortal flesh when we "walk not after the flesh, but after the Spirit," thus fulfilling the righteousness of the Law."[630] Christ dwells in our hearts by faith.[631] He accomplishes this by giving us His Spirit.[632] (Indeed, if any have not the Spirit of Christ, he or she is none of His.)[633] The body of the believer becomes the Temple of the Holy Ghost.[634] The Spirit comes into our hearts,[635]

---

[627] I Corinthians 12:27; 14:23-25

[628] To avert confusion, it should be made clear that, no matter what nation might at any time have the *dominion*, it is Christ that reigns from the heavens over the *kingdom of men*. Furthermore, the Spirit has made it clear that at last, Israel will have this dominion on the earth headquartered in earthly Jerusalem; the *Church* will be the "Bride of Christ," whose inheritance is as joint heirs with Him and whose city is heavenly Jerusalem.

[629] II Corinthians 4:10-11—The interested reader should compare II Corinthians 4:10-12 with Galatians 2:20 and Matthew 16:24. The word translated *life* in II Corinthians 4:10-11 is ζωή (*zoe*—(Strong No. 2222): used to speak of the essential aspect of *life*.) See also the verb form of this word, ζάω (*zao*—(Strong No. 2198)). It is the word Paul uses when he declares, "I am crucified with Christ: nevertheless I live (*zao*); yet not I, but Christ liveth (*zao*) in me: and the life which I now live (*zao*) in the flesh I live (*zao*) by the faith of the Son of God..." Therefore, we are dead, and our *life* (*zoe*) is hid with Christ in God (Colossians 3:3). Our *life* (*zoe*) is hid with Christ in God, and His *life* (*zoe*) is supposed to be manifested in our mortal flesh.

[630] Romans 8:1-4; Galatians 5:16-25

[631] Ephesians 3:17

[632] Romans 8:8-11

[633] Romans 8:9

[634] I Corinthians 6:19

[635] II Corinthians 1:22; Galatians 4:6

where He sheds abroad the love of God.[636] Although He never leaves our hearts, the Temple needs to be continually filled with the Spirit.[637] Jesus prophesied that through the belly of the believer, the Holy Ghost would flow into the world like "rivers of living water."[638]

Christ in the heart of the believer corresponds to Moses' Ark of the Covenant in the Holy of Holies. When the children of Israel walked in favor with God, satisfying the demands of the Law (which included a provision for obtaining forgiveness of sins, by the way),[639] God filled the Temple with a manifestation of His presence. Once, when Israel was a "nation under God" and the Assyrians rose up against her, the angel of the LORD wiped out 185,000 soldiers in one night's work.[640] Nations trembled when Israel walked in God's favor and the Ark of God was brought into battle.[641] However, when they rebelled against Him, He would write Ichabod over the Tabernacle—the word *Ichabod* means the "glory is departed."[642]

Believers must present their bodies a living sacrifice, holy, acceptable to God, so that He may manifest the life and power of Jesus in the kingdom of men through them. Those who surrender to Christ's reign will be delivered from the wrath to come; those who refuse will be destroyed. When the believer is filled and flowing, the power of Christ is active in the world, pushing back the spirit of Antichrist and advancing the kingdom of God. When believers grieve

---

[636] Romans 5:5
[637] Ephesians 1:13,14; 5:18-21
[638] John 7:38-39
[639] I John 1:7-9
[640] II Kings 19:35
[641] I Samuel 4:8
[642] I Samuel 4:21

or quench the Spirit,[643] the spirit of Antichrist grows strong and promotes the kingdom of darkness in this world.

Oh, woe is us! Look at any map and consider how much of the world continues under the power of darkness.

Conclusion

The book of Daniel testifies to the truth that God rules in the kingdom of men and gives it to whomever He will. This principle is as applicable today as it ever was. Only now, Jesus Christ as the Son of man, holds the kingdom of men in the kingdom of God as the Son of God.

As you continue, you will understand more about your essential role as servants of Christ under His present rule over the earth. All who force their will against Christ and usurp His authority in the world will be destroyed when He returns. Whereas, all who repent and believe on Christ Jesus are translated into the Kingdom of God's dear Son and receive a present appointment as kings and priests unto God in the kingdom of Christ. All God's king-priests are commissioned to represent Him in the present kingdom of Christ on Earth as His ambassadors. Our primary purpose is to declare the Lordship of Jesus Christ and His soon return. However, connected with the fulfilling of that purpose, Christ's king-priests have authority in the world and influence in heaven, and they play a pivotal role in the ongoing war over the dominion.

Most Evangelical Christians limit their role to only spreading the message of the Gospel. This is certainly the primary mission. But consider the success the Devil has at hindering our work,[644] and notice how the forces of darkness align against us all over the world, presuming to cancel the King's command.[645]

---

[643] Ephesians 4:30-31; I Thessalonians 5:19
[644] I Thessalonians 2:18
[645] Matthew 28:18-20

Few understand rightly the role of God's king-priests in the spiritual warfare played out among the nations, where Satan works to hinder the work of believers in this world. Again, look at any world map and consider the number of countries where Satan has contrived to make it unlawful to preach the Gospel. It is staggering how much territory in this world Satan has managed to bring under his power. Christians are to blame! And not only because so many who call themselves Christian refuse to depart from iniquity. Most Christians do not understand the significance of their influence on the outcomes of spiritual warfare. Consequently, they do not use their authority as kings under Christ in this Earth nor their power in heaven as priests unto God. Others have only a superficial understanding of these things and don't know what to do or how to go about it.

Beginning with the next chapter, I'm going to show how to use our authority as kings in this world and priests in heaven to do our part in God's War.

One of the most controversial aspects of Christian involvement in spiritual warfare is when it intersects with physical wars. Let's begin there.

~

"Providence has given to our people the choice of their rulers. And it is the duty as well as the privilege and interest, of a Christian nation to select and prefer Christians for their rulers."

~ John Jay

(John Jay to Jedidiah Morse February 28, 1797: Source: October 12, 1816. *The Correspondence and Public Papers of John Jay*)

Chapter Fifteen

God's Warriors:
King-Priests in Christ's Kingdom

Wars and Rumors of Wars

W AR! Sixties rocker Edwin Starr sang a song that asked, "What is it good for?" And answered, "Absolutely nothing!" The stupidity of that sentiment is exposed in one word: Hitler. War is made necessary when evil men aspire to take the place of God in the world. Invariably, such rulers view the Divinely endowed inalienable rights of men as a threat to their authority. When such men or nations begin to usurp the rights of their fellowman, resistance from good men is called for, which sometimes breaks out into war. To this end, God appointed the sword of vengeance to nations under GOD to execute wrath upon evildoers.[646] Of course, this includes the execution of Divine wrath upon tyrants. What is war good for? Liberty and justice—and freedom! That's what!

Jesus said there would be wars and rumors of wars throughout human history until He returned.[647] Wars come when some nation tries to take the dominion and control the resources of the earth. Inevitably, these powers usurp Christ's authority by seducing men out from under God to oppress them. This is where Christ steps in.

[646] Romans 13:1-6
[647] Matthew 24:6

With all power in Heaven and Earth in His hands, Christ gives stewardship of the dominion to whomever He will. The nation to which He has given stewardship of the dominion receives *the sword*: the right and power to execute wrath upon the evildoer. Christ uses His nation under GOD to execute Divine wrath upon tyrants.

How Does Christ Use His Nation Under God to Execute Wrath Against Tyrants?

Christ is the King, and all nations are subject to His rule. He has the prerogative to discipline this or that nation (or people) as He pleases. As pointed out above, Jesus uses His nation under God (the government to which He has given the dominion), as His sword when executing vengeance on evildoers.[648] We notice He will often hold back the hand that grips His sword until the oppressed are humbled and cry to Him for deliverance. This is illustrated clearly by the Exodus.

Israel suffered grievous oppression under the cruel hand of the pharaohs for at least eighty years.[649] From the beginning of their bondage, GOD was preparing their deliverance. However, He did not send their deliverer until they turned their hearts to Him in humbled petition.[650]

Moses recognized that he was providentially positioned to be the deliverer of his people. The unusual circumstances of his birth, his position in the palace as a prince in Egypt, his extensive training, and his impressive accomplishments, made him the obvious choice. He went out among his brethren and slew an Egyptian who was abusing a Hebrew

---

[648] Romans 13:1-6; Isaiah 34:5; Ezekiel 21:5; 30:24-25
[649] Moses was adopted by the daughter of Pharaoh soon after the oppression began. He lived forty years in the palace, then forty years in the desert of Midian, before he was called of GOD to deliver Israel from Egypt (Acts 7:23, 30; Exodus 7:7).
[650] Exodus 3:7

slave, presupposing that his Hebrew brethren would understand he was God's deliverer.[651] But Moses was rebuffed by the people he aspired to save—and by the GOD for Whom he thought to save them.[652] Israel would suffer forty more years of oppression before GOD would send Moses to execute His judgment upon Egypt and deliver His people.[653] It's not enough that this or that nation has the dominion under God; it must wait on the LORD.

God moves His nation-under-God to intervene when He is moved by what He sees as His eyes run to and fro throughout the earth, beholding the evil and the good.[654] Christ searches the hearts of men,[655] looking for those on whose behalf He might show Himself strong.[656] Although He was preparing Israel's deliverance from the moment their oppression began, He would not send their champion to deliver them until He saw the hearts of His people humbled and crying to Him for liberation.

Such things are within the purview of GOD, and frankly, they are "things too high"[657] for us. It involves matters of the heart and the mysterious way God turns the hearts of kings (or rulers).[658] Nevertheless, we can be sure God ponders the

---

[651] Acts 7:25

[652] Exodus 1-2

[653] God said He would not deed the land of Canaan to Abraham until the iniquity of the then current deed holder, the Amorite, had come to the full (Genesis 15:16). One reason God waited to send Moses because He was allowing the Amorites their "space to repent"—their iniquity had not yet come to the full. Many think God allowed His people to fall into oppression because He wanted to use that time to steel them for the battles they would face. However, the slave generation did not, in fact, have what it takes to complete their mission. Rather, the next generation, which grew up in freedom, did.

[654] Proverbs 15:3

[655] Proverbs 21:2

[656] II Chronicles 16:9

[657] Psalms 131:1

[658] Proverbs 21:1

hearts of all men and pays attention to the cries from the hearts of His own. Nations rise and fall, powers ebb and flow, great movements of men and angels come and go, all orchestrated by the Hand of God responding to the hearts of His people. We are often reminded that God moves to heal a land when those who are called by His name humble themselves and pray.[659]

America is the nation-under-God today. In its institutions and history, America acknowledges God and, as Patrick Henry said, it was founded upon the Gospel of Jesus Christ.[660] It serves as a modern example of how God uses the nation to whom He has given His sword to execute His judgment upon the nations. The U.S. usually intervenes when the matter is in one way or another related to ours or our Ally's national security interests. Examples include WWI and WWII, Korea and Viet Nam. Or more recently, we might offer Russia's intrusions upon the Sovereignty of Ukraine, or China's threats against Taiwan; North Korea's repeated threats, or Iraq's invasion of Kuwait, as examples. We should include Iran's effort to obtain a nuclear weapon, which concerns us because of its sponsorship of terrorism, and their threats against us and Israel.

National security is the foremost reason for intervention. The protection of our allies in a just dispute stands second. The third, which is truly the overarching concern underlying all U.S. intervention, is to advance or protect the cause of freedom at home and around the world. The first and second criteria are straightforward. The third, however, is more complicated. Usually, the nation under God will not get directly involved until some set of circumstances

---

[659] II Chronicles 7:14
[660] Morris, Benjamin in *The Christian Life and Character of the Civil Institutions of the United States,* presents the definitive proof of America's Christian roots.

develop that threaten that nation or its allies directly or indirectly. This is what finally brought us into WWII. Other times, it can be economic concerns—we can't allow a nation hostile to freedom to control oil reserves necessary for our economy, for example.

It's easy to say there is no justification for going to war over something like control of oil reserves. No Blood for Oil makes for a great anti-war sound bite. However, assuming you have read the first half of this book, you understand that every war is about control of the earth's resources—the dominion. Therefore, it's not about oil, per sé. It's about control of Earth's resources and the fact that some men attempt to take those resources into the power of evil empires, such as Iran or China. If good men sit back and do nothing, evil empires will grow sufficiently strong to bring the entire world into darkness. We understand that the stakes are far higher than oil. Ultimately, it's about justice and liberty. It's about Freedom! Religious liberty is the fountain of all our liberties. Ultimately, it's about the freedom to preach the Gospel.

Should the sword of vengeance[661] be used to advance the Gospel? Jesus instructed His disciples to procure a sword in preparation for His departure.[662] The disciples searched about and found two swords, and Jesus said that was enough. Later that night, Peter drew his sword and struck one of the soldiers that had come to arrest Jesus. Our Lord rebuked him, bid him put the sword away, and explained the time for that battle had not yet come. It's scheduled for day the Lord returns, "and all the holy angels with Him."[663] Believers are encouraged to keep and bear swords (arms)

---

[661] Romans 13:1-6
[662] Luke 22:36
[663] Matthew 25:31; see 26:53

for their self-protection, but not to advance the Gospel. However, God will use His sword of vengeance to advance the cause of liberty. And liberty will include the freedom to preach the Gospel. But the Gospel is advanced using another sword—the Sword of the Spirit, which is the Word of God.[664]

What brings a nation under God to war is sometimes very simple and straightforward. Sometimes it's ambiguous and even mysterious. God may openly direct a leader: as in the case of Moses, when he encountered GOD in a burning bush.[665] Or Gideon.[666] God will sometmes move a nation He intends to judge to rise against His nation under God, only to then use His nation to punish it. Usually it's obvious: this or that nation directly threatens our national security, which, effectively, compels us to intervene. Other times it becomes apparent that we cannot stand aloof while a tyrant rampages across the world, destroying innocent lives, a la Hitler.

God might turn the hearts of rulers to His purpose, and we don't readily see a connection between national interests and the conflict at hand. Sometimes the Divine purpose driving us to war will be hidden behind the glaring machinations of wicked men, and only those with great spiritual discernment can see what way the Hand of God is moving. One example easy for us to comprehend is the Civil War. Motivations ranged from the noble to the coarse—but we can be confident God's purpose was to free the slaves and end that abhorrent practice in this nation.

What Part Do Believer-king-Priests Have in Wars?

I have often sung the popular spiritual song, "This world

---

[664] Ephesians 6:17
[665] Exodus 3
[666] Judges 6

is not my home, I'm just a' passing through. My treasures are laid up, somewhere beyond the blue." But Satan uses such sentiment to wrap a lie in truth, and believers are unaware of the deceit they're swallowing.

Satan has done a masterful job of convincing Christians they have no part in this world. By convincing them they have no role to play, many Christians have withdrawn from any meaningful participation in this world's affairs. Perfect! That gives Satan a free hand. He can take over all the governments of the world and turn them against Christ—and the Gospel. The power ordained by God to execute wrath against evildoers is usurped by the spirit of Antichrist. When this happens, the government becomes the enemy of righteousness. Invariably, it will devolve into persecuting God's children, and for no other reason than they are Christians.[667] Think about this.

God ordained the sword of civil government to execute wrath against evildoers. How is it possible that so many governments have been able to usurp the power God ordained and use it to persecute God's children? In America, He placed that sword in the hands of Christians. And He gave America the stewardship of the dominion. But if the children of disobedience in America gain control of the power God ordained to government, they will do here what they have done everywhere they are in power. They will contrive laws that will put Christians in conflict with government—laws that are in many cases designed by them for this very purpose. Obviously, this is contrary to God's ordained purpose for governments. And it is only happening in America because Christians have relinquished the sword of civil government to men and women controlled by the spirit of Antichrist.[668] We have done what Judah did before

---

[667] Romans 13:1-6
[668] II Timothy 2:26

us: we have "set up kings, but not by [Jehovah]."[669] We have given power to ungodly men and women who are of the spirit of Antichrist and not of the Spirit of Jesus Christ.

Our vote plays a critical part in directing how the sword of civil government is deployed. We have the power in this country to choose our rulers and to cast them out of office. But we consistently vote in rulers who do not have a Christian worldview; in their philosophy of life or beliefs, they are Antichrist. So we kill babies.

We have given the power of our government to men and women who believe that murdering babies in the womb is a woman's right. And now they clamor for the right to kill them up to the time of their birth. Government has been given to promoters of the LGBTQ agenda, giving way to all the evils that spawn from that movement. Consequently, gender confusion, the breakdown of traditional marriage, and encroachments upon our freedoms of speech and religion are advanced as a matter of public policy in America. Even our freedom of thought is threatened. Increasingly in this country, Christians are being cast as social pariahs while wicked and ungodly men and women and their evil deeds are lauded. These people are slowly turning the sword of civil force against Christians in our country, the same way it has happened in almost every other nation today.

Nations come under the spirit of Antichrist when those responsible for releasing the Spirit of Jesus Christ into the world are grieving and quenching Him instead.

Christians grieve the Spirit when they vote into power persons whose loyalties are not to Christ. If this continues, the Spirit of liberty will be quenched! If our government remains under the influence of people whose lord is the

---

[669] Hosea 8:4

"prince of the power of the air, the spirit that now works in the children of disobedience,"[670] liberty will be lost! And this happens when foolish Christians vote selfishly or sentimentally and not according to the Word of God. But mostly it happens because of Christians who fail to vote at all— yielding our nation to Satan by default.

"This world is not my home"? Then whose home is it? The Devil's? Does it belong to him? That is what Satan wants us to believe. The truth is, it all belongs to Christ. He bought the field, which He explained represents the world, to secure to Himself the treasure that is in it.[671] He spoiled all principality and power, and received "all power in heaven and in earth."[672] Christians have a legitimate claim to Earth as their home while they tabernacle in this body. Indeed, the children of obedience have a greater claim to the earth than do the children of disobedience.

I said Satan uses the sentiment of the popular song, "This world is not my home," to wrap a lie in truth. We are passing through, and we are strangers and pilgrims, aliens to those who held it before Christ came.[673] We "love not the world, neither the things that are in the world,"[674] and our treasures are laid up in Heaven. The lie is not in any of the statements made in the lyrics of the song, but in the suggestion that we have no part in this world and, by implication, no legitimate place in it. But Jesus prayed that we would not be taken out of the world;[675] we are in this world by His authority.

---

[670] Ephesians 2:1-2
[671] Matthew 13:44
[672] Colossians 2:15; Matthew 28:18
[673] I Peter 2:11
[674] I John 2:15-16
[675] John 17:15

Remember, Satan could claim as his all the kingdoms of the world and the glory of them, but Jesus spoiled his house and took it all away. He gave to His disciples "His goods"[676] and went away to get another kingdom. Now we are strangers and pilgrims commissioned by the King of Heaven and Earth to hold His goods as stewards until He returns. Jesus left with His disciples the *goods* He spoiled from Satan's house. That includes *the dominion.*

All who inhabit the earth are Christ's citizens, whether they like it or not. Christ's enemies see us as an alien invasion, occupying what the spirit that operates in them convinces them is theirs. Do you begin to understand? We must not buy into that lie. The truth is Christians are the legitimate heirs of the kingdom. We are God's occupying force, with the keys of the kingdom granting us authority from Christ the King to preach the Gospel to every nation. We need to permeate every system—whether politics, education, economics, or entertainment—everywhere applying the salt of God's righteousness and the light of God's truth. Our mission is urgent! Christ Jesus died to save every one of His citizens from the wrath that is coming upon this world. And by all accounts, that wrath is coming soon!

When it comes to war, believers have a vested interest in taking their place on the side of the nation under God. Not only do believer-king-priests have a vested interest, but also a stated responsibility to defend their nation under God.

Does This Mean Christians Should Bear Arms in War?

In the church where I received Christ, my pastor encouraged me to believe it was never right for a Christian to kill. Others in the church thought he was mistaken in this matter. They believed Christians could and should participate

---

[676] Matthew 25:14; see also Matthew 12:29 and 24:47

in the military. Being a young Christian, I was confused about this. Years later, and after a careful study of Scripture on this question, the matter was settled. Christians, of all people, must participate in the execution of God's wrath upon evildoers via the sword of civil government. God uses His people to bear His sword.

Romans 13:1-6 tells us God ordains the sword of civil government; surely God's people should be the ones holding it. We need Christians in our military and serving on our police forces. These people are called God's ministers.[677] God's ministers ought to be under the influence and control of the Spirit of Jesus Christ and not the spirit of Antichrist.

What a great trick of Satan, to get Christians to allow the spirit of Antichrist to take control of our military and police. The Bible says Satan can take the children of disobedience captive at his will.[678] We need people holding these powers who are under the influence of the Spirit of Jesus Christ.

Besides, Jesus never discouraged His disciples from participating in the Roman army.[679] Before He left the Upper Room to begin His torturous slog to Calvary, He instructed His disciples to arm themselves.[680] In fact, He emphasized the need for a sword, saying, if necessary, "Let him sell his garment, and buy one."

This nation under God needs Christians throughout our government, in every capacity, and nowhere is this more important than in our military and police forces.

And yet, this is not the primary role of Christ's king-priests in the matter of "wars and rumors of wars."

---

[677] Romans 13:4
[678] II Timothy 2:26
[679] Acts 10
[680] Luke 22:36

The Primary Role of Believer-king-Priests in War

Believer-king-priests have an even more significant role in the rise and fall of nations than involvement in the military and law enforcement.

As we have shown, GOD rules in the kingdoms of men and gives the dominion to whomever He chooses. This involves the rise and fall of nations. And GOD deploys mighty angels to war with devils as He attends to this matter. Now, as we shall show, GOD moves in response to the prayers of His people. A few examples are thought necessary to set the table for this discussion.

Gabriel is one of God's archangels. He drew back the curtain that separates the physical from the spiritual and revealed to Daniel the involvement of GOD's angels and Satan's devils in the rise and fall of empires.[681] Consider the testimony I presented earlier showing the activity of angels in the wars of men. In every example, praying saints were involved. But the relationship between praying saints and the outcome of battles is portrayed nowhere better than when Israel fought the Amalekites. Moses stood before God on a nearby hill, and so long as his hands were raised in prayer, Israel prevailed over the Amalekites. But when his arms grew weary and his hands sunk, the enemy prevailed.[682] Aaron and Hur stepped in to hold up Moses' hands so that the Israelites prevailed over their enemies. You see in these stories that angels, devils, and men are active in every war; and that God determines the outcome based on the prayers of His people.

Jesus Christ gave power and authority to His disciples

---

[681] See Daniel 10:12-14, and 10:20-11:1
[682] Exodus 17:10-12

over devils.[683] He extended this power and authority to continue during His absence on the day of Pentecost.[684] He left us instructions on how to use this power and authority to uproot wicked men and women and bring down evil empires.

Jesus taught His disciples that they had the power to bring down Empires and uproot leaders. When He said if we had faith the size of a mustard seed, we could move mountains and uproot trees,[685] He was not talking about excavation or deforestation. The mountain is used in Holy Scripture to speak of kingdoms or nations, and empires.[686] The tree is used to represent leaders, of men, or families of men.[687] As king-priests, we have standing before the Throne of the Almighty, and by faith, we may call down evil empires and uproot wicked leaders.

Christ met with Elijah and Moses on what we call the Mount of Transfiguration.[688] Peter, James, and John were there with Him. Down below, His nine disciples encountered a devil they were powerless to cast out. This had never happened before. When Jesus and their three fellow Apostles returned, the disciples asked Jesus about the devil they could not command. Jesus explained that some kinds of devils require more than usual spiritual power to control. In those cases, it was necessary to include fasting with their prayer: "this kind goeth not out but by prayer and fasting,"[689] He said!

On the mountain of transfiguration, there assembled the three most powerful spiritual men the world has ever known: Elijah, Moses, and, greatest of all, Christ Jesus.

[683] Luke 9:1, Jesus gave His disciples *power* (*dunamin*—strength, capability) and *authority* (*exousian* — authority, one invested with authority to act).
[684] Acts 1:8
[685] Matthew 21:21; Mark 11:23; Luke 17:6
[686] Jeremiah 51:25; see Daniel 2:35, 44-45
[687] Daniel 4:10-15; Psalm 1; Romans 11:24
[688] Matthew 17
[689] Matthew 17:21

Interestingly, each of these men is renowned for surviving an ordeal of forty days and nights in prayer and fasting.[690]

As kings, believers have the authority in the physical world to command all men everywhere to repent and believe on Christ Jesus.[691] Also, we have the authority to declare sins forgiven to all who repent and believe, and the sins of all who refuse to remain.[692] As kings unto God, believers may extend the peace of God's kingdom upon a house or withdraw it,[693] and bless the city or kick the dust of rebellious cities from their feet, marking them for condemnation in the day of our LORD JESUS.[694] As kings unto God, believers have authority in the spiritual world to command devils and, indeed, to resist the Devil himself and so compel him to flee.[695]

God raises nations and puts them down. The spiritual authority of believer-kings is only impactful when exercised under God. Then the believer's actions bring the spiritual into an intersection with the physical world. The believer-king may command the proud mountain (nation or Empire) to be removed and cast into the sea. And he or she may command the proud trees (their wicked rulers) that sit upon these mountains, to join them there.

Here is where the believer-king-priest has his or her most significant impact on the kingdoms of men. If believers used their power and authority under God, every proud mountain that exalts itself against King Jesus would be

---

[690] Exodus 34:28; I Kings 19:8; Luke 4:1-2
[691] Acts 17:30; 16:31
[692] John 20:23
[693] Matthew10:13
[694] Matthew 10:14. It should be remembered that this is not a trivial matter and that God takes it very seriously. So much so, that He has decreed "the curse causeless shall not come" Proverbs 26:2).
[695] James 4:7

cast down, and the wicked trees with their evil fruit would be uprooted.

Every nation that exalts itself against King Jesus must yield to His authority or be destroyed. This is our message to the nations: repent, turn to GOD, confess Jesus is Lord, and believe on Him for the salvation of your souls, or be damned at His appearing.

Meanwhile, through spiritual warfare, we can engage by prayer and fasting to exert a powerful influence into the theater of God's War.

The devils supporting these evil regimes that bar the Gospel from being preached in their borders can be overcome by prayer and fasting. With their influence broken, their ability to protect their wicked leaders from justice is removed. These nations will fall! Their leaders removed from power. They cannot withstand the assault of the Church in fervent, earnest, and holy prayer, and the preaching of the Gospel with the Holy Ghost sent down from heaven.

Conclusion

Satan takes territory yielded to him by lazy, or worldly, or ignorant believers. He then sets a stronghold around it and appoints mighty devils to fortify that stronghold. From such fortifications, he extends his influence into surrounding areas, and weak, carnal, flesh-serving Christians yield yet more territory to Satan. He extends the territorial reach of his occupation, setting devils at the gates of his fortresses, and expands his kingdom of darkness in the world. Weak Christians attempt in vain to overcome these gates of hell while devils mock the Church of God.

But Jesus said the gates of hell shall not prevail against

the Church.[696] If the Church is revived, if it is awake to righteousness and shunning iniquity, if it is praying and fasting, and if it is stirring up its most holy power, then it can charge the gates of hell. And those gates will retreat! Then believers can pull down these strongholds[697] and reclaim lost territory.

But this must happen soon, ere it's too late and Christ must say to His churches, I will spew you from my mouth.[698]

Repent!

We begin now to turn our attention to what a believer-king-priest must do to use his or her influence in heaven to exercise his or her authority in the earth.

~

---

[696] Matthew 16:16-18
[697] II Corinthians 10:4
[698] Revelation 3:16

Chapter Sixteen

God's Warrior Kings

(Part One)

Kings in Christ's Kingdom

JESUS CHRIST THE LORD has made us kings and priests "unto God and his Father; to him be glory and dominion for ever and ever. Amen."[699] *Glory* (a manifestation of one's worth that excites adoration, honor, and worship) and *dominion* (the right of sovereign rule over a realm) are the prizes Satan covets. Fitting that Peter should use this expression in his letter: "To Him [Jesus Christ] be glory and dominion for ever and ever. Amen." For in that same letter, the Spirit warns us, "Be sober, be vigilant; because your adversary the devil, as a roaring lion, walketh about, seeking whom he may devour."[700] We are appointed kings and priests whose duty is to Him, to Whom are the glory and the dominion forever and ever, in opposition to him who would usurp it.

He said not that He *will*, or *shall*, but that He "*hath* made us kings and priests."[701] Furthermore, these kings and priests are the only obstacles to Satan's designs. Therefore, the Devil centers his attention on them. Indeed, we must be "vigilant; because (our) adversary . . . as a roaring lion, walketh about, seeking whom he may devour."[702]

[699] Revelation 1:6
[700] I Peter 5:8
[701] Revelation 1:6a (Emphasis added)
[702] I Peter 5:8

Capable spiritual warriors understand how to exercise their authority as kings and priests unto God in spiritual warfare. Therefore, we must learn how to war as kings and how to war as priests. We will begin by offering insights into the believer's role as kings in Christ's service.

Kings in Christ's Kingdom Service

Some reading this might remember the rock band KISS. Their vile behavior and rebellious persona inspired an urban legend that the letters of their band name denoted Kings In Satan's Service. They have consistently denied this; nonetheless, it is true—that is, regardless of the real meaning of their band name, if not kings, they are certainly kids in Satan's service.[703] Satan is called the prince of the power of the air, the spirit that works in the "children of disobedience."[704] He takes them captive at his will[705] and uses them to further his purpose in the earth. We identified that purpose above: to usurp the "glory" and "dominion" that God gave to His Son, Jesus Christ.[706] The spirit that operates in the world through the children of disobedience is the spirit of

---

[703] The following citations, taken from the video documentary *They Sold Their Soul for Rock-n-Roll,* produced by Good Fight Ministries, P.O. Box 2202, Simi Valley, CA 93062, will convince any reasonable mind that no matter what is the meaning of their name, the band members of KISS are undeniably in service to Satan. Gene Simmons (vocals-bass guitar) advised his young fans, "People are going to tell you, 'You can't do this. You can't do that.' They can all go (expletive) themselves … you don't need them around, and that includes your parents. Get rid of those leeches" (*Faces,* December, 1984). Obviously, the "spirit of disobedience" controls Gene Simmons (Ephesians 2:2). Satanist Thomas Thorn (co-founder of rock band *The Electric Hellfire Club,* and an ordained priest in Anton LaVey's *Church of Satan*) spoke of the influence KISS had on him: "KISS was rebellion incarnate, and we identified with that in the same way we would later align ourselves with Lucifer and his rebellion against God." In the song *God Of Thunder,* KISS sings of being the *lord of the flies* (an attribution to Satan), and of following the *left-hand path* that leads to the *father of lies*—both expressions are references to Satanism and Satan.
[704] Ephesians 2:2
[705] II Timothy 2:26
[706] Matthew 28:18

Antichrist.[707] Wherever Satan succeeds at gaining place in this world, he turns it over to his children of disobedience. Surely, at least some of these children of disobedience rank as kings in Satan's service.

Jesus is the King of kings, and He has commissioned every believer to be a king in His service. God the Father has given the glory and the dominion to the King of kings and Lord of lords.[708] Satan knows we are destined to inherit all things in Christ.[709] The Spirit that operates in us is the Spirit of Jesus Christ.[710] His Holy Spirit has been sent into the world to reprove it of sin, righteousness, and judgment.[711] He moves into the world through the belly of believers.[712] The Spirit that is in us is greater than the spirit that is in the world.[713] We are kings in the Savior's service. And we solemnly warn all men of this world that they had best "kiss the Son, lest He be angry, and [they] perish from the way, when His wrath is kindled but a little," and comfort them with the promise: "Blessed are all they that put their trust in Him."[714]

By the Holy Spirit, Paul taught us that everything that happened to Israel, "happened unto them for ensamples: and they are written for our admonition, upon whom the ends of the world are come."[715] Saul, David, Solomon, and the succession of kings that followed upon the division of the kingdom into Israel and Judah offer some insight into our kingship.

[707] I John 4:3
[708] Matthew 28:18
[709] Revelation 21:7
[710] Galatians 3:16; Romans 8:9-11
[711] John 16:7-13
[712] John 7:38-39
[713] I John 4:4
[714] Psalm 2:12
[715] I Corinthians 10:11

Of course, we cannot exhaust the store of revelations available to us in the stories of all the kings. However, what follows are examples and admonitions that are essential to every believer-king engaged in spiritual warfare.[716]

Basic Principles

First, in the Old Testament, God established a clean break between the kingship and the priesthood.[717] God combined these offices in us.[718]

Later, when we study the priesthood of the believer, we will develop the truth that we are a unique priesthood—of the order of Melchizedek and not of the order of Levi.[719] Here, we desire to point out that Melchizedek was both a king and a priest.[720] Interestingly, a Gentile[721] king-priest ruled in Salem (Jerusalem) in the days before Abraham, and the significance that Abraham paid tithes to him is explained in Hebrews 7:6-10. Essentially, it signifies the fact that his priesthood was before that of Levi. We should, therefore, understand that our kingship is prior too.

Second, any insights we derive from the examples and admonitions of the Old Testament stories of the kings must be understood spiritually, not carnally.[722] Their warfare was carnal, that is, physical. Ours is spiritual.[723]

Third, this is not to say the spiritual has no bearing upon

---

[716] I Corinthians 10:11
[717] II Chronicles 26:18
[718] Revelation 1:6
[719] Since Jesus is "our High Priest" and we are "made ... priests unto God" by Him (Revelation 1:6), it is justly reasoned that we are of His priesthood; that is, of the order of Melchizedek (Hebrews 7). (Hebrews 7:1-21)
[720] Genesis 14:18
[721] One of the great puzzles of Scripture is the identity of Melchizedek. This question is addressed thoroughly in Appendix: Melchizedek.
[722] John 6:63
[723] II Corinthians 10:4

the physical. Indeed, Satan and Christ war over the dominion, which, as said before, involves the kingdoms of this world. Instead, I'm saying that we do not "war after the flesh";[724] and therefore, the weapons we use in our warfare are "not carnal, but mighty through God to the pulling down of strongholds."[725] Our battle is against vain imaginations[726] that puff-up men and women to rage against the knowledge of God (the acknowledgment of His Sovereign rule over all creation).[727]

One of the vain imaginations we must draw the Sword of the Spirit against today is the lie that men need not repent toward God to be saved.[728] God commands all men everywhere to repent and believe on Jesus Christ.[729] All who disobey the Gospel command to repent and believe must be warned that God will "in flaming fire [take] vengeance on them . . . that obey not the gospel."[730]

There is a seducing spirit working an evil doctrine in the minds of believers today who suppose men are not required to repent of their sins for salvation.[731] But every sinner will

---

[724] II Corinthians 10:3
[725] II Corinthians 10:4
[726] Romans 1:21
[727] Psalm 2:1; Acts 4:25
[728] Acts 20:21
[729] Acts 17:30; I John 3:23; Acts 20:21
[730] II Thessalonians 1:8
[731] Catholics and most Protestants view repentance as a work of righteousness, a promise to do good works, a turning over of a "new leaf," and so forth. We are not saved by works of righteousness we have done, but according to His mercy (Titus 3:5; see Ephesians 2:8-10). Paul spoke of the repentance that is unto salvation in II Corinthians 7:10. And he described it in Acts 26:14-20. The sinner is commanded by God to turn from darkness to light, from the power of Satan to God (Acts 26:18), with evidence that this turning was genuine, sincere, or, another way to put it, that the fruit of this repentance is seen in "works meet for repentance" (Acts 26:20). The short of it is this: no one can get saved except by the only name given among men whereby we must be saved (Acts 4:12; see Romans 10:9), and every man that "names the name of Christ" is commanded to "depart from iniquity"

be held to account for every violation of God's Law. God is recording every infraction of His laws, and in the end, unless forgiven, sinners will be judged for every sin.[732]

Our message is the same as it was at the beginning of the Gospel: "Repent: for the kingdom of Heaven is at hand."[733]

We declare the Lordship of Jesus Christ, which recognizes the truth that God has given Him all power in heaven and Earth; and we herald God's command that all must repent and believe on the Lord Jesus Christ.[734]

God's kings seize upon every rebellious thought taking it captive, and call upon the spirit of every mind[735] to bow to the command of Christ.[736] They refuse at their peril, for we also stand in a "readiness to revenge all disobedience" when our own "obedience is fulfilled."[737]

Believer-kings, as children of obedience, battle against the children of disobedience. The Spirit in us resists the spirit that now works in them.[738] However, at present, we war against them with the Sword of the Spirit, the Word of God[739] by preaching the Gospel with the Holy Ghost sent down from heaven.[740] Believer-kings are authorized to do this in every nation.[741]

Fourth, the authority of believer-kings is limited. While

(II Timothy 2:19), and any who name His name and do not depart from iniquity will be barred entry into Heaven (Luke 13:27).

[732] Revelation 20:11-15
[733] Matthew 3:2; 4:17; Acts 26:20
[734] Acts 17:30; Romans 10:9-13
[735] Ephesians 4:23
[736] II Corinthians 10:1-5
[737] II Corinthians 10:6
[738] Ephesians 2:2
[739] Ephesians 6:17
[740] I Peter 1:12; Acts 1:8
[741] Matthew 28:18-20

we shall reign as kings on the earth with Christ, and we will judge angels,[742] our King sets the time of judgment, and we have no authority beyond His. The kingdom in which God has made us kings is the kingdom that is not of this world but from above.[743] Christ, as Son of God, is the ruler of Heaven; and as Son of man, He is the ruler of Earth. Every believer is presently a king unto God[744] and an ambassador for Christ, representing the King to this world.[745] However, our mission in this world limits our authority as kings— presently, we are here to "pray you in Christ's stead, be ye reconciled to God."[746]

For this reason, we must be careful to obey magistrates and to honor kings and all in authority,[747] with one exception. Jesus Christ declared that whereas to Him has been given all power (authority) in Heaven and Earth, we are commanded to preach the Gospel to every nation.[748] Therefore, if any

---

[742] I Corinthians 6:3

[743] John 19:11; see John 3:31; 8:23—Often, this is mistaken to mean believers ought not to participate in earthly warfare. Matthew 28:18 informs us that all power is given to Jesus Christ in Heaven and in Earth. Romans 13:1-6 makes it clear that all power comes from God (by Jesus Christ), and Christ Jesus ordains all the powers presently in the earth. Furthermore, Romans 13 informs us of His purpose for ordaining these powers: they are to bear the sword of vengeance to execute wrath upon evildoers. When governments forget God, they are turned into hell (Psalm 9:17); we believe this means they come under the power of Satan. It is acceptable for believers to participate in the military, as Cornelius, and many other early Christians who were never commanded to resign their military commissions or avoid military service. Indeed, since Jesus Himself ordains these powers, it is expected that He would direct some of His own to take up the "sword" of vengeance to wield it on His behalf. On the other hand, the role of the Church is to "teach all nations, baptizing them in the name of the Father, and of the Son, and of the Holy Spirit: teaching them to observe all things whatsoever [Christ Jesus has] commanded [us]" (Matthew 28:19-20).

[744] Revelation 1:6

[745] II Corinthians 5:20

[746] II Corinthians 5:20

[747] Titus 3:1; I Peter 2:13-17; Romans 13:1-6

[748] Matthew 28:18-20

power under heaven forbids us to preach, we must obey God rather than man.[749]

Fifth, as kings, we represent God to man. (While as priests, we represent man to God.) We are soldier-kings.[750] We wield the "sword of the Spirit," wearing the armor of God,[751] and battle against the enemies of God in this world. Although our weapons are spiritual, we engage God's enemies in the world, confronting them with the truth.

Sixth, as a king unto God,[752] we have the authority to act on God's behalf. God delegates this authority to us in the form of power (a right to act and an enabling to be effective) to fulfill Divinely appointed tasks in the Name of Jesus Christ the Lord.

The authority of the believer is a topic discussed at length in Dr. Beckum's book, *Prayer for Revival*.[753] He explains that the power that God has given to us has two critical aspects, like two sides of the same coin. The first aspect of the believer's authority is Divine authorization to act, and the second is Divine potency to make the action effective in accomplishing God's purpose. Understand that being a king unto God means He authorizes us to act on His behalf. And with this authorization comes a measure of His Divine potency—spiritual power.

God extends His potency only in support of what He has authorized.

Believer-kings are kings indeed. Jesus gave His disciples authority in this Earth over all sickness and devils, which

---

[749] Acts 5:29; see Acts 16:20-38. Only the Holy Ghost has the power to forbid us to preach in this or that place (Acts 16:6).

[750] II Timothy 2:3-4

[751] Ephesians 6:12-18

[752] Revelation 1:6

[753] Beckum, Dr. Benny L. *Prayer for Revival*, p. 141.

are unclean spirits.[754] He also granted to them Divine authority to preach the Gospel, an authority they appealed to over the heads of civil and religious authorities in the earth.[755] Our authority over sickness and devils is directly related to His instruction to preach the Gospel to every nation.[756] As believer-kings, we have authority from God to assault the kingdom of darkness in the spiritual realm (power over unclean spirits) and authority in the physical realm (power over sickness), with authority to preach the Gospel to every nation—an authority that eclipses that of earthly magistrates.

Conclusion

Controversy has divided the Lord's people over questions about the extent and use of this authority. In the next chapter, I will offer a summary of biblical teaching on the use of our authority as believer-kings.

~

---

[754] Matthew 10:1; Mark 3:15; 6:7; Luke 9:1
[755] Acts 5:29
[756] Matthew 28:18-20; Mark 16:15-17

"Whether our religion permits Christians to vote for infidel rulers is a question which merits more consideration than it seems yet to have generally received either from the clergy or the laity. It appears to me that what the prophet said to Jehoshaphat about his attachment to Ahab ["Shouldest thou help the ungodly and love them that hate the Lord?" 2 Chronicles 19:2] affords a salutary lesson." ~ John Jay

(John Jay [The Correspondence and Public Papers of John Jay, 1794-1826, Henry P. Johnston, editor (New York: G.P. Putnam's Sons, 1893), Vol. IV, p.365])

Chapter Seventeen

God's Warrior Kings
(Part Two)
The Manifestation of the Authority of Christ

JESUS commissioned us to go under His authority and preach the Gospel to every nation. Satan opposes Christ and has usurped the Divinely ordained power of governments in many countries to bar Christians from preaching the Gospel there.[757] We wrestle against these principalities and powers, against the rulers of the darkness of this world, against spiritual wickedness in high places.[758]

All power is Divinely ordained, and the prince of the power of the air has no legitimate jurisdiction over the powers of earthly governments since all this power was given to Christ. If we will submit to God, then all that is necessary is that we "resist the devil," and he will flee from us.[759] Believer-kings have authority over the principalities and powers. Indeed, the Spirit in us is greater than the rulers of the darkness of this world. Spiritual wickedness in high places must yield to the power of Christ.

The Manifestation of Christ Through Demonstrations of Power

With authority, Christ also gave us power, a Divine enabling to be peculiarly effective in our kingdom work.

[757] Romans 13:1-6
[758] Ephesians 6:12
[759] James 4:7

Evidence of this power manifests through the operation of spiritual gifts. I have written a book about spiritual gifts that thoroughly explores the topic.[760] My purpose here is served by pointing out a straightforward truth: Christ manifests to the world in and through His believer-king-priests by His Spirit. Controversy over this issue creates confusion, and Satan uses this to quench the manifestation of the Spirit. For that reason, I'll address a few of the controversial aspects of the demonstrations of Christ's power in the kingdom of men.

Jesus specifically gave us power in the spiritual and physical world: over devils (spiritual) and sickness (physical).[761]

Healing

James makes it clear that believer-kings can expect healing from the Lord.[762] However, it is equally clear that the power of healing is not granted carte blanche to any individual. The healing mentioned by James is invested in the Church and effected through prayer.

We notice that at the beginning of the Gospel, handkerchiefs or aprons that encountered Paul's body healed any who touched them.[763] As the churches became established, cases emerge where it appears that healing was unavailable when it would have been welcomed.

At Miletum, Paul left Trophimus sick.[764] Epaphroditus was "sick nigh unto death,"[765] and although it is apparent the Lord spared him, it seems evident that Paul did not supernaturally heal him.

---

[760] *Spiritual Gifts Unwrapped,* available as a PDFl from our Online bookstore. Go to booksatdbp.com, or the Lighthouse Baptist Church bookstore: baptistlighthouse.org.
[761] Luke 9:1
[762] James 5:13-16
[763] Acts 19:12
[764] II Timothy 4:20
[765] Philippians 2:25-28

Furthermore, Paul did not rebuke sickly Timothy for lacking faith for healing. Instead, he instructed Timothy to use a little wine for his stomach's sake and his customary infirmities.[766] And Paul spoke of a personal illness that God refused to heal, though he implored God for the healing three times.[767]

Contrary to the spirit operating upon or in many who claim the name Christian today, Paul humbled himself and said, "I take pleasure in infirmities."[768] The fact that Paul prayed for healing indicates it is available. The fact that God declined to oblige him tells us it is not always God's will to proffer it. Happily, Paul was not left to suffer his infirmities without his Father's aid: "My grace is sufficient for thee: for my strength is made perfect in weakness."[769]

The glorious manifestation of healing power that took place by the hands of the Apostles and some early saints, such as Philip,[770] was peculiar to the era Paul called "the beginning of the Gospel."[771] When God was establishing His covenant with Israel, He brought them out of Egypt with a glorious, open manifestation of kingdom power. While God continued to work mightily on behalf of His people, He did not display His might as He did then.

The same is true concerning the establishment of the New Testament. God continues to move in mighty ways today. But it is self-evident that at no time in the history of the Church, following the period identified as the beginning of the Gospel, do we find such a plethora of open

---

[766] I Timothy 5:23
[767] II Corinthians 12:7-10
[768] II Corinthians 12:10
[769] II Corinthians 12:9
[770] Acts 8:6
[771] Mark 1:1; Philippians 4:15

miracles. God continues to move in mighty ways today. But it is self-evident that at no time in the history of the Church, following the period identified as the beginning of the Gospel, do we find such a plethora of open miracles. Maybe this is owing to the lack of a Moses or Jesus. Perhaps the failure of God's people to believe accounts for the lack of open miracles today, for we understand that faith is a factor.[772] In any case, the Sovereign purpose of God during any Divine season[773] is the ultimate factor.

Nonetheless, it must be admitted that many sicknesses in the churches today fall into the category of I Corinthians 11:30, where we learn "many [were] sickly . . . and many sleep"[774] because some in Corinth disrespected the Lord's Supper. By the way, "many sleep" means many were dead. Furthermore, few Christians will submit to the Scriptures and call for the elders to pray over them for healing. They do not believe the Bible, and as we know, a lack of faith limits what God will do for us.[775] And, finally, it is not too much of a reach to say few elders today have their faith increased enough to "save the sick."[776]

The waning of powerful displays of spiritual power is because of the *season* principle explained above, but we must not hide our lack of faith and spiritual power behind that. In truth, God will move mightily in our midst right now if only we will follow the principles outlined in His Word. Indeed, so long as Christ's Spirit is active in our lives, "the power of the Lord [is] present to heal."[777]

[772] Matthew 13:58
[773] A "season" is used in the Scripture to speak of that span of time necessary for some purpose of God to come to fruition. Often, during a "season" God displays some manifestation of the heavenly into the earthly. These are the mysterious "times or the seasons, which the Father hath put in his own power" (Acts 1:7).
[774] I Corinthians 11:30
[775] Psalm 78:40-41; see Matthew 13:58
[776] James 5:15
[777] Luke 5:17

Power Over Devils

What about the authority God has given His disciples over devils? Was Christ keen to empower the church to preach the Gospel against the opposition of devils in the beginning, but is not so keen on it now? No! The Spirit in us is greater than the spirit that is in this world today as ever before.

When Paul was forbidden from preaching the Gospel in Asia, the Holy Ghost is the One Who forbad him.[778] However, when Paul was hindered from returning to the Thessalonians, he attributed the hindrance to Satan.[779]

The incident recorded in Acts 16, where the Spirit forbad Paul to preach in Asia, occurred in about A.D. 51. Paul's letter to the Thessalonians, in which he revealed that Satan had hindered him from coming to them, was written no more than two years later.[780] Both events occurred in the period Paul called "the beginning of the Gospel." How did Satan hinder Paul's ministry? We know there are times when God uses Satan in mysterious ways to further His purpose.[781] Sometimes Satan gets an advantage over us through our own or some other's failure to receive God's grace.[782] But James instructed us to resist the devil, promising he would flee from us; and that means the authority of the believer-king over devils is something that would continue until His return.[783]

The warfare we are called to engage in is spiritual and involves wrestling "against principalities, against powers, against the rulers of the darkness of this world, against

---

[778] Acts 16:6
[779] I Thessalonians 2:18
[780] Klassen, Frank R. and Reese, Edward, *The Chronological Bible*, p. 1446, 1451.
[781] II Samuel 24:1-25 with I Chronicles 21:1-30; see Isaiah 54:16
[782] II Corinthians 2:11; Hebrews 12:15
[783] James 4:7

spiritual wickedness in high places."[784] The principalities, as we have already shown, include powerful angelic personalities operating behind human rulers. The word *powers*, in Ephesians 6:12, translates the same word Jesus used when He told us that He gave His disciples "power against unclean spirits."[785] This tells us that God intended we would be wrestling against devils continuously until His return.

The idea is that God has given us jurisdiction, which refers to a sphere in which someone has the legal authority to act and make judgments.[786] Our jurisdiction includes the principalities that operate in both the spiritual and physical realms. Jesus spoke of the "power of darkness."[787] According to the Apostle Paul, the power of darkness is presided over by the "rulers of the darkness of this world,"[788] and these rulers serve the "prince of the power of the air."[789] Finally, the phrase *spiritual wickedness in high places* points our attention to the activity of devils that operate in the first heaven.[790] Since God charged us to engage in spiritual warfare, and since that warfare involves battling devils, God surely would provide us the power to do battle against our enemy.

[784] Ephesians 6:12
[785] Matthew 10:1
[786] Websters: *Jurisdiction* "Ju¿ris·dic¿tion, *n.* [L. *jurisdictio*; *jus, juris*, right, law + *dictio* a saying, speaking: cf. OF. *jurisdiction*, F. *juridiction*. See Just, *a.*, and Diction.] 1. *(Law)* The legal power, right, or authority of a particular court to hear and determine causes, to try criminals, or to execute justice; judicial authority over a cause or class of causes; as, certain suits or actions, or the cognizance of certain crimes, are within the *jurisdiction* of a particular court, that is, within the limits of its authority or commission. 2. The authority of a Sovereign power to govern or legislate; the right of making or enforcing laws; the power or right of exercising authority. ... 3. Sphere of authority; the limits within which any particular power may be exercised, or within which a government or a court has authority."
[787] Luke 22:53
[788] Ephesians 6:12
[789] Acts 26:18; II Corinthians 4:3-4; Ephesians 2:2; Colossians 1:13; Luke 22:53; see John 12:46
[790] Ephesians 6:12; see I Timothy 4:1-4

Jesus anticipated that our need for power to deal with devils would continue to His return.[791]

The Manifestation of Christ's Spirit of Liberty[792]

Believer-kings have authority (power) on the earth to do the work of God. However, our authority as kings in the earth doesn't mean that we may privately usurp public, that is, civil authority.[793] The day will come when we will rule and reign over the earth with Jesus Christ present as King of kings and Lord of lords.[794] Presently, we are kings commissioned as ambassadors of the returning King, declaring the mind of the Lord to His citizens during His absence.[795]

The Spirit of the Lord through the Bible reveals that all men are created equal and endowed by their creator with certain inalienable rights. Believers are king-priests unto God and are under the influence of the Spirit of liberty.[796] Only where the Spirit of the LORD is will you find liberty. Wherever the spirit of Antichrist is prevailing, you'll find tyranny.

The ordaining power behind the sword of civil government is "Our Father, which art in Heaven." And He has endowed all humankind with certain inalienable rights, and these rights are ours under God. Every nation under God

---

[791] Matthew 17:21

[792] II Corinthians 3:17

[793] What is wrong with vigilantism? Vigilantism is the private usurpation of public authority to enforce laws. The death penalty serves as a helpful example. God gave the power to execute the death penalty upon evildoers who take the life of another (Genesis 9:6). He did not give this power to an individual to act independently of public authority; He gave it to *man*—"Whoso sheddeth man's blood, by man shall his blood be shed." The requirement for evidences (witnesses) proves God did not intend this power would be in the hands of a private person (Deuteronomy 17:6; see also 19:15).

[794] II Timothy 2:12; Revelation 20:6; see 19:11-15

[795] II Corinthians 5:20; see Luke 19:11-27

[796] II Corinthians 3:17

will honor the Divinely endowed inalienable rights of man. Nations not under the Spirit of liberty, that is, the Spirit of Jesus Christ, will violate human rights and bring men into servitude to the government of the spirit of Antichrist.

The Church has the keys of the kingdom, and the Gospel message opens entry into the Kingdom of God's dear Son. Every nation that receives the Gospel and acknowledges Jesus Christ is Lord may enjoy Heaven's favored nation status[797] and receive stewardship of the dominion. Such a country must "set up kings (rulers)"[798] by God's direction. Godly men, in whom is the Spirit of Christ, must be appointed to rule. In such a nation, the inalienable rights of all men will be recognized and protected.

Furthermore, such a nation will serve as the Sword of the Lord , executing wrath upon evildoers.

When genuine Christians rule, freedom and liberty will be afforded to all. If the wicked take rule in any nation, they will eventually drag that nation out from under God, and the inalienable rights of humanity will be usurped. Liberty only prevails where you find the Spirit of the LORD in the ascendancy. Wherever the spirit of Antichrist prevails, there will be oppression.

To put it another way, wherever you see liberty, you can be sure the Spirit of the Lord is prevailing. And wherever you see tyranny, you can be confident the spirit of Antichrist is prevailing. This is also true in terms of the degree of liberty or tyranny. To the extent the Spirit of the Lord is prevailing, to that degree, there will be liberty; to the extent that the spirit of Antichrist is prevailing, to that degree, there will be tyranny.

---

[797] Psalm 33:12
[798] Hosea 8:4

The Spirit of liberty and the spirit of tyranny always work against one another. Christians, in whom is the Spirit of liberty, are the only vehicles through which genuine liberty will enter the world. This means; first, we must preach the Gospel to turn sinners from darkness to light, and from the power of Satan to God. And, second, Christians need to be filled with the Spirit of God and allow the Holy Ghost to move through them into the world.

Therefore, Christians have both the right and the responsibility to participate in civil government. After all, to Christ has been given all power in Heaven and Earth; so civic authorities derive their just power from Him. Christ has delimited the powers of government and stipulated its purpose in the commission given in Romans 13:1-6.[799]

There is no higher power than God's, and He has limited the reach of governmental authority. Nevertheless, our obligation to obey magistrates (public rulers) derives from the fact that *the powers that be are ordained of God.*

On the other hand, it is equally true that the power has no legitimacy if it supersedes its Divine Author—Christ. This is self-evident. As John Locke, in his essay on government,[800] observed: no father has absolute power over his

---

[799] God has placed the "sword" of civil government into the hands of earthly rulers, and not in the hands of the "Church" (Romans 13:1-6). The "sword" represents the power of life and death, the power of coercion, to enforce laws (Romans 13:4). These "rulers" are "ministers of God," commissioned specifically, not to be "a terror to good works, but to the evil" (Romans 13:3). Furthermore, they are charged with the duty to "execute wrath upon him that doeth evil" (Romans 13:4). Within the context of this declaration, *evil* would have to be understood as that which is contrary to God's will. If they violate their charge, they will be held accountable to the King of kings. Like John the Baptist of old, our duty is to declare to rulers their accountability to the Law (Mark 6:18). (See above, on vigilantism.)

[800] Locke, John, *An Essay Concerning the True Original, Extent and End of Civil Government,* 1690. http://www.let.rug.nl/usa/documents/1651-1700/john-locke-essay-on-government/

son, no king has absolute power over his subjects, and no government has absolute power over its citizens. Locke received his insight from Scripture, and his sentiments agree with the Spirit of Christ. The spirit of Antichrist, on the other hand, speaks of State sovereignty and promotes the subjugation of the individual to the collective. The Spirit of Christ is antithetical to the spirit of Antichrist, and vice versa.

America, founded upon the biblical truths articulated above, is unique in the world. Therefore, not only is it appropriate for believer-kings to participate fully in government, it is essential if we are to preserve our liberties. No people of any nation should appoint over them persons who are not under Christ. Indeed, no government can legitimately declare itself out from under God.

The principle of believer-kings is perfectly suited to the form of government our founders bequeathed to us. Every citizen is an equal partner in the body politic. We are a nation where no individual is king. Rather, *We the people* rule in the place of a king—a veritable nation of kings.

Conclusion

From George Washington to today, we have owned allegiance to the King of kings, Jesus Christ. In the last decade, for the first time in our history, this nation elected rulers who publicly denounce this principle. Believer-kings must rouse themselves, exercise their authority, and like warriors, engage the spiritual forces at work corrupting our culture and dragging our nation out from under God. For the prophecy of Ronald Reagan holds true—*when we are no longer one nation under God, we will be a nation gone under.*

~

Chapter Eighteen

God's Warrior Kings

(Part Three)

The Heart of the Believer-King

KING JESUS IS KING OF KINGS—and each believer is one of those kings.[801] He has given His kings authority under Him in the earth.[802] Believer-kings need to understand how to exercise their power under God. In this chapter, I'll point out the characteristics Christ Jesus is looking for in the heart of His kings.

God's Gold Standard: The Heart of King David

The Old Testament was written to provide examples and admonitions for His king-priests in these last days.[803] David had qualities that set him apart as a king, by which God would measure all others.[804] It seems fitting, therefore, that we should measure our kingly qualities by those of David.

David's heart interested God. He saw in it some reflection of His own, saying that David was "a man after mine own heart."[805] He often called it a perfect heart.[806] All others were measured by it.

The word in our text translated *after* is consistently used

---

[801] Revelation 19:16; 1:6
[802] Mark 3:15; Acts 1:8
[803] I Corinthians 10:11; see Hebrews 1:2
[804] I Kings 3:14; 9:4; 11:4-6, 33; 14:8; 15:3; II Kings 14:3
[805] Acts 13:22
[806] I Kings 11:4; 15:3

to speak of something that is *according to* or *after the manner of* something else. For example: Hebrews 7:11, 15, 16, 17, 21; 8:4, 5, 9; 12:10; James 2:8, and many more. The expression *a man after my own heart* comes from the Bible, and it has always been understood to mean someone with whom we can relate. But of course, we do not mean that they are identical to us.

Some will object to David being God's standard. Pointing to his failure with Bathsheba and the subsequent murder of her husband, they will protest his behavior betrays a heart most unlike God's. They will attempt to reconstruct the meaning of the verse to say David was a man who sought after God's heart. No doubt, David sought the heart of God. Yet we come to the same problem. For it is equally obvious that in the matter of Uriah and his wife, Bathsheba, David most certainly did not seek God's heart.

Included in those characteristics of David's heart that God found pleasing was that he prepared his heart to seek the Lord.

True! David's heart was not in every respect like God's. And although Jehoshaphat prepared his heart to seek the Lord, he stumbled into compromise once or twice. We might take a little comfort in the fact that God did not expect to find a man who was His equal in righteousness, integrity, honor, and purity. But He looks for a heart that pleases Him.

Our God ponders our hearts.[807] Does He find any reflection of His own? God searched the heart of every one of His kings, looking for a heart like His servant David's. Here is our first admonition: God expects His kings to be men and women "after his own heart."[808]

---

[807] Proverbs 21:2; 24:12
[808] I Samuel 13:14

What qualities did God see in David's heart that moved Him to make it the standard by which the hearts of kings are measured?

Characteristics God Seeks in the Heart of His Kings

Believer-kings must have integrity of heart.[809] The essential meaning of *integrity* is wholeness; the idea being that what has integrity is sound or unbroken.

We begin here because the qualities that follow are those expected to be in every whole-hearted king. One lacking in any of the following may be said to be lacking in integrity.

Believer-kings must be upright in heart.[810] The word *upright* speaks of rectitude, in this case, conformity to God's ways. Saul never committed adultery or murder, as far as we know. However, he disobeyed a direct order from God.[811] This is something David never did.[812]

(Once again, we must reconcile David's behavior regarding Uriah and God's testimony to his general character. We find it in the fifty-first Psalm. There is no such Psalm from Saul. Enough said!)

David's heart was upright. It was fixed,[813] erect—like a soldier standing at attention, showing respect for his superior officers and readiness to follow orders. David's

---

[809] I Kings 9:4; Psalm 78:72

[810] I Kings 3:6

[811] I Samuel 15:10-11

[812] It might seem strange to some that David disobeyed God's law so egregiously, and yet was forgiven and restored to his throne, while Saul offended in a matter that by comparison would to most seem slight, and yet for this he lost his throne. We might explain this by pointing out the fact that Saul received a direct command to perform a specific task and he failed to obey. However, the answer more likely lies in the fact that we do not find a Psalm 51 from Saul. In any event, it is sad that this contradiction in David's life continues to give occasion for some to scorn and even to blaspheme—a testament to the ruin sin brings into our lives and the way it continually frustrates grace.

[813] Psalm 57:7

heart stood at attention before God. The believer-king must call his heart to attention before his King.

Believer-kings must serve whole-heartedly.[814] Consider this commendation from the Lord concerning David: "as my servant David, who kept my commandments, and who followed me with all his heart, to do that only which was right in mine eyes."[815] Serving Him with all our heart includes keeping His commandments and doing *only what is right in His eyes*.

Perhaps David's critics will note that this did not always show up in his behavior. The accusers might remind us of his serious error that brought death to the camp when he arranged to convey the Ark of the Covenant in a manner forbidden by the Law.[816] David's *Shemei's*[817] might continue casting their dust into our faces with reminders of the devastation he wrought upon Israel when he numbered the people contrary to the Law.[818] Notwithstanding these

---

[814] I Kings 14:8

[815] I Kings 14:8

[816] II Samuel 6:1-11; I Chronicles 13:1-14

[817] II Samuel 16:13, Shemei cursed David while throwing stones and casting dust.

[818] Read II Samuel 24 carefully. The Spirit points out that what brought judgment upon Israel was the fact that God was angry at that nation, again (II Samuel 24:1). This story illustrates two mysterious truths regarding God's Sovereign rule in the kingdom of men (Psalm 103:19; Daniel 4:17, 25, 32) and how He exercises His prerogatives over earthly rulers. In Proverbs 21:1, we learn that "The king's heart is in the hand of the LORD, as the rivers of water: he turneth it whithersoever He will." Proverbs 16:10 says, "A divine sentence is in the lips of the king: his mouth transgresseth not in judgment." According to II Samuel 24:1, God was angry at Israel. Being angry at Israel, He "moved David against them to say, Go number Israel and Judah." Later, we find God rebuked David for numbering Israel (II Samuel 24:10-14). Apparently, it was not done according to the law, which required each man numbered to present an offering of a *half shekel,* which is ten *gerahs,* to the service of the Tabernacle (Exodus 30:12-16). (The *shekel* and the *gerah* refer to coins used by the ancient Hebrews for money.) The judgment that resulted from this sin fell hard upon the nation when 70,000 died of the plague of pestilence God sent among the people (II Samuel 24:15-17). God used David to bring occasion against the people who had provoked Him to anger, and He used David to bring relief (II

failures, God testified concerning what He saw in David's heart: "who followed me with all his heart, to do that only which was right in mine eyes."[819] How can God say such a thing, knowing the grave failures of His servant David?

Grace! God, Who looks on the heart, continued to see in David's what these occasional missteps mask. But we may see the justification for God's assessment of David's heart in the record of his response to the chastisement he received for his missteps.

In the case of the Ark, God chastened David sorely, but he never left the Lord. Instead, he drew nigh to the Lord and inquired of the Word of the Lord concerning the right way to convey the Ark.[820]

Regarding his failure to number the people according to the Law of Moses, he repented sincerely and petitioned the Lord in humility, and, once again, rather than move away from God, he drew nigh to the Lord, choosing for his chastisement what would put him into God's hands.[821] Contrast David's response to correction with Cain's. When God confronted Cain for his sin, Cain "went out from the presence of the Lord,"[822] never to return.

Like David, believer-kings may purify their hearts before the Lord by drawing nigh to Him.[823] Although they will stumble from time to time, if their heart is right toward

---

Samuel 24:17-25). While David's own heart was not right with God at this time, nonetheless, God turned that heart to His purpose, so that out of that mouth went forth a judgment from God upon Israel; indeed, the *king's* heart is in the hands of the LORD, and his mouth does not transgress in *judgment.* (II Samuel 24; I Chronicles 21; see Exodus 30:12-16)

[819] I Kings 14:8
[820] I Chronicles 15:2-13
[821] II Samuel 24:10-14
[822] Genesis 4:16
[823] James 4:8

God, they will humble themselves under His mighty hand, draw nigh to Him, and be restored. (We thank God for I John 1:7-9 and 2:1-2.) If believer-kings are not whole-heartedly sold out to Christ Jesus, they are vulnerable to becoming embittered against God when He chastises for sins.[824] Believer-kings cannot be effective if they refuse the chastisement of the Lord, for if they draw back in unbelief, the Lord takes no pleasure in them.[825]

How gracious is God? Even after David's failures, God looked into His servant's heart and testified concerning it: "my servant David, who kept my commandments, and who followed me with all his heart, to do that only which was right in mine eyes."[826] The secret lay in the fact that David was whole-heartedly devoted to God.

Believer-kings must be jealous for God's honor.[827] Brave men provoke the spite of prideful cowards. Mistaking their cowardice for reasonable caution, they mistake the boldness of the brave as prideful arrogance. Such was Eliab, David's elder brother.

Goliath was the champion of the Philistines. He stood about nine-and-a-half feet tall in full battle armor, carried a spear whose shaft was from two to two-and-a-half inches in diameter, a spearhead that weighed fifteen pounds and swung a sword unlike any other.[828] He bellowed his blasphemous challenge daily, defying the God of Israel.[829] Everyone, including King Saul and Eliab, the elder brother of David, cringed at the sight of this giant.

---

[824] Hebrews 12:5-15
[825] Hebrews 10:38
[826] I Kings 14:8
[827] I Samuel 17:29
[828] I Samuel 21:9
[829] I Samuel 17:4-11

David was but a lad at the time. His father sent him to check on how things went for his brothers, who had joined the king's army. When David heard the blasphemy of Goliath, his heart burned with valor, jealous for the honor of his God. He said, "What shall be done to the man that killeth this Philistine, and taketh away the reproach from Israel? for who is this uncircumcised Philistine, that he should defy the armies of the living God?"[830] When Eliab heard his young brother's words, his heart also burned, but with scorn, not valor. He cruelly mocked David's motives. But David did not back down. He cried, "What have I now done? Is there not a cause?" When Eliab saw Goliath, he saw a fearsome giant; when David saw him, he saw a cause worthy of his devotion—to defend the honor and glory of God.

Jealousy for the glory of God characterized David, but it was probably nowhere more dramatically displayed than when he set out to face Goliath. Being challenged to defend the honor of the God Whom we love stirs us to self-sacrificing feats of faith. No believer-king will amount to much unless God's honor is a cause worthy of extreme devotion, moving him or her to self-sacrificing feats of faith.

Believer-kings must be zealous about the House of God.[831] David carried in his bosom a great dream—that there would be a house for the name of God among His people. God honored the heart of David; that it cherished the desire to build Him a house pleased Him. Nevertheless, God did not give the building permit to David, but to his son instead. What did David do? He did not pout and doubt; he devoted his remaining years to preparing everything that would be needed for his son to build the House of God.[832]

[830] I Samuel 17:26
[831] II Chronicles 6:7-8
[832] I Chronicles 22:1-5

Another Son of David, the one whom David himself called Lord,[833] is building a House for a "habitation of God through the Spirit."[834] He is Jesus Christ, and the "House" He is building is called the Church.[835] Believer-kings are commissioned to labor together with Him in the building of His Church.[836] We have received the building permit: "Go ye therefore, and teach all nations, baptizing them in the name of the Father, and of the Son, and of the Holy Ghost: teaching them to observe all things whatsoever I have commanded you."[837] Believer-kings must support the church. It is the only institution in the earth that has the authority and power to charge the gates of hell and thwart Satan's agenda in the world today.

As our King, so believer-kings must be enthusiastic about the House of God. When Jesus went into the Temple and found in it those who would compromise its integrity, righteous anger stirred His heart, and the "zeal of [His Father's] house" ate Him up.[838] With a passion for defending His Father's honor, He took a whip and drove from the "House of God" those that defiled it—the House of God was to be known as a house of prayer, but they had made it a den of thieves. A fiery zeal for the purity and honor of the House of God will burn in the heart of a believer-king who has a "heart after [God's] own heart."

Sadly, today, a general contempt for the "House of God"

833 Matthew 22:41-46
834 Ephesians 2:22
835 Matthew 16:18; I Timothy 3:15
836 It goes beyond our immediate purpose to elaborate on the doctrine of the Church. Suffice it here to say, this author believes the *Church* is local, visible, and independent, and must be set square upon the foundation of the Apostles and Prophets—meaning the doctrines must be in conformity to the Word of God. (I Corinthians 3:5-17)
837 Matthew 28:18-20
838 Psalm 69:9; John 2:13-17

prevails throughout our culture. The spirit of Antichrist resists the presence of Christ's churches, and seducing spirits, in league with the prince of the power of the air, stir the minds of unbelievers to call for Christians to be invisible in their communities. At the same time, these seducing spirits turn the thoughts of God's people against the Church with all manner of false doctrines about it: churches ought not to have public buildings; churches ought not to evangelize their communities; the "true" church is invisible, they say. And many unwittingly serve the intention of Satan to keep it that way! When Christians don't take the church, which is the House of God, seriously, how can we expect the world to have any respect or reverence toward the House of God?

The prevailing attitude among God's believer-kings today is one of apathy, and even contempt, for the Lord's glory and honor, and His Church. The heart of believer-kings today is set on personal glory and honor. Service to God is rendered in exchange for their fame and recognition. This is because many are less like David and more like his grandson, Rehoboam, who did evil, "because he prepared not his heart to seek the Lord."[839]

If any reading this believes he or she lacks any of the vital characteristics named above, he or she is encouraged to do what Jehoshaphat did when he offended: repent and prepare your heart to seek the Lord.[840]

Conclusion

Christ Jesus, our Lord, has given authority and power to His kings who serve under Him. They have this power in the spiritual and physical realms of God's creation.

---

[839] II Chronicles 12:14
[840] II Chronicles 19:3

However, their authority is under God. Believer-kings have the authority to call down mountains (Empires) and uproot trees (call down rulers), but unless their heart is right with God, they are virtually powerless. Satan knows this, so he labors constantly to pollute the heart of Christ's kings. All believer-kings must prepare their hearts to seek the Lord.

In the next chapter, I will offer insight into preparing your heart to seek the Lord.

~

Chapter Nineteen

God's Warrior Kings
(Part Four)
Preparing the Heart of the Believer-King

S ATAN'S DEVILS TREMBLE when a truehearted believer-king takes the field of battle. This chapter offers insight into how Satan corrupts our hearts and how to prepare for battle.

As mentioned above, the essential characteristic of a truehearted believer-king is a heart that seeks after God. Every believer-king has a longing in his heart for God.[841] This longing is natural to the *new man* created by the Spirit of God.[842] But it is not native to the *old man*.[843] Because understanding the contrast between the old and new man is important to a proper understanding of how to have a heart for God, I'll take a moment to explain these terms.

The Old Man and the New Man

The old man is what we call the Adamic nature.

Humankind descended from Adam. Adam sinned; that is, he transgressed God's law. It is the nature of sin to corrupt the essence of whatever it touches. Sin corrupted Adam's nature. The word *nature* refers to the inherent features, or characteristics that are a natural part of being human, what

---

[841] Luke 17:22; Romans 8:15; John 10:3-27
[842] I Peter 1:23; II Peter 1:4; I John 3:9; 4:7; 5:1-4, 18
[843] Ephesians 4:22

we may call the human essence. Like all living things, the nature of mankind is in his seed. The essence of an apple (or any living thing) is in its seed, and the nature of that seed passes to all the fruit that follows. Likewise, Adam's corrupted nature has passed to all his posterity through his seed.

To illustrate this, we know that some diseases affect us superficially; they pass through our bodies but don't alter our nature. Other diseases corrupt our physical body at a cellular level and inflict permanent damage. In some cases, this permanent damage will pass to our posterity through our seed. When Adam sinned, permanent damage to his essence occurred, which altered his nature. Through his seed, the damaged essence passed to all his posterity. Because Adam sinned, we are all born sinners; and this Adamic nature is called *the old man*.

The wages (payment) for sin is death.[844] Proof that Adam's nature passed to his posterity is forced upon us when the consequence of sin afflicts children before they have become conscious of sin. Infants sometimes die in innocence and without any violent act committed against them. Because we know the consequence of sin passed to all mankind, we know its condition has also. Even those who have not sinned in the manner Adam did have a natural appetite for sin and a predisposition to disobey God.

Sin is natural to the old man because sinning is characteristic of its nature.

Other words are used in the Bible to speak of what we call the sin nature. For instance, the word *flesh* is used to

---

[844] God established death as the wages of sin partly to limit the progress of sin's corruption. Unchecked by death, sin would go on inflicting its misery indefinitely. On the other hand, if God collected on the wages of sin immediately in every case, no one would have the opportunity to receive His forgiveness and obtain the remedy, which takes us to the *new man* we will discuss later.

speak of the old man because sin resides in the members of our bodies.[845] The word *carnal* comes from the same word translated *flesh* and means something that corresponds to the desires of the flesh. In other words, saying something is *carnal* is another way of describing behavior that is consistent with the nature of the old man.

Humanity descended from Adam's seed, and so all are said to be in Adam. When Adam and Eve chose to follow the path of Satan and rebel against their Creator, their nature was altered so that Adam's entire race now has a nature akin to that of Satan. For this reason, they are called children of the devil.[846] Children are not identical to their natural fathers but share some features and characteristics. In the same way, all Satan's children are not identical to him, yet all share some elements of his nature. The most fundamental feature of the old man is a natural enmity against God.[847]

The new man is what we call the new nature of all who are born of the Spirit of God.

All who are born again receive a new nature. The expression *born again* refers to the act of God whereby a child of Satan becomes a child of God through faith in His Son, Jesus Christ.[848] This is possible because Jesus' death on the Cross paid the wages of sin in full on behalf of all mankind.[849] Now anyone can turn away from darkness to light and from the power of Satan to God. When any sinner repents and believes on God's Son, he is birthed into the family of God. This new birth generates a new life, a new man. Therefore, believers are new creatures in Christ Jesus.[850]

---

845 Romans 7:18, 23
846 I John 3:10
847 Romans 8:7
848 John 1:11-13; 3:1-6
849 I John 2:1-2; Romans 5:8-9
850 II Corinthians 5:17; see Ephesians 2:10

Jesus is called the last Adam.[851] All born of *Christ* are said to be *in Christ* in the same way all born of *Adam* are said to be *in Adam*.

The new man in Christ is a partaker of His nature, called the divine nature.[852] In the same way that we inherit the consequence and condition of Adam's sin from our natural birth, we inherit the consequence and condition of Christ's righteousness from the new birth: eternal life and the righteousness of Christ by His Spirit that dwells in us.

Accordingly, when we walk after the flesh, we are behaving according to the interests and desires of the old man, the sin nature, serving our old master, Satan. When we walk after the Spirit, we are behaving according to the interests and desires of Christ Jesus, the nature of the new man, and serving our new Master, the Lord Jesus Christ.

When we walk after the Spirit, our heart will be true; it will be right with God. When we walk after the flesh, our heart will be false; it will not be right before God. To have a true heart, we must walk after the Spirit.

To walk after the Spirit means we mind (give our attention to) the things of the Spirit. When we set our thoughts on the things of the Spirit, we are spiritually minded. To walk after the flesh means we are minding (giving our attention to) the things of the flesh. When we do this, we are carnally minded.

Now you will understand me when I speak of being spiritually minded or carnally minded. To have a true heart before GOD, we must be spiritually minded.

The carnal mind is enmity against God.[853] But the new

---

[851] I Corinthians 15:45
[852] II Peter 1:4
[853] Romans 8:7

man "is created in righteousness and true holiness."[854] If the believer-king is walking and warring after the flesh,[855] his or her heart will be filled with thoughts that are discordant to God's heart, contrary to His Spirit. This grieves the Spirit. Such believer-kings are in danger of quenching the Spirit—extinguishing His influence in and through them.[856] It is possible a believer-king's heart can be compromised but not entirely given over to the flesh (remember Jehoshaphat). Such believers are double-minded, and the remedy is to purify their heart.[857] In either case, the believer-king must prepare his or her heart to seek the Lord.

We are kings and priests unto God,[858] and it is our responsibility to set our heart upright before God.[859]

---

[854] Ephesians 4:24

[855] II Corinthians 10:3

[856] Matthew 15:19; Ephesians 4:30-31; I Thessalonians 5:19

[857] James 4:8

[858] Revelation 1:6

[859] The word translated *preparations* in Proverbs 16:1 is מַעֲרְךָ (*ma-arak,* pronounced *mah-ar-awk'* (Strong No. 4633 — "from 6186; an arrangement, i.e., (figuratively) mental disposition:—preparation"). The Hebrew expression transliterated *l'adam ma-arak leb* (literally *for adam arrangement of heart*) is translated by some as "To man belongs the preparations of the heart." First, the Hebrew does not provide any indication that the phrase intends to say that the preparations of the heart belong to men. To convey this idea in Hebrew, we would expect a definite article (*ha*) with *preparations,* or the syntax to have been different—the expression *preparations of the heart* would more naturally come before the expression *to man.* Furthermore, the Hebrew word at the beginning of Proverbs 16:1 is most naturally translated *for man.* In Hebrew, the sense is that *for man come the preparations of the heart, and, additionally from Jehovah, the answer of the tongue.* Of course, this would be torturous, hence the elegant translation in our KJV. The word that translates *prepared* in II Chronicles 12:14 (regarding Rehoboam's failure to *prepare* his heart) and II Chronicles 19:3 (regarding Jehoshaphat's commendation for *preparing* his) is כּוּן (*kuwn,* (Strong No. 3559 — "a primitive root; properly, to be erect (i.e., stand perpendicular); hence (causatively) to set up …")). Of course, the proper English word to translate each of these comes from the root *prepare.* The distinction between them noticed here is helpful to show that man's part in *preparing* the heart is to set it upright before God—then, God takes it from there and arranges what is necessary in the heart to produce the fruit He seeks. Finally, you might have noticed that the translators used the verb *is* rather than the plural verb *are.* That is

What Must We Do to Set Our Heart Upright?

First, understand what the heart is.

We tend to associate the heart with emotions. But the Bible mostly associates our emotions with our bowels or belly.[860] And it associates our heart with our thoughts.[861]

There are, however, at least two places in the Bible where the heart is associated with the bowels. In Psalm 22:14, we find a prophecy of Jesus' agony on the Cross. He cried, "My heart is like wax; it is melted in the midst of my bowels." And Jeremiah lamented, "My bowels, my bowels! I am pained at my very heart; my heart maketh a noise in me" (Jeremiah 4:19). Some things trouble the thoughts of our heart so deeply we feel it in our gut—to melt our heart into our belly,[862] to pain it,[863] and even to stop it.[864]

---

further testimony to their faithfulness to stay within the language of the text in their translation work, for *is* is correct. Imagine Jesus meditating on this passage and discerning from it the insight He reveals in Matthew 12:34. For the verb *is* is singular, and this requires us to see a one–to–one connection between the heart and the words spoken from it. Consider Jesus' own regard for giving this level of attention to verbs in His interpretation of the Hebrew passage translated, "I am the God of Abraham, Isaac, and Jacob" (Matthew 22:32; see Exodus 3:6). If one wonders that such things as Jesus named in Matthew 12:34 would come from God, understand that what comes from the mouth manifests the heart from which it comes. God merely *arranges* the exposé.

[860] Genesis 43:30; I Kings 3:26; Song of Solomon 5:4; Isaiah 16:11; 63:15; Jeremiah 4:19; 31:20; Lamentations 1:20; 2:11; II Corinthians 6:12; Philippians 1:8; 2:1; Colossians 3:12; Philemon 7, 12, 20; I John 3:17

[861] Brain cells have been found in heart tissue. From *Prevention Magazine*, June 2009, p. 29, "Researchers at the Institute of HeartMath claim to have discovered more than 40,000 neurons, or brain cells, in heart tissue, fueling speculation that the heart may be capable of intuitive guidance. In fact, a few heart transplant patients report inheriting memories from their donors. . . . " (Genesis 6:5; Judges 5:15; I Chronicles 29:18; Job 17:11; Psalm 33:11; Jeremiah 23:20; Daniel 2:30; Hebrews 4:12; see also Matthew 15:19; Mark 7:21)

[862] Psalm 22:14

[863] Jeremiah 4:19

[864] I Samuel 25:37

The heart is related to one's bent of mind (intentions),[865] and one's desires.[866] Three things shape our affections: our thoughts, our intentions (the will), and our desires. Because the thoughts of the heart trigger strong emotions felt in our belly, we connect our hearts to our feelings. While our affections are felt in our emotions, they are shaped by the thoughts of our heart.

The heart is the center of our inner life. Our life's blood is pumped throughout our body by the heart. The life (soul)[867] of the flesh is in the blood, according to Leviticus 17:11. The physical center of our blood's circulatory system is the heart. By extension, therefore, the heart is the center of our soul. And the soul is closely connected with our belly.[868] Remember this! You'll need this insight when we start connecting fasting and prayers to receiving spiritual power in your life.

The Holy Spirit dwells in our hearts,[869] and our spirit is also closely connected with our heart.[870] His Spirit bears witness with our spirit that we are the children of God.[871] This occurs in our heart, where the Holy Ghost sheds abroad the love of God.[872] No doubt, this is at least part of what is meant by the "communion of the Holy Ghost."[873]

---

[865] Hebrews 4:12, speaks of the *thoughts and intents of the heart.*

[866] Psalm 37:4, speaks of the *desires of the heart.*

[867] The word translated *life* in Leviticus 17:11 is נֶפֶשׁ (*nephesh,* (Strong No. 5315 — "properly, a breathing creature"). It's rendered *soul* 416 times, *life* (101x), *creature* (9x), *body* (8x), and *dead* (5x). Occasionally it is translated *one, any,* or *anyone.* Jesus distinguished between the *soul* and the *body* in Matthew 10:28 (see also Isaiah 10:18 and I Thessalonians 5:23). Yet, often the *body* and the *soul* are very closely connected (Deuteronomy 12:15, 20, 21; 14:26; Leviticus 7:18, 21, 25, and etc.). The relationship of the *soul* and the *belly* will be explored later (Psalm 35:13).

[868] Psalm 31:9; 44:25; Proverbs 13:25

[869] Galatians 4:6

[870] Deuteronomy 2:30; Psalm 34:18; Psalm 78:8; 143:4; Proverbs 15:13; to name only a few.

[871] Romans 8:16

[872] Romans 5:5

[873] II Corinthians 13:14

The heart is the place where our soul, through our spirit, intersects and interacts with the spiritual. The belly is the place where our soul, through our body, intersects and interacts with the physical.

Now that you understand what the heart is, we can go on to the next principle in preparing your heart to seek God. As we proceed, keep one essential truth in mind. The thoughts of God's heart must shape the thoughts of ours. Otherwise, the thoughts of our hearts will be deceitful. The Word of God (the Bible) expresses the thoughts of God's heart to our hearts.

Second, do not trust in your own heart.

"He that trusteth in his own heart is a fool."[874] The Spirit, by Jeremiah, warns us, "The heart is deceitful above all things, and desperately wicked: who can know it?"[875] The heart is the place where our spirit functions to shape the thoughts of our hearts. We are warned not to trust our thoughts; beware the vanity of our mind.

Our fallen nature cannot be trusted, and so we do not lean on the "arm of flesh."[876] Our carnal mind will not be subject to the Law of God, nor can it be, even if it would.[877] However, we have a promise that if we walk after the Spirit, we will not fulfill the lusts of the flesh.[878]

Remember, to walk after the Spirit means we mind (give attention to) the things of the Spirit.[879] We can be spiritually minded,[880] or we can think and behave carnally.[881] To be *carnally minded* is to *walk after the flesh*.[882] If we allow the

---

[874] Proverbs 28:26
[875] Jeremiah 17:9
[876] II Chronicles 32:8
[877] Romans 8:7
[878] Galatians 5:16
[879] Romans 8:5
[880] Romans 8:6
[881] I Corinthians 3:3
[882] Romans 8:5; Colossians 2:18

old man to control our thinking, carnal thoughts will fill our hearts. Therefore, we must be spiritually minded to prepare our hearts to seek the Lord.

Third, the believer-king must set his or her affections on things that are above.

"Set your affection on things above, not on things on the earth."[883]

The word *affection* is curious. According to Webster (1828), the first definition of the word is "the state of being affected."[884] After that, he lists passion, but informs us that "more generally" it refers to "a bent of mind towards a particular object" and explains that this word holds "a middle place between disposition, which is natural, and passion, which is excited by the presence of its exciting object." Finally, Webster explains that the word refers to an attribute, quality, or property that is inseparable from its object. He illustrates this by pointing out, for example, that love, fear, and hope are affections of the mind while figure (shape) and weight are affections of physical bodies.[885]

The command to set your affections on things above, I hope, is now more understandable to you. What follows will clarify it further.

---

[883] Colossians 3:2
[884] Webster, Daniel, *American Dictionary of the English Language,* np, *Affection.* The 1913 edition includes "The act of affecting or acting upon." Other differences between the 1828 and 1913 editions follow: 1828 notes this use is rare, and offers "Passion" as the second, whereas 1913 offers it ninth, and includes "violent emotion" noting this use is obsolete. 1828—the more common use begins with the third entry, "A bent of mind . . ." followed by "4. . . . a settled good will, love or zealous attachment . . . ," "5. Desire . . . "—and notes the word indicates an ". . . attribute, quality or property (of a thing) which is inseparable from its object." 1913 presents this notion of the word as the second entry.
[885] Ibid.

The English word affection is chosen to translate seven different Greek words.[886] As noted above, it is a subtle word with multiple nuances. In summary, the word encapsulates all the attributes of our heart—bent of mind (thoughts and intents), desire (as that which influences our will in a particular direction—Proverbs 18:1), and sensibilities (often called feelings), including kind regard, sympathy, tenderness, esteem, and passion. Passion is often considered negatively, as inordinate lust or vile affection—however, not all passion is low. The word *affection* includes all that relates to our heart and is, therefore, worthy of our attention. Jesus wants all our affection set on things that are above. To do that we must disentangle them from the things of this world. In short, He wants our whole heart.[887]

Much of what we call affection is experienced as emotion. However, affection goes beyond feelings.

There is an intellectual aspect to affection, such as the *thoughts of our heart* in which we set the attention of the mind to some object or idea. Then there is the sentient aspect of affection, our response to what occupies our

---

[886] 1. πάθος—*pathos* (Strong No. 3806—"properly, suffering . . . a passion (especially concupiscence)") (Romans 1:26—*vile affection*, and Colossians 3:5—*inordinate affection*); 2. πάθημα—*pathema* (Strong No. 3804—"something undergone, i.e. hardship or pain; subjectively, an emotion or influence") (Galatians 5:24—*affections* and lusts); 3. ἄστοργος—*astorgos* (Strong No. 794—"to cherish affectionately. . . hard-hearted towards kindred") (Romans 1:31; II Timothy 3:3—*without natural affection*); 4. φιλόστοργος—*philostorgos* (Strong No. 5387—"cherishing one's kindred, especially parents or children") (Romans 12:10—*kindly affectioned*); 5. σπλάγχνον—*splagchnon* (Strong No. 4698—"the spleen . . . pity or sympathy: — bowels, inward affection") (II Corinthians 7:15—*inward affection*); 6. φρονέω—*phroneo* (Strong No. 5426—"to exercise the mind, i.e. entertain or have a sentiment or opinion ... to be (mentally) disposed") (Colossians 3:2—*affections* on things above); 7. ἱμείρομαι—*himeiromai* (Strong No. 2442—"a yearning . . . to long for") (I Thessalonians 2:8—*affectionately* desirous).
[887] Deuteronomy 4:19; 6:5; 10:12; 11:13; 13:3; 26:16; 30:2, 6, 10; and repeated over 100 times

mind—usually experienced as emotion or sensation, which generally generates desire. Desire calls upon our will or volition to work out a way to satisfy the desire. Our desires will be good or evil, depending on the character of the thoughts that inspire them.

To "set your affections on things above," you must arrest the thoughts of your heart and bring them into the obedience of Christ.[888] Only then will the believer-king's responses to the thoughts of his or her heart generate pure desires, which will act upon the will to motivate him or her into holy actions.

Believer-kings must "humble [themselves] . . . under the mighty hand of God"[889] and zealously bring "into captivity every thought to the obedience of Christ"[890] if they hope to do "the will of God from the heart."[891] In no other way can we surrender all our earthly ambitions (desires) and "seek . . . first the kingdom of God" in service to the King.[892]

Devils will labor to occupy our thoughts with what will give rise to evil desires which will seduce our will away from God and bring us under their control.

Conclusion

We must rouse ourselves to battle, like a truehearted king, against whatever giants Satan sends against us, and quit sniveling and quaking in fear, hiding in the shadows with the cowardly "Christianette soldiers" who swell our ranks today. Like Eliab and like Saul—or like David? Will you prepare your heart to take the challenge of spiritual warfare, and like a king in the Saviour's service, charge the gates of

---

[888] II Corinthians 10:5
[889] I Peter 5:6
[890] II Corinthians 10:5
[891] Ephesians 6:6; Luke 22:42
[892] Matthew 6:33

hell as David charged Goliath? God is searching among His believer-kings for one who has a heart like David's. He is pondering your heart right now.

Unto God, we are made kings and priests. As kings, we have authority in this world. We can, by faith, pull down the strongholds of Satan. We can call down mountains (kingdoms) and uproot mighty trees (earthly leaders). We can command devils and make Satan flee. A truehearted believer-king exerting his or her influence in the world by speaking truth to devilish lies and resisting the enemy's efforts to silence his or her voice, can release the Spirit of Christ into the world and overcome the spirit of Antichrist. As kings in Christ's service, we command all men everywhere to repent, to believe on Jesus Christ to be saved from the wrath to come, proffering to all Christ's terms of surrender: Confess with your mouth the LORD Jesus, and believe in your heart God raised Him from the dead.[893]

However, unless believer-kings understand and fulfill their role as believer-priests, all will be lost. The believer-king's authority and power come from the indwelling of the Spirit of Christ. Rightly understanding how to conduct ourselves as believer-priests is critical to releasing the Holy Ghost to flow from our belly like rivers of living water. In the next chapter, I will begin to explain how we should perform our duties as believer-priests unto God.

~

---

[893] Romans 10:13

Chapter Twenty

God's Warrior Priests

(Part One)

God's Priests and His Temple

JESUS CHRIST THE LORD has made us kings, and He made us priests.[894] To do our part in spiritual warfare, we must rightly understand the role of believer-priests in God's War.

Peter said, "Ye also, as lively stones, are built up a spiritual house, an holy priesthood, to offer up spiritual sacrifices, acceptable to God by Jesus Christ."[895] Jesus Christ is our High Priest.[896] (He makes our sacrifices acceptable.) We are made priests under Him, and we are charged to offer up spiritual sacrifices.

Christ's priesthood is not after the Levitical order. It is after the "order of Melchizedek."[897] We must not understand our priesthood in terms of the Levitical order. We do not wear the holy garments, nor offer the Old Testament Temple sacrifices, nor are we to encumber ourselves with the myriad of ordinances pertaining to that priesthood.[898]

Indirectly, however, we are instructed to gain insight into the conduct of our priesthood from the examples provided by the Old Testament priest.[899]

[894] Revelation 1:6
[895] I Peter 2:5, see 6-9
[896] Hebrews 10:21
[897] Hebrews 7:17; see Psalm 110:4
[898] Colossians 2:14; Hebrews 10:4; all of Hebrews 9
[899] I Corinthians 10:11

Generally, believers have little understanding of the New Testament Priesthood. The doctrine was defined in the context of debate against Catholic notions of a mediator priest empowered by Christ to absolve sins, and as having sole authority to interpret the Scriptures for Christians.[900] We should be grateful to the faithful martyrs and heroes of our faith who stood against these evils and broke the power of Rome off the neck of genuine Christianity. Every believer is a priest, and Christ alone is our mediator.[901] However, this doctrine has a whole lot more to offer.

First, I shall establish the importance of the priesthood in spiritual warfare. Second, you will be introduced to the New Testament Temple and to the New Testament priesthood that serves God in that Temple. Finally, we shall be challenged to sanctify the Temple and the priest. Old Testament examples will be used when necessary or helpful. All of this takes us to the heart of what it means to be engaged in spiritual warfare.

The Importance of the Priesthood in Warfare

The priests were more significant in determining the

---

[900] The *priesthood of the believer* means every believer is a priest unto God (Revelation 1:6). It was developed within the context of the controversies regarding the authority of the Papacy during the Protestant Reformation. The Reformers emphasized the truth that every believer is a *priest unto God,* and therefore, in no need of a mediating priest, but each believer has the privilege of direct access to God through Jesus Christ, the only Mediator between man and God (I Timothy 2:5). Furthermore, the doctrine called the *priesthood of the believer* was associated with the truth that every believer has a responsibility to "Study to shew (himself) approved" (II Timothy 2:15), and has an equal share in the graces of God that are communicated to us by the Holy Spirit to help us understand the Scriptures (John 16:13; Acts 1:8). This meant the believer-priest is not dependent upon another priest to know the mind and will of God. Every believer has access to the mind and will of God through the Scriptures. Hence, the doctrine of the *priesthood of the believer* was key in breaking the power of the Catholic Church over the conscience of believers. However, beyond that, the doctrine is woefully underdeveloped.

[901] Revelation 1:6; I Timothy 3:5

outcome of wars for the first nation under God than were its kings and soldiers.

Most of Exodus, Leviticus, Numbers, and Deuteronomy are devoted to instructing and establishing the priesthood. The Levitical priesthood was limited to Israel.[902] Jesus is our High Priest, and He has commissioned us to minister to every nation.[903] Nonetheless, the books of Moses, along with the history books of Joshua through II Chronicles, offer insights into the critical role of our priesthood in warfare.[904]

When Israel moved into their Promised Land, the priests played a very significant role in conquering it. The battle of Jericho offers a classic example.[905] Joshua was instructed to appoint seven priests to blow seven trumpets, followed by the priests who bore the Ark of the Covenant. The men of war were instructed to march in front of the seven trumpet priests. Following behind the Ark would be the rear guard. They circled the city one time a day for six days. Each day, the seven priests blew on their trumpets, but not a word was spoken. On the seventh day, they circled the city seven times, and when the priests blew the trumpets very loudly, the walls of Jericho fell, and the men of war overtook the city. To conquer Jericho, the priests had to carefully obey the LORD spiritually before Israel could conquer it physically in the name of the LORD.

Not only did the priesthood play a significant role in Israel's successes, but it also figured significantly in her

---

[902] However, God did use Israel to influence the nations and, through Israel, called all nations to "praise the LORD" (Psalm 117:1).

[903] II Chronicles 15:3; Matthew 28:18-20

[904] Not that we should regard the functions of the Levitical priesthood as parallel to our function before God among the nations. Rather, as Paul said, the things that were written afore time were written for our learning, admonitions and exhortations (Romans 15:4; I Corinthians 10:11).

[905] Joshua 6

failures. Eli was God's high priest. His two sons were evil. They "lay with the women that assembled at the door of the tabernacle of the congregation."[906] Among their responsibilities, they made sure the lamp in the Holy Place had enough oil necessary to burn perpetually. They let the fire die in the Temple lamp. The folly of these priests brought much grief to Israel.

Because of the sins of Eli's sons, and Eli's failure to restrain them, God rejected Eli's family from the priesthood. He placed Samuel under Eli to be trained to take his place.[907] By the time Samuel was grown, all Israel regarded Samuel as a prophet.[908] Eli and his sons remained in their service as priests, and his sons continued in their wickedness—until war broke out between Israel and the Philistines.

Israel lost the first battle. Perhaps they remembered the epic battle of Jericho and superstitiously thought they could overcome the Philistines if they carried the Ark of God into battle before them.[909] The Philistines were also superstitious about the Ark. When the Levites brought the Ark of God into the camp, all Israel gave a great shout, and the Philistines said, "Woe unto us! who shall deliver us out of the hand of these mighty Gods? these are the Gods that smote the Egyptians with all the plagues in the wilderness."[910]

But God was not with Israel! The character of the priesthood had sunk so low the people despised the offerings of the Lord. Israel drifted away into a backslidden condition. The Philistines triumphed and captured the Ark as spoils of war.[911]

---

[906] I Samuel 2:22
[907] I Samuel 1-3
[908] I Samuel 4:1
[909] I Samuel 4:3-6
[910] I Samuel 4:8
[911] I Samuel 4:10-22

Hophni and Phinehas were killed. Eli listened with concern when told about the death of his sons. But when he received news that the Ark of God was lost, he fell backward off his seat, broke his neck, and died.[912] Phinehas' wife was pregnant. When she received news of the death of her husband and her father-in-law, she went into labor. At the birth of her son, just before she died, she said, "The glory is departed from Israel: for the ark of God is taken."[913] The glory departed when her husband and brother-in-law filled the Temple with their debauchery in years gone by until finally the flame in the Holy Place died, and darkness filled the Temple of God.[914]

Samuel became the priest and prophet of God for Israel. He was faithful! Under his leadership Israel returned to the LORD and prevailed over her enemies.

See the pattern. The priesthood secures the blessing of God, and the soldiers are strengthened and made prosperous in battle. If the priesthood is degenerate, the glory departs, and God delivers His people to the power of their enemies. This is what is happening in America today.

Consider another story that illustrates the importance of the priesthood during a time of war. A vast army rose up against Judah from "beyond the sea."[915] Jehoshaphat sought the Lord and was told not to fear, but "to morrow go out against them: for the Lord will be with you."[916] The priests "stood up to praise the Lord God of Israel with a loud voice on high."[917]

---

[912] I Samuel 4:18
[913] I Samuel 4:22
[914] We don't know exactly how old Samuel was when God called him; we only know that he was a child.
[915] II Chronicles 20:2; see v. 22-23
[916] II Chronicles 20:17; see 20:5-17
[917] II Chronicles 20:19

After the king consulted with the people, it was decided that he should appoint singers who would "praise the beauty of holiness." (Singing to the Lord is one of the functions of the priesthood in the worship of the Temple.)

Jehoshaphat sent these priests out in front of his army, singing praise to the beauty of holiness and saying, "Praise the Lord; for his mercy endureth for ever."[918] We cannot find that God instructed Jehoshaphat to do this. Nevertheless, his faith certainly did impress the Lord—for "when they began to sing and to praise, the Lord set ambushments against the children of Ammon, Moab, and Mount Seir, which were come against Judah; and they were smitten."[919]

From the Old Testament examples above, we can see that the actions of today's believer-priests have a profound influence on what God does in the physical world.[920] When believer-priests function properly, God works mighty wonders on behalf of His people. When believer-priests become corrupt, the glory (God's manifest presence) withdraws, and our enemies prevail over us.

Alas, today the New Testament priesthood is overrun with covetous priests, like Eli, and whoremongers, like Hophni and Phinehas. Such priests neglect the "lamp of God" (the Word of God)[921] and let it flicker out and die "in the Temple of the Lord."[922] In such times the Lord seeks a Samuel. His eyes are set upon your own heart as you read these words.[923] He called, "Samuel, Samuel."[924] Do you hear Him calling your name?

---

[918] II Chronicles 20:21
[919] II Chronicles 20:22
[920] I Peter 2:5
[921] Psalm 119:105
[922] I Samuel 3:2-3
[923] Proverbs 15:3; 24:12
[924] I Samuel 3:10

Introduction to the New Testament Temple

The believer's physical body is the Temple of the Lord.[925] God (by the Holy Ghost) dwelt between the cherubim over the Ark of the Covenant in a room called the holy of holies in the Old Testament Temple.[926] Today, He dwells in the heart of the believer.[927] By analogy, therefore, the heart is the holy of holies of the New Testament Temple.

The Ark of the Covenant was kept in the Old Testament Temple, as mentioned above, and represents Christ in us, for Christ is the Ark of the New Covenant. In the Ark the golden pot of true manna from heaven was kept; Jesus said that manna represented Him.[928] Also kept in the Old Testament Ark of the Covenant was the rod that budded, which certified Aaron's authority as God's High Priest. Finally, the Law of God, which is the Word of God, was kept in the Ark.[929] Christ is God's manna,[930] God's High Priesthood,[931] and God's Law in our hearts.[932] Today, Christ in us is the Ark of the New Covenant in the New Testament Temple.[933]

The body of the believer is the Temple of God.

The heart of the believer is the holy of holies in the New Testament Temple.

In the Old Testament Temple, there was a golden censer that burned incense continually. This represented prayer,

---

[925] I Corinthians 6:19
[926] Psalm 99:1; 80:1; Isaiah 37:16
[927] Galatians 4:6; Ephesians 3:17
[928] John 6:31-59; see Hebrews 9:4
[929] Numbers 17:3-10
[930] John 6:31-59
[931] Psalm 110:4; Hebrews 5:6-20; 7:1-21
[932] John 1:1
[933] Colossians 1:27; Romans 8:10-11

and prayers are to be made in the New Testament Temple continuously.[934]

The golden censer in the Temple of God indicated the priest's authority to come before God with the prayers of the people. The incense was directly associated with prayer: "Let my prayer be set forth before thee as incense; and the lifting up of my hands as the evening sacrifice."[935] However, for that incense (prayer) to be acceptable to God, it must be burned in the golden censer with holy fire.[936]

The New Testament also identifies the golden censer of incense with the prayers of the saints.[937] This illustrates the New Testament principle that Jesus Christ, our High Priest, makes our sacrifices acceptable.[938] Our prayers, like incense, must be presented to God in Christ Jesus—the golden censer—to be consumed by the fire of God.[939]

Prayer is the primary function of the believer-priest. Constant communion with God is maintained only by earnest, fervent praying.[940] Intimacy with God in the communion of the Holy Ghost[941] is developed in the prayer closet of God's priests,[942] where, by His Spirit, we cry Abba, Father.[943] The Old Testament Tabernacle, the "house of God," was to be, above all else, a house of prayer.[944] No

---

[934] Revelation 8:3; Romans 8:26; see Leviticus 10:1; 16:12-46; I Thessalonians 5:17; see Hebrews 9:4

[935] Psalm 141:2; Luke 1:10

[936] Nadab and Abihu "offered strange fire before the LORD, which he commanded them not" (Leviticus 10:1). God's holy fire went out from the LORD, "and devoured them, and they died before the LORD" (Leviticus 10:2).

[937] Revelation 8:3-5

[938] I Peter 2:5

[939] Hebrew 12:29

[940] James 5:16

[941] II Corinthians 13:14

[942] Matthew 6:6

[943] Romans 8:15

[944] Isaiah 56:7; Matthew 21:13

wonder believer-priests are called upon to "pray without ceasing" in the New Testament Temple.[945]

Christ dwells in the heart of the believer-priest by the Holy Spirit. In Him, we have the true manna from heaven.[946] He is our High Priest after the order of Melchizedek.[947] Jesus has made us priests.[948] Therefore, His presence in our heart is the certification of our priesthood. Christ is the budding rod in the New Testament Ark of God.

The letter of the Law was kept in the Ark of the Covenant on tables of stone.[949] In Deuteronomy 31:26, God commanded Moses to inscribe the Law into the walls of the Ark of the Covenant of the Lord.[950] (When anyone faced the mercy seat, he was confronted, face-to-face, with the Law of God.) The epistle (letter) of Christ is inscribed upon the fleshy tables of our hearts.[951] May all who meet us come face-to-face, as it were, with Christ.[952]

In summary, the body of the believer-priest is the Temple of God. Christ, by the Holy Ghost, dwells in that Temple, but

---

[945] The exhortation applies with even greater force to the Lord's churches, which are specifically called "the house of God" (I Timothy 3:15). Indeed, if *believer-priests* are the Temple of God (I Corinthians 6:19), and His *Church* is made up of *believer-priests,* it follows that the exhortation concerning the "House of God" would have its fullest application to the *Church.*

[946] Ephesians 3:17

[947] Psalm 110:4; Hebrews 5:6-10; 6:20; 7:11-21

[948] Revelation 1:6

[949] Romans 7:6; Hebrews 9:4c (The word *epistle* means letter.)

[950] The "book of the law" was "put … in the side of the ark of the covenant of the LORD" (Deuteronomy 31:26). The expression, *in the side,* was used to instruct Noah to build a door it into the side panel of the Ark (Genesis 6:16). In every other place but one (I Samuel 24:3) the expression is found the idea expressed is *where* inside of this or that something is to be found: as, for example, *"in the sides* of the hole's mouth" (Jeremiah 48:28). The various Hebrew words translated by this English expression are never translated *within* or *inside.* It appears, therefore, that the book of the Law was inscribed in the walls of the Ark of the Covenant.

[951] Jeremiah 31:33

[952] II Corinthians 4:11

He resides, particularly, in the heart of the believer-priest. He has made us priests unto God. Our primary function as priests in this Temple is to offer prayer, as incense, in the golden censer, which is Christ, to be consumed by our God, Who is a consuming fire.

We have a duty to sanctify the Temple of GOD.

Nadab and Abihu offered their incense in their golden censers with strange fire.[953] God killed them!

O, listen: this is the reason that the reproach of Sardis rests upon us. The church in Sardis had a name that it was alive when in truth, it was dead.[954] Believer-priests today do routinely offer prayers to be consumed in the strange fire of their lusts.[955] That is why it may be said of so many of His churches today, "thou hast a name that thou livest, and art dead."[956] They have no potent influence in the spiritual realm, and so sinners and devils mock their influence in the physical.

I dare say most churches, small and large, stink with decay. Some of our larger churches are nothing more than dog-kennels, goat farms, and pig pens. But in our medium-sized and smaller churches too, members revel in the world like sows wallow in muck, gleefully squealing as they flaunt their filthy lifestyle in the name of grace. Dogs dressed like sheep in the pasture lick the vomit of their shame, while goats feed on anything, and everything, put before them.

If revival comes, and the Lord walks into our camp, how many *Nadab's* and *Abihu's* will drop dead in our churches

---

[953] Leviticus 10:1-3
[954] Revelation 3:1
[955] James 4:3
[956] Revelation 3:1

like Ananias and Sapphira?[957] Will not the Holy Saviour Who took a whip to Temple defilers soon purge the priesthood of Phinehas and Hophni, whose fornication makes the ministry of the Lord to stink. And the lazy covetous elders too, such as Eli who, prospering by their service, refused to restrain them?[958]

If these reproofs have rebuffed your conscience, be not overwrought with grief. Repent, rather, and turn to God. Fall before His mercy seat, and there, face-to-face before the Holy Law of God, beg His mercy. Perhaps you may petition His Throne on the ground that you "did it ignorantly in unbelief."[959]

~

---

[957] See Acts 5:1-11
[958] I Samuel 1-3
[959] I Timothy 1:13

"Nothing is more certain than that a general profligacy and corruption of manners make a people ripe for destruction. A good form of government may hold the rotten materials together for some time, but beyond a certain pitch, even the best constitution will be ineffectual, and slavery must ensue."

~ John Whitherspoon

(John Witherspoon, *The Dominion of Providence Over the Passions of Men*, 1776)

Chapter Twenty-One

God's Warrior Priests
(Part Two)
The Body, the Spirit, and the Soul

THE BELIEVER'S BODY IS GOD'S Temple. Within our bodies, there is our soul and our spirit.[960] Our soul through our spirit is the priest in God's Temple, responsible for offering spiritual sacrifices unto God.[961] To understand how our soul through our spirit functions as God's priest in His Temple, we need to know the relationships between the body, the spirit, and the soul.

Introduction to the Body, Spirit, and Soul

There are three distinct and yet wholly interrelated and dynamic aspects of our being: the body, the spirit, and the soul.[962] These combine to form a unity so that the individual is identifiable with each one, both separately and collectively. In other words, my soul is me, my spirit is me, and my body is me, and yet there is only one me.

---

[960] I Thessalonians 5:23

[961] I Peter 2:5

[962] I Thessalonians 5:23, "And the very God of peace sanctify you wholly; and *I pray God* your whole spirit and soul and body be preserved blameless unto the coming of our Lord Jesus Christ." Jesus differentiated between the *soul* and the *body,* when He said, "And fear not them which kill the body, but are not able to kill the soul: but rather fear him which is able to destroy both soul and body in hell." The Bible distinguishes between the *soul* and the *spirit* in Hebrews 4:12, where it says, "For the word of God is quick, and powerful, . . . dividing asunder of soul and spirit . . . ."

Furthermore, each of the three aspects of our being is comprised of two features or properties.[963] Understanding the interrelationships between the body, the spirit, and the soul—and the vital role the two properties of each play in our spiritual life—is powerful. Hang on, because the spiritual is about to become as real to you as the physical.

I need to use some technical terms to explain our spiritual anatomy. This is because, for example, in our Bible, the words *soul* and *life* are sometimes used interchangeably to identify the conscious personality of an individual—that part of us that is aware. Most of the time, the word *life* translates another word that refers to that part of the soul that animates our body. Sometimes, I will need to direct your attention to the property of your soul that makes you

---

[963] A *property* is a feature or characteristic of a thing that manifests without requiring some chemical change. One could say steam is a *characteristic* of water, but this requires a chemical change, usually induced by heat, to manifest, and therefore steam is not a *property* of water. Liquidity, however, is a feature of water that manifests without any chemical change, and so *liquidity* is a property of water. Each separate aspect of our being has two properties.

self-aware, your consciousness. Other times I will need to direct your attention to the property of your soul that gives you life, the ability to move your body, or animation. To do this, I give each a unique name. The name for the property of the soul that provides us with awareness is called by the Greek word that means *awareness*, or *consciousness*. The name for the property of our soul that gives us animation is the Greek word that has that meaning.

The Greek word that refers to our awareness is *psuche* (soo-kee). The Greek word that refers to our animation is *zoe* (zo-ee).

The same thing is true when we discuss the body and the spirit.

Please treat these new words like the names of newly met friends. And, like meeting new friends, first we are introduced; then later we get to know them.

The soul has two properties.

Meet Zoe and Psuche. Zoe is the animating property of the soul. Psuche is the property of the soul that makes us aware. The animating property is straightforward. It's that property of the soul that gives our bodies the ability to move. *Awareness* might need a little clarification.

The word *Psuche* refers to that aspect of our soul that makes us self-aware, our consciousness. It refers to what we call our conscious personality. To keep it simple, I name this property of soul awareness.

The soul has two properties: animation (Zoe) and awareness (Psuche).

Self-consciousness, or awareness, is where our mind comes into our discussion. As we shall see, the mind is the place where our soul and spirit connect.[964] For that reason, we will talk about mind when we discuss how our spirit functions in God's Temple.

You have met Zoe (animating principle) and Psuche (conscious personality). These are the two properties of our soul. Now let's meet two more new friends.

The body has two properties.

Meet Soma (*body*) and Sarke (*flesh*). The body has two properties: first, corporeality (physicality); and second, the sin nature. I discussed the sin nature earlier when I explained the expressions *old man* and *new man*. (See chapter Nineteen.) The sin nature resides in our body of sin.[965] Often, I will need to differentiate between the *body* in general and the *body of sin* specifically.

Sarke

Soma

---

[964] The word *psuche* is translated *mind* three times in the Bible. Besides, it is obvious that our consciousness is a function of our mind. In fact, our soul engages in thought through our spirit, and by its thoughts gives shape and direction to our spirit. Understanding the nature of *spirit* is challenging because whatever language is used to explain it requires constant clarification in order to avoid confusion or misunderstanding. Therefore we must begin with a flat statement: the *spirit* is distinct from the body and the soul even though, like the body, its existence dependent upon the soul. For example, if the body looses its soul, it returns to dust. In a similar manner, if the soul and spirit are separated, the spirit immediately returns to God. Another way of looking at this is to notice that the word *spirit* means, literally, breath. If the *soul* leaves the body, it takes the breath of that body away; that's because the soul and the spirit are inseparable, except by the sharp knife of the Word of God (Hebrews 4:12). If the spirit is separated from the soul, the spirit will dissipate; similarly to how the body returns to dust, the spirit returns to air. Our *spirit* emanates from our soul in our mind, and is shaped by the thoughts of our heart. And our *spirit* intersects and connects our soul to God by His Spirit. It's our point of connection with GOD. The doctrine is called *spiration* in theology; and we do not need to go deeper into this matter here.

[965] Romans 6:6

Soma is an abbreviation of the Greek word that means body. When I need to direct your attention to the body (as a whole), I'll use the word *Soma*.

The Bible sometimes uses the word *flesh* to speak of that part of our body where the sin nature resides.[966] The Greek word that means flesh is *sarke* (sar-kee). This is the word I will use when I'm talking about the sin nature. That's because the Bible says the law of sin resides in the members (the fleshly parts) of our bodies.[967]

Soma refers to the body, but Sarke refers specifically to the fleshly parts of the body. The distinction is important. Because sin nature resides in the flesh parts of our bodies, I distinguish it from the body (*Soma*) by calling it *Sarke*.

To conclude our introduction to the body, you need to know that the soul acts in this world through the body.

You met *Soma* and *Sarke*; let's meet two more new friends.

The Spirit is closely associated with the mind.

Meet *Pneuma* (new-mah) and *Nous* (noose). The Greek word for spirit is *pneuma*. *Nous* is the Greek word for mind.

The relationship between Pneuma (our spirit) and Nous (our mind) is a little bit different than those we have discussed so far.

I mentioned earlier that the mind is the place where our spirit connects with our soul. I also

---

[966] See Romans 7:5, 18, 25; see Romans 8:1-13; 13:14; and Galatians 5:16-24. Also Romans 7:23. The law of sin resides in the members, the flesh, of our body.
[967] Romans 7:23

explained that the Bible shows a very close connection between the spirit and the mind. Because of this, I wanted to discuss the mind in its connection with the spirit. Let's do that now.

The essential property of spirit is spirituality, which means it is non-corporeal; it does not have physicality.[968]

Our spirit expresses itself through the mind and manifests in thoughts. Another way to put it is to say our thoughts are the actions of our spirit.

Our souls do things in the physical realm through our bodies.[969] In the spiritual realm, our souls act through our thoughts.[970] The spirit (pneuma) and the mind (nous) are closely connected. And the Nous is where our spirit and soul intersect. Our soul interacts with the spiritual realm of God's creation through our spirit.

Thoughts are the actions of our soul through our spirit.[971] The very close relationship between

[968] The amazing thing is that while our spirit does not have physicality it does take the shape and form of our physical body. See I Corinthians 15:44. When speaking of our bodily resurrection, the Spirit explains, "There is a natural body, and there is a spiritual body." A *spirit* can, and sometimes does, manifest in the form of the body it inhabits. Samuel's spirit once manifested in the physical form of his body (I Samuel 28:11-16). In the resurrection, the properties of physicality and spirituality will be fused; which will allow us to manifest physically or spiritually at will. The way Jesus did after His resurrection (see John 20:26-30).

[969] Leviticus 17:18, for one of many examples.

[970] Ephesians 4:23, I Chronicles 29:18; see Matthew 15:19 and Hebrews 4:12

[971] In fact, the word *mind* is used to translate the Greek word *psuche* five times: Philippians 1:27; Acts 14:2; James 1:8; 4:8; and Hebrews 12:3. Added to the fact that the word *mind* is never used to translate the Greek word *pneuma* (*spirit*), and you can see that the *mind* is part of our awareness and so is more properly understood as a property of the soul. The reason it is set here, with *spirit*, is because the soul and the spirit are connected at the mind. The soul through the spirit engages spirituality, and this takes place in the mind.

our spirit and our thoughts may be seen in the following Scriptures: Romans 8:27 ("the mind of the Spirit"); Ephesians 4:23 ("the spirit of your mind"); Philippians 1:27 ("in one spirit, with one mind"); and indirectly by I Timothy 4:1-4, where we are warned about seducing spirits that plant heretical thoughts in our mind.

I hope you enjoyed meeting your six new friends. We'll get to know them better later.

Our being is comprised of three aspects: body, spirit, and soul. Let's talk about how they interconnect.

The Relationship of the Body, the Spirit, and the Soul

Paul mentions the three distinct aspects that together make up the whole person: "I pray God your whole spirit and soul and body be preserved blameless unto the coming of our Lord Jesus Christ."[972] What do we mean when we say that each of these is distinct, and each is dynamic? In this chapter, I'll address the fact that each is distinct. The dynamic aspect of body, spirit, and soul is discussed in chapter twenty-five.

Each aspect of our being (the body, the spirit, and the soul) is distinct.

Jesus differentiated between the body and the soul when He said, "Fear not them which kill the body, but are not

---

[972] I Thessalonians 5:23—Good men debate the question of *trichotomy* versus *dichotomy*. *Trichotomists* view man as consisting of three distinct aspects. *Dichotomists* view man as consisting of only two. The debate is over whether the *soul* and the *spirit* are distinct or whether these words merely describe the nature of the spiritual part of our being. Some argue that man was originally tripartite, but when Adam sinned, the *spirit* died and man became a bipartite being. When one receives Christ, these argue, either his human *spirit* is quickened, or made alive, or, according to others, the Holy Ghost enters in to restore man's tripartite nature. Nevertheless, on the question of a distinction between the spiritual and the physical, there is no debate among Bible believing Christians.

able to kill the soul: but rather fear him which is able to destroy both soul and body in hell."[973]

The Apostle Paul differentiated the soul from the spirit when he said, "For the word of God is quick, and powerful, and sharper than any twoedged sword, piercing even to the dividing asunder of soul and spirit, and of the joints and marrow, and is a discerner of the thoughts and intents of the heart."[974] At the same time that this verse reveals a distinction between the soul and the spirit, it also shows the impossibility of discerning that distinction apart from the revelation of God's Word.

According to the Bible, man is comprised of three distinct aspects of his being: a body, a spirit, and a soul.

The body, which functions as God's Temple, is distinct from the spirit and the soul.

Earlier, we established that according to Scripture, the believer's body is the Temple of the Holy Ghost. [975]

The Holy Spirit dwells in our hearts[976] and

---

[973] Matthew 10:28. The Watchtower Bible and Tract Society cult, following the teachings of the false prophet, Charles Taze Russell, deny the distinction Jesus identified between the body and the soul. Numbers 19:22 tells us the *soul* touches; Leviticus 7:18-25 and 17:10-15 tell us the *soul* eats; and Leviticus 4:2 tells us the *soul* sins. Russell attempts to confuse Bible students by inferring from these verses that the *soul* and the *body* are identical. Jesus made it clear that the soul and the body are not identical, and Jesus is a greater authority than Russell. See Genesis 35:18, "And it came to pass, as her soul was in departing, (for she died) that she called his name Benoni: but his father called him Benjamin." It is clear that *death* occurs when the *life* (soul) departs from the *body*. After death, the *life* (soul) continues to have an existence (Luke 16:22-23 and Revelation 6:9).

[974] Hebrews 4:12

[975] I Corinthians 6:19-20

[976] II Corinthians 1:22

bears witness with our human spirit that we are God's children.[977] The Holy Spirit and our human spirit live together in the Temple.

Christ in His Temple

Our God has placed His Spirit in the Temple as the earnest of His purchase of it, securing the believer's natural body as His purchased possession. He will redeem it at His coming for His saints, called the glorious appearing when He will transform our natural body into a body like His.[978]

As we have already seen, the natural body of the believer is designated God's Temple on the earth today. Hence, it is true that God's Spirit inhabits this body and is the presence of Christ in us.[979]

According to the Bible, the Holy Spirit dwells in our bodies together with our human spirit.

Our soul, through our spirit, functions as God's priest in the New Testament Temple, and our spirit is distinct from our soul.

Priest

Spirit

The distinction between the spiritual and physical aspects of our being is evident. But the difference between the soul and the spirit is not intuitively perceived. As noted above, the Scripture clearly distinguishes between soul and spirit; yet, in

[977] Romans 8:16
[978] Ephesians 1:13-14; Philippians 3:19-21; I Corinthians 15:44-58; I John 3:2
[979] Romans 8:9-11

the Scriptures, we find that the functions of intelligence, affection, and volition—the distinguishing qualities of personality—are ascribed to each.[980] For this reason, it is impossible to perceive a distinction between them in our experience. Scripture, however, reveals that our soul intersects with the physical world through our bodies, and with the spiritual world through our spirit. Furthermore, from Scripture, we know our soul acts in the spiritual realm by our mind, where it chooses to walk after the flesh, or after the Spirit of God. But we get ahead of ourselves.

Conclusion

Each person, created in the image of God, is comprised of a body, a spirit, and a soul. This corresponds with the Godhead: the Father, the Son, and the Holy Ghost. The Father is the invisible, eternal essence of God, which corresponds to the soul of man, his fundamental essence.[981] The Son is the image of the invisible God,[982] corresponding to the body, which is the visible aspect of our invisible self. The Holy Ghost is the Spirit of God and corresponds to our spirit.[983]

Similar to how the Godhead is comprised of three separate personalities but one eternal being, the body, spirit, and soul are distinct, yet together comprise one entity. Obviously, the Godhead is more profound in both the distinctions and the

---

[980] For example, we notice that the *spirit* and the *soul* are identified with affection (emotion) (*spirit:* Psalm 34:18, 51:17, Isaiah 57:15, 66:2, Daniel 2:3, Acts 18:25, and I Kings 21:5; *soul:* Isaiah 53:11, 58:3, Ezekiel 24:21, Psalm 42:5,6,11 and 43:5 — see also Job 7:11). The same is true concerning *volition,* or the *will* (*soul:* Ezekiel 18:4,20, Micah 6:7, Leviticus 26:15, and Deuteronomy 12:20; *spirit:* Matthew 26:41, Exodus 35:21, see also II Chronicles 18:20,21 and Isaiah 26:9). The *spirit* and the *soul* are also associated with *intelligence* (*spirit:* Ephesians 4:23, Romans 8:27, see also Isaiah 11:2 and I Corinthians 2:11; *soul:* Proverbs 19:2, 2:10, 24:14, and Psalm 139:14).

[981] Matthew 16:26
[982] Colossians 1:15
[983] Romans 8:16

union of the three Persons of the Godhead. Nonetheless, we are created in God's likeness, and we need to understand how each aspect of our being functions. This is especially true when we engage in spiritual warfare as soldiers for God in God's War.

Toward that end, in the next few chapters, I will sort out the biblical distinctions between the soul and the spirit.

~

"Republics are created by the virtue, public spirit, and intelligence of the citizens. They fall, when the wise are banished from the public councils, because they dare to be honest, and the profligate are rewarded, because they flatter the people, in order to betray them." ~ Joseph Story

(Joseph Story, *Commentaries on the Constitution*, 1833.)

Chapter Twenty-Two

God's Warrior Priests
(Part Three)
The Soul of God's Warriors

R EMEMBER THE GREEK friends you met earlier, Zoe and Psuche? Let's get to know them better.

Our soul has two properties: zoe (pronounced zo'-ee) and psuche (pronounced soo'-kee).[984] Now, you'll begin to understand how these distinctions are helpful.

---

[984] Including those related etymologically, Strong identifies ten Greek words and six Hebrew/Aramaic words translated *life*. There are one primary and one secondary word used to express the idea of *life*. The primary Greek word is ζωή–*zoe* (Strong No. 2222, 2198, 2227). Including all occasions where *zoe* is translated *life, live,* or *living,* it is used 225 of the 294 times these words are found in the New Testament. The secondary Greek word that is translated *life* but never translated *live* or *living* is ψυχή—*psuche* (Strong No. 5590, 895). It is translated *life* 35 times and *soul* 39 times. The word generally translated *spirit* is *pneuma*. It is translated *life* only 1 time (Revelation 13:15), and never translated *live,* or *living.* Together, *zoe* and *psuche* account for 93% of all occurrences of the word *life* in the New Testament. The Greek words *zoe* and *psuche* correspond to the Hebrew words *chay* and *nephesh,* and identify the same two properties. In the Old Testament, the words *life, live,* or *living* are found 550 times. The primary root word is חַי - *chay* (Strong No. 2416, 2417, 2421, 2425), accounting for 413 of the 550 occurrences, and the secondary word is נֶפֶשׁ - *nephesh* (Strong No. 5315), 101 times. It is never translated *live,* or *living. Chay* and *Nephesh* account for 97% of the times the words *life, live,* or *living* are found in the Old Testament. The Greek word *zoe* (never translated *soul,* and consistently referring to the animating principle of a created being) corresponds to the Hebrew word *chay* (never translated *soul* and consistently used to speak of the animating principle) while the Greek word *psuche* is the only word translated *soul* in the New Testament and almost evenly translated *life.*

Our essential life, or animating principle, is zoe; and our self-awareness and consciousness is psuche. These are properties of the soul.

The soul is the fundamental essence of a man's being. Jesus made this clear when He asked, "What shall a man give in exchange for his soul?"[985] and said we should not be concerned about man, who may kill the body, but rather fear Him who has the power to destroy "both soul and body in hell."[986] The soul is that part of our being without which we would cease to be. Notice that we believe for the saving of our soul.[987] The salvation of our spirit and our body, depends entirely upon the salvation of our soul. The soul is the core of our being.

I'll explain all this later. But when we got saved, God saved our Soul.[988] Because our soul is saved, our body will be glorified and made like His resurrected body and our spirit will be saved in the day of the Lord Jesus—when He returns for us.[989]

When Christ saved our soul, He removed it from our body and then separated our Zoe from our Psuche. He then placed our Zoe safely with Him in God the Father. Then He attached His Zoe to our Psuche. Christ became, literally, our life. (That's why when we do sinful things, we drag Him into it.)[990] This is the answer to Christ's prayer given in John 17 when He prayed:

---

[985] Mark 8:37
[986] Matthew 16:26; 10:28
[987] Hebrews 10:39
[988] Hebrews 10:39
[989] Philippians 3:20-21; I Corinthians 5:5
[990] I Corinthians 6:15

Neither pray I for these alone, but for them also which shall believe on me through their word;

That they all may be one; as thou, Father, art in me, and I in thee, that they also may be one in us: that the world may believe that thou hast sent me.

And the glory which thou gavest me I have given them; that they may be one, even as we are one:

I in them, and thou in me, that they may be made perfect in one; and that the world may know that thou hast sent me, and hast loved them, as thou hast loved me. — John 17:20-23

As we shall see, our soul is made alive by the life of Christ, and it interacts with the physical world through our bodies and with the spiritual world through our spirit.

All living creatures have a soul. But there is something about a man that separates him from all other animals. This brings us to a discussion of the spirit in man.

~

"No people will tamely surrender their Liberties, nor can any be easily subdued, when knowledge is diffused and Virtue is preserved. On the Contrary, when People are universally ignorant, and debauched in their Manners, they will sink under their own weight without the Aid of foreign Invaders." ~ Samuel Adams

(Samuel Adams, letter to James Warren, November 4, 1775.)

Chapter Twenty-Three

God's Warrior Priests

(Part Four)

The Spirit of God's Warriors

YOU MET PNEUMA AND NOUS earlier. Let's get to know them better.

Pneuma is the Greek word for spirit. The root of this word means to breathe.

Breathing certainly indicates the presence of the spirit of life.

But having a spirit means more than breathing. The spirit and the soul share all functions of personality.[991] When Paul instructed the Corinthians to discipline a member of that church, he encouraged them to do so assured that although Satan would destroy his flesh, his "spirit may be saved in the day of the Lord Jesus."[992] The Bible speaks of the "spirits of just men made perfect."[993] And, finally, when the Apostle Paul exhorted us to "cleanse ourselves from all filthiness of the flesh and spirit, perfecting holiness in the fear of

---

[991] Generally, we say that personality is made up of *mind, will*, and *emotions*. In Scripture we find both *soul* and *spirit* share all three—*soul:* mind: Psalm 139:14; will: Acts 3:23; Leviticus 20:6; 26:15; and Lamentations 3:24; emotions: Psalm 42:6-11; Psalm 35:9; *Spirit:* mind: Romans 8:27; Ephesians 4:23; will: Exodus 35:21; Matthew 26:41; and emotions: I Kings 21:5; and Luke 1:47.

[992] I Corinthians 5:5)

[993] Hebrews 12:23

God,"[994] he was not talking about using a better mouthwash. Obviously, the word *spirit* means more than breathing.

While breathing does not complete the meaning of the word *spirit*, using the root word for breath to identify the spirit of both God and man reveals something important to us about its nature.[995]

First, the word *breath* speaks to the fact that our spirit moves invisibly, and it is expressed from within us and manifests through our bodies into the world around us. Generally, others experience our spirit in our disposition, our attitudes, or our moods, our -*aires*.

Second, our spirit connects us with God. When God breathed into man the breath of life,[996] He formed "the spirit of man within him."[997] This set man apart from the animals,

---

[994] II Corinthians 7:1

[995] The Hebrew word that is translated *spirit* 240 times out of the 244 times the word *spirit* appears in our Bible is also translated *breath* 28 times. That's more than half the number of times the words *breath, breathe,* or *breathing* occur in our Bible.

[996] The word translated *breath* in "breath of life" (Genesis 2:7) is not *ruwach* (רוּחַ (Strong No. 7307, 7308)), the primary word for *spirit*. In fact, it is נְשָׁמָה (*nesh-aw-maw'* (Strong No. 5397)), and is usually translated *breath* (used 24 times, translated variously as follows: *breath, breathed, etc.* (18x), *blast* (3x), *inspiration* (1x), *soul* (1x), and *spirit* only twice (Job 4:9 and Proverbs 20:27). Notice that in at least one Scripture (Isaiah 57:16) the word is translated *soul*. Of further interest is the fact that the word translated *breathed* (נָפַח—*naphach'* (Strong No. 5301)) in Genesis 2:7 ("And the LORD God formed man of the dust of the ground, and *breathed* into his nostrils ...") is a word very closely associated with the Hebrew word that is the primary word for *soul* (נֶפֶשׁ (Strong No. 5315)). This shows that the idea of *breathing* is not the primary significance of the word *spirit* (*ruwach*).

[997] I believe God generated into existence man's *spirit* (*ruwach*) when He *breathed* into his nostrils the *breath* of life. By this, He gave to man a unique *spirit*. All animals are *living souls* (Genesis 1:21—*living creature* translates *chay nephesh;* Revelation 16:3—*living creature* translates *zoe psuche*). Also, all animals have a *spirit* (Ecclesiastes 3:21 and Ezekiel 1:21,21; 10:17). However, the *spirit* of the animal is distinguished from that of man in Ecclesiastes 3:21: "Who knoweth the spirit of man that goeth upward, and the spirit of the beast that goeth downward to the earth?" Clearly, the *spirit of man* relates to the *spiritual* aspect of God's creation while the *spirit of the beast* is limited to the physical. (Zechariah 12:1)

for "the spirit of man . . . goeth upward, and the spirit of the beast goeth downward to the earth."[998] The idea is that man's spirit is not bound to the earth in the way of the spirit of beasts. Ours moves upward, toward God.

The spirit is the unique quality of human nature that gives humankind the capacity to relate to God on a personal level.[999] What separates a man from all other earthly creatures is his spirit.[1000] God is a Spirit, and those who worship Him must do so "in spirit and in truth."[1001] Only spiritual beings can worship Him. God gave us a spirit so we may worship Him. His Spirit communes with our spirit. For example, by His Word of truth, the Holy Spirit bears witness with our human spirit that we are God's children.[1002] It is by His Spirit that we cry "Abba Father."[1003] God made all the other creatures for man, but He made man exclusively for Himself. GOD is a Spirit, and He connects with us through our spirit. This involves the mind.

Nous is the essential Greek word for mind.[1004]

---

[998] Ecclesiastes 3:21

[999] Romans 8:16

[1000] Some suppose lost men do not have an active *spirit.* The Scripture testifies that the *spirit* of unbelieving Pharaoh was troubled (Genesis 41:8). The confusion comes partly from a mistake regarding death. While it is true that lost men are *spiritually dead* (Ephesians 2:1), it is certainly not true that therefore their *spirit* cannot function. Notice, for example, that the believer's *body is dead* because of *sin,* yet it continues to function, and even to function in sin (Romans 8:10; Romans 6:13-19; I John 1:7-9). Death is the separation of *life* from the body (Genesis 35:18); hence, *spiritual death* is separation from the ultimate *life source,* that is, from God. This explains the nearly irresistible urge in man to *worship.* Chimpanzees do not worship, and while many men might be said to be like chimpanzees in this, as well as in other traits, the fact remains, most men do worship yet most do not worship God.

[1001] John 4:24

[1002] Romans 8:16

[1003] Romans 8:15

[1004] The words *mind* and *minds* are found 67 times in the New Testament. There are 26 different forms translated *mind* (56) or *minds* (11). Only *Nous* consistently speaks of the function we associate with the word *mind,* and this is the word translated *mind* far more often than any of the other forms (15 times, as compared with

The spirit and the mind are closely related. For example, the Bible speaks of the *mind of the Spirit*, suggesting the Holy Spirit is directly connected to God's mind.[1005] Paul exhorted us, "Be renewed in the spirit of your mind,"[1006] suggesting the same thing is true of us—our spirit and mind are connected. Other Scriptures indicate this relationship, although indirectly. One example is where Paul warns us to beware of seducing spirits that teach us the doctrines of devils,[1007] planting thoughts in our minds. Another example is when the Scriptures suggest that being of one mind is equivalent to being of one spirit.[1008]

God's Holy Spirit connects and communes with our spirit.[1009] Our soul interacts with God through our spirit. The "mind of the Spirit" connects with our soul through "the spirit of our mind." Our spirit might also connect with other spirits through our thoughts. We must try the spirits and direct our thoughts after the Holy Spirit. It's called walking after the Spirit. (We understand what it means to walk physically. We walk spiritually by our thoughts. Our spirit moves along on the feet of our thoughts.)

---

7 as the next highest, and the rest are between 1-4 occurrences each). Furthermore, the rest are descriptive of the activity we associate with mind, forming opinions, remembering, thinking, and so forth. Understood in this way, the essential word for *mind* is **νοῦς** nous, "Probably from the base of 1097; the intellect, i.e. mind (divine or human; in thought, feeling, or will); by implication, meaning: — mind, understanding. Compare 5590." It is worthy of our notice that the word *psuche* is translated *mind*, or *minds*, three times: Philippians 1:27; Acts 14:2; and Hebrews 12:3. Also, the word *pneuma* (spirit) is never translated *mind*.

1005 Romans 8:27
1006 Ephesians 4:23
1007 I Timothy 4:1-4
1008 Philippians 1:27
1009 Romans 8:16; II Corinthians 13:14

Our thoughts and imaginations are the actions of our spirit. Each thought is an action of our soul through our spirit. To illustrate, when a man looks on a woman with lust in his heart, he has committed an act of adultery.[1010]

Remember that our soul connects with God through our spirit. When our soul through our spirit conceives thoughts in our heart, God is there, watching.[1011] God ponders the thoughts of the heart and weighs the spirit of man.[1012] He is drawn to a humble and contrite spirit but repulsed by pride and fleshly lusts.[1013]

Conclusion

In summary, the body, the spirit, and the soul are distinct aspects of our being that fulfill separate but interconnected functions. The soul is the fundamental aspect of our being. It engages both the spiritual and physical in God's creation. It engages, interacts, and experiences the physical in God's creation through the body. It engages, interacts, and experiences the spiritual in God's creation through the spirit. Finally, the soul acts upon the world both spiritually, through its spirit, and physically, through its body.

~

[1010] Matthew 5:28
[1011] Galatians 4:6 with II Chronicles 16:9
[1012] Proverbs 16:2; 21:2; 24:12
[1013] Isaiah 57:15; Ecclesiastes 7:8; see James 4:6; I Peter 5:5

"The general principles on which the fathers achieved independence were the general principles of Christianity. I will avow that I then believed, and now believe, that those general principles of Christianity are as eternal and immutable as the existence and attributes of God."

~ Samuel Adams

(Thomas Jefferson, *The Writings of Thomas Jefferson* (Washington D. C.: The Thomas Jefferson Memorial Association, 1904), Vol. XIII, p. 292-294. In a letter from John Adams to Thomas Jefferson on June 28, 1813.)

Chapter Twenty-Four

God's Warrior Priests

(Part Five)

The Body of God's Warriors

Sarke

YOU'VE MET SOMA AND SARKE. Now it's time to get to know them.

The word *body* translates the Greek word *somatos* (σῶματος).[1014] The Greek for *flesh* is sarkos (σάρκος).[1015] I'll abbreviate them: soma and sarke. Soma (body) is related to Sarke (the flesh) like Zoe is to Psuche.[1016]

Remember our earlier discussion of the *old man* and the *new man*? The word *flesh* is used to speak of the natural man, with the nature of Adam;[1017] that is the old man. The flesh is where the law of

Soma

[1014] Strong No. 4983, *somatos,* from σῶμα—*soma,* "From 4982; the body (as a sound whole), used in a very wide application, literally or figuratively: — bodily, body, slave."

[1015] Strong No. 4561, *sarkos,* from σάρξ—*sarxhe* (sarx), "Probably from the base of 4563; flesh (as stripped of the skin), i.e. . . . the meat of an animal . . . , or (by extension) the body (as opposed to the soul (or spirit), or as the symbol of what is external, . . . or (by implication) human nature (with its frailties (physically or morally) and passions), or . . . : — carnal(-ly, + -ly minded), flesh(-ly)."

[1016] The use of the Greek words to differentiate between the two properties of the soul is helpful to avoid confusion. Using the Greek words *Soma* and *Sarke* to differentiate between the *body* and the *flesh* provides for consistency, but it's not necessary in order to avoid confusion. I can use the words *body* and *flesh* to speak of the distinction that exists between them. For that reason, I'll use the simpler terms, *body* and *flesh* in our discussion from this point forward.

[1017] Romans 1:3; 2:28; 4:1; 7:5

sin resides. Holy Scripture says the law of sin operates in the members of our bodies.[1018] The members of our bodies are flesh. The flesh is so ruined by the Fall of Man that there is nothing good in it.[1019] Nevertheless, God has taken ownership of our body (Soma) and desires to manifest Jesus in our mortal flesh (Sarke).[1020]

Let's do a double take on that thought. God has made Soma, our natural body) the Temple of the Holy Ghost, and desires Jesus to manifest in Sarke (our mortal flesh). How this is even possible will be explained when we discuss something called spiritual circumcision.

The Floor Plan of God's New Testament Temple

There were some who desired to show Jesus around the Temple; apparently, they were in awe of that stone and mortar construct.[1021] Jesus surprised them when He prophesied, "There shall not be left one stone upon another, that shall not be thrown down."[1022] The New Testament Temple also will decay, and unless Christ gathers us to Himself before we die, it will, one day, return to dust. He will one day transform our body into a glorious body, like His own— but for the present, the New Testament Temple of God, like the old one, is earthly and susceptible to corruption.

The Old Testament Temple had rooms, and each room served a purpose. Likewise, the New Testament Temple has rooms, and a purpose for each. If we took a tour of the Old Testament Temple, we might begin at the brazen altar, move across the yard to the laver of washing, and then enter the Temple. In the first room, we would see the

---

[1018] Romans 7:23
[1019] Romans 7:18
[1020] I Corinthians 6:20; II Corinthians 4:11
[1021] Luke 21:5
[1022] Luke 21:6

table of shewbread on our right and the golden candlestick to our left, and before us, the altar of incense. Walking up to the altar of incense, we would come to a great veil, and behind that veil, another room called the Holy of Holies. In this room, we would find the Ark of the Covenant, in which was the manna, Aaron's rod that budded, and the tables of stone on which were inscribed the Laws of God. Now let's tour the New Testament Temple.

Outside the Temple proper, at the Brazen Altar, we meet Christ our Saviour, Who was sacrificed for us on the Cross. There too is the laver of washing, where whatever will enter the Temple must first be washed, that is, sanctified unto God. Then we come to the Temple itself: the body of the believer. As we shall see, the door into the first room of the New Testament Temple is at the belly, which is the first room, corresponding to the Holy place of the Old Testament Temple. The second room is the heart, where Christ dwells, corresponding to the Old Testament Holy of Holies.

The Body of the Believer Is the Temple of God

Later, I'll explain how God sanctified the body to be His Holy Temple. For now, it's enough for us to understand that God has taken ownership of the body (Soma) of every believer: "What? Know ye not that your body is the Temple of the Holy Ghost which is in you, which ye have of God, and ye are not your own? For ye are bought with a price: therefore glorify God in your body, and in your spirit, which are God's."[1023]

[1023] I Corinthians 6:19-20—The *body* spoken of here is not the *body of Christ, the Church.* Paul tells us believers are built upon the foundation of the apostles and prophets, Christ being the Chief Cornerstone, and he calls this a Temple: "in whom all the building fitly framed together groweth unto an holy Temple in the Lord" (Ephesians 2:20-22). But this Temple is under construction. When we are gathered to meet Jesus in the air, the building will be "fitly framed together," and we will be an habitation of God through the Spirit. In I Corinthians 6, however,

The body is the "purchased possession" spoken of by Paul when he explained that when we received Christ as Lord and Saviour, God sealed us to Himself by putting His Holy Spirit inside of our bodies.[1024] The presence of the Spirit in us is the token of His earnest payment (a pledge that confirms or secures a contract of ownership). His Spirit in us marks our body as God's property.

In the future, God will redeem His purchased possession. At that time, He will change our vile body to be like His own glorified body.[1025] Until then, the sin nature continues to reside in Sarke (the flesh) of Soma (the body), which is the Temple of God. Nevertheless, God has commanded us to present Soma to Him as a living sacrifice. And we must offer it holy, or it will not be acceptable.[1026] It's the vessel He uses in this Earth right now to accomplish His will in the earth, as it is done in Heaven.[1027]

We enter the Temple through its door and into the first room.

The First Room of the New Testament Temple: The Belly

Jesus said His Spirit would flow into the world through the belly of His disciples.[1028] That sounds strange to us. It helps if we take a moment and think about how we use the word *heart*.

---

the Spirit is talking about our human body: "Flee fornication. Every sin that a man doeth is without the body; but he that committeth fornication sinneth against *his own body*" (I Corinthians 6:18). Following this, Paul asks, "Know ye not that your body is the Temple of the Holy Ghost?" (I Corinthians 6:19). The *body* that is "the Temple of the Holy Ghost" right now is the body of the believer.

[1024] Ephesians 1:13-14

[1025] Philippians 3:20-21; I Corinthians 15:50-58

[1026] Romans 12:1-2

[1027] See II Timothy 2:20-21

[1028] John 7:38-39

Physically, the heart is an organ in the approximate center of our chest that pumps our blood throughout our body. However, we use the word *heart* to speak of our inner life and think of it as the center of our affections. The Bible uses word *belly* the way we use the word *heart*. Only, the belly represents the center of our appetites, while the heart represents the center of our affections. So, the word *belly* represents our physical, or flesh life, and the word *heart* speaks of our inner or spiritual life.

The first room of the New Testament Temple is the belly. This room is nearest to the physical world; it's where our soul, which inhabits the body, intersects, and interacts with the physical world around us.

The belly is indicative of the flesh, or what we sometimes call the self-life or the carnal life. It represents the center of our fleshly appetites.[1029]

Our belly is like the door of God's Temple. Physically, the stomach receives what we put into our bodies. Needed nutrients are obtained, and the waste excreted.[1030] Spiritually, what is in the world comes into God's Temple through the *flesh*. And what is inside of us passes through it into the world around us.[1031] Jesus depended on our knowledge of this to understand what He meant when He said His Spirit would flow through our belly like rivers of living water. His Spirit moves through our belly, that is, through our flesh.

The Bible speaks of us feeding on His Word.[1032] What we eat spiritually is also digested, and the nutrients feed the soul and the spirit. When we taste God's Word, it rejoices

---

[1029] Philippians 3:19; Romans 16:18; see Galatians 5:19-21
[1030] Matthew 15:17
[1031] John 7:38-39
[1032] I Peter 2:2; Hebrews 5:12

the heart;[1033] but it can make the belly bitter.[1034] Of course, we would not liken what passes into the world from digested spiritual food as "spiritual waste." Our spiritual digestive system is so efficient that nothing of God's Word is wasted. But what we take in from the world is different.

Remember the context of the comment Jesus made about what passes from us into the drought from the belly. He said what comes out of us spiritually comes from the heart.[1035] Solomon said "the issues of life" come from the heart. This means our behavior originates in our hearts.[1036] Jesus described what comes out of the heart of the natural man: evil thoughts, murders, adulteries, fornications, thefts, false witness, and blasphemies.[1037]

Jesus likened what comes from the sinful heart to what comes out of the bowels into the toilet. Sometimes these things are called the works of the flesh.[1038] In one Scripture, it's called the filthiness of the flesh.[1039] These behaviors are the vile waste product of the sin nature.

However, if the heart is full of the Spirit of God, and the vessel (the body—God's Temple) cleansed[1040] and presented to God holy, acceptable to Him,[1041] then His Spirit can flow from our heart, and through our belly, and into the world like rivers of living water.

The Spirit of God flowing through us into the world is what Paul was talking about when he said God wants Jesus to manifest in our mortal flesh.[1042]

[1033] Jeremiah 15:15-16; Ezekiel 3:1-6
[1034] Revelation 10:9-10
[1035] Matthew 15:18-19
[1036] Proverbs 4:23
[1037] Matthew 15:19
[1038] Galatians 5:19-21
[1039] II Corinthians 7:1-2
[1040] I John 1:7-9; II Corinthians 7:1-2
[1041] Romans 12:1-2
[1042] II Corinthians 4:11

The Bible uses the word *belly* to represent the center of the fleshly appetites of our physical life and the word *heart* to speak of the center of the affections of our spiritual life. And that takes us to the second room.

The Second or Inner Room—the Heart

Remember the analogy of the Old Testament Temple? In the first room, we found the candlestick to our left and the table of shewbread to our right, and straight before us we found the altar of incense. In the New Testament Temple, we are guided by the light of the candlestick (the Light of God's Word—Psalm 119:105, and His true churches—Revelation 1:19-20), and then nourished by the bread (the milk and meat of God's Word—I Peter 2:2; Hebrews 5:12), and we approach the altar of incense: the place of prayer. There, by prayer, our soul through our spirit connects with the Holy Spirit, Who prays for us;[1043] and thus we enter the second room, the Holy of Holies, the place where the Shekinah[1044] glory (the abiding presence of GOD) dwells in the New Testament Temple—the heart.[1045] Here is where we find Christ (the Ark of the New Testament Covenant).

Christ dwells in our heart[1046] by the Holy Ghost,[1047] and He beseeches us to present this body (His Temple)[1048] to Him as a living sacrifice,[1049] that He might fill His Temple.[1050]

[1043] Romans 8:26

[1044] The word *Shekinah* refers to abiding presence of God. It comes from the Hebrew word that means to dwell: Strong No. 7931, שָׁכַן shakan, *shaw-kan'*; "a primitive root (apparently akin (by transmission) to 7901 through the idea of lodging; compare 5531, 7925); to reside or permanently stay (literally or figuratively):—abide, continue, (cause to, make to) dwell(-er), have habitation, inhabit, lay, place, (cause to) remain, rest, set (up))."

[1045] II Corinthians 4:6; Ephesians 3:17

[1046] Ephesians 3:17

[1047] Galatians 4:6; Romans 8:9

[1048] I Corinthians 6:19

[1049] Romans 12:1-2

[1050] Ephesians 5:18-21

When the Holy Spirit fills His Temple, He manifests Christ to the world through our mortal flesh.[1051] This fulfills His vision of the Spirit of Christ flowing through our belly like a river of living water.[1052]

The presentation of the body as a living sacrifice is coupled with an important exhortation: "Be not conformed to this world: but be ye transformed by the renewing of your mind."[1053] For this reason, victory in spiritual warfare hinges on the work of "casting down imaginations, and every high thing that exalteth itself against the knowledge of God, and bringing into captivity every thought to the obedience of Christ."[1054]

Conclusion

What is the role of the New Testament priest in spiritual warfare? The Antichrist spirit is in the world opposing the Spirit of Jesus Christ. The objective is for Christ to fill His Temple and manifest in our mortal flesh. When this occurs, the Holy Ghost begins to flow through our belly (our physical life) like rivers of living water. For this to happen, the New Testament priest must attend to the sacrifices of the Temple. The key is our soul (the priest) through our spirit (mind) in God's Temple (the body) dutifully presenting the sacrifices of the New Testament Temple.

~

[1051] II Corinthians 4:11
[1052] John 7:38-39
[1053] Romans 12:2
[1054] II Corinthians 10:5

Chapter Twenty-Five

God's Warrior Priests
(Part Six)
The Dynamic of the Body, Soul, and Spirit

DYNAMITE IMPACTS its environment by the sudden release of intense energy! A related word, *dynamic*, describes something that is continually impacting its environment. Dynamite impacts its environment only once. The body, spirit, and soul of each believer-priest are dynamic; they are separately and collectively influencing their environments constantly.

When I say the body, spirit, and soul are dynamic, I mean all of them together, and each individually, is always, actively, impacting its environment. Each—the body, the spirit, and the soul—contributes something specific to our overall experience of life. And together they affect our experience of the world and our impact upon it, both physically and spiritually.

The Physical and Spiritual Elements of the World Are Part of the Same Environment

The earth is one, but it has many environments. Each environment has unique aspects, but they share the same planet. Every environment has a physical and spiritual element. Material things and spiritual things are different elements that are part of every environment on the same planet.

Both spiritual and physical events occur together at the same time and in the same space in which we live, and they are interrelated. We are kings and priests. As kings, we interact with the physical aspect of the world as ambassadors for Christ to the nations. As priests, we interact with the spiritual aspect of the world before God's Throne on behalf of men and nations.

Our appointment as kings unto God relates to our authority in the earth to act on God's behalf. We preach the Gospel, commanding all men everywhere to repent and believe in the risen Saviour. We declare the terms of surrender: confess Him as Lord and receive free salvation by grace through faith in Jesus' name. Our function as kings unto God relates mostly to our physical interaction with men and nations.

Also, God made us priests. As priests, we have authority in heaven to approach the Throne of the Almighty on behalf of men and nations. This is our spiritual function. We offer spiritual sacrifices that are made acceptable to God by our Saviour, Jesus Christ.[1055] When we fulfill the obligations of our priesthood, the Holy Ghost fills His Temple.[1056] Only when we are filled can the Spirit flow through us, extending the power (Divine function and authority) of God into the world, impacting the affairs of men and nations.[1057]

Therefore, we must understand the relationship between physical and spiritual events that occur in the world. The first thing to understand is that material and spiritual events happen at the same time and in the same space.

Physical and Spiritual Events Occur Together

[1055] I Peter 2:5
[1056] I Corinthians 6:19; Ephesians 5:18
[1057] John 7:38-39; 16:7-13

God created all things. He created all physical things and all spiritual things. The physical and the spiritual occupy the same time and space. All spiritual activity occurs in the same created universe in which physical events occur.[1058]

Examples of Physical and Spiritual Events Occurring Together in the Same Environment

The king of Syria thought to take God's prophet prisoner.[1059] One morning, while staying in a city called Dothan, the prophet Elisha and his servant Gehazi rose early and discovered a great host of the Syrian army had encircled the city. Elisha's servant was distressed and cried, "Alas, my master! how shall we do?"[1060] Elisha said, "Fear not: for they that be with us are more than they that be with them."[1061] The young man looked quizzically about him, for he saw only the Syrian army.

[1058] *Time* and *space*: *Time* or *space* are intrinsic to the creation of matter and motion. Imagine absolutely nothing exists. Next, imagine you created a rock, and there it is. It is alone; there is nothing else but the single rock. The dimensions of the rock define all the space there is. So long as there is nothing other than the rock, there can be no space between the rock and anything else, for the simple reason that there is nothing else. Next, imagine you create another rock. You can see that you did not have to "create space"—it is the definition of area between the two rocks. Space, therefore, is conceptual, and takes no "place" in reality except as a measurement between objects. The phenomenon of time is the same. First, you have the measurable interval between the two acts of creation—rock one and rock two. That constitutes a passage of time, no matter by what arbitrary means you measure it. *Time* is only conceptual, until events occur in sequence. One does not have to create *time*—it is intrinsic to the occurrence of sequential events. We reckon time by measuring the movement of the earth around the sun and the moon around the earth. Time is a phenomenon that occurs as a by-product of the creation of matter and motion. The fact that the phenomena of *time* and *space* have an existence conceptually but not in reality until matter is, and is set in motion, helps us understand how iniquity was "found" in Lucifer's heart. Iniquity took on a conceptual possibility of existence when God granted to another being the power of free will. Yet, it did not appear in reality until Lucifer corrupted himself in his heart (Isaiah 14:12-17; Ezekiel 28).

[1059] II Kings 6:13-14
[1060] II Kings 6:15
[1061] II Kings 6:16

Elisha prayed that the Lord would open the eyes of his servant to see the "horses and chariots of fire" that were there creating a wall of defense between them and the Syrian host.[1062] The young man was then able to see the angelic beings that were already there, in the same time and place in which Elisha and the young man lived. The spiritual and physical exist and operate in the same time and space.

The Scripture tells us God's angels are ministering spirits sent to "minister for them who shall be heirs of salvation."[1063] They are spiritual beings "sent" to minister to us in this physical world, and their actions impact it.

The angel of the Lord visited Peter in prison and executed a *jailbreak*.[1064] The angel, a spiritual being, hit Peter on his side, released Peter from physical chains, and opened solid doors.

Earlier, we learned about the relationship between the spirituality of the priesthood and the success of God's people in their physical conflicts. While Peter was in prison, "prayer was made without ceasing of the church unto God for him."[1065] The spiritual intersects the material; the spiritual and the physical are interrelated. Physical events interconnect with spiritual events, and spiritual events always intersect with physical ones.

The spiritual aspect of our being must engage the spiritual aspect of the world if we are to have any God-honoring impact on the physical aspect of it.

The critical relationship between the spiritual and the physical is nowhere more profoundly indicated than when

---

[1062] II Kings 6:17
[1063] Hebrews 1:14
[1064] Acts 12:7-11; see Acts 5:19
[1065] Acts 12:5

Jesus stood in the Temple and cried, "If any man thirst, let him come unto me, and drink. He that believeth on me, as the scripture hath said, out of his belly shall flow rivers of living water."[1066] The Holy Spirit explained that when Jesus said this, He was speaking of the Spirit of God Who would flow through the belly of believers (our physical lives) into this world.[1067] The belly of the believer is the physical vehicle through which the Spirit moves into the world with impact.

The Spiritual Impacts the Physical

What will the Holy Spirit do when He moves into the world through us? Jesus said He would "reprove the world of sin, and of righteousness, and of judgment."[1068] Profound! God exerts His influence upon this world by His Spirit moving through the belly (physical life) of believers into the material world.

Conclusion

The fact that the body, the spirit, and the soul are dynamic means each contributes to the dynamic impact of the believer's life upon this world. The truth that God's Spirit moves into the world through His Temple on Earth, the believer's body, makes it imperative that we understand how this works.

But first, how can the Holy Spirit of GOD use the vile body of a sinner? To understand that, you need to understand something called spiritual circumcision.

~

[1066] John 7:37-38
[1067] John 7:39
[1068] John 16:8

"The Holy Ghost carries on the whole Christian system in this earth. . . . There is no authority, civil or religious — there can be no legitimate government but what is administered by this Holy Ghost. There can be no salvation without it. All without it is rebellion and perdition, or in more orthodox words damnation."

~ John Adams

(Letter from John Adams to Benjamin Rush, from Quincy, Massachusetts, dated December 21, 1809, from the original in our possession.)

Chapter Twenty-Six

God's Warrior Priests
(Part Seven)
Understanding Spiritual Circumcision

C IRCUMCISION involves cutting off the foreskin.[1069] Spiritually speaking, the body of this flesh is the foreskin of the soul and spirit (hereafter, soul/ spirit). Spiritual circumcision involves cutting away or separating the material (physical) from the immaterial (the soul and the spirit).[1070] Understanding spiritual circumcision is essential to understanding how the New Testament priesthood functions.

What Is Spiritual Circumcision?

God circumcises with "the circumcision made without hands."[1071] This is not a physical circumcision, which is done by the hands of men. Christ performs this circumcision by His Holy Spirit, which is why we call it spiritual circumcision.

Physical circumcision was a shadowy reflection of spiritual circumcision. In physical circumcision, the foreskin is cut away. In spiritual circumcision, the body of the sins of the flesh is cut away.[1072]

[1069] Genesis 17:11
[1070] Colossians 2:11
[1071] Colossians 2:11
[1072] Colossians 2:11-12. Verse 12 suggests that this circumcision occurs in connection with *baptism*. Some suppose *spiritual circumcision* is effected by *water*

When we received Christ Jesus, we believed to the saving of our soul.[1073] At the moment of our salvation, the Spirit of Christ entered our hearts.[1074] By an operation called the circumcision of Christ, God separated our soul/spirit from our flesh[1075] so that the body is dead because of sin.[1076]

By His Word, which is sharper than any two-edged sword, piercing even to the dividing asunder of soul and spirit, Christ separated our soul from our spirit.

Then, He took our soul (Zoe-Psuche) and separated the Zoe (animating property— also called our life) from the Psuche (our conscious self). Scripture defines physical death as the soul departing from the body.[1077] At this point, our soul lost its life. Its *Zoe* was taken from us by the Holy Ghost; we were dead—crucified with Christ.[1078]

---

baptism. Water baptism does not wash away sins (I Peter 3:21 with II Corinthians 7:1), or place us *in Christ*. Colossians 2:9-10 tells us it is related to our being "complete in him." That occurs when we are placed *into Christ:* "*In whom* also ye are circumcised" (Colossians 2:11). We are placed *in Christ* when Christ's Spirit comes *into us* (Romans 8:9-11). This occurs when we *believe* on the Lord Jesus Christ (Ephesians 1:13-14; 3:17; John 7:39). The *baptism* mentioned in Colossians 2:12 is that spoken of in I Corinthians 12:13. That *baptism* is by the Spirit and places us in a body where there is neither Jew nor Gentile. In the body of Christ, the Church, these distinctions are recognized (Acts 10:45; 11:2; Romans 3:30; 4:9-12; Galatians 2:7-8; see Acts 15:19-22). In the *body* of Christ seated on the right hand of God, there is neither male nor female (Galatians 3:28).

[1073] Hebrews 10:39
[1074] Galatians 4:6
[1075] Colossians 2:11
[1076] Romans 8:8-10
[1077] Genesis 35:18
[1078] Galatians 2:20

You might imagine Psuche watching as its Zoe is carried away by the Holy Ghost.

Our Zoe (animating life) was then placed into Christ (baptized by the Spirit into Christ's resurrected body.)[1079] Our life (Zoe) was connected to Christ and hidden with Christ in God.[1080] This is how it came to be that we are now no longer in the flesh but in the Spirit[1081] and seated together with Christ in heavenly places.[1082]

Jesus' Spirit then attached His Zoe to our Psuche and reunited our soul with our spirit. We became partakers of the Divine nature.[1083]

The Holy Spirit returned our soul/spirit to our mortal bodies on the earth. The body that was dead because of sin is made alive by His Spirit because of His righteousness.[1084] Indeed, if the "Spirit of Him that raised up Jesus from the dead [dwells in us], He that raised up Christ from the dead shall also quicken [make alive our] mortal bodies by His Spirit that dwelleth in [us]."[1085] This is the quickening of the mortal body, not the resurrection of the glorified body in the likeness of Christ, which is yet future.[1086]

[1079] I Corinthians 12:13; Galatians 3:27
[1080] Colossians 3:3
[1081] Romans 8:8-9
[1082] Ephesians 2:6
[1083] II Peter 1:4
[1084] Romans 8:9-11
[1085] Romans 8:11
[1086] Philippians 3:20-21

Therefore, "I am crucified with Christ: nevertheless I live; yet not I, but Christ liveth in me: and the life which I now live in the flesh I live by the faith of the Son of God, who loved me, and gave himself for me."[1087]

Of course, all of this transpires in the twinkling of an eye. To dramatize the event, consider the following description of what this would look like in slow motion.

A sinner repents and believes in Jesus Christ. At that moment, the power of darkness is broken, and Satan is compelled to relinquish any claims he had on the sinner.

The Holy Ghost quickly cuts away the foreskin of the flesh. The spirit and soul of the sinner remain joined together but stand naked before God, yet alive. The body, however, collapses to the ground. Anyone checking his pulse would find him dead.

With the two-edged S w o r d   of the Spirit, the Word of God, the Spirit then severs the soul and the spirit. Now the spirit is standing there, alone, separated from his or her soul. Imagine them looking at one another in shock.

After the Holy Spirit has separated the sinner's soul from his or her spirit, He then carefully takes the sinner's soul and separates zoe from psuche.

[1087] Galatians 2:20

At this point, the psuche and the zoe die. (It's important here to understand that death means separation, not the cessation of existence.)[1088]

Christ's Spirit flies off to Heaven with the sinner's zoe and places it into Christ's glorified body where it is eternally secure with Christ in God. Meanwhile, the body is laying there, back on Earth, motionless, and all the sinner's friends are weeping.

With the sinner's zoe safe in Christ, the Spirit returns to the soul and attaches Christ's Zoe to the sinner's psuche. Immediately, the Life (Zoe) of Christ makes the sinner's soul alive—a new creation is birthed to God.[1089] From now on, Christ's life is the animating principle of the new man created in Christ, and the sinner is now a saint. The Holy Spirit seals the sinner's life to Christ for eternity.

Next, the Holy Spirit takes the soul, made alive by the Life of Christ, and recombined with the saint's spirit, He returns them to the corpse that has been lying on the ground. The mortal body is quickened—it comes back to life, stands up, and waves at everybody. God immediately claims it as His Temple.

[1088] Death is the separation of the soul from our body. This is illustrated in Genesis where Rachel's death is described as her soul departing from her body: "And it came to pass, as her soul was in departing, (for she died) . . . ." (Genesis 35:18). Rachel did not cease to be when she died. The body continued to be, although lifeless. The soul departed and went to be gathered with her people (a la Genesis 25:8, 17; 35:29; 49:29; plus over 100 more; see Luke 16:22-23; and II Corinthians 5:1-8, especially v. 8).

[1089] II Corinthians 5:17

Of course, the transaction described above occurs instantaneously, making the believer's body God's Temple on Earth.

I hope your faith is bold, and you'll not compartmentalize these truths into spiritual and physical as if those categories are separate realities or separate spheres. The believer-priest must embrace the spiritual reality of these things as part of his or her physical life and experience.

Remember that both spiritual and material things occupy the same space and time in which we live our daily lives. The spiritual truth that you are dead in trespasses and sins, but made alive by the Spirit, is a spiritual event in your physical reality. For this reason, we are commanded to "reckon [ourselves] to be dead indeed unto sin, but alive unto God through Jesus Christ our Lord."[1090]

When Paul declared he was "crucified with Christ," he was not speaking metaphorically. Let's go over this again, but this time I'll explain more clearly the implications of these truths.

Paul said, "I am crucified with Christ, nevertheless I live, but not I, but Christ liveth in me: and the life which I now live in the flesh I live by the faith of the Son of God, who loved me and gave Himself for me."[1091] The words *live* and *liveth* in Galatians 2:20 translate *zoe*. Remember, zoe is the essential animating property of soul (psuche). Colossians 3:3 tells us our life (translates *zoe*) is hid with Christ in God. This means it was detached from our psuche and placed into Christ.

[1090] Romans 6:11
[1091] Galatians 2:20

When Christ entered our body by His Spirit, He attached His Zoe (Life) to our psuche (soul). Therefore, Christ's eternal Zoe (eternal life) presently is the animating property of our psuche, and the life of our bodies. This means our bodies are the "members of Christ," not figuratively, but literally, which is the basis for Paul's rebuke against believers who commit fornication: "Shall I then take the members of Christ, and make them the members of an harlot? God forbid."[1092] Do you see how these spiritual things have real consequences in the physical world? By the way, we will give an account for what we have done in this body, whether it be good or bad.[1093]

At the same time, His Spirit baptized (immersed) our zoe into Christ's body in heaven,[1094] making us one with Him and with the Father.[1095]

Since the Holy Spirit connected Christ's Zoe to our psuche, Christ has become the life (Zoe) of our soul (psuche). Our soul is saved by the attachment of Christ's eternal life to our soul. The animating power of our soul comes from Christ, Who now dwells in us. This is possible because the circumcision of Christ has cut off the body of the sins of the flesh.[1096]

Conclusion

The body is God's Temple. The soul is God's king and priest. And the soul engages the physical world through our bodies and the spiritual world through our spirit. With this knowledge, you are ready to learn how to execute your duties as God's priest in His Temple.   ~

[1092] I Corinthians 6:15
[1093] II Corinthians 5:10
[1094] Colossians 3:3; Ephesians 2:6
[1095] See John 17:21-23—this is what Jesus prayed for
[1096] Colossians 2:11-12

"The Christian religion is, above all the religions that ever prevailed or existed in ancient or modern times, the religion of wisdom, virtue, equity and humanity."

~ John Adams

(John Adams, Works, Vol. III, p. 421, diary entry for July 26, 1796.)

Chapter Twenty-Seven

God's Warrior Priests

(Part Eight)

New Testament Spiritual Sacrifices—Insights From the Five Old Testament Offerings

J ESUS HAD A VISION—that out of our belly would flow rivers of living water.[1097] He has done His part in sending the Holy Spirit into the hearts of believers, just as He promised. We must do our part! In this chapter, we begin learning how to do the work of the New Testament priesthood that will release this fantastic power into the world. We will start by considering valuable insights available to us from the example of the Old Testament sacrifices.

Insights from the Five Old Testament Sacrifices

Five Old Testament offerings correspond to the five New Testament sacrifices.[1098] Essential insights into our priesthood can be gleaned by considering what God set before us as examples in the Old Testament Priesthood.[1099] Before we consider those insights, understand that all these offerings are representations of Christ's work for us accomplished on the Cross and that He fulfilled them physically and spiritually. The Old Testament saints presented these offerings looking forward to the Cross. Those who serve in the New Testament Temple offer their sacrifices looking back to it.

[1097] John 7:38-39

[1098] Exodus, Leviticus, Numbers and Deuteronomy offer details on these offerings. Hebrews explains how they relate to the New Testament.

[1099] I Corinthians 10:11

Additionally, we are priests unto God, and Christ is our High Priest. Since we are in Christ, when we present the offerings He has prescribed, God receives them as from Christ. Jesus Christ makes our offerings acceptable.[1100]

Each of the twelve tribes of Israel was instructed to present the five Old Testament offerings identified in Numbers 7:12-17. They are as follows: the Meat Offering (fine flour, etc.—no blood and no leaven), and the Offering of Incense (no blood). These are followed by those offerings that involve the shedding of blood: the Burnt Offering, the Sin Offering, and the Peace Offering.

God required three of the five offerings to be presented at the altar of sacrifice that was at the door of the Tabernacle. This is where God met with His people.[1101] He wanted the other two presented within the Temple of the Tabernacle. The five offerings are listed alternately: first, one offered at the door, followed by one sacrificed within the Temple, then one presented at the door, followed by one offered within the Temple, and so on.

The three offerings presented at the door are the Meat, Burnt, and Peace offerings. The two offerings presented within the Temple are the Offering of Incense and the blood of the Sin Offering. (The sin offering was sacrificed at the door, but the blood was taken within the veil to be sprinkled on the mercy seat).

The Tabernacle in its entirety was called the House of God; and the Temple was within the House. Today, the church is the House of God; and the body of the believer is the Temple in the House.[1102]

[1100] I Peter 2:5
[1101] Exodus 29:42
[1102] I Timothy 3:15; I Corinthians 6:19

The "door" to the House of God is Christ.[1103] His death on the cross gave us entry into the Household of God—making us part of God's family. As a member of His Household, we are welcomed in His House.

Three of our New Testament sacrifices are presented to God "at the door": the Meat Offering, the Burnt Offering, and the Peace Offering.

These correspond to the New Testament sacrifices in the following way: the Meat Offering is indicative of that which we present to provide "food for God's House."[1104] This corresponds to the sacrifice of our offerings to the ministry, called a sweet savor sacrifice well-pleasing to the Lord.[1105] Our giving, inclusive of our tithes and offerings, and our service to the House of God would correspond to the Meat Offering. That the Meat Offering is presented at the "door" of the House of God tells us all our giving to ministry is offered upon the sacrifice Christ made for us on Calvary. We bring our tithes and offerings into the "storehouse that there might be meat in [God's] house."[1106]

The next offering presented at the door is the Burnt Offering. We remember that before the law—before Moses received the Law and the Commandments—Abraham was instructed to present his son, Isaac, as a Burnt Offering.[1107] God intervened and provided a substitute offering to take Isaac's place. Isaac was released to serve the LORD as a living sacrifice: one who was counted dead, but given life, and now owes his life to the one who delivered him. Isaac illustrates the truth that the payment for sin is death,[1108] and

---

[1103] John 10:7
[1104] Malachi 3:9-11; see Leviticus 2:2-3
[1105] Philippians 4:18
[1106] Malachi 3:9-11; I Corinthians 9:14
[1107] Genesis 22
[1108] Romans 3:23

we have all sinned, but God commended to us His great love by sending His own Son to die for us.[1109] He released us, and now we who are counted dead serve Him who took our place in death. This corresponds to the living sacrifice we are called upon to present to the LORD: "I beseech you therefore, brethren, by the mercies of God, that ye present your bodies a living sacrifice, holy, acceptable unto God, which is your reasonable service."[1110]

Jesus told us we must take up our cross daily and follow Him.[1111] Like the Meat Offering mentioned above, this is a daily sacrifice. We come to the *door*—to Christ Who died for us on the Cross—and present ourselves to Him as worthy of death. But because He took our place on that altar, we are released to go forward, serving Him as a living sacrifice, which is our reasonable service. The body is His, and we are obliged to yield it to His use in service.

The Burnt Offering requires the shedding of blood. Happily, Christ took our place, so it is His blood that makes our offerings acceptable to Him.[1112]

The third sacrifice presented at the door is the Peace Offering. The Old Testament Peace Offering was another offering made by the shedding of blood.[1113] Many think blood is not part of the sacrifices of the New Testament priesthood. This is not true! Blood is required for our New Testament offerings! Only the source of the blood is the primary difference between the Old and New Testament sacrifices. Our offerings are made acceptable to God by the blood already shed by Christ on the Cross. Christ supplied the blood!

[1109] Romans 6:23; 5:8-9
[1110] Romans 12:1
[1111] Matthew 16:24; Mark 8:34; Luke 9:23
[1112] I Peter 2:5
[1113] Hebrews 9:22

The Peace Offering of the Old Testament was peculiarly connected with thanksgiving,[1114] which is the New Testament sacrifice of praise.[1115] As New Testament priests unto God, we present our sacrifices of praise in His church, the fruit of our lips giving thanks to His name.

These are the offerings sacrificed at the door, in our case, in the Lord's churches. Two are offered within the Temple structure that stood within the House of God. These are the Offering of Incense and the Sin Offering. We offer the New Testament counterparts to these offerings within the New Testament Temple, our body.

The first offering to be presented within the Temple is the Offering of Incense.[1116] The altar of incense represented prayer.[1117] Only fire from the brazen altar was to be used to burn the incense, and this fire was to burn continually.[1118] God was very jealous in this matter. Any strange fire touching His incense provoked Him severely.[1119] In other words, all prayer must ascend to Him from the sacrifice of His Son.

The New Testament sacrifice of prayer is represented in the Old Testament by the altar of incense. Our prayers can only be acceptable to God when they are offered in the fire that consumed the sacrifice of Christ on the Cross.[1120] Our God is a consuming fire; Christ is the Lamb of God. He presented Himself to God on the Cross, and the Father received the sacrifice of His Son on our behalf. The first critical insight we get from this Old Testament analogy is that our prayers are offered up to God in the same fire in which Christ was

---

[1114] Leviticus 7:11-12
[1115] Hebrews 13:15
[1116] Exodus 30
[1117] Psalm 141:2; Luke 1:10; Revelation 8:3-4
[1118] Exodus 30:8
[1119] Exodus 30:9
[1120] Leviticus 16:12

offered up to God. The bottom line is all these offerings point to Christ and His death for us on the Cross, and it is His blood that makes our offerings acceptable to God.

Another insight into the New Testament sacrifice of prayer from this Old Testament example: this fire must continually burn on the altar of incense in God's Temple today. We must keep that fire burning, lighting the first room of the New Testament Temple, which is our belly, that is, our self-life. We do this, in part, by taking up our cross daily and following Christ. And we must pray without ceasing unto the LORD.[1121]

The second Old Testament Offering presented within the Temple is the Sin Offering. The Sin Offering was sacrificed upon the altar at the door of the Tabernacle. The High Priest carried the blood from that sacrifice into the Temple, where he went behind the veil into the Most Holy place. Here the blood was sprinkled upon the altar to atone for our sins. The High Priest was the only person allowed to enter the Holy of Holies and only one time each year.

All New Testament priests are invited to approach God through the veil that separates the Holy Place from the Holy of Holies in the New Testament Temple. The veil of the Old Testament Temple represented the incarnate body of Christ.[1122] That Old Testament veil is taken away. When Christ died on the Cross, the veil was rent physically[1123] and spiritually.[1124] Today, all believer-priests are invited to enter through the veil and approach the Throne of the Almighty GOD.[1125] The veil is still there, the resurrected flesh of the

---

[1121] Luke 18:1; I Thessalonians 5:17
[1122] Hebrews 10:19-23; see John 1:1, 14; I Timothy 3:16
[1123] Luke 23:45
[1124] Hebrews 10:19-22
[1125] Hebrews 4:16

flesh and bone body of our risen Lord.[1126] Our access to the throne of Grace is through our Lord Jesus Christ.

Christ, our High Priest, has presented the blood atonement for our sins once for all.[1127] No New Testament priest brings any blood into the Holy of Holies—Christ's blood has opened the way for us to enter His presence. This is the second room of the New Testament Temple, the Holy of Holies, the heart, where Christ by His Spirit dwells. By the wonder of God's omnipresence, when our soul enters into communion through our spirit with God's Spirit, we move directly into the presence of our Father. The blood of His Son warrants our access. The Spirit describes the place where we approach God in Revelation 4-5.

It is here, in His presence, that we offer the sacrifice of a broken and contrite spirit. Here we humble ourselves before Him, and yield our will to His, and bow before Him, placing ourselves under His Mighty Hand.[1128] And it is here that we confess our sins, trusting He is indeed faithful and just to forgive us our sins and to cleanse us from all unrighteousness.[1129]

Conclusion

Remember that when the Old Testament priest faithfully executed his priesthood duties, God filled His Temple, and the power of God was manifested to the assembly (the congregation). Israel was invincible when the glory of the LORD was upon the Tabernacle. The New Testament priest must learn how to fulfill his or her priesthood duties so that GOD will fill His Temple and manifest His glory to the world today.

[1126] Hebrews 10:20; Luke 24:39
[1127] Hebrews 10:18
[1128] John 5:30; I Peter 5:6
[1129] I John 1:7-9

In the next chapter, we will begin learning how the New Testament priest fulfills his or her priestly duties.

~

Chapter Twenty-Eight

God's Warrior Priests

(Part Nine)

New Testament Spiritual Sacrifices— Dedicating the Temple

J EREMIAH IS THE PROPHET who declared to Judah that the kingdom would be taken from her and given to Nebuchadnezzar, king of Babylon.

In the days of Jeremiah, the prophet, GOD lamented: "Woe is me for my hurt! my wound is grievous: but I said, Truly this is a grief, and I must bear it. My tabernacle is spoiled, and all my cords are broken: my children are gone forth of me, and they are not: there is none to stretch forth my tent any more, and to set up my curtains."[1130]

How could this have happened? He went on to say, "For the pastors are become brutish (meaning dull, or dumb like an ox),[1131] and have not sought the LORD: therefore they shall not prosper, and all their flocks shall be scattered."[1132] Because of this, the LORD warned, "Behold, the noise of the bruit is come, and a great commotion out of the north country, to make the cities of Judah desolate, and a den of dragons."[1133]

[1130] Jeremiah 10:20

[1131] *Brutish* translates נִבְעֲרוּ (*niv-'aru,* from Strong No. 1197 בָּעַר *ba'ar* "a primitive root; to kindle, . . . also (as denominative from 1198) to be(-come) brutish:—be brutish, . . . waste." The idea seems to be inflamed by wine (Isaiah 5:11; Jeremiah 51:7) they gave themselves to their appetites (Proverbs 23:2) so they became dull and beast-like.

[1132] Jeremiah 10:21

[1133] Jeremiah 10:22

Judah had backslidden and turned away from the God of their fathers. The priests neglected the Tabernacle, and God lamented they had long neglected their duties. And this developed because the pastors (those the Holy Ghost appointed to feed the flock of God) had become dumb oxen, feeding themselves and not the flock of God.[1134] America has followed the path of Judah.

In a house on the street called Jaboneria, in Bell Gardens, California, the LORD visited me most unusually. It was 1971. My dad lived in the house, and one of my brothers lived there with him. I was in Bible College at the time, and stopped by to see my brother, Ronald. No one was home. I sat on Ron's bed, waiting for him to return and decided to read my Bible. It was about 7 a.m.. I opened to Jeremiah 10 and began to read.

When I got to the passage cited above, I noticed something I never had before: the one speaking in verse 19, saying, "Woe is me for my hurt" was not Jeremiah—it is the LORD saying, "Woe is me for my hurt." God was opening-up to His prophet and sharing His personal heartache. The idea stunned me.

His rebuke struck me: I had become brutish and had neglected the service of God's Temple. I didn't have the understanding that God has since given me. Nevertheless, I knew that we are priests of the New Testament Temple responsible to set it in order today. And God's priests neglect His Temple today, and it grieves Him deeply. A thought fixed itself in my mind! For this cause, our nation teetered on the precipice of judgment.

I finished my reading, and Ron had not returned, so I decided to go on about my day. When I walked from his

---

[1134] Ezekiel 34:2

room into the hallway, I was suddenly overwhelmed with a sense of sorrow. I collapsed to the floor, crying to God on behalf of my country and begging Him to spare us. I heaved convulsively and prayed till I was physically and emotionally exhausted. I began to calm down and regain my composure, and wondered at the encounter, not sure what to make of it. Since then, I've had such encounters but none so intense as this. That experience set me on the course that led to the writing of this book and to my efforts to call Christ's church to prayer and fasting for revival in America.

What follows is the result of much prayerful study of GOD's Word on the subject it addresses, and I hope you will understand the importance of it. We must revive the New Testament priesthood in American churches and "stretch forth [His] tent . . . and set up [His] curtains," or else we will surely be destroyed.

There are five New Testament sacrifices: the living sacrifice,[1135] the sacrifice of praise,[1136] the sacrifice of prayer,[1137] the sacrifice of giving,[1138] and the sacrifice of a broken spirit and a broken and contrite heart.[1139] To order the New Testament Temple correctly, each of these sacrifices needs to be presented faithfully by the New Testament priesthood. To get started, let's consider the first of the five New Testament sacrifices: the presentation of this body as a living sacrifice.[1140]

The body is God's Temple, and it must be presented holy!

How Do We Defile the Temple of God?

[1135] Romans 12:1-2
[1136] Hebrews 13:15
[1137] Psalm 141:2
[1138] Philippians 4:18
[1139] Psalm 51:17
[1140] Romans 12:1-2

The body of the believer-priest is God's Temple today. It is the vessel God desires to use in this world to do His work.[1141] We are stewards of this vessel and responsible for preparing it for the LORD's use.[1142] However, He will not use it if it is defiled. How do we defile the Temple of God?

Something defiled is unfit for its intended use. For example, a fork that is badly bent or otherwise damaged will not be fit for your use. You will likely set it aside and ask for another to replace it. Furthermore, if it falls to the floor, you would probably not want to use   i t for fear some filthiness had contaminated it. However, if you intended to use the fork to dig in your garden, you would not care if it fell to the floor. And the damaged fork might serve some other purpose. In that case, it would not likely be considered defiled for its intended use.

God's intended use for your body is to represent Him in this world and to serve as a vehicle through which He will manifest Himself to the world. A body publicly identified with the lust of the flesh, the lust of the eyes and the pride of life, creates an identification problem. The world is at "enmity with God."[1143] God is not going to send the message that He is a friend of the world by identifying publicly with someone who is.

There is another problem. Our soul is made dirty when it touches the filthiness of the flesh. The filthiness of the flesh involves the lust of the flesh, the lust of the eyes or the pride of life; these things make us unclean. God's Holy Spirit will not flow through an unclean vessel.

[1141] II Timothy 2:21
[1142] John 7:38-39
[1143] James 4:4

Fleshly lusts "war against the soul."[1144] Satan stirs up fleshly lusts through various temptations, hoping to attract your soul to set the spirit of your mind upon the things of the flesh, making your spirit filthy. When you set your mind on the things of the flesh, the thoughts of your heart will be evil, set on things contrary to God and that brings evil into the world. In this case, the soul/spirit of the believer begins acting out the works of the flesh through the body.

The works of the flesh are listed in Galatians: "adultery, fornication, uncleanness, lasciviousness, idolatry, witchcraft, hatred, variance, emulations, wrath, strife, seditions, heresies, envyings, murders, drunkenness, revellings, and such like."[1145] All these things are sinful; they are transgressions against God's law and contrary to His will. These are things that God hates because of all the evil these behaviors set loose in the world.

When we set our thoughts on the lust of the flesh, the lust of the eyes, and the pride of life, the heart becomes filled with evil thoughts, and, as Jesus said, these are the things that defile us.[1146] They make us unfit for service. God will not identify Himself with these behaviors, and so He will not manifest His glory through such a vessel.

Consider! The body is the Temple of God, the belly is its first room, and the heart is its innermost room. God dwells in the innermost room; His Spirit is in our hearts. When God's priests surrender to Satan's temptations, they commit evil in front of God. We are defiling the Holy of Holies. When the Temple is defiled, all that comes out of us is tainted by filthiness. That is what it means to defile the Temple.

[1144] I Peter 2:11
[1145] Galatians 5:19-21
[1146] Matthew 15:17

Be forewarned, "If any man defile the Temple of God, him shall God destroy; for the Temple of God is holy, which Temple ye are."[1147]

How Do We Dedicate the Temple?

The body must be dedicated and set aside exclusively for Christ's use. He will not use a filthy vessel, as noted above. Therefore, the body must be presented holy. What does this mean?

To be holy, remember, means to be separated from that which defiles, or offends God, and identified publicly with GOD. This is called sanctification, which is a process by which someone or something is set apart for holy uses.

The first step in preparing the vessel for God's use is to cleanse yourself of all filthiness of the flesh and spirit, perfecting holiness in the fear of God.[1148] You must confess your sins before God, humbly and honestly, agreeing with God about every sin for which you are guilty. And believe His promise to cleanse you from all unrighteousness.[1149]

Holiness involves separation from sin, but it also requires identification with God. Romans 12:2 speaks to the identification aspect of holiness—"not conformed to this world, but . . . transformed, by the renewing of your mind." The believer-priest must prepare his or her body so that it is identifiable with God and not with the world.

Sanctification has to do with identification. According to Romans 12:2, we prepare the body to be presented a living

---

[1147] I Corinthians 3:17
[1148] II Corinthians 7:1-2
[1149] I John 1:7-9

sacrifice by not identifying the body or our mind with the world. We are to achieve this by renewing our minds by bringing every thought into the captivity of Christ. One of the major changes of mind every believer must accept is that you (including your body) are not your own; you are "bought with a price."[1150] This will affect how you dress and how you present yourself to the public.

God's priests must "draw nigh"[1151] unto Him with their bodies appropriately prepared for presentation. But before you draw close to God, "cleanse your hands, ye sinners; and purify your hearts, ye double minded."[1152] This requires that we cleanse ourselves of all filthiness of the flesh and spirit, perfecting (completing) holiness in the fear of God.[1153] So, confess your sins before God, humbly and honestly, agreeing with God about every sin for which you are guilty, believing His promise to cleanse you from all unrighteousness.

We cannot overestimate the living sacrifice. It is critical! Consider the brokenness of God over Judah's neglect of the Tabernacle and their failure to prepare it for God:

> My tabernacle is spoiled, and all my cords are broken: my children are gone forth of me, and they are not: there is none to stretch forth my tent any more, and to set up my curtains. — Jeremiah 10:20

God was lamenting the neglect of His Temple in the days leading up to its destruction by Nebuchadnezzar. Who can doubt God weeps today; His New Testament Temple is abandoned? Beware—

[1150] I Corinthians 6:19-20
[1151] Hebrews 7:19; James 4:8
[1152] James 4:8
[1153] II Corinthians 7:1-2

> He that despised Moses' law died without mercy
> under two or three witnesses: Of how much sorer
> punishment, suppose ye, shall he be thought worthy,
> who hath trodden under foot the Son of God, and hath
> counted the blood of the covenant, wherewith he was
> sanctified, an unholy thing, and hath done despite
> unto the Spirit of grace? — Hebrews 10:28-29

Consider: When the Spirit of God contemplated the contrast between the law and grace, He expressed concern about the fact that since grace is greater, those under it are more, not less, accountable. How many Christians would state the contrast between the Old and New Testaments in the words of Hebrews 10:28 (see above)? Do you not see that we have turned it all around backward? Indeed, we have "done despite unto the Spirit of grace."

The body must be presented "holy, acceptable unto God."[1154] God imparts His holiness to us through chastisement.[1155] Gracey (the name I give to a typical contemporary Christian) does not understand this. Gracey supposes holiness is imputed by grace through faith, like righteousness.[1156]

But holiness (separation from the world and identification with God) is not imputed. It is imparted. And it is not imparted as something bequeathed; it is imparted as something added to another through diligent effort, as when a teacher imparts knowledge to his or her students. One way we become partakers of His holiness is through the Father's chastisement.[1157]

Yet, Gracey, you "gaddest about . . . to change thy way,"[1158] and "trimmest . . . thy way to seek love?"[1159]

[1154] Romans 12:1
[1155] Hebrews 12:10
[1156] Romans 4:6-22
[1157] Hebrews 12:5-11
[1158] Jeremiah 2:36
[1159] Jeremiah 2:33

To *gad about* is to flippantly chase after whatever catches one's fancy in the moment. To *change thy way* means this gadding about led them away from the paths God had prepared for them. To trim one's way means to make accommodations to please present company, or to gain favor from someone we desire to impress. The motivation is to seek love. Judah sought the love of the world and adjusted her ways to secure it. The examples of this in contemporary Christianity are so many it would be impossible to document them here, and so obvious it is not necessary.

Every day we hear about some old Christian denomination moving away from biblical morality and adapting themselves to the political correctness of our modern culture: ordaining sodomites (homosexuals) to ministry, calling prayer meetings to support the practice of legalized abortion—which is the shedding of innocent blood, to name a few. Widely embraced Evangelical leader Rick Warren supposes he will mitigate the enmity between Islamofascism and Christianity by claiming their Allah is our Allah. But their god is not our GOD.[1160]

Have we time or space to name the Evangelical churches that *gadabout* seeking to procure the favor of the world by adopting its methods and manners in worship? Many contemporary churches strive to create a worship environment that looks like the bar scene or a rock concert. These

---

[1160] When I preached with Dr. Feghaly in Lebanon, I had the very great pleasure to meet many wonderful Arabic Christians. The word for *God* in the Arabic language is *Allah*. But they stress that the Allah of Islam is not the Allah of Christianity. You know that today all religions use the word *God* to identify what or who they worship. But our GOD is not their God. Jesus made this clear to the woman at the well when He explained to her that although she supposed the God she worshiped was the same as the God the Jews worshiped, the truth: "Ye worship ye know not what: we know what we worship: for salvation is of the Jews" (John 4:22). The same thing that has happened in America has happened in the Arabic world: their *God* is not our GOD, and their *Allah* is not our *Allah*.

that go gadding about to seek love, favor, acceptance with the world cannot "reprove, rebuke, and exhort" it.[1161] They are not of the Spirit Jesus sent into the world to "reprove the world of sin, righteousness, and judgment."[1162] (I have a book that speaks to this more particularly. It's titled *The New Cart Church*. I recommend it to fervent believers who have a passion for holiness and understand that it's possible to do the right thing the wrong way and that this matters to God.)

Conclusion

The New Testament Temple is neglected, and this is a condition not likely to change apart from a severe fall of judgment from God.[1163] To avert that judgment, we must set the New Testament Temple in order. All its rooms must be cleansed of all filthiness of the flesh and spirit, perfecting holiness in the fear of God.[1164] We must begin by presenting this body to God as a living sacrifice, holy, set apart to Him—separated from the world and identified with God.

~

[1161] II Timothy 4:2
[1162] John 16:7-13
[1163] I Peter 4:17
[1164] II Corinthians 7:1-2

God's Warrior Priests

(Part Ten)

New Testament Spiritual Sacrifices—
Presenting the Sacrifices of the New Testament Temple

W HEN GOD WAS PLEASED with the sacrifice of His people, He moved in their assembly and manifested His glory. Is that what this is about, to have an exciting manifestation of God in our midst? It's thrilling when God works among us, but it's about a lot more than merely getting GOD to show Himself in our meetings, or even in our lives.

Does God have an interest in manifesting in and through us beyond His desire to fellowship with man? In the days of Moses, it was critical to know God was in their camp because they needed God to provide for them and guide them through the wilderness. Also, they needed God to fight for them when they encountered enemies that sought to destroy them. Does God have an interest in manifesting in and through us beyond fellowship?

We need God to move through believers and bring down the many strongholds Satan has established in our country. The Devil holds significant territory in education, politics, and our churches; and he is disseminating much evil into our culture from these strongholds.

Satan has established a stronghold corrupting our elections. I recently learned as many as 900,000 fraudulent votes were cast in our last election. Voter fraud has become entrenched in our nation. Satan uses it to plant his own wicked and unreasonable leaders in places of power. They use these positions to erode the integrity of our nation under God further. Such rulers will undoubtedly trifle away our liberties in their attempt to destroy America as founded.

We need America's believer-priests to stretch forth the tent and set up the curtains so that Almighty God will move through the believer like rivers of living water crashing down Satan's strongholds. Imagine the Holy Ghost washing over America, the healing stream, restoring liberty. For where the Spirit of the Lord is, there is liberty.

Only by prayer and fasting can we overcome the devils holding territory and defending satanic strongholds today. And God will not hear the prayers nor receive the fasts of faithless priests.

We are at a crossroads in this country, and we must get this right, or God's judgment will fall from Heaven upon us.

On God's part, remember, He is at war with Satan who is trying to dispossess Christ's rule over the dominion. And Christ requires a nation under God in the earth through whom He will execute His wrath when necessary and through whom to extend His favor and blessing.[1165] But why is this important to God?

God desires all mankind to be saved and come to the knowledge of the truth.[1166] Men are saved when they receive His Word into their hearts. Jesus referred to the Word as God's seed, and men's hearts as the soil. He saves men by the seed of His Word, and He works in the earth to prepare the soil for that seed.[1167] The preparation of the soil

---

[1165] Romans 13:1-6; Genesis 12:1-4
[1166] I Timothy 2:4
[1167] Matthew 13:1-9, 18-23

is accomplished through chastisement[1168] and blessing.[1169] He sends these things among men through His people, who are called by His name. God wants *a nation under God!* America is that nation today. But He warned us through Paul that if He spared not the natural branches, do not be so vain as to suppose He will not cut us off if we, like them, offend in unbelief.[1170]

Therefore, we must understand how to perform our duties as God's priests in His Temple. In the last chapter, we considered the importance that we present our bodies a living sacrifice. In this chapter, we will discuss the sacrifices we make in and through this dedicated body.

All New Testament Sacrifices Have a Public and a Private Expression

Earlier, we considered insights available in the example of the five sacrifices of the Old Testament priesthood, and how they correspond to the five New Testament sacrifices. It will be helpful now to remember one of those insights.

Remember that the entire Tabernacle is the House of God, and the New Testament Church is the House of God today. The Old Testament Temple was, properly speaking, a building within the Tabernacle. It had two rooms: the Holy Place, and the Holy of Holies. The body of the believer is the Temple of the House of God today: the belly corresponds to the Holy Place, and the heart corresponds to the Holy of Holies. Of the five Old Testament offerings, three were presented outside of the Temple, at the door of the House. Two were presented within.

[1168] Divine judgment—Ezekiel 20:26
[1169] Divine favor—Romans 2:4
[1170] Romans 11:21

Also remember: all the Old Testament offerings were connected to the brazen altar at the entrance of the House. The brazen altar points to Christ's death on the Cross. This means every sacrifice is directly linked to the Cross. They are all interrelated.

When we consider sacrifices presented by the New Testament priest in and through the Temple, we understand that each has a public and a private component. Three of the New Testament sacrifices are public offerings, presented in the fellowship of the believers and before men. However, these offerings have a private component—for example, any praise we give to God before men must come from a heart that is pure and sincere.

Likewise, essentially private offerings, such as prayer, also have a public component: while we "enter into [our] closet"[1171] to pray, we are also mindful that the Bible supports public prayers.[1172]

The Sacrifice of Praise

The first offering every priest must present is his or her body as a living sacrifice (see chapter twenty-eight). The body is God's Temple today. Now we begin learning about the offerings we present in and through God's Temple. And that takes us to the second through fifth sacrifices.

The second New Testament sacrifice we are called upon to present before God is the sacrifice of praise, the fruit of our lips, giving thanks to His Name.[1173]

Our souls offer the sacrifice of praise to God in our hearts. But we also praise God publicly, in the assembly of the believers, and the world at large.

[1171] Matthew 6:6
[1172] Acts 12:5; 13:1-2; etc.
[1173] Hebrews 13:15

We declare our thanksgiving to GOD as a sacrifice of praise. And while we do this always in our hearts, keep in mind that this offering is about declaring to others our thankfulness to God. This is the sacrifice of praise, the fruit of our lips giving thanks to His Name.[1174]

God inhabits the praises of Israel.[1175] Psalm 22 records the cry of our Saviour's heart from the cross. In the throes of agony, Christ reflected on this great truth and cried: "But thou art holy, O thou that inhabitest the praises of Israel." It's humbling to think such a thought would cross the holy mind of the precious Lamb of God at such a moment. Nevertheless, in the extreme anguish of His body and soul, He remembered where to find God—in the praises of His people.

God makes an appearance in the praises of Israel. We may claim the honor, for we are grafted into that trunk.[1176] God invites us to join with Israel in praise.[1177]

The Old Testament mentions the sacrifice of praise.[1178] *Praise* translates תּוֹדָה (todah,[1179] from a root that signifies extending one's hands to God in adoration). It is the common Hebrew word for *thank you*, and hence, it is generally translated *thanks* or *thanksgiving*.[1180] In the Scripture, it is

---

[1174] Hebrews 13:15
[1175] Psalm 22:3
[1176] Romans 11:17-24
[1177] Romans 15:11
[1178] Jeremiah 17:26; 33:11
[1179] Strong No. 8426
[1180] תּוֹדָה (*todah* (Strong 8426)) comes from a root that signifies extending the hands, in the current context, a gesture of adoration. Found 32 times in the Old Testament, twice rendered *confession* (Joshua 7:19 and Ezra 10:11), five times *praise* (Psalm 42:4; 50:23; 100—*in the title of the Psalm*—Jeremiah 17:26; 33:11), one time *praises* (Psalm 56:12), and three times *thank offerings* (II Chronicles 29:31; 33:16). *Thanks* or *thanksgiving* covers the rest. In every instance, it refers to an offering of thanks to God. On one occasion, it is translated *sacrifice of thanksgiving* (Amos 4:5); and five times, it is coupled with זֶבַח (*zebach* (Strong 2077), "a

always used to refer to an offering of thanks, which God said glorifies Him.[1181] The Holy Spirit calls this offering a "sacrifice of praise to God continually," and defines it as "the fruit of our lips giving thanks to his name."[1182]

The New Testament priest is expected to present his body (the Temple of God) as a living sacrifice, holy, acceptable to God, and then to fill that Temple with the sacrifice of praise, the fruit of our lips, giving thanks to His Name.[1183]

Imagine a child, his hands extended high and waving, while he runs to greet his daddy upon his return home from work, excitedly squealing, "Daddy, Daddy, Daddy." Our Heavenly Father delights when His children run to Him, waving their hands, elatedly crying, "Abba, Father."[1184]

It honors God when we maintain a thankful attitude amid our trials and tribulations. It proves our faith and does not allow Satan to get the advantage and use our grief to turn others away from God and His Gospel.

We are called upon to present the sacrifices of joy.[1185] The language of Psalm 7:6 does not justify signaling this out as a separate or distinct sacrifice. We must submit all our sacrifices to God with joy, but this one especially. For joy and praise are inseparable.

We notice that the sacrifice of praise (thanksgiving, see

---

slaughter, i.e., the flesh of an animal; by implication, a sacrifice") and is translated *sacrifice of thanksgiving* (Leviticus 7:12, 13; 22:29; Psalm 107:22; 116:17). God said those who do this *glorify Him* (Psalm 50:23; see 69:30). We are instructed to enter His presence with this offering (Psalm 95:2; 100:4). It is often accompanied with singing (Nehemiah 12:27; Psalm 147:7; Isaiah 51:3), and is connected with the *sacrifice of joy* (Psalm 27:6, see 42:4).

[1181] Psalm 50:23; 69:30
[1182] Hebrews 13:15
[1183] Psalm 119:108
[1184] Romans 8:15
[1185] Psalm 27:6

above) is connected with joy and the sacrifice of joy is connected with singing.[1186] Singing within our hearts with joy to the Lord is paramount to New Testament Temple worship.[1187] It's the private component of this public sacrifice. When we fill the Holy of Holies (heart) with joyful praise, it will flow out of our lips in expressions of thanksgiving to His name.

Don't underestimate the power of praise—genuine admiring adoration. Not fleshly praise, not praise that is generated by fleshly emotion, but authentic, Holy Ghost inspired worship of GOD. One day, a king of Judah, named Jehoshaphat, sent out the praise-singers against the enemy of God. The LORD "set ambushments"[1188] against Judah's enemy, and God's angel destroyed the threatening army. We need to harness the power of praise, remembering, GOD inhabits the praises of His people.

Let's go forward, praising God against the stronghold of election fraud, against the stronghold of perverse education, against the stronghold of abortion—baby murder!

The Sacrifice of Prayer[1189]

The sacrifice of prayer is made aloud in church and publicly. However, essentially, this is a sacrifice God looks for in the closet.[1190] We are to be in continual communion with God in our hearts.[1191]

Earlier, we considered the truth that prayer is the essential duty of the New Testament priest. If the Old Testament House of God was to be a house of prayer, surely the New

---

[1186] Psalm 42:4; Nehemiah 12:27; Psalm 147:7; Isaiah 51:3
[1187] Ephesians 5:18-21
[1188] II Chronicles 20:22
[1189] Psalm 141:2
[1190] Matthew 6:6
[1191] II Corinthians 13:14

Testament House of God must be more so.[1192] The church cannot be a House of Prayer unless those who make up the church will pray.

Interestingly, the appeal to pray without ceasing is a New Testament exclusive.[1193] Unless we infer it from I Samuel 12:23, where Samuel vowed, "God forbid that I should sin against the Lord in ceasing to pray for you," or from the requirement to keep the fire on the golden altar of incense lighted continually before the Lord in His Holy Temple. And consider the golden candlestick of the Old Testament Temple. If it points to the seven golden candlesticks, which are the seven churches, perhaps the exhortation to pray without ceasing is also suggested by the requirement to keep that fire lighted in the Temple. Indeed, Jesus said His Father's House would be called the house of prayer.[1194]

The fire that lighted the Church in Acts 2 must be cherished, and nurtured, and fed the beaten olive oil that it might burn continually before the Lord of glory.

The beaten olive oil[1195] is the fruit of the olive tree. The olive tree is a symbol representing Israel. We are grafted into that tree.[1196] The fruit that the Lord seeks from us is the fruit of righteousness.[1197] We may beat out this oil to the Lord willingly. Paul testified: "But I keep under my body, and bring it into subjection."[1198] The expression, *keep under* translates a word that means to beat, to treat with severity, to subdue.[1199] (Fasting is an effective way to bring the body

---

[1192] I Timothy 3:15
[1193] I Thessalonians 5:17
[1194] Leviticus 24:2-4; Revelation 1:20
[1195] Leviticus 24:2
[1196] Romans 11:17-23
[1197] Amos 6:12; James 3:18
[1198] I Corinthians 9:27
[1199] The expression *keep under* translates ὑπωπιάζω (*hupopiazo* (Strong No.

under subjection.) However, if we refuse to yield this fruit to God willingly, He will beat (chastise) out the needed oil from the olives. Take heed! "Now no chastening for the present seemeth to be joyous, but grievous: nevertheless afterward it yieldeth the peaceable fruit of righteousness unto them which are exercised thereby."[1200] This olive oil is strained, and purged of impurities in our prayer closets. Selah! (*Means to pause and consider!*)

What has the fruit of righteousness to do with offering the sacrifice of prayer? The Spirit said, "The Lord is far from the wicked: but he heareth the prayer of the righteous."[1201] Again, "Awake to righteousness, and sin not; for some have not the knowledge of God: I speak this to your shame."[1202] And again, "Know ye not, that to whom ye yield yourselves servants to obey, his servants ye are to whom ye obey; whether of sin unto death, or of obedience unto righteousness?"[1203] It's true that our salvation is a gift received by faith and "not by works of righteousness which we have done."[1204] But that does not mean we have no obligation to bring forth the fruit of righteousness through obedience.[1205]

Verily, verily, the reverse is true; for we who have the Spirit are exhorted to "Walk in the Spirit," and promised if we do so, "Ye shall not fulfill the lust of the flesh."[1206] "If

---

5299)—"from a compound of 5259 and a derivative of 3700; to hit under the eye (buffet or disable an antagonist as a pugilist), i.e., (figuratively) to tease or annoy (into compliance), subdue (one's passions):—keep under, weary"). Hence, if we *beat* the oil (fruit of righteousness) from the *olives*, well, but if not, then the rod of correction will fall upon us to produce it (Hebrews 12:11).

[1200] Hebrews 12:11
[1201] Proverbs 15:29
[1202] I Corinthians 15:34
[1203] Romans 6:16
[1204] Titus 3:5
[1205] Romans 16:19; II Corinthians 7:15; 10:5-6
[1206] Galatians 5:16

we live in the Spirit, let us also walk in the Spirit."[1207] To walk in the Spirit requires we yield the body to the Spirit's control. To do this we must follow Paul's example, who said he brought his body into subjection.[1208] Or else we will need to submit God's chastening, by which He imparts to us holiness and produces the desired fruit of righteousness.[1209]

God's Spirit is the fire that is fed by olive oil—the fruit of righteousness. It fuels the fire that illuminates the world with the Light of His glory through us. Did He not say the world would "see [our] good works, and glorify [our] Father which is in heaven?"[1210]

The prayers of the righteous man are the prayers that avail much.[1211] The imputed righteousness of Christ affords us a place before the Throne;[1212] the imparted righteousness of Christ affords integrity to our petitions.

Why does the LORD connect such earnest exhortations to personal holiness and righteousness with His instruction to present before God our prayers like the evening incense? That we must pray is evident to most. Too many pray with dirty hands and impure hearts.[1213]

Gracey thinks of God as though He were a vending machine, a Genie, or an indulgent grandfather. While some are heedless of the need for prayer and go on after the flesh, vainly supposing "gain is godliness,"[1214] others think of prayer superstitiously, like casting a spell or unleashing

---

[1207] Galatians 5:25
[1208] I Corinthians 9:27
[1209] Hebrews 12:11, see 5-11
[1210] Matthew 5:16
[1211] James 5:16; I Peter 3:12
[1212] Hebrews 4:16
[1213] James 4:8; Isaiah 59:1-2
[1214] I Timothy 6:5

a Genie. Some "ungodly men, turning the grace of our God into lasciviousness,[1215] have crept into our churches and corrupted many. These creepers teach *Gracey* to cry "legalist" any time we recommend holiness, especially in dress and manners. It's a favorite term of the *creepers*, useful to dismiss any expectation of righteousness that would be a condition of fellowship with God.

The Sacrifice of Giving[1216]

If the reader presumes this sacrifice less important than the others only because it receives less attention here, he or she makes a grave error. All New Testament sacrifices are designed to do one thing ultimately: present our hearts to God in holy worship. Jesus said, "Where your treasure is, there will your heart be also."[1217] The treasure of most believers follows their heart. This is backward. The believer must direct his or her heart to the Lord, and the sacrifice of giving is essential to that end.

When Paul received a ministry offering from the Philippians,[1218] the Spirit moved him to write, "I am full, having received of Epaphroditus the things which were sent from you, an odour of a sweet smell, a sacrifice acceptable, wellpleasing to God."[1219]

The great Apostle referred to giving to support the ministry as communicating.[1220] The word translated *communicate* is κοινωνέω (koinoneo).[1221] Essentially it means to share with others. But the full meaning includes the idea of

---

[1215] Jude 4
[1216] Philippians 4:18
[1217] Matthew 6:21
[1218] I Corinthians 9:14
[1219] Philippians 4:18
[1220] Philippians 4:14-15; Galatians 6:6; I Timothy 6:18; Hebrews 13:16
[1221] Strong, *Strong's Greek Dictionary of the New Testament,* Entry No. 2841.

partaking, partnering, and connecting with another in his or her work. Taking this together with Jesus' observation that our heart follows our treasure, we understand that through our sacrifices of giving, we connect our hearts to the work of the Lord.[1222]

Beware you do not despise this sacrifice.[1223]

The Sacrifice of a Broken and Contrite Spirit[1224]

A broken spirit is always connected with one who has been humbled. It is equated with a broken heart.[1225] The spirit and heart are dynamically linked so that when the heart is overwhelmed with sorrow, the spirit is broken.[1226]

Our spirit is the invisible expression of our soul. It manifests in our attitude and affects our bearing, our tone of voice, and our countenance.[1227] Our spirit is expressive of our character, which shapes our motives; that is, the intents of the heart.[1228] Our spirit takes on the shape of these intentions.

[1222] Tithing is thought to be among those ordinances of the Law that are not a part of New Testament worship. Abraham tithed before the Law (Genesis 14:20); Moses incorporated it into the Law (Leviticus 27:30; Numbers 18:24). The tithe belongs to the LORD (Leviticus 27:30), and He gave it to the Levites for the work of the ministry (Numbers 18:24; Malachi 3:9-11). Paul instructed the churches to support the Gospel ministry in the same way (I Corinthians 9:3-14). Because Paul refused support from the Corinthians, some think Christian ministers should follow his example (I Corinthians 9:15-18). I agree; we should follow his example. Paul refused to receive support from the carnal-minded Christians at Corinth, and so turned to other churches to help him in their place: "I robbed other churches, taking wages of them, to do you service. . . . for that which was lacking to me the brethren which came from Macedonia supplied" (II Corinthians 11:7-9). It is a general spiritual principle that ten percent (a *tithe*) belongs to GOD. Howbeit, God desired all giving was and is to be *free will* (Deuteronomy 23:23; Ezra 7:16; see also Psalm 119:108).
[1223] Malachi 1-3
[1224] Psalm 51:17
[1225] Psalm 34:18
[1226] Proverbs 15:13
[1227] Proverbs 15:13
[1228] Hebrews 4:12

We use the expression *high–spirited* to speak of one who is full of vigor for life, but it can also describe the prideful. One may be said to have a prideful spirit, a selfish spirit, a lascivious spirit, or an arrogant spirit, and so forth. Daniel was a man who had an excellent spirit.[1229] This was because he had understanding.[1230] The "knowledge of the holy is understanding."[1231] Daniel understood the fear of the Lord and, not fearing man, he walked in holiness (separation from the world and public identification with God). By this, he developed an excellent spirit. Therefore, we understand that when we talk about one's spirit, ultimately, we are talking about what characterizes their personality.

To be *full of spirit* means one is full of himself. The world, which is always contrary to God, applauds a highly spirited individual—someone who is self-confident, self-reliant, and self-assured. Jesus was speaking to this when He said, "Blessed are the poor in spirit."[1232] Those who are poor in spirit are not full of themselves. They despise vanity. The poor in spirit stand before God empty of all self, as a beggar for His mercy and grace.[1233]

God is attracted to humility. He dwells in the "high and holy place," but condescends to come alongside those with a contrite and broken spirit.[1234] To whom shall He Who inhabits eternity look? "Even to him that is poor and of a contrite spirit, and trembleth at my word," GOD answered.[1235] This sacrifice will never be despised.[1236]

[1229] Daniel 5:12; 6:3; see Proverbs 17:27
[1230] Proverbs 17:27
[1231] Proverbs 9:10
[1232] Matthew 5:3
[1233] Psalm 40:17
[1234] Isaiah 57:15
[1235] Isaiah 66:2
[1236] Psalm 51:17

The flesh and the spirit must be subordinated. The body, wherein operates the law of sin in our members (flesh), must be vigorously taken and brought under subjection to Christ Jesus.[1237] The spirit must be humbled and turned to walk no more after the flesh, but after the Spirit instead.[1238] You (the soul) must "cleanse [yourself] from all filthiness of the flesh and spirit, perfecting holiness in the fear of God."[1239] Away with this lukewarm, contemporary Christianity— away with this wicked religion of devils that delights to be spotted (marked, identified) with the world.[1240] Back to the true religion, that is pure and undefiled, that visits mercy upon the unfortunate in their affliction, and that motivates the truehearted soldier of Christ to "keep himself unspotted from the world."[1241]

Let us carefully, prayerfully, prepare this precious sacrifice to set before God—the sacrifice of a broken spirit. How shall the spirit be broken? "A merry heart maketh a cheerful countenance: but by sorrow of the heart the spirit is broken."[1242]

There are two ways to produce brokenness of spirit and encourage God to draw nigh to us.[1243] We may heed the exhortation of James: "Be afflicted, and mourn, and weep: let your laughter be turned to mourning, and your joy to heaviness."[1244] In other words, we may judge ourselves and repent, and do the work of the priesthood faithfully: preparing and

---

[1237] I Corinthians 9:27
[1238] Romans 8:5-12; Galatians 5:16
[1239] II Corinthians 7:1
[1240] James 1:27
[1241] James 1:27
[1242] Proverbs 15:13
[1243] Psalm 34:18
[1244] James 4:9

presenting the Temple to God, and humbly offering our sacrifices to Him in the Spirit. Or else, God will lay the rod of correction upon us; indeed, He will afflict us and so bring our heart to such sorrow as will break our spirit.[1245]

Remember, our soul through our spirit functions as God's priest in the New Testament Temple. It is called the "ministration of the spirit," and the Spirit said it is "rather glorious."[1246] We often sing, "Our God is Holy." Amen, for He is indeed Holy! We might also sing, "Our God is Humble!"

Paul said we "labor together with God."[1247] To get any kingdom work done, we must labor together with God: not merely for God, but with God. To pull down the strongholds of Satan in our land by which devils hold captive the souls Jesus died to save, we must go forward with God. To advance the cause of Christ's kingdom is to build His House by preaching the Gospel to every man, woman, and child in this world. To accomplish this, we must labor together with God. Yea, without Him, we can do nothing.[1248] Indeed, "Except the LORD build the house, they labor in vain that build it."[1249] We must stand watch over our cities and sound the alarm at every encroachment of the enemy against our soul's liberty, ready at all times to defend our rights against Satan's unreasonable and wicked men and women who would take them from us. But we must have God with us, for "except the LORD keep the city, the watchman waketh but in vain."[1250] To have God with us, we must be humble and holy.

[1245] Psalm 107, especially verse 39
[1246] II Corinthians 3:8
[1247] I Corinthians 3:9
[1248] John 15:5
[1249] Psalm 127:1a
[1250] Psalm 127:1b

The more honor granted to God's creatures, the more responsibility they bear, and the greater need there is for humility. God resists the proud, but He gives grace to the lowly.[1251] Since our soul brings these spiritual offerings before the Lord of Glory through our spirit, everything depends on our spirit being humble and our body being holy.

Conclusion

It bears repeating. There are devils holding territory and defending satanic strongholds today that we cannot overcome except by much prayer and fasting. And God will not hear the prayers nor receive the fasts of faithless priests. The New Testament priest must fulfill his or her duty in the Temple of God by faithfully presenting the five sacrifices: the living sacrifice, the sacrifice of praise, the sacrifice of prayer, the sacrifice of giving, and the sacrifice of a broken spirit.

If you are like me, you are probably impatient to get to the practical, tactical aspect of our warfare. You want instruction regarding what exactly are the "weapons of our warfare" and how do we use them to cast mountains and mighty trees into the sea. That is, how do we wrestle against the principalities and powers that reject Christ's rule in the earth, opposing His command to preach the Gospel in every nation? More specifically, how do we use the weapons of our warfare to break the powers of darkness in America? How do we wrest the power of government from those who use it to support the murder of babies in the womb right up to birth, who advance the life-destroying practice of sodomy, and who force us to subject our children to an education that is systematically undermining our beliefs and values, while training them to be subversives against

---

[1251] James 4:6; Proverbs 3:34

the kingdom of Christ? How do we push back against the rising power of the Antichrist spirit in America? And, beyond America, how do we break the power of darkness in countries like China, where our brothers and sisters in Christ suffer brutal oppression for the cause of Christ? And in other lands also—.

You are anxious, perhaps, to learn how we pull down Satan's strongholds and advance the kingdom of Christ on Earth. We will begin that discussion in the next chapter and proceed as follows:

First, I will clarify our primary or strategic objective, and second, our tactical objectives. These chapters will be short. And because you must have certain essential principles fresh in your mind as we proceed, I will review where necessary. But every review will include something new. Then third, what are the weapons of our warfare? Then fourth, how do we use those weapons to advance the Kingdom of Christ in the kingdoms of this world? And finally, you'll find training exercises for God's warriors.

~

"In the chain of human events, the birthday of the nation is indissolubly linked with the birthday of the Savior. The Declaration of Independence laid the cornerstone of human government upon the first precepts of Christianity"

~ John Quincy Adams

(John Quincy Adams, An Oration Delivered Before the Inhabitants of the Town of Newburyport at Their Request on the Sixty-First Anniversary of the Declaration of Independence, July 4, 1837 (Newburyport: Charles Whipple, 1837), pp. 5-6.)

Chapter Thirty

God's Warrior Priests
(Part Eleven)
The Primary Objective of Our Priesthood

THE FAMOUS FIRST QUESTION of the Westminster Confession[1252] asks and answers: "What is the chief and highest end of man?—to glorify God and enjoy Him forever." Our chief end? Indeed! But this is not our strategic objective in God's War. It is too broad for our purpose. We are interested in the primary, or strategic objective of the New Testament priesthood that concerns our daily lives as we engage in spiritual warfare against the spirit of Antichrist.

It might be appropriate to say that our primary objective is to fulfill the Great Commission: to go into all the world and preach the Gospel to every creature.[1253] This is the primary mission of the churches, and it defines the ultimate life purpose of every believer. It does not, however, answer the question of this chapter.

What is the primary objective of the New Testament

[1252] Westminster Confession, 1646, The *Westminster Confession* is a statement of faith, or a *doctrinal statement.* Virtually all Reformed Theologians use it. (A *reformed theologian* follows the tenets of John Calvin.) Some Baptists, being influenced by the Protestant Reformers, have used it, or adapted it for their use as a doctrinal statement. Baptists, such as this author, who identify as Independent, and Fundamental, reject the Calvinistic aspects of this confession. (ONLINE) http://www.reformed.org/documents/index.html?mainframe=http://www.reformed.org/documents/westminster_conf_of_faith.html (As of 12/30/09).
[1253] Mark 16:15

priesthood, relative to the fulfillment of our ultimate purpose in creation and our essential mission in the earth? The answer is found in John 7:38-39.

The Jews were puzzled by something Jesus said: "What manner of saying is this that he said, Ye shall seek me, and shall not find me: and where I am, thither ye cannot come?"[1254] Soon after, Jesus cast a glorious vision: "He that believeth on me, as the scripture hath said, out of his belly shall flow rivers of living water." The very next verse explains His meaning: "(But this spake He of the Spirit, which they that believe on Him should receive: for the Holy Ghost was not yet given; because that Jesus was not yet glorified)." Jesus spoke of His departure, and then, in connection with this, He spoke of the coming of the Holy Ghost.

Jesus gave His disciples clear instructions about what they were to do during the time they waited for Him to return. He explained that He would send the Holy Ghost upon them Who would empower them to be His witnesses.[1255] It happened at Pentecost, beginning the fulfillment of His prophecy about the Holy Spirit flowing into the world through the belly of those who believe in Him.[1256]

Old Testament priests were responsible to present their sacrifices according to the Word of God, by this securing the manifestation of the shekinah glory (the visible appearing of the Holy Ghost) in the Tabernacle. Likewise, the New Testament priest must present the sacrifices of the New Testament so that the Holy Ghost may fill and then flow through the Temple, manifesting Christ to the world.[1257]

[1254] John 7:36
[1255] Acts 1:5-9
[1256] John 7:38-39
[1257] II Corinthians 4:11

Jesus' primary objective for the New Testament priesthood is to release the Holy Ghost to flow through our belly into the world like rivers of living water. O, that there might be a second flood, but not by the water that condemns, rather by the water that saves. The Spirit of Jesus Christ flowing mightily into the world, manifesting the power and glory of Christ, driving back the spirit of Antichrist, pushing back against the robbers of liberty. That all might know Satan's power is broken, that Christ reigns Supreme over Heaven and Earth. That all might hear the command of God: Repent and believe on His Son or be destroyed in the day of His visitation. This is the primary objective: the flowing of the Holy Spirit through believers into this world.

Conclusion

The New Testament priesthood is responsible to maintain the Temple through which the Holy Ghost moves into this world because the primary objective of the priesthood is to extend into the world the influence of the Spirit of God.

~

"[Alexander] Hamilton suggested that it be named the Christian Constitutional Society, and listed two goals for its formation: first, the support of the Christian religion; and second, the support of the Constitution of the United States. This or-ganization was to have numerous clubs throughout each state which would meet regularly and work to elect to office those who reflected the goals of the Christian Constitutional Society."

~ *The Works of Alexander Hamilton*

(Alexander Hamilton, The Works of Alexander Hamilton, John C. Hamilton, editor (New York: John F. Trow, 1851), Vol. VI, p. 542, to James A. Bayard, April, 1802; see also, Alexander Hamilton, The Papers of Alexander Hamilton, Harold C. Syrett, editor (New York: Columbia University Press, 1977), Vol. XXV, p. 606, to James A. Bayard, April 16, 1802.)

Chapter Thirty-One

God's Warrior Priests

(Part Twelve)

The Tactical Objective of Our Priesthood

T HE STRATEGIC OBJECTIVE is to release the Holy Ghost into the world through the belly of the believer (the Holy Place of the New Testament Temple). Therefore, the tactical objectives are related to preparing the Temple to be filled with the Holy Spirit of God so that He will then flow through the Temple into the world.

The New Testament Temple priest need only follow the simple instructions found in two key passages of Scripture to fulfill Christ's objective. These are Romans 12:1-2 and Ephesians 5:18-21.

The Dedication of the Temple

I discussed this at length earlier, but there are a few things more to say that are critical to rightly fulfilling this obligation. Remember:

> I beseech you therefore, brethren, by the mercies of God, that ye present your bodies a living sacrifice, holy, acceptable unto God, which is your reasonable service. And be not conformed to this world: but be ye transformed by the renewing of your mind, that ye may prove what is that good, and acceptable, and perfect, will of God. — Romans 12:1-2

There is something more to presenting the body holy,

acceptable to God than the requisite constant cleansing of our hands and purifying of our hearts.[1258] God wants us to be non-conformists: "Be not conformed to this world." The conformance that concerns Him includes the way we think and the behavior that reflects those thoughts. Dismissed as irrelevant by many, fashions matter to God, chiefly regarding gender distinction[1259] and modesty,[1260] but any worldly style that identifies a believer with the spirit of this world. Extensive use of the Scriptures will sharpen the tastes and senses of believers so that they may discern these things correctly.[1261]

It is perhaps helpful to remember when we dress our bodies that we are preparing the Temple of God for public presentation. The governing rule is the glory of God, and the guiding principle should be appropriateness. For example, it would be inappropriate to dress in a suit to work in our gardens; and it would be inappropriate to wear our gardening clothes to church.[1262] We should respect what is holy.

Of course, not being conformed to this world entails more than how we dress our bodies; it involves every aspect of our lives. Probably the best definition of what it means to be not conformed to this world is in the following

---

[1258] James 4:8

[1259] Deuteronomy 22:5; I Corinthians 11:14

[1260] I Timothy 2:9

[1261] Hebrews 5:14

[1262] Christ looks not on the outward appearance, but rather He looks on the heart (I Samuel 16:7). But remember the wedding guest that was not dressed appropriately who was dismissed (Matthew 22:11-12)? Whether one argues that this is mere metaphor, it does not change the fact that Jesus used for His illustration a man dressed inappropriately for an occasion. The exhortation that God looks on the heart and not the "outward appearance" (II Corinthians 10:7) is not speaking of the appropriateness or inappropriateness of one's attire, but that, in the case of I Samuel 16, the youthfulness, and smallness of David should not be thought by Samuel to mean he would not be God's choice for king.

entreaty: "As obedient children, not fashioning yourselves according to the former lusts."[1263] These former lusts refer to our fleshly appetites that are fed by the following behaviors, called works of the flesh: "Adultery, fornication, uncleanness, lasciviousness, idolatry, witchcraft, hatred, variance, emulations, wrath, strife, seditions, heresies, envyings, murders, drunkenness, revellings, and such like."[1264]

Rather than be conformed to this world, we are to be transformed. The word *transfigured*[1265] translates the same word here rendered *transformed.* When Jesus was transfigured, He manifested the Glory of God. We are to be transformed in such a way so that Jesus will manifest in our mortal flesh.[1266]

Our transformation is accomplished by renewing our minds. The Holy Ghost teaches us that the work of putting on the "new man" and putting off the "old man" is something that results in our being "renewed in the spirit of (our) mind."[1267] This happens when we yield ourselves "unto God, as those that are alive from the dead, and [our] members as instruments of righteousness unto God."[1268] To yield is to let pass, or to surrender to the influence or control of something or someone. We are to yield to the control of God. God claims our bodies, and we are to yield to His authority and surrender it to His control. The principal thing to understand here is that God is active, He is working, He is moving—our part is to yield. Unfortunately, we spend most of our time resisting.[1269]

[1263] I Peter 1:14—see I Corinthians 7:31 and I John 2:15-17
[1264] Galatians 5:19-21
[1265] Matthew 17:2
[1266] II Corinthians 4:11
[1267] Ephesians 4:22-32
[1268] Romans 6:13
[1269] Acts 7:51; see Ephesians 4:30-31

This yielding to God is equivalent to our walking after the Spirit and not after the flesh.[1270] The experience of walking after the Spirit is one that affects a renewing of the spirit of our mind. When our mind is compelled to think in the patterns of the Spirit of God, which would mean to have our thoughts shaped by the words of God, the spirit of our mind is renewed. The mind is reset to its original settings. The specific thing we do to make this happen is to bring every thought to the obedience of Christ.[1271] We will discuss this thoroughly in the next chapter.

Our mind has long been shaped into conformity to this world's lusts. When we walk after the Spirit, our spirit is transformed. The Bible puts it this way; *we are renewed in the spirit of our mind.* When our minds are renewed, our lives are transformed.

Essentially, it is a battle we fight in our minds, and when we win there, the victory shows up in our body. The Holy Spirit begins flowing through our belly—that's when Jesus begins manifesting in our mortal flesh—and that's when things start getting done. This brings us to the next key passage.

The Filling of the Temple

> And be not drunk with wine, wherein is excess; but be filled with the Spirit; speaking to yourselves in psalms and hymns and spiritual songs, singing and making melody in your heart to the Lord; giving thanks always for all things unto God and the Father in the name of our Lord Jesus Christ; submitting your-selves one to another in the fear of God.
> — Ephesians 5:18-21

Jesus took a whip and drove the moneychangers from

[1270] Romans 8
[1271] II Corinthians 10:5

the Temple, accusing them of turning His Father's House into a house of merchandise.[1272] Toward the end of His earthly ministry, He did it again, crying against those who would make the Temple of God a den of thieves.[1273] We must cleanse the Temple of any thought that defiles it. As New Testament priests, the zeal of the Lord's House ought to eat us up.[1274]

Ephesians 5:18-21 is eminently priestly. In it, the Apostle Paul instructs us what to do to be filled with the Spirit.

Ephesians 5:18-21 is one sentence, which may be divided into four significant segments headed by each of the four participles we find in it: *speaking, singing, giving,* and *submitting.* These participles identify four specific things the New Testament priest does in the Temple of God to be filled with the Spirit.

Each of the four things the believer-priest does to be filled with the Spirit is related to the thoughts of our hearts and affects the attitude (spirit) of our minds: 1. Speaking to yourselves in psalms, hymns, and spiritual songs; 2. Singing and making melody in your heart to the Lord; 3. Giving thanks always for all things unto God and the Father in the name of our Lord Jesus Christ; and 4. Submitting yourselves one to another in the fear of God.

These four activities are critical to being filled with the Spirit. However, in connection with these activi-ties— speaking, singing, giving, and submitting—the believer-priest must ask to be filled with the Spirit.

Ask to be filled with the Spirit.

The point of Ephesians 5:18-21 is to instruct us on how

[1272] John 2:14-17
[1273] Matthew 21:12-13; Mark 11:15-17; Luke 19:45-48
[1274] Psalm 69:9

to be continually filled with the Spirit. It is a command, "be filled with the Spirit."[1275] Being filled with the Spirit is juxtaposed to being drunk with wine. Instead of being under the intoxicating influence of wine, we are to be under the empowering influence of God's Spirit. To come under the control and influence of wine, one must drink it to excess. (Believers are not to look at wine when it stirs itself aright, which is the first sign of fermentation—Proverbs 23:31.) For the believer to come under the controlling influence of the Spirit of God, he must *drink into (the) Spirit.*[1276] Remember that Jesus introduced His vision of the Spirit flowing through the belly of believers by crying, "If any man thirst, let him come unto me, and drink. He that believeth on me, as the Scripture hath said, out of his belly shall flow rivers of living water."[1277]

We spiritually *drink* by believing!

When Jesus breathed on His disciples, the Holy Ghost entered into them, and for the first time in the history of the world, the Holy Spirit of God took up residence in the heart of a believer.[1278] Jesus instructed the disciples to receive the Holy Ghost, Whom He had sent into them.[1279]

God's Spirit filled the saints at Pentecost.[1280] The same group gathered later and were filled with the Holy Ghost again.[1281] There is no indication that they backslid in the time intervening between Pentecost and the experience recorded in Acts 4. We must understand the need to be filled with the Spirit is continuous; it is not a onetime experience.

[1275] Ephesians 5:18
[1276] I Corinthians 12:13
[1277] John 7:37-39
[1278] John 20:22; Galatians 4:6
[1279] John 20:22
[1280] Acts 2:4
[1281] Acts 4:31

The evidence that one is drunk with wine is apparent. This is also true of those filled with the Spirit. Paul lists the characteristics of those filled with the Spirit in Galatians 5:22-23: love, joy, peace, longsuffering, gentleness, goodness, faith, meekness, and temperance.

Of course, being filled with the Spirit is critical to our purpose as New Testament priests. There are clear instructions in this passage, which, if followed, will result in our being continually filled with the Holy Ghost.

The first thing the believer-priest must do is to obey the command: "Be filled with the Spirit." This suggests that the Spirit of God naturally moves to fill His Temple. The believer-priest is obligated to surrender his or her body to Him for this purpose. It also suggests that the believer-priest must do something to be filled with the Spirit. The first step to obey this command is to ask God for the Spirit; that is, ask the Lord to fill you with His Holy Ghost.

Luke 11:1-13 is a lesson on prayer. At the end of that lesson, Jesus applied what He taught to meeting our most vital need—the Holy Spirit. The first step is to ask the Father to fill you with His Spirit; something God is very willing to do. Therefore, we know that when we ask to be filled with the Spirit, the Father immediately responds.

Only one thing can get in the way of us receiving the filling of His Spirit immediately: We "ask amiss, that [we] may consume it upon [our] lusts."[1282] Some want the power of God for personal gain. Many think it is something their good works or gifts to the Church can purchase. Some imagine that their good works or donations can be used to negotiate with God for this favor. One character in the Bible

---

[1282] James 4:3

illustrates the "believer" who asks amiss for the power of the Holy Ghost.

Simon, the sorcerer, believed and was baptized, and desired to have the power of the Holy Spirit; but he wanted it for personal gain.[1283] Peter rebuked Simon:

> Thou hast neither part nor lot in this matter: for thy heart is not right in the sight of God. Repent therefore of this thy wickedness, and pray God, if perhaps the thought of thine heart may be forgiven thee. For I [Peter is speaking] perceive that thou art in the gall of bitterness, and in the bond of iniquity. — Acts 8:21-23

Simon illustrates another reason some Christians ask but do not receive the filling of God's Spirit. He foolishly thought he could purchase the power of God. Some believers mistakenly suppose the power of God is something earned by good works. Believers have difficulty understanding the difference between works of the flesh and works of faith. Good works that are the product of our faith in Christ are the effect of the "new man" manifesting the fruit of God's Spirit. Good works that are the product of the flesh arise from the "old man" attempting to obligate God. God's Spirit will not fill the Temple so long as the "old man" has it under his control.

Being continually filled with the Spirit.

When you receive the filling of the Spirit, you want to maintain the constant filling and flowing of the Spirit of God. You must be careful to neither "grieve the Spirit"[1284] nor "quench the Spirit."[1285] The most effective way to avoid grieving or quenching the Spirit is "being continually filled" with the Spirit.

[1283] Acts 8:18-19
[1284] Ephesians 4:30-31
[1285] I Thessalonians 5:19

Believer-priests must be continually doing four things in the Temple of God. As mentioned above, these are indicated in the passage by four participles: *speaking, singing, giving,* and *submitting.* The significant thing about participles is that they show ongoing activity. If someone speaks, it's something they are doing. If they spoke, it's something they did. But if we say they are speaking (a participle), we understand they are presently engaged in the activity. The believer-priest must be doing four things continuously to maintain the filling of the Spirit of God.

The Four Actions Necessary for Maintaining the Filling of the Spirit

Speaking to yourself:

We must be continually speaking to ourselves.[1286] When you have asked in faith to be filled with the Spirit, you need to start talking to yourself. We notice the word *speaking* is a specific direction given following a command. This means "speaking to yourselves" is what you do to obey the direct order to be filled with the Spirit.

What should you be saying to yourself? The Spirit says we must continually speak to [ourselves] in psalms and hymns and spiritual songs. The Psalms are Scripture, and hymns and spiritual songs are expressions of worship to God through praise and admonishments to godly living through lyrics set to a melody.[1287] It is reasonable that we should extend this to include speaking to ourselves the words of God. Our Lord said, "If ye abide in me, and my words abide in you, ye shall ask what ye will, and it shall be done unto you."[1288] To hide God's Word in our hearts requires us to repeat them in our hearts until they are memorized.[1289]

[1286] Ephesians 5:19a
[1287] Colossians 3:16
[1288] John 15:7
[1289] Psalm 119:11

The Spirit instructs us to speak to ourselves in Psalms, and Psalms are Scripture. He also tells us to speak hymns and spiritual songs to ourselves, and this includes songs of praise and exhortation written by other saints. We legitimately may infer from this that we are to fill our mind and heart with all wholesome words. Paul said, "Finally brethren, whatsoever things are honest, whatsoever things are pure, whatsoever things are lovely, whatsoever things are of good report; if there be any virtue, and if there be any praise, think on these things."[1290]

I've puzzled over why the Spirit tells us to speak psalms, hymns, and spiritual songs, and then follows with, singing and making melody in your heart to the Lord.[1291] Are we not speaking the psalms when we sing them? No doubt about it! One way to speak God's words, and the wholesome lyrics of hymns and spiritual songs, is to sing them in our hearts. But I think these are intended to be separate, albeit interrelated, actions.

For example, if I only sing the Psalms in my heart, I don't necessarily memorize them in a way that allows me to meditate on the meaning of the words and phrases. Try to recite the words of a Psalm you often sing. You'll find that you need the melody to remember the words. That's okay! But until you can recite the words without the tune, you have not fully integrated that Psalm into your heart. Force yourself, from time to time, to quote the words of a Psalm, hymn, or spiritual song, and take time to meditate on those words and phrases.

Another insight to bring forward is that one way to be speaking Psalms, hymns, and spiritual songs in our hearts

---

[1290] Philippians 4:8
[1291] Ephesians 5:19b

is by singing them. These activities, speaking and singing, are interrelated. We are speaking while we are singing, and we should be both speaking and singing.

Remember that your soul is God's priest, who through your spirit communes with God's Spirit in His Holy Temple. The spirit of your mind directly engages the Mind of the Spirit.[1292] If your soul and spirit are humble when you approach the Father, He will by His Spirit draw near to you. And you will enter the communion of the Holy Ghost.[1293] This communion is broken if the mind wanders away to carnal thoughts.[1294] It can be restored if you take captive the straying thoughts and bring them back under the obedience of Christ.[1295] It is the constant work of the New Testament priest to maintain this communion.

Perhaps this sounds odd—but speaking to yourself is what you must do to maintain the filling of the Spirit. Speak to yourself in psalms, hymns, and spiritual songs.[1296] We may extend this to include quoting Scripture, particularly from the Psalms, and pondering lyrics of hymns and spiritual songs, and to other wholesome words of godly saints as well.

Singing and making melody in your heart:

We must sing and make melody in our hearts to the Lord.[1297] Like the word *speaking*, the word *singing* is a participle; it's an ongoing activity of our soul through our spirit in the Temple of God. As pointed out above, the construction of the sentence suggests we speak to ourselves by singing. The two phrases, "Speaking to yourselves in

---

[1292] Romans 8:27
[1293] II Corinthians 13:14
[1294] Romans 8:6
[1295] II Corinthians 10:5
[1296] Ephesians 5:19a
[1297] Ephesians 5:19b

psalms and hymns and spiritual songs" and "singing and making melody in your heart to the Lord" are connected: we *sing* what we *speak*. Therefore, we are to be continually speaking and singing in our hearts through psalms, hymns, and spiritual songs.

The Holy Ghost resides in our hearts; He is our audience! Because the Holy Spirit is omnipresent, when we sing in the Spirit, we are singing in the immediate presence of the Almighty. Since the Spirit dwells in our hearts, when we sing in our hearts, the Spirit of God is our audience. By filling the Holy of Holies (the heart) with holy melodies, we drown out the noise of seducing spirits that are trying to distract the spirit of our mind away from the mind of the Spirit. On the other hand, if we turn our thoughts to the flesh, we break the connection, and grieve the Spirit. The faithful priest who is diligently attending to the sacrifice of praise leaves no opening for those things that grieve the Spirit to enter in: "bitterness, and wrath, and anger, and clamour, and evil speaking [and] malice."[1298]

Ask to be filled with the Spirit. Then start speaking to yourself in psalms, hymns, and spiritual songs—and by extension, recite verses and even passages of Scripture to yourself. And while you are speaking, fill your heart with singing to the Lord; sing a "new song" to the Lord by creating melodies in your heart as you recite or read the Psalms.[1299]

Giving thanks for all things:

This is the sacrifice of praise to God: "giving thanks always for all things unto God and the Father in the name of our Lord Jesus Christ,"[1300] which we are exhorted to give to

---

[1298] Ephesians 4:30-31
[1299] Psalm 33:3
[1300] Ephesians 5:20

God "continually," described as "the fruit of our lips giving thanks to His Name."[1301] We spoke of this New Testament sacrifice earlier.

The phrase *giving thanks always* also begins with a participle. So we understand that the action it describes is part of the ongoing activity of the believer-priest. However, the phrase starting with *giving* is separated from the one before it by a semicolon, indicating it is a separate action, albeit intimately connected, and related to what came before it.

In other words, being continually filled with the Spirit is what we must do. To obey that command, we speak to ourselves in psalms, hymns, and spiritual songs by singing and making melody in our hearts to the Lord. In connection with that activity, and even while we proceed with it, we present before the Throne of God sacrifices of praise, speaking thanksgiving unto God for all His marvelous works. Of course, we may do this by singing psalms of thanksgiving, or hymns or spiritual songs that present thanksgiving to God.

It is allowable, therefore, to understand from our text that we 1. ask to be filled, 2. speak Scripture in our heart, 3. sing praises to our God, and 4. present, formally and purposely, specific sacrifices of praise to Him.

Imagine a priest standing before God's Presence, lifting his or her hands in worship: quoting Scripture, psalms, hymns, and spiritual songs, all while reflecting on the meaning of the words and phrases. From time to time, he or she pauses to prepare a special presentation of thanksgiving to God, and places that thank-offering before Him, releasing it to Him with praise. Then the priest sings in his or her heart, filling

---

[1301] Hebrews 13:15

up the room—the inner room, the holy of holies of the New Testament Temple—His dwelling place! Then God moves into the praise and fills the sacred place!

We are specifically instructed to respond to all that God has brought into our lives with thanksgiving. Therefore, as we identify this or that, we sanctify it unto the Lord, receive it from Him with thanksgiving, and then formally and purposely present that thanks to Him as an offering.

Satan attempts to provoke the believer-priest to grieve and even quench the Holy Spirit. Misery and conflict and clamor serve to distract the priests of God's Temple from their priestly duties—and so draw away their affections from things above to attach to things below. Satan's purpose is first to provoke murmuring and complaining until the Temple rooms are filled with wrathful clamor, which will grieve the Spirit[1302] and finally quench Him.[1303] The saint is then susceptible to an assault against the soul by fleshly lusts.[1304] Once entrenched in some carnal sin, the saint comes under the control of Satan.

It is imperative to Satan that he distracts the believer from his or her priestly duties. Otherwise, a faithful priest will release the flow of the Holy Ghost through the door and into the world like rivers of living water. Nothing is a greater danger to Satan and his designs in this world. He must keep the door of God's earthly Temple shut, and the Spirit grieved and, if things go particularly well, quenched.

There is a sacrifice the believer-priest can present to thwart Satan's scheme. It's called the sacrifice of praise described as the fruit of our lips, giving thanks to His name.

[1302] Ephesians 3:30-31
[1303] I Thessalonians 5:19
[1304] I Peter 2:11

And we must give thanks for whatever comes. For only giving thanks *always* for *all things* unto God and the Father in the Name of our Lord Jesus Christ breaks the power of Satan's attack and releases the power of God compelling the Devil to flee.[1305]

This offering is to be presented "in the name of our Lord Jesus Christ."[1306] Our preparation is critical. Nothing can be acceptable to God that does not come to Him through His Son, our Lord, the Saviour, Jesus Christ. Additionally, "all things" include what is not savory to us. But when we present thanksgiving for these things in the "Name of our Lord Jesus Christ," His Cross savors our sacrifice. Remembering He suffered the Cross for the joy set before Him helps us give thanks for even our most difficult trials for the joy set before us. His joy was us. Our joy is Him.

Finally, while Ephesians 5:20 instructs us to present our offering in His Name, notice that Hebrews 13:15 teaches us to give our thanks to His Name. We might take up the various names of God and present a special thanksgiving to Him relative to each one. I recommend Dr. Benny Beckum's book, *Prayer for Revival*, in which he provides an excellent study of the Names of God.[1307]

Submitting yourselves one to another:

We must submit ourselves one to another. Many believers fail to be filled with the Spirit because they refuse to accept

---

[1305] James 4:7

[1306] Ephesians 5:20

[1307] Beckum, Benny, Dr. *Prayer for Revival,* pp. 70-87. The names he lists are as follows: *El-Shaddai* (God–Almighty), *Jehovah–jireh* (the LORD will provide), *Jehovah–nissi* (the LORD our banner), *Jehovah–rapha* (the LORD that healeth), *Jehovah–shalom* (the LORD is our peace), *Jehovah–roi* (the LORD my shepherd), *Jehovah–tsidkenu* (the LORD our righteousness), *Jehovah–sabaoth* (the LORD of Hosts), *Jehovah–shammah* (the LORD is there), *Jehovah–El Elyown* (the LORD, God Most High), *Jehovah–qahdosh* (the LORD that sanctifieth thee).

accountability to one another. This grieves the Spirit and robs the believer of His filling.[1308]

We must submit to one another "in the fear of God."[1309] For example, read Hebrews 10:24-25, which says, "And let us consider one another to provoke unto love and to good works: not forsaking the assembling of ourselves together, as the manner of some is; but exhorting one another: and so much the more, as ye see the day approaching." Accountability is critical to spiritual growth and success in spiritual warfare. Indeed, the Spirit attaches accountability inextricably to those things we must do if we are going to be continually filled with the Spirit.

God connects fellowship between saints to their fellowship with Him. Consider how strongly God feels about this matter. If we do not love the brethren, according to the Apostle John, we are not of God: we abide in death, and we are under the influence of the father of lies.[1310] Jesus said we are to love one another as He loved us.[1311] Paul makes it clear that loving our brethren is not merely affectionate regard, but a sincere commitment to their well-being.[1312] Indeed, if we are to love one another as Christ loved us, we must be sacrificially committed to their best interests.

Loving one another is the foundation of accountability.

Submitting to one another is often the point of failure

[1308] Ephesians 4:30-31

[1309] The fact that this is followed by specific exhortations to husbands and wives (Ephesians 5:22-35) should not lead us to conclude the command to submit ourselves to one another only applies to husbands and wives. It would be equally in error to fail to apply it to husbands and wives, however. Husbands and wives are heirs together of the grace of life (I Peter 3:7), obligated to show mutual respect and honor. The specific responsibilities of each party in marriage are detailed in the passage that follows the exhortation to be filled with the Spirit. (Ephesians 5:21)

[1310] I John 3:10, 14; 4:20

[1311] John 13:34; 15:12-17

[1312] I Corinthians 13:1-9

in the New Testament priesthood. Because of pride, many believer-priests prefer to be alienated from the fellowship of God's people rather than accept accountability to the disciplines of church life. Every believer-priest is obliged to connect his or her body (the Temple of God) to a church, the body of Christ, which is the House of God.[1313]

The believer-priest must submit him- or herself to the Holy Ghost appointed overseers of Christ's local assembly.[1314] No New Testament priest that refuses to submit him- or herself to the authority of the Scripture is going to be filled and flowing with the Holy Ghost. Such persons are pretenders, obstinate, and rebellious—which is as the sin of witchcraft.[1315] Seducing spirits may provide any number of excuses to bolster the rebellion of such believer-priests,[1316] but nothing excuses them from obedience to Christ.

Do not underestimate the importance of accountability. It is a way of life for the believer-priest. For example, we must submit ourselves unto God before we can "resist the Devil" with any expectation that he will "flee" from us.[1317] God purchased the Church with His blood[1318] and made Christ its head.[1319] It's His.[1320] He organized it.[1321] It is His body in the earth.[1322] His Spirit appoints its overseers to feed the flock of God in the churches, which He purchased with His own blood.[1323] Of course, the overseer's authority is

---

[1313] I Timothy 3:15
[1314] Acts 20:28; I Timothy 3:1-13; Hebrews 13:7, 17
[1315] I Samuel 15:23
[1316] I Timothy 4:1-4
[1317] James 4:7
[1318] Acts 20:28
[1319] Ephesians 5:23
[1320] Matthew 16:18
[1321] I Timothy 3:1-14; read the entire epistle of I Corinthians
[1322] Ephesians 1:22-23
[1323] Acts 20:28; see 13:1-2)

limited and under Christion.[1324] But that is all the more reason every believer-priest must place him- or herself under the authority of Christ by accepting accountability to His appointed overseers.

Satan hates godly authority, and so does every servant in his kingdom of darkness. Invariably, the same ones who despise God's ordained authority will place themselves in the service of tyrants.

Conclusion

God has commanded every believer-priest to be filled with the Spirit. He has clearly explained what must be done to obey that command. He must ask to be filled, speak Scripture in his heart, fill his heart with worshipful singing of psalms, hymns, and spiritual songs, present sacrifices of praise in thanksgiving to God continually, and establish accountability with his fellow believer-priests. If the believer-priest will be obedient and faithful in the execution of his or her responsibilities, the Temple of God will be filled with the Spirit. The Holy Ghost will flow through the door of God's Temple into the world, working God's will in the earth as it is done in Heaven. Satan will be routed. The spirit of Antichrist will be pushed back. And territory long held by Satan will be brought back under the rule of Christ Jesus the King!

~

[1324] I Peter 5:1-3

Chapter Thirty-Two

The Weapons of our Warfare

(Part One)

The Nature of Our Weapons, the Front Line of Every Battle, and the Primary Tactical Maneuver

WARS ARE FOUGHT WITH WEAPONS. They are decided by who has the best weapons and the soldiers with the will and skill to use them.

It's God's War, and we know that He that is in us is greater than he that is in the world.[1325] We know that there are more with us than with them.[1326] We know our weapons are superior: "With [Satan] is an arm of flesh; but with us is the LORD our God to help us, and to fight our battles."[1327] Therefore, "Be strong and courageous, and be not afraid nor dismayed."[1328]

I said the outcome of virtually every war is determined by who has the best weapons. We have the best weapons, so why are we losing? The Gospel is banned in much of the world; unreasonable and wicked men and women control most of the resources of the earth and employ them in service to Satan; Christians are trampled upon in the earth, and this last-standing "one nation under God" is under siege by the children of disobedience, and they are gaining in power. Only very lately have believer-priests begun to

---

[1325] I John 4:4
[1326] II Kings 6:16-17
[1327] II Chronicles 32:7-8
[1328] II Chronicles 32:7

stir, and we can hope it is not too little, too late. But why is Satan winning? Not only is the outcome of war determined by who has the best weapons, but also by which army has soldiers with the will and the skill to use those weapons.

God's warriors are inept at using the weapons of our warfare. They don't understand what those weapons are, and they don't know how to use them. In this chapter, you are going to learn about the weapons of our warfare.

> For though we walk in the flesh, we do not war after the flesh: (for the weapons of our warfare are not carnal, but mighty through God to the pulling down of strongholds;) casting down imaginations, and every high thing that exalteth itself against the knowledge of God, and bringing into captivity every thought to the obedience of Christ; and having in a readiness to revenge all disobedience, when your obedience is fulfilled. — II Corinthians 10:3-6

We Do Not War After the Flesh

The first thing the Spirit wants us to understand about our warfare is that, although we walk in the flesh in this world, we do not engage in combat after the flesh.

Paul said, "We walk *in the flesh*" (italics added for emphasis). Earlier, when I explained spiritual circumcision, I brought out the fact that in Romans 8:8-9, Paul said those of us who are in Christ are no longer in the flesh but in the Spirit.[1329] If Paul, in Romans, told us we are not in the flesh, why does he, in II Corinthians 10:3, say we walk in the flesh? Because we do! Allow me to explain.

Romans 8:8-9 tells us that if the Spirit of Christ dwells in us, we are no longer in the flesh, but in the Spirit. The believer-priest's life (zoe) was separated from his or her

---

[1329] Romans 8:8-9

soul (psuche) and baptized into Christ.[1330] Therefore, we are not in the flesh but in the Spirit.[1331] By the Spirit's omnipresence, we are presently seated with Christ in heavenly places,[1332] where our life is "hid with Christ in God."[1333] This left the body dead[1334]—"If Christ be in you, the body is dead because of sin."

Manifestly, however, our body continues to live in this world.[1335] How? The Zoe (life) of Christ was attached to our psuche (soul) when the Spirit, which is Christ in us, quickened (made alive) our mortal body[1336] and claimed it for His Temple.[1337] So, there is the "I" that is in Heaven, seated together with Christ, my zoe, or life, that is hid with Christ in God; and then there is the "I," my soul made alive by Christ's life, that is on Earth in this body, serving as the priest in His Temple.

For as long as I dwell in this "earthly tabernacle"[1338] (my body), my soul continues to walk in flesh. For this reason, we have reason to lament with Paul, "I know that in me (that is, in my flesh) dwelleth no good thing,"[1339] and cry with him, "O wretched man that I am! who shall deliver me from the body of this death?"[1340] And then rejoice with him, "I thank God, through Jesus Christ our Lord."[1341] And finally, from Paul, we learn how to live victoriously over

---

[1330] Romans 6:3; Galatians 3:27
[1331] Romans 8:8-9
[1332] Ephesians 2:6
[1333] Colossians 3:3
[1334] Romans 8:10
[1335] Galatians 2:20—*nevertheless, I live*
[1336] Romans 8:10-11
[1337] I Corinthians 6:19-20
[1338] II Corinthians 5:1
[1339] Romans 7:18
[1340] Romans 7:24
[1341] Romans 7:25

the wretched flesh—we do it by walking after the Spirit, and not after the flesh.

Therefore, I (my life "hid with Christ in God") am not in the flesh.[1342] But I (my soul in this present body)[1343] walk (live out my life) in the flesh. But Paul goes on to say we do not war after the flesh. The keyword is *after*.

We are in the flesh in this world. Therefore, whatever we do is necessarily done in this flesh. However, we don't war after the flesh. What does this mean? In Romans 8, the Apostle Paul explained that we must make a choice, with our mind, to walk *after the flesh* or *after the Spirit*. To walk *after* the flesh or the Spirit means to walk under the influence of either. Because our soul lives in this flesh, we walk *in* the flesh. But we do not live or walk *after* the flesh.

Therefore, although we walk in the flesh, we do not war after the flesh. For our weapons are not carnal; that is, they are not after the flesh.[1344] The phrase *not after the flesh* tells us our weapons are not physical, but spiritual. It also tells us the weapons of our warfare neither serve the lusts of the flesh nor utilize any of its works: "The works of the flesh are manifest, which are these; Adultery, fornication, uncleanness, lasciviousness, idolatry, witchcraft, hatred, variance, emulations, wrath, strife, seditions, heresies, envyings, murders, drunkenness, revellings, and such like."[1345] All these things are in Satan's arsenal; indeed, these are his weapons for his is the arm of flesh. But none of these things are in our arsenal.

[1342] Romans 8:8-9

[1343] II Corinthians 5:1-9

[1344] Some resist the concept of *carnal Christian*. But that is like saying there are no "illegal aliens": an alien (non-citizen) here illegally. The expression *carnal Christian* identifies a believer who is carnally minded (Romans 8).

[1345] Galatians 5:19-21

We Are at War, and Our Flesh Is the Front Line of Every Battle

Warrior-priests must always remember they are always engaged in spiritual warfare. The front line of every battle is at the door of the Temple, represented by the belly, identified with the flesh—the *old man*. The reason Satan attacks at the door of the Temple is plain to see; it is through this door that the Holy Ghost has entrance into the world, and his primary objective is to stop the Spirit of Jesus Christ from flowing into the world like rivers of living water, overwhelming and restraining the spirit of Antichrist.[1346] He knows God's plan is for Jesus to manifest in our mortal flesh.[1347] Therefore, Satan concentrates his attack on the flesh. Also, the flesh (belly) is the weakest point of our defenses. Often the "spirit is willing," but the "flesh is weak."[1348] Our flesh is the front line of every battle because it is the door of the Temple, the entrance to the Holy Place, where Christ manifests, the portal through which His Spirit moves into this world.

The Primary Tactical Maneuver in Every Battle

The primary tactical maneuver in our warfare is to bring every thought to the obedience of Christ.[1349] The language might seem a bit odd at first—bringing into captivity every thought to the obedience of Christ. We might expect it to read something like bringing every thought into obedience to Christ. However, the idea is that we take every thought into captivity, and then bring it to the obedience of Christ.

First, what does it mean to bring into captivity every thought? The carnal mind is enmity against God. The Spirit

---

[1346] John 7:38-39
[1347] II Corinthians 4:11
[1348] Matthew 26:41; Mark 14:38; see Romans 8:3
[1349] II Corinthians 10:5

tells us that "it is not subject to the law of God, neither indeed can be," which was our condition when we were in the flesh and could not please God.[1350] However, now we are in the Spirit, and if we walk in the Spirit, we will not fulfill the lusts of the flesh.[1351] Now we must choose whether we will mind the things of the flesh or the things of the Spirit. It's where we direct our mind. Our mind is where thoughts happen. The work of the believer-priest is to arrest every thought, take it captive; that is, bring it under control, seize it, and command it. Every thought must be taken captive.

Thoughts are the soldiers in the battle at the door. The fleshly thoughts of our old nature war against the soul, and hold closed the door of the Temple against Christ's Spirit. Seducing spirits stir up doctrines (teachings) of devils[1352] by stirring thoughts and imaginations that deceive the believer-priest into exalting him- or herself against the knowledge of God,[1353] and being prideful, such priests grieve and even quench the Spirit so that He does not come through that door. The faithful believer-priest must rise and take every thought into captivity.

When a soldier takes captives, the captured are brought under the power of their captors. The believer-priest takes every thought (soldier) captive in the Name of Jesus Christ and brings it under God's command.

Second, what does it mean that every thought is to be taken into captivity to the obedience of Christ?

What was the obedience of Christ relative to His thoughts? Philippians 2:5-8 answers this question:

[1350] Romans 8:7-8
[1351] Galatians 5:16-17
[1352] I Timothy 4:1-4
[1353] II Corinthians 10:5

> Let this mind be in you, which was also in Christ
> Jesus: who being in the form of God, thought it not
> robbery to be equal with God: but made himself of no
> reputation, and took upon him the form of a servant,
> and was made in the likeness of men: and being found
> in fashion as a man, he humbled himself, and became
> obedient unto death, even the death of the cross.
> — Philippians 2:5-8

Jesus often urged us to be of this mindset: "If any man will come after me, let him deny himself, and take up his cross, and follow me."[1354]

The primary tactical maneuver in every spiritual battle is to take every thought to the Cross. Every thought is to be subject to the rule: dead to sin, alive to God.[1355] Every idea, every imagination, is to be compelled to kneel at the foot of the Cross. Every fantasy must be made to bear His Cross.

Practically speaking, we must let this mind be in [us] that was also in Christ Jesus, Who, 1. Thought it not robbery to be equal with God, but made Himself of no reputation (gave up concern for His reputation), and 2. Took upon Him the form of a servant (came not to be served, but to serve others), and 3. Being found in fashion as a man, He humbled Himself unto death, even the death of the cross (He denied Himself, and took up His cross).

Satan will try to seduce us, and if he cannot do so, he will try to torment us into turning our thoughts loose from the obedience of Christ. Remember, first; Satan tried to bribe Jesus by offering to give Him the kingdoms of the world if only He would bow to Satan. This failing, Satan used everything in his power to provoke Jesus and to get

---

[1354] Matthew 16:24-25; Luke 9:23; see Galatians 2:20; John 12:24-25; Matthew 10:37-39; Mark 8:34-38
[1355] Romans 6:11

Him to refuse the cup of ultimate humiliation. Emotional torment, physical torture, cruel mocking, hatred, wrath, and sedition—all of it unleashed upon our LORD. Jesus understood this was allowed by His Father to fulfill His purpose to redeem humankind. God uses some believers in the manner of a Moses or an Elijah, who like great warriors overcame their enemies and did not die by their hands. Others, like Stephen and Paul, are martyred for the cause— like God's own Son.

We must remember not to fear him who can kill the body only; rather fear Him who has power over both body and soul.

Lest I be misunderstood, allow me to explain that God does not want Christians, like His Son, to suffer and physically die for the sins of man. Christ died as the only atonement for our sins. Christians do not die to atone for their sins or the sins of others. Children of disobedience who murder Christians are not serving God or fulfilling His will. They are treasuring up for themselves wrath against the day of wrath.[1356] Jesus will judge the nations based on how they have treated His brethren explicitly.[1357]

And remember: although Paul was martyred, during his life the Spirit of Jesus Christ moved through him so mightily that the spirit of Antichrist was forced to retreat, and all Asia "heard the word of the Lord Jesus."[1358] Indeed, the devils knew Paul and stood down at his rebuke.[1359] Sadly, however, Satan used two of his children of disobedience, Phygellus, and Hermogenes, to seduce Paul's followers in Asia to turn away from him.[1360] And Satan was able to

---

[1356] Romans 2:5
[1357] Matthew 25:40
[1358] Acts 19:10-27
[1359] Acts 19:15
[1360] II Timothy 1:15

reestablish his "seat" in the world, in a city of Asia named Pergamos.[1361] This happened toward the end of Paul's life, and he lamented it only a week or so before he was beheaded.

Did Paul ultimately lose? Of course not! He will receive the martyr's crown, and fruit continues to accrue to his account almost 2,000 years later. It is primarily from the Apostle Paul that we learn what is needed to release the Spirit of Jesus Christ into the world to overcome the spirit of Antichrist—to allow the Gospel to be preached throughout the world. Nevertheless, we learn from Paul's loss of Asia something important about the spiritual warfare we are called on to engage.

As in any war, there are both victories and defeats. We are foolish if we don't take every battle seriously because, while we are assured victory, some battles are lost, and the consequences are real. Paul experienced his most significant victories in Asia during his ministry in and from Ephesus. I described this earlier; it was truly amazing what God was doing in Asia. However, when God's people listened to the false teachings of the two false prophets that Satan used to deceive them, the revival stopped, and the spirit of Antichrist was able to prevail. This is because the believer-priests in Ephesus, and especially in Pergamos, Thyatira, Sardis, and Laodicea, were not faithfully executing their priestly duties. Satan took full advantage of these unfaithful priests.

To restore the liberties that came to this nation in the days leading up to the American Revolution, we must return to the Spirit of liberty: the Spirit of Jesus Christ. Because, where the Spirit of the Lord is, there is liberty. Jesus' vision was that His Spirit would flow from our belly like rivers of living water. And that is what you are learning in this book.

[1361] Revelation 2:13

It is our only hope for our liberties to be restored.

Conclusion

Now that we understand the nature of our weapons is spiritual and not carnal, that the front line of every battle is our flesh, and that the primary tactical maneuver of every soldier in Christ's army is to bring every thought to the obedience of Christ, it is time to get acquainted with the weapons themselves.

~

Chapter Thirty-Three

The Weapons of our Warfare
(Part Two)
The Armory

B ATTLES ARE FOUGHT with weapons. Victory turns on the skill of the soldiers and their will to use them.

The soldier must be willing to use his weapons. In WW II, a certain sergeant watched his men with care. If he noticed a soldier paralyzed in shock, he would slap his helmet and yell in his ear: SHOOT THE ENEMY OR HE WILL SURELY SHOOT YOU!

First, the soldier must be willing to shoot the enemy. But understanding his weapons and the principles of physical warfare enhances his skills and increases his effectiveness. Christian soldiers must not only be ready to engage the enemy, but they must learn how to engage their peculiar enemy with skill.

The Bible puts it this way: "Cursed be he that doeth the work of the LORD deceitfully, and cursed be he that keepeth back his sword from blood."[1362]

Sadly, many believer-warriors do the work of the LORD deceitfully. Like Hermogenes and Phygellus, spoken of in the previous chapter, these deceive God's people either into inaction in God's War or to become traitors—to join the side of the spirit of Antichrist.

[1362] Jeremiah 48:10

Satan's favorite lies are these: there is no ongoing war, Jesus might come someday, but until then, it's the Devil's world. These unwittingly deny that Christ has come in the flesh. They play into the hands of Satan and yield the world Christ bought for Himself to the control of the children of disobedience.

Some are squeamish about using the Sword of the Spirit, so they cringe, and will not stand up for God's truth. Oh, they are brave enough in church, but in the world, they are silent as lambs. Many are easily intimidated by the reaction they get from the children of disobedience who hate God and refuse to bow to the Lord Jesus. So, they *keep back* the Sword. They have now been rebuked: God's curse is upon them. Other king-priests are overwhelmed; the raging of the heathen[1363] stuns them into paralysis with fear and bewilderment. These had better start swinging the Sword, or the enemy will surely overcome them and take away their liberties. What it means, practically speaking, to "swing the Sword" is explained later.

Not only must God's warriors be willing to engage the enemy, but they must also use their weapons skillfully. To do that, first, they must know their weapons.

Introduction to the Armory of God's Warriors

Our weapons are spiritual, but that does not mean they do not have a physical component. What I mean is, for example, prayer is one of our primary weapons, and prayer is a spiritual exercise. However, prayer is done in this body, which is God's Temple. There is a physical component to praying. You will see that this is true of all our weapons. It goes to what we learned earlier about the spiritual intersecting with the physical. After all, it's all about the Spirit

---

[1363] Psalm 2

moving through our physical body into the material world to engage spiritual enemies—so that we may reclaim physical territory.

Ephesians 6:10-18 speaks particularly of the armor of God that we must wear when we enter spiritual warfare against the principalities and powers of this world. Remember, the principalities and powers refer to the spiritual entities (devils) along with their physical counterparts (the children of disobedience) that hold positions of authority in the world.

Paul uses the word *wrestle* to describe our engagement of Christ's enemies in this world. Wrestling is up-close and personal. Paul explains that this wrestling is not physical; it is not "against flesh and blood." We wrestle with the spiritual powers behind our physical opponents—we wrestle devils.

Paul, by the Spirit of God, used a Roman soldier's armor as an analogy to our spiritual armor. Most see only one weapon in this armor—the Sword of the Spirit. But Paul speaks of *weapons*, plural.[1364] The Sword is primarily a weapon for attacking an opponent, but it is also used to defend. And while the helmet, shield, and even the shoes are mostly defensive, they were sometimes employed as weapons in battle.

Our primary weapon in spiritual warfare is the "sword of the Spirit, which is the Word of God."[1365] However, the shield of faith is an essential weapon in spiritual warfare. Indeed, the Sword of the Spirit and the shield of faith are closely related and of critical importance in spiritual warfare. Our effectiveness with the Sword is dependent entirely upon the strength of our faith.

[1364] II Corinthians 10:4
[1365] Ephesians 6:17

Once the disciples tried but failed to help a devil-possessed child by the Sword of the Spirit: they commanded the devil to depart, but it refused. Jesus explained they failed because of their unbelief.[1366] Christ often lamented His disciples' little faith.[1367]

Earlier, we established that ground zero in our battle is the mind. As you will see, when we battle the Devil over our thoughts, every article of our armor will come into play.

We must wrestle against principalities, powers, and spiritual wickedness in high places.[1368] We must battle the seducing spirits that attempt to seduce our thoughts away from Christ[1369] by vain philosophies[1370] and by fake science.[1371] We war against whatever might inspire our imagination to exalt itself against the knowledge of God.[1372] In the Name of Jesus Christ, we arrest such thoughts and bring them humbled to the Cross, where the self is crucified, and Christ is lifted up.

Seducing spirits stir our thoughts to resist arrest. They war against us and hurl at us the fiery darts of the devil. We throw up our shield of faith to quench those darts. Then slashing and thrusting at those seducing spirits with the Sword of the Spirit, we advance, swiping at them with our shield and kicking at them with our Gospel shoes. If a devil gets too close, we head-butt it with confidence in our Captain and His power to deliver. Be forewarned: if you engage such enemies without having firmly in place the breastplate of righteousness and your loins girt with truth,

---

[1366] Matthew 17:20
[1367] Matthew 6:30; 8:26; 14:31; 16:8
[1368] Ephesians 6:12)
[1369] I Timothy 4:1-4
[1370] Colossians 2:8
[1371] I Timothy 6:20
[1372] II Corinthians 10:5

your enemy will prevail. Yea, except first you submit to God, your resistance, though ever so valiant, will fail.[1373]

The Weapons of God's Warriors

Six items are listed in Ephesians 5:14-18: the belt, the breastplate, the shoes, the shield, the helmet, and the Sword. The language of the passage suggests that we always wear the belt, breastplate, and shoes. The other three articles are to be taken up by the believer: the shield of faith, the helmet of salvation, and the Sword of the Spirit.

When a Roman soldier was on the march to war, he might rest from time to time. He would lay down his sword and shield and remove his helmet. When it was time to resume his march or engage the enemy, he would "take up" his helmet, his shield, and his sword; when on a war footing, he never removed his belt, breastplate, or shoes. The way Paul describes our armor tells us we are on a war footing.

We receive our armor from the Lord's armory. The breastplate of righteousness and the helmet of salvation are expressly identified as God's own:[1374] He "put on righteousness as a breastplate, and an helmet of salvation upon His head."[1375] But the sword is the Sword of the Spirit, the Word of God, and Daniel called it the Scripture of truth.[1376] Christ is the truth.[1377] Our Creator has dealt to every man the measure of faith,[1378] which makes up the shield. And since the preparation of the Gospel of peace is His, then the shoes are His, too. It is humbling to think Christ has bequeathed us His armor.

[1373] James 4:7
[1374] Isaiah 59:17
[1375] Isaiah 59:17
[1376] Daniel 10:21
[1377] John 14:6
[1378] Romans 12:3

The Belt

Our loins are to be girt about with truth.[1379] To gird (to encircle) is to put on a belt. The loins, by analogy, refer to our mind. Peter said, "Gird up the loins of your mind."[1380] The Greek word translated *mind*[1381] refers specifically to our deepest thoughts, our imagination, our understanding: the thoughts and intents of the heart.[1382] We gird the thoughts and intents of our hearts with God's truth.

We use a belt to hold something in place, and we use God's Word to hold our thoughts and intentions accountable to the truth of God's Word. As I have already shown, the primary tactical maneuver in spiritual warfare is to take every thought into captivity to the obedience of Christ. The activity of taking every thought into the obedience of Christ is making sure our belt is in place and tight. This action sanctifies us; that is, it sets us apart to God. Jesus said, "Sanctify them through thy truth: thy word is truth."[1383]

We gird our loins by reading, meditating on, and memorizing Scripture, and subordinating every thought to the Scripture of truth.

The Breastplate

The breastplate protects both the heart and belly—the Holy Place and the Most Holy Place of the New Testament Temple. And this breastplate is of righteousness. The righteousness of God is sometimes represented by gold and as a mighty impenetrable fortress. If I said, "Here is a breastplate of gold," you would think it was precious and

---

[1379] Ephesians 6:14b
[1380] I Peter 1:13
[1381] *Mind* translates the Greek word διάνοιας (*dianoias,* Strong No. 1271).
[1382] Hebrews 4:12
[1383] John 17:17-19

beautiful, but not particularly useful for protection. Such a breastplate would be more for a show of status than for warfare. But ours is a spiritual breastplate, and it is made of righteousness. This breastplate can secure the weakest soldier against the most powerful of Satan's blows.

Even if our enemy gets past our shield and our sword, and lays upon us the mightiest of blows, we may take comfort in knowing our inner breastplate, the righteousness of Christ, will not fail us. However, there is something we must understand about this breastplate.

Two aspects of righteousness make up our breastplate: the imputed righteousness of Christ and the personal righteousness of the saints.

Imputed Righteousness

The imputed righteousness of Christ refers to the great truth that our eternal salvation rests not upon our righteousness, but upon the righteousness of Christ Jesus, our LORD. Our acts of righteousness are as "filthy rags"[1384] to God, so that "there is none righteous, no not one."[1385] No amount of deeds we deem righteous could deliver us from God's judgment. Paul wrote, "Not by works of righteousness which we have done, but according to His mercy He saved us."[1386]

Imputed righteousness speaks of the fact that God assigned to us the righteousness of His Son; that is, God ascribed Christ's righteousness to our account. He did this without regard to our works.[1387] Christ has provided the breastplate of righteousness; it protects the Holy place (our body as a whole) and the Holy of Holies (our heart) of the New Testament Temple.

[1384] Isaiah 64:6
[1385] Romans 3:10
[1386] Titus 3:5
[1387] Romans 4:6

Even when in our own heart, we judge ourselves unworthy, and Satan accuses our conscience, "God is greater than our heart, and knoweth all things."[1388] When our failures trouble our conscience, it is comforting to know, "Nevertheless the foundation of God standeth sure, having this seal, The Lord knoweth them that are His."[1389]

However, the Apostle John—who told us that if our heart condemns us, God is greater than our heart—also said, "Beloved, if our heart condemn us not, then have we confidence toward God. And whatsoever we ask, we receive of Him, because we keep His commandments, and do those things that are pleasing in His sight."[1390]

If we do not those things that please God, Satan will land multiple, powerful blows upon the breastplate of righteousness. And while he cannot hope to break through the righteousness of Christ, the mighty blows upon the breastplate can shake our confidence and cause our heart to cower in doubt. So Satan can hinder our prayer life, and stop the flow of the Holy Ghost from His Temple into the world.

A condemning heart will rob our confidence toward God; and this will negatively impact our effectiveness as prayer warriors. We cannot come boldly before the Throne of grace to find the mercy required for our time of need.[1391] This could be the cause of devastating losses in our current battles in God's War.

Probably the worst of all consequences is when the believer's heart becomes dead to the blows. These hearts have gone beyond grieving the Spirit;[1392] they have quenched

---

[1388] I John 3:20
[1389] II Timothy 2:19
[1390] I John 3:21-22
[1391] Hebrews 4:16)
[1392] Ephesians 4:30-31

Him.[1393] Sometimes Satan seduces the Christian warrior to believe grace is God's permission to sin when the truth is grace is God's provision to overcome. Deceived Christians permit themselves to live after the flesh. Having become puffed up, they have long lost any fervent passion for holiness.[1394] They turn the "grace of our God into lasciviousness"—sensuality.[1395] Other times it is accomplished by establishing a root of bitterness that springs up and defiles all around them.[1396] This leads me to the next aspect of the breastplate of righteousness.

Immediately after Paul assured us the foundation of God is sure, sealed by the fact that, "The Lord knoweth them that are His," he said, "Let every one that nameth the name of Christ depart from iniquity."[1397] God expects His children to do right. The second aspect of the breastplate of righteousness is the personal righteousness of the saints.

Imparted Righteousness

We have made the doctrine that we are saved by grace the enemy of the truth that we are saved "unto good works."[1398] Believer-priests, aka, God's warriors, aka, God's soldiers, are expected to honor their heritage and aspire to the ranks of those, "Who through faith subdued kingdoms, wrought righteousness, obtained promises, stopped the mouths of lions, quenched the violence of fire, escaped the edge of the sword, out of weakness were made strong, waxed valiant in fight, [and] turned to flight the armies of the aliens."[1399] Confusion results when believer-priests fail to distinguish

---

[1393] I Thessalonians 5:19
[1394] I Corinthians 5:2; II Corinthians 7:1-2
[1395] Jude 4
[1396] Hebrews 12:15
[1397] II Timothy 2:19
[1398] Titus 3:5; Ephesians 2:8-10; Romans 4:6
[1399] Hebrews 11:33-34—emphasis added

the righteousness that is through faith from that which is of the flesh. Allow me to clarify.

The righteousness that is of the flesh is self-righteousness—an arrogant presumption that God would or even could receive anything that is after the flesh. The Scriptures say those who are in the flesh cannot please God. But we are not in the flesh, and so we can please Him. But only by faith: for "without faith it is impossible to please Him."[1400]

By faith, we acknowledge that "in me (that is, in my flesh,) dwelleth no good thing."[1401] And so we repudiate the arm of flesh and follow after Christ's Spirit, and walking in the Spirit, we do not fulfill the lusts of the flesh.[1402] Our faith in Christ directs us to obey Him and do what is right in His sight; this is our righteousness.

Some who are jealous for Christ do err in their zeal. Zealous to affirm the absolute inability of man to please God by his own righteousness, they confuse the saint by suggesting he can do nothing right. It's true that in our flesh there is nothing good.[1403] But it's also true that by faith we can please God.[1404]

Hundreds of Scriptures attest to God's expectation that His children do works of righteousness. It is astonishing anyone should think Christians cannot do such works. Flabbergasting that some suggest God doesn't expect this from His children. Shocking that anyone should think it does not please the Heavenly Father when His children perform good works. It's utter nonsense, and this false teaching has done much damage to the cause of Christ and

---

[1400] Hebrews 11:6
[1401] Romans 7:18
[1402] Galatians 5:16
[1403] Romans 7:18
[1404] Hebrews 11:6; Romans 8:8-9; I Thessalonians 4:1

His kingdom. The fact that no works of righteousness that we do can save us is an important truth. But the idea that God does not expect or reward the works of righteousness of His children is devilish.

The daunting task of assembling the hundreds of Scriptures that show God expects good works from His children and rewards them for the same is unnecessary. All the work is done in one passage.

> For by grace are ye saved, through faith; and that not of yourselves: it is the gift of God: not of works, lest any man should boast. For we are His workmanship, created in Christ Jesus unto good works, which God hath before ordained that we should walk in them. — Ephesians 2:8-10

All who name the name of Christ must "depart from iniquity" and bring forth the fruit of repentance, which is good works.[1405]

The breastplate of righteousness is the righteousness of Christ; indeed, "He put on righteousness as a breast-plate."[1406] But we compromise the integrity of our witness for Christ if we live unholy, or ungodly before the world. Satan knows how to pound on the breastplate, protesting his just accusations against us loudly. This weakens our faith. Weak faith reduces our influence with God, and so reduces Christ's influence in the world through us.

When the soldier is compromised—with Satan pounding on the breastplate—and his heart is weak, what shall we do? The answer requires that I borrow insights revealed later regarding the shield of faith. It begins with our belief that "God is greater than our heart!" God

[1405] II Timothy 2:19; see Luke 13:27; and Psalm 6:8; with Matthew 3:8; with Acts 26:20
[1406] Isaiah 59:17

is our judge, not our heart. There is a certain vanity in the notion that we are qualified or disqualified by the standards and expectations we create. The Spirit will correct us: "God is greater than our heart." And He has provided for us to confess our sins, with the promise that He is "just and faithful to forgive us our sins, and to cleanse us from all unrighteousness."[1407] We come to the Father under the Blood of the Lamb of God, and at the sight of that Blood, Satan must back away in defeat.[1408]

The Shoes

Our feet are to be "shod with the preparation of the gospel of peace."[1409] To shod is to put on, and to "shod with the preparation of the gospel of peace" means to put your shoes on in readiness to preach the Gospel. The Gospel is the message that when preached if believed, effects the salvation of the souls of men.[1410]

We understand that to shod our feet in preparation to preach is not itself the act of preaching. To put on our Gospel shoes speaks to our readiness to preach the Gospel to sinners.

The Gospel threatens Satan. It removes men and women out from under his power[1411] and turns them into a potential threat to his ability to hold his usurped place in this world. Remember, he has no legal right to hold any place in this world. Christ Jesus defeated him, spoiled all principality and power, and made it all His own. Christ's unfaithful priests have yielded to Satan any "place" in this Earth that he presently holds.[1412]

[1407] I John 1:9
[1408] Revelation 12:11
[1409] Ephesians 6:15
[1410] I Corinthians 15:1-3
[1411] Acts 26:18
[1412] Ephesians 4:27

Understand that Christ draws all men to Himself.[1413] He does this by the Holy Ghost manifesting Jesus in our mortal flesh, and through our belly moving into this world to reprove it of sin, righteousness, and judgment.[1414] We can put our Gospel-ready shoes on, but our effectiveness is reduced if we are not filled and flowing.

Many who evangelize today are walking after the flesh and not after the Spirit. For this reason, they must depend on the arm of flesh to gain their converts. They are reduced to using the techniques of the salesman. Fleshly, sentimental appeals, and carnal-minded psychological manipulation are used to recruit sinners to join their churches. Sincere but mislead Christians are taught to hustle non-Christians into repeating a prayer with the promise that, if they do, they'll go to heaven when they die. The Gospel is elegantly simple. And all who repent and believe on Jesus as alive and as Lord will certainly be saved when they "call upon the Name of the Lord." But many conversions today are spurious. Often sinners are unwittingly recruited into the ranks of those that will protest in amazement when, expecting to be received into Heaven, Jesus says, "I never knew you: depart from me, ye that work iniquity!"[1415]

No one is saved who did not become so when responding with godly sorrow to the drawing of the Holy Ghost: reproving his or her conscience for sin, righteousness, and judgment.[1416] Only godly sorrow will work repentance unto salvation, which Paul described as the sinner turning from darkness to light, and from the power of Satan to God.[1417] No

---

[1413] John 12:32
[1414] John 16:7-11
[1415] Matthew 7:23
[1416] John 12:32, 16:7-9; Acts 24:25
[1417] II Corinthians 7:10; see Acts 17:30; 26:14-20

sinner is saved until he confesses with his mouth that Christ Jesus is LORD and believes in his heart that Christ rose from the dead. Then, in that case, when the sinner "calls on the name of the LORD," he will be saved.[1418]

There is no formula prayer. One sinner smote his breast and lamented, "God, be merciful to me, a sinner."[1419] Another prayed, "Lord, remember me when thou comest into thy kingdom."[1420] In every case, the sinner was responding to conviction with a sincere heart, acknowledging their sin, and turning to God for forgiveness.

Every sinner saved is made a saint. And every saint receives a pair of Gospel shoes: Jesus commands us to go "into all the world and preach the gospel to every creature."[1421]

The shoes are essential in spiritual warfare. They protect our feet from the filth of the world, and from what might harm them. God cares about taking care of our feet. He describes the feet of those who preach the Gospel to others as beautiful.[1422] Jesus washed the feet of His disciples.[1423] Our feet get dirty very quickly when we walk about in this world without our shoes on.

Believer-priests must never take these shoes off; they are responsible for preaching the Gospel wherever they go, whether or not they want to. Their own testimony is all that is needed to be an effective witness. But if they drag their feet through the muck (fleshly sins) of this world, they will bring reproach upon the Gospel and make their feet dirty.

[1418] Romans 10:9-13
[1419] Luke 18:13
[1420] Luke 23:42
[1421] Mark 16:15
[1422] Romans 10:15; Isaiah 52:7
[1423] John 13:12

We also use our shoes to kick and stomp on the enemy. A readiness to speak the Word of God to sinners gives you a sound footing in any enemy attack. When you encounter any situation, if you are prepared to use it for a witness, that is an excellent advantage to you when wrestling any devil. When you maintain your stand and don't compromise the truth, you will then have a sure footing to stand against the wiles of the Devil.[1424]

Jesus said we have power (authority) to tread on serpents and scorpions, and over all the power (might) of the enemy.[1425] This authority is in the "Gospel of peace" that we preach. We need to get our feet out of the muck of this world and onto the soul-winning trail—to go forward daily, ready to preach the Gospel.[1426] In our Gospel shoes, we may go kicking and stomping on "serpents and scorpions" and prevailing over "all the power of the enemy."

The Shield

Faith is our shield. Jesus repeatedly encouraged us to believe that whatever He does in or through our lives, it will be according to our faith.[1427] Whatever of God's grace (His goodness responding to our need) enters this world, it comes through our faith.

The strength of this article in our armor is almost totally dependent on us. We are all given "the measure of faith" at conception,[1428] but we are responsible for its growth and strength.[1429] Jesus chastised those with little faith.[1430] And He

---

[1424] Ephesians 6:11
[1425] Luke 10:19
[1426] Romans 1:15
[1427] Matthew 9:29
[1428] Romans 12:3; see John 1:9
[1429] II Thessalonians 1:3
[1430] Matthew 6:30; 8:26; 14:31; 16:8

praised those who had "great faith."[1431] Being "full of faith" is directly connected with having the power of God upon one's life.[1432]

Much study and practice in using the Word of God are how we grow and strengthen our faith.[1433] The Scripture is our faith. Understand that faith is not the subjective feeling you might have of confidence in God; it is your commitment to and confidence in the verity of God's Words.

Jesus used the shield of faith each time He quoted Scripture to quench the fiery darts Satan threw at Him in the desert.[1434]

The shield of faith appears to be the most vital of all the items of our armor: "Above all, taking the shield of faith," indicates that this item is most important.[1435] We use it to quench all the fiery darts of the devil. In Jesus' time, the Romans used bamboo shoots dipped in a flammable material, set ablaze and shot by bow or hurled by hand at an opponent. The devil has such darts, and he is deft at using them.

What a picture! Satan is hurling fiery darts at you, one after the other. And he is relentless. The tip of each dart is

---

[1431] Matthew 8:10; 15:28

[1432] Acts 6:8

[1433] Romans 10:17

[1434] Luke 4:1-8

[1435] In Dr. Beckum's excellent book, *Prayer for Revival,* you will find a footnote on page 177 that explains why we do not agree with those who argue that the Spirit intends here to inform us the shield of faith covers all the body of the soldier. Beckum writes the following: The language "above all" consistently indicates the idea of first in order or greater in importance or regard [Genesis 3:14; Exodus 19:5; Numbers 12:3; Deuteronomy 7:6, 14; 10:15; 14:2; 26:19; 28:1; I Kings 14:9, 22; 16:30; II Kings 21:11; I Chronicles 16:25; 29:3, 11; II Chronicles 2:5; 11:21; Nehemiah 8:5; 9:5; Esther 2:17; 3:1; Psalm 57:11; 99:2; 138:2; Ecclesiastes 2:7; Jeremiah 17:9; Ezekiel 31:5; Daniel 11:37; Luke 3:20; 13:2, 4; John 3:31; Ephesians 1:21; 3:20; 4:6, 10; Colossians 3:14; James 5:12; I Peter 4:8; III John 2]. In fact, of the 53 times the expression is used in the KJV, in every instance, it communicates the idea of first in order, or greater in importance or regard. Dr. Beckum addresses the so-called argument from *the Greek* very effectively, but I will refer you to his work if you are interested in pursuing this further.

dipped in some inflaming lust and shot in rapid succession, one evil thought after another, each calculated to stick on your body anywhere and set the whole aflame with anger, wrath, lust for adultery, fornication, or greed-inspiring thoughts of theft. With each arrow, the Devil targets the flesh, warring against the soul.[1436] He hopes to provoke the priest of God's Temple to turn from his or her duties and attend instead to the lusts of the flesh. In this way, the Devil can draw God's priest-king into service to one or more of the works of the flesh. The strategy, of course, is to provoke you to grieve the Spirit. When under such an assault, the believer-priest, God's warrior, must spot the incoming dart and throw up the shield of faith in its path: the words of God—a promise, a command, an exhortation from Scripture.

We hold up the shield as we charge the enemy, and we thrust the Sword of the Spirit at him as we advance. Backing him off, slamming the shield into him, until he is down, and then taking him captive by faith, we subdue that devil and make him flee.

But beware! Every soldier with a trace of rebellion in his or her spirit will fail. Heed the injunction to "submit yourselves therefore unto God." Then when you "Resist the devil . . . he will flee from you."[1437]

Perhaps you would like to see how this looks.

I pray with my Bible open before me. Sometimes I take my atlas also and lay it out before me on the floor while I'm praying. I make sure that I'm surrendered to God, in every area submitted. Then I will lay my hand over China and begin to assault the devils that hold that nation's leaders in their grip. I challenge their authority in the Name of Jesus

[1436] I Peter 2:11
[1437] James 4:7

Christ and start declaring the Word of God concerning the authority of Jesus Christ over Heaven and Earth. I declare His right of power (authority) by the blood He shed on Calvary, whereby He broke the power of Satan over all principalities and powers. And in the Name of Jesus Christ, by the authority invested by Him in His king-priest, I command that these devils vacate their strongholds.

A counterattack from Satan always comes. Strange, bizarre thoughts suddenly flood my mind, inexplicable fatigue, and damning accusations from my past hit me like bullets. Pressing forward, I hold up the shield of faith, and can almost hear the fiery darts quenching as the shield absorbs them. Thrusting the sword of the Spirit (quoting Scripture), every accusation of the accuser is defeated. Fervently I proclaim the LORDSHIP of Christ and His command and promise that His Gospel will be preached in every land. And standing upon that authority, I demand the devils holding China in darkness to flee—for the light of the glorious Gospel is coming to China.

The Helmet

The expression *helmet of salvation* is literally in Hebrew *a helmet of Yeshuah*.[1438] *Yeshuah* is Hebrew for Jesus. The helmet of salvation is literally a helmet of Jesus.

The preposition *of* indicates a relationship between the helmet and salvation, or the helmet and our Lord Jesus.

Helmets protect and identify. The helmet of Jesus protects our head and identifies us as soldiers in His army.

The warrior-priest wearing this helmet is identified as a soldier who wars under the command of Jesus for the salvation of sinners.

[1438] Isaiah 59:17

However, the primary purpose of the helmet is to protect the head. The breastplate (which is righteousness) protects the heart and the belly, the two rooms of the New Testament Temple. Every soldier under the command of Jesus wears salvation as a covering to protect his or her head.

I pointed out earlier that, from a biblical point of view, our thoughts are the activity of our soul by our spirit in our hearts. We never find the expression *thoughts of the head*, but the phrase *thoughts of the heart* appears twenty-three times. However, we experience our thoughts in our heads; or, better, we see our thoughts with our heads. Nebuchadnezzar said, "I saw a dream which made me afraid, and the thoughts upon my bed and the visions of my head troubled me."[1439] Daniel spoke of the visions of his head: "I Daniel was grieved in my spirit in the midst of my body, and the visions of my head troubled me."[1440] The visions of the head are constructed by the thoughts of the heart, and they inform the direction we take in all our physical actions.

The word translated *head* identifies the principal part of something, the chief or captain. The idea is that the head gives direction to the body. It's the decision center.

The confidence we have in our salvation protects our head from being wounded by seducing spirits that will cause us to lose our direction. These blows upon the head can cause us to respond slowly. Satan can provoke our head to direct the spirit of our mind into forming negative thoughts that will fill our hearts with doubt.

Remembering that the primary tactical maneuver in our warfare is to bring every thought into captivity to the obedience of Christ, we can appreciate the importance

[1439] Daniel 4:5
[1440] Daniel 7:15

of this helmet. Satan will try to beat upon the head with clever lies, evil suspicions, and distractions that divert our attention, and finally, our affections, away from our Lord. Always embrace the memory of His death for us on the Cross. Remember His sacrifice; His love commended to us there, His faithfulness in saving our soul. These thoughts will deflect those blows and protect our heads. Never go into battle without salvation wrapped around your head like a helmet.

The helmet is used as a weapon, too. When Satan attacks our thoughts, we can, and should, head-butt him with Jesus' helmet—the helmet of Yeshuah, the Helmet of Jesus: I am an ambassador of Christ, a soldier of the Cross; by the authority of Jesus Christ, I resist the Devil and any devils he sends against me. Head-butt!

And remember, when we put on this helmet, we identify ourselves as soldiers in the army of our Saviour—it is the Helmet of Yeshuah. Put it on! Mindful of the exhortation:

> Let this mind be in you, which was also in Christ Jesus: who being in the form of God, thought it not robbery to be equal with God: but made Himself of no reputation, and took upon Him the form of a servant, and was made in the likeness of men: and being found in fashion as a man, He humbled Himself, and became obedient unto death, even the death of the cross. — Philippians 2:5-8

In *Band of Brothers*, a lieutenant explains to a soldier that the only hope he had was to accept the fact that he was already dead. "And the sooner you accept that," said the lieutenant, "the sooner you'll be able to function the way a soldier is supposed to: without mercy, without compassion, without remorse. All war depends upon it." This was intended to be a cynical look at warfare and was served up as an indictment against it. Indeed, the careful observer will note the undercurrents of pacifist sentiment woven into the narrative of that otherwise great dramatic representation of the Great War! But there is a truth buried in the cynicism. The reason most Christians never perform as the soldiers Christ commissioned them to be is that they hang on to this life and refuse to give it up.[1441] They will not "deny themselves" and "take up their cross" and follow Christ.[1442]

A lie is also hiding in the lieutenant's advice, for the truly great soldier never forgets mercy or compassion. These are the chief motivations for the genuinely great soldier— mercy and compassion for the oppressed to be free, and a sense of executing wrath upon evildoers, satisfying the vengeance of God upon oppressors.[1443] But ours is a spiritual war, and we war on behalf of the mercy of God and with compassion for the lost.[1444]

Putting on the "helmet of salvation" is obedience to the command to "let this mind be in you, which was also in Christ Jesus."[1445]

The Sword

Each item in our armor is both defensive and offensive in its design and use. The same is true of the Sword of the Spirit. But before we look at the defensive and aggressive use of the Sword, let's consider the fact that it is the Sword of the Spirit.

<u>It is the Sword of the Spirit.</u>

The preposition *of* in the phrase *Sword of the Spirit* means

---

[1441] Luke 9:24; 17:33
[1442] Matthew 16:24; Luke 9:23
[1443] Romans 13:1-6
[1444] Jude 22
[1445] Philippians 2:5-8

it is the Spirit's Sword. We are told this Sword is the Word of God.[1446] The Word of God is called a two-edged sword that comes from the mouth of Christ, "And out of His mouth went a sharp twoedged sword."[1447] The Spirit uses the words that come from the mouth of our Lord like a two-edged sword.

We are urged to *take up* this Sword. We take up the Sword of the Spirit when we read or hear the Word of God, and when we heed it and speak it.

For example, when we received the Gospel, the Word of God divided our soul and our spirit,[1448] performing the spiritual circumcision we discussed in an earlier chapter.[1449]

When Christ's soldiers preach and teach the Scriptures to the unbeliever, the Spirit uses that Sword to cut to the heart,[1450] discerning the thoughts and intents of the heart[1451] and exposing its secrets.[1452] Indeed, it is a two-edged sword, for when believers read or hear the Word, the Spirit uses it this way in their hearts also.

We use the Scripture of truth as a weapon to advance the cause of freedom.

Satan keeps those that are lost bound in darkness by lies.[1453] Jesus referred to His Word as light and declared, "The truth shall make you free."[1454] When believers "take" up the Sword of the Spirit, that is, when they read it and heed it and speak it to others, the Holy Spirit uses the "Scripture

---

[1446] Ephesians 6:17
[1447] Revelation 1:16
[1448] Hebrews 4:12
[1449] Colossians 2:11
[1450] Acts 5:33; 7:54
[1451] Hebrews 4:12
[1452] I Corinthians 14:25
[1453] II Corinthians 4:4
[1454] John 8:32)

of truth" to expose the lies that shroud the hearts of the lost in darkness.

The Spirit was sent into the world to reprove it.[1455] The word *reprove* means to make or lay bare, to expose. The Holy Spirit uses the Sword of the Spirit to cut away the lies that blind men's minds, and to expose and destroy the lies that, like chains, bind them in darkness.

This is critical! Jesus explained the reason men do not believe is not because of insufficient evidence to convince a reasonable mind of the truth. It is because they love darkness rather than light. And the reason they love darkness rather than light is that their deeds are evil.[1456] The Sword of the Spirit blows their cover and exposes them to the truth.

Jesus said only those who *do truth* will come to the light.[1457] So Soldiers in Christ's army need to swing the Sword of the Spirit (read, heed, and speak the Scripture of truth) against every lie Satan uses to blind men. This will accomplish two things.

First, by this, the Spirit will fulfill His mission to reprove the world of sin, righteousness, and judgment.[1458] And second, by this, the Spirit will draw all men to Christ, and those who are doers of the truth will come to the light and be saved. See John 3:17-21.

The Spirit was sent into the world to reprove it of sin, righteousness, and judgment. Jesus explained that men love darkness because their deeds are evil. Satan deceives men and women into believing lies that will encourage them to

---

[1455] John 16:8
[1456] John 3:17-21
[1457] John 3:21
[1458] John 16:8

sin bringing evil into the world; it will fortify their resolve to resist the Gospel.

The more grievous the sin, the better. Satan sears the conscience of men and women so they will feel no compunction, no guilt, about it. Then when they hear the word of truth, they will ignore it or despise it. Then, when their conscience is seared, he recruits them to speak his "lies in hypocrisy having their conscience seared with a hot iron."[1459]

Beware, Satan wants to pollute the conscience of children; he wants to get them corrupted at an early age. By sexualizing children, he breaks down their instinctive resistance to sexual sins. Then they are more easily seduced into more vile behaviors that finally will impair their natural revulsion against sin. This will destroy their ability to discern right from wrong, to judge between good and evil. Finally, sinners with a seared conscience not only can violate their conscience without guilt, but they will become Satan's evangelists, "speakers of evil things," "having their conscience seared with a hot iron."

When Christians fail to speak the truth about adultery, fornication, and deviant sexual practices, such as sodomy, pedophilia, and bestiality, our children are given to Satan; our communities are given to darkness.

Children at the age of accountability have an instinctive, intuitive sensitivity to good and evil, and when exposed to such evils, they naturally feel shame and confusion. Even as young as 5 to 7, children exhibit shame when their nakedness is exposed to strangers. It's a natural thing.

The spirit of Antichrist wants our children to become

[1459] I Timothy 4:2

confused, so confused they can't even discern between male and female. Because when he can do this, he can raise a generation that will virtually erase all lines that divide evil from good. Finally, they will call good evil, and evil good, and bring upon US the curse of the Prophet Isaiah:

> Woe unto them that call evil good, and good evil; that put darkness for light, and light for darkness; that put bitter for sweet, and sweet for bitter! . . . Therefore as the fire devoureth the stubble, and the flame consumeth the chaff, so their root shall be as rottenness, and their blossom shall go up as dust: because they have cast away the law of the LORD of hosts, and despised the word of the Holy One of Israel. — Isaiah 5:20

Satan has co-opted our education system in America. He is using the unreasonable and wicked lovers of darkness that are under his control in our culture in places of power and influence to promote the corruption of our children's innocence by their perverted sex education programs.

Teaching children that sexual practices the Bible calls an abomination are acceptable is contrary to the values and traditions of Americans, and threatens the health and happiness of our children. These behaviors are destructive to their health and ruinous to their lives. Teaching a boy that he might be a girl trapped in a boy's body or vice versa fosters confusion, resentment, and often encourages self-destructive behavior.[1460] They aggressively teach our children to view sodomy as acceptable, and that to say otherwise is sinful, evil, hateful, and so forth. Yet this is a disease-ridden lifestyle that shortens the lives of those who

---

[1460] There are literally hundreds of science-based articles addressing concern about the increased suicide risk for LGBTQ youth. Here is a source that provides a large sampling of such articles: https://www.ncbi.nlm.nih.gov/pmc/articles/PMC3662085/#R20.

live it.[1461] Why are we promoting this in our culture? "The thief [Satan] cometh not, but for to steal, and to kill, and to destroy."[1462]

Children of disobedience under the control of the spirit of Antichrist are calling good evil and evil good.

All of this has developed in American culture because Christians have failed to fulfill their role assigned to them by Christ Jesus. They have been tricked into believing they have nothing to say about any of this. Duped by the perversion of separation of church and state, Christians have shrunk into the shadows, afraid to speak the Word of God in the public square. Having intimidated Christians into silence by railing against "imposing our morality," they now impose their immorality on us with arrogance and hatred.

But what is the truth? Christians have been tolerant to a fault of the audacious effronteries cast upon them by the LGBTQ community. Gay-rights activists, on the other hand, have attempted to pass laws that infringe upon the rights of free speech and free association, and even on the religious liberty of Christians. The wicked legislate their immorality. Not content to legalize their vile behavior, they are using the formidable powers of government to force us to approve of their behaviors. But their most egregious effrontery is their effort to steal the hearts of our children. They require us to expose our children to their vile practices without our consent.

[1461] For documentation supporting this concern see the following: Council on Scientific Affairs, "Health care needs of gay men and lesbians in the United States," *JAMA*, May 1, 1996, p. 1355; M. Frisch, "On the etiology of anal squamous carcinoma," *Dan Med Bull*, Aug. 2002, 49(3), pp. 194-209; M. Frisch and others, "Cancer in a population-based cohort of men and women in registered homosexual partnerships," *Am J Epidemiol*, June 1, 2003, 157(11), pp. 966-72; D. Knight, "Health care screening for men who have sex with men," *Am Fam Physician*, May 1, 2004, 69(9), pp. 2149-56; and at least twenty more such sources. Go to http://ww.home60515.com/4 for more information.

[1462] Luke 18:20

The truth is every human being is created in the image and likeness of God and is subject to His will. Every violation of God's laws committed by every man, woman, and child on this planet is written down in His books.

The truth is Christ Jesus is the King of this Earth right now, and every person is subject to His rule and owes allegiance to Him. Every subject of the Crown of Christ will be judged by God's righteousness and not by anyone's personal ideas of right and wrong.

The truth is homosexuality is an abomination to God; it is unnatural, perverse, and extremely unhealthy, as noted above. Nature itself abhors the practice. It's killing those who practice it. Those living that lifestyle are in bondage, oppressed even by their own community.

For example, in California, the State Assembly passed a resolution condemning anyone offering to counsel homosexuals who want to overcome their same-sex-attraction. Those supporting this evil oppression tried to make it a law, but because the outcry against it was so great, they opted instead to pass it as a resolution. Outrageous! These people would oppress a homosexual stuck in an unwanted lifestyle.

Satan lies about the sin of homosexuality constantly, but the truth is, it is a miserable lifestyle. Evil brings sickness, depression, suicide, drug addiction, and domestic violence. In all these categories, homosexuals suffer far more than others. Nothing is more hateful and hurtful to our children than to promote this lifestyle in our culture.

Underneath all the hype about sexual freedom and civil rights, the undertow of the LGBTQ movement is dragging America toward criminalizing Christianity. Making that movement one of two main fronts in our battle with the

Antichrist spirit in America today. The other is abortion. The spirit of Antichrist is using the controversy surrounding these issues first to marginalize and then to criminalize Christianity in America. We must not allow that to happen.

Men do not have children. The absurdity that people reputed to be intelligent and reasonable are advocating the notion that men can have babies reveals the insanity prevailing in America today. Apart from a sinister, devilish plot on the part of Satan to destroy America, the phenomenon is inscrutable.

The only way to fight against this deranged capitulation of common sense, or natural, intuitive understanding, is to speak the Word of God—swinging the Sword of the Spirit against these lies.

Christians must speak the Scripture of truth to all humanity. God's Law and Christ's righteousness must be taught to our children. The Gospel must be preached: all men everywhere must be commanded to repent and believe on Jesus Christ to be saved from the wrath to come. Liberty only thrives where the Gospel survives. We need to teach them "to observe all things whatsoever [Christ has] commanded."[1463]

Meanwhile, Satan does everything in his power to stop Christians from swinging the Sword of the Spirit against his lies. Because when we declare God's truth, the Holy Spirit becomes active in this world and reproves—that is, exposes—the evil that lurks in the darkness. It alone has the power to awaken the conscience of men, especially of our children—and only the truth can set them free.

We must speak the word of truth to our young people about economic systems that defy God and His order. We

---

[1463] Matthew 28:18-20

must warn them against systems that put men under the control of wicked and unreasonable men and women who will use the power of government to oppress them.

Socialism is evil! Not only because it's a failed economic system but because it is a tool whereby Satan takes the place of God in the lives of the people and corrupts them.

More murder has happened under the banner of socialism and communism than any other ideology. Only Christianity has afforded men inalienable rights endowed to them by their Creator. Every other religion, along with every other political ideology, oppresses men, and refuses to acknowledge that their rights are inalienable and endowed by GOD.

It all goes back to the opening chapters of this book: Satan wants to rule men under his children of disobedience. He uses lies to gain this power. Christians have the truth, and they are the only ones who can show mankind the way to liberty and justice for all. The more faithful Christians there are in any country, the more influence the Holy Spirit will have in that culture. And "where the Spirit of the Lord is, there is liberty."[1464]

We use the Sword of the Spirit defensively.

Jesus illustrates using Scripture defensively.[1465] When being tempted by Satan, each time the Devil used the Scripture out of context, Jesus responded by quoting another Scripture that corrected Satan's misuse of it.

When Satan attacks us, we resort to Scripture to find solace and wisdom. When he confuses us, we look to Scripture for clarity and understanding.

When anyone attempts to use the Word of God deceitfully,

[1464] II Corinthians 3:17
[1465] Luke 4:1-16

we correct the error by using the Sword of the Spirit to declare the Word of God truthfully.[1466]

Every lie Satan is using to corrupt our culture today must be answered by the Scripture of truth. Every use of Scripture to combat the lies of Satan is defensive against the assault of the spirit of Antichrist. If used skillfully, it takes the offense in advancing Christ's rule in the earth and puts the spirit of Antichrist on the defense, in retreat.

Conclusion

Paul's description of our warfare, and the armor we must wear in battle, concludes in this very important way:

> Praying always with all prayer and supplication in the Spirit, and watching thereunto with all perseverance and supplication for all saints. — Ephesians 6:18

In other words, we stand with our loins girt about with truth, wearing the breastplate of righteousness and the Gospel shoes. Then we take the helmet of salvation, the shield of faith, and the Sword of the Spirit. Now we are ready. What are our marching orders? Paul said we go forward praying always with all prayer and supplication and speaking the truth to Satan's lies.

Specifically, we must pray for all the saints: Jesus taught us to pray, "Our Father, which art in Heaven, hallowed be thy name," and "give us this day our daily bread," and "forgive us our sins, as we forgive," and so on. We spend too much time on me and mine and not enough on our and us. We must pray for our ministers: "And for me," Paul said, "that utterance may be given unto me, that I may open my mouth boldly, to make known the mystery of the gospel."[1467] In other words, pray God's ministers will be enabled to have boldness as they swing the Sword of the Spirit in their work.

[1466] II Corinthians 4:2
[1467] Ephesians 6:19

Praying is key to successful spiritual warfare. In the next chapter, we will begin talking about prayer warfare. We will learn how to bind the strong man in a stronghold and break his power over the territory he holds. We will learn how to charge the gates of hell and understand what these are.

~

"[P]ublic utility pleads most forcibly for the general distribution of the Holy Scriptures. Without the Bible, in vain do we increase penal laws and draw entrenchments around our institutions."

~ James McHenry

In other words, the answer to increased violence in America is not fewer guns, but *more Bibles and Bible reading.*

(Revolutionary officer; signer of the constitution; ratifier of the u. S. Constitution; secretary of war under presidents George Washington and John Adams. Bernard C. Steiner, *One Hundred and Ten Years of Bible Society Work in Maryland*, 1810-1920 (Maryland Bible Society, 1921), p. 14.)

Chapter Thirty-Four

Spiritual Warfare
(Part One)
Attacking the Gates of Hell

HELL'S GATES cannot withstand the assault of a Spirit-filled church. Jesus commissioned His Church, promising the gates of hell shall not prevail against it.[1468] He gave to it "the keys of the kingdom," which gave her power on Earth to bind and loose with the authority of heaven.[1469] What are the gates of hell and the keys of the kingdom, and what does it mean to bind and loose?

In this chapter, I will explain how to deploy against the enemies of our liberties, how to act on what we have learned, how to identify and pull down strongholds, and how to "resist the devil," causing him to retreat, in short, how to charge the gates of hell and win.

Ground Zero in God's War Today

Satan knows that "The wicked shall be turned into hell, and all the nations that forget God."[1470] A nation turned into hell has been given over to the power of darkness; it has come under the control of Satan. All Satan must do to gain power over a nation is seduce men into wickedness until the nation reaches the tipping point (defined later). Then God turns them over to Satan's power.

[1468] Matthew 16:18
[1469] Matthew 16:19
[1470] Psalm 9:17

A nation does not suddenly fall into Satan's hands. It's a process that can take decades, even centuries. We saw this earlier in those chapters on the history of God's War. But some things are different now. Then, the Spirit of God dwelt between the Cherubim over the Ark within one Temple of God on Earth. Satan had only to neutralize one Temple. Today, Christ has a Temple in the body of each believer, and they are spread all over the earth. Satan must contend with the Spirit of Jesus Christ, which is the Spirit of liberty, in millions of *Temples*, each with the potential to unleash rivers of living water into the world.

It's even worse for Satan. He has lost the power of death. His kingdom has lost all right to power in the earth. And he has been banished from both Heaven and Earth. Today, he operates in between, as the prince of the power of the air.

For all the above reasons, ground zero in Satan's attack has shifted.

After Satan succeeded to compromise the Temple of God fully, and before Christ came into the world, ground zero for God's War was in the power centers of world Empires. Remember? Gabriel and Michael fought the princes of Persia and Grecia over the control of those Empires. But Christ has come, defeated Satan, received all power in Heaven and Earth, and cast out the prince of this world. Ground zero in God's War is no longer in the throne rooms of great rulers. It's the churches. Jesus bequeathed to His churches the keys of the kingdom, and into His disciples the Spirit of Christ.

Today, the King of Earth walks among the churches, which serve as the center of His global operations—this is ground zero in God's War today.[1471] He established His Church in

1471 Revelation 1:19-20; 2:1-2

the earth and bequeathed to her the keys of the kingdom.[1472] Christ gave to His disciples His goods, the spoils of His victory over Satan's kingdom of darkness.[1473] And He commissioned them to declare to all the world His terms for their surrender.[1474] He empowered them to overcome devils and diseases[1475] and charged them to hold what is His, to occupy, until He returned.[1476] He warned them, "Be ye angry, and sin not: let not the sun go down upon your wrath: neither give place to the devil."[1477]

Meanwhile, Satan prowls the air seeking any on Earth he may devour. Sadly, he has found plenty to eat. Many Christians are only too willing to give him a place on this planet. Satan has gained so much place in the earth that Christians are about to lose their place in it.

Everywhere Satan has been given place in the earth, he sets up the gates of hell to enclose and protect the usurped territory.

What Are the Gates of Hell?

Scripture uses the words *gate* or *gates* as a reference to the seat of power (authority) of a city.[1478] It refers to the defenses of a

---

[1472] Matthew 16:16-19

[1473] See Matthew 12:29, and Colossians 2:15—Jesus spoiled all the "goods" held by Satan, and those "goods" included all "principalities and powers." Then see Matthew 25:14 where we see He "delivered unto [His servants] his goods."

[1474] See Mark 16:15; Matthew 28:18-20; etc. — Jesus charged His disciples to preach the Gospel; see Romans 1:16 — the Gospel is the power of God unto salvation; see Romans 10:16; II Thessalonians 1:8; I Peter 4:17 — sinners must "obey the gospel" to be saved from the flaming fire vengeance of God; see Acts 17:30 and 16:31 — the Gospel command is that all men everywhere repent and believe on the Lord Jesus Christ; see Romans 10:9-13 — the terms of surrender include: "Confess with thy mouth the Lord Jesus," and "believe in thine heart that God hath raised Him from the dead."

[1475] Mark 3:15; James 4:7; 5:15

[1476] Luke 19:13

[1477] Ephesians 4:25-26

[1478] Jeremiah 37:13; Nehemiah 1:3; 2:3; 3:3; and of Sodom in Genesis 19:1; and Gaza in Judges 16:3

kingdom or its strength and power to resist invasion. When an army takes the gate of its enemy, it has overcome the enemy's defenses and taken control of their territory. The conquering army will, usually, fortify the gate to secure and defend their newly acquired possession.[1479] In the case of the gates of hell, they mark territory held by the powers of hell—the kingdom of darkness, Satan and his devils.

The gates of hell are the fortifications Satan sets up in the world to mark and hold territory he has usurped in it. From these fortifications, he sometimes launches covert and sometimes open assaults against Christ and His churches. He defends these fortifications against any effort to reclaim that territory for Christ or to resist his efforts to expand his control. These fortifications are Satan's strongholds.

Spiritual and physical entities guard Satan's strongholds. The spiritual entities that protect a stronghold are devils. These devils have physical counterparts—individual children of disobedience under the control of one or more of Satan's devils.

Christians, and especially the Church, are the only real threats to a satanic stronghold. To neutralize the threat from Christians, Satan tempts them into sinning and then accuses them to God. To neutralize the threat of a church, he stirs up dissension, encourages apathy, plants false doctrine, and attempts to seduce the leadership into his control. Christians and churches that give place to Satan play into his hands. The church becomes lukewarm, or so compromised in the spiritual community that devils laugh and mock them, and thus compromised in the physical community, so no one takes them seriously. This serves to undermine their ability to resist the Devil and it gives the world what it needs to

---

[1479] Genesis 22:17; see also Nahum 3:13

justify its scorn of the Christian and the churches. It leads, finally, to God casting His own into the streets to be trampled under the feet of men, as Jesus warned.[1480]

Compromised Christians and churches are without God's power, and so easy prey for Satan, who is continuously prowling about seeking to make a meal of us.[1481] The more Christians he can devour, the more territory he gains in this world. The more territory he gains, the stronger he becomes to tempt, and then accuse, and then abuse, and finally to devour more Christians, gaining greater territory in the world.

As Satan gains control of territory in this world, he places unreasonable and wicked men and women into positions of power who are under his control.[1482] Satan greedily takes up any power Christians are willing to give him. When he gains control of some area of a nation—say education, religion, the economy, politics, entertainment, or science—he establishes strongholds, advancing hell's gates. Then he appoints powerful devils to guard and defend those gates.

Genuine Christians find themselves increasingly marginalized and then pushed out of any territory Satan controls. The ultimate objective is to rid the earth of the influence of the Spirit of Jesus Christ[1483] so that Satan can reclaim power over all the kingdoms of the earth. Christians and churches are the primary targets of these devils, and so they are the targets of the children of disobedience who serve those devils.

Satan focuses on Christians and the churches because only in them is the power to charge the gates of hell and overcome them. Christians and Christ's churches have the keys of the kingdom.

[1480] Matthew 5:13; see also Romans 11:21
[1481] I Peter 5:8
[1482] II Timothy 2:26
[1483] Psalm 2

What Are the Keys of the Kingdom? *How are they used in binding and loosing, and what does it mean?*

The expression *keys of the kingdom* speaks of having access to the power (authority) of the dominion. Jesus explains that this authority is used for binding and loosing.

When Jesus healed a woman on the Sabbath day, the Pharisees objected, accusing Him of breaking the law of the Sabbath.[1484] Jesus charged them with hypocrisy: "Doth not each one of you on the Sabbath loose his ox or his ass from the stall, and lead him away to watering?" It's what He said next, however, that provides a vital insight into our discussion: "And ought not this woman being a daughter of Abraham, whom Satan hath bound, lo, these eighteen years, be loosed from this bond on the Sabbath day?" Satan had bound this woman for eighteen years and Jesus, exercising His kingdom authority and power, *loosed* her.

Jesus spoke of the need to bind the strong man before we could spoil his house.[1485] The context of the passage stipulates Satan as the strong man He is talking about binding.

Christ gave the power of loosing and binding to His churches.[1486] The Church has the power to loose sinners from the bondage of Satan and to bind Satan so that his house may be spoiled. Every soul can be saved from the wrath to come, and whatever territory Satan has taken in this world may be recovered for the glory of Christ.

Ultimately, the Gospel is the power of God to break men free from Satan's power. And it is the responsibility of the believer to declare the Gospel to every person in the world.

[1484] Luke 13:13-15
[1485] Matthew 12:25-29
[1486] Matthew 16:19

The Gospel commands all men to repent and believe on Jesus Christ.[1487] When sinners repent, they turn from darkness to light, and from the power of Satan to God.[1488] Satan held the power of death over mankind because of sin—God declared the wages of sin is death, and all have sinned.[1489] But when Jesus died on the Cross, He paid the wages of sin for all humankind.[1490] His blood was shed not only for those who believe but also for the sins of the whole world.[1491] When Jesus died on the cross, He took the power of death from Satan and set all mankind free. Now any sinner who turns from Satan to Christ can be saved from the judgment GOD has prepared for the Devil and his angels.[1492] The terms of surrender to King Jesus are simple: "Confess with [your] mouth the Lord Jesus, and believe in [your] heart that God raised Him from the dead."[1493]

Therefore, when someone repents and believes on Jesus Christ, we have the authority to declare them loosed from Satan's power—their sins are remitted.[1494] And we have the authority to declare sins retained against every sinner that refuses to confess with their mouth the Lord Jesus and believe on Him for the remission of their sins.[1495] They are bound to Satan—their sins are retained.

We take this authority with us into spiritual warfare. Earlier, we learned that all believers are called upon to wrestle against principalities and powers and spiritual

---

[1487] Acts 17:30; 16:31
[1488] Acts 26:14-20
[1489] Hebrews 2:14; Romans 6:23; 3:23
[1490] I John 2:1-2
[1491] I John 2:1-2
[1492] Matthew 25:41
[1493] Romans 10:9-13
[1494] John 20:23
[1495] John 20:23

wickedness in high places. We have the keys of the kingdom, and we may use them to bind and loose. We can overcome the devils that guard strongholds in our nation, state, counties, and cities—over education, entertainment, and the economy, over science, politics, and religion—and bind Satan and his devils, restraining the spiritual power that supports Satan's human resources.

Two things occur. First, the reproof of the Holy Ghost falls upon the sinner's conscience, and the light of the glorious Gospel penetrates the darkness that holds them in its power. Second, those that refuse to yield to the authority of the Holy Ghost will be brought into confusion, and their efforts to hinder the work of Christ will be frustrated and defeated. Often, the very machinations they attempted to use to hinder the work of Christ will turn on them. They will fall into their own snares.

Conclusion

Satan's gates are strongholds where he defends territory that unfaithful Christians have given him. These spiritually dull, lazy, carnal-minded Christians have sold out to Satan to satisfy the lusts of their flesh. Now it is time to learn more particularly how to pull down these strongholds.

∼

Chapter Thirty-Five

Spiritual Warfare
(Part Two)
Attacking the Gates of Hell—Pulling Down Strongholds

ATAN'S GATES are strongholds protecting the area he has been given by believers who are under his influence in this world. These gates give him an outpost station in the world. From this outpost station, he can launch attacks on Christ's Temple and neutralize the children of obedience and take even more territory into his control. He posts powerful devils at these gates to protect his newly acquired territory. These are Satan's strongholds. In this chapter, we will learn more particularly how to pull them down.

Identifying Strongholds

A stronghold is a gate of hell reinforced by Satan to hold territory yielded to him by weak, backslidden, worldly Christians. When Christians surrender to the lusts of their flesh or follow the seducing spirits that teach devilish doctrines, Satan gains territory in their life, and through their life, into this world. This grieves and quenches the Holy Spirit so that He doesn't enter the world, which allows Satan to go about his evil deeds unchecked.

A stronghold, therefore, is any area Satan holds under his power.

Satan Can Seduce Believers Into Becoming A Tool He Uses to Oppose Christ

Satan uses every believer he controls to hinder the Gospel ministry. Take Peter as an example.

Once when Jesus spoke of His crucifixion and resurrection, Peter confronted and rebuked Him, effectively saying he would never allow that to happen.[1496] Jesus said to Peter, "Get thee behind me, Satan."[1497] Satan used Peter to oppose Christ's plans and purpose.

Satan uses believers in this way when they allow themselves to be deceived by him. These believers are under the power of Satan, enclosed within the gates of hell, and those who are spiritual must attempt to restore them, but they need to be careful. Jesus warns this must be done in humility lest those attempting to rescue a snared believer find themselves tempted into one of Satan's snares.[1498] If we attempt to restore a brother snared by Satan in a spirit of pride, we can end up stuck in the same snare.

Satan Has Manipulated Believers Into Yielding Territory to Him In Almost Every Area of Life

Education,[1499] entertainment,[1500] science,[1501] and politics[1502] are territories held by Satan in America today.

The education and entertainment industries champion abortion, which is the shedding of innocent blood,[1503] and the so-called Gay-Rights agenda, which is against nature

---

[1496] Matthew 16:21-24
[1497] Matthew 16:23
[1498] Galatians 6:1
[1499] Colossians 2:8
[1500] Ezekiel 8:12; Genesis 6:5
[1501] Falsely so-called—I Timothy 6:20
[1502] Hosea 8:4
[1503] Deuteronomy 19:10; II Kings 21:16

and nature's God.[1504] Even science is co-opted to buttress these evils. With fake science,[1505] they claim that homosexuals are born that way, that there are more than two genders, and that the baby in the womb is not a human being.

Also, the politicians wielding their influence to manipulate our laws are using the powers of government to endorse and support these evils. Using the government to encourage these evils gives clear evidence that Satan holds these politicians under his authority.

Add the evidence that Satan has made significant gains into religion, where groups of denominations gather together to stand with the unreasonable and wicked and lend their support to the power of Satan. Rather than "Get thee behind me, Satan!" these denominations are bidding Satan lead the way.

Jesus gave power to His disciples to overcome Satan. The only reason he has been able to obtain so much influence in the world is that Christ's disciples have betrayed the King.

Satan's strongholds are relatively easy to identify. You see them wherever darkness prevails over the minds and hearts of men, wherever Satan's agenda is being served, supported, and advanced in our culture. And these strongholds are guarded by powerful devils working through strategically placed children of disobedience to advance his agenda. His primary objective, to stop the Holy Ghost from moving into the world through the Temple of God. He must! In no other way can he bring the world under his power and raise the man of sin, leading all nations into a one-world government and a final confrontation with Christ in his dispute over control of the dominion.

[1504] Romans 1:18-31
[1505] I Timothy 6:20

Pulling Strongholds Down Or Charging the Gates of Hell

Paul said the "weapons of our warfare are not carnal, but mighty through God to the pulling down of strong holds."[1506] I call this the weapons clause in Paul's statement on spiritual warfare. He was rebuking the Corinthian believers who proudly assumed he was acting according to the flesh. The Apostle explained that he was at war, that the weapons he used were not carnal, but "mighty through God," and that his focus was not on the flesh; instead, he was "casting down imaginations, and every high thing that exalteth itself against the knowledge of God, and bringing into captivity every thought to the obedience of Christ."

The weapons clause in Paul's statement is set off from the sentence in parentheses. It is relevant to the point of the sentence; however, the fact that it is set off in parentheses tells us it is a stand-alone statement of truth. In other words, our weapons have a broader range of uses than what is represented in this passage. And the general purpose of these weapons is to pull down strongholds.

Nevertheless, the specific use Paul made of the weapons is a primary use of the weapons of our warfare in God's War.[1507] Remember, our mind is the front line in our battle with devils. And every thought must be examined in the light of God's Word, and if exposed as evil, it must be arrested and brought into the obedience of Christ. However, we also use the weapons of our warfare against the vain thoughts devils stir up in the minds of their human agents, too. We must examine every notion expressed by others in the light of truth.

Indeed, we use the weapons Paul spoke of to expose and cast down the vain imaginations and the arrogant notions that

---

[1506] II Corinthians 10:4; see 3-6
[1507] II Corinthians 10:5

come out of Hollywood and public education. Scriptwriters cleverly craft their evil scripts to support every imaginable Antichrist abomination which pollutes the innocence of children and perverts the soul of our nation. Teachers pressure eight-year-old boys to imagine themselves as girls instead.[1508] Schools force evolution upon our children and continue to include in textbooks discoveries admitted by all to be false. Yea, we use these weapons to cast down the devils, the seducing spirits that inspire these wicked ideas and promote them through their agents until they become accepted commonly in our ever-increasingly darkening society.

When we pull down strongholds, the spiritual supports standing behind the human agents of Antichrist are broken, leaving these children of disobedience without the protection of Satan's cover. They are exposed; the hidden things are brought into the light. When that happens, when the light of truth breaks in on these areas of darkness, then justice and equity can enter.

For example, when Christians pull down strongholds, teachers like the example mentioned above are exposed. When Christians exercise their spiritual authority in speaking the truth against Satan's lies, the evil oppression of unreasonable and wicked men and women is exposed. Light makes it hard work for devils to deceive. When God's truth shines in the darkness of this world, those once blinded in the dark of lies can see. The conscience of the people is set free from the influence of the lies Satan has used to dull them and lure them into a spiritual sleep.

My testimony regarding this will illustrate what I'm

[1508] Newman, Alex, *Freedom Project Media,* May 13, 2019. Nellie Muir Elementary School teacher in Woodburn, Oregon, badgered 8-year-old boy into becoming confused about his gender identity. Parents are suing the school.

saying. I had taught on prayer and fasting at Lighthouse Baptist Church off and on throughout my ministry there. But in 2008-2009, I led the church to engage in spiritual warfare seriously with a "40 Days of Fasting" program. We placed a calendar on a sign-up table, and members were encouraged to select a meal or meals, a day or days, that they would set aside for prayer and fasting. Our goal was that someone in the church would be in prayer and fasting during every meal for forty days.

The church responded wonderfully to the challenge, and we filled the calendar within a few weeks. Then, in May 2010, I began a series of messages on prayer and fasting in spiritual warfare and began challenging the church to "charge the gates of Hell" during a series of specially called prayer meetings on Sunday nights. From this, we launched our spiritual assault prayer teams in July. We specifically targeted abortion and the so-called Gay-Rights agenda as the strongholds we wanted to pull down.

I challenged the church to pray against the strongholds Satan used to support Barbara Boxer and Kevin Jennings. Barbara Boxer was a state Senator from California. Kevin Jennings, a homosexual, appointed by Obama's Secretary of Education to be Assistant Deputy Secretary for the Office of Safe and Drug-Free Schools, used his position to aggressively promote the "Gay Agenda" in our public schools. Specifically, I challenged the Spiritual Assault Teams and the church, in general, to pray God would expose the horrors of abortion to the American people.[1509]

Kevin Jennings' service ended in 2011. Barbara Boxer decided not to run for reelection and served out her last term with Republicans in control of both houses of Congress.

[1509] See www.santamarialighthouse.org: "Spiritual Assault Teams" for a sample of the letters we used and the strongholds we targeted in July 2010.

As for the abortion industry, in 2019, you have seen what amounts to a pro-life revolution sweeping our country. Alabama has banned all abortions except when a mother's life is in danger. Mississippi, Ohio, Georgia, and Kentucky have passed what are called heartbeat bills, making it against the Law to perform an abortion if the baby's heartbeat is detectable. Louisiana, South Carolina, West Virginia, and Florida are working to pass legislation that restricts abortion when a heartbeat is detectable. Texas tried but failed to pass a heartbeat bill into Law. Arkansas and Utah increased restrictions on abortion, but judges in their respective states blocked them. It all began when God heard our prayers and He began exposing the real heart of abortion to the general public. Project Veritas exposed Planned Parenthood's monstrous practice of selling baby body parts. New York's governor and all who supported him revealed the real character and heart of abortion, calling for the murder of the unborn to be legal up to birth. There is no longer any pretense about *fetuses* or *blobs of tissue*. They are murdering babies.

We are far from any victory dance! The battle is raging with higher intensity than ever before. The country is almost wholly polarized between the Left and the Right. Hostility is increasing! As conservative Christians enter the culture war, becoming public in their opposition to the Antichrist agenda, many on the Left are becoming increasingly hostile, even physically aggressive. Finally, once-sleepy Christians are waking up and joining their fellow warriors long in the fight against those that are dragging our nation out from under God. Biden recently said the upcoming election is a fight for the soul of America. He is right! There is a tug-of-war over the soul of our nation.

One side is trying to pull us out from under God. They have been winning for several decades. The other side is trying to pull us back. Lately, enough have grabbed the rope on the side of the God and Country patriots that we have begun to pull this nation back toward our Founders' vision for America. We'd better step it up. Dig in—PULL! We must fight for every inch!

Like other conservative pastors, I have for years preached and taught against the sins of abortion, sodomy, the sexualization of our youth, the corruption creeping into our politics. Many faithful shepherds have raised the alarm against the efforts of secularists to silence Christian voices of dissent. We have been appalled by the effort to criminalize our faith—evidence the spirit of Antichrist in our country is prevailing. In 2008, Obama's declaration that "America is no longer a Christian nation," was followed by a significant pause, before he clarified, "at least not just." The statement was a signal indicating an epochal course change was ahead. His was the first presidency in America to show open disdain for Christians, evidenced by disparaging remarks, like the infamous God and gun-clingers statement; his refusal to enforce the Defense of Marriage Act, and his open encouragement of the abominable and life-threatening homosexual lifestyle, to name a few. By 2010, Christians were feeling disenfranchised; but nothing seemed to change until Lighthouse Baptist Church, and many other like-minded churches, began to fast and pray. That is when we started to see significant results.

How Do You Pull Down Strongholds in Spiritual Warfare Through Prayer?

Spiritual Assault Teams require warrior priests. We call them Prayer Warriors! It's an expression we use a lot at

Lighthouse Baptist Church. It's not unique to us; we did not coin the phrase. But we sure use it! You've learned enough by now to understand the concept. We do war by prayer.

After Paul, by the Spirit, challenged us to enter spiritual warfare and described the armor of our weaponry, he charged us to go forward into battle, "praying with all prayer and supplication in the Spirit, and watching thereunto with all perseverance and supplication for all saints."[1510] He commissioned us to be prayer warriors.

What does it mean to pray in the Spirit? The expression *in the Spirit* (capital *S*) is used eight times in the New Testament.[1511] The key verses are Romans 8:9; Galatians 5:25; Romans 8:1, 4; and Galatians 5:16.

In Romans 8:9, we are told that we are not in the flesh but in the Spirit. This was clarified earlier when I explained spiritual circumcision. Essentially, it means the Spirit separated our flesh from our life, and then hid our life with God in Christ. Because the Holy Ghost is omnipresent, our placement in the Spirit allows us to have an immediate presence in Heaven. And Christ, being in us by His Spirit, has a direct presence in the earth through our bodies.

Another key verse is Galatians 5:25, where Paul challenges us: "If we live in the Spirit, let us also walk in the Spirit." His Spirit places our life in Christ; therefore, we live in the Spirit. Since we live in the Spirit, we are challenged to walk in the Spirit. To *live* means we dwell or have our being in the Spirit. To *walk* means we live out our lives filled with the Spirit; that is, we take steps to do this or that in the Spirit.

[1510] Ephesians 6:18
[1511] Romans 8:9; Galatians 3:3; 5:16, 25; Ephesians 6:18; Colossians 1:8; I Timothy 3:16; Revelation 1:10

The crucial third verse brings it all together. It does not use the expression *in the Spirit*, but it gives clarity to what it means to walk in the Spirit. It's Romans 8:1, where Paul tells us those who "walk not after the flesh, but after the Spirit," are not condemned. In verse 4, we learn that if we walk "after the Spirit," we will fulfill the righteousness of the Law. This takes us to the fourth essential verse: Galatians 5:16.

If we walk in the Spirit, we will "not fulfill the lust of the flesh."[1512] The idea is that because we live in the Spirit, we are enabled to order the way we behave so that we fulfill the righteousness of the Law and not the lust of the flesh. Remember, we walk physically by putting one foot before the other toward our destination. You move forward on your feet. Similarly, we walk spiritually by directing our thoughts, one after the other, toward the things of the Spirit or those of the flesh. You move forward, spiritually, on your thoughts. Your mind is the steering wheel.

To pray in the Spirit, you must first be in the Spirit. So, first, you need to receive the Holy Spirit, and to do that, you must be saved from the wrath to come. To be saved from the wrath to come, you must humble yourself to the LORD Jesus, confessing with your mouth that He is LORD and believe in your heart that God has raised Him from the dead. Having met these conditions, you must call upon the Name of the LORD. When you do, God will forgive all your sins. You must, by faith, receive His promised forgiveness and salvation. Then you'll have His assurance that He has saved you from the wrath that is coming upon this world.

As a saved person, you have received the Holy Spirit into your heart. Now to pray in the Spirit, you must mind the things of the Spirit. Minding the things of the Spirit means

---

[1512] Galatians 5:16

you have set your mind on what is of interest to Him, and not on the sinful interests of your flesh. When you mind the things of the Spirit, you will take care of your spiritual duties, those things that are of the Spirit. This would include the five New Testament sacrifices we discussed earlier. When you conduct yourself in the New Testament Temple, minding your duties, the Spirit will fill your body. So long as the Spirit fills you, then your spirit will be in the Spirit and not in the flesh. You will live in communion with the Holy Ghost.[1513]

When you pray in the Spirit, the *spirit of your mind*[1514] will come into communion with *the mind of the Spirit.*[1515] Ephesians 6:18 tells us to pray in the Spirit, making supplication for "all saints"; and Romans 8:27 tells us, "He that searcheth the hearts knoweth what is the mind of the Spirit, because He maketh intercession for the saints according to the will of God."[1516]

One clear indication that you are praying in the Spirit is fervency in praying for your fellow believers. It pleases God when He sees His children praying for one another. When you are obeying His command to pray for one another, God will move on you to pray earnestly and fervently in spiritual warfare against principalities and powers. You will begin pulling down strongholds, casting down mountains, and uprooting trees.

What is that about—this business of casting down mountains and uprooting trees? That is the topic of the next chapter.

[1513] II Corinthians 13:14
[1514] Ephesians 4:23
[1515] Romans 8:27
[1516] Romans 8:27

Conclusion

You have learned how to identify a stronghold of Satan. You have been warned that Satan can gain control of believers if they are not minding the things of the Spirit—and you've learned what that means. You have been introduced to the gates of hell and given some basic instruction on how to charge those gates. Let's learn more about how we can reclaim territory Satan has usurped in our personal lives, the lives of our families, our churches, our cities, our states, and our beloved country.

~

Chapter Thirty-Six

Spiritual Warfare
(Part Three)

*Attacking the Gates of Hell—Casting Down
Mountains and Uprooting Trees*

J ESUS LAMENTED the weak faith of His disciples. After giving them power over devils, they encountered one they could not master.[1517] Jesus rebuked the devil, and it departed. The puzzled disciples approached Jesus and asked Him, "Why could not we cast him out?" Jesus said, "Because of your unbelief."[1518] Then He said something remarkable: "For verily I say unto you, if ye have faith as a grain of mustard seed, ye shall say unto this mountain, Remove hence to yonder place; and it shall remove; and nothing shall be impossible unto you."[1519]

In the context of dealing with devils, Jesus spoke of faith that can remove mountains. Was He using hyperbole to make a statement about the weakness of His disciples' faith? Possibly. But my experience with the Scripture inclines me to believe there is more to it.

In another place, Jesus said, "If ye had faith as a grain of mustard seed, ye might say unto this sycamine tree, Be thou plucked up by the root, and be thou planted in the sea; and it should obey you."[1520]

[1517] Matthew 17:14-18
[1518] Matthew 17:19-20a
[1519] Matthew 17:20b
[1520] Luke 17:6

You might wonder what casting down mountains and uprooting trees has to do with God's War! The Scripture reveals that these mountains and trees represent nations and individuals that have arrogantly positioned themselves in opposition to Christ's rule on the earth. Jesus taught us that with faith the size of a mustard seed, we could cast down these mountains and uproot these trees. Jesus taught us that with faith the size of a mustard seed, we could cast down these mountains and uproot these trees.

First, The Master Strategy By Which Satan Neutralizes Our Power To Cast Down Mountains And Uproot Trees

As mentioned above, Jesus told us we could cast down mountains in the context of dealing with devils. We have learned much about Satan's interest in gaining control of governments. We need to learn about how Satan neutralizes our power before we consider how we use our power to resist the Devil's effort to take over nations. We learn that from what He taught us about uprooting trees.

Jesus' promise that we could command a tree to be uprooted and planted in the sea might seem unrelated to our purpose: overcoming Satan's influence in the world. But pay attention to what follows, and you will learn about the incredible power we have over devils and their human agents, and how Satan has effectively neutralized the power Jesus gave to us.

Our Lord had told the disciples they must forgive an offending brother every time he repents. He said that even if an offending brother trespassed against them seven times in a single day if he turns again and says, "I repent," they were to forgive him. Understandably, the disciples exclaimed: "Lord, increase our faith." He responded, "If ye had faith as a grain of mustard seed, ye might say unto this sycamine tree, Be thou plucked up by the root, and be thou planted in the sea; and it should obey you." What can this possibly have to do with the faith required to forgive? More importantly, what has this to do with wielding spiritual power in God's War? One use Jesus said we are to make of the authority that is ours to bind and loose is in the area of church discipline.[1521]

Jesus gave us explicit instructions regarding how to handle offenses. The offended must go to the offender and make an honest effort to reconcile. That failing, he or she must confront the offender again with one or two witnesses, once again in a sincere attempt to be reconciled. If reconciliation is not secured, the matter must be brought before the church, and the decision of the church is final. All of this is laid out in Matthew 18:15-17. What has this to do with binding and loosing?

Immediately after Jesus explained what to do about offenses, He said, "Verily I say unto you, Whatsoever ye shall bind on Earth shall be bound in heaven: and whatsoever ye shall loose on Earth shall be loosed in heaven."[1522]

Remember, when Jesus gave the keys of the kingdom of Heaven to His Church, He said, "Whatsoever thou shalt bind on Earth shall be bound in heaven: and whatsoever thou shalt loose on Earth shall be loosed in heaven."[1523] This is the exact expression used in connection with handling offenses in His churches.[1524]

Unity in the churches is vital to our Lord. If an offending brother merely says, "I repent," His disciples were instructed

---

[1521] Matthew 18:15-18
[1522] Matthew 18:18
[1523] Matthew 16:19
[1524] Matthew 18:18

to forgive him, even if he does this seven times in a single day. Why is this so important to our Lord? I mean, beyond the undeniable fact that our Father wants His children to love one another.

Paul warned the Corinthians that unless they were willing to forgive an offending brother who had repented, Satan would get an advantage over them.[1525] Earlier, the same offending brother was sinning openly, unrepentant and unrebuked.[1526] Paul chastised them for failing to confront the offending brother, whose sin was so egregious Paul instructed the congregation to turn the man over to Satan for the destruction of his flesh.[1527] The church obeyed Paul's instructions, and the man's conscience stirred and moved him to repent. But then the church was in danger of falling into the snare of the devil because they were reluctant to forgive him after he repented.

The whole business is about protecting the Lord's churches from the wiles of Satan, keeping them safe from the devices devils use to destroy the witness of a church. Satan provokes weak members to offend, and proud members to ignore or cover up the offense, positioning the church, awkwardly, even ironically, to have to turn a brother over to their enemy, Satan. And then Satan goes to work provoking the self-righteous in the church to harden their hearts in bitter unforgiveness after a brother does repent. By these means, Satan sets up a stronghold in the church that he uses to neutralize its influence in Heaven and on Earth.

The Lord's Church is the only institution on the earth that has the power to charge the gates of hell and prevail: no wonder Satan concentrates his attack on the churches.

[1525] II Corinthians 2:10-11
[1526] I Corinthians 5:1-2
[1527] I Corinthians 5:3-5

When Jesus talked to His disciples about casting down mountains and uprooting trees, the context was spiritual warfare: using the spiritual authority He gave to His church over devils. In one case, it was about casting out a devil that held territory in the life of a child. In the other, it was about protecting the churches from the Devil's dirty tricks. This business of casting down mountains and uprooting trees has to do with spiritual warfare.

Casting Down Mountains and Uprooting Trees

What are the mountains?

A mountain is used in the Scripture to represent an earthly kingdom. Earlier, we discussed Nebuchadnezzar's dream. In that dream, he saw an image that Daniel explained was a prophecy concerning Nebuchadnezzar's kingdom and the progression of history to the coming of Christ.[1528] At the end of the dream, Nebuchadnezzar saw a stone fall upon the feet of the image and crush it to powder. Then the stone grew and became a "great mountain, and filled the whole earth."[1529] Daniel explained that the "great mountain" was the kingdom Christ would establish in the earth when He returns. A mountain is used to speak of a kingdom.

We see this used elsewhere in the Scripture: For example, the prophet Jeremiah identified Babylon as the "destroying mountain."[1530]

Jesus commissioned us to go into the entire world and preach the Gospel to every nation.[1531] Also, He gave us the

---

[1528] Daniel 2

[1529] Daniel 2:35

[1530] Other Scriptures employing the symbolism of a mountain to speak of a nation or a kingdom are as follows: Isaiah 41:15; Isaiah 52:7 with Matthew 28:18-20 and Romans 10:15; and Isaiah 55:12 with Genesis 18:18, among others. (Jeremiah 51:25)

[1531] Mark 16:15; Matthew 28:18-20

power needed to accomplish our work.[1532] The power He gave us includes the authority to cast down mountains—kingdoms—that rise up proudly against Him and attempt to countermand His instruction.

What about the trees?

God uses trees to represent men or families. For example, Daniel interpreted a dream in which a tree was used to represent King Nebuchadnezzar.[1533] God uses olive trees to represent the Israelites and the Gentiles.[1534]

Men are represented as trees walking. Jesus often healed the blind.[1535] Once a blind man was brought to Him, and Jesus healed him, but the way He did it was very unusual. He led the blind man outside the town, then "spit on his eyes, and put His hands upon him."[1536] Then Jesus asked him what he saw. The man said, "I see men as trees, walking."[1537] Then Jesus put "His hands again upon his eyes, and made him look up." When he did this, the Bible says, "and he was restored, and saw every man clearly."[1538]

Did Jesus have an off day? That seems unlikely. We are not told, expressly, why Jesus did not heal the man so that immediately he saw clearly as He had done so many times before. So, we are left to speculate, and when we speculate, we must do so from within the context of what we know to be true. We are certain Jesus did not have an "off day," and we are likewise sure all that He did He did with purpose.[1539]

[1532] Acts 1:5-8
[1533] Daniel 4:5-33; especially 20-22
[1534] Jeremiah 11:16; Hosea 14:6; Zechariah 4:3-11; Romans 11:17-24; see also Revelation 11:4
[1535] Matthew 11:5
[1536] Mark 8:23
[1537] Mark 8:24
[1538] Mark 8:25
[1539] Luke 19:10

What can we learn from this strange story?

I think Jesus purposely adjusted this man's sight to see men as trees walking because, spiritually, men are trees walking. The first Psalm describes the righteous man as a tree planted by the rivers of water, bringing forth its fruit in season.[1540] Repeatedly, God calls for fruit from men.[1541] Once, Christ rebuked a fig tree that failed to provide its fruit to Him when He came for it.[1542] This represented His complaint against Israel that failed to bring forth the fruit of the kingdom.[1543]

What does it mean to cast down mountains and uproot trees in spiritual warfare?

Remember when we spoke of king Herod killing James and putting Peter into prison? You can read about this in the Scripture of truth; see the book of Acts, chapter 12. The story of Peter's jail-break illustrates Christ's present rule over nations (mountains) and men (trees). It also illustrates the role of the Church exercising her authority in the earth, bringing Christ's kingdom authority to bear upon both nations (mountains) and men (trees).

Herod was able to kill James, but when he put Peter into prison, God sent His angel to deliver him. What was the difference? The Scripture tells us that the church prayed without ceasing for Peter while he was in prison.[1544] To underscore the authority of Christ over kings, later in this same chapter,[1545] Herod gave an oration, inspiring the people of Tyre to call him God.[1546] Because Herod refused

---

[1540] Psalm 1
[1541] Romans 7:4; John 15; etc.
[1542] Matthew 21:19-20
[1543] Matthew 21:43
[1544] Acts 12:5
[1545] Acts 12
[1546] Acts 12:22

to give God the glory, the Angel of the Lord smote Herod: worms ate him as he sat on his proud throne, and died.[1547] Immediately after the Scripture tells us worms ate Herod, the Holy Ghost observed: "But the word of God grew and multiplied."[1548] All these things happened—and were written down—for a reason: these things instruct us in the matter of kingdom power and our use of it in spiritual warfare. A praying church defeated the evil plans of a wicked king.

Paul exercised extraordinary power against men (trees) who would presume to interfere with the Gospel ministry. When Paul and his company came to the Isle of Paphos, the deputy of that country, Sergius Paulus, called for Barnabas and Paul to speak the Word of God to him. A sorcerer was there with Sergius when Barnabas and Paul arrived. This sorcerer was a false prophet, a Jew, whose name was Barjesus,[1549] called *Elymas the sorcerer*. The name *Elymas* is a proper noun constructed from the word that means wizard. This wizard attempted to "turn away the deputy from the faith."[1550] Paul was "filled with the Holy Ghost" and fixed his eyes upon the sorcerer and said, "O full of all subtilty and all mischief, thou child of the devil, thou enemy of all righteousness, wilt thou not cease to pervert the right way of the Lord?" Then Paul declared a curse upon that child of the devil: "Thou shalt be blind, not seeing the sun for a season."[1551] Immediately, *Elymas the sorcerer* was blind and "went about seeking some to lead him by the hand."[1552] That man (tree) was uprooted and set aside from interfering with the preaching of the Gospel.

[1547] Acts 12:23
[1548] Acts 12:24
[1549] Acts 13:6-7
[1550] Acts 13:8
[1551] Acts 13:11
[1552] Acts 13:11

Jesus knew that kingdoms and men under the influence of Satan would do all in their power to hinder His Church from preaching the Gospel throughout the world. This is the reason He gave us the power of the Holy Ghost when He commissioned us to be "witnesses" of His Gospel.[1553]

Conclusion

Consider! Jesus commissioned His Church to preach the Gospel to every nation and equipped her with the power to get it done. That included spiritual power to cast down mountains (kingdoms) and uproot trees (men) that attempt to stand in our way. Regardless, the children of disobedience (evil trees) control almost every nation (mountain) and effectively bar the Gospel from being preached in most of the world today. How? You already know the answer: because Christians have given "place to the devil."[1554] In fact, we have given so much place to the Devil in this world that we are about to lose our place in it. Right now, Christians are the number one most persecuted people in the world. Right now, America is becoming increasingly Antichrist.

If an Antichrist-controlled leader takes hold of the White House, and the Legislature, they will soon retake the Judiciary, and believers will lose their liberties in America. In the next chapter, I explain what we must do. We have the power, but we must understand how rightly to use it.

~

[1553] Acts 1:5-8
[1554] Ephesians 4:27

"There must be religion. When that ligament is torn, society is disjointed and its members perish... [T]he most important of all lessons is the denunciation of ruin to every state that rejects the precepts of religion."

~ Gouverneur Morris

(Revolutionary officer; member of the continental congress; signer of The Constitution; "penman of the Constitution"; diplomat; U. S. Senator: Letters of Delegates to Congress: February 1, 1778-May 31, 1778, Paul H. WallBuilders 11/11/09 6:11 PM http://www. wallbuilders.com/LIBprinterfriendly.asp?id=8755 Page 30 of 34 Smith, editor (Washington DC: Library of Congress, 1982), Vol. 9, pp. 729-730, Gouverneur Morris to General Anthony Wayne on May 21, 1778.)

Chapter Thirty-Seven

Spiritual Warfare
(Part Four)

Attacking the Gates of Hell—America at the Tipping Point

THERE IS NEITHER TIME, nor space, nor need to catalog here all that ails America. You would not likely be reading this book if you were not aware of the dangers we face as a nation. Her problems are from one root: America has forgotten or is in the process of forgetting God. The Scriptures of truth warn: "The wicked shall be turned into hell, and all the nations that forget God."[1555] It is happening: Satan is gaining more territory in this country, setting up strongholds and advancing his control over every sphere of our society—we are in the process of being turned into hell.

It is a process! It happens gradually. A nation steps away from God, not all at once, but incrementally. However, at some point God breaks out in open wrath, and judgment falls. Call it the tipping point, when suddenly all supports give way, and the nation free-falls into hell.

Israel is the model. She trucked along in and out of God's favor throughout her career as one nation under God. Anyone reading through Judges will see the cycle: God's favor and blessing is followed by growing apathy and drift from God, and incrementally they move away from Him until

---

[1555] Psalm 9:17

they reach the tipping point; then the nation free-falls into sin, which leads to judgment, which is followed by repentance and restoration to God's favor. The cycle repeated throughout the history of that first "one nation under God" . . . until finally, God cast off His people. It's important to understand, God provides His nation a generous "space to repent," but it is limited. Judgment will finally fall—and fall hard—upon a nation that forgets God. What criteria triggers the fall of God's wrath upon a nation? What is the tipping point?

Jeremiah laid out God's indictment against Judah at the time He removed the kingdom from Judah and Israel and gave it to Nebuchadnezzar and the Gentiles. The indictment reveals two grievous evils that develop in a nation that forgets God that push it to the tipping point: the shedding of innocent blood and sexual perversity.[1556]

Of course, innocent blood is shed from time to time along the way throughout the history of any nation; and as for sexual perversity, we know that adultery, fornication, and lasciviousness afflict every community. These things are evil, and God has ordained *the power* (the government) to execute His judgment against these evildoers.[1557] And that is the key!

The tipping point occurs when the divinely ordained power not only fails to judge these and other evils, but also becomes a facilitator of them. When the divinely ordained power becomes a defender of evil, it will necessarily be an enemy to good. That's the tipping point!

God gives His nation a "space to repent." The Apostle John mentions the concept in Revelation 2:21: "And I gave

[1556] Jeremiah 5:7; 13:27; 23:14
[1557] Romans 13:1-6

her space to repent of her fornication; and she repented not." Also, illustrations of the principle appear throughout the Scripture of truth. The longsuffering of God with Israel is an example. For almost 900 years He strove with them, sending His prophets and chastising them before He finally removed the kingdom from her and scattered His people all over the world.[1558]

How can we identify America as a nation under God?

First, the kingdom is in the power of Christ to give to whomever He will. He offered it to Israel, but she rejected Him, and so He withdrew the offer and declared He would give it to a nation that brought forth the fruit of the kingdom.[1559] The fruit of the kingdom is repentance toward God and faith toward our Lord Jesus Christ. This character-ized our nation in the period leading up to the Revolution.

Second, we are in the period Jesus called the times of the Gentiles, so the nation that will have the kingdom under God (Christ Jesus) will be a Gentile nation.

Third, it will be a nation founded upon the Gospel of Jesus Christ, where the Spirit of Liberty reigns, and where the God of Abraham, Isaac, and Jacob, the God and Father of our Lord Jesus Christ, is acknowledged.

Fourth, it will be a nation given immense power in the earth, that has been exalted among the nations to be a light of liberty, justice, judgment, and equity. God has exalted America and given her the kingdom.

[1558] God has begun already to fulfill His promise to regather Israel to her land in preparation to restore the kingdom to her. Nevertheless, even now, she continues to be partially blinded spiritually (Romans 11:25), and her beloved Jerusalem will continue to be trampled under the feet of Gentiles until the times of the Gentiles are fulfilled (Luke 21:24).

[1559] Matthew 21:43

Finally, it will not be a nation of perfect, sinless people. Israel had flaws, but she was publicly identified with God and as God's people. And God was willing to favor Israel until she reached what was described above as the tipping point.

When will America reach the tipping point?

America has run through the cycle, identified earlier, several times. We have had lapses into grievous sin as a people, with Divine judgment that was followed by repentance, leading to revival and restoration. However, the difference today is that the government of America is sanctioning evil and becoming an enemy of the good. Our government is increasingly coming under the control of God's enemies. Once this is complete, God will release this *one nation under God* to the power of Hell.

The year 2020 marks a pivotal election in America. The two trigger issues are being clarified right now in America: shedding innocent blood and sexual perversion.

America now knows the truth about abortion; it is the murder of innocent babies. Abortion advocates have shrouded the issue with lies. They told us, "It's okay because it is only a fetus"; they said, "it's only a glob of tissue"; and "it's not a person." Their favorite lie has been, "it is the woman's body, and so it's the woman's choice." But the light of truth has exposed these lies. A doctor who has performed abortions for forty years admitted the fetus is only a word we use to describe a phase in the development of a human being—he acknowledged that the fetus is a baby! As for the argument that the baby is part of a woman's body, science, from the beginning of this debate, has known that the baby is genetically distinct from the mother.

It is clear the abortionist has no regard for the life of the child in the womb, and now openly calls for the murder of babies right up to full term. They cannot call a nine-month-old infant a lump of tissue. Add to this the recent revelation that Planned Parenthood was engaged in selling baby body parts. We learned later that in some cases, the baby needed to be alive at the time the organs were harvested for them to be viable for use. It has become evident that the hellish spirit of Antichrist drives the abortion industry.

Sexual promiscuity in America has blighted our society. Three million teenagers contract a sexually transmitted disease each year. The commercialization of sex encourages a general casual and even flippant attitude about sexuality. Today, there is virtually nothing exclusive about marriage. The family, once regarded as the backbone of the "body politic," the bedrock of our communities, is weakened. Rampant promiscuity has given rise to open perversity. Breaking sexual taboos in the natural expression of our sexuality has opened the door to the acceptance of unnatural sexual deviancy: sodomy (homosexuality), pedophilia, and bestiality are beginning to gain greater acceptance in our society.

According to the Bible, there is a line that divides natural and unnatural sexual sins. The fact that we are abusing God's rules governing the natural expressions of intimacy between a man and a woman is bad enough. He warned that the marriage bed is undefiled, but He will judge whoremongers and adulterers.[1560] Furthermore, He warned

---

[1560] Hebrews 13:4. Under the Old Testament, adultery was punishable by death: "And the man that committeth adultery with another man's wife, even he that committeth adultery with his neighbour's wife, the adulterer and the adulteress shall surely be put to death" (Leviticus 20:10). In the New Testament, we believe this judgment is left to God (Hebrews 13:4; see John 8:11),

that harlotry increases the transgressors among men.[1561] However, sins that are consistent with our nature is one thing, but unnatural deviancy is far worse. America is crossing that line.

Another critical choice America faces in the upcoming election (2020): Will we fully embrace the acceptance and promotion of unnatural affections leading to abominable practices? The Holy Scriptures warn us, "If a man also lie with mankind, as he lieth with a woman, both of them have committed an abomination."[1562] The Gay Rights agenda seeks to normalize a behavior that God calls an abomination. If we capitulate to this agenda, God will undoubtedly answer with judgment.

Paul, by the Spirit, outlined the trajectory of a nation that departs from God, and it ends in Divine judgment.[1563] He showed us that a nation reaches the end of this path when it accepts and endorses unnatural sexual perversion: "For this cause God gave them up to vile affections: for even their women did change the natural use into that which is against nature: and likewise also the men, leaving the natural use of the woman, burned in their lust one toward another; men with men working that which is unseemly, and receiving in themselves that recompense of their error which was meet."[1564] God considers this behavior an abomination. That means He has declared a curse upon it.

The curse of homosexuality is physical. The diseases

[1561] Proverbs 23:28

[1562] Leviticus 20:13. Under the Law of Moses, the penalty for sodomy was death. However, as with adultery, see footnote no. 1560, the judgment for sodomy (homosexuality) is left in the hands of God. Notice that when Paul spoke of the evil of this sin, he did not call for a civil punishment, but said they receive "in themselves that recompence of their error which was meet (fitting)" (Romans 1:27).

[1563] Romans 1:17-32

[1564] Romans 1:26-27; read 1:17-32

associated with this behavior are many, and they are very disturbing, and, of course, many of them are life-threatening. The average life span of practicing homosexuals is almost half that of their heterosexual counterparts.[1565]

The curse of homosexuality is also political. Demanding special rights for homosexuals encroaches upon the natural, inalienable rights of everyone else. As the homosexual agenda advances, we see increasing encroachments upon our religious and civil liberties.

The curse of homosexuality is also spiritual: God gives such people over to a reprobate mind. A culture that embraces this evil is delivered over to the control of fleshly passions, "to do those things which are not convenient; being filled with all unrighteousness, fornication, wickedness, covetousness, maliciousness; full of envy, murder, debate, deceit, malignity; whisperers, backbiters, haters of God, despiteful, proud, boasters, inventors of evil things, disobedient to parents, without natural affection, implacable, unmerciful: who knowing the judgment of God, that they which do such things are worthy of death, not only do the same, but have pleasure in them that do them."[1566]

In the darkness of deceit, the homosexual agenda has been able to gain momentum in our society. The truth about LGBTQ lifestyles is being exposed, albeit slowly. "LGBTQ persons are born that way," "LGBTQ behavior is a natural, alternative, sexual orientation," and "LGBTQ people are victims of bigotry arising from homophobia"— all lies exposed by the truth. There is no scientific basis for concluding that anyone is born gay. Same-sex attraction is not natural, but in fact, it is contrary to nature and

[1565] See Footnote No. 1461 for a detailed list of documentation supporting this claim.
[1566] Romans 1:28-32

nature's God. Resistance to the unnatural practices of the LGBTQ community is a natural societal check against the encouragement of behavior that is socially alienating and life-threatening.

Homosexuals are not only demanding they be free to pursue their lifestyle choice unfettered by our laws and customs. They go beyond and insist everyone agrees with their lifestyle choice, affirms it, and concede to the lie that it is normal. But more egregious than this, the homosexual activist demands that we teach our children the lie that homosexuality is a normal alternative lifestyle choice.

A transgender woman has been hired by a public library to teach teenagers how to do drag. They are already teaching this philosophy to our children in sex education classes in California. When we give our children over to these unreasonable and wicked men and women, we come into direct confrontation with God Who warned: "But whoso shall offend one of these little ones which believe in me, it were better for him that a millstone were hanged about his neck, and that he were drowned in the depth of the sea."[1567]

We are rushing toward the tipping point. So long as the divinely appointed power is in place to check the spread of these egregious evils, God will continue to be temperate in His judgment. Jesus said His followers were the salt and light of the earth. So long as God's salt and light can speak to the conscience of the nation, there is hope. So long as believers have recourse to law, so long as they can appeal for a remedy against the abuses of these unreasonable and wicked men and women against their liberties, then we may hope God will extend the space to repent. However, if the divinely appointed power (the governing institutions

---

[1567] Matthew 18:6

of a nation under God—see Romans 13:1-6) employs that power to promote, facilitate, and protect these evils, and turns its power against the righteous, that nation will be destroyed: God will fulfill His promise and turn that nation into hell.[1568]

America is very close to the tipping point. I believe this upcoming election (2020) will close or continue the space to repent. In this election, Americans will push this nation under God into judgment or turn it back from the maw of hell.

By the way, it is not about personalities; it's about principles of governance. Christians must use their influence as salt and light by voting their conscience. Christians must vote for principles of governance that protect the sanctity of life and the sanctity of marriage. Christians must vote for candidates that promise, and deliver on their promises, to steer this ship-of-state back under the protective wings of the Almighty. We must repent for the wholesale shedding of innocent blood and the defiling of the conscience of our youth by encouraging them to engage in sexual perversity.

Conclusion

Prayer is the key! However, there are other activities that, as we like to put it, put feet to our prayers.

In the next chapter, I will talk about the steps Christian soldiers must take in spiritual warfare to save this "one nation under God."

~

[1568] Psalm 9:17

"To the kindly influence of Christianity we owe . . . civil freedom and political and social happiness . . . . All efforts made to destroy the foundations of our Holy Religion ultimately tend to the subversion also of our political freedom and happiness. In proportion as the genuine effects of Christianity are diminished in any nation... in the same proportion will the people of that nation recede from the blessings of genuine freedom... Whenever the pillars of Christianity shall be overthrown, our present republican forms of government – and all the blessings which flow from them – must fall with them."

~ Jedidiah Morse

(Jedidiah Morse, A Sermon, *Exhibiting the Present Dangers and Consequent Duties of the Citizens of the United States of America*, Delivered at Charlestown, April 25, 1799, The Day of the National Fast (MA: Printed by Samuel Etheridge, 1799), p. 9.)

Chapter Thirty-Eight

Spiritual Warfare
(Part Five)
Attacking the Gates of Hell—SavingAmerica

JUDAH HAD LOST HER WAY and forsaken the LORD. Like her sister did before her. Jeremiah cried: "Stand ye in the ways, and see, and ask for the old paths, where is the good way, and walk therein, and ye shall find rest for your souls."[1569] Judgment was about to fall hard upon that nation under God, and Jeremiah's message was God's last call for repentance before it fell. Their answer back was, "We will not walk therein."[1570] Judah fell!

The call is not for the wicked in our nation to return to the old paths. The wicked are commanded to repent and believe on Jesus Christ to be saved from the wrath to come. Christians are the key to save this "one nation under God."

The Spirit of Jesus Christ is in believers. And when the Spirit fills a believer, He flows through them into the world. The Holy Spirit of Jesus Christ in the believer is the only power on Earth that can overcome the spirit of Antichrist that is in the world. Believers are the key to saving America because in them resides the only power on Earth that can charge the gates of hell and compel devils to retreat. Therefore, Christians are the ones called to stop what they are doing, look at where they are spiritually,

---

[1569] Jeremiah 6:16a
[1570] Jeremiah 6:16b

inquire about the old paths, and then set themselves onto those paths that lead us back under God. What will we answer?

I have written a book titled *The New Cart Church* that I recommend to all Christians who are willing to heed the call to stop what they are doing, look at where they are spiritually, and, if necessary, seek an old paths ministry where they can get involved and do their part to move this nation back under God.

Forward to the charge! How shall we advance?

Prayer changes things. The spiritual and the physical occupy the same space and time; these are two aspects of one reality. I've mentioned this before. Why is it so important? Spiritual events occur in the same time and space that physical events do, and spiritual events impact physical events and vice versa. For example, when you do the physical act of praying, spiritual events occur. These spiritual events impact physical events. To put the point more plainly: prayer changes things.

We will consider four specific things we must do prayerfully in order to save America.

Pray the Prayer of Faith

James spoke of the prayer of faith.[1571] Remember, faith is used both as a noun and a verb. As a noun, the word *faith* refers to the truth of God's Word.[1572] As a verb, faith refers to the actions one takes in response to the Word of God.[1573]

[1571] James 5:15

[1572] The following Scriptures use the word *faith* as a noun identifying the truth of God's Word: Acts 6:7; 13:8; 14:22; 16:5; Romans 1:5; 14:1; I Corinthians 16:13; II Corinthians 13:5; Galatians 1:23; Ephesians 4:13; Colossians 1:23; 2:7; I Timothy 1:2; 3:9; 4:1; 5:8; 6:10, 21; II Timothy 3:8; 4:7; Titus 1:13, 15; I Peter 5:9; Jude 3.

[1573] The following Scriptures use the word *faith* to speak of the activity of believing, that is actions that are in accordance with God's Word: (there are well over 100 such verses in the Gospels alone; I'll offer a sampling from the Gospel of Matthew)

Faith is not a feeling or a sense that something is true. It is common for us to imagine something is true that is not. Yet the feeling or sense that it is true is equally as strong as when we believe something that is. A feeling or sense that something is true does not make it true. Faith, as a noun, refers to the Word of God, and the right apprehension of it, and this must be the ground of any activity that can be called faith.

Therefore, the prayer of faith refers to praying in accordance with the Scripture of truth.

Later in the same passage, the prayer of faith is described as "The effectual fervent prayer of [the] righteous man,"[1574] which, James said, "availeth much"—that is, it gets a lot of work done.

The words *effectual* and *fervent* are necessary to translate one Greek word that is the base of our word for *energy*.[1575] It speaks of energetic, efficient activity that is effectual; that is, it's productive.

The experssion *prayer of faith* means more than that someone prays in a manner consistent with orthodox beliefs. The prayer of faith must be based upon the Scripture of truth, submitted to the commandments of God, and confident in His promises; but it also must be fervent.

Jesus spoke of great faith and weak or little faith. The Gentile woman who refused to give up seeking Jesus' help for her daughter despite His seeming reluctance to hear her prayer illustrates great faith. Jesus exclaimed: "O woman,

Matthew 8:13; 9:28; 18:6; 21:25; 21:32; 24:23, 26; 27:42.

[1574] James 5:16b

[1575] ἐνεργουμένη, Strong No. 1754: ἐνεργέω energeo, *en-erg-eh´-o;* "from 1756; to be active, efficient:—do, (be) effectual (fervent), be mighty in, shew forth self, work (effectually in). Strong No. 1756 "ἐνεργής energes, *en-er-gace´;* from 1722 and 2041; active, operative: — effectual, powerful."

great is thy faith."[1576] Peter illustrated great faith when he walked on water with Jesus, but it quickly turned to little faith when he saw the winds and threatening waves and began to sink. Jesus rebuked him, saying, "O thou of little faith, wherefore didst thou doubt?"[1577]

Happily, it does not require great faith to pull down the strongholds that Satan has established in America. We can cast down mountains and uproot trees with faith the size of a mustard seed. It only requires enough faith to embolden the believer to come confidently before the throne of grace, to obtain mercy and "find grace to help in time of need,"[1578] and then, believing God, "Say unto this mountain, be thou cast into the sea."

Candidate Obama's logo included a symbol of Mount Olympus. The stage upon which he received the nomination of his party eerily resembled the Pergamum altar of Zeus—mentioned in the Bible and called the "seat of Satan." At this altar, Christ's beloved martyr, Antipas, was burned alive in a hollow bronze bull. Obama was a disciple of Saul Alinsky, who dedicated his book *Rules for Radicals* to Lucifer.

It is not surprising, therefore, that Obama governed according to the principles of the spirit of Antichrist: he promoted globalism as well as government sanction and support for the two tipping-point sins—shedding of innocent blood (abortion) and sexual perversity (promoting the homosexual agenda).

Of course, the proud mountain of Olympus could not have risen in America unless Satan had already established

---

[1576] Matthew 15:28—"great is thy faith"
[1577] Matthew 14:31—"O thou of little faith"
[1578] Hebrews 4:16

strongholds throughout, with powerful devils assigned to defend them. Obama's outrageous and open displays of the Antichrist spirit served to awaken many Christians from their slumber.[1579] They began to pray.

We have prayed that Mount Olympus would be cast down, and we have seen much progress to that end; but there are yet many strongholds that must be pulled down.

Many sincere believers have prayed earnestly and fervently that the proud mountain of Olympus would come down; we have boldly voiced our disapproval of his agenda and called for his legacy to unravel. We have prayed, and we have said out loud to that proud mountain, "Be thou cast into the sea." Nevertheless, the Antichrist spirit that has risen in America continues to pull this nation out from under God. Recently, it has nested in the "shadow government," promoting the globalist agenda, subordinating American interests to that agenda, and pulling America out from under God. In some ways, it appears to be gaining rather than waning in strength. How is this possible?

Some kinds of devils are more potent than others. To cast them out requires something more. This takes us to the second thing we must do to save America.

Prayer and Fasting

Sometimes, prayer is not enough. Some devils can only be cast out by prayer and fasting. We need to revisit the story of the stubborn devil.

Jesus had taken Peter, James, and John with Him onto a mountain, leaving the other nine apostles below. While they were gone, a man approached the nine apostles, hoping they would cast out the devil that tormented his son. Jesus

---

[1579] I Corinthians 15:34; Romans 13:11

had expressly given all His disciples the power to cast out devils. Exercising this power had become routine for the Apostles, but, inexplicably, they were unable to cast out this especially stubborn devil.

When Jesus returned with Peter, James, and John, the distraught father ran to Jesus, begging Him to cast the devil from his son, explaining that he had brought him to Jesus' disciples, but "they could not cure him."

Jesus rebuked them: "O faithless and perverse generation, how long shall I be with you? how long shall I suffer you? bring him hither to me." Judgment always begins with God's own House. So, after Jesus rebuked the faithlessness of His disciples, He then turned His attention to the devil. He rebuked the devil; the devil departed immediately; and "The child was cured from that very hour."[1580]

Jesus' disciples approached Him and asked, "Why could not we cast him out?" He explained: "Because of your unbelief: for verily I say unto you, If ye have faith as a grain of mustard seed, ye shall say unto this mountain, Remove hence to yonder place; and it shall remove; and nothing shall be impossible unto you."[1581]

However, Jesus added something He had not before mentioned: "Howbeit this kind goeth not out but by prayer and fasting."[1582]

There are different kinds of devils? *Kinds* translates the root from which we get the word *generation*.[1583] It's used to speak of something derived from another by which it

---

[1580] Matthew 17:18

[1581] Matthew 17:19-20

[1582] Matthew 17:21)

[1583] Strong No. 1085 "γένος genos, *ghen'-os;* from 1096; "kin" (abstract or concrete, literal or figurative, individual or collective):—born, country(-man), diversity, generation, kind(-red), nation, offspring, stock."

gets its identity. There are, obviously, various *kinds* of devils, and this one was surprisingly resistant to the spiritual power of the disciples. This sort of devil is exceptionally strong; therefore, it requires exceptional spiritual power to overcome it.

We get peculiar power through prayer and fasting. Remember, when Jesus was on that mountain, Moses and Elijah stood on either side of Him. Before Peter, James, and John stood the three most spiritually powerful beings the world has ever or will ever know: Each of them is noted for having fasted 40 days and nights.

How does fasting increase our spiritual power? Earlier, you learned about the New Testament Temple and its priest-hood. You learned that the belly is a metonym for our flesh and refers to that part of us where the sin nature resides. You learned about Jesus' prophecy that out of our belly would flow rivers of living water, symbolic of the flowing of the Holy Spirit through our lives into the physical world. You learned that the belly is the door to the Holy Place; it is the point of intersection between our soul and the physical world. It's the place where our Saviour, Jesus Christ, manifests to the world.[1584] This occurs when the Spirit of Jesus Christ is flowing through our belly.

Furthermore, you learned there is a close correspondence between our belly and our soul. Indeed, our soul interacts and intersects with the physical world through our belly/ flesh. The belly is the door of the New Testament Temple. When our soul gets puffed up with pride, we bar the Spirit of Jesus Christ from flowing through our belly and manifesting Jesus to the world around us. For "God resisteth the proud."[1585]

[1584] II Corinthians 4:11
[1585] James 4:6

God resists the proud, but He gives grace to the lowly. When we become prideful, we cannot have fellowship with God; and His Spirit will not fill the Temple of God, nor will He flow through us. We must humble ourselves under the mighty hand of God.[1586] Sometimes this requires fasting. Because of the connection between our soul and our belly, we may humble our soul by humbling our belly.[1587]

Depriving our belly of its necessary food has a direct impact on our soul. By bringing our belly under subjection to our will through fasting, we weaken the influence of the flesh (belly) over our soul. Decreasing the influence of the flesh increases the influence of the Holy Spirit. As the soul becomes humble, the spirit becomes contrite. God is attracted to a humble and contrite spirit, and He will draw close to us and revive us.[1588]

When our spirit is contrite, it is moldable and more easily conformable to holiness (separation from sin and identification with God). In humility, submitting ourselves to God, we can then resist the Devil with much-increased power and influence.[1589]

However, all of this begins with honesty. It is only in the honest and good heart that the Word of God will bring forth fruit.[1590] An honest heart will confess that it is not good, for there is none good but God.[1591] When Jesus spoke of the honest and good heart in Luke 8:15, He was not speaking of the goodness that defines God's perfect nature.[1592] He used the word to speak of what functions properly. In this

---

[1586] I Peter 5:6
[1587] Psalm 35:13
[1588] Isaiah 57:15
[1589] James 4:7
[1590] Luke 8:15
[1591] Matthew 19:17
[1592] Mark 10:18

case, He was talking about a heart that responds to God's Word sincerely. The first evidence that a heart is properly functioning is a willingness to be honest about itself and God.

Honesty continues to be critical throughout our Christian lives. It is always when we fail to be honest with God, ourselves, and with others that we begin to function incorrectly. Honesty is essential because God will not respond to an insincere prayer. Honesty continues to be critical throughout our Christian lives. It is always when we fail to be honest with God, ourselves, and with others that we begin to function incorrectly. And if God will not hear us, He will not empower us. The power we need to overcome the devils that defend Satan's strongholds today requires us to get honest, humble, and holy; and it all begins with honesty.

Humility is the second essential characteristic of the heart that will draw nigh to God, which will attract Him to us.[1593] As I said, it begins with honesty. Often, however, to humble ourselves under the mighty hand of God requires the extraordinary measure of prayer and fasting.

Now we come to the third essential quality God requires of those to whom He will impart His power. Having gotten honest before God, and humbled ourselves, and softened our spirit before GOD, He will draw near to us, and call us into deeper levels of holiness. He will call us to cleanse ourselves of all filthiness of the flesh and spirit, so that we may set about to perfect (complete) holiness in the fear of God.[1594] This will make us a vessel meet (fit) for the Master's use.[1595] We can then present our body to God as a

---

[1593] James 4:8
[1594] II Corinthians 7:1-3
[1595] II Timothy 2:21

living sacrifice, holy, acceptable to Him.[1596] He will then take up this body and manifest greater measures of His power through us than ever before.

Sometimes this involves the Holy Spirit exposing sin in our lives that we have ignored. We often rationalize away the conviction of the Spirit by believing lies, like, God understands I'm only human. Of course, that is true. However, to excuse disobedience to God in this way denies the truth that God has provided for us to overcome and empowered us to obey. Others have gone so far as to justify their sins with carefully crafted lies that justify them. But when we get honest with God and begin confessing our sins, we are made holy.

Unless God's people will sincerely engage in earnest prayer and fasting—honestly, humbly, surrendering to His holiness—we are doomed as a nation. For the kinds of devils holding our nation hostage to Satan's will can only be cast out by prayer and fasting.

I have written a small book titled *Kingdom Power by Prayer and Fasting* that I recommend to any who desires to get started at this level of spiritual warfare.

Now you are ready to learn about the third thing we must do to save America.

Prayer and Preaching

Up until now, we have talked about actions that are private and personal. We do not pray or fast to be seen by men. However, this does not mean we do not pray or fast publicly. The saints pray in the assembly, and Jesus prayed aloud before His disciples. The issue is motivation. If we pray to be seen by men, God will not hear us; and that defeats

---

[1596] Romans 12:1-2

the object of praying. The same is true of fasting. Jesus anticipated we would be in public when we fast. That is the reason He instructed us not to disfigure our faces, so we appear unto men to fast. So, up until now, we have talked about those things we do spiritually, unto God, in order to influence the spiritual world to make a physical impact.

Now I will begin talking about those things we do in the physical world before men.

Under "Pray the Prayer of Faith," I talked about the fact that we must speak to the mountain we want to be removed and the tree we want to uproot. This is what preaching is all about.

When we talk about preaching, typically, we think of the man behind the pulpit holding forth, as we say, or proclaiming the Word of God to a congregation or other assembly. However, preaching should be understood to include speaking the Word of God to individuals as well as to crowds. Also, preaching is not exclusively the work of the pastor. Every Christian is called upon to preach, which includes speaking God's truth against the lies of Satan to our friends, family, associates, and neighbors.

Christians must speak up! Believers must speak up against corruption, against wickedness, and against the unrighteousness of those who commit evil. When we refuse to stand up to the lies Satan uses to advance his agenda, we are inviting him to take over. So, we must speak up in the public square about these things.

For many years, Satan had Christians hoodwinked into believing they were not supposed to speak up on political issues. This was always wrong! God's prophets spoke against the wickedness of kings, rulers, and sinners wherever and whenever it manifested. Nevertheless, Christians who accepted this wicked lie did not create much of a problem back when our government was guided more than less by Christian principles. The danger was not noticed, so long as our social customs continued to be influenced by Christian mores. However, when society began to opebnly reject Christian principles of morality, believers found themselves increasingly marginalized. Satan had turned their world upside down. What was right was now wrong, and what was wrong was now right. And now, when they try to speak up, often they are shouted down.

Our government began acting on principles contrary to the Christian faith, and Antichrist beliefs were being adopted by society, reshaping culture into a hostile place for Christians. Today, the children of disobedience are pushing Christians out of society. If they speak up, they are roundly criticized, and cajoled, and openly mocked for their beliefs. They are shamed into silence, being told, "You cannot push your morality on us."

The wicked regularly push their immorality onto all the rest of us. But if we object or protest or speak out, the secularists rise and, with open hostility, attack us with slander: bigot, fascist, hypocrite. Lately, the assaults have become increasingly physical. The violent are indeed taking the kingdom by force.

Even those who call themselves Christians join in the attack. A favorite in-house tactic to either silence or neutralize the influence of Christians who care about holiness (separation from sin and identification with God) is to call them Pharisees or legalists.

The spirit of Antichrist is boiling today. Through Christians and non-Christians alike, the Antichrist spirit rages: "Let us break their bands asunder and cast away their cords from us."[1597] This spirit has overcome entire so-called *Christian Denominations.*

The children of disobedience are shouting us down in the public square and pushing us out.

You hear the same stories I do. High School teachers humiliate conservative students in their classrooms; college professors verbally attack Christian students; teachers fail students because they refuse to accept their lies. Many Christian conservative students today say it is dangerous for them to be open about their faith on campus.

Christians struggle to break through the resistance of the children of disobedience who control social media outlets (Facebook, Twitter, Instagram, and Google, to name a few) that are well known for censoring conservative speech. Satan has strongholds at every door of public communication, working to stop our message from penetrating the darkness.

On the other hand, the children of disobedience are given a megaphone to amplify their message.

The mainstream media (MSM) have conspired to control the shaping of public opinion. Spinning virtually every story in favor of the principles and beliefs of the spirit of Antichrist and against the principles and beliefs of the Spirit of Jesus Christ, they contrive to control public perception.

Satan has strongholds at every avenue of public discourse, and he uses them to discourage Christian participation in the public debate over political and social conscience issues. When he fails to discourage us from speaking up, he tries to distort our message. When our message breaks through, those under the control of the spirit of Antichrist become vicious and even violent.

[1597] Psalm 2

Some Democrat representatives have openly called for barring Christians from serving on our courts because of their beliefs. Some have insinuated, and others have openly declared that Christians have no business holding government positions of power.

Political correctness has created an unofficial police force commissioned to stop Christians from making their voices heard in public debate.

There is not a sphere of public life in which Christians do not have to fight to be heard. Conservative Christians routinely are pushed out of science, education, politics, and even entertainment. It got so bad for a while that many people came to believe it was against the law to mention God on so-called secular public radio stations.

I host a radio/podcast show that airs on a secular station in our town. It is called The Brain Massage® show. A few months after I got started in this new venture, the station manager called me to his office. He kindly explained that while many people enjoyed my show, some complained when I mentioned Jesus, used the word God, or quoted from the Bible on public airwaves. I had already received personal threats from listeners, warning me they were going to "take away my tax exemption" or "report me to the FCC." By the way, I also got a few death threats and other ominous warnings intended to intimidate me into silence about my Christian conservative points of view.

Very politely, our station manager asked me to consider toning down what he called the "God talk." He said he was confident I could make my point without mentioning Jesus or quoting directly from the Bible. The manager and I had become friendly, and I asked him to trust me to handle the problem. He agreed.

On the next show, I mentioned it had come to my attention that some in my audience objected when I made mention of, "Well, let's just say, certain religious leaders, and when I quoted from a certain religious book." Then I became playful and asked the audience to participate in an experiment. I instructed them to place their finger on their wrist so they could read their pulse. Then I explained I would mention the names of certain religious leaders, and they were to note whether their heart rate accelerated.

All this happened before 9/11, so when I mentioned Mohammed, I said, "Hmmm, no response, no change in your heartbeat? Good!" Then I mentioned others: "Joseph Smith, Buddha, Confucius—no change? Good." Then I said—"Jesus: Oh no, call 911, heart rates are spiking all over the city; lady, you, yeah, you, get a bag, quick, place it over your mouth and breath slowly two or three times, yeah, that's it! Goodnight, folks, some of you are hyperventilating." I laughed. The radio personnel who heard this little rant laughed too. It was all tongue-in-cheek, but it made an important point. I asked, quietly, but seriously—"Why do you suppose that name, among all others, has the power to disturb you so deeply?"

For several weeks, I regularly said things like, "Okay, folks, I'm about to use a name that causes some to have heart attacks, and others to hyperventilate, so, consider yourself forewarned, ready? Here it is, *Jesus*." I would say stuff like, "I'm about to quote from the most hated book in America, which is weird since this is the book our Forefathers quoted from more than any other single book. This book has guided our courts in law and our schools in education; it has been a source text for archaeology and the foundation of our social customs from our founding.

What book am I talking about? The Bible!" I introduced something we call the Bible Thump Alert. I put together a sound bite that sounded like the dive signal for a submarine (Aroogah) with my announcer saying, "Bible Thump Alert, Bible Thump Alert!"

Within a short time, all the complainers melted away. Some called to apologize for complaining. Others expressed how embarrassed they were that they had a problem with this. You see, it is true! If we submit ourselves to God, when we resist the devil, he will flee from us.

Paul sometimes got arrested illegally in order to stop him from preaching. When this happened, he challenged the arrest on the grounds that he was a Roman citizen and, as such, was afforded certain rights. Paul used his citizenship rights to check the efforts on the part of the spirit of Antichrist to interfere with his liberty.[1598] He resisted the devil!

We must resist every effort to silence us or to deny us our God-given liberties. Understand that in America, we live under a Constitution that recognizes our rights, and we must take full advantage of the privileges of our citizenship. We must stand up to the bullies trying to take these liberties from us, and in standing up to them, we must speak up and aggressively appeal to the protection of our laws.

So, we must pray and preach, and by that, I certainly mean we need to preach the saving Gospel of Jesus Christ. Every sinner saved becomes a soldier of the Cross. However, it also means we need to speak righteousness to our neighbors. We need to speak God's truth to whatever lie Satan is using to blind the minds of men and women.

One last comment on this point: Many years ago, pastors and evangelists preached against sin, and they preached

---

[1598] Acts 22:25-28

hard on moral issues. They followed Paul's example, who preached "repentance toward God, and faith toward our Lord Jesus Christ."[1599] Today, most preachers avoid preaching repentance toward God. They do not do what I call the soil work—plowing up hard hearts with confrontational preaching that challenges the conscience of sinners with the Law of God. It has gotten to the place where many preachers today forgo preaching against adultery, fornication, hatred, wrath, strife, and so forth, and many who will preach about these things do so only to Christians. But every sinner is obligated to obey God's law. Every sinner will give account for his or her sinful lifestyle. Jesus sent His Spirit into the world, specifically to reprove it of sin, righteousness, and judgment.[1600]

The idea has crept into our churches that the only thing sinners need to hear is that Jesus loves them and wants to save them. But the Bible says God is angry at the wicked every day,[1601] and His wrath abides upon him or her right now.[1602] So right now, God commands all men everywhere to repent.[1603] Preachers used to prepare the soil (the heart) for the seed (the Word of God) by hard preaching against sin. But today, most of what is called "Gospel preaching" serves more to harden than to prepare hearts for the Gospel.

To conclude this point, here is the bottom line. We must put feet to our prayers, and that means we must charge the gates of hell with the Sword of the Spirit. Let us go forward, swinging the Spirit's sword of truth against every lie Satan uses to hold men's minds in darkness.

[1599] Acts 20:21
[1600] John 16:7-9
[1601] Psalm 7:11
[1602] John 3:36
[1603] Acts 17:30

Pray and Resist the Devil In Every Sphere of Our Society

The fourth thing we must do to save America is to resist the Devil in this country. I have touched on this already. Let us look more directly at what it means to pray and resist Satan.

Believers must get involved in politics, in science, in education, in every sphere of life. Our call is to go into the entire world, and that includes every facet of life on this planet—including entertainment, by the way. We are not "of the world," but we are certainly called to go "into all the world" as salt and light.

The Spirit of Jesus Christ is supposed to be moving through us into the world, all of it: politics, science, education, and so on—reproving the world of sin, righteousness, and judgment. How do you suppose this happens? It happens when we speak God's Word to sinners everywhere sinners are sinning. It also happens when we touch the lives of others with the mercy and love of Jesus Christ. It happens when we speak truth to the lies, reproving the wicked for their wickedness. And it happens when we demonstrate the love of God by our love for one another and our fellow man. In short, it happens when we submit to God and resist the Devil.

We are not to use the methods of the world: deceit, hatred, and violence. These are the ways of the world. Remember, the "violent take it by force."[1604] We do not need to take the kingdom by force; it is ours already. We need only to assert our possession of the kingdom on behalf of the King. We rise, and speak up, state our claims, insist on our liberties, defend them, and rebuke, reprove and exhort with all longsuffering.

Time and space do not allow me to talk about how critical

[1604] Matthew 11:12

it is that the Church clean up her act, to remind us all that God's "judgment begins with the House of God,"[1605] which today is the "Church of the living God."[1606] I must assume anyone reading this who is a Christian already knows these things. Besides, if the Church will take heed to the message of this book and respond in obedient faith to Christ's challenge presented in it, she will be moved by God's Spirit toward revival soon enough.

Practical Things You Can Do to Save America.

First and foremost, find a Bible-believing, Gospel preaching church where the pastor is not a *Christianette*, but a true champion in spiritual warfare. Start supporting men of God who take a stand in the field of battle.

Along with the above, support programs like The Brain Massage® radio/podcast and our friends in this fight: Rush, Hannity, Shapiro, Candace, Allie, Diamond & Silk, Chicks On The Right, Levin, Bongino, and many more. You will not likely agree with everything I say, or with every opinion expressed by the others I mentioned; but these are America-loving, God-fearing patriots. And, as Jesus said, "He that is not against us is on our part."[1607]

Support with your time, talent and treasure, organizations active in the culture war: such as Capitol Connections, Awake America, Judicial Watch, American Center for Law and Justice (ACLJ), Christian Law Association, American Family Association, Citizens United, Family Research Council, and the American and Conservative Union. There are several others, but these are ones with which I am most familiar.

[1605] I Peter 4:17
[1606] I Timothy 3:15
[1607] Mark 9:40; see also Luke 9:50

Get on Twitter, Facebook, Instagram, LinkedIn, and whatever other social networking platforms you can access to express your point of view and engage with others on the topics important to you.

Contact your representatives: your mayor and city council members, your governor and state representatives, your House representatives and your senators, and let them know who you are and what concerns you have.

Write letters expressing your concerns to all your representatives.

Run for office. Start at the local level and work your way up. Find leaders in your community that are worthy of your support and stand behind them financially and with your services: phone calls, canvassing, surveys, and the like. Contact your local conservative leaders and offer to volunteer. Learn what help is needed and lend a hand where you can.

Finally, above all else, live out your Christian life filled with the Spirit and be personally involved in witnessing to others of Christ's salvation, and supporting ministries dedicated to this vital work.

Conclusion

Probably only a very few can take on more than a handful of the suggestions given above, but be determined to do all you can. You will be surprised how much you can do if you'll make the sacrifice necessary to be available.

Beware, do not go forward without being fully dressed in the LORD's armor, and don't go in your own strength.

~

Chapter Thirty-Nine

Rules of Engagement in God's War

RULES OF ENGAGEMENT (ROE) enforced upon our military sometimes expose our soldiers to risk. We know some of our own have been killed directly as a result of these rules. On the other hand, bombing a village taken hostage by our enemies presents a dilemma. Do we ignore the innocent lives being used as a shield by our enemies? Whatever your sentiment about ROEs, the fact is, every military of a civilized nation in modern history operates under stipulated rules of engagement.

Furthermore, these rules of engagement have always been a matter of frustration and consternation among troops. It is the same in God's army. In this chapter, I want to talk briefly about the rules of engagement in God's War!

Be Honest

"Cursed be he that doeth the work of the LORD deceitfully."[1608]

The First Rule of Engagement in God's War Is Honesty.

Groan! That is likely the sound you will hear coming from my office on Friday morning as I cull through my Inbox, looking for news I can use for my radio/podcast show:

[1608] Jeremiah 48:10

The Brain Massage®. It grieves me every time I begin show-prep and find sizzling hot, tantalizing lies perpetrated by a "conservative patriot" sounding the alarm.

Here are a few examples. A picture of Biden holding a young boy by his chin, pulling him close to his face: shocking, discomforting. Wrong! This is a picture taken at the funeral services of Biden's son; he was comforting his grandson who had just buried his father. That one would only cost me about ten minutes to run down.

Omar Ilhan said, "White men should be enslaved in chains if they refuse to convert to Islam!" Really? Wow! I'll have to check that out! Glad I did! Bogus—an impure invention!

Here is a doozy: a picture of Bill Clinton chumming it up with a convicted child-porn perpetrator. Nope! Not the same guy. That one would take about twenty minutes of my time. (Let us talk about his twenty plus rides on Epstein's Lolita-Express—you see, it's not as if there is a shortage of truth we can use to expose these people.)

One more. Kamala Harris said as President she would give the Congress 100 days to come up with "reasonable gun safety laws," or she would implement them by executive order. A self-described conservative created a paraphrase of her statement and represented it as a quote. "If elected and you don't surrender your guns, I will sign an executive order and the police will show up at your door." I teasingly refer to such conservatives as *CON*-servatives. Using dishonest distortions to make a point snuggles close to defamation.

I am a fervent supporter of our God endowed inalienable right of self-defense, and the right to keep and bear arms that arises from that natural right of man. Furthermore, I am aware that the *Left* today seem *hell-bent* on infringing upon that right. I don't doubt the paraphrase mentioned above might be a fair representation of Kamala's sentiment—although, it sounds much more like Feinstein than Kamala. Nevertheless, I strongly object to the practice of using lies to defend the truth.

We despise these same tactics when they are used to caricature conservatives negatively and dishonestly. Remember, Jesus said, "Do unto others as you would have them do unto you." We cannot win against the Devil using the Devil's tactics.

We should retweet, share, repost, and repeat any truthful exposé of the wicked machinations of the enemies of our liberties. Reproving the world of sin, righteousness, and judgment involves exposing the subterfuges of the spirit of Antichrist by the light of truth. However, please take the time to verify the story. If you cannot verify it, do not use it. In the end, it only hurts our cause; and besides, our King has very harsh penalties for lying. We can get in serious trouble for violating His rules of engagement.

There are hundreds if not thousands of these circulated every year, and it is a shame. Some of these stories are so obscene; I wonder if the children of disobedience place them as decoys to trap unsuspecting conservatives into making themselves fools in repeating them. Defamation of character by false accusation is the tool of the father of lies, and should never be used by Christ's soldiers in fighting God's War!

I know: they lie about us all the time. And I know that a lie circles the world before the truth gets its shoes on. I also know that Jesus said we are to be wise as serpents. Let's look at these common rationalizations for compromising the integrity of the conservative movement.

Avoid the excuses used to justify violating this ROE.

<u>They lie about us all the time.</u>

Like my momma told me when I complained that Donny does it: "If Donny flushed his head in a toilet, would you?" The fact that devils lie is not a reason for us to do so.

<u>The lie runs around the world before the truth gets its shoes on.</u>

As for how quickly lies run, it is the reason we keep our shoes on. We must be vigilant (watchful) and diligent in our response. Remember, while lies run faster than truth, lies also peter out more quickly. The truth runs forever; it never gets exhausted.

<u>Jesus said we should be wise as serpents.</u>

True, Jesus said be wise as serpents; but He followed that with be harmless as doves.[1609] We are to be wise as the serpent, but that does not mean we are to be a snake. I don't think we should assume when Jesus said be wise as serpents that He was telling us to be wise in the way devils are. The serpent is closely associated with the Devil and his devils. However, in no case are we to adopt satanic cunning.

Jesus complained that the children of this world are wiser in their generation than are the children of light.[1610] He did not mean we are to adapt their wisdom to our uses.

There is wisdom from below and wisdom from above.[1611] We are instructed to avoid the wisdom from below.

[1609] Matthew 10:16
[1610] Luke 16:8
[1611] James 3:13-18

The characteristics of wisdom from below (worldly wisdom) include bitter envying and strife. God warns us that this wisdom "descendeth not from above, but is earthly, sensual, devilish."[1612] Wherever this wisdom is used, there is "confusion and every evil work."[1613] When Jesus encouraged us to be wise as serpents, He did not recommend we adopt the Serpent's wisdom.

Jesus lamented the children of Satan understand how to work the kingdom of darkness better than the children of God understand how to work the kingdom of Heaven. The wisdom He is looking for is that given to us by God.[1614]

The wisdom Jesus recommends is from above, characterized by Kingdom attributes. It is first and foremost pure; then peaceable, gentle, and easy to be entreated (approached, questioned, petitioned). It is full of mercy and good fruits, and it is without hypocrisy.[1615]

Never do the work of the LORD deceitfully—that's the first rule of engagement.

Now let us consider the second ROE (rule of engagement) number two in God's War.

Use the Sword of the Spirit

In Jeremiah's warning against doing the work of the Lord deceitfully, he also declared a curse on all who hold back their sword from blood:

> Cursed be he that doeth the work of the Lord deceitfully, and *cursed be he* that keepeth back his sword from blood. — Jeremiah 48:10 (Emphasis added.)

[1612] James 3:15
[1613] James 3:16
[1614] James 1:5-6
[1615] James 3:17

Peter said we must answer all who have a question about the hope that is in us, with meekness and fear.[1616] The first part of Peter's exhortation picks up on Jeremiah's second curse. The first curse is upon any that do the work of the LORD deceitfully. The second curse is upon any that drawback the sword from blood. Peter instructs us to draw and apply the sword of the Spirit, the Word of God, and use it to answer those who have a question about our faith. It is not inappropriate to extend this to the instruction we have received to reprove the unfruitful works of darkness.[1617]

The Spirit, through the Apostle Paul warned us to "have no fellowship with the unfruitful works of darkness, but rather reprove them."[1618] To reprove means to point out a fault, to rebuke an error, to convince someone of wrongdoing.[1619] In short, it means to shine the light of truth on their evil deeds. Many Christians today loathe obedience to this instruction. They hold back; they refuse to use the Sword of the Spirit, the Word of God, to reprove the unfruitful works of darkness. Seeking the love and favor of the world, they spurn the love and favor of God. They choose to have fellowship with the darkness of this world, and forsake fellowship with God: for "God is light, and in him is no darkness at all," and only "if we walk in the light, as he is in the light, [do] we have fellowship one with another."[1620]

Christians who refuse to swing the Spirit's Sword against the works of darkness are under the curse of God.

[1616] I Peter 3:15
[1617] Ephesians 5:11
[1618] Ephesians 5:11
[1619] Our English word *reprove* is defined in Webster's' 1913 as follows: "1. To convince; . . . 2. To disprove; to refute . . . 3. To chide to the face as blameworthy; to accuse as guilty; to censure . . . 4. To express disapprobation of; as to *reprove* faults." In Ephesians 5:11, the word translated *reprove* is ἐλέγχετε, from Strong No. 1651. "ἐλέγχω elegcho, el-eng´-kho; of uncertain affinity; to confute, admonish: — convict, convince, tell a fault, rebuke, reprove."
[1620] I John 1:5-7

Some employ the Sword of the Spirit while they war according to the flesh. These willingly slash at others with Bible verses, but they are in disobedience to Christ's rules of engagement. Often, they do significant damage to the cause of Christ Jesus.

The second part of Peter's exhortation stipulates a rule of engagement when applying the sword of the Spirit. When we deploy the Spirit's Sword to reprove the unfruitful works of darkness, we must do it in meekness and fear.

Use the Spirit's Sword With Meekness.

Meekness does not mean weakness. It does mean mildness, but not timidity. It does indeed call for humility, but not passivity. Moses was reputed by God to have been the meekest man on the earth in his day.[1621] Yet it was Moses who melted golden calves, ground them to powder, mixed the powder into the drinking water, and made the idol-worshiping children of Israel drink it.[1622] There is no doubt about it. So far as God is concerned, meekness is not weak, timid, or passive.

Essentially, meekness is an attitude of humility toward God that positions us to reflect His attitude toward men.

Christians should be known for their charity (love); even when we speak the "truth that hurts," we must follow this essential rule of engagement: "speaking the truth in love."[1623]

Use the Spirit's Sword With Fear.

Peter attached to the rule of meekness the rule of fear. These are connected as if they are one thing: meekness and fear.

[1621] Numbers 12:3
[1622] Exodus 32:1-20
[1623] Ephesians 4:15

God warns us against the fear of man.[1624] Jesus instructed us not to fear those able to kill the body, but rather to fear Him that can destroy both body and soul in hell.[1625] Indeed, we are repeatedly exhorted to fear God.[1626] We are to give an answer concerning the hope we have in Christ in the fear of God, not in the fear of man.

It comes down to motivation!

Do we swing the Sword of the Spirit against the unfruitful works of darkness out of frustration and anger? Remember that the wrath of man does not work the righteousness of God.[1627] When motivated by our love for God and for the souls He sent His Son to die to save, we will reprove in meekness, not harshness.

Are we speaking the truth to reprove the unfruitful works of darkness out of fear of man? In other words, are we moved to attack those who commit evil in our communities because we are afraid of them? Remember that the fear of man brings us into a snare.[1628] "There is no fear in love." We can confidently trust God to answer the prayer Jesus prayed for us: "I pray not that thou shouldest take them out of the world, but that thou shouldest keep them from the evil."[1629] There is no need to fear what man can do to us.

This leads us into the third rule of engagement: boldness.

Be Bold Not Brazen!

Boldness is the third rule of engagement.[1630] It is the natural by-product of being filled with the Spirit of God.

[1624] Proverbs 29:25— it brings a snare
[1625] Matthew 10:28
[1626] II Corinthians 7:1; Ephesians 5:21; see I Peter 2:17; Revelation 14:7
[1627] James 1:20
[1628] Proverbs 29:25
[1629] John 17:15
[1630] Acts 4:29 and Philippians 1:20

Boldness is neither brash nor crass. It is assertive, but not rude. By no means does it lack sensitivity. Boldness makes no pretense of a refinement that lacks the character to speak out against evil, or that is a respecter of persons, or that exalts him- or herself above speaking plainly about sins committed openly. When the righteous are not bold, the wicked are emboldened. Famously, it is said, the only thing necessary for the triumph of evil is for good men to do nothing.[1631]

Indeed, the righteous are bold as a lion, whereas the wicked flee though none pursue.[1632]

Boldness gives one confidence that inspires frankness, a willingness to confront others with directness and clarity when necessary, but not a pugnacious audacity, eager to fling railing insults.

Our boldness arises out of our confidence in God and commitment to our cause. When David heard the insults of the giant, he was stirred in his spirit to respond; and when he met with resistance from God's people, David cried out: Is there not a cause? When he charged the giant with his sling and his stone, he declared to the giant his confidence in GOD: "Thou comest to me with a sword, and a with a shield: but I come to thee in the name of the LORD of hosts, the God of the armies of Israel, whom thou hast defied."[1633]

The most determined resistance you will likely face will come from those who call themselves by the name of Christ. Like David, you must not lose heart, but be bold;

[1631] Often attributed to Edmund Burke, but the first to phrase this notion was John Stuart Mill, who in 1867 said, "Bad men need nothing more to compass their ends, than that good men should look on and do nothing." https://www.independent.co.uk/voices/the-top-10-misattributed-quotations-a7910361.html
[1632] Proverbs 28:1
[1633] I Samuel 17:45

and remind them of the cause. When the wicked berate you and threaten and cajole you as Goliath did David, you must remember that you fight under the banner of Jesus' name.

Elijah on Mount Carmel is an excellent example of boldness. The great prophet challenged the prophets of Baal to a prayer duel: "Call ye on the name of your gods, and I will call on the name of the LORD [Jehovah]: and the God that answereth by fire, let Him be God."[1634] The people of Israel had forgotten the true God and began serving Baal. They were confused. Elijah desired to clarify the distinction between the true God of Israel and the false gods of the heathen.[1635]

Elijah's successor was Elisha. Once Elisha was called to stand before both Ahab, king of Israel, and Jehoshaphat, king of Judah. Ahab was a wicked king who led Israel out from under God; he was despised by God and by his true prophets. Elisha said to Ahab, "As the LORD of hosts liveth, before whom I stand, surely, were it not that I regard the presence of Jehoshaphat the king of Judah, I would not look toward thee, nor see thee."[1636]

These things are mentioned to dispel the myth that Christians are supposed to be milquetoast, sycophants, and servile, groveling before earthly kings, princes, prelates, and principalities.

On the other hand, we are to give honor to whom honor is due and show respect for the power, even when we despise the person holding it, which brings us to the last rule of engagement we need to consider for this present work.

[1634] I Kings 18:24
[1635] [I Kings 18:39
[1636] II Kings 3:14

Honor to Whom Honor Is Due

Peter instructed us to "Honour all men. Love the brotherhood. Fear God. Honour the king."[1637] He said this when Nero was emperor of Rome (c.AD 64-67). He added the injunction that we "let nothing be done through strife; but in lowliness of mind let each esteem other better than themselves."[1638]

Remembering that Jesus sometimes looked on those self-righteous, offending Jews "with anger, being grieved for the hardness of their hearts,"[1639] and recounting His strong words of reproof against them, "Whited sepulchres . . . beautiful without, but . . . full of dead men's bones," and the "woes" He pronounced upon the cities that rejected His ministry,[1640] we are compelled to understand the instruction to honor all men does not mean we are to ignore their foolishness and sin. Indeed, John the Baptist did not "hold back the sword" of truth against Herod regarding his "brother's wife."[1641]

On the other hand, both Jesus and Paul submitted to the duly constituted power, understanding God ordained it: "Thou couldest have no power at all against me," said Jesus, "except it were given thee from above."[1642] And Paul humbled himself before the high priest: "I wist (knew) not, brethren, that he was the high priest: for it is written, Thou shalt not speak evil of the ruler of thy people."[1643]

We must honor the position even when we despise the person holding it.

[1637] I Peter 2:17
[1638] Philippians 2:3
[1639] Mark 3:5
[1640] Matthew 11:21
[1641] Mark 6:18
[1642] John 19:11—Jesus to Pilate
[1643] Acts 23:5—Paul to the High Priest after rebuking him for hypocrisy

Primarily, this rule of engagement speaks to the attitude we should have when confronting anyone about sin. We must honor all men and esteem others as better than ourselves. We do not consider ourselves above the law, nor do we see ourselves as better than anyone else.

Conclusion

These rules restrain us from becoming proud and haughty, or arrogant in our spirit, while we boldly proclaim the truth against every lie Satan has used to deceive the hearts of men. Jesus' rules of engagement check our fleshly desire to "win an argument," and keep us focused on winning the soul to Christ instead. These rules of engagement keep us under Christ while we represent Him as kings and priests unto God. These rules of engagement shape us into humble servants of the Most High God and serve as a guard against exhibiting an attitude of superiority; they keep us mindful that our mission is to show God's love to humanity, Who said, "As many as I love, I rebuke and chasten."[1644]

These rules of engagement, if followed sincerely, will ensure that we speak the truth in love.

∼

[1644] Revelation 3:19

Chapter Forty

The Return to Piety and Old Time Religion

T O CONCLUDE GOD'S WAR, understand that everything depends on the strength of Christ's soldiers. Of course, we are talking about spiritual rather than physical strength. To increase our spiritual power, we exercise ourselves unto godliness.

Paul said, "Refuse profane and old wives' fables, and exercise thyself rather unto godliness. For bodily exercise profiteth little: but godliness is profitable unto all things, having promise of the life that now is, and of that which is to come."[1645]

Godliness (piety, religious devotion to God)[1646] is something developed through exercise. It is not produced by bodily exercise. Nevertheless, it requires exercise to develop; it's not something imputed to us as a grant from God. We must put forth an effort to improve it. The fact that godliness is the product of exercise is something most believers do not understand.

[1645] I Timothy 4:7-8

[1646] The word translated *godliness* is εὐσέβειαν (*eusebeian,* from εὐσέβεια—*eusebeia* (Strong No. 2150)). The root refers to someone noteworthy for reverence and piety. It is not used exclusively for Christians. Cornelius was identified as *devout* (translates the same Greek word) before he was converted (Acts 10:2). Yet, it seems to speak of God-fearing persons since another word is used when referring to the *devoutness* of merely religious persons (Acts 13:50; 17:4, 17)—σέβομαι (*sebomai* (Strong no. 4576)).

Much teaching in the churches today has effectively robbed the believer of a proper understanding of holiness and personal piety.

Webster informs us that piety—the keyword in the definition of godliness—refers to "veneration or reverence of the Supreme Being, and love of His character, or veneration accompanied with love; (together with) . . . piety in practice, (which) is the exercise of these affections in obedience to His will and devotion to His service."[1647]

Webster adds to the above, "Duty: dutifulness; filial reverence and devotion; affectionate reverence and service shown toward parents, relatives, benefactors, country, etc."[1648] He refers us to a synonym, religion, which he defines as "The outward act or form by which men indicate their recognition of the existence of a god or of gods having power over their destiny, to whom obedience, service, and honor are due . . ."[1649] Seducing spirits have succeeded to develop very scornful attitudes in the hearts of believers toward the three most important words related to our understanding of godliness: piety, duty, and religion.

What Is Piety?

"Pious gasbag" and other equally denigrating epithets are regularly used to ridicule Christians who speak out against ungodliness, whether or not they are sincerely devoted to their faith. The wily Devil encourages scorn in the hearts of unbelievers against the pious with such degrading slurs. He does this to counter the influence their piety might have upon the conscience of those in Satan's power.

The Importance Of Duty

[1647] Webster, Daniel *American Dictionary of the English Language*, 1828, *piety*
[1648] Ibid. See "*Piety*, 2. Duty" in the 1913 edition.
[1649] Ibid—*religion.*

Consider how duty is practically a dirty word among many Christians today. Speak of duty, and you are very likely to be attacked with charges that you are a legalist, or that you are trying to bring believers back under the Law. Of course, it is a wicked lie designed to counteract the influence that truly pious believers might have upon the minds and hearts of unbelievers and carnally minded saints.

Difficult as it might be for some to hear, in the Sermon on the Mount, Jesus raised the bar for personal righteousness; He did not lower it.[1650] He made it clear that it must exceed what is stipulated in the Law. Law and grace are not antithetical.[1651] Indeed, when the Apostle Paul declared his emancipation from the Law[1652] he did not mean he was without law to God.[1653] Paul was not under the Mosaic ordinances such as circumcision,[1654] or Sabbath-keeping,[1655]

[1650] Matthew 5-7

[1651] We are saved *by grace* and not *by the law*. But *grace* and *law* are not antithetical. The idea that there was no *grace* during the *law* or that there is no *law* during what we call"the age of *grace*" is absurd, on the face of it. The provision of God's Law through Moses was an act of wonderful *grace*, as it provided to them the schoolmaster that would bring them to Christ (Galatians 3:24). The Old Testament sacrifices provided for forgiveness that was premised upon the substitutionary sacrifice of another on behalf of the sinner—the very essence of the terms of grace by which we come to God through Christ Jesus. Paul, a *grace preacher* by any honest reckoning, declared that he was *not without law to God, but under law to Christ.* Consider how some use John 1:17, which informs us that the law came by Moses, but grace and truth came by Jesus Christ. Some say this verse means that first there was Law, by Moses, and then later came grace by Jesus. If it were not so serious a matter, we might dismiss such superficial handling of the Scripture as the work of a novice, a babe, unused to handling the word of truth (Hebrews 5:14). Yet, men long acquainted with the Scriptures put this silly argument forward. Consider, therefore, that in the context of the very passage they cite, we are told that the Word was long before Moses. The obvious point of the verse is that *grace* and *truth* preceded the Law—something Paul points out in Galatians 3:17.

[1652] Romans 7:6-25

[1653] I Corinthians 9:21; see Romans 7:25 and consider the significance of Galatians 5:16

[1654] Galatians 6:15

[1655] Colossians 2:16

or the Old Testament sacrifices.[1656] Christ nailed these ordinances to His Cross.[1657] However, Paul recognized that every believer had a duty to depart from iniquity and do right.[1658]

The Role of Religion

Against religion, so much evil has been said, and so many Christians shun it, that it virtually no longer exists in the evangelical Christian community. Strange that some believers are eager to side with Satan in his hatred of pure religion, which is defined by James as "to visit the fatherless and widows in their affliction, and to keep [ourselves] unspotted from the world."[1659]

Of course, we may legitimately infer from the text that there is a sort of religion that is impure and defiled. Such religion deserves our scorn. However, the word *religion* itself is scorned and ridiculed; indeed, the concept of religion is hated, sometimes more viciously by Christians than by atheists.

Religion does not save; Jesus does! But religion is vital to the purpose of the New Testament priesthood, for it provides the form of godliness through which the Holy Ghost exerts His influence and power in this world.

The Spirit decried those who have a form of godliness but denied the power thereof.[1660] He did not object to the form of godliness. He objected only that some presented it empty, devoid of the presence and power of the Holy Ghost, which is the power thereof.

Religion is the form by which godliness is expressed in the world, and through which the Holy Ghost exerts His

[1656] Hebrews 8-9
[1657] Colossians 2:14
[1658] II Timothy 2:19; I Corinthians 15:34; Ephesians 6:6
[1659] James 1:27
[1660] II Timothy 3:5

holy influences upon the conscience of our communities. But it must be pure religion and undefiled.

The Holy Spirit, through James, did not offer an exhaustive or comprehensive definition of religion. He provided two key characteristics to look for in a pure and undefiled religion. The two features of pure and undefiled religion are 1. Ministry to the afflicted and, 2. Separation from the filthiness of this world.[1661] He made it clear that religion involves us in activities that honor God in public ministry.

Religion provides a form for the expression of godliness in the world. Godliness is often assumed to mean God-likeness. But the word speaks of persons who are passionate about God, whose life testifies to their devotion to Him and adoration of Him. Therefore, the form through which this godliness might express itself may vary from time to time and from place to place.

Daniel established a form of godliness, which consisted of him opening a window in his home in Babylon that faced Jerusalem and praying three times each day in full view of the public. Neither Moses nor any other prophet gave any such instruction. Nevertheless, it was consistent with all that Moses and the prophets had revealed. Daniel's prayer habit was a form of godliness that was acceptable to God and honored by Him.

We may study the New Testament for indications of ways the early disciples established various forms through which they expressed their godliness to their communities. They worshiped in public meetings and preached in the streets, for example.[1662]

Exercises Unto Godliness

[1661] I John 2:15-17
[1662] I Corinthians 14:22-25 and Acts 2, 4

What exercises might we do to develop godliness? The word *exercise*, as it applies to the body, refers to strenuous physical activity intended to increase bodily strength or agility. In our text, as it applies to spiritual matters, exercise conveys the idea of doing the things that promote godliness in our lives. It's all quite practical. If you want to be godly, you must do the things that increase godliness in your life.

Personal Abstinence (or Will Worship)

Personal abstinence is all but lost among Christians today. Indeed, Christians indulge their flesh freely and immerse themselves into our entertainment-crazed culture with abandon. Paul spoke to the value of will-worship. Will-worship includes exercising will power over fleshly appetites that are not necessarily sinful, but that might interfere with our testimony, or that become sinful in excess.

Any believer who avoids certain things in this world that he or she finds compromising had better prepare for resistance from fellow believers. Some well-meaning but unwise believers will likely chastise him or her with warnings about falling into the trap of "touch not; taste not; handle not" Phariseeism.[1663] But the Bible does say, to New Testament Christians, "Touch not the unclean thing."[1664]

Gracey, as usual, does not read her Bible carefully. Colossians 2:20-23 does indeed discourage believers from getting tangled up in the spirit of the law and putting too much emphasis on externals. However, read verse 23 in the passage cited above: "Which things have indeed a shew of wisdom in will worship, and humility, and neglecting of the body." There is wisdom in will-worship. Which the Spirit

---

[1663] Colossians 2:21
[1664] II Corinthians 6:17

indicates is conducive to humility, which is encouraged by neglecting the body.

There is wisdom in adopting at least some rules that govern our appetites for entertainment. Such abstinence exercises our will in obedience, and our spirit in humility, by checking and regulating the insatiable demands of the body for pleasure.

However, none of this brings any honor to the flesh. Also, except where Scripture speaks plainly to something believers ought to avoid, these rules are preferential and should not be imposed upon the Church at large. Nevertheless, as the Spirit has said, they can be useful exercises unto godliness.

Prayer, Scripture Reading, Church Attendance, Giving, Witnessing, Good Works In the Community, etcetera.

Reading the Scripture is mentioned explicitly as an exercise that sharpens our spiritual sensibilities.[1665] Prayer,[1666] attending church,[1667] giving to ministry,[1668] witnessing,[1669] doing good works in the community[1670]—all these things are essential spiritual duties by which we exercise ourselves unto godliness.

Final Words On Spiritual Exercises That Are Unto Godliness

Paul, by the Spirit, told us that developing godliness is beneficial in the world in which we now labor and in the world to come.[1671]

[1665] Hebrews 5:14
[1666] I Thessalonians 5:17
[1667] Hebrews 10:24-25
[1668] Romans 15:27
[1669] Acts 1:8
[1670] Matthew 5:16; Ephesians 2:10
[1671] I Timothy 4:7-8

Whatever benefit godliness has in this world must disturb the Devil greatly, for he has devoted a great deal of energy to the work of compromising it in the life of Christians. Indeed, it seems most Christians today have no real regard for the sort of godliness that has a practical manifestation in righteousness and in departing from iniquity. It seems most believers today are happy to revel in a perverted notion of grace that they imagine permits them to live loose, undisciplined lives.

God's grace is not His permission to sin; it is His provision to overcome. But it goes beyond our immediate purpose to delve further into that matter at present.

Finally, while the form is essential, without the power of God, it is nothing but an empty shell. The New Testament priest must, above all else, be filled with the Spirit. And that matter has been discussed at length in this present work.

Conclusion

Satan controls much place in our nation and our churches, but only because he first gained it in our lives and our homes. We must take the scourge of God's Word, zealously purge the Temple of God of all that defiles and exercise ourselves in godliness. Only then will we be soldiers fit for the war that is before us. For strong soldiers are needed to take back the place Satan has usurped. Indeed, if we fail to do our duty as God's kings and priests, if we do not exercise the authority He has given to us, if we defile the Temple of God, beware the scourge of His chastisement: "If any man defile the Temple of God, him shall God destroy; for the Temple of God is holy, which Temple ye are."[1672] Remember, "Judgment must begin at the house of God."[1673]

[1672] I Corinthians 3:17
[1673] I Peter 4:17

~ End ~

"By renouncing the Bible, philosophers swing from their moorings upon all moral subjects... It is the only correct map of the human heart that ever has been published."

"[T]he only means of establishing and perpetuating our republican forms of government is the universal education of our youth in the principles of Christianity by means of the Bible.

~ Benjamin Morris

(Benjamin Rush, Letters of Benjamin Rush, L. H. Butterfield, editor (Princeton, NJ: Princeton University Press, 1951), Vol. II, p. 936, to John Adams, January 23, 1807. Benjamin Rush, Essays, Literary, Moral & Philosophical (Philadelphia: Thomas & Samuel F. Bradford, 1798), p. 112, "A Defence of the Use of the Bible as a School Book.")

~ E p i l o g u e ~

JESUS IS THE KING, and all mankind His subjects! Evangelical Christians are looking for the return of our Lord, but few fully comprehend the significance of His first coming. God's War explores the meaning of Christ's first coming. And it can be summarized in the opening sentence of this paragraph: Jesus is the King, and all men are His subjects. The implications of this statement are profound.

God's War is a conflict between the kingdom of God and the kingdom of darkness. Fought on battleground earth, the spoils of this war are the souls of men. Mighty angels and devils clash in this conflict as on Earth kingdoms rise and fall. Wars and rumors of wars rumble across the planet as one or another nation strives to control something called the dominion.

In the beginning, God created the Heaven and the earth. He began by creating an audience—the angelic hosts. They watched and sang as He proceeded to expand space with billions of stars and planets and moons and comets. One world got special attention—Earth. He gave it to a mighty angel, named Lucifer. Lucifer set his heart on his glory, power, and riches; and turned his affections away from the

One Who gave him his glory. His heart filled with pride, and he announced his intention to set his throne above the stars of God, to be like the Most High. God rejected his prideful boast and cast him down—"and the earth was without form and void, and darkness was upon the face of the deep."

God formed the earth to be inhabited by a new creature. Mankind was created male and female in the image and likeness of God and given the power to procreate—this is the kingdom of man, and God was its only King. He gave to mankind mastery of the earth and all its resources—this is called *the dominion*. He warned them death was the wages for sin.

Lucifer was outraged! He determined to remove the kingdom of man out from under God, to usurp God's place in the earth, and take control of the dominion. To do this, he seduced men into sin, gaining the power of death over mankind. Lucifer came to be called Satan—the accuser! When mankind fell into sin and came under the power of Satan, God promised to send a deliverer.

Satan set out to seduce men to follow him in his rebellion. The first human to call himself a king was Nimrod, and he founded Babel, the first kingdom out from under God, later called Babylon. God intervened and scattered the people. They followed Nimrod's example and set up kings over kingdoms all over the earth. From then forward, God would give the dominion (the right to rule the earth under God) to whomever He pleased. He settled it on Israel! Israel was God's people, a nation under God. Satan strove against God's angels and Israel attempting to provoke God to surrender Israel to his power and give him the dominion.

Satan finally corrupted Israel so that God removed the

dominion from her and gave it to a servant of God that ruled Babylon whose name was Nebuchadnezzar. At that time, through the prophet Daniel, God foretold how the dominion would pass from one nation to another until Satan had it all in his hands. His prophecy revealed that during the fourth kingdom Satan would rule Earth through a king called the *son of perdition*, that is, the son of Satan. Finally, the promised deliverer would come and destroy Satan's kingdom and replace it with His eternal kingdom. Satan planned to destroy all mankind before Christ could set up his kingdom on Earth. The prophecy began fulfillment when the dominion passed from Babylon to Persia.

Satan corrupted Babylon until God transferred the dominion to His shepherd, Cyrus, king of Persia. Satan corrupted Persia so that God would not allow her to continue holding the dominion. However, by that time, God did not have a servant or a shepherd to whom He would give the dominion. The next world ruler, Alexander the Great, called himself god, the Son of Zeus—he was under the power of Satan. God relinquished the dominion to Alexander, who was the first king of the third kingdom. He brought all the kingdoms of the world under Satan's power.

Alexander conquered the world then died, and his Empire was divided among his generals. Satan knew the prophecy of Daniel. He expected his man of sin, someone we call the Antichrist, to appear at the beginning of the fourth kingdom. Satan would use his power to destroy all humanity. So, he watched for the prophesied Antichrist to appear. But something happened he did not expect. God sent His Son, the Christ, into the world. The heir of the dominion had arrived. Christ appeared in flesh, which alarmed the kingdom of darkness. It meant that Christ Jesus could rule

Heaven as the Son of God and Earth as the Son of man. Jesus could combine the kingdom of God with the kingdom of men. Thus, the kingdom of God invaded the kingdom of darkness to save the kingdom of men.

As soon as John the Baptist began declaring the kingdom of God had come, Satan rebelled and refused to yield the dominion to Him. He refused to return the kingdoms of this world to God's power. Jesus bound Satan and spoiled his house—breaking his power over all the kingdoms of this world, and removing the dominion from his control.

Jesus is the Christ of God in the flesh of men. He removed the dominion from Satan's power, and banished the Devil from Earth. Satan has no right to rule the earth or to hold humanity in his kingdom of darkness. Anyone who will may turn from darkness to light and from the power of Satan to God. Furthermore, Jesus removed the dominion from Adam's race and took it into His power as the Son of man, the last Adam. Therefore, neither Satan nor sinners descended from Adam have any claim to the dominion.

Jesus is the King, and all mankind are His subjects. After taking the dominion of Earth from Satan and sinners, He left His church with the keys of the kingdom and ascended into Heaven to receive another kingdom, the eternal kingdom. He sent His Spirit into the world to reprove it of sin, righteousness, and judgment, and to draw all men to their only Saviour.

Under His authority, we are instructed to preach the Gospel of His kingdom to all mankind, declaring His terms of surrender. The terms of surrender are as follows: confessing with your mouth the LORD Jesus and believing in your heart that God raised Him from the dead, you must call on the name of the Lord to be saved. That's it! All who surrender to the Gospel command to repent and believe will be saved from the wrath to come. All who do so are called the children of obedience because they obeyed the Gospel. Those who refuse to obey the Gospel are called the children of disobedience. Jesus promised to return for the children of obedience and receive them into Heaven with Him. Then He will return with His saints following when He comes to destroy all earthly kingdoms and establish His eternal kingdom in the earth.

Meanwhile! Satan has reasserted his influence on the earth through the children of disobedience. He is called the prince of the power of the air, the spirit that now works in the children of disobedience. He deceives them into denying that Christ has come in the flesh, convinces them that the earth belongs to them, and that only they have the right to rule the dominion. They rail against God and His anointed. They declare they will not have Jesus to be their Lord; they will not have him to reign over them. These are under the control and influence of the spirit of Antichrist. Their objective is to bring the world under Satan's power, to unite the world into a global dictatorship ruled by Satan through the man of sin, the Antichrist.

However, the Spirit of Jesus Christ in believers works through them to resist the spirit of Antichrist. The children of obedience oppose the agenda of the spirit of Antichrist. Christians get in the way of this world's efforts to create a one-world government ruled by the children of disobedience. They interfere with their desire to rid the world of the influence of Jesus Christ. But so long as the Spirit of Jesus Christ is in the world, the spirit of Antichrist cannot reveal the man of sin. We keep getting in their way!

One day, Jesus will remove the children of obedience from the earth, and it will fall entirely into the hands of the Antichrist. While we are being prepared to return with Him to destroy the kingdoms of this world and set up His eternal Kingdom, Satan will wreak havoc upon humanity on Earth. He will attempt to kill every living human being on the planet, but Christ will stop him when He returns with us to establish His Kingdom on the earth.

This is God's War! The Spirit of Jesus Christ is the spirit of liberty; the spirit of Antichrist is the spirit of tyranny. When the children of disobedience get their way, tyranny prevails. When the children of obedience are in control, liberty prevails. Because the Gospel promotes liberty and delivers men from the power of Satan, every country controlled by the spirit of Antichrist hinders the Gospel from being preached freely. In every country where the children of obedience hold power, the Gospel is preached freely. Where the Gospel is preached freely, you will notice that all the people enjoy greater liberty. Where the Gospel is restricted, you will see that the freedoms of the people are limited.

The controversy between the children of obedience and the children of disobedience has reached a critical juncture in America. From our founding, the children of obedience (those in whom Christ's Spirit dwells) have held sway in the government and society. Americans were renown for their love of freedom. They made famous the principle that God has endowed inalienable rights to all humanity. To the degree that we have given control of our government to the children of disobedience, we are progressively losing our liberties. Hostility from the children of disobedience against the children of obedience has broken out into open and even physical violence. The upcoming election will determine whether we finally pull this nation out from under God, or reestablish our nation under God.

The spirit of Antichrist convinces the minds of those it controls to believe Christians have no voice in the affairs of government. But the opposite is true. Christians have as much right to voice their opinions on matters affecting the government as anyone else. Indeed, Christians have a greater right to govern in this world, since the earth belongs to Jesus Christ and not to Satan. God is the ordaining authority behind all government power. The dominion belongs to Christ, the Last Adam, and all who are born of His Spirit are made heirs together with Christ Jesus. Under His authority, we are commanded to preach the liberating Gospel and no power on Earth has the authority to counter that command.

Furthermore, every sinner is obliged to obey Christ as their King and commanded to bow the knee to Him as LORD.

Christians are kings and priests unto God, now, and responsible to represent God before men, and men before God. Christians not only have the same human rights as anyone to engage in the politics of whatever government they live under, but they also have a divinely appointed responsibility to do so. Satan does not want men and women to know this. He does not have the right to govern in the earth over men. Any authority he has attained he has usurped. The violent "take the kingdom" by force. It's never given to them. Christians have a divine right to rule the world under Christ. However, Heaven's current policy requires men to choose to surrender to Christ. This policy will continue in force so long as Christ's Spirit is present in the earth withholding the spirit of Antichrist.

Christians will rule the world with Christ when He returns to the earth. The wicked will have no choice in the matter at that time. Now, however, men have a choice. They can accept the terms of surrender to King Jesus, or join with those who declare they will not have that man to reign over them. If they accept the terms of surrender, the Spirit of liberty will govern them. If they reject Christ, the spirit of Antichrist will prevail, and tyrants will oppress them.

The upcoming election in 2020 is a choice between the Spirit of liberty and the spirit of tyranny. According to the Bible, people don't always choose their leaders wisely. Hosea complained that Israel had set up kings contrary to the will of God. Let's pray Americans will elect leaders who follow biblical principles, who accept the terms of surrender to King Jesus, who are motivated and moved by the Spirit of Liberty. But we do not cast spells with our prayers. God will not dismiss man's free will. Men must choose whom they will serve. So, where do our prayers come in?

Greater is the Spirit of Jesus Christ in us than the spirit of Antichrist in them. What we want is a fair and honest election. Christ Jesus gave us power over devils, and we can use our ability to restrain the influence of Satan in the upcoming election. We can pray that truth will prevail, and the people will be able to decide based on facts. We can pray that voter fraud will be exposed and that it will not determine the outcome of our election. We can labor to preach the truth, and make it clear to our fellow Americans what is at stake—Liberty! We are choosing between liberty and tyranny in 2020. Choose liberty!

Jesus' Spirit is the Spirit of Liberty, and He wants His Spirit to flow through us like rivers of living water. His

Spirit moves through us to reprove the world of sin, righteousness, and judgment. Believers release the flow of the Spirit of God into the world by prayer, fasting, preaching, and shining the light of truth on Satan's lies. If we perform our duty as light and salt, at least Americans will have a clear choice set before them. If America chooses the Democrat Party, they will have chosen to side with the spirit of Antichrist.

It is time for Christians to rise and take America back! The children of disobedience have undermined the Founders' vision for this great country. They are assaulting our liberties daily. They have turned common sense upside down, opened the doors of our land to the pollutions of vice and evil, and pushed Christians out of public life. They parade perverse men and women before our children advocating a dangerous and vile lifestyle. They are mocking our values and beliefs, and it's time that we had enough!

Political correctness is an affront to our liberties. Gender fluidity is an affront to our natural sense. The assaults of the Left are past insulting, beyond dumb, over the boundary of the far side of nonsense; it has become dangerous. The Left today is dangerous. Not to our liberties only, which is bad enough. The Left has become vicious in their raging against Christians. Stand up now, or be silenced forever.

We can no longer support church leaders who betray King Jesus and throw in with Satan and the spirit of Antichrist. Christ's soldiers must leave Denominations that forsake the Bible and bow the knee to political correctness. They must do it now! Or they are guilty for crimes against the kingdom of Christ. He will render them their justice. But we must not support them in their betrayal.

Christian soldiers must take the field of battle with the Sword of the Spirit—the Word of God. We must not back down when the children of disobedience bristle and rail against us with their scorn and vicious insults.

Christ's ambassadors need to make their presence known at government forums. If the children of disobedience twist our words, untwist them. If they accuse us falsely, stand up against their accusations. If they misrepresent our beliefs, expose their lies.

Killing babies in the wombs of their mothers is a travesty and it has come to its end! It's time for God's people to stand up for the lives of the unborn children. Forcing our children to be exposed to the unnatural and life-endangering lifestyle of the homosexual is over! Take our children back from these people who would pervert their souls. Our children do not belong to them! They cannot have our children! Enough!

I think you get the idea! We are soldiers, and it's time we take the initiative in this battle and engage. The enemy has been aggressively taking more and more territory in education, politics, science, and entertainment! Christians have yielded so much place in this world to the Devil we are about to lose our place. It's time for Christians to stand and push back against the spirit of Antichrist and to reaffirm America as "one nation under God."

~

Appendix-1: Melchizedek

One of the great puzzles of Scripture is the identity of Melchizedek. By the rule of first mention (which says that the first mention of a subject sets forth the essential truth concerning it), we are compelled to accept that Abram, and the rest of the kings of Canaan, recognized Melchizedek as the king of Salem. The natural assumption is that this king, like the rest, was a human being. Two lines of argument presented below support this conclusion. The first is grammatical, and the second is textual. It is the belief of this author that these lines of argument work together to show that Melchizedek is not a pre-appearance of the Son of God, but rather a type, or a representation, of the Son of God.

Grammatical Argument: Hebrews 7:3 has encouraged many Bible students to think Melchizedek was a Theophany (an appearance of God in the physical world) or a Christophany (a pre-incarnate appearance of Christ in the physical world): "Without father, without mother, without descent, having neither beginning of days, nor end of life; but made like unto the Son of God; abideth a priest continually."

Yet, the verse depended upon to make this claim is the verse that denies it. The Scripture says not that Melchizedek is the Son of God, but that he is "made like unto" the Son of God. The phrase *made like unto* translates ἀφωμοιω-μένος (aph–omoio–me'nos (Strong No. 871— ἀφωμοιοω "assimilate closely: — make like")). This word, as it is found in our text, occurs only in this text. It is an enigmatical term, but we may trust the translators of the KJV—the word is rightly translated *made like unto*. Nevertheless, the exercise of parsing this word can be helpful in dissolving any doubts about its meaning.

There is no question that the etymological root of the term is ὅμοιος (homoios (Strong No. 3664) "similar (in appearance or character): — like, + manner)." However, the spelling in the word points to ὁμοιόω — homoioo, (Strong No. 3666) "from 3664; to assimilate, i.e., to compare passively, to become similar: — be (make) like, (in the) liken(–ess), resemble." In other words, it is the same word; only in this case it indicates that something (Melchizedek) has been "made in likeness unto." Hence, the essential idea of the word is *to be made like.*

Strong identifies the prefix as *apo* (see Strong No. 575), saying that it "usually denotes separation, departure, cessation, completion, reversal, etc." It generally communicates the idea of *from.* This Greek preposition always takes the genitive case, and in our text, it modifies the indirect object, *Son of God.* The idea is that the Son of God stands as the model from which Melchizedek is made a likeness.

The suffix μεν-οσ (*men-os*) indicates that the word is a passive participle, nominative, singular, and masculine. The fact that it is passive indicates that Melchizedek is the subject being acted upon or made like unto. That it is a participle indicates it takes, in this case, properties of a verbal adjective in its function. That is, the verbal phrase, made like unto, points to the Son of God as the model from which the likeness is made. That it is nominative indicates it is directed to the subject who is made like unto the Son of God; that is, Melchizedek. The fact that it is singular and masculine is obvious in its portent.

The parts of the word, taken together, indicate that Melchizedek is purposely set forth in Scripture in a manner intended to convey a close resemblance to the Son of God. Further, the word in this text conveys the idea that the Son of God is the model, the actual, if you will, from which Melchizedek is made the likeness. In other words, the Son of God actually possesses the characteristics that are ascribed to Melchizedek for the purpose of making him like unto the Son of God.

The translators rendered the expression *made like unto*, and in the context of the passage, it is clear the Spirit intends us to understand not that Melchizedek is the Son of God, but rather, that he is presented in Scripture in such a manner as to purposely present him as a representation of the Son of God.

It is clear, therefore, that Melchizedek is not the Son of God. However, we do not fault any who take the view that Melchizedek is a pre-appearance of Christ in human form. We do, however, offer the following general observations.

Textual Argument: Whenever a Theophany (or Christophany) occurs in Scripture, He is identified as God, or called Lord. For example, when God appeared to Abram, the Scripture clearly identifies Him as LORD (Jehovah).[1674] Nowhere in Genesis 14 do we find any reference to Melchizedek as Lord, nor does Abram refer to him as such.

Some have suggested that Melchizedek must be a Christophany because Abraham paid tithes to Melchizedek. The reasoning is that Abraham could only pay tithes to Christ, who presently receives them from us.[1675] However, Levi received tithes and that did not make Levi Christ. Indeed, all tithes, including those presented under the Levitical priest-hood, are rendered to God—the Bible declares plainly that the tithe is holy unto the LORD.[1676] A correct understanding of the language of Hebrews 7:3 (see above) reveals that

---

[1674] Genesis 18:13
[1675] Hebrews 7:8
[1676] Leviticus 27:30, 32; Numbers 18:26; Deuteronomy 14:23; II Chronicles 31:6

the idea is that when Abraham paid tithes to Melchizedek, he—that is, Melchizedek—was standing as a likeness unto the Son of God. The point is that Christ is preeminent over Melchizedek, Aaron, Levi, Abraham . . . .

Finally, the Apostle Paul, whom we believe the Holy Ghost used to give us Hebrews, complained that the Jewish believers were unable to receive what light he had regarding Melchizedek.[1677] One wonders why the Jewish believers, who accepted the testimony of John 1:1-14, would have any problem receiving the notion that Melchizedek was a pre-appearance of Christ in the physical world. Surely, every Jew who received *Jeshua Ha Mashiach* would rejoice in such a revelation.

On the other hand, if in fact Melchizedek was a Gentile king-priest ruling in Salem (Jerusalem) before Abraham,[1678] especially if Melchizedek was a descendant of Ham, an Amorite,[1679] it is easy to understand why the Holy Spirit would judge these Jewish believers unable to receive it. Consider the implications to a Jewish believer if, in fact, Melchizedek was a king-priest unto God ruling in Jerusalem before Abraham received the promise.

Genesis 14:13 reveals that the Amorites originally dwelt in the land of Canaan and that they were confederate with Abram. From Genesis 15:16 we discern that, from God's point of view, the Amorites possessed the land of Canaan by His divine decree. Ezekiel 16:3,45 informs us that the Amorites founded Jerusalem. Those who dwelt in the city of the Amorites, called Salem,[1680] were called Jebusites.[1681]

[1677] Hebrews 5:10-11
[1678] Genesis 14:18-24
[1679] Genesis 10:15-16; with 14:13
[1680] Jerusalem—Psalm 76:2
[1681] Judges 19:10

The Jebusites held Jerusalem before Abraham's day and continued to hold that city during and after the invasion of Israel into Canaan.[1682] It was not until David took the city that Jerusalem became the capital of Israel.[1683] However, in Genesis 10:15-16, we learn that the Amorite was a descendant of Ham.

Finally, we notice that God has determined to take the land away from the Amorites and give it to Abraham, but Abraham would have to wait until the iniquity of the Amorites was full. Did God demote Melchizedek? It appears not. Melchizedek is indicative of that priesthood established from eternity in Christ Jesus, the Son of God. That priesthood is made up of king-priests.[1684] He lost earthly Jerusalem but gained the heavenly Zion.

We may be sure that informing Jewish believers that Melchizedek was Christ Jesus in a pre-incarnate manifestation would have been easily received. However, informing them that God had a Gentile son of Ham serving Him as king-priest in Jerusalem before Abraham would have been difficult. To have a son of Abraham paying tithes to a son of Ham would be very difficult, indeed, for Jewish believers to receive. What believer is not surprised at these revelations? The fact is, however, that God intends to reconcile unto Himself all in Christ Jesus—including Ham. Have you not read the prophecies concerning Egypt, and noted God's intention to gather them to Himself? Indeed, some of these prophecies speak of Egypt with a tenderness usually reserved for Israel.[1685]

[1682] Judges 19
[1683] I Chronicles 11:5
[1684] Revelation 1:5-6; I Peter 2:5
[1685] Isaiah 19:18-25

Therefore, we conclude that Melchizedek was made like unto the Son of God but was not in fact the Son of God.

To recap:

The language of Hebrews 7:3 makes it clear that Melchizedek is neither to be promoted above Christ, which is blasphemy, nor to be elevated to the status of Christ; he is presented in Scripture in a manner intended to convey him as a likeness, a resemblance of Christ Jesus, the Son of God. The text in which he is introduced does not offer any support for the idea that he is a pre-incarnate appearance of Christ.

The fact that the Spirit deemed the Jewish believers unprepared to receive what He had to say about Melchizedek indicates that there was something about the subject that would be difficult for Jewish believers to receive. They would certainly have no problem receiving the revelation that Melchizedek was a pre-incarnate appearance of Christ. On the other hand, the revelation that he was, in fact, a Gentile king-priest, descended from Ham, ruling in Jerusalem before Abraham, to whom Abraham paid tithes, would most assuredly choke the faith of Jewish Christians. Indeed, our attitude toward Ham and his descendants is such that it is difficult for any Christian to receive.

We should not choke on this! God intends to reconcile to Himself all things through Jesus Christ the Son of God:

> And having made peace through the blood of His cross, by Him to reconcile all things unto Himself; by Him, I say, whether they be things in earth, or things in heaven — Colossians 1:20

~

Appendix-2: Kingdom of God and Kingdom of Heaven

Many believe the phrases *kingdom of God* and *kingdom of Heaven* identify entirely separate kingdoms. The author held this opinion for many years until he noticed that the phrases are used interchangeably in the Scripture. This appendix offers a closer look at this question. In the text, we encourage the Bible student to compare Mark 1:15 with Matthew 3:2 and 4:17; Mark 4:1-2 with Matthew 13:1-2; then compare Mark 4:11, 30-32 with Matthew 13:11, 31-32; Mark 10:23-24 with Matthew 19:23; Luke 6:20 with Matthew 5:3; Luke 7:28 with Matthew 11:11-12; and Luke 13:29 with Matthew 8:11. While it is possible to offer a reasonable, if somewhat strained, argument for the idea that the kingdom of God and the kingdom of Heaven are separate kingdoms, most of the above comparisons will not allow an honest student to avoid what is obvious—these expressions are used interchangeably.

First, the two expressions are clearly used interchangeably in the following examples:

Matthew 4:12-20

> Now when Jesus had heard that John was cast into prison, he departed into Galilee;
>
> And leaving Nazareth, he came and dwelt in Capernaum, which is upon the sea coast, in the borders of Zabulon and Nephthalim:
>
> That it might be fulfilled which was spoken by Esaias the prophet, saying,
>
> The land of Zabulon, and the land of Nephthalim, by the way of the sea, beyond Jordan, Galilee of the Gentiles;
>
> The people which sat in darkness saw great light; and to them which sat in the region and shadow of death light is sprung up.

From that time Jesus began to preach, and to say, Repent: for the kingdom of Heaven is at hand.

And Jesus, walking by the sea of Galilee, saw two brethren, Simon called Peter, and Andrew his brother, casting a net into the sea: for they were fishers.

And he saith unto them, Follow me, and I will make you fishers of men.

And they straightway left their nets, and followed him.

Mark 1:9-18

And it came to pass in those days, that Jesus came from Nazareth of Galilee, and was baptized of John in Jordan.

And straightway coming up out of the water, he saw the heavens opened, and the Spirit like a dove descending upon him:

And there came a voice from heaven, saying, Thou art my beloved Son, in whom I am well pleased.

And immediately the Spirit driveth him into the wilderness.

And he was there in the wilderness forty days, tempted of Satan; and was with the wild beasts; and the angels ministered unto him.

Now after that John was put in prison, Jesus came into Galilee, preaching the gospel of the kingdom of God,

And saying, The time is fulfilled, and the kingdom of God is at hand: repent ye, and believe the gospel.

Now as he walked by the sea of Galilee, he saw Simon and Andrew his brother casting a net into the sea: for they were fishers.

And Jesus said unto them, Come ye after me, and I will make you to become fishers of men.

And straightway they forsook their nets, and followed him.

The passages are clearly parallel accounts of the beginning phase of Jesus' public ministry. Herod had John the Baptist imprisoned, and Jesus began His public ministry, picking up where John left off, with the message John had preached: "Repent, for the kingdom . . . is at hand."[1686] The correspondence between the two passages makes it clear that what Jesus taught regarding the kingdom of God is the same thing He taught regarding the kingdom of Heaven. In Mark, we read that the expression He used was Kingdom of God, and in Matthew, we are told the expression He used was Kingdom of Heaven. Nothing in either passage offers any reason to assume He was talking about separate kingdoms. No matter how one puts this together, the point is clear: Jesus used the expressions *kingdom of God* and *kingdom of Heaven* interchangeably.

Certainly, no one reading this book would imagine that one of the Gospel writers made an error and remembered Jesus saying *kingdom of God* while the other remembered Him saying *kingdom of Heaven*. It does not seem likely that Jesus used only one of the two phrases, and the Holy Spirit is merely offering an alternate but equivalent phrasing. However, if that is the case, it means the Spirit is providing a commentary on His words—in other words, showing us that when Jesus said kingdom of God, He meant the same thing John meant when he said kingdom of Heaven. Third, assuming Jesus used both expressions, the impress upon the mind is clear—both expressions refer to the same thing.

Nevertheless, it is conceded that when God uses different words to speak of the same thing, He desires to bring forward a different aspect of it. In other words, a distinction between the two phrases does exist, but only as different aspects of the same kingdom.

[1686] Matthew 3:1-2

Truly, no further examples are needed, but more examples are available. Notice that Mark and Matthew ascribe the same parables to the kingdom of God and kingdom of Heaven, respectively. In other words, Jesus' kingdom parables describe both the kingdom of God and the kingdom of Heaven in the same way. If the descriptions match in every way, the titles used to identify it are equivalent, or synonymous.

Mark 4:1-2 and Matthew 13:1-2 both set up the Lord's dissertations on the mysteries of the kingdom. In Mark, the Spirit refers to this kingdom as the kingdom of God, and in Matthew, He refers to it as the kingdom of Heaven.

When the disciples asked the Lord why He spoke in parables, His answer in Mark was that it was because it was given to them, and not to the world, to know the mysteries of the kingdom of God.[1687] In Matthew, He said it was because it was given to them, and not the world, to know the mysteries of the kingdom of Heaven.[1688]

Mark does not present the Parable of the Wheat and Tares. However, he does include the Parable of the Mustard Seed.[1689] That parable is virtually identical to the one recorded in Matthew 13:31-32. In both cases, the grain of mustard seed is used as a symbolic representation of the kingdom; in both cases, its smallness is noted; and both accounts state the facts that when it is planted and grows, it becomes the "greatest among herbs" and the birds lodge in its branches. Yet, as pertinent to our discussion, there is one difference. In Mark, we are told the Lord is likening the kingdom of God to the mustard seed; in Matthew, we are told He is likening the kingdom of Heaven to the mustard seed.

[1687] Mark 4:11
[1688] Matthew 13:11
[1689] Mark 4:30-32

In Mark 10:23-24, Jesus remarked on how difficult it is for the rich to enter the kingdom. In Matthew 19:23, Jesus reflects on the same subject. In Mark, He refers to the kingdom as the kingdom of God. In Matthew, He refers to the kingdom as the kingdom of Heaven. If any man be contentious and argue that it is certainly possible that the rich face the same difficulty in both the kingdom of God and the kingdom of Heaven, we only reply that the assumption most natural to the text, especially when the prior evidence is considered, is that Jesus is talking about one and the same kingdom.

The same argument is applicable to the comparison of Luke 6:20, "Blessed be ye poor, for yours is the kingdom of God" with Matthew 5:3, "Blessed are the poor in spirit: for theirs is the kingdom of Heaven." Likewise, concerning John the Baptist, in Luke 7:28, Jesus said, "He that is least in the kingdom of God is greater than he" while in Matthew 11:11, He said, "He that is least in the kingdom of Heaven is greater than he."

There is clearly no argument that can explain away Luke 13:29 with Matthew 8:11.

In Luke 13:29, Jesus says, "And they shall come from the east, and from the west, and from the north, and from the south, and shall sit down in the kingdom of God." According to Matthew 8:11, this gathering occurs "in the kingdom of Heaven." Clearly, the kingdom of God and the kingdom of Heaven are identifying the same kingdom.

Add to this the observation that these are never presented juxtaposed to one another. In other words, you never read the kingdom of God and of heaven, for example.

Second, the argument of those who conclude that these phrases identify distinct kingdoms is not compelling.

It will be shown that the distinction is not of two separate kingdoms, but rather, of two aspects of one kingdom.

It is usually argued that the kingdom of God is spiritual, while the kingdom of Heaven refers to the physical manifestation of God's kingdom rule on Earth. With this, our author agrees wholeheartedly. However, this does not mean there are two separate kingdoms: one spiritual and one physical. Rather, the spiritual rule of God (the kingdom of God) is extended from His heavenly throne over all His creation, including the earth—and this rule of God from Heaven is called the kingdom of Heaven.

The distinction that the kingdom of God refers to the spiritual and the kingdom of Heaven refers to the physical is taken from Luke 17:19-21, where we are told that the kingdom of God is within you, and that it does not come "with observation." First, let's address the fact that the kingdom of God is within us.

The kingdom of Heaven is rightly understood to be the manifestation of the Sovereign rule of God over the earth, but it should not be limited to the earth. The kingdom of Heaven is the kingdom Jesus went to heaven to receive. He has received it and will return to the earth to establish this kingdom in the earth—so that, at last, His will will be done in Earth, as it is in heaven. Meanwhile, the kingdom of God, which is in us, exerts the influence of the kingdom of God's dear Son through us into this world, serving the soon-to-return King of kings and Lord of lords. We represent the kingdom of Heaven in the earth today as ambassadors to the King in absentia.

Christ bought the "field" (world), and "all power is given unto (Him) in heaven and in earth"—He is Lord of all; however, He has not "taken unto himself His great power."[1690] His citizens are crying with the rage of the heathen[1691] and responding to our declaration that Jesus is Lord, with the answer, "we will not have that man to reign over us."[1692] Nevertheless, one day soon, He will remove His servants from the earth and then return with us to establish the kingdom of God in manifestation of His glorious King in the kingdom of Heaven on Earth. Meanwhile, the parables explaining the mysteries of the kingdom of Heaven (of God) clearly indicate that kingdom is present in what we might call its mystery form. In other words, every parable Jesus gave concerning the kingdom of Heaven (of God) is about how that kingdom is operating here, on the earth, during our dispensation.

To settle this in your heart, remember that our Lord refers to those parables as the mysteries of the kingdom of Heaven and of God. Read the parables. Each of them describes His work as it proceeds during our time as wheat (believers planted as seed) in the field (the world). We apply those lessons to our work in the earth today. Likewise, all the parables describe our work now. This proves that, in its mystery form, the kingdom of Heaven is present in the earth today—within you. Which brings us to the next question: how is it that the kingdom of God comes "without obser-vation" if in fact the kingdom of God and the kingdom of Heaven are the same kingdom?

John the Baptist, as well as Jesus, the Son of the living God, heralded, "The kingdom of Heaven is at hand."

[1690] Revelation 11:17
[1691] Psalm 2
[1692] Luke 19:11-27

After Christ died on the Cross, was buried, and on the third day rose from the dead, He conquered the prince of this world and took the kingdoms of the earth into His power; hence, He declared: "All power is given unto me in heaven and in earth." He translated all who receive Him as LORD into the kingdom of God's dear Son, and through them, He exerts His kingdom authority in this world. This is the form of the kingdom as it is operating in the world today, and it is described in the kingdom parables.

In other words, the kingdom was *at hand* during the days of John the Baptist and Jesus Christ and is present in the believer now. However, believers are commanded not to take the kingdom authority to themselves, but rather, like Christ, to take up our Cross and follow Him—preaching the Gospel to everyone in the world, declaring Jesus is Lord and commanding all men everywhere to repent and believe the Gospel. This form of the kingdom, indeed, did not come "with observation." Instead, this form of the kingdom is "within you." When Christ returns to Earth, we will come with Him, and then the Kingdom of God/Heaven will take over all the kingdoms of the world.

~

Appendix-3 — Dating the Beginning of Rome

Dating the first three transitions is relatively simple. God took the kingdom of Israel and transferred it to Nebuchadnezzar when the prophet Jeremiah declared it from the mouth of God to Israel (c.608 B.C.). The next transition was also clear-cut: when Persia defeated Babylon—we know the name of the first king of that kingdom was Cyrus (Isaiah 48:17; 45:1-2) and we can confidently date it at 539 B.C. The third transfer is also easy to mark: we know the first ruler was Alexander, and although some debate arises regarding the date, we know it was when he finally conquered Persia and became the undisputed ruler of the world—c.331 B.C.

Historians will confess to the difficulty of identifying a clear beginning of the Roman Empire. The rise of Rome to a world power happened slowly.

Some date it with the annexation of Greece, or much of it, to Roman control in c.149-146 B.C. But the war was inconclusive, and the Greeks continued to resist, with some of the regions reasserting independence from Rome. It was not until c.88 B.C. that Greece was finally and fully subdued by Rome. However, Alexander's Empire was divided into four kingdoms, and this only accounts for one of them— Macedon. What about the rest of Alexander's Empire?

The region we call Turkey was the second of the four divisions of Alexander's Empire. It includes what was then called Asia and Galatia. This was the second kingdom to form out of Alexander's divided Empire. Asia came under Roman power in 133 B.C., when Attalus III of Pergamum bequeathed his kingdom to Rome, but Galatia did not become a Roman province until Augustus established it in 25 B.C. And that's two years after Caesar Augustus was proclaimed Emperor of the Roman Empire, c.27 B.C., which is the usual date used to mark the beginning of the Roman Empire.

Then we have the third and fourth kingdoms into which Alexander's empire was divided to account for—Syria and Egypt. These came under Roman power earlier.

The Seleucid Empire dissipated after the fall of Antiochus III (c.186 B.C.), predecessor of the infamous Antiochus IV Epiphanes—the prototype of Antichrist. Epiphanes fulfilled Daniel 11:13-19, and his heir established the "estate" in which Daniel's prophesied little horn will rise to power (Daniel 11:21-45). When Antiochus IV died in c.164 B.C., Rome exerted significant influence over Egypt; but it did not gain total control until about 83 B.C. Successive rulers in Syria, and Israel were mere vassals, but the area continued to be troublesome until Pompey settled it firmly under the power of Rome in 64 B.C.

Rome exerted significant influence in Egypt from the time of Ptolemy VI, securing him in his throne and providing protection to Egypt against invasion by Antiochus IV (169-164 B.C.). A little over 80 years later, Ptolemy XI was placed on the throne of his father by the Roman General Sulla, after he awarded both Egypt and Cyprus to Rome in 88 B.C. Nevertheless, Egypt did not yield to Roman power until the death of Cleopatra VII in 30 B.C.

As you can see, essentially, Rome did not become a world Empire until Octavian rose to power under the name *Augustus Caesar* and coalesced the Empire under his sole rule. This was made formal in 27 B.C., and so that is the date most use as the beginning of the Roman Empire.

∼

Appendix-4 — *The Temptation of the Christ*

There are two accounts of the temptation in the desert. One is found in Matthew 4:1-11. The other is in Luke 4:1-14. Both accounts describe events that occurred while Jesus was being tempted in the wilderness, but they are not parallel accounts.

First, the order of the temptations: In Luke's account the order is 1. command the stone to be made bread, 2. the offer of the kingdoms of the world if Jesus would bow and worship Satan, and then 3. leap from the pinnacle of the Temple; whereas in Matthew's account the order is 1. command the stone be made bread, 2. leap from the pinnacle of the Temple, and then 3. the offer of the kingdoms of the world if Jesus will bow to Satan.

Second, in Luke's account the suggestion is that Jesus was tempted throughout the forty days of fasting (Luke 4:1), but in Matthew's account it is clear the round of temptations recorded there occurred at the end of His forty days of fasting (Matthew 4:2-3).

When the accounts are read carefully, the following scenario emerges: The Holy Ghost drove Jesus into the wilderness to be tempted of the devil, and Satan was given access to tempt Him. Satan began right away working on Jesus, taking advantage of His physical weakness brought on by the fasting.

The effort to provoke Jesus to turn stone to bread was an obvious attempt to provoke Jesus to answer a physical need by using His power independently from His Father.

The temptation to leap from the pinnacle of the Temple was an attempt to seduce Jesus into acting on His allegiance to His Father and desire to honor His Word, but to do so independently of His Father.

These efforts failed.

But our interest is in Satan's offer to give Jesus all the kingdoms of the world. Satan had to know Jesus was the heir and would inherit all the kingdom of men anyway. The only way this could have been thought to be a temptation to Jesus is if Satan knew what cup His Father had given Him to drink in order to obtain the kingdoms of the world. Satan is, by all accounts, extraordinarily intelligent, and although he, like all others, was blinded to the first coming of Christ when it occurred, Satan heard John refer to Jesus as "the Lamb of God," and it seems to me very unlikely that Satan did not put this together and realize what was going on. I think Satan figured out that Jesus would die for the sins of mankind and "take away the sin of the world," thereby breaking Satan's hold on the kingdom of men.

Furthermore, I think Satan understood how Jesus would die: by crucifixion. It became his mission to stop that from happening. I think Satan was offering Jesus an alternative to the Cross, a compromise offer.

Finally, we notice that in Luke's account Lucifer makes a run at this in the middle of his temptations of Christ, and then, in Matthew's account, we learn that he comes at Jesus with all three temptations, only this time hits him with this one last, when Jesus has been worn down physically, mentally, and emotionally.

One last observation of interest: we notice that earlier, when Satan attempted to get Jesus to bow to him in exchange for all the kingdoms of the world without having to suffer the Cross, Jesus said, "Get thee behind Me, Satan" (Luke 4:8). But at the end of the temptation ordeal, when Satan made his last grand effort to get Jesus to compromise and take the kingdoms of the world in exchange for transferring His worship from the Creator to His arch enemy, Satan, Jesus said, "Get thee hence, Satan" (Matthew 4:9).

Was the first an invitation extended to Satan to take his proper place behind the Son of God? Was this moment of exchange between God manifest in the flesh and Satan even more profound than we have before perceived? Did God in flesh (Immanuel) make a counteroffer to Satan?

Lucifer offered to give the kingdoms of the world up if the God-Man would bow and worship Satan; did the God-Man counter by commanding Satan to take his place behind the Son of God? Having refused to yield, at his second effort, did Jesus withdraw the offer and commanded Satan to "get thee hence"?

This becomes even more intriguing when we consider that later, Satan will attempt to use Peter to dissuade Jesus from going to the Cross, and Jesus will say to Peter, "Get thee behind Me, Satan" (Matthew 16:21-23). And then, toward the end of His ministry on Earth, Jesus declared that the "prince of this world" would be "cast out" (Get thee hence!). And Jesus said, finally, ". . . the prince of this world is judged" (John 16:11).

~

Topical Index

Jesus:

~ T ~

~ U ~

~ V ~

~ End of Topical Index ~

Scripture Index

~ End of Scripture Index ~

THE KEY TO RELEASING GOD'S POWER INTO THE WORLD

KINGDOM POWER

by **PRAYER & FASTING**

(Second Edition)

JERRY SCHEIDBACH

The prequel to *God's War! Kingdom Power by Prayer and Fasting* will impact your life like it has thousands. A great Bible study guide for small groups on the subject of prayer and fasting.

Go to www.booksatdbp.com (special pricing for bulk orders)

~ 533 ~

PRAYER FOR REVIVAL

A Textbook on Prayer, Fasting, and Revival

DR. BENNY BECKUM

Prayer For Revival is a modern day classic! Dr. Beckum presents a textbook on prayer that reads like a powerful devotional. This book does not merely teach you about prayer, it moves you to do it. ***Go to http://www.theintercessor.org***

Prayer First is a vital truth every believer needs to understand rightly. This little book presents a sermon put together in collaboration with Dr. Beckum and Dr. Scheidbach to prove from the Bible that prayer is first.

Go to www.booksatdbp.com (special pricing for bulk orders)

THE
NEW CART
CHURCH
Doing the Right Thing the Wrong Way

Jerry Scheidbach

The New Cart Church presents a call to return to the "old paths" where, as God said in Jeremiah 6:16, is the "good way." A must read for any who seek revival in our day!

Go to www.booksatdbp.com (special pricing for bulk orders)

he Visions Of Daniel

Comprehensive Commentary On The Remarkable Prophecies of Daniel

SCHEIDBACH

God's War makes much use of Dr. Scheidbach's knowledge in bib-
ical prophecy. This is the most insightful commentary on Daniel
o come along in more than a century.

Go to www.booksatdbp.com (Only available as a PDFI)

THE
BOOK OF THE
HORSE

THE
BOOK OF THE
HORSE

Exeter Books

NEW YORK

Consultant Editor
Pamela Macgregor-Morris
Technical Consultant
Jane Starkey

Contributing Editors
Peter Churchill · W. S. Crook · Jane Kidd · Dr Bruce Macfadden B.S. PhD.
Pamela Macgregor-Morris · Jonathan Powell · Fiona Scott
Colin Vogel · Toni Webber

A QED BOOK
Copyright © 1979 QED Publishing Limited
First published in USA 1982
Reprinted 1986
by Exeter Books
Distributed by Bookthrift
Exeter is a registered trademark of Bookthrift Marketing, Inc.
Bookthift is a registered trademark of
Bookthift Marketing New York, New York
ALL RIGHTS RESERVED
ISBN 0 671 05546 1

Filmset in Britain by Vantage Photosetting Co. Ltd.
Colour origination in Italy by Starf Photolito SRL., Rome
Printed in Hong Kong by Lee Fung Asco Ltd.

This book was designed and produced by
QED Publishing Limited
6 Blundell St., London N7 9BH
Editorial Director Jeremy Harwood
Art Director Alastair Campbell
Production Director Edward Kinsey
Art Editor David Mallott
Editors Jenny Barling, Marion Casey, Alastair Dougall,
David MacFadyen
Art and editorial co-ordinator Heather Jackson
Designer Marnie Searchwell
Illustrators Kai Choi, Harry Clow, Christopher Forsey,
Tony Graham, Rory Kee, Elaine Keenan, Edwina Keene,
Abdul Aziz Khan, Kathleen McDougall, John Woodcock,
Clive Haybal, Martin Woodford, Kathy Wyatt, Jim Marks
Photographers Mike Busselle, Mike Fear, Colin Maher,
Jay Swallow, Jon Wyand
Picture Research Maggie Colbeck, Linda Proud
Paste up Jean Kelly

QED would like to thank the many individuals and
organisations who have helped in the preparation of this
book. Invaluable assistance was given by: Mr H. J.
Cooper F.W.C.F.; Gill Ennis; Melanie Gee; Diana
James; Mr Martin Kiley of the Santa Sleigh Stud; Mr A.
S. Laing, Hon. Sec. of the Vale of Aylesbury Hunt;
Leslie Lane; Mr Lanigan of the Coolmore Stud; Sheana
MacFadyean; Marcia McCloud; Patricia Monaham; Bill
Nicholls; Sue Peach; Carol Rodwell; Warner Shepherd,
Leicester; Miss Pauline Voss and Mrs G. M. Taylor of
the Huntersfield Farm Riding Centre, Sutton, Surrey;
The British Horse Society; The British Show Jumping
Association; The Department of Palaeontology at the
Natural History Museum, London; The Diamond
Centre for the Handicapped, Carshalton, Surrey;
National Equestrian Centre, Kenilworth, Warks.; S
lers Ltd.; The Riding Department of Austin Re
Regent St. London W1; The Royal College Veterin
Library; The Worshipful Company of Farriers; Rosal
Billingham.

Contents

Foreword
Lucinda Prior-Palmer

Contents

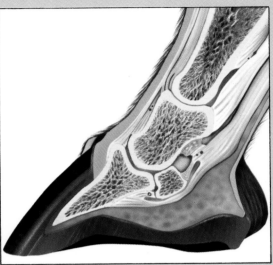

Foreword
by Lucinda Prior-Palmer

Lucinda Prior-Palmer, with her horse 'Be Fair', after winning the 1975 European Individual Three Day Event Championship. She is one of the most distinguished and successful event riders in the world.

It is with genuine appreciation that I write the foreword to this book. The Book of the Horse is, I believe, revolutionary of its kind. It is the first time that I have read an encyclopedia of the horse which lays out in such a modern and captivating formula all the various subjects connected with this, the greatest of all animals.

A great deal of magic is attached to the horse. If you like him, you love him. There is an obsessive attraction in his personality, his adroitness and courage and in his ability to reciprocate human communication. Such qualities go unremarked by non-believers. They may acknowledge that one end bites and the other kicks, but it seems as if they do not wish to understand more than that. More the pity for them; they will never know what a wealth of fascination and happiness they are missing.

The Book of the Horse serves a dual purpose. I personally find it intriguing, as it gives a wealth of vital information, precisely and imaginatively presented. Many fascinating pictures and illustrations take the place of the cumbersome mass of text normally associated with instructional literature. Following the modern trend of thought that the mind retains visual images better than verbal ones, the practical sections contain many lessons and rules of equitation in accurate and appealing diagrams. Anyone wishing to learn about horses from the beginning would be well advised to start their pursuit of knowledge here.

One question remains to be answered. Books on horses exist in abundance and have done so for many years. Why? Why do people read so much about horses, especially when many have very little connection with them?

The answer is anyone's guess, but I would like to believe that it represents a tribute to the animal that has featured through the ages with such vital importance. From the earliest days of recorded history, the horse took part in sport and war; for thousands of years he was the everyday means of transport. Later, with the advent of mechanization, a stronger emphasis was placed on sport and leisure.

There is no animal in the world as versatile. Horses are involved in many different spheres – polo, jousting, steeplechasing, flat racing and hunting in many different forms being but a few. The horse takes part in no less than four separate Olympic contests – show jumping, dressage, pentathlon and horse trials. Such extensive involvement, even though his use as a means of transport has declined, surely explains at least a part of the reason why so many people are interested in reading about the horse.

Many spectators must watch in awe and envy the top-class exponents of equestrian sport. Among them Lester Piggott and Eddie Macken are two artists who spring immediately to mind. They have come as near to perfection as nature will permit. Such heights seem unattainable. To some, it may seem barely worth learning or continuing to ride. The maestros have obviously been born with something that normal people do not possess. That, however, I do not believe. As the introduction to the chapter on Basic Riding states: 'The key to learning to ride is basically one of confidence.' The rider needs faith in his or her ability to communicate with the horse. Equally, the horse needs such confidence in the rider.

Confidence and communication. This forms the basis of success with horses from the beginning right through to the star of the show. It may be many years before such confidence takes sufficient root. Work, perseverance and patience are the secret of the search. Luck, of course, is a transient quantity important to everyone in anything they undertake.

Every step is worth it, even though it is frequently two steps forward and one step back. It is an education in life as well as in horses, and the learning lasts forever.

Horses carry the history of mankind on their backs. If you should find one is carrying you as well, acknowledge your good fortune and indeed your honour. When trust and respect, the foundation rock of any satisfactory partnership, is formed between you and your horse, an unexpected dimension will be added to your life.

Chapter One

The origins of the horse

Man's partnership with the horse dates back some 5,000 years or so to the time when the animal was first domesticated in Asia. However, the history of horses themselves goes much further back than that – to the remote prehistoric past. The present-day horse species – these include the domestic horse and its close relatives, the zebras, asses, kiang and Przewalski's horse – are only the remains of a once much bigger collection belonging to the group, or genus, *Equus* that lived during the Ice Age, or Pleistocene Epoch. Many of these species became extinct at the end of the Pleistocene some 12,000 to 15,000 years ago.

But even the Pleistocene is not the starting point for horse history. In fact, *Equus* was preceded by a spectacular history of numerous kinds of fossil horses spanning some 55 million years of geological time. The story of this evolutionary process, leading up to the present-day *Equus*, is the theme of this chapter.

Palaeontologists and horses

The major source of knowledge as far as the evolution of the horse is concerned is based on the very rich fossil deposits of western North America. However, the story begins during the first half of the nineteenth century in England. There, in 1840, the great British palaeontologist Sir Richard Owen was the first to describe a genus of fossil horse, to which he gave the name *Hyracotherium*. This horse had been collected the previous year from the Eocene clay deposits that surround London; these are about 55 million years old.

In the latter half of the nineteenth century, the focus of the science switched to North America, with the foundation of many of the now prominent natural history museums there. The establishment of these museums increased public interest in palaeontology and numerous expeditions were sent out by them to explore and collect the rich fossil deposits in the west. As a result, numerous fossil horses were collected and sent back to the museums for study by some of the founders of North American palaeontology. Such early studies were very influential; for example, they had a profound influence on the acceptance of Darwin's Theory of Evolution, because of the palaeontological support they provided for it.

One of the most prominent students of horse evolution during the second half of the nineteenth century was O. C. Marsh, the Professor of Palaeontology at Yale University. The Yale expeditions to western North America were frequently both exciting and successful, and, as a result, one of the largest collections of fossil horses was amassed there.

In these studies, Marsh was aided by fellow scientists such as Oscar Harger, Max Schlos-

The British palaeontologist Sir Richard Owen. In 1840, he discovered and described the first genus of fossil horse.

ser, George Baur and Samuel Wendell Williston – all of whom worked under him at Yale. He also was aided by the vast private fortune of his uncle, George Peabody; part of this was used to establish the Peabody Museum of Natural History at Yale and part of it financed the various collecting expeditions.

In 1876, Marsh named a new genus of

fossil horse, *Eohippus*, or the During Marsh's time, this wa known horse collected in No and it still is today. It is kno Paleocene and early Eocen western North America, whicl million years old – roughly th the Eocene London Clay de the twentieth century, promine American palaeontologists c collections of *Hyracotherium* and Europe with those of *E* North America and concluded t different names actually repr one form. Based on the accept rules, Owen's genus *Hyracotheri* 1840, has priority over Marsl named in 1876. But the name the 'dawn horse' is still in genera vernacular for *Hyracotherium*.

After the early flowering of horse evolution by Marsh and became apparent that the North deposits contained the principal li history of the subject. As a result, American palaeontologists have co greatly to the understanding of tl These major figures include Henry Osborn of the American Museum o

Fossil horses, particularly Eohippus or 'dawn horse' **(below),** *played an important part in confirming Charles Darwin's revolutionary theory of evolution, contained in his monumental treatise 'On the Origin of Species' published in 1859. A quarter of a century later in 1876 the great British naturalist Thomas Huxley* **(near right),** *a prominent supporter of Darwin's theory, came to the USA and studied the major palaeontological collections of the time. He was particularly impressed by the collection of fossil horses that O. C. Marsh* **(far right),** *Professor of Palaeontology at Yale University, had amassed as a result of his expeditions into western North America. Huxley felt that this collection gave considerable support to Darwin's views.*

During a discussion between the two men, Huxley began sketching his idea of the then hypothetical ancestral horse, Eohippus, and then added a rider, which Marsh christened Eohomo ('dawn man'). Later that year, Marsh was able to scientifically describe the horse, if not its rider.

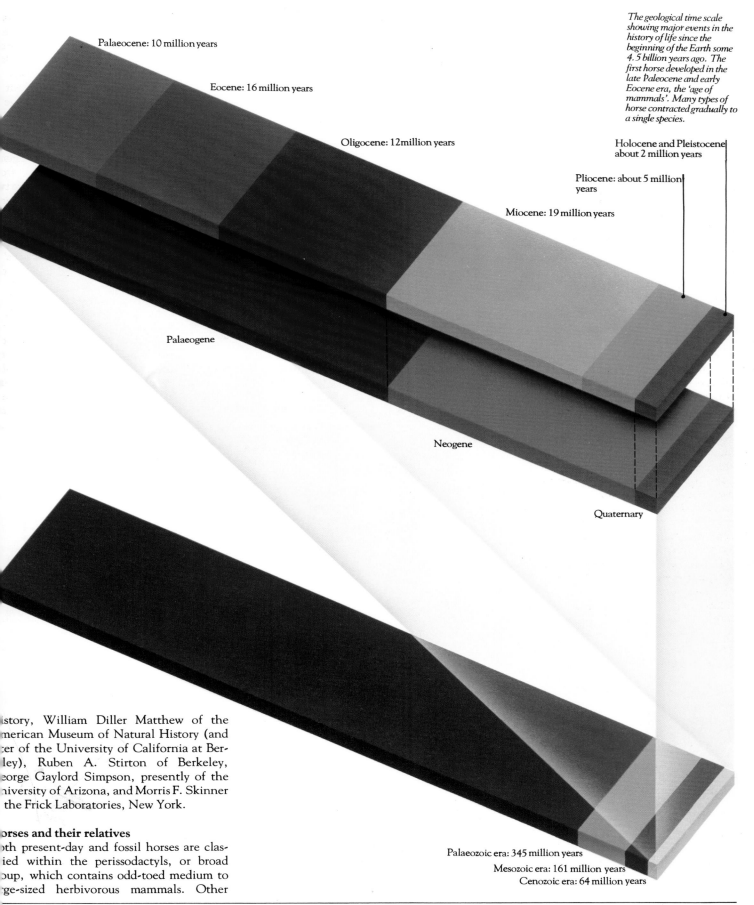

Palaeocene: 10 million years

Eocene: 16 million years

Oligocene: 12million years

The geological time scale showing major events in the history of life since the beginning of the Earth some 4.5 billion years ago. The first horse developed in the late Paleocene and early Eocene era, the 'age of mammals'. Many types of horse contracted gradually to a single species.

Holocene and Pleistocene about 2 million years

Pliocene: about 5 million years

Miocene: 19 million years

Palaeogene

Neogene

Quaternary

story, William Diller Matthew of the merican Museum of Natural History (and er of the University of California at Berley), Ruben A. Stirton of Berkeley, eorge Gaylord Simpson, presently of the niversity of Arizona, and Morris F. Skinner the Frick Laboratories, New York.

orses and their relatives
oth present-day and fossil horses are clasied within the perissodactyls, or broad oup, which contains odd-toed medium to ge-sized herbivorous mammals. Other

Palaeozoic era: 345 million years

Mesozoic era: 161 million years
Cenozoic era: 64 million years

odd-toed ungulates (hoofed animals) include the tapirs and rhinoceroses, as well as some extinct groups which include the largest land mammals that ever lived, the brontotheres. These ungulates derive their name from the fact that there are an odd number of digits – five, three or one – on each limb. In contrast, the artiodactyls, or even-toed ungulates, such as cows and sheep, generally have two digits, plus, in many cases, the reduced remains of two additional side toes.

The ancestry of the perissodactyls appears to have been within a wholly extinct group of primitive ungulates called the condylarths. The relatively well-known condylarth *Phenacodus* lived at the same time as *Hyracotherium*, and certain species of *Phenacodus* showed perissodactyl-like trends. However, the actual direct perissodactyl ancestor is not known from older Paleocene deposits.

For a long time, *Hyracotherium* was in fact considered to be the basic stock from which all the major groups of perissodactyls were ultimately descended. In a sense, therefore, *Hyracotherium* was thought to be as much a tapir or rhinoceros as it was a horse. Recent work, based on the structure of *Hyracotherium*'s skull, however, shows that it is indeed a horse.

Four-toed horses
Throughout the history of horse evolution,

Below *The present-day tapir (**left**) and rhinoceros (**right**). Both these animals are close perissodactyl relatives of the horse.*

several general trends can be seen related to the progressive adaptations of different types of horses to their own environment. Most of these have concerned their feeding and locomotion.

As has been seen, the earliest, or 'four-toed', horses, including *Hyracotherium*, first appear in late Paleocene deposits some 55 million years ago and range throughout the Eocene epoch until about 38 million years ago. These horses were already relatively advanced over their condylarth ancestors in many of their skull and skeletal adaptations. They had four digits (meaning both fingers and toes) in their fore foot – hence the name of this group – and three toes in their hind foot. The presence of four digits on the fore

feet of these early horses represented a transitional perissodactyl stage in the reduction from five to three toes – not a trend toward an even number of digits as seen in artiodactyls. Condylarths and many other mammals have five digits on each limb.

Besides a reduction in the number of digits, the four-toed (and later) horses also showed a trend towards elongation of the limbs, allowing for a longer stride while running; this, of course, would be especially important in evading predators. Their skull showed that trends were developing toward specialization for feeding on leafy material or for browsing. Evidence for this included the elongation of the molar grinding series of teeth and their deepening, along with

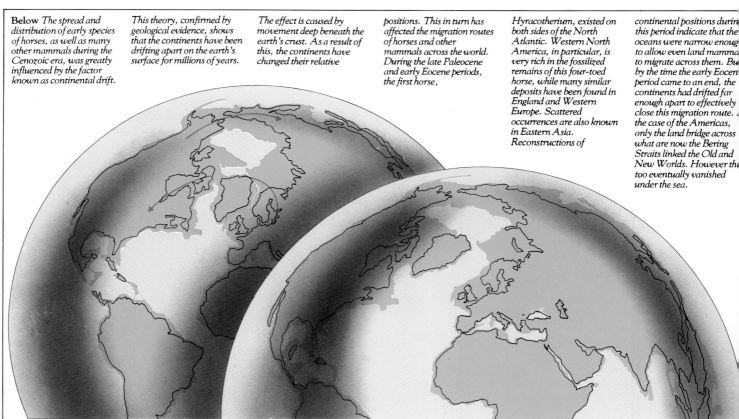

Below *The spread and distribution of early species of horses, as well as many other mammals during the Cenozoic era, was greatly influenced by the factor known as continental drift.*

This theory, confirmed by geological evidence, shows that the continents have been drifting apart on the earth's surface for millions of years.

The effect is caused by movement deep beneath the earth's crust. As a result of this, the continents have changed their relative

positions. This in turn has affected the migration routes of horses and other mammals across the world. During the late Paleocene and early Eocene periods, the first horse,

Hyracotherium, existed on both sides of the North Atlantic. Western North America, in particular, is very rich in the fossilized remains of this four-toed horse, while many similar deposits have been found in England and Western Europe. Scattered occurrences are also known in Eastern Asia. Reconstructions of

continental positions during this period indicate that the oceans were narrow enough to allow even land mammals to migrate across them. But by the time the early Eocene period came to an end, the continents had drifted far enough apart to effectively close this migration route. In the case of the Americas, only the land bridge across what are now the Bering Straits linked the Old and New Worlds. However this too eventually vanished under the sea.

ɔve *The Condylarth
ɔnacodus and* (**right**) *the
-toed horse Dinohippus,
ɔ late Miocene deposits
ɔorth America.*

ɔpening of the skull and jaws. In addition,
ɔent and very interesting work on fossil
ɔin endocasts (internal mud fillings) of
ɔracotherium* and other horses has shown
ɔt even the earliest horses were progressive
ɔ their brain evolution relative to more
ɔmitive mammals like condylarths.

ɔThe four-toed horses were of very small
ɔture in contrast to *Equus*: for example,
ɔracotherium* was about the size of a fox
ɔrier. Geographically, they were wide-
ɔead. Though their best-known remains are
ɔm North America, they are also well re-
ɔsented in early Eocene deposits in England
ɔd western Europe.

ɔThis geographical dispersion, together
ɔh the great similarity in *Hyracotherium* in
the Old and New Worlds, also shared by
many other mammals that lived at the same
time, implies that it was possible to migrate
between these areas before the middle
Eocene (about 49 million years ago). One
probable migration route at that time was
across the then much narrower Atlantic
Ocean. After early Eocene times, however,
the North Atlantic migration route seems to
have been inactive, due to the ever-
increasing width of the ocean as a result of
continental drift. Furthermore, after about
49 million years ago, it appears that horses
and other land mammals could only have
crossed between the Old and New Worlds via
the land bridge over what are now the Bering
Straits.

With the exception of one little-known
genus from the western USA, found in early
Oligocene sediments, the four-toed horses
became extinct some 38 million years ago, at
the end of the Eocene period. At this time,
one kind of four-toed horse seems to have
given rise to primitive three-toed horses.

Three-toed horses
The three-toed horses flourished during the
middle portion of the Cenozoic Era. This
group consisted of the primitive browsers,
feeding on leafy vegetation, and the advanced grazers, feeding on grassy vegetation.

The three-toed browsers, represented by
Mesohippus, appeared at the beginning of the
Oligocene Epoch some 38 million years ago.
When contrasted with four-toed horses,
these animals show a general increase in size.
Obviously, as their name implies, they had
three digits on each limb. The fourth digit on
the forelimbs had gradually become reduced
in the four-toed horses until it was a vestigial
splint, or completely lost, as in the three-toed
horse. There was also a relative elongation of
the limbs.

All of these features, as well as other ones,
were indications that the horses were further
adapting to a diet of leafy material and a more
efficient way of running. During the
Oligocene, they were confined to North
America; however, during the early Miocene
(some 20 million years ago), the anchithere
three-toed browsers, represented by *Anchitherium*, also spread to the Old World. The
browsers ultimately became extinct about 12
million years ago.

It is the development of three-toed grazers,
as well as browsers, that makes the Miocene
an important time in the history of horse
evolution, for this division represents an
important diversification of feeding habits.
Both at this time and later during their fossil
record, the most important evidence for this
change comes from developments in the
three-toed grazers' skull and teeth. Grazing
generally implies the eating of grasses as opposed to leafy material, and this means that a
grazer's dental structure will experience a
significant amount of wear, as grasses have a
high content of very abrasive minerals. Thus,
the early three-toed grazers show an increased
trend towards a deepening of their grinding
molars, jaws and skulls, which apparently was
a response to this then newly-acquired source
of food.

The history of the three-toed grazers is
located principally in North America,
though one very successful member of this
group, the hipparions, migrated from the
New World to the Old World during the late
Miocene. This was some 10 to 11 million
years ago. Hipparions were relatively diverse

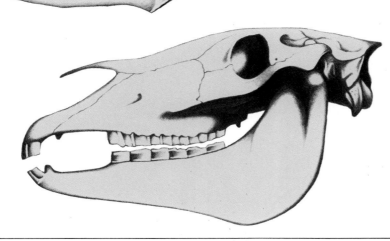

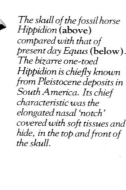

*The skull of the fossil horse
Hippidion* (**above**)
*compared with that of
present day Equus* (**below**).
*The bizarre one-toed
Hippidion is chiefly known
from Pleistocene deposits in
South America. Its chief
characteristic was the
elongated nasal 'notch'
covered with soft tissues and
hide, in the top and front of
the skull.*

Left *The distribution of
Equus during the Pleisto[ce]
era and today. The genu[s]
originated in North Ame[rica]
during the Pliocene era s[ome]
3 – 4 million years ago an[d]
subsequently migrated i[nto]
South America and the [Old]
World. During the
Pleistocene, Equus was
geographically more
widespread than any oth[er]
fossil horse. However at [the]
end of the era, many spec[ies]
became extinct, and the
present-day distribution [of]
wild Equus is limited by
comparison.*

in kinds and very abundant at most late
Miocene localities on both sides of the
Atlantic. They became extinct during the
early Pleistocene.

One-toed horses

One-toed horses first appeared during the
middle Miocene, about 15 million years ago.
These grazing horses apparently descended
from one type of three-toed grazer in North
America.

The transition from three toes to one was
the result of a gradual reduction in the size of
the side digits during the course of evolution,
until only the central digit on each limb
played any role in running. Advanced one-
toed horses, like those of the present day,
have small splints on each limb that represent
the vestiges of the side toes. The dental
structure of the one-toed horses was also
advanced over that of their predecessors,
with further deepening of the molars, jaw
and skull. With some exceptions, there was a
general trend towards increased body size
relative to most earlier horses.

Most of the fossil groups of one-toed
horses were confined to North and Central
America, where the horse originated. However, one bizarre group, represented by such
forms as *Hippidion*, did migrate into South
America during the Pleistocene some two to
three million years ago.

It was the one-toed horse *Dinohippus* that
was apparently ancestral to the Pleistocene
representatives of the present-day genus,
Equus; these first appear in middle Pliocene
deposits in North America between three

and four million years ago. There followed a
surprising evolution of different species
during both the Pliocene and the Pleistocene, resulting in the ancestors of many of
the types of horses that we know today.

Pleistocene representatives of *Equus* were
the most geographically widespread of all
fossil horses. It appears that about three million years ago they were very abundant in
North America and that they also migrated
into Central and South America, Asia,
Europe and Africa. But, by the end of the last

Ice Age, about 12,000 to 15,000 years ag[o]
many of the fossil species of *Equus* had b[e]
come extinct and only a few survive today.

The reasons for the extinction of la[rge]
Pleistocene *Equus* are as enigmatic as for [all]
the other large mammals, including t[he]
mammoth, mastodon and sabre-toothed ca[t]
that became extinct at the same time. So[me]
have suggested the reason lay in the chan[ge]
of climate, the influence of man, or perha[ps a]
combination of these and other facto[rs.]
Whatever the cause, the process was e[...]

Above *Early Equus. After
many million years of
development, this is the
ancestor of all present-day
horses.*

Right *Przewalski's horse, or
the wild horse of Mongolia.
The ancestors of this animal
were among the first horses
to be domesticated in
Southern Russia about
3,000 BC.*

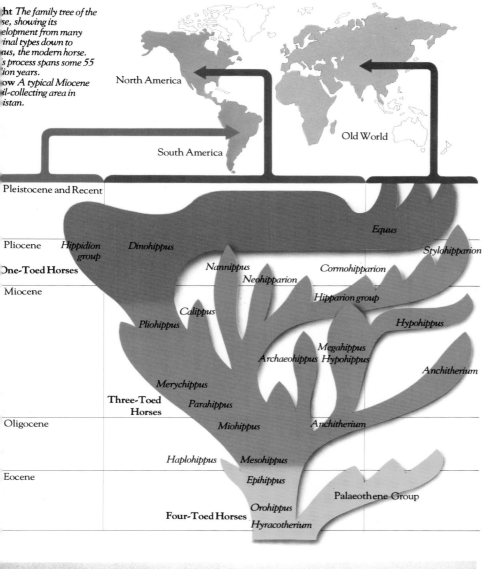

*ht The family tree of the
se, showing its
elopment from many
nal types down to
us, the modern horse.
s process spans some 55
ion years.
ow A typical Miocene
il-collecting area in
istan.*

North America

South America

Old World

Pleistocene and Recent

Pliocene — *Hippidion group* — *Dinohippus* — *Equus* — *Stylohipparion*

One-Toed Horses — *Nannippus* — *Neohipparion* — *Cormohipparion*

Miocene — *Calippus* — *Hipparion group*

Pliohippus — *Hypohippus*

Megahippus
Archaeohippus Hypohippus — *Anchitherium*

Merychippus

Three-Toed Horses — *Parahippus*

Oligocene — *Miohippus* — *Anchitherium*

Haplohippus — *Mesohippus*

Eocene — *Epihippus*

Orohippus — **Palaeothene Group**
Four-Toed Horses — *Hyracotherium*

treme, particularly in the New World. There, horses became totally extinct until their subsequent re-introduction to the region by the Spanish *conquistadores*.

Changes through time

As the fossil record of horses is reviewed, several changes or evolutionary trends are apparent, as the process of natural selection led to the development of forms better able to survive in a given environment. One of the most striking changes is a general increase in size from the earliest *Hyracotherium* to the present-day *Equus*, though there were some exceptions to this during the Miocene and Pliocene, when some horses remained the same size or even became smaller. Other changes seen during the course of horse evolution specifically relate to feeding and locomotion. Particularly in the grazers there was a deepening of the skull and jaws along with the evolution of the higher crowned molars needed to grind abrasive grass. As far as locomotion is concerned, horses show a trend toward relative elongation of the limbs and reduction or loss of the side toes. The most advanced form of this is the present-day one-toed horse *Equus*.

Domestication of the horse

The evidence for domestication of the horse comes principally from archaeological sites in the Old World. It includes skeletal remains of horses themselves, as well as cultural artifacts that depict horses, such as sculptures, carvings and coins. However, there is by no means universal agreement as to the origins of the domesticated horse.

For a long time, archaeologists have asked two interrelated questions: Were horses originally domesticated in one, or more than one, general region of the Old World? Was one, or more than one, kind of horse originally domesticated? In answer to the first question, there seems to be some agreement that the horse was first domesticated in Asiatic Russia around 3,000 BC, and that the process spread rapidly. By about 1500 BC there is evidence that the domestic horse was part of cultures throughout the Old World. It was found in cultures as far apart as those of Greece, Egypt, India and the Far East. The second question has proved harder to answer. Firstly, there is no general agreement as to what constitutes a distinct horse breed, variety, race, or even species. Some scientists feel that two different kinds – Przewalski's horse and the extinct tarpan – were involved in the original Russian domestication event. Others argue that the tarpan is merely an extinct form of Przewalski's horse, and therefore only one kind of horse was involved in the process.

Chapter Two

The horse and man

The first horse peoples

It has been suggested that among the first animals to be domesticated was the reindeer, which in North-east Asia was both ridden and used to draw sleds, as well as to provide milk, meat and leather. In this area, the habitats of both horse and reindeer overlapped to some extent, and it may be that, at some distant date, the horse first became domesticated as a kind of reindeer substitute. The theory does have possibilities, because even at a primitive level of technology, it would not have been too difficult for a reindeer-keeping people to begin taming wild horses. In poor weather conditions, such as heavy snow, the wild horse would not be able to attain, or sustain its usual speed of flight, so enabling a man driving a light reindeer sledge to come within roping range. During the summer, however, the only animals likely to be caught uninjured would be unweaned foals which, though deprived of their mothers, could be fostered instead by reindeer, whose milk is perfectly digestible by young horses. That of the cow, curiously enough, is not.

But probably it will never be known who the first true horsemen were. Some authorities suggest the ancient Chinese, others the Brahmins of India. In Brahmin mythology, Manu, the first human, is given a horse to ride, making it clear that the tradition of equitation in the sub-continent is a very ancient one indeed. On the other hand, Chinese ceramics of 3500 BC show horses both ridden and harnessed; perhaps, therefore, they were the first people to master both riding and driving.

To whichever nation the honour of first domesticating the horse properly belongs, it is certain that by the third millennium BC, similar skills of horsemanship were being developed by many different peoples in Asia, Europe and North Africa – in fact, in almost any area where the wild horse occurred. Persians, Assyrians and Sumerians had all learned to master the horse at a very early period, or so it would seem from the scanty written and archaeological evidence available at the present time.

The early horse peoples

The first literary mention of the animal occurs in a text of the Third Dynasty of Ur, dating from about 2100 BC, in which it is described as having 'a flowing tail', so distinguishing it from the onager or the ass. Mention is also made of it 'at the caravan route' – a colloquial phrase apparently meaning that the creature had been tamed. But for the next thousand years or so, pictorial or written records of the horse that have survived are rare indeed.

The first people to domesticate the horse in Europe may have been a hardy, resourceful and aggressive group of Aryan tribes who lived in the Great Steppes to the north of the mountains that border the Black and Caspian Seas. About 2000 BC, bands of these Steppe people began to migrate east, west, and south, taking with them great herds of cattle and horses. Seeking new homes was for them a necessity, since their native pastures and ranges had become virtually barren – probably through overgrazing. Recent discoveries of settlements in different parts of northern and western Europe, all containing horses' bones and all dating back to about 1700 BC, help lend weight to the theory.

Oddly enough, in some parts of the world, it would seem that harnessing and driving the horse actually preceded riding. The chariot seems to have been the usual way of going to the hunt, or to war, for the Hittites, for example, whose war-chariots were the scourge of the ancient world, and for the Egyptians, to whom the notion of riding a horse does not appear to have occurred.

A prehistoric cave painting from Lascaux in southern France. Primitive man hunted the horse for food, and such paintings were probably a plea to the gods to bring him fortune and success in the hunt.

Perhaps the chariot was a development from a domestic cart, though there is no evidence for this. Certainly, once it was invented, no army could afford to be without it, and by 2000 BC, the chariot was standard equipment throughout the Mediterranean and even as far as India.

On some peoples, of course, especially to wandering hunters and herdsmen, the idea of riding dawned at a very early period. Neolithic cave-paintings depict men riding four-legged equines, but unfortunately not in sufficient detail to positively identify the animals – they may in fact be onagers, which were domesticated before horses. But the original wild horses were small animals, no bigger than 12 or 13 hands high, and it is at least feasible that they could have been controlled by a man with a rope halter. After all, the American Indians required no further tack when they re-domesticated the feral

mustang, which they rode with neither sa dle nor bit right up to the present da

The earliest written reference to hor riding is a rather disparaging one. It occurs a letter written by King Zimm-Linn Mari – a vassal state of Babylon – to his so 'My lord should not ride upon a horse. Let r lord ride on a chariot or even on a mule, a let him know his royal status'. Presumably this time – about 1800 BC – the m and the chariot were considered more rigueur than the horse.

Certainly, during the Bronze Age the u and ownership of the horse drawn chariot v the prerogative of rank and seemed to almost a badge of aristocracy among the a cient nations of the Near East.

Somewhere in the region, unknown gen devised the light mobile vehicle which sup ceded the heavy solid-wheeled Sumerian c ager drawn chariot. Extraordinary skill a balance were required to drive the new, lig one, two or three man chariots, in which t charioteer looped the reins around his wai leaving his hands and arms free to work wi bow, spear or sword.

Probably the greatest of the chariote were the Hittites, whose empire, in the fo teenth century BC, reached across Kurc tan, Armenia and Syria. Surviving Hitt writings show a surprisingly modern approa to the training, breeding, feeding, exerc ing, grooming and veterinary care of hors What appears to be the foundations of indoor riding school have been discovei near the ancient city of Ugarit. The skeletal remains and the dimensions of t stables seem to indicate that Hittite hor were probably about the size of a mode pony. Somewhat endearingly, according the texts, their stallions were given nam like 'Foxy', 'Starry', 'White' and 'Piebal White horses were especially prized in t ancient Near East, where it was believed th after death, they drew the chariots of t gods.

Incidentally, it was also in Assyria th something approaching modern tack see to have been first invented – at least, so fa the Near East is concerned. Though th chiefly preferred the chariot both for ridi and for hunting, relief sculptures depict A syrian noblemen at the hunt riding hor fully equipped with saddle, bridle and eve martingale to prevent the horse from raisi its head too high. They did not, howeve possess stirrups, which were probably vented by nomadic Huns on the Chine border in about 500 AD; their use did r penetrate into Europe for at least anoth three centuries.

Throughout early history, Chinese hor manship was generally far in advance of th

elief of an early horse-
n, dressed for war, from
balace of Guzana in west
1.

in the West. As long ago as 1000 BC, the Chinese were using horses for almost every modern purpose – as battle chargers, as mounts for herdsmen, as draught and pack animals, and in all manner of farm work. Even at this early period, they had mastered the principles of selective breeding and raised different types of horse for particular purposes. Many of their skills had been learned, and then improved upon, from those practised by the Mongols, who had raided over the Chinese borders since time immemorial.

Horses had been domesticated in Egypt since about 1650 BC, the breed being largely

Top left King Ashurbanipal of Assyria leading his horses and below grooming and feeding in the royal stables. Assyrian horses were among the first to be equipped with saddles and bridles, though their riders had no stirrups. The horse, too, had its role in Assyrian religion as well as on the battlefield.

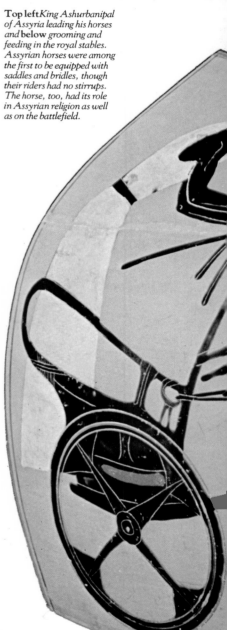

much improved by Libyan stock captured by the great Rameses, one of the most accomplished generals of antiquity – himself a brilliant charioteer, if his portraits are to be believed. In these, he is depicted driving an open-fronted chariot balancing with one foot on the chariot pole.

As Egypt declined, so the Persian Empire rose, to become supreme military power of the western world in about 600 BC. Much of Persian success was due to their horses, specially bred to carry heavy arms and armour. Despite their efficiency, they were not, however, elegant animals, and their gen-

erally unrefined appearance suggests a certain admixture of Przewalski blood.

The writings of Xenophon

Though the ancient Greeks were excellent horsemen, they were never as successful with cavalry as were the Persians. All the same, out of Greece came Xenophon, one of the most original writers on horses and horsemanship who ever lived. Xenophon was born of a wealthy family in Athens in 430 BC. Famous as a soldier and poet while still a young man, he also wrote the first known book on equitation. One of his main points

x collector's wagon,
n with corn collected
Egyptian peasants.
horse soon made its
e in transport as well as

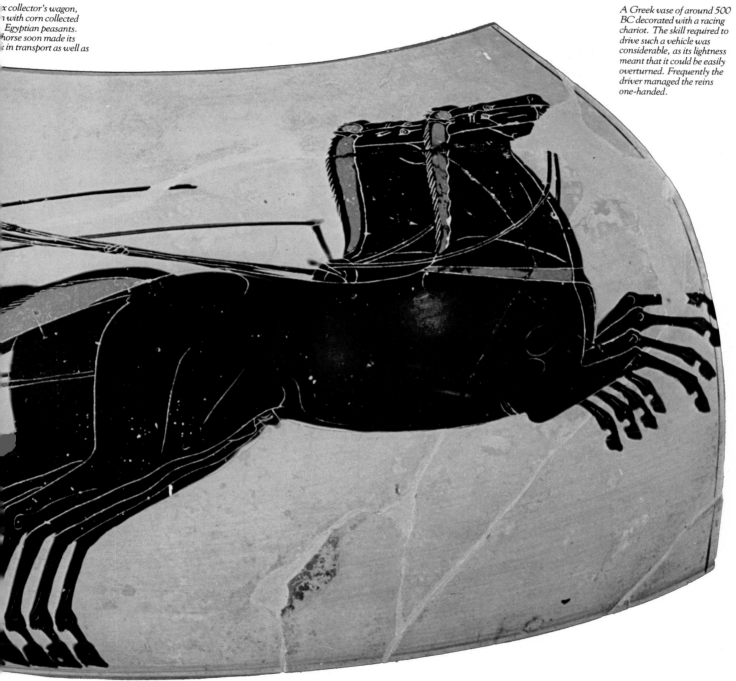

A Greek vase of around 500 BC decorated with a racing chariot. The skill required to drive such a vehicle was considerable, as its lightness meant that it could be easily overturned. Frequently the driver managed the reins one-handed.

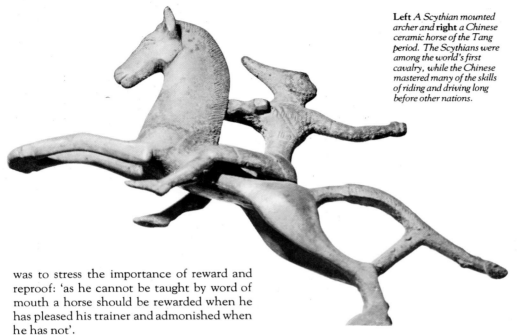

was to stress the importance of reward and reproof: 'as he cannot be taught by word of mouth a horse should be rewarded when he has pleased his trainer and admonished when he has not'.

Horsemen of today are unlikely to agree with Xenophon's views on head-carriage: 'The horse's neck should rise straight to the poll and thus the crest will then be in front of the rider.' Although he also wrote that the neck should bend at the poll, most Greek horses are depicted with virtually no bend at all. Nevertheless, he had a certain amount of reason on his side, for as he said: 'A horse with this type of conformation would be least able to bolt even if he was very spirited. For it is not by flexing the neck but by stretching it out that horses endeavour to bolt.'

In Xenophon's day, a roughened snaffle style of bit was used for training the young horse, and when sufficiently schooled, it progressed to a smooth, less severe type of snaffle. Concerning the rider's seat on the horse, Xenophon advised: 'I do not approve

A relief of a four-horse chariot from Cyprus. One of the main uses of horses was in war and, in it, chariots were the backbone of many armies.

of the seat as in a chair, but that which is like a man standing upright with his legs apart. For the thighs in this way have a better grip of the horse, and with the body erect one can with more force hold the javelin and strike from horseback if necessary.' Until the twentieth century, this was to remain the orthodox seat in Europe and remains so in the Western riding style of the United States. At this time, saddles with trees did not exist and although saddle cloths were sometimes used, they were considered to be suitable only for 'soft-bottomed' Persians, who, Xenophon observed, 'lay more coverlets upon the backs of their horses than upon their bodies, for they think of sitting softly rather than securely'.

Xenophon wrote that one must never lose one's temper when dealing with horses. 'When a courageous horse is unwilling to approach some object, it must be explained to him that it is not so awful, and if this fails, you must lead him gently to it and touch it yourself. Those who compel a horse with blows, make him more frightened than ever, for horses believe whenever they receive harsh treatment in such circumstances, that the feared objects are responsible for their discomfort.'

When or how the horse first arrived in Italy is uncertain; the earliest known record is a painted vase of the seventh century BC which depicts an Etruscan army on the march accompanied by horses. Although the Romans of the Republic and early Empire followed the Greek style of equitation, they were not really great horsemen. The Roman army consisted almost entirely of heavy infantry, and such cavalry as it pos-

sessed were largely ancillaries recrui[ted] from different parts of the Empire.

From Xenophon to Alexander the Gre[at] the quality of riding did not develop to a[n] large extent. On the other hand, the qual[ity] of horses was improved by crossing the B[ac]trian horse with the Macedon Tarpan-type[s] local stock.

In the ancient world, mares were k[ept] mainly for breeding and soldiers almost[al]ways rode stallions. Although the practice[of] gelding slaves was considered acceptable a[nd] even necessary, it was thought to be [too] painful and dangerous for stallions. For h[un]dreds of years the Scythians were the o[nly] people who denied this rule. Living on [the] plains north of the Danube, they used b[oth] mares and geldings in war. The reason[ing] behind this is very sound, as a stallion in [war] can become quite unmanageable if he dete[cts] the presence of a mare in season.

Celts and Arabs

It was probably the Scythians who chased [the] Celts out of the Danube valley and set [in] motion the migration which was to lead th[em] eventually to the Atlantic coast and to [Bri]tain. On the way, through raiding and bar[ter] they acquired many horses, the most imp[or]tant of which were the large, heavy ho[rses] from the Alpine foothills. These they cros[sed] with their own Tarpan type chariot pon[ies] and the resulting stock was crossed yet ag[ain] with the aboriginal ponies of Britain to p[ro]duce what has become known as the 'anci[ent] British horse'.

Despite Xenophon's brilliance, it was ac[tu]ally the Celts who developed a pain[less] method of compelling the horse to bend [its] neck at the poll. They invented the curb-[bit] which enabled them to control their mou[nts] not by force, but through gentle pressure [on] the reins. Nevertheless, the remainder of [the] ancient world stuck to their original bits.

At the beginning of the Christian e[ra] horses were very rare animals among [the] Arabs. Camels were used for war and tra[ns]port and donkeys for domestic work. T[he] Bedouin had begun to breed horses before [the] days of the Prophet, but it was he, realiz[ing] the necessity of cavalry in the expansion [of] the Muslim world, who gave the first gr[eat] impetus to Arab horsebreeding. Breed[ers] were promised 'The horse shall be for a ma[n a] source of happiness and wealth; its back sh[all] be the seat of honour and its belly riches, a[nd] every grain of barley given to it shall purch[ase] the indulgence of a sinner and be entered [in] the register of good works'. Out of su[ch] splendid promises was born 'the drinker [of] the wind', the Arab horse that is arguably t[he] finest, the most intelligent and courage[ous] animal ever created.

The horse at war

*'In dreary, doubtful waiting hours
Before the brazen frenzy starts
The horses show him nobler powers:
O patient eyes, courageous hearts'*

Thus wrote the British poet Julian Grenfell of the feelings of many an apprehensive cavalry soldier, standing beside his horse in the anxious moments before the crash of action. The emotions he describes must have been felt by almost all horse warriors.

Probably the world's first cavalry were the Mongolians, who, in about 5000 BC, began to break and train the little red, brown and dun wild horses of the steppes, descendants of those which had crossed the land bridge from North America. These horses were about 13 hands high, with upright manes and dorsal stripes. By all accounts, the Mongolians were incredibly skilful horsemen – their mounted archers, standing on the saddle, could split an apple at twenty paces while riding at full gallop. Hordes of Mongolian cavalry repeatedly invaded China, to which they incidentally introduced the horse, and, from there, the knowledge and use of horses

spread along the trade routes further into Asia, Europe and Africa.

Charioteers and bowmen

Though the Chinese were quick to appreciate the advantages of the horse in war, they chose at first to harness the animals to chariots, rather than to ride them. Chinese war lords were doing battle in chariots in 2300 BC; by 1200 BC, the custom had spread westwards to Egypt. There, the ruling Pharaohs – notably Rameses II in his campaigns against the Hittites – frequently fought in this way.

The Chinese, however, had learned many other lessons in fighting horsemastership from their ferocious Mongol neighbours, which were to take another twenty centuries to reach the Middle East and Europe. They learned to live close to their horses, to drink

Top right The Norman cavalry go into action at the Battle of Hastings, from the Bayeux Tapestry. Right Uccello's depiction of the Battle of S. Romano and below a Japanese screen painting of the rival generals at the Battle of the Uji river in 1184. The medieval period was the great age of the horse at war, when the armoured knight and his charger dominated the battlefield. This dominance lasted until first archery and then gunpowder came to challenge their invincibility. A whole mystique grew up around the age.

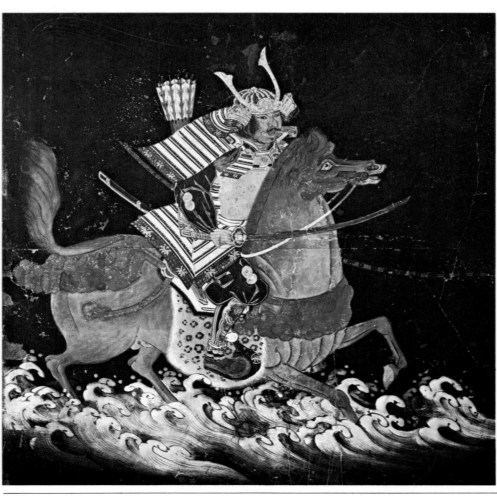

mare's milk and to make a strong liquor—*kummis*—from it. From them they copied the saddle and the stirrup—devices that were almost unkown in Europe until AD 400. They also adopted the Mongols' rigid horse collar. This was probably the first harness to take the weight of the load off the horse's windpipe and jugular vein. The innovation had an immense impact on the logistics of war, since it more than doubled the horse's draught potential.

In the Middle East, the chariot took its place in Egyptian and Persian battle lines as the first form of mobile fire-power. The lumbering carts of earliest times were soon replaced by lighter vehicles, drawn by powerful purpose-bred armour-clad horses. These horses, perhaps the ancestors of the purebred Arabian, gave the chariots a speed and momentum that had a devastating effect on

enemy foot soldiers. The armoured drivers stood in turrets of strong timber, from which they fired fusillades of arrows, while three-foot scythes on the axle trees wrought fearful execution as they crashed into the infantry.

The first cavalry outside Mongolia were the mounted bowmen of the Assyrians and Scythians who took to the field in about 1200 BC. Later, mounted spearmen or lancers were incorporated into the armies as well. Most interestingly, their horses—Arab types with fine, slightly-dished faces and clean well-boned legs—were being bred even as early as this for their speed and boldness in battle, while baggage train animals ·were stockier, more workmanlike and commoner. Selective breeding at this time already included gelding; grain feeding, too, for better performance, was the rule.

Much military horse lore was passed to the

Greeks by the Egyptians but, despite Xenophon and his remarkably perceptive treatises on horsemanship, their most persistent enemies, the Persians, had by far the greater cavalry strength. In 500 BC Xerxes had under his command 80,000 chariot and ridden horses in all, an almost unbelievable equine army for the time. The best horses were those of the Niceans, which came from Media and Armenia. These were the biggest horses then known, standing between 14 and 15 hands high.

Tales of the awesome ferocity in battle of these early war horses may not be all fable. The animals ridden in action were invariably stallions, and they were often schooled to use their natural foreleg 'boxing' action to batter at the infantry before them.

Greeks, Persians, Romans and Chinese

However Greek horsemanship should not be underestimated, largely because of Xenophon. His treatises on cavalry training and horsemanship written in 360 BC were designed to produce a horse useful in battle, and contained advice on how to judge and buy a horse. Xenophon advocated precision of pace, balance, proper carriage, acceptance of the bit, flexion and considerate application of the aids. These precepts and preoccupations are still fundamental to the art of horsemanship today, even after twenty three centuries.

At about this time—the 3rd century BC—the Chinese, too, were perfecting an 8,000-strong cavalry force to confront the Huns along the Great Wall of China. At first this force was mounted on shaggy little Mongolian ponies, but gradually these were re-

Above A gaily-caprisoned officer of Napoleon's Imperial Guard and below the charge of the Scots Greys at the battle of Waterloo in 1815. With the introduction of firearms and artillery, the role of the horse on the battlefield changed, as cavalry became more of a fast-moving blitzkrieg weapon. Hussars, Dragoons and Lancers all had their respective roles to play, and in all the European armies of the day, the cavalry became regarded as the élite striking force, its membership being largely aristocratic. Nowhere was this more true than in the British army during the

Napoleonic Wars. Then, the cavalry tended to treat the order to charge as though starting a fox-hunt. This was certainly the case in the Greys' charge at Waterloo, when, their blood being up, they pursued their fleeing foes into the heart of the French position heedless of loss. In contrast, Napoleon's cavalry were usually more professional.

The horse had its other uses too. **Far right** *A romantic view of the 'Remnants of an Army,' as the sole survivor of a British disaster on the Indian north-west frontier is saved by the courage, speed and stamina of his horse.*

placed by bigger and stronger animals, br from Niceans imported from what is no Samarkand. This war horse breeding pro ramme reached a major climax in AD 104 Until then the Chinese armies had relied ponies from the Mongolian plateau to t north, where they were, and are, still, mass in great herds. In a drive to end dependen for such essential war material on a potenti enemy-controlled region, the authorities i stituted a Horse Breeding Law, which d creed that every rural family had to keep least one horse. This was such a success that realized 30,000 cavalry remounts in just fi years.

The cavalry of the early Romans was th on the ground—for example, they field only 3,000 against Hannibal's 8,000 sw Barbs (ridden without bridle or rein, bei guided by a short whip), and they were nev a great success. Only after the defeat Carthage did the Roman cavalry achie high standards and effectiveness, althoug according to Caesar's account of his Gal wars, most of his 10,000 mounted soldie were German, Spanish and Numidian me cenaries. The cavalry, however, was still match for the 40,000 Parthians on their fas nimble Nicaean horses, ridden with t noseband and single rein of five centuri before. These were the first fully armour horses in the world, though the amount metal they carried was not yet heavy enou to necessitate special breeding for ext strength.

By this time, the principal nations we producing two main types of horse in th military horse-breeding programmes, ea for its own particular qualities. T

rmblood' was the more volatile, spirited, er-made horse and the 'coldblood' was re placid, phlegmatic, and thus suitable draught and load-carrying. Although the mans appeared to appreciate the impor- ce of this, their cavalry was allowed to ome decadent, and the army depended re and more on mounted mercenary aux- ries. As a result, Alaric the Goth's cavalry ked Rome with the same ease that Attila's ns, on their medium-sized, hardy Steppes ies, were able to invade Italy. The roots his Roman decline, however, dated back ch further. The failure of Caesar's first ault across the Channel was largely due to speed and flexibility of the Celtic unted archers and charioteers. The credit his success in 54 BC belongs almost en- ly to his 2,000 Gaulish cavalry, mounted their heavy, 15-hand horses.

e age of chivalry

m the fall of the Roman Empire to the rman conquest of England, little is known the war horse. In Saxon Britain, for ex- ple, though the English kings Alfred and helstane imported stallions and imposed ort restrictions on good horses, no de- opments of military significance took ce.

n the Arab world, however, the picture s very different. The Prophet Mohammed tilled his people with his own respect for influence of the horse on war. In conse- nce, the Arab cavalry horse developed in p with the burgeoning Saracen Empire; acen cavalry swept across Arabia, North rica and up into Spain, and not until they ountered Charles Martel's powerful, il-clad Frankish cavalry at Poitiers in AD was their advance halted.

The tenth century saw the opening of the at age of chivalry in Europe. This was to minate in the breeding of huge battle rses, capable of carrying up to 400 lb of noured knight. The Norman invasion of 6 introduced the forerunners of the mas- e Percheron and Shire to a cavalryless glish army. William of Normandy's war- rs were mostly mounted, they knew how to ht on horseback, and in their thundering ves they broke and routed the gallant con infantry. The Norman horses were not massive, being about 14 hands high, but der William's imaginative command at stings, their shock effect was more than ough to win the day.

The Crusades for the first time contrasted battle qualities of fleet Arabs and Barbs h those of the European knights on their vier horses. Here, considerations of mo- ty, protection and striking power had to weighed against each other with infinite

care and thought. This too—the twelfth century—was the age of the largest cavalry force in history—Ogtai Khan's one and a half million superbly organized and disciplined Mongol cavalry who, on their tough 13-hand Mongol ponies, swept through Asia and east- ern Europe until they were eventually stop- ped by heavily armoured cavalry on the bor- ders of Poland.

By the end of the fifteenth century, the massive European *destrier,* or charger, had to carry in tournament and battle nearly 500 lb of armour, as well as its noble knight. But with the spread of firearms, most armour became obsolete. The sixteenth and seven- teenth centuries heralded the beginnings of a new kind of cavalry—fast, manoeuvrable and lightly armoured—the kind of formations typified by Cromwell's Ironsides in the En- glish Civil War. Thus, firearms by no means heralded the end of cavalry, but they changed its role from battering ram to swift, shock attack and reconnaissance.

Dragoons, Lancers and Hussars

The development of the English Thor- oughbred which began during the reign of Charles II (1660–85) infused the blood of the existing English horse with that of the Arab. This had a considerable influence not only on the British cavalry, but on that of most of the Western world. In Russia, for instance, the Cossacks were remounted and trained on Arab and Throughbred- influenced stock from the breeding farms of the great Steppes; by the eighteenth century, Peter the Great was commanding a mounted force of 84,000 men.

New horse-breeds, too, led to the develop- ment of three very distinct kinds of cavalry throughout the armies of Europe: the Dragoon, primarily a foot soldier, but mounted for movement on solid, cobby horses; the Lancer, riding a much finer ani- mal suited for fast flanking movements and sudden charges; and the galloping, sabre- wielding Hussar, the *Blitzkrieg*-weapon of battlefield and campaign.

The Napoleonic Wars furnish the first

authentic records of the difficulties of sus- taining horses through a major campaign. The Emperor took 30,000 cavalry, and prob- ably as many pack and draught horses, into Russia in 1812. But through cold, starvation and the savage attacks of the Cossacks, he re-crossed the River Niemen after the terrible retreat from Moscow with fewer than 2,000 animals. Thereafter his cavalry was almost always inferior to that of his enemies, and it was indeed the charge of Blücher's Prussians that finally swung the day against him at Waterloo.

From Waterloo to World War

After Waterloo canister, shrapnel and the advent of automatic weapons began to force the massed cavalry charge into obsolescence. But the golden age of cavalry was far from over, and until the end of the nineteenth century at least the fast, flexible and efficient horse artillery batteries, whose drivers rode as postillions on the nearside horses, played a highly important part in battle.

In the British Indian campaigns of the nineteenth and early twentieth centuries, the English hunter type was soon replaced by tough little Arabs from Persia, and by the big Australian Arab and Thoroughbred cross from New South Wales. These Walers, as they were called, made excellent troop and artillery horses, and eventually more than 120,000 of them served with British and Empire forces in the First World War.

To this period, too, belongs one of the most catastrophic cavalry charges in all his- tory. The Charge of the Light Brigade at Balaclava in the Crimea in 1854 was the nadir of British horse campaigning and man- agement. The entire campaign was a chapter of dreadful privation for both horse and man, which came to a climax that October day, when of the 673 horses which, on a misun- derstood order, charged 2,000 yards into the muzzles of the Russian artillery, only 260 survived. The remainder, those that were not killed outright, still struggled on in their parade places until they fell. One charger, dreadfully lanced, carried its badly wounded rider a full mile to safety before collapsing.

In the USA, the great Indian Comanche and Kiowa tribes, who had learned to break and ride the feral descendants of the horses of the Conquistadores (the 16th-century Spanish invaders of America), had become as skilled as the Mongols in mounted archery, though they never compared with them in respect of other aspects of horsemastership. By the 1860s, however, the white settlers had begun to push westwards, and the stage was set for the great cavalry campaigns of the Indian wars. In these, the Indians found worthy opponents in the US cavalry, but, in the end, it was overwhelming technological superiority, rather than particular tactical brilliance, that won the day for the expanding white man.

Technological development, too, was one of the factors behind the revolution in cavalry tactics that took place in the US Civil War; the barrel superceded the blade, and much of the actual fighting took place dismounted. As far as the mounted man was concerned, it was a war of long hard marches and sudden shock actions—'Git thar fustest with the mostest.' It was a sudden and intense metamorphosis from tradition to pragmatism, and, once again, the equine suffering at least equalled the human. In one veterinary hospital alone, in a period of five months, no more than a half of the 7,000 horses could be saved, and in the last year of the war 180,000 Northern cavalry horses alone died of starvation.

World War and after

As weaponry grew ever more complex, so the horse's battlefield privations increased – often as a result of outdated tactical dogma and die-hard worship of brilliant mounted reviews and drills. In the South African War of 1899–1902 the carbine-armed Boers on their hardy ponies ran rings round the British regulars. In the last phase of the war, one regiment of Dragoons could muster, of their original complement of 775 horses, a mere 27—the losses being due almost entirely to privation and disease. In the war as a whole, out of more than half a million horses, 350,000 died.

Even after 1900, the cavalry horses of most European nations were still expected to carry some 300 lb, which included rider and weapons—sabre or lance, rifle, ammunition — and campaign kit. During the First World War millions of horses were employed on all the many fronts at any given time—draught and pack animals as well as cavalry mounts. Again, losses were appalling, those from privation and exposure being five times greater than those incurred in battle itself. Seven thousand horses were killed in one day alone

Left *The Charge of the Light Brigade at Balaclava during the Crimean War;* below *and* right *two views of Custer's legendary last stand at the Little Big Horn by Indian and American artists respectively. Both these actions were disasters for both the horses and the men concerned. At Balaclava the bravery of the Light Brigade in charging straight in to the face of the massed Russian artillery in blind obedience to a mistaken, misunderstood, order inspired one of Tennyson's finest poems. It also prompted a French general to comment 'It is magnificent, but it is not war.' Similarly, Custer's cavalry, surrounded by Indian foes fought to the last man.*

during the Battle of Verdun (1916) – and not one single major cavalry action was fought in four years on the Western Front.

On the Eastern Front, until 1917, Cossacks, German and Austro-Hungarian cavalry engaged in corps-strength battles reminiscent of wars a century earlier, while in the Middle East General Allenby's 20,000-strong Desert Mounted Corps of Australian, New Zealand, British and Indian cavalry made forced marches of up to 60 miles a day, often without water or forage. In one action, 172 Yeomanry charged and routed four Turkish infantry battalions and three batteries of artillery. This action is still held as an example of the capabilities of determined cavalrymen.

The story of the horse in war does not end in climax. After the armistice in 1918, mechanization gradually replaced the operational cavalry, artillery and draught horse. But even as late as 1939, Poland fielded almost 90,00 horses on active service, the Germans – supposedly the most mechanized army in the world – 800,000 (including five SS cavalry divisions), while the Russians had a million and a quarter animals available for battle.

What was probably the last full-scale cavalry charge was made by the Russians in November 1941, near Moscow. Squadron after squadron of horsemen charged the astounded German 106th Infantry Division, 'stirrup touching stirrup, riders low on their horses' necks, drawn sabres over their shoulders' – straight into a storm of modern small arms and artillery fire. Thirty reached the German ranks, and were there machine-gunned. All 2,000 horses and men of the 44th Mongolian Cavalry Division lay fallen in the snow. There were no German casualties.

However, draught and pack animals were critically important in Second World War campaigns that took place in mountainous or forested areas – in Italy, for example, and in the jungles of Burma. The British and Americans regularly air-lifted pack horses and mules, many 'muted' by painless operation to preserve secrecy on clandestine missions, and the Japanese too relied heavily on animal transport.

Today, other than in China, which still maintains four full cavalry divisions, only a few operational horsed formations still remain – notably in the USSR, India, South America and South Africa.

The story of the horse in war is a brave one. Paradoxically, now that its day is past, many soldiers feel mankind has lost, in this age of mechanized combat, a valuable dimension of feeling and of sacrifice inspired by the selflessness, loyalty and affection of man's oldest military ally.

Scenes from modern war.
Left cavalry pick their way
around a mine crater on the
Western Front in 1917,
while **below** an ammunition
wagon moving up to the
front at the Battle of the
Somme (1916); German
First World War transport
with horses and drivers both
in gasmasks; loading a
packhorse; and a scene from
the Eastern Front in 1941
as Soviet horse artillery
pursues the fleeing
Germans, with air support.
The twentieth century saw
the final disappearance of the
horse from an active role on
the battlefield, with the
advent of machine guns,
barbed wire and tanks.
Below right a legacy from
the past, as Soviet cavalry
emerge from concealment to
attack the advancing
German panzers in
September 1941.

The horse at work

Speed, sure-footedness and spiritedness, rather than horse-power, were the qualities demanded by the men who first broke horses to harness. Heavy work, especially ploughing, was accomplished by oxen. Their steady, plodding gait and sheer brute strength were particularly suited to the heavy beam ploughs that hardly changed from the Middle Ages to the eighteenth century. Where speed did not matter, ox-power was paramount, and indeed, teams of oxen – six to a plough – were fairly commonplace in many parts of Europe until the Second World War. Another advantage of the ox was that after hauling a plough for four years, it could be fattened during the ensuing summer and then slaughtered for meat, so providing a double return for the farmer.

Through more than a thousand years of European farming, probably until the seventeeth century, most of the horses available to agriculture were far too light to attempt much more than carting and harrowing, though in the latter task especially they excelled. They did not object to the skittering of the harrow over broken ground that would have driven oxen, used to the steady drag of the plough, into hysteria; but being little more than ponies, the heavy work of the farm was beyond their strength.

Yet the ideal horse for this work did exist, and had done so since the Normans swept across Europe in the eleventh century. A principal factor in their spectacular military success was the *destrier,* the great war horse, that could carry an armoured knight through opposing infantry like a reaper through grain. Of Andalusian and northern European descent, the 'Great Horses' became the ancestors of every modern breed of draught horse – the Percherons and the Brabants, the Shires, Clydesdales and many others. Later, an Arab strain was introduced into some of these to give them lightness and speed.

For centuries, it would have seemed sacrilege to have put such animals to any employment other than that of war; they were the knight's proudest, and most expensive, possession, and there were other factors too that limited their wider distribution and use. One was the shortage of sufficiently good grassland to support such enormous beasts in any great number, while another was the slow development of suitable harness. The hard collar, for example, was not introduced into western Europe until the late Middle Ages; until then, horses hauled from a breastband that constricted their breathing and prevented them from throwing their full strength into their work.

But it was the invention of gunpowder and finally, the cavalry pistol that released

heavy horses from war. A pistol ball could penetrate any armour; in consequence, it became obsolete and speed and manoeuvrability replaced weight-carrying as the most desirable qualities in cavalry mounts.

Carts and waggons

Curiously, it was not in agriculture that the demobilised heavy horses first made their mark, but as draught animals for royalty. In 1564, Queen Elizabeth I ordered a travelling wagon – to be drawn by six great horses. In this, she journeyed from London to Warwick, but, so it was reported, was unable to sit down for a week afterwards. Nevertheless, she persisted, and on her famous progresses became accustomed to moving about the country in wagon trains drawn by 400 heavy horses. Only these, with their great strength, were capable of hauling over, or rather through, the abominable road surfaces of the period.

Encouraged by royal example, both in England and Europe, the first public stage wagons, each dragged along by eight massive draught horses, were carrying passengers and freight between cities before the close of the sixteenth century. But it was to be many a long year before road surfaces improved sufficiently to allow such vehicles to compete on equal terms with the ridden horse, the pack horse and the pack horse trains.

Not until the eighteenth century did the draught breeds make their first real impact on agriculture. Better land drainage, improved grazing and selective breeding methods greatly increased the number and strength of draught horses available. At the same time, the revolution in farm machinery necessitated the use of an animal more intelligent and more adaptable than the ox.

The hey-day of the agricultural draught horse, and of the specialized craftsmen who served it was from the end of the eighteenth century until the outbreak of the First World War in 1914.

Prince of these was the wheelwright, who

Left *A horse and plough medieval illuminated manuscript and* **below** *a Etruscan urn of about 15 to 100 BC, depicting a couple taking their last journey to the underworl a horse-drawn wagon. It was in transport and agriculture that the horse proved its indispensibility though it did not become major force in European farming until the inventic of a suitable collar in the Middle Ages. Until then, too, the horse's value in w was too great to allow its for civilian labour on a la scale.*

nbined the crafts of blacksmith, joiner
l woodsman in creating not only wheels,
: entire farm carts and wagons which, by
: end of the period, had developed into
sterpieces of rural engineering. In Au-
lia, Europe and the New World, wheel-
ghts built carts and wagons great and small
erbly adapted to the soil, work and condi-
ns of the particular area. Probably the
st glorious glimpse of the draught horse is
t afforded by a matched team of Shires or
cherons hauling a Suffolk wagon, with its
-dished wheels and blazing colours. But
: the clipper captains who flourish-
at the very end of the era of sail, so

perhaps the greatest of working horsemen
evolved almost as the tractors moved in.
These were the mule-skinners of Australia
and the western plains of the USA and Canada who drove combine harvesters powered by
30-strong teams of horses or mules. It was said
of the drivers that they could remove a fly
from the ear of the lead horse with a 40 ft
whip; it may even have been true.

Carriages and coaches
The earliest vehicle extant that might be
described as a carriage is the State Chariot of
King Tutankhamen. This dates back to the
fourteenth century BC, but so far as our own

era is concerned, the ancestry of both carriages and coaches reaches no further back
than the massive public stage wagons of the
sixteenth century. One such vehicle of the
period was named after the town of Kotze in
Hungary where it was built, and this in turn
may have lent its name to the whole breed of
coaches that followed. However, coaches
and carriages as we think of them – light,
well-strung vehicles with independently
turning front axles and drawn by teams of
speedy horses – were an impossible dream
before the great road engineering schemes of
the eighteenth century. Nevertheless, once
these had been accomplished, coach design

Right *Harvesting in Australia and* **inset** *a barge horse at work. As the Australian wheat fields grew ever larger, vast teams of horses, drawing combine harvesters, were set to work in them. Their role in the nation's agriculture lasted until the Second World War. In England, too, barge horses played a vital part in the canal era of the Industrial Revolution, but with the advent of railways their usefulness declined.*

improved almost overnight and the great draught horses were relegated to the farm. Their places between the shafts were usurped by lighter, faster breeds such as the Cleveland Bay, the Kladruber, the Oldenburg and the Fredricksborg.

As early as 1784, the British post office made transport history by setting up staging posts every ten miles or so between London and Bath. Changing horses at each stage, the mail coach accomplished the journey – about a hundred miles – in the then incredible time of 15 hours at an average speed of 6⅔ mph. Within a very few years, a complex system of coaching inns and staging posts was established throughout Britain and Europe. Some idea of the size of the operation may be gathered from Hounslow, the first staging post on the Great West Road out of London; at its peak, just before the coming of the railways, 2000 horses were stabled there.

In the new countries, most notably in Australia with its vast distances of virgin territory, the stagecoach remained a major means of transport for much longer than in Europe. The most famous Australian coachmen were Cobb & Co., who in the 1880s controlled a coaching network covering some 6000 miles of road. They bred their own type of hardy 'coacher' horses to pull their 14-passenger vehicles that continued to drive through the night by the light of powerful acetylene lamps.

The improvement of roads in Europe also led to a proliferation of private coaches and carriages until, by the end of the first quarter of the nineteenth century, there were almost as many types on the road as there are makes of car today. Heavier vehicles were driven by a coachman and drawn by four or six horses – in the latter case, one of the lead horses was often ridden and guided by a postillion. Lighter carriages, such as the two-wheeled gig, the high-cocking cart, with a box beneath the seat for fighting cocks, and the crane-necked phaeton, the 'high-flyer', whose high sprung seat towered over the two or four horses between the shafts, were owner-driven. These were the sports cars of the age, the property of young bloods with a taste for speed and thoroughbred, matched horses. For the more sober-minded, there were enclosed broughams and landaus, and open victorias for those who wished to see and be seen; for moving children from one place to another, there were governess carts

and dog carts.

Each country evolved light carriages according to its needs. Some of the most famous were those developed in the USA, such as the four-wheeled buggy with a fixed or folding roof, fringe-top surreys for well-turned out families and buckboards for the rough trails of the West.

Cities and industry

Like mankind, horses first became acquainted with industry on a large scale in about the middle of the eighteenth century. Since Biblical times they had been used to operate wine and olive presses and to grind corn, while for hundreds of years they had powered windlasses at mine pitheads and worked ore-crushing machinery. Pit ponies, however, were not used until the nineteenth century, when the first horizontal drifts or galleries were constructed in coal mines; the last pit ponies working in a major coal mine

in the UK went into honourable retireme in 1972.

Probably the first major equine contri tion to the Industrial Revolution was in ca transport, which for 50 years before the co ing of the railways was the fastest possi means of moving raw materials and finish goods between market, port and facto Barges worked most efficiently at h speeds, with their noses lifted on to their o bow waves; to achieve this, relays of drau

Top left *Perils of the city are vividly shown in this* Punch *version of a nineteenth-century traffic jam.* **Top** **right** *A highwayman, one of the perils of the road, and* **inset** *US stage coaches meet in the wilds of the west. In* *both the Australian outback and the wild west there was a constant threat of highway robbery from bush rangers or* *outlaws; in the UK, however, the highwayman was a vanishing breed.*

ses were stationed along towpaths. The ses moved at a fast trot between one stage the next, never pausing, except at locks. The advent of the railways and the growth industry actually raised the demand for rkhorses to an unprecedented peak. As ching companies went gradually out of siness and the canals silted up, more and re horses were drafted into the cities, ere, indeed, the railway companies were ong their biggest employers. Teams of two

or four hauled heavy wagons between factory, dock and railhead; well within living memory, it was possible to see apparently endless queues of patient Shires and Clydesdales waiting outside dock gates in the rain, their drivers muffled in sacking and tarpaulins against the weather.

For short-haul shifting of heavy loads in cities, draught horses were sufficiently economical to carry their supremacy well into the age of the internal combustion engine.

Only after a long struggle did the city draught horse finally yield to the falling price of petrol. To prove the point, in 1935, two Shires employed by Liverpool Corporation in the UK turned and moved with ease a load of 16½ tons over sleet-slippery granite setts.

Most of the lighter horses had gone long before, not entirely to the regret of many city-dwellers. Exhaust fumes and motorised jams are bad enough, but manure-filled streets and a tangle of irascible horses and

iron-shod wheels was probably infinitely worse. All the same, the dashing hansom cabs and the four-wheeled growlers, the fiacres of Paris, the smart equipages of the rich parading in the parks, the racing, bell-ringing fire engines, the beautifully matched horses of the brewers' drays and even the humble milk float, possessed a romance with which—at least in retrospect—no motorised vehicle could possibly compete.

Work horses and the future

A very few years ago most people would have said that the draught horse had no future at all; that apart from a few retained by enthusiasts for old times' sake, it was doomed to vanish from the Earth. This process started at the beginning of the century with the development of the internal combustion engine and the oil price wars that dramatically re-

duced the cost of petrol. It continued at the close of the First World War, when the tens of thousands of American, Australian and British horses that had hauled guns and supplies up to the lines, were left to celebrate Armistice Day in the knacker's yard. It accelerated between the wars as farms became steadily more mechanised. There was a brief hiatus during the Second World War, at least in Europe where horses resumed their old roles in agriculture, city haulage and barge towing. Then, as petrol became plentiful and cheap once more, the steady march of mechanisation resumed.

It was during the oil crisis of the early 1970s that it began to occur to some people that perhaps the draught horse had a place in our economy after all. Farmers wondered if they were over-mechanised, if perhaps their tractors and combines were over-adequate to

the acreage they worked, and it was covered that in certain jobs and on cert soils, especially heavy clays, the horse actually more efficient. Oddly enough, of these is harrowing, one of the earliest t that the first farmers to use the horse ever the animal to. Tractors compact wet, he soil while horses, though slow, harrow cleanly as ever their forebears did.

In the cities too, horses are making so thing of a comeback. British brewers, v cut down on their superbly matched te only with infinite reluctance, are r reopening their stables. As the price of pe rises, it becomes ever more economica make city deliveries involving long halt dray, rather than by truck.

Such ventures have led to the resumpt of draught horse breeding, not out of se ment but in the belief that these creat

ove *Horse power was
...essential in the new
...m age, as this picture of
...'Nig' on the US North
...fic railroad shows. Such
...sive engineering feats
...ld have been impossible
...out the horse as a hauler
...en, machinery and
...erials.*

Above right *A fire engine
races through the New York
streets; in the cities, too, the
horse for long remained the
sole source of motive power.
Gradually, however,
mechanisation took over;* **far
right** *UK pit ponies leave
their mine for the last time in
1971.*

...ve a real part to play in the modern world.
...s doubtful if the ploughman, walking a
...fectly straight furrow behind his team of
... great horses controlled by a single rein,
...l ever gain much more than the applause
...crowds at agricultural shows. But all lovers
...nature will rejoice that such skills are kept
...e.

e saddle-horse
...e working saddle-horse's role as a means of

Below *A horse at work on a Brazilian peasant farm,* **bottom** *a prize-winning team of Clydesdales hauling a brewer's wagon in the USA,* **right** *clearing trees in an Australian forest and* **below right** *pony transport for seaweed on the Patagonian coast.* **Far right** *A hay-making scene in Norfolk, UK;* **inset** *, a Norwegian Fjord pony at work and a horse-drawn plough toiling over a field.*

The horse has never lost its importance to poorer societies, where it is still one of many farmers' most valuable assets. Their entire living can well depend on it. Now, even in the industrialised nations of the west, the rising cost of oil and petrol has led to its reappearance on the scene. Farmers, for example, have realised that the horse is actually more efficient at certain tasks, such as harrowing, than the tractor. In both Canada and Australia, lumberjacks frequently prefer to use horses for hauling fallen timber, because of their greater ability to cope with heavy ground and confined spaces.

In cities, too, the horse is reappearing on the streets — and in a working role, not solely for purposes of display. Brewers, in particular, have always favoured horses as the ideal traction for their drays; even in the days of cheap diesel fuel, many of them kept on their carefully-matched teams, though in many cases, their main role was in the showing arena rather than actually at work. Now, however, the horse-drawn wagon, according to enthusiasts, is proving its superior versatility over the truck that once brought it close to extinction; horses, for instance, do not eat fuel in traffic jams.

It is unlikely, however, that the working horse will ever again play the same essential role as it did only half a century ago, though some speculative writers have predicted the opposite.

everyday conveyance for ladies, gentlemen and soldiers is now largely a nostalgic memory. So too, in many parts of the world, is its role as a pack animal; as roads improved, the best pack horses were promoted to carriage work where their special qualities of apparent tirelessness and endurance continue to be valued to this day. One of the finest breeds to undergo the transformation in the UK was the Chapman's horse, which during the seventeenth and eighteenth centuries travelled between fairs and markets all over Britain, carrying the wares of the Chapmen, the travelling salesmen of the day. Moving at the pace that suited them best, 'walk five miles in the hour and trot sixteen', Chapman horses could carry up to 700 lb over 60 miles in 24 hours. This ability that was to stand them in good stead when they were bred into Cleveland Bays, and became one of the most sought after of ca riage horse breeds.

Better roads and the spread of the railways also put an end to the saddle horse's centuries-old service as a speedy carrier of mails and despatches. In Europe, one of the earliest of such services was in the hands of the Praetorian Guard who, at the height of the Roman Empire and using relays of riders and horses, carried messages from London to Rome in five days, a record that was scarcely improved upon for the best part of two thousand years. But the most celebrated of all mail-riding epics was surely that of the Pony Express in 19th-century America. So famous has this become, that it is hard to believe that it lasted for little more than 18 months between 1860 and 1862. The service ran from St Joseph, Missouri, through Kansas, Nebraska, Colorado, Wyoming, Utah and Nevada, to Sacramento, California – a distance of 1,966 miles which the company guaranteed to cover in ten days. Four hundred horses–or rather, ponies, since none were more than 14 hands–stood ready in the relay stations established along the route, saddled and waiting for the mails to be slung across their backs and to gallop on to the next staging post. The riders too, were small and wiry, but heavily armed with pistols and carbines against bandit and Indian attack. Like their ponies, they were a special breed, and almost before Wells Fargo had taken over most of their route, their exploits had become legend.

Ranching and cowboys

Only in one task does the working saddle horse still reign supreme–that of helping to guard and control livestock in remote plains and great grasslands. In the Camargue, for example, the salt-marsh delta of the Rhône in France, the *guardiens,* or cowboys, ride a local breed of horses–virtually unchanged

since Roman times–in pursuit of the wild black bulls that are exported to the bull-rings of Spain. In Australia, despite such recent innovations as the light aeroplane, the cattle truck and the jeep, the bulk of ranch work is still accomplished by the stockman on horseback. Generally, he rides a Waler, a tough, hardy crossbreed first developed in New South Wales as a remount for the British cavalry in India.

But the most famous of all working horsemen was, and probably still is, the cowboy of the south-western United States. As with the Pony Express rider, film and fable have combined to give the notion that he dominated a very large portion of American history. In fact, the 'Golden Age' of the cowboy lasted little more than 25 years, from the end of the Civil War in 1865, to the arrival of the railroads in Texas in about 1890.

Conversely, his antecedents are considerably more ancient than most film fans suspect, for they reach back to the cattle ranches of medieval Spain and Portugal. In the sixteenth century, Cortes and his Conquistadores brought this style of farming to Mexico, from which it spread to what would later become the south-western states of the USA. The language, equipment and dress of the modern cowboy are all traceable to those early beginnings. Even the deep, comfortable Western saddle, rising fore and aft, is only a slight adaption from the war-saddle of the Conquistadores. When roping a steer, the rider takes a turn of the lariat (*reata*–leather thong) round the horn of the saddle, which is secured by cinches (*cincha*–girth). The cowhand's broad-brimmed hat and jingling, rowelled, spurs are adapted from the dress of the Mexican *vaquero,* whose very name has been anglicised to 'buckaroo'.

Oddly enough, it is only the cowboy's horse, the renowned Quarter horse, that comes from the eastern USA. Its name and ancestry stemmed from Virginia, where in the eighteenth century, racehorses capable of phenomenal speeds over a quarter of a mile were bred. Short bursts of speed, hardiness, good bone and muscle, was exactly what was required in cattle country, and the Quarter horse was moved west, to breed there in thousands.

Until the Civil War, there was no demand for, or at least no means of transporting, western beef to the markets of the east. The cattle's only value lay in their hides and tallow; the meat, as often as not, was left to rot. But as the railroads drove ever farther west, to Missouri, Kansas and Colerado, it became feasible and highly profitable to drive Texas cattle north on the hoof. Each Longhorn that reached the railheads at Kansas City, Abilene, Dodge, or Denver fetched an

Far left *A mounted policeman in New York,* below *Magyar riders at a Hungarian horse festival and* left *the first US Pony Express rider leaves for the west in 1860. The saddle horse, too, has its role as a working horse. Even today, it is still used on the cattle ranches of the USA, South America and Australia.*

average of $10; and they arrived in millions. It was out of these drives, over trails 1,500 miles and more long, with names such as Chisholm and Shawnee, Western and Goodnight-Loving, that the legend of the cowboy was born.

'Take 'em to Missouri!'

During this period, it is estimated there were about 40,000 men engaged in the business of moving beef from the scrublands of Texas to the railheads, not counting those who were working to the north in Wyoming, Montana and Oregon. They were paid $30 a month, and were expected to supply their own clothing, bedding, boots and saddles; on the last two items, beautifully stitched and ornamented, they would cheerfully spend two years' pay. Food and horses were provided by the rancher or the trail boss; generally, it was reckoned that each cowhand required about ten horses to see him through a drive. This might last six months or more and during it both horse and rider might easily work eighteen hours a day. Breaking and training this vast number of horses was considered an inferior trade to that of cowhand; a horse-breaker was paid $25 a month, or $3 a horse.

Tough though trail work was, moving at a snail's pace during the day with occasional wild dashes after strays, and riding herd over the bedded-down cattle for half the night, it did at least have the compensation of an occasional visit to a town along the route. There were few such compensations for the ranch hand, who for weeks on end might ride round the boundaries of the range digging fence post holes, repairing barbed wire, branding, castrating and dehorning calves, with only a horse for company. However, it was on such expeditions that both horse and rider learned their trades – cutting out a single calf from a herd, hauling fences taut, or roping a runaway steer.

Modern conditions have changed much of this vigorous and demanding way of life. Today, for instance, cowhands' horses, ready-saddled, are transported to the more distant ranges by trailer. Glamorous, blond maned palominos, and dappled Appaloosas, descended, so it is said, from the horses of Cortes, now work alongside the great-grandchildren of the Quarter horses that blazed the cattle trails. But the standard of horsemanship, and of rapport between horse and rider, remains as high as ever.

The horse in human imagination

For thousands of years, up to the present day, man has credited the horse with wisdom, courage, loyalty, strength, dignity and mystery. For us, with a dozen means of fast communication at our disposal, it is easy to forget that until a relatively short time ago, and for millenia before that, the greatest speed at which even the most vital message could be delivered was limited to that of the galloping horse. Or that the fate of nations and entire civilizations were decided by the presence on the battlefield of a number of herbivorous quadrupeds.

By easy transference, the horse became more than the mere bearer of messengers and warriors. It became instead a partisan, an active arbiter in the destinies of men. From there it was but a short step to divine status, though in Western mythology there is only one horse god, or rather goddess, as such – Epona of the Celts, whose representation is probably carved into the chalk hillsides of southern England. But as lesser divinities, and as the favoured means of transport of the gods, horses have an unrivalled role. The Greeks believed that the sun was a horse-drawn chariot, driven daily across the sky by the god Helios, while the Hindus assigned a similar role to Surya; virtually the same legend appears in the mythologies of almost every early civilization.

Divine tidings and death

Horses brought divine tidings to men, both good news and bad. The Norse spring began as Freya rode across the world, scattering flowers. This story is echoed in British folklore in the tale of Lady Godiva who lifted the burden of taxation imposed on the people of Coventry by riding naked through the streets. As with Freya, to look upon her on her mission brought heavenly retribution, instant and terrible.

Horses carried the messengers of Death and often conveyed the dead themselves to their ultimate destination. The Valkyries, the 'choosers of the slain', rode across Norse battlefields selecting the bravest of the brave for inclusion among the immortals of Valhalla. Later, the Four Horsemen of the Apocalypse of St John – War, Famine, Pestilence and Death – haunted the imagination, and the art, of the Middle Ages.

Satan, or the Devil, on the other hand, was always thought of as riding a black horse, a convention followed by super-villains all the way through history down to the early days of Western movies. The Devil's horse breathed fire, however, and was covered with scales, spikes or other unusual accoutrements. In this it resembled the mount of Woden, the northern god who led his Wild Hunt across Europe on nights of wind and storm, snatching up any mortal who dared to raise his face from the earth. According to legend, he rides still through the forests of Windsor Great Park that surround Queen Elizabeth II's principal residence. There he is known as Herne the Hunter; to glimpse him or his horse, both with antlers sprouting from their brows, means death within the year.

Similar penalties are incurred by those who have the misfortune to encounter any one of a whole range of phantom horses and horsemen, indicating perhaps, that the legend of the Wild Hunt is more deeply entrenched in our collective subconscious than we would like to think. Sometimes, horse and rider are invisible, as in the case of the Wicked Lady Ferrers, England's only highwaywoman, whose horse's hoof-beats are still reputedly heard in the quiet lanes of Hertfordshire. In other instances they are only too visible; Ghost Riders in the Sky, a popular song of a few years ago, recounts the legend, firmly believed in by many old-time cowhands, that evildoers in their profession are condemned to ride some spectral range for ever, in desperate pursuit of a herd they can never catch. But audible or visible, the fate of those who meet the phantom riders is the same; death or some great misfortune within the year.

Horses and heroes

Otherworld denizens apart, there are a large number of horses whose deeds – or those of their riders – have brought them an immortality that hovers somewhere between legend and history. The Duke of Wellington's Copenhagen, whose imperturbability in battle was equalled only by that of his master, is one example, and Napoleon's Marengo, the

The Amazons – the mythical warrior women of ancient Greek history – were superb riders, as this gold tracing on a silver panel shows. Depiction of combat between Amazons and Classical heroes, such as Theseus, was a favourite subject for Greek artists.

Carried off in a chariot,
Persephone faces rape at the
hands of Pinax. Winged
horses – the most celebrated
being Pegasus – were a
major force in Greek
mythology, being credited
with many magic properties.

Emperor's inseparable companion in victory and defeat, is another. Deeper into the realms of legend was Bayard, on which Sir Roland and his three brothers fled the anger of the great Emperor Charlemagne, and Bucephalus, favourite charger of Alexander the Great who after the animal's death, built the city of Bucephala, in present-day Pakistan, over his grave. A different immortality was awarded to the horse of Emiliano Zapata, the Mexican patriot. When his master was shot down in ambush, the horse escaped and, so it is said, still wanders the hills awaiting Zapata's return.

All in all, heroes are much improved by the presence of a horse; as status symbols and supporting players in ballad and legend they

can hardly be improved upon. King Arthur, his knights and their chargers sleep an entranced sleep in a cave, save for one night in the year – May Day Eve – when they ride proudly together over the hills of Somerset and Wales. The life of Cuchulainn, the Celtic folk-hero, was saved by the prescience of the Gray of Macha, who anticipating disaster, refused to be yoked for battle. Young Lochinvar galloped into the sunset, safe from outraged parents and bridegroom, with Fair Ellen mounted on his saddlebow.

Creation myths
Such wondrous beasts, our ancestors felt, could have sprung from no ordinary beginnings. According to the ancient Greeks, they

were created by Poseidon, God of the Se and first appeared to men out of the ocea Perhaps this belief arose out of some long a invasion, when horses and warriors sw ashore together; if so, it would go far explain the origins of the Centaur, half-ma half-horse, whose lustful kidnapping women was offset, to some extent, by wisdom. Mistaking horse and rider for a sir le creature was an error made much later the Aztecs of Mexico, who appalled by t mounted Conquistadores, allowed them achieve their bridgehead unmolested. similar invasion may also account for t Ting-ling, centaur-like beings which, a cording to Chinese legend, once inhabit the island of Formosa. Like the Greek var

Left The familiar myth o George and the dragon is captured by an African artist in an Ethiopian sett **Above right** the domina figure of Napoleon crossi the Alps, captured by J. David, the apostle of Romanticism in art, and **right** a myth is translated into music. Amalie Mate poses as Brunnhilde in th Bayreuth premiere of Richard Wagner's opera Walküre ('The Valkyrie one of whose most famou scenes is the 'Ride of the Valkyries.' In this, Wag tried to capture the rhyth galloping horses in his mu
Horses have always be closely linked with heroes and heroines of the past. Knightly figures, such as George, always had a faithful charger, while Marengo, Napoleon's fie steed, inspired almost as many legends as his maste Wagner's Brunnhilde ha Grane as her companion. the last act of Gotterdämerung ('The Twilight of the Gods'), sł rides him into the flames o Siegfried's blazing funera pyre to join her beloved in death.

Everyone, however, was aware of its beauty and of its proud and imperious nature which made it very difficult to tame. The only means of doing so was to induce a virgin to sit alone and naked under a tree. The unicorn would then approach, and overcome by the girl's loveliness and purity, would lay its head peacefully in her lap. It could then be seized and bridled without further trouble.

Capturing or killing a unicorn was well worth while, since its horn, if dipped into cup or food, had the effect of neutralising any poison. This made it much in demand by royalty. Queen Elizabeth I bought such a horn, and exhibited it at Windsor Castle during the later years of her reign. It was valued at £100,000, despite the comments of some of her more well-travelled subjects who thought it might have been the horn of a narwhal.

Smiths, magic and ritual

Some of the magic of horses has settled upon those who handle them – especially blacksmiths, whose dealings with fire and iron gave them invulnerability against all forms of enchantment and witchcraft. This belief persisted well into the Christian era, as can be seen from the story of St Dunstan, who as well as being a great and good man, gave us the protection of the horseshoe against evil.

Sometime in the 16th century, or perhaps even earlier, a secret society was formed in England, Scotland and other parts of Europe.

these too were renowned for their ...dom.

...Not content with the speed of mortal ...ses – or the sagacity of the centaur – ...eek myth also created Pegasus, the winged ...se sent by Poseidon to reveal the source of ...h water to Man. It was tamed by the ...rior Bellerophon, with the aid of ...ene, Goddess of Wisdom, who gave him ...olden bridle for the purpose. Thus Bel...phon became the first horseman and, ...eed, the first cavalryman, since mounted ... Pegasus, he fought and overcame both ...dusa and the Gorgons.

...t is not surprising that the Arabs, among ... greatest horsemen in the world, should ...e their own version of how their superb ...d of horses originated. The first horse, ...y believe, was created out of a handful of ... south wind by Allah, who declared: ...y name shall be Arabian, and virtue ...nd into the hair of thy forelock and ...nder on thy back. I have preferred thee ...ve all beasts of burden inasmuch as I have ...le thy master thy friend. I have given thee ... power of flight without wings, be it in ...laught or in retreat. I will set man on thy ...k that shall honour and praise Me and sing ...leujah to My Name.'

...Never was a promise more brightly fulfil... and its first rider was Ishmael, son of ...raham and first ancestor of the Bedouin.

...One of the most widely known but least ...erved horses of antiquity was the unicorn. ... Greeks believed that it lived in India, ...le the Hindus were convinced that it was ...ive to Ceylon, or perhaps somewhere else.

Variously known as the Horse Whisperers or the Horseman's Word, its members were ploughmen and head horsemen, the most valued of skilled farm-workers. Membership gave a power over horses that amounted almost to witchcraft; it was believed by outsiders that the members of the society had the power to tame the most savage horse by a whisper, or that they could induce one to stand stock-still.

The society flourished until well within living memory, and in districts where the horse continues to play a part in the economy, may flourish still.

Such secret societies, it is thought, could be among the last manifestations of the Celtic horse cult that existed in Europe up to, and well into, the Roman occupation. On the great Celtic festivals of Samain (November 1), Imbolc (February 1), Beltane (May 1) and Lugnasad (August 1), which were based on key dates in the agricultural and pastoral year, with Samain as New Year Day, horse-races were run in honour of horse-goddess Epona or Rhiannon. Traces this preoccupation with horses, perhaps mingled with memories of Woden and Wild Hunt, may still linger on in the mumming plays that are performed in many villages of Europe on November 1, known now as All Saints' Day. A central character in number of these is the Obby Oss, a grotesque creature, half man, half horse, with a great

Eclipse by the ...eenth-century artist ...rge Stubbs, probably ...in's most celebrated ... painter, **right** *'Bronco ...er', captured in action ... US artist Frederic ...ington (1861–1909) ...elow Eadweard ...bridge's sequential ...ping horse. For many ...ries, artists found it ...ssible to depict a moving ... at speeds greater than a ... Even Stubbs, whose interest in horses was such that it led him to make detailed anatomical studies of them, was unable to reveal the true rhythm of a galloping horse. Like all artists of the period, his studies are formalised.*

It was the pioneer photographic work of Muybridge that made realism possible. Taken at high speed to achieve clarity, his studies had a profound influence on Remington.

...g wooden head and gaping jaws.

...e horse and the arts

...ere is little doubt that one of the chief ...es of the horse in art—painting, literature, ...ns—as in life, is that of servant, compan- ...and prop to the ego of Man. We can have ...y little idea of how a horse feels in its ...ural state, but left to itself, it is unlikely ...t it would pull a plough, bear a knight or ...alryman into a situation that would al- ...st certainly lead to death or dismember- ...nt for horse or rider, prance picturesquely ...er the guiding hand of an emperor, or do ...st of the other things that have attracted ...nters and writers to the animal since the ...n of history. The horse has been ...ken—an apt term—to the will and wishes ...man. Consequently, by an odd transfer- ...e, we ascribe to it the virtues and qualities ...most admire in ourselves—courage, loyal- ...intelligence and diligence—and it is as the ...odiment of these that it has been so often ...ised by painters and poets. To these qual- ...s are added the horse's own beauty, speed ...strength, so that what we are frequently ...ved by in both art and literature, is actual- ...centaur-like being that combines all the ...antages of both man and beast. An out- ...ding example of this is provided by the ...ounted Emperor' school of sculpture and ...nting, in which the dignity, authority and ...sonality of the man is magnified by his ...ng mounted on a horse. The earliest of ...n portraits surviving is that of Marcus ...relius, the second century Roman em- ...or, whose colossal equestrian statue domi- ...es the Capitoline Hill in Rome.

...his statue, or the symbolism it rep- ...nted, so influenced sculptors and portrait

painters that until our own time, it was almost impossible to envisage a 'Great Man' in any situation other than on horseback. Titian's Charles V, Van Dyck's Charles I, and Falconet's bronze of Peter the Great, all enhance royal dignity astride a horse. Napoleon, not surprisingly, preferred something more spirited. His favourite painter was J. L. David, a founder of the Romantic movement, who depicted his patron in a number of epic situations in which the Emperor is shown directing operations from the back of a rearing horse. The most dramatic, perhaps, is *Napoleon crossing the Alps*. The horse's hooves plunge against a darkening sky crisscrossed by lightning. Its eyes start and its nostrils flare; but the fact that Napoleon is in charge of both horse and the situation is made apparent by his firm seat, his stern visage and his outstretched arm.

Horses at war, or in swift movement have challenged artists since the earliest times.

convention that appealed to a great many artists and sculptors among the ancients. Even the Greeks, superb horsemen and strivers after realism in art though they were, could not quite capture the movement of a galloping horse – as can be seen from the otherwise glorious Parthenon frieze. Despite the anatomical drawings of the horse by Leonardo da Vinci, artists of the Renaissance and after continued to be blind to any equine movement more rapid than a sedate walk. The famous English sporting paintings and prints of the eighteenth and early nineteenth centuries persisted in portraying galloping hunters and racehorses with all four legs outstretched – an anatomical and mechanical impossibility. It was the American pioneer cinematographer, Eadweard Muybridge, who by means of freeze-action photographs, was able to prove that at canter and gallop, the horse draws its feet together, and at one point of the action, all four feet leave

Two views of horses seen by artists from different times and cultures. **Left** *A Chinese handscroll on silk of polo players, painted by Lin-Lin in about 1635 and* **right** *Le Petit Cheval Bleu (The Little Blue Horse) by the German expressionist painter Franz Marc (1880–1916). In their different ways, both artists reveal their sympathy with their subject – Lin-Lin in his vivid appreciation of one of China's oldest games and Marc in his warmth and depth of colour.*

Marc's sympathy with horses lasted until his death. One of his diary entries before he was killed near Verdun in 1916 expressed sympathy for the sufferings of the artillery horses.

The wild, springing creatures drawn on the cave walls at Lascaux are probably a prayer of our ancestors of 20,000 years ago that the swift horse might stay within range of their spears; by painting a picture of the animal, they captured its spirit and so gained ascendancy over it.

The artists made their living by hunting; exact observation of animal behaviour and movement was of vital importance to them. Consequently, though executed in swift, simple strokes, the horses that graze, gallop and wheel across the cave walls precisely mirror the living creatures. This was an ability that was to escape many artists for thousands of years to come.

The challenge of movement

In the magnificent Assyrian stone relief *The lion hunt of King Assurnasipal*, the sculptor depicted all the horses of the royal chariot lifting their forefeet at the same time, a

the ground at once. George Stubbs, doyen of horse-painters, had begun to appreciate this in the eighteenth century, and 100 years later, Toulouse-Lautrec seized upon the point in paintings such as *Jockeys* and *Mail Coach to Nice*. But the realism of the horse portraits of Sir Alfred Munnings, and the true appreciation shown in the work of Frederic Remington, pioneer recorder of the life of the US cowboy, was only made possible through the observations of Muybridge.

Portraits and sporting paintings apart, the role of the horse in the art of the machine age has been largely symbolistic. Innocence is the theme of the red and blue horses of Franz Marc, and happiness is inherent in the quickly glimpsed race meetings of Raoul Dufy. But in his massive *Guernica*, Picasso assigns the animal to a different twentieth-century role. At the focus of the painting, a horse struggles among the ruins of the bombed town, screaming in uncomprehending terror at the

aircraft raining death from the jagged sky.

The horse in literature

'On your imaginary forces, work. . . .' suggests Chorus in Shakespeare's *Henry V*, 'Think, when we talk of horses, that you see them, printing their proud hooves i' the receiving earth. . . .' As so often in his work, Shakespeare in this play uses the horse as an

image to convey a sense of urgency, of great deeds a-stirring, of their culmination in triumph or tragedy. On the sleepless, uneasy night before Agincourt, the opposing armies stir restlessly as across no-man's land 'steed threatens steed with high and boastful neigh', while the Dauphin of France bores his companions with praises of his horse, which he likens to a mistress. 'Methought your

mistress shrewdly shook your back yesterd... comments the Constable sarcastically, ... resumes his brooding on the morrow.

Richard III's oft-quoted cry of 'My K... dom for a horse!', if taken within the con... of the play, sums up the king's final s... realisation and sense of bitter betrayal. ... also the moment when the audience, hav... followed Richard through his innumer...

...ainies, begins to sympathise with his ...ght and has a reluctant admiration for his ...rage. Again, in *Richard II*, a king's down... ...is emphasised by a horse – 'a jade hath eat ...ad from my royal hand' – Richard's own ...oved charger, that, without a thought for ...old master, carries his supplanter to his ...onation.

...hroughout the ages the horse has been a ...ourite subject for writers from almost all ...r the world. The horses of fiction ...legion, from Don Quixote's steed which ...act he loved much better than his lady, ...cinea, to Black Beauty, whose an-...pomorphous musings did much to reveal ...condition of horses in the cities of ...eteenth-century England; and to The Pie, ...horse that Velvet Brown, heroine of ...*ional Velvet* rode to victory in the Grand ...tional. Human vision is inspired by the ...se, like that of the little boy who could ...' the winners of future races whenever he ...e his rocking-horse in D. H. Lawrence's ...y *The Rocking-horse Winner*. In his fable, ...*mal Farm*, George Orwell presents two ...horses as epitomising working-class vir-..., but whose labour and loyalty do them ...e good in the end. Curiously enough, ...id Low, the British political cartoonist of ...same epoch, also used a cart horse image, ...to personify what he saw as the plodding ...des Union movement of his time.

...he great horse writers of the nineteenth ...tury, such as Surtees, creator of Jorrocks, ...e actually more concerned with horsemen ...n with animals. To them, the horse was a ...ns of transport and a beast of burden, ...ch was referred to, if at all, in words of ...al insult. It is left to us, in the jet era, to ...ore to the animal some of the awe felt for ...our farther-off ancestors. This is expres-...n Peter Shaeffer's play, *Equus*, in which a ...ly, disturbed boy blinds the horse that ...become to him part god and part keeper

of his conscience.

The horse, it seems, exercises its magic still, even if many of us seldom see one except on cinema or television screens. There at least, in a line of John Ford's cavalrymen against the sky, or in the slow, menacing advance of the French knights in Olivier's *Henry V*, we can feel again the stir in our blood that must surely be ancestral.

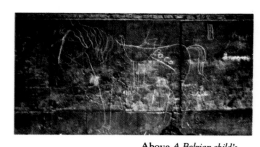

Above *A Belgian child's wall drawings of a horse and* **left** *the young Elizabeth Taylor, playing the heroine of 'National Velvet', mounts The Pie. This film, the story of a young girl and her horse winning the British Grand National, is one of the most popular of all time in countries all over the world.*

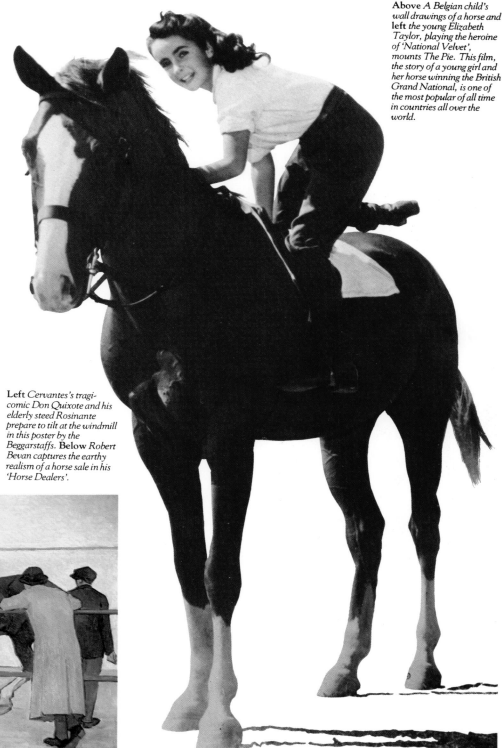

Left *Cervantes's tragi-comic Don Quixote and his elderly steed Rosinante prepare to tilt at the windmill in this poster by the Beggarstaffs.* **Below** *Robert Bevan captures the earthy realism of a horse sale in his 'Horse Dealers'.*

Chapter Three

The points of the horse

The most striking feature of the horse is that it can perform the many tasks asked of it by man, though its physical make-up is in many ways unsuited to such demands. In its main period of evolution, the horse developed from a four or even five-toed marsh dweller to take the basic form it has today at a relatively early date; and even though it has somewhat changed its shape and improved its performance, the basic working mechanism remains the same.

Such basic physical facts should always colour the rider's attitude to the horse, and what he or she expects of it. With a basic understanding of the so-called points of the horse, it should be possible, for example, to go some way towards lessening the risk of muscular strains. These are all too common and, in extreme cases, can lead to a horse having to rest for weeks, if not months. More important still, knowledge of these points acts as a valuable guide in deciding what is a suitable or unsuitable horse for the prospective rider. The most vital attribute of any riding horse is depth of girth, which denotes toughness and strength. Tall, leggy horses invariably lack stamina. Short legs and a deep body, with plenty of heart room, are the signs to look for.

The most important points of the horse are its limbs and feet. Both in the wild and in domesticity, the horse depends on its means of locomotion for survival.

Feet and legs require therefore to be as correctly conformed as possible, if the horse is to remain sound and mobile. Correct conformation is, indeed, the most valuable asset any horse can possess.

The hind leg

Experts differ as to whether the most important single asset is a good hind leg or a good foreleg. As the hind leg is the propelling force, it is usually given priority. At the point

Body colours of horses vary. The principal ones are black, brown, bay and chestnut, though Thoroughbreds can be bay/brown, grey and roan as well. Non-Thoroughbred horses and ponies can also be dun, cream, piebald, skewbald, odd-coloured, whole coloured, palomino and Appaloosian. Within all these colours there are variations of shade. If there is any doubt about the colour of a horse, the deciding factor is the colour of its points – that is, the muzzle, tips of the ears, mane, tail and the lower parts of all four legs. Some body colours, correctly pointed, are shown (below).

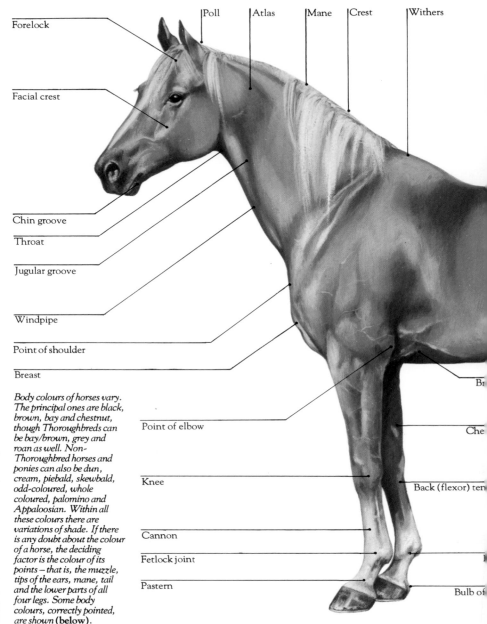

Forelock · Poll · Atlas · Mane · Crest · Withers · Facial crest · Chin groove · Throat · Jugular groove · Windpipe · Point of shoulder · Breast · Point of elbow · Knee · Cannon · Fetlock joint · Pastern · Back (flexor) ten · Bulb of

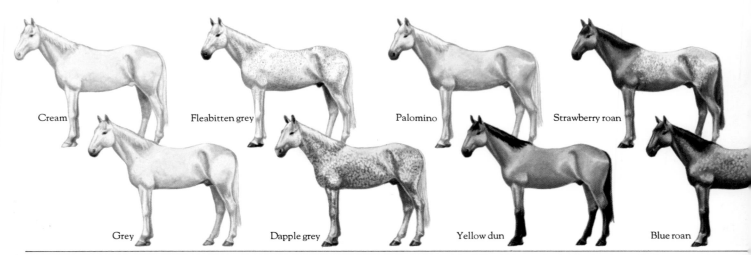

Cream · Fleabitten grey · Palomino · Strawberry roan · Grey · Dapple grey · Yellow dun · Blue roan

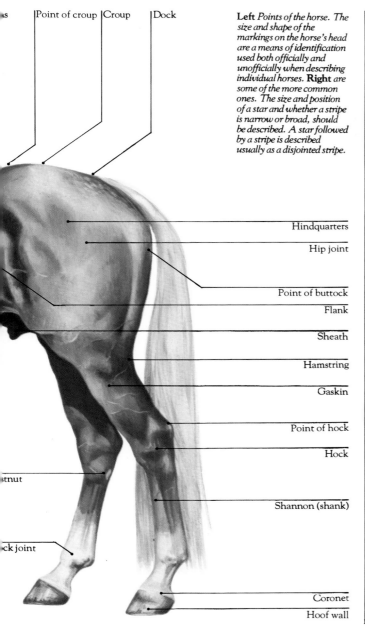

Point of croup | Croup | Dock

Hindquarters

Hip joint

Point of buttock

Flank

Sheath

Hamstring

Gaskin

Point of hock

Hock

Shannon (shank)

Coronet

Hoof wall

Left *Points of the horse. The size and shape of the markings on the horse's head are a means of identification used both officially and unofficially when describing individual horses.* **Right** *are some of the more common ones. The size and position of a star and whether a stripe is narrow or broad, should be described. A star followed by a stripe is described usually as a disjointed stripe.*

White face

Stripe

Blaze

Snip

Star

Right *White leg markings are an important means of identification. A sock covers the fetlock and part of the cannon, while a stocking extends to the knee or hock. Other marks take the name of their site.*

Bay

Piebald

Odd coloured

Liver chestnut

Brown

Skewbald

Black

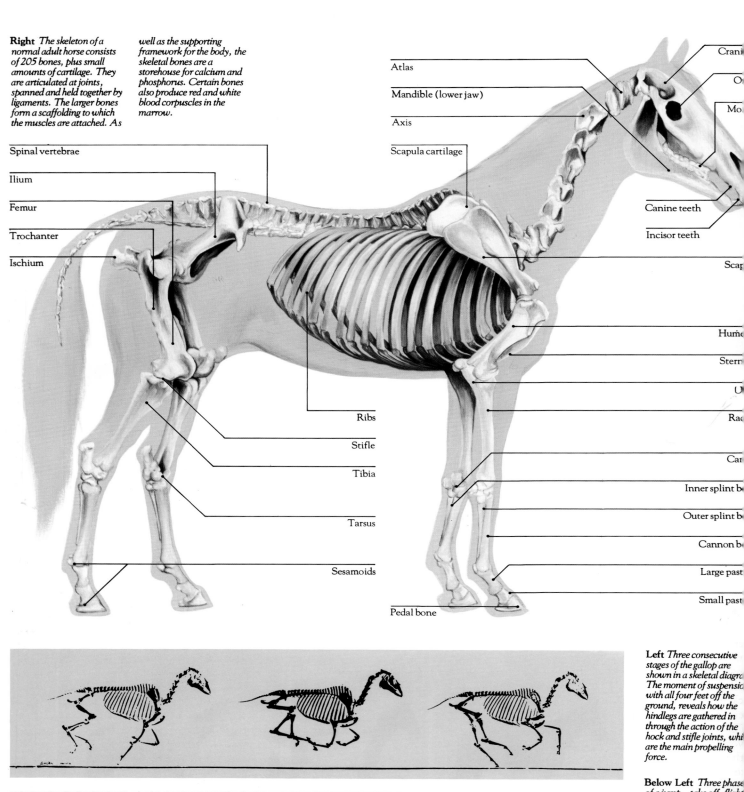

Right The skeleton of a normal adult horse consists of 205 bones, plus small amounts of cartilage. They are articulated at joints, spanned and held together by ligaments. The larger bones form a scaffolding to which the muscles are attached. As well as the supporting framework for the body, the skeletal bones are a storehouse for calcium and phosphorus. Certain bones also produce red and white blood corpuscles in the marrow.

Atlas

Mandible (lower jaw)

Axis

Scapula cartilage

Crani

O

Mo

Canine teeth

Incisor teeth

Scap

Spinal vertebrae

Ilium

Femur

Trochanter

Ischium

Hume

Stern

U

Rac

Car

Inner splint b

Outer splint b

Cannon b

Large past

Small past

Ribs

Stifle

Tibia

Tarsus

Sesamoids

Pedal bone

Left Three consecutive stages of the gallop are shown in a skeletal diagra The moment of suspensio with all four feet off the ground, reveals how the hindlegs are gathered in through the action of the hock and stifle joints, whi are the main propelling force.

Below Left Three phase of a jump – take off, flight and landing – show hock stifle joints in action again powering the spring and gathering up the hindlegs clear the obstacle. The unique structure of the foreleg, which is attached the upper body solely by muscles and ligaments, cushions the spine from th concussive shock of the landing.

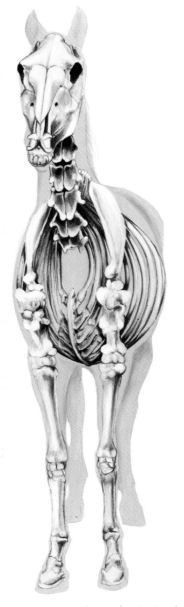

Far Left *This view of the horse's skeleton from the front shows the thoracic inlet – the bony ring through which the trachea and oesophagus enter the chest cavity. From the rear* (**Left**) *the pelvic bones are shown.*

able ride, they, too, are a sign of weakness that could lead to future trouble.

The foot

The size of foot varies with the type of horse. Thoroughbreds usually have small, rounded feet and, often, low heels. Heavy breeds, such as Clydesdales, Shires and Percherons, have larger, flatter feet.

The foot should be wide and open, not narrow, 'boxy' and contracted. The horn should look healthy and be free from unsightly cracks or ridges. Under it lies the sensitive laminae.

When the foot is lifted up, a well-developed frog should be visible on the underside. Starting at the bulbs of the heel and running upwards to end in a point near the toe, the frog acts as an anti-slip device and also helps to absorb concussion.

Each hoof is surmounted by the coronary band, which lies between the foot and the pastern.

Proper care of the feet is vital. In jumping, for instance, one forefoot has to take the whole weight of both horse and rider at the moment of landing. Good shoeing is therefore essential, or lameness will result. A young horse, too, can develop a form of lameness called pedal ostitis, caused by an excess of pressure on the sensitive sole of the foot by the os pedis – the terminal bone. This comes about largely through overwork, particularly in jumping.

The foreleg

The unique feature of the horse's foreleg is that it is attached to the upper part of the body by nothing more than muscle and ligamentous tissue. The horse has no equivalent to the human clavicle, or collar bone. The chief advantage of this is that the muscle is able to absorb a great deal of the concussion that would otherwise be transmitted to the spine. However, if undue strain is placed on the muscle, the horse can easily break down. This is particularly the case in race horses – often because the horse is what is known as 'back at the knee' (the shape is concave rather than convex).

The foreleg extends from the body below the point of the shoulder. The forearm runs down into the knee, which, like the hock, should be big, flat and prominent. Then the cannon bone, with tendons standing out clear and hard, runs down into the fetlock. The pastern separates this from the foot.

The legs have one final individual feature – the horny growths inside the legs above the knees. These are called chestnuts, and are, like fingerprints, completely individual. They are thought to be the remains of a digit.

ere it emerges from the body the stifle t is situated. This corresponds to the nan knee and is similarly equipped with a ella, or kneecap. This acts like a pulley ck to give added strength to the muscles ending the stifle.

he stifle itself is synchronized in its vements with the hock, as it is controlled he same muscles and ligaments. As one es, so does the other.

hen comes the gaskin, or second thigh. s should be muscular and well-developed ugh to stand up to the work and strain anded of it. This runs down into the k – probably the most important part of leg as the main propelling agent which bles the horse to gallop and jump.

he hock is made up of a whole series of ts, tightly bound together by ligaments. rticulates directly with the tibia (another vital bone) only through one bone – the astralagus. The feature as a whole should be big, flat and free from unsightly lumps, bumps or swellings. These can be indications of various types of unsoundness, such as curbs, spavins or thoroughpins.

The hock should also be near to the ground; short cannon bones from hock to fetlock and from knee to fetlock are a sign of strength. The tendons should stand out sharply and there should be no thickening of the lower leg.

The fetlock joint should also be well-defined and not puffy – a puffy fetlock resembles a human swollen ankle. This leads on to the pastern, which should be of medium length and slope. Very short pasterns cannot fulfil one of their main tasks – absorbing the concussion produced by movement. Though over-long pasterns give a springy, comfort-

The body

The shoulder runs from the withers – the bony prominence dividing the neck from the back and the highest part of the dorsal spine – down to the point of the shoulder. The shoulder itself should be long and sloping, especially at the upper end. An upright shoulder reduces endurance, as the horse has to do more work to cover the ground, and it cannot help to reduce concussion, which instead is passed on to the rider, making the horse uncomfortable to ride. This is particularly the case if the horse is ridden downhill.

The breast lies to the front of the shoulder, between the forelegs. It should be broad and muscular; narrow-breasted horses are weak and lack stamina. The underside of the neck should be concave and not unduly muscular.

The jaws run down to the muzzle. Well-defined, slightly distended nostrils and a large, generous eye are a sign of quality and good breeding. So are alert, well-pricked ears, which should not be too large. Between them lies the poll, leading to the top of neck, the crest, which runs down to the withers and back. The back consists of about eleven of the eighteen dorsal vertebrae, as well as the arches of the corresponding ribs. Behind it lie the loins, which should be strong and well-muscled. These extend to the croup, or rump, which runs down to the tail and its underside, the dock.

Standing behind the horse, the points of the hip can be seen projecting outwards on either side of the backbone, above the flanks. This outwards projection means that they can easily be injured.

Just below the loins, a triangular depression, known as the 'hollow of the flank', is located. This is the highest point of the flank, which stretches downwards from the lumbar spine. The condition of the flank often acts as a guide to the health of the horse; if the horse is sick, it may well be 'tucked up' or distended.

Teeth and age

Age in the horse is determined by examining the six incisors (grinding teeth). The two central incisors are cut when a foal is ten days old and are followed within a month or so weeks by the lateral incisors. The corner incisors follow between six and nine months to complete the horse's full set of milk teeth.

The trot (below) is an active, two-time pace, the legs moving in diagonal pairs with a moment of suspension. The rider rises in the saddle for one stride, then sits again.

The walk (right) is the slowest pace of the horse. The animal moves one leg after another in the sequence, left fore, right hind, right fore, left hind, in a regular four-time rhythm.

Trot

Canter

Gallop

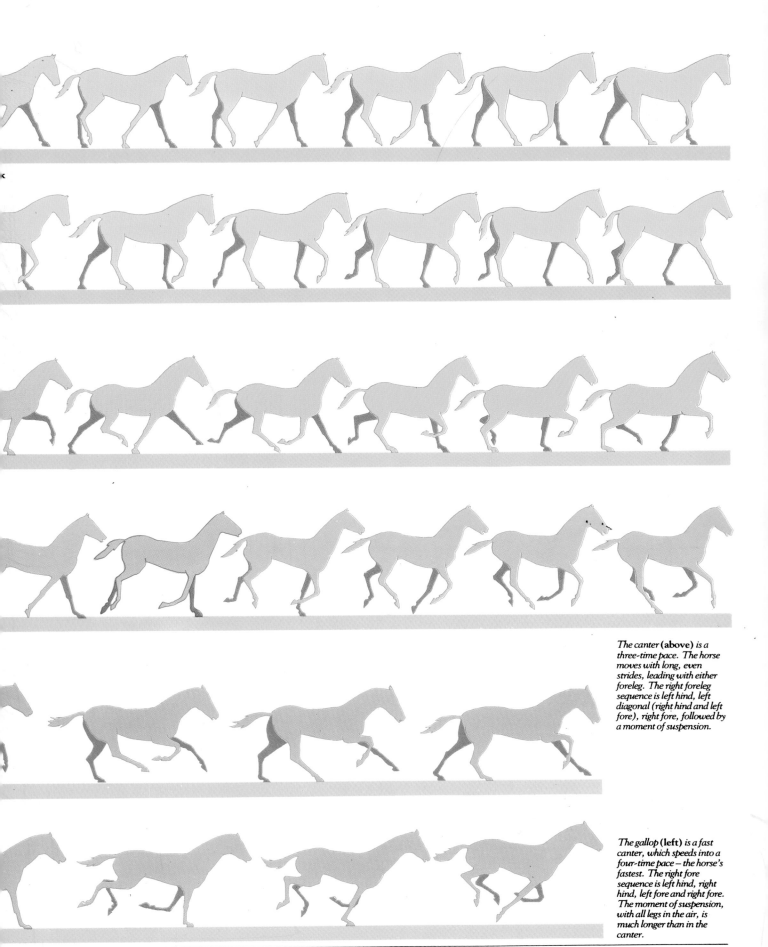

The canter (above) is a three-time pace. The horse moves with long, even strides, leading with either foreleg. The right foreleg sequence is left hind, left diagonal (right hind and left fore), right fore, followed by a moment of suspension.

The gallop (left) is a fast canter, which speeds into a four-time pace – the horse's fastest. The right fore sequence is left hind, right hind, left fore and right fore. The moment of suspension, with all legs in the air, is much longer than in the canter.

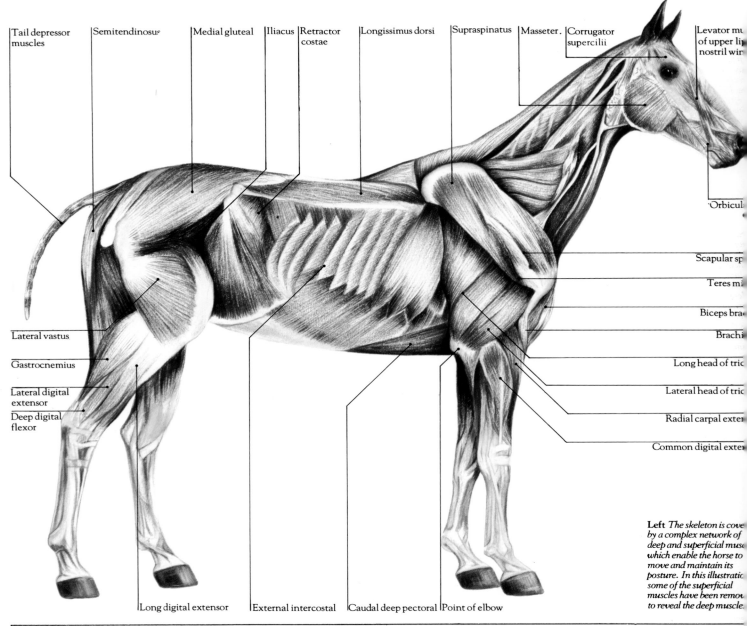

Tail depressor muscles

Semitendinosus

Medial gluteal

Iliacus

Retractor costae

Longissimus dorsi

Supraspinatus

Masseter.

Corrugator supercilii

Levator mu of upper li nostril wir

Orbicul

Scapular sp

Teres m

Biceps bra

Brachi

Long head of tric

Lateral head of tri

Radial carpal exter

Common digital exter

Lateral vastus

Gastrocnemius

Lateral digital extensor

Deep digital flexor

Long digital extensor

External intercostal

Caudal deep pectoral

Point of elbow

Left *The skeleton is cove by a complex network of deep and superficial muse which enable the horse to move and maintain its posture. In this illustratic some of the superficial muscles have been remou to reveal the deep muscle.*

A horse depends on its legs for survival, but unfortunately, the system which it has evolved for moving legs is not ideal. All the muscles are grouped together at the top of the leg, and the force from their contractions is transferred by tendons to the appropriate bone or joint. These stretched lines of communication are very prone to injury.

Tendons consist of thousands of collagen fibres lying in a groundwork of connective tissue. These fibres lie in the approximate direction of the force which is transmitted along the tendon. The connective tissue consists of an inert matrix with a network of blood vessels, elastic fibres and various individual cells. Chief among these cells are

the fibroplasts which are responsible for forming the collagen fibres.

Each tendon is surrounded by a smooth membrane, the peritendineum, and enclosed in a tendon sheath which also has a smooth lining. Movement of the tendon within its tendon sheath is further facilitated by the presence of tenosynovial fluid as a sort of lubricant.

If a tendon is strained the collagen fibres slip and rupture. There is also haemorrhage and tissue fluids collect at the site of the damage. New collagen has to be formed to repair the damage, and the orientation of these new collagen fibres is vitally important. If scar tissue is formed, then the materials and cells involved arrive at the site by migration

from the synovial sheath around the tendon and so consist of Collagen Type 3. If, instead of scar tissue, the existing collagen is regenerated, then this consists of Collagen Type 1 – a stronger type.

The extra fluid which is released at the site of the tendon injury is important for three reasons. Firstly, if it contains a great deal of fibrin it may clot rather like blood and form adhesions which will affect future movement. Secondly, the pressure which the fluid causes, both between the fibrous bundles and in the tendon sheath, is a major cause of pain. Finally, if the 'filling' of the leg becomes chronic it is an unsightly blemish. Regeneration always takes time, during which the horse should be completely rested.

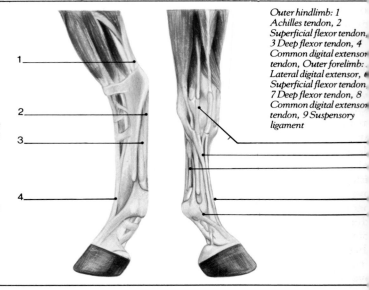

1

2

3

4

Outer hindlimb: 1 Achilles tendon, 2 Superficial flexor tendon, 3 Deep flexor tendon, 4 Common digital extensor tendon, Outer forelimb: Lateral digital extensor, Superficial flexor tendon, 7 Deep flexor tendon, 8 Common digital extensor tendon, 9 Suspensory ligament

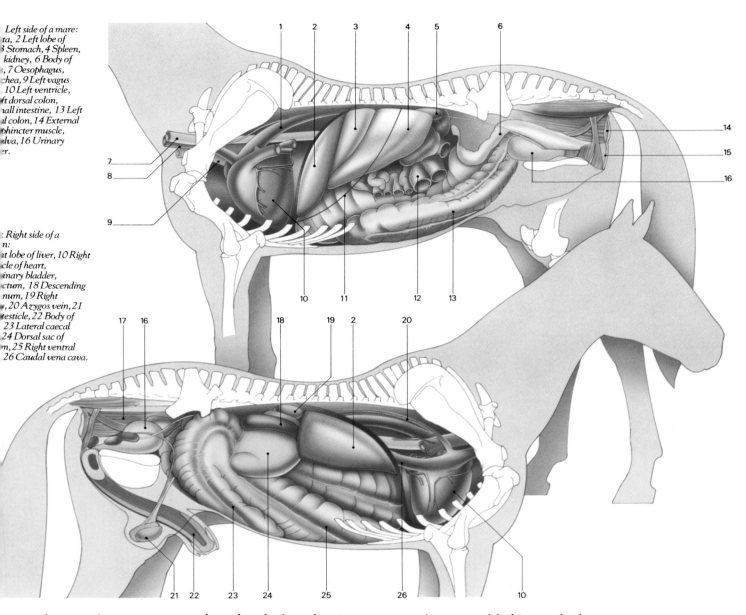

Left side of a mare:
...ta, 2 Left lobe of
...3 Stomach, 4 Spleen,
... kidney, 6 Body of
..., 7 Oesophagus,
...chea, 9 Left vagus
...10 Left ventricle,
...t dorsal colon,
...all intestine, 13 Left
...l colon, 14 External
...phincter muscle,
...lva, 16 Urinary
...er.

Right side of a
...n:
...t lobe of liver, 10 Right
...cle of heart,
...inary bladder,
...ctum, 18 Descending
...num, 19 Right
..., 20 Azygos vein, 21
...esticle, 22 Body of
...23 Lateral caecal
...24 Dorsal sac of
...m, 25 Right ventral
...26 Caudal vena cava.

...se are white in colour, in contrast to the ...ow of the permanent teeth, and taper to a ...t at the base.

...hese last the horse until the age of three, ...n the central incisors are replaced by ...nanent teeth. At four, the lateral incisors ...similarly replaced, and male horses also ...y a tush, or canine tooth. At five the last ...t teeth, the corner incisors, give way to ...nanent teeth.

...t six, the corner incisors have worn level, ...le by the age of seven they will have ...eloped a hook shape. At nine a dark line ...sible on the biting edge and Galvayne's ...ve, a longitudinal furrow, appears on the ...er teeth, near the gum. At ten, the slope ...he teeth increases and at fifteen this ...omes even more pronounced; this process ...hes its climax between the ages of twenty ...twenty-five. At twenty, too, Galvayne's ...ve reaches the lower edge of the teeth,

though, from that time, it starts to disappear at the same rate it first appeared.

All these factors – length, slope and the increasingly triangular shape – make it possible to estimate a horse's age reasonably accurately. After the age of eight, however, when the horse is said to be aged, it is not possible to be exact.

Measuring height
The horse's height is measured from the highest point of the withers to the ground. On the European continent, it is measured in centimetres, while in the UK, Ireland, North America and Australasia, it is measured in hands. A hand is officially defined as 4 in (10.16 cm) – the distance across a man's knuckles; 14 hands 3 inches, or 14.3 hands, is the accepted breakdown for fractionalised measurement. The common abbreviation 'hh' stands for 'hands high'.

Markings and colours
Markings on the head of the horse are described as a star (a small white patch of hair on the forehead); a stripe (a white line running down the face); a blaze (a broad white mark); a white face (like a Hereford cow); and a snip (a white line running into the nostril or around it). White markings on the legs are either socks (short) or stockings (long). These definitions have been established by the various breeding authorities.

Colours of the horse vary. They range from bay (the colour of a horse chestnut, with a black mane, tail and, usually, black lower legs, described as black points); black; brown; chestnut (varying shades of red, from bright to liver chestnut); dun (cream-coloured, shading to yellow, with black points, dorsal stripe, mane and tail); cream (with light mane and tail); palomino (varying shades of gold, with flaxen mane and tail); blue or red

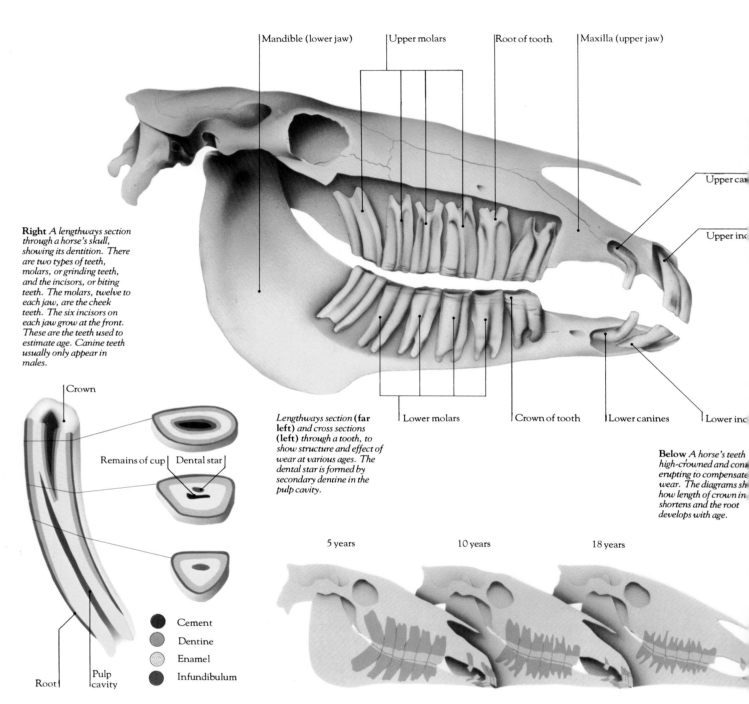

Mandible (lower jaw) | Upper molars | Root of tooth | Maxilla (upper jaw)

Upper ca

Upper inc

Right *A lengthways section through a horse's skull, showing its dentition. There are two types of teeth, molars, or grinding teeth, and the incisors, or biting teeth. The molars, twelve to each jaw, are the cheek teeth. The six incisors on each jaw grow at the front. These are the teeth used to estimate age. Canine teeth usually only appear in males.*

Crown

Remains of cup | Dental star

Lower molars | Crown of tooth | Lower canines | Lower inc

*Lengthways section (**far left**) and cross sections (**left**) through a tooth, to show structure and effect of wear at various ages. The dental star is formed by secondary dentine in the pulp cavity.*

Below *A horse's teeth high-crowned and con erupting to compensate wear. The diagrams sh how length of crown in shortens and the root develops with age.*

Root | Pulp cavity

● Cement
● Dentine
● Enamel
● Infundibulum

5 years | 10 years | 18 years

roan (grey or chestnut, with a white fleck throughout); piebald (black and white); skewbald (red or chestnut or bay and white); to pinto (piebald, skewbald, or odd-coloured, grey or roan and white, for example).

Gaits of the horse

The four basic gaits of the horse are the walk, the trot, the canter and the gallop. In addition, US saddle horses can have four extra gaits – the pace, the stepping pace, the slow gait and the rack.

The walk is a marching pace in which the four legs follow one another in the following sequence – left hind, left fore, right hind, right fore, left fore, right hind, right fore and left hind. When the four beats cease to be well accented, even and regular, the walk is termed disunited or broken. The gait itself is further sub-divided into ordinary walk, collected walk, extended walk and free walk.

The trot is a two-time pace on alternate diagonals (near fore and off hind and vice versa), separated by a moment of suspension. The gait can be ordinary, collected or extended, as can the canter.

The canter is a three-time pace. Leading with the off fore, or right foreleg, the horse follows this sequence: near hind, left diagonal (right hind and left fore), right fore, fol-

lowed by a period of suspension with all legs in the air before it takes the next st forwards.

The gallop is the horse's fastest pace, ing which it never has more than two fee the ground, and, more often than not, During a forward leap, all the feet leave ground and the horse is, literally, flying. legs can be lifted in one of two sequenc either left fore, right fore, left hind and r hind, or right fore, left fore, right hind left hind.

Common faults

With the exception of obvious faults of

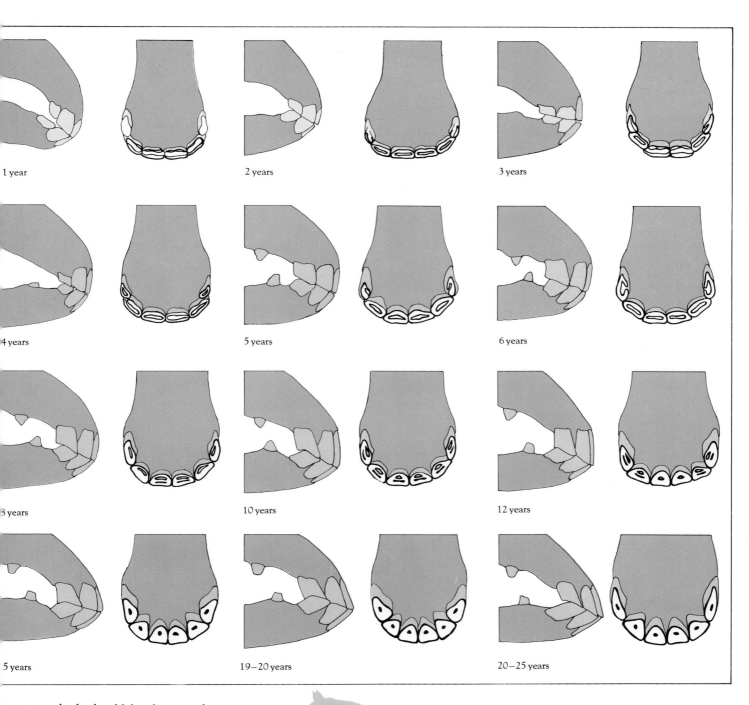

1 year

2 years

3 years

4 years

5 years

6 years

8 years

10 years

12 years

15 years

19–20 years

20–25 years

mation, which should be discovered on
ial examination, few horses are bad – if
y are, they have generally been made so by
lty handling and training. It is important
realize that a horse's brain is small com-
ed to its body size, that it cannot reason,
l that it should not be given credit for a
nan-type intelligence. Weaknesses such
rushing (striking one foot with the shoes
he opposite foot) and forging (striking the
efoot with the toe of the hind)
usually caused by faulty action or
eral unfitness. A fit, well-fed and careful-
xercised horse will seldom have to face
h problems.

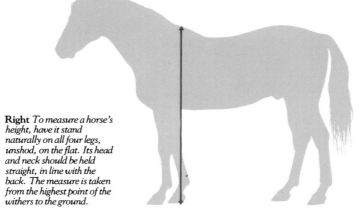

Right To measure a horse's
height, have it stand
naturally on all four legs,
unshod, on the flat. Its head
and neck should be held
straight, in line with the
back. The measure is taken
from the highest point of the
withers to the ground.

Above Changes in
dentition, signs of wear and
marks of age are used to
estimate the age of a horse.
The replacement of
temporary incisors with
permanent ones is an
accurate gauge up to five
years. From then until eight,
wear on cups and corner
teeth is a useful indicator.
After this, the growth of
Galvayne's groove on the
upper corner incisor, the
appearance of dental stars,
wearing away of cups and
the increasing forward slope
of incisors are the best
guides.

Chapter Four

Types and breeds

In this chapter, a breed is defined as one that has a stud book. There are two main types. Many stud books are open, that is, stock is registered in the breed stud book on condition that the parents are approved by the relevant breed society and are of pedigree stock themselves. The stallion and mare concerned need not necessarily be both of the same breed. The Hanoverian, for example, often has Arab, Thoroughbred or Trakehner ancestors. However, most of the older breeds – Arab and Thoroughbred, for instance – have closed stud books. This means that stock is only registered if both parents are registered members of that breed.

In addition, there are horses that are not registered in any stud book; most of these are defined as types. Hunters, hacks and cobs all come under this category, though it is possible to have a registered Thoroughbred hunter or hack.

There are also horses that are difficult to place within this system. The Australian Brumby, for instance, is the feral descendant of horses which escaped from captivity when the first European settlers came to Australia in the late eighteenth century. Thus, it is not a true breed, nor is it really a type. Nevertheless, it is cross-bred with domestic horses to produce very sturdy off-spring.

In the subsequent pages, each breed is discussed under its place of origin.

North America

America is now thought to be where the modern horse (*Equus caballos*) evolved. Before the land bridge linking North America and Asia was submerged to become the Bering Straits, horses probably migrated across it, to spread through Asia and, eventually, Europe. Some almost certainly stayed in America, but what happened to them is uncertain. No equine remains have been found dateable to any period after the Ice Age, so it seems that for 7000 years there were no horses in America. They re-entered the continent in 1511, when the Spanish adventurer Hernan Cortes landed in Mexico with a small force of conquistadores and 16 Andalusians.

The North American Indians were poor breeders of horses, taking no pains to breed selectively. The one exception was the Nez Percé tribe. By the end of the eighteenth century, they had developed high-quality, spotted horses which they christened Appaloosas. The other horses used by the Indians were the Mustangs, which escaped from the early settlers to run wild.

The colonists of the Atlantic coast also brought horses with them. The first distinct native breed to emerge from these imports was the Narrangansett Pacer, which was developed on Rhode Island mainly from Nor-

folk Trotter stock. However, losses through export and cross-breeding led to the purebred Narrangansett dying out.

In the mid-nineteenth century, cross-breeding produced one of the greatest of the US breeds, the Standardbred. The name comes from the standards set for horses to achieve during the selective breeding process. Today the Standardbred is the basis of the major sport of trotting, and has played a crucial part in improving foreign breeds.

The Quarter-horse is the oldest surviving American breed. It is also the most numerous in the USA; 800,000 are registered worldwide. The horse was developed by the seventeenth century settlers in Virginia and the Carolinas as an all-purpose animal. Its ability was tested by racing it over a quarter of a mile, and from this comes its name. As the Americans expanded westwards, the Quarter-horse proved to be an excellent cow pony.

Galiceno

Garranos

Galiceno

Pony
Height: 12.2 hands.
Colour: bay, black or dun.
Physique: short-coupled, narrow frame.
Features: versatile, natural running walk.
Use: ranch work and transportation.

Standardbred

Thoroughbred
Canadian Trotter
Hackney
Narrangansett Pacer
Arab
Barb
Morgan

Standardbred

Warmblood
Height: 15.2 hands.
Colour: solid colours.
Physique: varies as it is bred for speed; usually muscular Thoroughbred type with longer back, short legs and powerful shoulders.
Features: stamina, speed.
Use: driving and racing.

Pinto
Warmblood
Height: varies.
Colour:: black with white or white with any colour

but black.
Physique: varies.
Use: ranch work, riding or showing.

Quarter-Horse

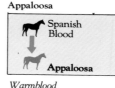

Arab
Barb
Turk
Andalusian
Thoroughbred

Quarter-Horse

Warmblood
Height: 15.3 hands.
Colour: solid colours, usually chestnut.
Physique: short head,

powerful, short-coupled body, large round hindquarters and fine legs.
Features: fast and versatile.
Use: riding, racing, ranch work and rodeos.

Appaloosa

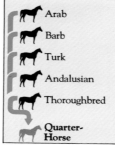

Spanish Blood

Appaloosa

Warmblood
Origin: Western States.
Height: 15 hands.
Colour: six basic patterns of spots usually on roan or white, white sclera around eye.
Physique: short-coupled, thin mane and tail, hard feet which are often

The Morgan is another of the established American breeds. It was the duct of a single foundation sire – eith Welsh Cob or a Thoroughbred, foale 1793. The horse was the property of innkeeper called Justin Morgan, hence name.

With the Thoroughbred and the Nar gansett Pacer, it was also the founda stock for the Saddlebred. This breed developed by the nineteenth century pla tion owners of the South, who wanted sh animals that were comfortable to ride. result was the Saddlebred, a spectacular h with three or five gaits. It is very popula the show ring, where it is ridden or show harness. Then in Tennessee a horse was veloped with an even smoother gait than of the Saddlebred – the Tennessee Walk Horse. It was officially recognized as a b in 1935.

striped.
Use: as a cow pony, a pleasure and parade h and in the circus.

Mustang

Spanish Blood

Mustang

Warmblood
Origin: Western State and Mexico.
Height: 14.2 hands.
Colour: most colours.
Physique: sturdy, tough lightweight frame, go bone and tough feet.
Features: hardy and fr
Use: riding, showing, riding, endurance tria competitions and stoc work.

Quarter-Horse

Appaloosa

Galiceno

Canadian Cutting Horse

Pinto

Standardbred

The USA also has registers for horses that are defined according to colour, but do not yet breed true to type. Of these, the most attractive is the Palomino, the glamorous Hollywood cowboy pony. The Pinto was the Indians' favoured horse; its two colours were supposed to aid camouflage. The Albino, however, is a more recent development. Its genes appear to be prepotent.

As far as imported stock is concerned, the Thoroughbred is the most numerous, racing being a major industry in the USA. Second in number is the Shetland. This is used in halter and fine harness classes, as well as in trotting races. Other imported breeds with their own stud books are the Welsh, Hackney, Cleveland Bay, Percheron, Belgian, Trakehner, Clydesdale and Arab.

The only native American pony is of recent origin. It is the Pony of the Americas, which was developed in the 1960s, using an Appaloosa sire (with Arab and Quarter-horse ancestors) and Shetlands.

Canada has no native breed of horse, the Canadian Cutting Horse being classed only as a type. Horse-breeding, however, has flourished, ever since the first horses were brought across the Atlantic by French settlers in 1665. Some of the descendants of these horses are to be found in the Sable Islands where they have roamed semi-wild since the eighteenth century.

Palomino

Saddlebred

Tennessee Walking Horse

Morgan

nnessee Walking rse

- Narrangansett Pacer
- Standardbred
- Canadian Pacer
- Saddlebred
- Morgan
- **Tennessee Walking Horse**

...mblood
...in: Tennessee.
...ht: 15.2 hands.
...ur: solid colours.
...sique: common head,
red neck, strong,
ing shoulder,
erful loins and
dquarters, clean legs
full mane and tail,
ed artificially high.
...ures: kind
perament; has a
ing walk with the
feet raised high and
ind legs moving with
strides.
showing and riding.

adian Cutting Horse

...mblood
...ht: 15.2–16.1 hands.
...ur: almost any
ur.
...ique: like the
erican Quarter Horse.
g body, short legs,
erful hindquarters.
...ures: intelligent, fast
agile.
: competition and
k work.

ino

- Arab
- Morgan
- **Albino**

...mblood
...ht: any.
...ur: white with pink
, pale blue or dark
n eyes.
...ique: lightweight
e, otherwise varies.
riding.

mino

...mblood
...n: California.
...ht: 14 hands.
...ur: golden, with no
ings other than white
ce or below the
s. Mane and tail
e, silver or ivory; dark
...ique: varies; registered
olour, so does not yet
d true to type.
riding, driving and
k work.

Pony of the Americas

- Shetland Pony
- Appaloosa
- **Pony of the Americas**

Pony
Height: 12.1 hands.
Colour: Appaloosa patterns.
Physique: Arab-like head, short back and round body.
Use: trail riding, competitions and as a children's pony.

Missouri Foxtrotting Horse

Warmblood
Origin: Tennessee.
Height: 15.2 hands.
Colour: sorrel.
Physique: compact, strong body, long neck and intelligent head tapering to muzzle.
Features: broken gait called 'foxtrot', walking with forelegs and trotting with hindlegs at speeds of 10 to 15 mph
Use: riding and stock work.

Morgan

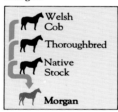

- Welsh Cob
- Thoroughbred
- Native Stock
- **Morgan**

Warmblood
Origin: Massachusetts.
Height: 15 hands.
Colour: bay, brown, black or chestnut.
Physique: short, broad head, thick neck, strong shoulders, back and hindquarters, good bone and full mane and tail.
Features: versatile, tough and good-tempered with a high action.

Saddlebred

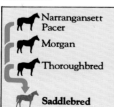

- Narrangansett Pacer
- Morgan
- Thoroughbred
- **Saddlebred**

Warmblood
Height: 15.2 hands.
Colour: black, brown, bay, grey or chestnut.
Physique: small head with straight profile.
Features: five-gaited
Use: showing and riding.

Scandinavia

Denmark's equine history revolves around the Fredericksborg. This was popular in the late sixteenth and seventeenth centuries as a High School horse, and in the eighteenth century as an improver of other breeds. However, today there are only a few of the animals left. They were named after Frederick II, who originated the breed at the Royal Fredericksborg Stud, founded in 1562.

The most popular Danish breed today is the Fjord Pony, followed by the Jutland, which has been bred in the peninsula for hundreds of years.

From the 1960s, the Danes, too, have had a stud book for a national riding horse – the Danish Sports Horse – based on imported pedigree stallions from Germany, Sweden, France and the UK, and local mares.

Sweden has been meeting the demand for riding horses with pedigree blood for over one hundred years. A stud book was started as early as 1874 for the Swedish Halfbred, which excells in dressage and eventing. Hanoverian, Trakehner, French, British and Arab blood has also been used, with the proviso that it is truly pedigree and that the stallions involved all pass performance tests.

For working the land and hauling timber, the Swedes use the Swedish Ardennes. This breed was established a century ago, when the Belgian Ardennes and the North Swedish were cross-bred. The Gotland is Sweden's pony. It is thought to be a direct descendant of the Tarpan, having run wild on Gotland Island since the Stone Age.

Norway, too, has a primitive pony type – the Norwegian Fjord – which has been bred for centuries. It was used by the Vikings, and now is popular all over the world. Its strength, toughness and good temperament make it suitable for all types of work, in addition to riding and driving.

The other Norwegian breed – the Døle – is not as internationally popular as the Fjord, but is more numerous in its homeland. Its offshoot, the Døle Trotter, was developed in the nineteenth century, to meet the demand for a fast carrying horse. It is now used in trotting races.

In Finland, the Finnish Horse (formed by the amalgamation of the Finnish Universal and Finnish Draught) is declining in numbers, largely due to the mechanization of agriculture, transport and timber hauling. However, imported warmbloods, used for riding, competitions and trotting, are on the increase.

Horses were introduced into Iceland over a thousand years ago, and the Icelandic Pony still breeds there freely. Even today, it still has a major role to play in the country's economy.

SWEDEN

Swedish Halfbred

- Oriental
- Spanish
- Friesian
- Trakehner
- Hanoverian
- Thoroughbred
- Arab
- **Swedish Halfbred**

Warmblood
Height: 16.1 hands.
Colour: Any solid colour.
Physique: smallish, intelligent head, large, bold eye, longish neck, deep girth and straightish back.
Features: intelligent, with an extravagant, straight action.
Use: general riding and competitions.

Gotland

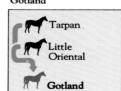

- Tarpan
- Little Oriental
- **Gotland**

Pony
Origin: Gotland Is.
Height: 12.1 hands.
Colour: dun, black, brown

or chestnut.
Physique: light frame, small straight head, long back and low set tail.
Features: hardy, active, sometimes obstinate.
Use: light agricultural work, trotting races, and as a children's pony.

Swedish Ardennes

- Ardennes
- Swedish Horse
- **Swedish Ardennes**

Coldblood
Height: 15.3 hands.
Colour: black, brown, bay or chestnut.
Physique: similar to but smaller than the Belgian Ardennes.
Features: active, good-tempered.
Use: agricultural work and timber hauling.

DENMARK

Fredericksborg

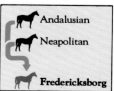

- Andalusian
- Neapolitan
- **Fredericksborg**

Warmblood
Height: 15.3 hands.
Colour: chestnut.
Physique: strong, plain harness horse, big chest, strong back.

Features: good-tempered, active.
Use: light draught, riding.

Jutland

- Ancient Stock
- Yorkshire Coach Horse
- Cleveland Bay
- Suffolk Punch
- **Jutland**

Coldblood
Origin: Jutland Is.
Height: 15.3 hands.
Colour: chestnut or roan.
Physique: massive, compact horse; plain head and short, feathered legs.
Features: good-tempered.
Use: draught.

Danish Sport Horse

- Hanoverian
- Native Halfbred
- Thoroughbred
- Trakehner
- Polish
- Anglo-Norman
- **Danish Sports Horse**

Warmblood
Origin: Denmark – developed by crossing various breeds from Northern Europe with locally bred mares
Height: 16.1 hands
Colour: all colours
Physique: varies, middleweight build
Use: general riding

Knabstrup

- Flaebehoppen
- Fredericksborg
- **Knabstrup**

Warmblood
Height: 15.3 hands.
Colour: spotted, Appaloosa patterns on roan base.
Physique: similar to but lighter than the Fredericksborg.
Use: circus.

NORWAY

Fjord

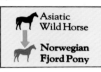

- Asiatic Wild Horse
- **Norwegian Fjord Pony**

Pony
Height: 14 hands.
Colour: dun, cream or yellow with dorsal stripe and upright black and silver mane.
Physique: small head, strong, short neck and powerful, compact body.
Use: work in the mountains; agriculture, transport, riding and driving.

Døle

- Danish Cold Blood
- Thoroughbred
- Trotter
- **Døle**

Warmblood
Height: 15 hands.
Colour: black, brown or bay.
Physique: two types; heavy draught – similar to the Dale; pony type – upright shoulder, deep girth, short legs with good bone and little feather.
Features: tough, versatile.
Use: agricultural work, riding and driving.

Døle Trotter

- Trotter
- Døle
- **Døle Trotter**

Warmblood
Height: 15 hands.
Colour: black, brown or bay.
Physique: lighter version of Døle with no feather.
Use: trotting races.

FINLAND

Finnish

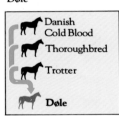

- Indigenous Forest pony
- Finnish Draught
- **Finnish**
- Finnish Universal

Coldblood
Height: 15.2 hands.
Colour: chestnut, bay and brown.
Physique: short neck, upright shoulder, deep, strong legs, light feather.
Features: tough, long-lived, even-tempered and fast.
Use: timber hauling, agriculture and trotting races.

ICELAND

Iceland Pony

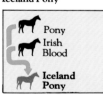

- Pony
- Irish Blood
- **Iceland Pony**

Pony
Height: 12.2 hands.
Colour: grey, dun.
Physique: stocky, compact body, full mane and tail.
Features: independent, tough and able to amble.
Use: mining, pack and communications.

Fjord

Iceland Pony

Finnish

Knabstrup

Fredericksborg

Døle

Swedish Halfbred

The Middle East and Africa

The world's oldest and most influential pure bred is the Arab, descended, it is believed, from Asiatic wild stock that ran wild in the desert lands of the Middle East as long ago as 5000 BC. Some experts claim that this original desert home was in either Persia, Syria or Egypt, but the majority hold that it was in the Yemen in the Arabian peninsula. From these origins, the Arab's special features – speed, endurance, fine coat and toughness – developed.

The main reason for the Arab's vast influence is because its equine virtues proved to be prepotent, that is they have been transmitted from one generation on to the next.

Today, Arabs are found all over the world, and their breeding is a flourishing industry. In the Arab's homeland, the Middle East, the most celebrated is the Persian – the oldest domesticated Arab – and the Egyptian, which, like the Polish Arab, is in heavy demand for export. This prepotency developed through the selective in-breeding pursued for centuries by the Bedouin tribesmen.

In Iran, too, there are other breeds of horse, which the recently formed Royal Horse Society is doing much to promote. Vast sums are being invested in both Thoroughbreds (mostly imported) and Turkomans for racing. The Turkoman itself has very early origins, which, in the adjacent USSR, played a part in the development of the Akhal Teké and Iomud. Most of the other strains of the Persian horse have now been amalgamated into one stud book for the Plateau Persian.

Under the Ottomans, Turkey produced many fine Arab strains from the sixteenth to twentieth centuries. The Byerley Turk played its part as a foundation sire for the Thoroughbred (see p. 84), but, during this century, the native stock deteriorated. This has led to the importation of the Nónius from Hungary to improve it and breed the Karacabey.

The other foundation stock for the Thoroughbred – the Barb – has its home in North Africa. It is often confused with the Arab, but experts claim that its origins lie with European, rather than with Asiatic, wild stock. It is distinguished from the Arab by its ram-like head, a lower-set tail, and its wilder temperament, but frequent crossing since the Arabs conquered North Africa has meant that there are few pure breeds surviving.

The rest of Africa, with one exception, has no native horses. The only native horse in South Africa – the Basuto Pony – developed from Barbs and Arabs imported in the mid-seventeenth century.

ARABIAN PENINSULA

Arab

Asiatic Wild Stock
↓
Arab

Thoroughbred
Height:14.3 hands
Colour: bay, chestnut (original colours), grey.
*Physique:*small tapering head, concave face, broad forehead, large, dark eyes, small ears, arched neck.
Features: fast, free floating action, stamina toughness.
Use: improving other breeds, riding

EGYPT

Egyptian Arab
Thoroughbred
*Height:*14.3 hands.
Colour: grey.
Physique: two types; th Kuhaylan is more rang than the short coupled Siglavy.
Features: speed
Use: racing, general ri and breeding.

Arab

Barb

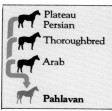

with Arab and
Thoroughbred
Use: riding

Plateau
Persian
Thoroughbred
Arab
Pahlavan

Persian Arab

Tarpan
Persian Arab

Thoroughbred
Height: 15 hands
Colour: grey or bay.
Physique: elegant,
compact body, otherwise
as Arab.
Features: possibly older
than the desert Arab.
Use: similar to the Arab.

sian Pony

n: Iran
ht: 10–11.2 hands
ur: grey, brown, bay,
tnut
ique: Arab-type head,
boned
ures: sure footed
transport, riding

avan
mblood
n: Iran
ht: 15.2–16 hands
ur: solid colours
ique: strong, elegant
ures: developed by
ing Plateau Persian

Plateau Persian

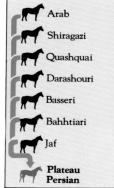

Arab
Shiragazi
Quashquai
Darashouri
Basseri
Bahhtiari
Jaf
Plateau Persian

Warmblood
Origin: Central Persian
Plateau.
Height: 15 hands.
Colour: grey, bay or
chestnut.
Physique: Arab features,
but this varies as this breed
is an amalgamation.
Features: good action,
strong and sure-footed.
Use: riding.

Turkoman (Turkmen)

Mongols'
Horse
Scythians'
Horse
Turkoman

Warmblood
Height: 15.2 hands.
Colour: solid colours.
Physique: narrow chest,
light but tough frame.
Features: floating action,
speed and endurance.
Use: foundation stock for
other breeds, riding,
cavalry and racing.

ALGERIA & MOROCCO

Barb

European
Wild Stock
Barb

Warmblood
Height: 14.2 hands.
Colour: bay, brown,
chestnut, black and grey.
Physique: long head,
straight profile, sloping
quarters, low set tail and
long strong legs.
Features: frugal and tough.
Use: improving other
breeds, riding and
transport.

SOUTH AFRICA

Basuto

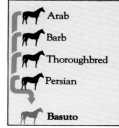

Arab
Barb
Thoroughbred
Persian
Basuto

Pony
Height: 14.2 hands
Colour: chestnut, bay,
brown and grey.
Physique: quality head,
longish neck and back,
strong, straightish
shoulder, short legs and
hard hooves.
Features: sure-footed,
tough with great stamina.
Use: racing, polo and
riding.

Persian Arab

Basuto

Caspian

East Asia and Australia

India's native stock is mostly 'country bred' (not selectively bred), but there are several distinct types. Of these, the Manipur has the best claim to fame, for it was the original polo pony. In the 1850s, English planters discovered this native game in Assam, which they then took up and spread around the world.

China is the home of the oldest surviving breed of horse – the Mongolian Wild Horse – originally bred by the Tartars, and rediscovered by Colonel Przewalski in 1881.

The working, and most numerous, pony in China is the Mongolian. It is similar to the Japanese native breed, the Hokaido.

Poor communications on the 3000 islands that make up Indonesia mean that ponies are vital for transport and agriculture. As they make such an important contribution to the economy, the government supports their breeding – the Batak being most supported. In Sumatra the best of the Batak mares are put to Arab stallions to improve quality.

Another of the Indonesian ponies which has a more unusual, romantic use is the Sumba, bred as a dancing pony. Bells are tied to its knees and it 'dances' to tom-tom rhythms.

Australia has no native horse of its own, and the first horses there were imported by the early British settlers some 200 years ago. The horses came first from South Africa and South America, and later from Europe and the USA. The country proved to be an excellent one for rearing horses, as did New Zealand later. Today, from originally having been importers, both nations are major exporters.

The first major Australian breed was the Waler. This was developed by crossing Arab, Thoroughbred and Anglo-Arab stallions with local mares and cobs, but, until fairly recently, the breed was still defined as 'country bred'. A stud book was not formed until 1971, when the Waler was given the new title of the Australian Stock Horse. In contrast, the Australian Pony's stud book was started as early as 1929, for stock which could be traced back to the Welsh Mountain stallion Grey Light.

The breeding of Thoroughbreds too, has flourished in Australasia. The descendants of the stock which originally came from France, the UK and the USA now underpin one of the most prosperous racing industries in the world. Trotting is also popular; Standardbreds have been imported from the USA since 1869.

Riding breeds are overseen by the Light Horse Breeders Association, which holds an annual all-breeds show. Since 1957, the Arabian Horse Society of Australasia has encouraged Arab breeding.

Burma Pony

Manipur

INDIA

Spiti and Bhutia

Mongolian Pony

Spiti Bhutia

Height: Spiti, 12 hands; Bhutia, 13.1 hands.
Colour: grey.
Physique: thickset and short-coupled.
Features: sure-footed and tough.
Use: transportation in mountains.

Manipur

Asiatic Wild Horse

Arab

Manipur

Pony
Height: 12 hands.
Colour: most colours.
Physique: thickset with high-set tail.
Features: quick and manoeuvrable.
Use: riding and polo.

Kathiawari and Marwari
Pony
Origin: Kathiawar and Marwar provinces.
Height: 14.2 hands.
Colour: most colours.
Physique: light, and narrow with some Arab features.

Features: frugal and to with great stamina.
Use: pack, transport a riding.

Arab

Native Pony

Kathiawari Marwari

CHINA

Mongolian Wild Hor
(Asiatic Wild Horse)
equus przewalskii poliakov)
Pony
Origin: Mongolia.
Height: 13.1 hands.
Colour: black, brown,

Mongolian Wild Horse

Australian Stock Horse

dun.
Physique: thickset, short-
coupled, good bone.
Features: tough, frugal,
with great stamina; fast
over short distances.
Use: work pony of
nomadic tribes; mares
provide milk for cheese,
which if fomented
provides a national drink,
called kumiss.

Foreign
Stock
Asiatic
Wild Horse
→ **Mongolian**

JAPAN

Hokaido (Hocaido)

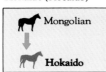
Mongolian
↓
Hokaido

Pony
Similar to Mongolian.

BURMA

Burma

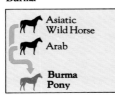
Asiatic
Wild Horse
Arab
↓
**Burma
Pony**

Pony
Height: 13 hands.
Colours: all colours.
Physique: larger version of
Manipur.
Use: polo and general
work.

TIBET

Native Tibetan (Nanfan)

Mongolian
Pony
↓
**Native
Tibetan**

Pony
Height: 12.2 hands.
Colour: all colours.
Physique: sturdy frame.
Features: energetic and
tough.

Use: riding and general
work.

AUSTRALIA

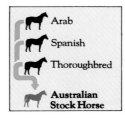

Australian Pony

Arab
Welsh
Pony
Exmoor
Pony
Shetland
Pony
Thoroughbred
↓
**Australian
Pony**

Height: 13 hands.

Colour: most colours.
Physique: Arab head,
longish neck, sloping
shoulder, deep girth, round
hindquarters.
Use: riding.

Australian Stock Horse

Arab
Spanish
Thoroughbred
↓
**Australian
Stock Horse**

Warmblood
Origin: New South Wales
Height: 16 hands.
Colour: all colours.
Physique: varies; usually
alert head, deep girth,
strong back.
Features: hardy, with a
strong constitution.
Use: herding and cavalry.

INDONESIA

Timor

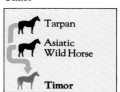
Tarpan
Asiatic
Wild Horse
↓
Timor

Pony
Origin: Timor.
Height: 11.1 hands.
Colour: dark colours.
Physique: fine but sturdy
frame.
Features: agile, good-
tempered.
Use: agricultural work and
transportation.

Java

Sumba

PUERTO RICO

South America

It was on the vast, fertile plains of Argentina that the Criollo – the horse of the *gaucho* (cowboy) – developed from horses imported by the Spanish settlers in the sixteenth century. The basic stock is supposed to have come from a shipload of 100 Andalusians and some light draught horses that arrived in 1535, and escaped to run wild on the pampas after Buenos Aires was sacked by the Indians. Through their adaptation to the rough native conditions, the Criollo was born.

Various attempts to improve the Criollo with outcrosses have proved failures, and the Argentinians now breed them selectively. One of the tests used for potential breeding stock is an annual 470-mile ride, during which the horses must carry 17 stone and may not be fed.

The world-famous Argentine polo pony is an off-shoot of the Criollo, being a cross between it and the Thoroughbred. The former provided the toughness and stamina, the latter the speed.

Argentina is also one of the world's largest producers of Thoroughbreds. However, the home demand is so great that relatively few are exported.

Brazil has 9 million horses, one of the largest equine populations in the world. Its native horse is the Crioulo, a smaller version of the Criollo.

Much of this vast work force is used by the army, which finds the horse invaluable in the rough, mountainous areas of the country. Stallions are made available by the army either at its own remount centres, or horses are lent to large breeders. Arabs and Thoroughbreds are used to produce riding horses and Bretons for draught horses.

Some of the Crioulo stock has been improved with outcrosses from Spanish and Portuguese horses, and, in the last century, this foreign blood was used to found the larger Mangalarga. This breed, in turn, was selectively bred by Cassiano Campolino in the 1840s to produce the Campolino.

Peru was the main Spanish base in South America and therefore few horses were allowed to escape and run wild. The most famous Peruvian horse is the Stepping Horse, developed from Barb and Arab stock 300 years ago. It has a unique lateral gait, which it can maintain at up to 14 mph.

Peruvian Stepping Horses were exported to Puerto Rico, where they acted as foundation stock for the Paso Fino. This is now found in large numbers in the USA.

Venezuela, like most South American countries, has its own Criollo type, derived from adapting imported Spanish and Portuguese stock to the hot, rough local conditions. This is known as the Llanero.

Paso Fino

Spanish
Peruvian Stepping Hors

Paso Fino

Warmblood
Height: 14.3 hands.
Colour: most colours.
Physique: Arab-like head strong back, loins and quarters and hard legs which are light of bone.
Features: spirited; extra four beat gaits, of which the slowest is the paso fino, then the paso cort and the paso largo.

BRAZIL

Crioulo

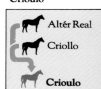

Altér Real
Criollo

Crioulo

Warmblood
Height: 15 hands.
Colour: lighter Criollo colours.
Physique: prominent withers, high set tail an longish neck.
Features: frugal and tou
Use: riding and herding

Mangalarga

Altér Real
Andalusian
Crioulo

Mangalarga

Warmblood
Origin: Meiras Gerais.
Height: 15 hands.
Colour: grey, sorrel, roa

Sandalwood

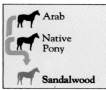

Arab
Native Pony

Sandalwood

Pony
Height: 13 hands.
Colour: dun with dorsal stripe, dark mane and tail.
Physique: lighter frame, finer coat and more elegant than other Indonesian ponies.
Features: fast.
Use: bareback racing and general work.

Sumba

Mongolian

Sumba

Pony
Height: 12.2 hands.

Colour: dun with dorsal stripe, dark mane and tail.
Physique: primitive type.
Use: dancing pony, general work.

Bali

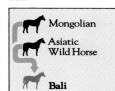

Mongolian
Asiatic Wild Horse

Bali

Pony
Origin: Indonesia/Bali
Height: 12.2 hands
Colour: dun with dorsal stripe and dark points
Physique: sturdy frame
Features: frugal and strong
Use: riding and general pack work

Java

Pony
Origin: Java.
Height: 12.2 hands.
Colour: most colours.

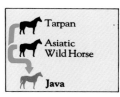

Tarpan
Asiatic Wild Horse

Java

Physique: strong frame.
Use: pulling 'sados' (two-wheeled taxis).

Batak

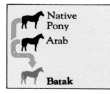

Native Pony
Arab

Batak

Pony
Origin: Indonesia Sumatra.
Height: 12.2 hands
Colour: most colours
Physique: comparatively refined, good conformation
Features: frugal, good temper
Use: agriculture, transport.

que: longish head,
back, powerful
-quarters, low set tail
ong legs; lighter
than the Criollo.
res: hardy; gait called
cha', between a
er and a trot.
riding and ranch

polino

- Mangalarga
- Andalusian
- **Campolino**

mblood
ht: 14.3 – 15.4 hands
que: similar to the
galarga but with a
ier frame and more

riding and light
ght.

J

vian Stepping Horse

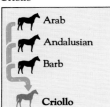
- Andalusian
- Spanish Blood
- **Peruvian Stepping Horse**

mblood
ht: 15 hands.
ur: bay or chestnut.
que: broad chest,

short-coupled, and
strong, round
hindquarters.
Features: endurance and a
special extended gait
similar to an amble.
Use: riding and stock
work.

ARGENTINA

[map of Argentina]

Falabella

- Shetland Pony
- Thoroughbred
- **Falabella**

Pony
Height: 7 hands.
Colour: all colours.
Use: harness pony and
pet.

Criollo

- Arab
- Andalusian
- Barb
- **Criollo**

Warmblood
Height: 14.2 hands.
Colour: dun with dark
points, dorsal stripe with
dark snippets; red and blue
roan, sorrel and skewbald.
Physique: short head

tapering to muzzle, short-
coupled, sturdy frame,
strong, sloping shoulder,
short legs, good bone and
small, hard feet.
Features: tough and
manoeuvrable.
Use: long distance riding
and ranch work.

VENEZUELA

[map of Venezuela]

Llanero

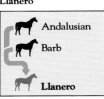
- Andalusian
- Barb
- **Llanero**

Warmblood
Height: 14 hands.
Colour: dun, yellow with
dark mane and tail, white
and yellow cream or
pinto.
Physique: lighter frame
than the Criollo; head
similar to the Barb.
Feature: tough.
Use: ranch work and
transport.

Peruvian Stepping Horse

Falabella

Criollo

Mangalarga

The USSR

Within the boundaries of the present-day USSR is thought to lie the region in which the horse was first domesticated in about 3000 BC. Russian horse-breeding therefore has an exceptionally long history. Different foundation stock has been important in varying parts of the country, the Arab having most influence in the west and the Mongolian Wild Horse further to the east. Striking variations of geography and climate have also led to the emergence of many different types of horse, and it is therefore no surprise that 40 breeds and breed groups are officially recognized. Currently, the Soviet government stipulates that each region should produce two or three breeds,

This development has largely taken place since the last war. During this time, the USSR has tried to establish its horse-breeding on a more rational, scientific basis – a task undertaken by the All-Union Research Institute of Horse Breeding. Some breeds have been selected for improvement with outside crosses. Those needing some refining influences have had Thoroughbred and Arab blood added – these include the Cossack Steppe horse, the Don, and the Kabardin, a tough mountain horse. When toughening-up was needed, the Russians then used Don blood.

New breeds have been developed, and, at the same time, some of the famous nineteenth-century breeds have been allowed to die out – but not before they were used as foundation stock for the replacement breeds. Thus the Strelets (a large Arab) was used as a basis for the Tersky (established 1948); and the Klepper (a tough, preponent pony) for the Toric and Viatka.

The most important influence on the Russian ponies has been the Asiatic Wild Horse, though some have had Arab blood added as a refining influence. This use continues the traditional Arab involvement in Russian horse-breeding.

More recently, too, the Thoroughbred has also played its part in refining other breeds, but its chief role has been in the establishment of the Russian racehorse. The best of these have headed westwards and Anilin was good enough to come second in the 1966 Washington D.C. International.

Trotting is an equally popular equestrian sport, with 42 studs producing Orlov and Russian Trotters. This began a century ago, when, in 1877, Count Orlov crossed an Arab stallion with a Dutch/Danish mare to found the breed that bears his name. However, the Orlov did not prove as fast as its foreign competitors, and American Standardbreds were therefore crossed with Orlovs to creat the speedier Russian Trotter.

Karabakh

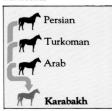

Warmblood
Origin: Karabakh mountains.
Height: 14.2 hands.
Colour: dun, bay or chestnut with metallic sheen.
Physique: tough mountain horse with a small, fine head, low set tail and good feet.
Features: energetic and good-tempered.
Use: riding, equestrian games and racing.

Russian Trotter

Warmblood
Height: 15.3 hands.
Colour: black, bay or chestnut.
Physique: the breed resulted from crossing Orlovs and Standard breeds.
Features: faster than the Orlov.
Use: trotting races.

Orlov Trotter
Warmblood
Height: 16 hands.
Colour: grey, bay or black.
Physique: thickset, upright shoulder, broad chest, deep girth and long straight back.
Features: active and fast.
Use: trotting races, riding, harness.

Orlov Trotter

Zemaituka (Pechora)

Pony
Origin: Baltic States.
Height: 13.2 hands.
Colour: brown, palomino or dun with dorsal stripe.
Physique: straight face, smallish ears, short neck and straight back.
Features: hardy, good-tempered and frugal.
Use: riding and work.

Akhal Teké

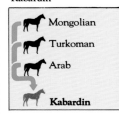

Warmblood
Origin: Steppes.
Height: 15 hands.
Colour: bay, chestnut, grey or black, usually with metallic sheen.
Physique: elegant, long head, straight profile, long, thin neck, long back, low set tail, long legs with light, strong bone and silky tail.
Features: hardy,

temperamental, fast and versatile; some pace.
Use: riding.

Kabardin

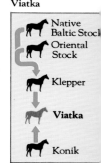

Warmblood
Origin: Northern Caucasus.
Height: 15 hands.
Colour: bay or black.
Physique: sturdy frame, short legs and long, straight back.
Features: good-tempered, sure-footed, tough and long-lived.
Use: mountain work as pack or riding horse, local equestrian games and racing.

Don

Warmblood
Origin: Central Asia (steppes).
Height: 15.2 hands.
Colour: chestnut, bay or grey.
Physique: deep body, long, straight neck and back and long legs.
Features: versatile, frugal

with great stamina.
Use: the original Coss horse; now driving, ri and long distance raci

Viatka

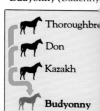

Pony
Origin: Viatsky territo Baltic States.
Height: 13.2 hands.
Colour: dark, sometim with dorsal stripe.
Physique: plain head, sturdy frame, broad, straight back, short le with good bone.
Features: frugal, tough fast.
Use: all-purpose pony

Budyonny (Budenny

Warmblood
Height: 15.3 hands.
Colour: chestnut or ba with golden sheen.
Physique: strong frame crested neck, close-coupled and deep-bod
Features: good temper fast and enduring.
Use: riding, competiti and steeplechasing.

Karabakh

Orlov Trotter

Akhal Teké

Don

Budyonny (Budenny)

Tersky

- Indigenous Ukraine stock
- Turkoman
- Arab
- Persian
- Strelets
- **Tersky**
- Arab

Warmblood
Origin: Stavropol region.
Height: 15 hands.
Colour: grey.
Physique: Arab features.
Use: racing, competitions and the circus.

Russian Heavy Draught

- Swedish Ardennes
- Percheron
- Orlov Trotter
- Indigenous Ukraine stock
- **Russian Heavy Draught**

Coldblood
Origin: Ukraine.
Height: 14.2 hands.
Colour: chestnut, bay and roan.

Physique: smallest coldblood; thickset, massive neck, broad back and sloping croup.
Features: strong, active and fast.
Use: agricultural work.

Novokirghiz

- Kirghiz
- Don
- Thoroughbred
- **Novokirghiz**

Warmblood
Origin: Kirghiz and Kazakhstan.
Height: 15 hands.
Colour: bay, grey, or chestnut.
Physique: long neck, long, straight back, sloping croup, short legs.
Features: tough, sure-footed and frugal.
Use: mountain work – harness and saddle.

Lithuanian and Latvian Heavy Draught

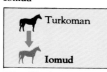

- Zemaituka
- Oldenburg
- Finnish Draught
- Swedish Ardennes
- **Lithuanian and Latvian**

Warmblood

Coldblood
Origin: Lithuania and Latvia – Baltic States.
Height: 15.3 hands.
Colour: bay, black, or chestnut with flaxen mane and tail.
Physique: large head, strong, long neck, sloping, bifurcated croup and little feather.
Features: good-tempered.
Use: draught.

Iomud

- Turkoman
- **Iomud**

Warmblood
Origin: Central Asia
Height: 14 hands.
Colour: grey, chestnut, or bay.
Physique: similar to but more compact than the Akhal Teké.
Features: great stamina, although not as fast as the Akhal Teké.
Use: riding, racing.

Lokai

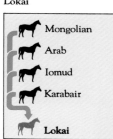

- Mongolian
- Arab
- Iomud
- Karabair
- **Lokai**

Warmblood

Origin: Uzbekistan.
Height: 14.3 hands.
Colour: grey, bay or chestnut often with golden tint.
Physique: varies, but usually sturdy frame with tough hooves; hair may be curly.
Features: a strong, sure-footed mountain horse.
Use: riding, pack, and racing.

Bashkirky

- Native Pony
- Budyonny
- Don
- Trotter
- **Bashkirsky**

Pony
Origin: Bashkiria.
Height: 13.2 hands.
Colour: bay, dun or chestnut.
Physique: thickset, prominent wither, longish back, low set tail and short legs.
Features: tough.
Use: riding and pulling sleighs; mares are milked for kumiss, a medicinal and alcoholic drink.

Vladimir Heavy Draught
Coldblood
Origin: Vladimir district.
Height: 16 hands.
Colour: any solid colour.

Physique: strong frame, good conformation, with feather on legs.
Features: active, good-tempered and powerful.

- Cleveland Bay
- Suffolk Punch
- Shire
- Ardennes
- Percheron
- **Vladimir Heavy Draught**

Toric

- Klepper
- Thoroughbred
- Trakehner
- Orlov Trotter
- Hanoverian
- Ardennes
- Hackney
- East Friesian
- **Toric**

Warmblood
Origin: Estonia.
Height: 15.1 hands.
Colour: chestnut or bay.
Physique: long, muscular

body, short strong legs with light feather.
Features: strong, good-tempered, with great stamina.
Use: light draught.

Karabair

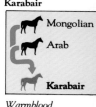

- Mongolian
- Arab
- **Karabair**

Warmblood
Origin: Uzbekistan.
Height: 15.2 hands.
Colour: bay, chestnut, grey.
Physique: similar to the Arab but stouter. Two types – the Saddle and Harness.
Features: versatile
Use: agriculture, riding and driving, mounted sports.

Kazakh

- Mongolian Wild Horse
- Don
- **Kazakh**

Pony
Origin: Kazakh.
Height: 13 hands.
Colour: bay, chestnut or grey.
Physique: Mongolian.
Features: tough.
Use: riding and herding, milk and meat.

Vladimir Heavy Draught

Tersky

ern Europe

ematic breeding in Bulgaria began when
kish rule ended in 1878. Arabs and
roughbreds were imported from Hungary
Russia to improve the local stock, and,
he beginning of the twentieth century,
e halfbreds had been established. These
: the Pleven – the most Arab-like – the
ubian, which had Nonius features, and
East Bulgarian, which was closest to the
roughbred. Apart from these halfbreds,
Russian Heavy Draught and the Arab are
bred at the state studs.

ungary's horse-breeding history dates
. to the coming of the Magyars in the 9th
ury AD. Their tough horses later bene-
l from cross-breeding with Arabs,
ght into this country during the Turkish
sions of the Middle Ages, and the Arab
remained a major influence ever since.
:oo, has British blood.

orses have also been imported from the
Thoroughbreds arrived as racing in-
sed in popularity and one of Hungary's
important warmblood strains – the
oso – also originated there. The other
r warmblood breed is the Nonius.

he work horse of Hungary – the Murakosi
borderline warmblood/coldblood. It was
loped in the 1920s to meet the demand
fast, strong horse, so Oriental, as well as
blood, foundation stock was used.

zechoslovakia is the home of the oldest
ational stud in the world, Kladruby, near
ubice, where the original stud was
ded by Emperor Maximillian II in the
-sixteenth century. The Spanish horses
mported were the ancestors of today's
e Kladrubers. Czechoslovakia also breeds
roughbreds, Furiosos, Noniuses and
s. The last-named now have a large
re on the 2,323-acre stud at Topolcianka
lovakia. It is mainly stocked with Shagya
Polish Arabs, many of which are ex-
ed.

oland has been a horse-breeding country
many centuries. Today, there are 42
r studs, each housing between 50 and
stallions. As a result, the country has the
st horse population in Europe – about 3
ion.

s in other East European countries, the
ernment controls the state studs. Horses
riding and sport (mainly of Trakehner
ns) are bred in the largest quantities,
wed by the Arab.

oland is also the home of the Tarpan, a
y whose origins date back to the Ice Age
is the ancestor of most warmbloods.
ls of Tarpan roam wild in the forests of
elno, but they are not thought to be
-bred, the last true Tarpan having died in
ivity in 1887. The modern Tarpan of

Poland today is an act of skilled recreation by
the Polish government in a selective breeding
programme.

Naturally, the Tarpan has greatly influenced the other Polish pony breeds. The
Huçul, which roamed wild in the Car-
pathians for centuries, has its primitive features, as does the larger and more manageable
Konik, the foundation stock for many East
European breeds.

In the highland areas of Yugoslavia, the
work horse still has an important role to play
on the land and in transport. The state promotes its breeding at national studs, where
Noniuses, Belgians, Norics, Arabs and Lipizzaners are all produced. It is, however, the
Bosnian Pony – a descendant of the Tarpan –
that makes up a third of the horse population;
it is selectively bred by the state studs.

Shagya Arab

Murakosi

POLAND

Konik

Pony
Height: 13.1 hands.
Colour: yellow, grey or blue dun, usually with dorsal stripe.
Physique: similar to the Huzul.
Features: long-lived, frugal, hardy and good-tempered; the foundation stock for many Polish and Russian breeds.
Use: agricultural work for lowland farmers.

Huzul

Pony
Origin: Carpathian mountains.
Height: 13.2 hands.
Colour: dun or bay.
Physique: Tarpan head and robust body.
Features: good tempered, tough and frugal.
Use: pack and agricultural.

Tarpan

Pony
Height: 13 hands.
Colour: brown or dun with dorsal stripe, dark mane and tail, and stripes on the forelegs and inner thighs. Coat may change to white in winter.
Physique: long head, longish ears, short neck, longish back and fine legs.
Features: tough and fertile.
Use: exhibited in zoos and also roams wild.

Sokolsky

Warmblood
Height: 15.2 hands.
Colour: chestnut, brown or grey.
Physique: large head, sturdy frame, short, straight back, short legs and large round feet with little feather.
Features: good tempered, frugal.
Use: agricultural work.

Wielkopolski

Warmblood
Height: 16 hands.
Colour: chestnut or bay.
Physique: a compact, well-proportion horse.
Features: good-tempered; formed by amalgamating the Masuren and Poznan.
Use: riding competitions and light draught.

Polish Arab

Warmblood
Height: 14.3 hands.
Colour: grey, chestnut and bay.
Physique: similar to the Arab, but with more sloping quarters and with tail carried lower.
Use: racing, breeding and riding.

HUNGARY

Shagya Arab

Warmblood
Height: 15 hands.
Colour: grey.
Physique: Arab features, small head.
Features: hardy, frugal active.
Use: cavalry, general riding and driving.

Murakosi

Coldblood
Height: 16 hands.
Colour: chestnut with flaxen mane and tail.
Physique: strong frame little wither, dip in back round hindquarters an little feather.
Features: strong and active.
Use: general draught a agricultural work.

Nonius

Warmblood
Height: Large Nonius,

Tarpan

Konik

Kladruber

15.3 hands; small
...us, under 15.3
...ds.
...que: elegant head,
...neck, strong back.
...res: versatile, long-
... and active.
... riding and
...ultural work.

- English
  Halfbred
- Norman
- Turk
- Spanish
- Lipizzaner
- Holstein
- Arab
- **Nonius**

...so

...*mblood*
...t: 16 hands.
...r: dark colours.
...que: muscular body,
...htish back, sloping
...quarters and low set

- English
  Halfbred
- Arab
- Thoroughbred
- **Furioso**

tail.
Features: robust.

CZECHOSLOVAKIA

Kladruber

Warmblood
Origin: Kladruby,
Bohemia.
Height: 16.2 hands.
Colour: grey.
Physique: larger Andalusian.
Use: agriculture and
harness.

- Andalusian
- Anglo-
  Norman
- Hanoverian
- Oldenburg
- **Kladruber**

BULGARIA

Danubian

- Anglo-
  Arab
- Nonius
- **Danubian**

Warmblood
Height: 15.2 hands.
Colour: black or dark
chestnut.
Physique: short-coupled,
deep girth, high set tail
and fine strong legs.
Features: strength.
Use: light draught, riding
and competitions.

East Bulgarian

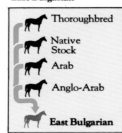

- Thoroughbred
- Native
  Stock
- Arab
- Anglo-Arab
- **East Bulgarian**

Warmblood
Height: 15.3 hands.
Colour: chestnut or black.
Physique: smallish head,
straight profile, deep girth
and longish straight back.
Features: energetic, hardy,
fast and versatile.
Use: riding, agriculture,
competitions and
steeplechasing.

Pleven

- Local Arab
- Hungarian
  Gidran Arab
- Strelets
  Anglo-Arab
- Gidran
  Anglo-Arab
- Local Anglo
  Arab
- **Pleven**

Warmblood
Height: 15.2 hands.
Colour: chestnut.
Physique: sturdier version
of the Arab.
Features: robust.
Use: an all-purpose horse.

YUGOSLAVIA

Bosnian

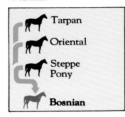

- Tarpan
- Oriental
- Steppe
  Pony
- **Bosnian**

Pony
Height: 12.2 hands.
Colour: dun, brown
chestnut, grey, black.
Physique: compact
mountain pony, similar to
the Huzul.
Features: endurance.
Use: agricultural work.

Bosnian

Wielkopolski

Furioso

France

The French government is more actively involved with horse-breeding than the governments of all other Western countries. Its involvement dates back to the days of Louis XIV, who created a government department responsible for providing officially-approved stallions for French breeders. This department developed into the Service des Haras, today a part of the Ministry of Agriculture and responsible for the French horse industry.

The Service runs 23 stallion depots, which are scattered throughout France. In the best breeding areas, such as Normandy, the depots house as many as 200 stallions. Each depot keeps a selection of stallions, ensuring that suitable sires are available to breed for racing, competitions, pleasure, work – and even for meat. Each one is strictly selected according to its conformation, athletic ability, pedigree and the success of its progeny.

The main competition horse in France is the Selle Français. The stud book for this breed was started only in 1965, when it took over from 45 different breed groups. Previously, there were many different warmbloods in France, although the Anglo-Norman (the French carriage horse, refined with Norfolk Trotter and Thoroughbred blood during the last century) and the Anglo-Arab (bred by crossing Thoroughbreds, Arabs and Oriental stock from south-west France) were the most numerous and successful.

The Arab has played an important part in French breeding since the conquering Moors brought them into the country 1200 years ago. They are the ancestors of all current French breeds, and are still extensively used for cross-breeding.

The French Thoroughbred has its origins in stock imported from the UK, but, since Gladiateur crossed the English Channel to win the Derby in 1865, French home-breds have challenged the best in the world. French trotters have also been internationally successful. Their home country is Normandy, where they were developed at the turn of the nineteenth century by crossing Norfolk Trotters with Thoroughbreds and Norman mares. Today, they are used both for trotting and for cross-breeding.

Of the French heavy horses, the Percheron is the most numerous nationally and internationally. The best-known pony is the Camargue, which roams wild in the marshlands of that district in southern France. The shape of its head implies that the Oriental influence was of Barb origin. The little Basque pony is also found running wild in the Pyrenees and Atlantic cantons. The most domesticated of these native breeds is the Landais, while the Shetland is the most popular imported pony.

Landais

Pony
Origin: The Landes region.
Height: 13.2 hands.
Colour: dark colours.
Physique: varies – usually fine frame with an Arab-like head.
Features: frugal.
Use: riding and driving.

Anglo-Arab

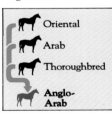

Warmblood
Height: 16 hands.
Colour: solid colours.
Physique: good shoulder and well-proportioned, powerful hindquarters.
Features: stamina and good movement.
Use: riding, competitions and racing.

Comtois

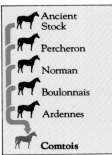

Coldblood
Origin: Franche-Comté.

Height: 15.1 hands.
Colour: bay or chestnut.
Physique: largish head, straight neck, long, straight back and little feather.
Features: active and sure-footed.
Use: agriculture.

Breton

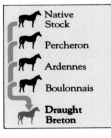

Coldblood
Height: 16.1 hands.
Colour: grey, chestnut or bay.
Physique: the Postier Breton – close-coupled, elegant head and short legs with little feather. The Draught Breton – larger, more elongated body.
Features: strong and active, although the Draught is less energetic.
Use: agricultural work.

Boulonnias

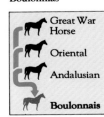

Coldblood:
Origin: Northern France.
Height: 16.1 hands.
Colour: grey, chestnut or bay.
Physique: similar conformation to the Percheron; silky coat.
Features: active and good-tempered.
Use: draught.

Basque

Pony
Origin: Basque region.
Height: 13 hands.
Colour: most.
Physique: primitive, with head slightly concave, small ears, short neck and long back.
Features: stamina and toughness.
Use: mining, riding; also runs wild.

Camargue (Camarguais)

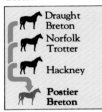

Pony:
Origin: The Camargue, Rhone delta.
Height: 14 hands.
Colour: grey.
Physique: Oriental-type head, straightish shoulder, short body, fine legs with hard bone.
Features: hardy.
Use: herding, trekking; also roams wild.

French Trotter

Warmblood
Origin: Calvados.
Height: 16.1 hands.
Colour: any solid colour.
Physique: tall, light-framed horse with a fine head, prominent wither, strong back and sloping hindquarters.
Features: athletic and fast.
Use: trotting, riding and cross-breeding.

Selle Francais

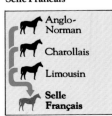

Warmblood
Origin: Northern France.
Height: 16 hands.

Colour: solid colours.
Physique: robust frame, powerful shoulder, stro longish back, deep girt and powerful hindquarters.
Features: good-tempere and athletic.
Use: riding and competitions.

Poitevin

Coldblood
Origin: Poitiers.
Height: 16.3 hands.
Colour: dun.
Physique: plain conformation, large b long body, big feet wi heavy feather.
Features: docile.
Use: mares put to Bau Poitevin (jackasses of about 16 hands) to bre large mules.

Percheron

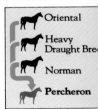

Coldblood
Height: 16.1 hands.
Colour: grey or black.
Physique: Oriental-ty head, strong, well-proportioned body, f mane and tail and cle hard legs without fea
Features: a good actio and great presence.
Use: draught.

Ardennais
Coldblood
Origin: France – Lorr Champagne, foothill Vosges
Height: 15.3 – 16 han
Colour: bay and roan
Physique: short, more thick set than any ot carthorse, stocky, compact, heavyweigh very muscular with a bone structure, stron head and broad face
Features: docile, gent hardy
Use: agriculture – 'th carthorse of the nort

Breton

Camargue (Camarguais)

French Trotter

Ardennais

Percheron

Anglo-Arab

Western Europe

Belgium was the home of one of the most celebrated horses of medieval times – the Flanders Horse – a coldblood which is the ancestor of many modern heavy horses. Its direct descendant is the Belgian, a breed now found throughout the world. The country's other heavy horse, the Ardennes, is shared, like the area in which it is bred, with France. It is thought to be a descendant of the medieval Great Horse. The Belgian Warmblood is a more recent innovation.

In Holland, stud book societies exist for Arabs, Hackneys, five pony breeds, Trotters, Racehorses, Dutch Warmbloods, and for the three native breeds. These are the Gelderland, a popular carriage horse, the increasingly rare Gronigen, and the Friesland, which is one of the oldest breeds in Europe.

Austria's most celebrated horse is the Lipizzaner, famous as the mount of the internationally-known Spanish Riding School in Vienna. The horse's name comes from its original home – Lipizza, near Trieste – but it is now bred at Piber, in southern Austria. Its origins date back to 1580, when the Hapsburg Archduke Charles imported Spanish horses (with Arab, Barb, and Andalusian forebears) from the Pyrenees. Italian, German and Danish blood was added to improve the stock in the eighteenth century, and Arab in the nineteenth. Today, there is no such out-breeding, but some in-breeding is practised.

Home-produced halfbreds, Hanoverians and Trakehners, are used to breed the Austrian riding horse. State aid is also given to support the breeding of the other famous Austrian horse, the Halflinger, bred originally in the district of Halfling, near Merano.

The Noriker takes its name from the Roman province of Noricum, where it was originally bred by the Romans. It is now used in both Austria and Germany.

Switzerland's state-financed national stud has produced work horses for agriculture and the army since the nineteenth century. The two main types were the Einsielder, originally bred by the monks of Einsiedeln Abbey in the eleventh century, and the Freiberger, a light draught horse from the Jura Mountains. With the fall in demand for these work horses, the stud started to breed a Swiss Halfbred in the 1960s. Stallions and mares were imported from Germany, France, Sweden and the UK; all breeding stock was put through rigorous performance tests, and stud books were started. This development had the desired effect of cutting down the previously high number of imported riding horses, and the breed is proving itself capable of holding its own with other European warmbloods.

AUSTRIA

Noriker (South German Coldblood)

Coldblood
Height: 16.1 hands.
Colour: chestnut, bay, sometimes spotted.
Physique: largish head, short thick neck, straight shoulder, broad back and short legs.
Features: sure-footed.
Use: agricultural and mountain work.

Lipizzaner

Warmblood
Height: 15.1 hands.
Colour: grey.
Physique: largish head, small ears, crested neck, compact body, short, strong legs and full fine mane and tail.

Features: intelligent, athletic
Use: high school equitation and driving.

Halflinger

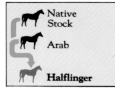

Pony
Origin: The Tirol.
Height: 14 hands.
Colour: chestnut with flaxen mane and tail.
Physique: head tapers to muzzle, broad chest, deep girth, long, broad back and short legs.
Features: kind temperament, frugal, tough, sure-footed.
Use: mountain work.

BELGIUM

Ardennes (Ardennais)

Coldblood
Origin: The Ardennes.
Height: 15.3 hands.
Colour: bay, chestnut or roan.
Physique: muscular, short-coupled body, crested neck, broad chest and

short, feathered legs.
Features: strong, active and good tempered.
Use: agricultural work.

Belgian Heavy Draught (Brabant)

Coldblood
Origin: Brabant.
Height: 16.2 hands.
Colour: red roan with black points or chestnut.
Physique: heavy, large frame, shortish back, short legs with feather on fetlocks.
Features: strength, presence and good action.
Use: draught.

HOLLAND

Gelderland

Warmblood
Origin: Gelderland.
Height: 15.1 hands.
Colour: chestnut, or grey.
Physique: plain head, crested neck, short-coupled with a high set tail.
Features: extravagant action and great presence.
Use: carriage work, riding.

Groningen

Warmblood
Origin: Groningen.

Height: 15.3 hands.
Colour: dark colours.
Physique: straight profile, long ears, deep, powerful body and high set tail.
Features: frugal with a stylish action.
Use: light draught, riding and driving.

Friesian

Warmblood
Height: 15 hands.
Colour: black only.
Physique: longish head, crested neck, round hindquarters, good body feather and full mane and tail.
Features: good temperament.
Use: in the circus, riding and driving.

Dutch Draught

Coldblood
Height: 16.1 hands.
Colour: bay, chestnut or black.
Physique: tall with a powerful front and deep strong body.
Features: strength, stamina, and a kind but spirited temperament.
Use: draught.

SWITZERLAND

Franches Montagnes (Freiberger)
Warmblood
Origin: Avenche.
Height: 15.1 hands.
Colour: blue roan or grey solid colours.
Physique: powerful, compact frame.

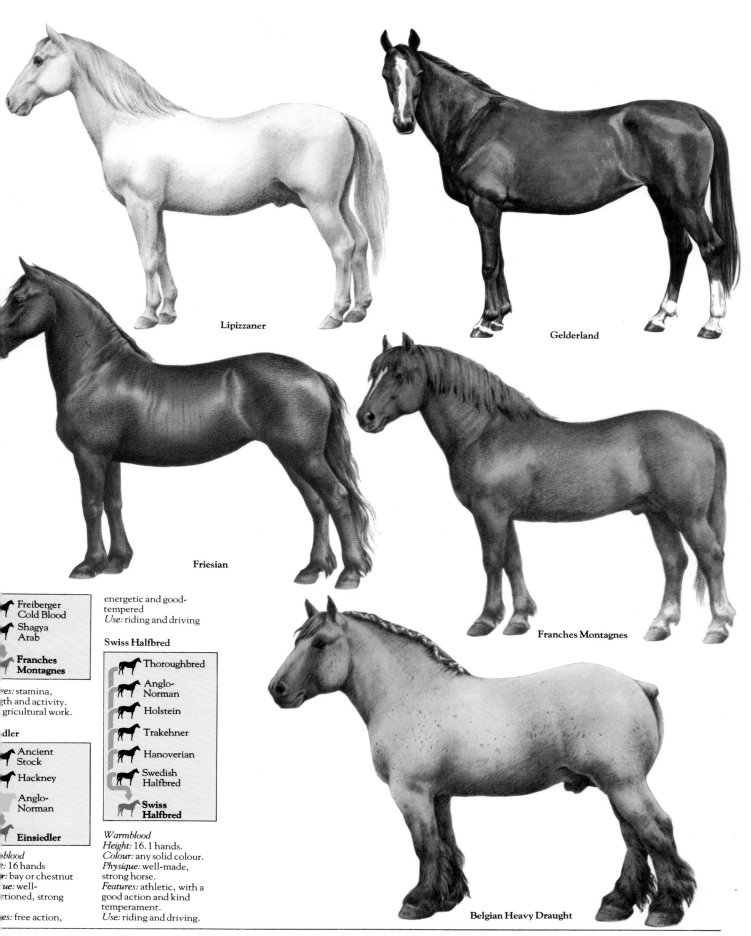

Lipizzaner

Gelderland

Friesian

Franches Montagnes

Belgian Heavy Draught

energetic and good-
tempered
Use: riding and driving

Swiss Halfbred

res: stamina,
th and activity.
gricultural work.

dler

Ancient
Stock

Hackney

Anglo-
Norman

Einsiedler

blood
: 16 hands
: bay or chestnut
ue: well-
tioned, strong

es: free action,

Thoroughbred

Anglo-
Norman

Holstein

Trakehner

Hanoverian

Swedish
Halfbred

**Swiss
Halfbred**

Warmblood
Height: 16.1 hands.
Colour: any solid colour.
Physique: well-made,
strong horse.
Features: athletic, with a
good action and kind
temperament.
Use: riding and driving.

Britain and Ireland

Britain and Ireland share a long history of horse breeding. Ireland, in particular, has produced some of the finest horses in the world; for its part, the UK's great contribution to horse breeding has been the development of the Thoroughbred, the world's most valuable and fastest breed.

On the west coast of Ireland, the tough but handsome Connemara pony has run wild for centuries. Its origins are said to be the same as those of the Highland; the difference between the two lies in the cross-breeding that took place between the native ponies and the Spanish jennets and Arabs which came ashore from the shipwrecked Spanish Armada in the sixteenth century.

Ireland has no true native coldblood, for the Irish Draught is a borderline warmblood/coldblood. Its origins are obscure, but it is thought to descend from medieval war horses and some European warmbloods. It was originally a dual-purpose horse – farmers both hunting on it and using it for work in the fields – but, with mechanization, this latter use has dwindled. It was then crossed with the Thoroughbred to produce a high-class riding horse, which now receives considerable government support. This was largely achieved through the Irish Horse Board, formed in 1971 to look after the non-Thoroughbred horse industry.

The foundations for the future British Thoroughbred were laid in the century following the Stuart Restoration to the throne in 1660; during this period, more than 200 Arabs, Turks and Barbs were imported to improve British racing stock. It is still uncertain whether these imports were crossed with the native racing mares – the now extinct Galloway ponies – or whether the foundations were purely Oriental. There is no question, however, that the three greatest influences were the stallions Darley Arabian (originator of the Blandford, Phalaris, Gainsborough, Son in Law and St Simon lines); the Byerley Turk (Herod line); and the Godolphin Barb (Matcham line).

The original Thoroughbreds were only 14.2 hands high, but, over the years, they grew in height to today's average of about 16 hands. During these formative years, the horse also changed in other ways as well. At first, stamina took precedence over sheer speed, but, by the nineteenth century, speed and quicker maturity was deemed to be essential. By this time, too, the British Thoroughbred had established itself all over the world. As no other country could produce a faster horse, all resorted to importing Thoroughbreds from Britain.

The UK's other main export in the horse world has been its native ponies. Nine dis-

Thoroughbred

- Arab
- Turk
- Barb
- Galloway
- **Thoroughbred**

Thoroughbred
Height: 16 hands.
Colour: solid colours.
Physique: varies from close-coupled sprinters with large, powerful hindquarters to big-framed, longer backed, big-boned chasers. Must have an elegant head, long neck, sloping shoulder, prominent wither and silky coat.
Features: fast and spirited.
Use: racing, riding and improving other breeds.

Suffolk Punch

- Native Great Horse
- Norfolk Trotter
- Norfolk Cob
- Flanders Horse
- **Suffolk Punch**

Coldblood:
Origin: East Anglia.
Height: 16.1 hands.
Colour: chestnut, with no white markings.
Physique: short, clean legs, massive neck and shoulders and square body.
Features: good action, long-lived, frugal and good-tempered.
Use: draught.

Hackney

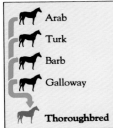

- Hackney Horse
- Fell
- Dales
- **Hackney Pony**

- Norfolk Roadster
- Thoroughbred
- **Hackney Horse**

Warmblood and Pony
Height: Horse, 15.1 hands; pony, under 14.2 hands.
Colour: dark colours.
Physique: smallish head, strong straightish shoulder, powerful hindquarters and tail set and carried high.
Features: spirited, with a high-stepping action.
Use: driving.

Fell

Pony
Origin: Cumbria (Westmorland and Cumberland).
Height: 13.2 hands.
Colour: black, brown or bay.
Physique: great substance, minimum 8 inches of bone, fine hair on heels and long curly mane and tail.
Features: strength and stamina; a fast trotter.
Use: all-purpose; driving, agricultural work, pack and trekking.

Irish Draught

- War Horse
- European Warm Bloods
- **Irish Draught**

Coldblood/Warmblood
Height: 16 hands.
Colour: bay, brown or grey.
Physique: straight face, short, muscular neck, longish back, strong, sloping hindquarters, good bone, little feather and large round feet.
Features: good-tempered and a good jumper.
Use: multi-purpose, but mainly breeding riding horses.

New Forest

- Welsh Pony
- Galloway
- Thoroughbred
- **New Forest Pony**

Pony
Origin: The New Forest, Hampshire.
Colour: solid colours.
Physique: great variety – type A, lighter, under 13.2 hands; type B, heavier, between 13.2 and 14.2 hands.
Features: hardy, frugal and friendly.
Use: riding.

Welsh Cob (section D).

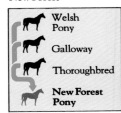

- Oriental
- Welsh Pony
- Trotter
- **Welsh Cob**

Warmblood:
Height: 14 to 15.1 hands.
Colour: solid colours.
Physique: compact, great substance, quality head, strong shoulder, deep,

- Celtic Pony
- Galloway
- Friesian
- **Fell**

powerful back and silky feather.
Features: high knee action, stamina, strength and versatility.
Use: all purpose; driving and riding.

Irish Halfbred

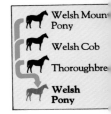

- Irish Draught
- Thoroughbred
- Connemara
- **Irish Halfbred**

Warmblood
Height: 16.1 hands.
Colour: most colours.
Physique: varies.
Features: strong, good-tempered and athletic.
Use: riding.

Welsh Pony (section

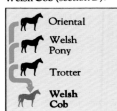

- Welsh Mountain Pony
- Welsh Cob
- Thoroughbred
- **Welsh Pony**

Pony
Height: 12 to 13.2 hands.
Colour: solid colours.
Physique: larger version Section A.
Features: good action and kind temperament.
Use: riding.

Welsh Pony (section

Pony:
Height: under 13.2 hands.
Colour: solid colours.
Physique: cob type, with silky feather.
Features: hardy, active, frugal.
Use: driving and trekking.

Welsh Mountain (see A).

Pony
Height: under 12 hands.
Colour: grey, brown or chestnut.
Physique: Arab-like head, long, crested neck, sloping shoulder, short back and high set tail.
Features: spirited, intelligent, with great powers of endurance.
Use: riding; foundation stock for children's riding ponies.

Welsh pony

Suffolk Punch

Shire

Thoroughbred

Irish Draught

Hackney

tinctive types have emerged, of which the Exmoor claims to be the oldest. Its origins are thought to date back to prehistoric times, when the ancestors of today's Exmoors crossed the land bridge that then linked Britain and Europe.

The Exmoor's near neighbour, the Dartmoor, is larger and not as purebred. However, it still has fewer out-crossings than the New Forest Pony, which, largely because it lives in a more inhabited area, has received admixtures of Arab, Thoroughbred and Galloway blood. Oriental influence can also be clearly seen in the elegance of the Welsh Mountain Pony.

The Welsh Cob was established by the fifteenth century. Since then, these cobs have served Welsh farmers well, working in the fields, drawing carriages, hunting and running in trotting races.

The Fell Pony's home is the Pennines. These ponies stem from the Celtic Pony; the most influential subsequent crossing came with the Friesian blood added in Roman times. Their neighbour to the east, the Dale, has similar origins, but is more of a harness pony. This development came about in the nineteenth century, when a Welsh Cob stallion injected size and strength into the breed, now the largest of the British ponies.

The Highland's ancestry has the same roots as the Fell and Dale. However, additions of Arab and French blood, and Clydesdale to the Garron, has made the Highland quite distinct. Even further to the north are the Shetlands; the ancestry of this small, sturdy breed – a major British export – dates back to 500 BC.

Britain's native ponies also gave rise to a very influential, but now extinct, breed – the Norfolk Trotter or Roadster. Many of these horses were at one time exported, and they served as the foundation stock for most breeds of trotting horse, as well as many riding horses. The closest surviving relation is the eye-catching Hackney, with its spectacular high action.

The only recognized breed of riding/driving horse is the Cleveland Bay. Bred in Yorkshire for more than 200 years, and used, like the Irish Draught, as a dual-purpose horse, its greatest value today is for driving and for crossing with Thoroughbreds, to produce competition horses and hunters.

The largest horse in the UK is the Shire. This is said to be a descendant of the Great Horse of England of medieval times. The smaller, rounder Suffolk Punch, however, has a more definite ancestry. Every member of the breed can be traced back to a horse foaled in 1760. Scotland's heavy horse, the Clydesdale, is thought to share the Shire's ancestry.

Dale

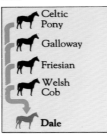

Pony
Origin: Eastern Pennines.
Height: 14.1 hands.
Colour: dark colours; no white, except star.
Physique: powerful frame, straightish shoulder, fine hair on heels and thick mane and tail.
Features: strong, good-tempered and sure-footed.
Use: pack, agricultural work and riding.

Exmoor

Pony
Origin: Exmoor, Somerset and Devon.
Height: 12 hands.
Colour: bay, brown or dun with black points, light mealy muzzle, no white.
Physique: prominent 'toad' eyes, wide chest, strong quarters and thick, springy coat with no bloom in winter.
Features: strength and endurance.
Use: riding.

Clydesdale

Coldblood
Origin: Lanarkshire.
Height: 16.2 hands.
Colour: dark with white on face and legs.
Physique: long, crested neck, high withers, straightish hind legs, much feather.
Features: active.
Use: draught.

Connemara

Pony
Origin: County Connaught
Height: 13.2 hands.
Colour: grey.
Physique: compact, intelligent head, crested neck, sloping shoulder and deep, strong, sloping hindquarters.

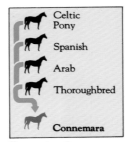

Features: intelligent, sure-footed, hardy; a good jumper.
Use: riding and driving.

Cleveland Bay

Warmblood
Origin: Yorkshire.
Height: 16 hands.
Colour: bay or brown; white markings not desirable.
Physique: large head, convex profile, longish back, high set tail and good bone.
Features: versatile, long-lived and strong.
Use: riding and driving.

Shetland

Pony
Origin: Shetland and the Orkneys.

Height: 9.3 hands (6.2 hands the smallest recorded).
Colour: black, brown or coloured.
Physique: small head, face usually concave, small ears, short, strong back, full mane and tail; winter coat very thick.
Features: hardy and strong.
Use: general.

Dartmoor

Pony
Origin: Dartmoor, Devon.
Height: 12.1 hands.
Colour: bay, black or brown.
Physique: small head, strong shoulders, back and loins, high set tail, and full mane and tail.
Features: long-lived, sure-footed and tough.
Use: riding.

Highland

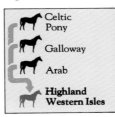

Pony
Origin: Western Isles and mainland.
Height: Mainland (Garron), 14.2 hands; Islands (Western Isles), 13.2 hands.

Colour: Mainland, bla or brown varying to du and grey; Islands, dun with a dorsal stripe.
Physique: Mainland, s ears, powerful loins, strong, short legs, on Islands, smaller.
Features: strength.
Use: Mainland, deer stalking and work for crofters. Islands, children's pony.

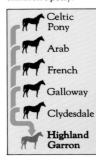

Highland Garron

Shire

Coldblood
Origin: Central Count
Height: 17 hands.
Colour: dark with whit markings.
Physique: face nearly convex, broad forehea long, crested neck, bro back, sloping croup an much fine silky feathe
Features: strength; the tallest breed in the wo
Use: draught.

Dale

Exmoor

Cleveland Bay

Shetland

Highland

Connemara

Irish Halfbred

Dartmoor

Southern Europe

Italy was one of the world's first major horse-breeding areas; the Etruscans bred horses there more than 2500 years ago. It was in medieval times, however, that Italy produced its most famous horse – the Neapolitan. Bred from Barb, Arab and Spanish stock, the Neapolitan was used for Haute Ecole in all the major courts of Europe during the sixteenth and seventeenth centuries. It also became the foundation stock for many other breeds.

Nowadays, imported breeds are the most popular ones in Italy. Of the native breeds, the Avelignese is popular for mountain work, but riding horses, such as the Murghese, Salerno and Calabrese are on the decline. Most Italian riding stock now comes from West Germany, France and Ireland.

The horses of Spain have marked Oriental features derived from the Arabs and Barbs brought into the country by successive conquering armies from the Middle East in the Middle Ages. The most celebrated Spanish breed, the Andalusian, is thought to have Oriental, Noriker and Garrano ancestry. It owes its survival largely to the monks of the Carthusian monasteries of Jerez de la Frontera, Seville and Cazello, who continued to breed the horse after it was replaced by the heavier Neapolitan in the Spanish court in the fifteenth century. The Zapata family did much the same at their Andalusian stud, and the two strains have been kept relatively pure up to the present day.

The breeds of Portugal have much in common with those of Spain, for both countries came under the same Moorish influence. Thus the Altér-Real comes from the same basic stock as the Andalusian, and the other Portuguese breed, the Lusitano, also has Andalusian connections. It is a tougher horse than the Altér-Real.

The mountains of northern Portugal are the breeding grounds for the Minho, or Garrano, Pony. The breed has Arab origins and has survived with little change for thousands of years. Close to the Spanish border, in the plains between the Sor and Raio rivers, the tough Sorraia Pony is found. This was one of the first ponies to be domesticated; it is strong enough to be used for herding and agriculture.

Greece was famous for its horses and horsemen in Classical times, but now the country has only a few native pony breeds. The Peneia is used on the farms of the Peloponnese, the Pindos is used in the mountains of Thessaly and Epirus, and the Skyros is a children's pony. Riding horses are usually Arabs or Lipizzaners, though, as riding becomes more popular, a variety of types are being imported.

ITALY

Avelignese

Pony
Origin: Alps and Appennines.
Height: 14 hands.
Colour: chestnut.
Physique: heavy-frame.
Features: sure-footed.
Use: pack, agricultural.

Italian Heavy Draught

Coldblood
Origin: Italy.
Height: 15.2 hands.
Colour: sorrel or roan.
Physique: fine, long head, shortish neck, flat back.
Features: fast, strong.
Use: meat and agricultural.

Calabrese

Warmblood
Origin: Calabria.
Colour: solid colours.
Physique: middleweight, short-coupled riding horse.
Use: riding.

Salerno

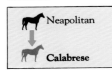

Warmblood
Origin: Maremma and Salerno.
Height: 16 hands.
Colour: solid colours.
Physique: large, refined head.
Use: riding.

GREECE

Murghese

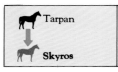

Warmblood
Height: 15.2 hands.
Physique: Oriental features but heavier frame.
Features: versatile.
Use: dual-purpose horse for agricultural work or riding.

Skyros

Pony
Origin: Island of Skyros.

Height: 10 hands.
Colour: dun, brown or grey.
Physique: light of bone, upright shoulder and often cow-hocked.
Use: pack, carrying water, agricultural work and riding.

Peneia

Pony
Origin: Peneia, Peloponnese.
Height: 10 to 14 hands.
Colour: most colours.
Physique: Oriental.
Features: frugal, hardy.
Use: pack and agricultural

Pindos

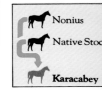

Pony
Origin: Mountains of Thessaly and Epirus.
Height: 12.1 hands.
Colour: grey or dark.
Physique: tough.
Use: riding and light agricultural work.

SPAIN

Andalusian

Warmblood
Origin: Andalusia.
Height: 16 hands.
Physique: largish head, almost convex profile, strong, arched neck.
Features: intelligent and athletic.
Use: high school and general.

Hispano Anglo-Arab

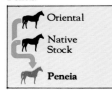

Warmblood
Origin: Estramadura a[nd] Andalusia.
Height: 15.3 hands.
Colour: bay, chestnut [or] grey.
Use: competitions, ri[ding] and testing young bul[ls]

TURKEY

Karacabey

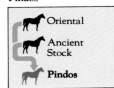

Warmblood
Height: 16 hands.
Colour: solid colours.
Physique: tough.
Use: riding, light drau[ght] agricultural work, cav[alry] and pack.

MAJORCA

Balearic

Pony
Height:
Colour: bay or brown.
Physique: fine head, usually Roman nose.
Features: good-tempe[red]
Use: agricultural wor[k,] driving.

PORTUGAL

Skyros

Italian Heavy Draught

Altér Real

Lusitano

Salerno

Andalusian

...ia

Tarpan

Sorraia

...in: River Sorraia
...ict.
...ht: 13 hands.
...ur: dun with a dorsal
...e and stripes on legs.
...ique: primitive
...arance, long head,
...ght profile, long ears.
...ures: tough and frugal.
... runs wild.

... Real
...mblood
...n: Alentejo
...nce.
...ht: 15.2 hands.

Andalusian

Arab

Thoroughbred

Norman

Hanoverian

**Altér
Real**

Colour: chestnut, bay or
piebald.
Physique: smallish head
with straight profile.
Features: spirited.
Use: riding.

Garrano (Minho)
Pony
Origin: Garranho do

Arab

Garrano

Minho, Traz dos Montes.
Height: 11 hands.
Colour: dark chestnut.
Physique: light frame.
Features: strong.
Use: riding and pack.

Lusitano
Warmblood
Origin: Southern and
Central Portugal.
Height: 15.1 hands.
Colour: grey.
Physique: small head,
small ears, large eyes,
thick neck.
Features: frugal.
Use: bullring.

West and East Germany

West Germany is famous for its riding horses, particularly the Hanoverian and Trakehner. Its success stems primarily from the considerable financial support given by both the national and regional governments to the breeding industry, and the thought and control with which breeding has been directed.

The breeds of riding horse in West Germany are defined according to area – hence the Hanoverian in Hanover and the Holstein in Schleswig-Holstein, for instance. The only breeds to be organised on a national basis are the imported breeds – the Thoroughbreds, the Trotters, various breeds of pony, and the Trakehner, whose original home now lies in East Germany.

The most numerous and successful warmblood is the Hanoverian. Originally a heavy war horse, it has been refined for various uses over the centuries.

Before the war, the Trakehner, named after its home of Trakehnan, was thought to be the Hanoverian's superior. The stud was established in 1732, and it survived until 1944, when the advancing Russians forced evacuation. A few stallions and 700 mares reached the west to form the nucleus of today's Trakehner breed.

The Holstein is the other main German breed in international demand. It has been raised on the marshlands of Schleswig-Holstein since the fourteenth century, when Neapolitan and Spanish blood was first imported to improve the local Marsh Horse. More recently, Cleveland Bays and Thoroughbreds have been used to further refine the breed.

The other German warmbloods have relied extensively on these three breeds for foundation stock, and, together with Arab and Thoroughbred blood, still use them for improvement. None of the German warmbloods are pure-bred; outside blood (always pedigree) has been brought in to improve a breed when necessary. Neither is there a pure breed of pony, and, in fact, there is only one native one – the Dolmen, bred on the Duke of Croy's estate.

The heavy horses of Germany, too, were developed largely through the use of imported stock. The Rhineland and the Schleswig Heavy Draught were established during the nineteenth century by crossing foreign breeds.

East Germany is rather isolated as a horse-breeding nation, and, unlike other Eastern bloc countries, makes no great effort to export horses to the west. The two main breeds produced are offshoots of those found in West Germany, the Mecklenburg having similar origins to the Hanoverian and the East Friesian to the Oldenburg.

Hanoverian

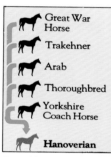

Warmblood
Origin: Hanover and Lower Saxony.
Height: 16 hands.
Physique: powerful.
Features: athletic.
Use: competition and riding horse.

Hessen, Rheinlander and Pfalz-Saar

Warmblood
Height: 16 hands.
Physique: strongly built.
Features: good temperament, action.
Use: riding.

East Friesian

Warmblood
Height: 16.1 hands.
Colour: solid colours.
Physique: similar to the Oldenburg but lighter.
Use: riding and light draught.

Dulmen

Pony
Origin: Westphalia.
Height: 12.3 hands.
Colour: black, brown or dun.
Physique: various.
Use: riding.

Württemburg

Warmblood
Height: 16 hands.
Colour: black, brown, bay or chestnut.
Physique: cob type.
Features: hardy.
Use: riding and driving.

Schleswig Heavy Draught

Coldblood
Colour: chestnut, flaxen mane and tail.

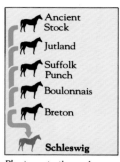

Physique similar to the Jutland.
Use: draught.

Holstein

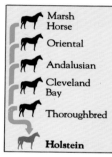

Warmblood
Origin: Holstein.
Height: 16.1 hands.
Colour: black, bay, brown.
Physique: heavier frame than the Hanoverian
Features: a good action.
Use: general uses

Trakehner

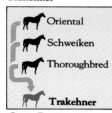

Origin: East Prussia.
Height: 16.1 hands.
Colour: dark colours.
Features: intelligent with an extravagant action.
Use: riding and competitions.

Bavarian

Warmblood
Origin: Lower Bavaria.
Height: 16 hands.
Colour: solid colours.

Physique: medium-size frame, deep girth.
Use: riding.

Rhineland Heavy Draught

Coldblood
Height: 16.1 hands.
Physique: heavy and compact.
Features: strength, early maturity.
Use: draught.

Mecklenburg

Warmblood
Height: 16 hands.
Colour: solid colours.
Physique: smaller version of the Hanoverian.
Use: riding, cavalry.

Westphalian

Warmblood
Origin: Westphalia.
Height: 16.1 hands.
Colour: any solid colour
Physique, *Features*
Use: Similar to Hanoverian.

Oldenburg

Warmblood
Origin: Oldenburg and East Friesland.
Height: 16.3 hands.
Physique: largest of the German warmbloods;
Use: riding and driving

Trakehner

East Friesian

Oldenburg

Holstein

Schleswig Heavy
Draught

Hanoverian

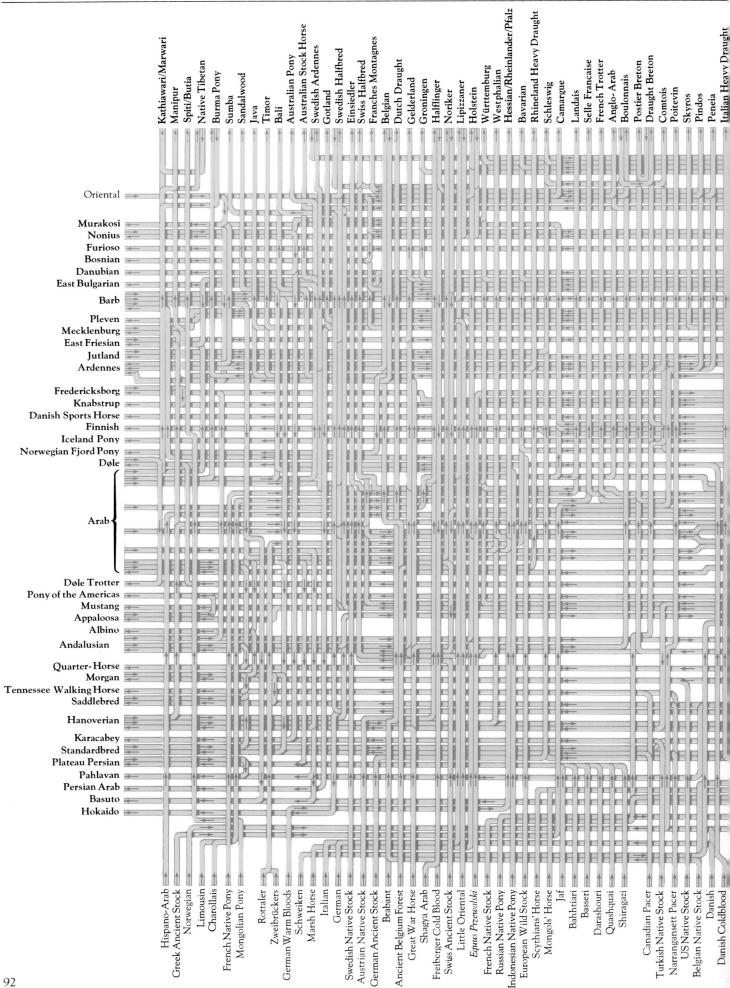

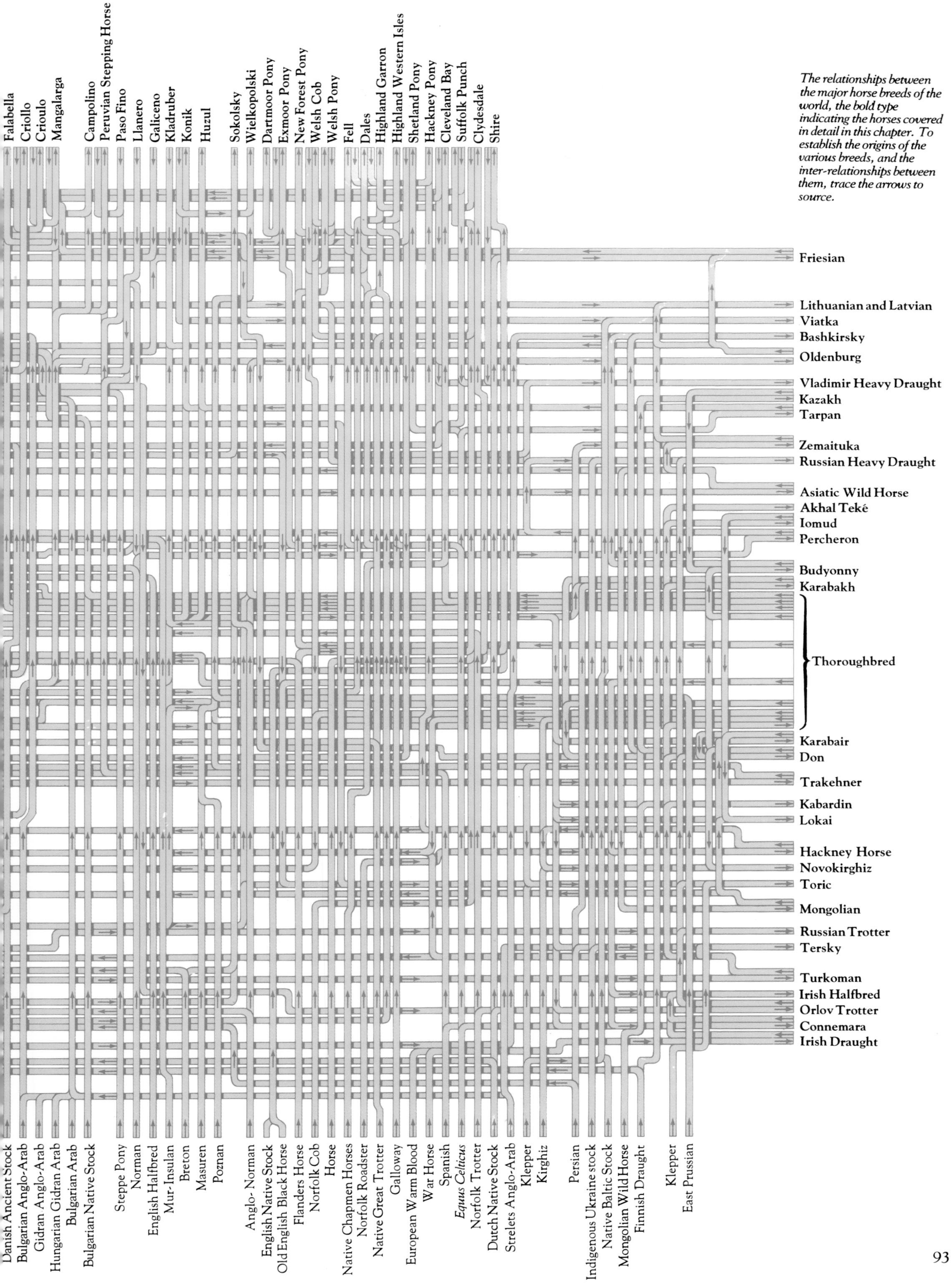
Falabella
Criollo
Crioulo
Mangalarga
Campolino
Peruvian Stepping Horse
Paso Fino
Llanero
Galiceno
Kladruber
Konik
Huzul
Sokolsky
Wielkopolski
Dartmoor Pony
Exmoor Pony
New Forest Pony
Welsh Cob
Welsh Pony
Fell
Dales
Highland Garron
Highland Western Isles
Shetland Pony
Hackney Pony
Cleveland Bay
Suffolk Punch
Clydesdale
Shire
Friesian
Lithuanian and Latvian
Viatka
Bashkirsky
Oldenburg
Vladimir Heavy Draught
Kazakh
Tarpan
Zemaituka
Russian Heavy Draught
Asiatic Wild Horse
Akhal Teké
Iomud
Percheron
Budyonny
Karabakh
Thoroughbred
Karabair
Don
Trakehner
Kabardin
Lokai
Hackney Horse
Novokirghiz
Toric
Mongolian
Russian Trotter
Tersky
Turkoman
Irish Halfbred
Orlov Trotter
Connemara
Irish Draught
Danish Ancient Stock
Bulgarian Anglo-Arab
Gidran Anglo-Arab
Hungarian Gidran Arab
Bulgarian Arab
Bulgarian Native Stock
Steppe Pony
Norman
English Halfbred
Mur-Insulan
Breton
Masuren
Poznan
Anglo- Norman
English Native Stock
Old English Black Horse
Flanders Horse
Norfolk Cob
Horse
Native Chapmen Horses
Norfolk Roadster
Native Great Trotter
Galloway
European Warm Blood
War Horse
Spanish
Equus Celticus
Norfolk Trotter
Dutch Native Stock
Strelets Anglo-Arab
Klepper
Kirghiz
Persian
Indigenous Ukraine stock
Native Baltic Stock
Mongolian Wild Horse
Finnish Draught
Klepper
East Prussian

The relationships between the major horse breeds of the world, the bold type indicating the horses covered in detail in this chapter. To establish the origins of the various breeds, and the inter-relationships between them, trace the arrows to source.

Buying a horse

For even an experienced rider, buying a horse can be an operation fraught with hazards. For example, the horse can turn out to be unsound, 'nappy', a rearer or a runaway, traffic-shy, bad in the stable, or difficult in company with other horses or when left alone. It may, on the other hand, be a paragon of virtue, but simply not what you are looking for. Buying a horse is as highly personalized a procedure as choosing a wife or a husband.

There are many methods of buying a horse – riding magazines, for example, list horses for sale. But generally, if you are buying a horse for the first time, the soundest course of action is to find a reputable dealer and rely on his judgement. This is far preferable to purchasing a horse at a sale. Sales are sometimes used to unload undesirable horses – the chronically sick, for instance, which have to be kept going on drugs, or those which have serious vices. Of course, if a horse is warranted sound when it is sold and then turns out not to be, the purchaser can return the horse and get the money back. But it is simpler and safer not to get into this situation in the first place.

Few reputable dealers will take advantage of someone who confesses their ignorance. The beginner should therefore admit his lack of experience and trust in the dealer's judgement, though an experienced friend is by far the greatest asset.

Points to watch for

There is a saying that a good horse should 'fit into a box'. This means that a classically conformed horse should, excluding its head and neck, be capable of fitting into a rectangle. A horse of this type is most likely to be, and remain, sound.

Good limbs are, of course, essential. The foreleg should give the overall impression of being 'over', rather than 'back' of the knee. Pay attention, too, to the horse's centre of gravity – the part of the creature on which the greatest strain devolves. Points before or behind the centre are also liable to strain, but a well-conformed horse is far less at risk.

To assess the horse's personality, look it squarely in the eye; the character and intentions of a horse are fairly easy to read and interpret with a little experience. A bold but kind eye, generously proportioned, indicates a reliable, sympathetic temperament. Piggy little eyes, especially if the skull is convex between them and runs down to a Roman nose, are sure signs of an untrustworthy beast.

The role of the vet

Before any purchase is made, always have the horse examined by a veterinary surgeon, who should be first told what the horse is required

Top left Bidding for a horse at an auction, top right a horse being displayed to potential buyers in the sale ring and below a successful purchase. Far left The veterinary examination – an essential stage in any transaction – and left trying out a horse's paces prior to purchase. When buying a horse, the important things to check are the animal's conformation, movements, soundness and suitability for the prospective rider, both in temperament and the uses intended for it.

A vet can help assess the first three points, but the rider is the best judge of the other two. Whenever possible, try out a horse thoroughly. Take it into a large field to test its paces and to make sure that it can be easily controlled, past its stable to check that it is obedient and along a road to ensure that it is not traffic-shy.

for. A general hack, for instance, will not make an event horse. The examination should begin with the horse being 'run up in hand', in order to check that the horse moves straight, and that it is sound. A sound horse can be heard to be going level and evenly, as well as seen to be. An unsound horse will favour the lame leg, keeping it on the ground for as little time as possible. If very lame, it will nod its head as it drops its weight on to the sound leg.

The feet and limbs are then examined, the vet being on the watch for any heat or swelling, exostoses (bony enlargements such as spavins, sidebones, or ringbones), and signs of muscular unsoundness, such as curbs, thorough-pins, or thickened tendons.

If all appears satisfactory, the horse's eyes are examined for cataract; it is then mounted and galloped to check its wind. This is to ensure that there are no latent troubles with breathing or lungs – defects that are betrayed by a 'roar' or a 'whistle'.

Horses with wind afflictions may also have cardiac problems, for the effort of breathing

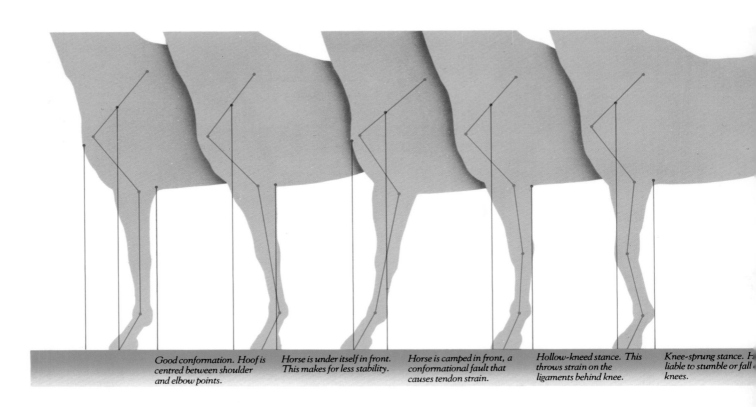

Good conformation. Hoof is centred between shoulder and elbow points.

Horse is under itself in front. This makes for less stability.

Horse is camped in front, a conformational fault that causes tendon strain.

Hollow-kneed stance. This throws strain on the ligaments behind knee.

Knee-sprung stance. H liable to stumble or fall knees.

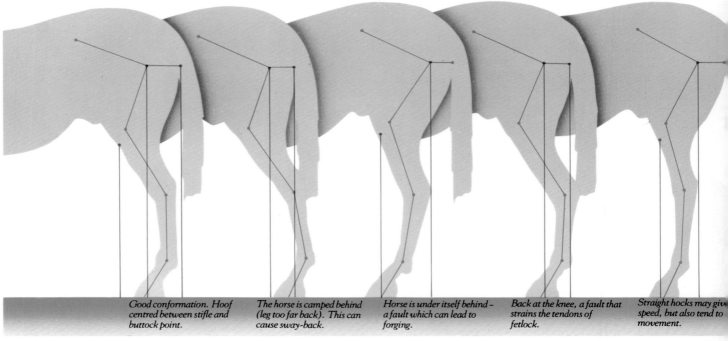

Good conformation. Hoof centred between stifle and buttock point.

The horse is camped behind (leg too far back). This can cause sway-back.

Horse is under itself behind – a fault which can lead to forging.

Back at the knee, a fault that strains the tendons of fetlock.

Straight hocks may giv speed, but also tend to movement.

in such cases naturally imposes an added strain on the heart. For this reason, after the gallop, the heart is tested with a stethoscope.

The general condition of the horse is also examined and checks made for worms or other parasites. Finally, the vet submits a report of his findings.

Trial before buying

It is sometimes possible to have a horse on trial for a limited period to see if horse and rider are compatible, though usually only if the dealer has a personal knowledge of the buyer. Horses are prone to all kinds of ailments and afflictions, and no dealer should be expected to entrust a horse to an inexperienced prospective purchaser.

A trial period is exceptionally valuable when buying a pony for a child. Here, the normal problems can be further compounded

by the child's lack of strength, as well possibly, of experience. The safety of child must be the first priority. Children been killed when their ponies take fright bolt – a particular hazard when riding near roads. It is therefore of the ut importance only to buy from people impeccable credentials. The outgrown fa pony is ideal, but often hard to find, as t animals are often passed on to the ow

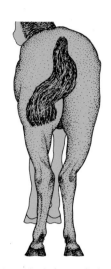

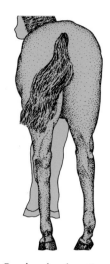

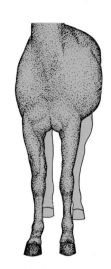

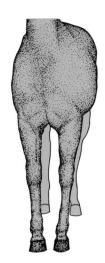

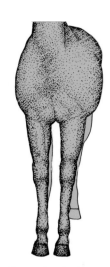

conformation. Point ck is in line with hock of.

A cow-hocked stance looks awkward, but is no problem if legs strong.

Bow-legged conformation puts strain on hock bones and ligaments.

Good conformation. Point of shoulder is in line with knee and hoof.

Pigeon-toed stance puts strain on the knees. The horse may tend to stumble.

Horse is closed in front. Has little heart room, may tend to brush.

Below *A shallow-bodied horse has little stamina as it lacks lung capacity.*

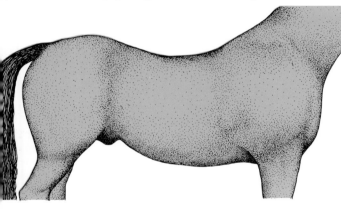

e A hollow back lacks h and flexibility. It a sign of age.

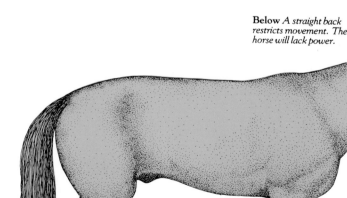

Below *A straight back restricts movement. The horse will lack power.*

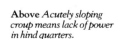

Above *A straight croup means little flexibility and less power in jumping.*

Above *Acutely sloping croup means lack of power in hind quarters.*

ds and relations. Ponies are also sold by breeders, and breed societies will supply ames of studs.

r a first horse, do not make the mistake ying too young an animal A well-trained that knows its job and is a willing and perative ride, is a much better buy than a g, inexperienced one. Two novices to- r is a bad combination; the horse is very to dominate its inexperienced rider.

Thus, a horse of four, five or six years of age is not a beginner's ride. At eight years, it is mature, and, providing it is sound and healthy, it should be useful and active until aged well over twenty. The more nervous the rider, the more docile the horse should be.

It is possible that as a rider becomes more proficient, he or she will look for a horse with more quality. This is a natural and correct progression, but resist the temptation of buy-

ing a horse with too much 'fire in its belly'. This may well pull your arms nearly out of their sockets when, say, in company with other horses. Remember, too, that well-bred horses are far more expensive to keep than, say, a cob, for they usually have to be stabled in winter. A cob, on the other hand, can winter out in a New Zealand rug quite happily, as long as it has access to a shelter and is given hay and one or two feeds a day.

Chapter Six

Breeding a horse

Breeding and raising a foal is one of the most satisfying things involved with horses, but it is a complex business, and should never be undertaken without careful consideration of all the problems involved. For instance, a foal cannot be produced simply for the amount of the stud fee; the additional expenses of veterinary fees, upkeep, and of transporting the mare to and from the stud all have to be taken into account. The vet must be consulted, both to check for hereditary defects and also to ensure that the animal is free from disease – the usual method is to take a cervical and clitoral swab. Most studs require a veterinary certificate to this effect. So, unless the facilities are right and time and money are of no object, think twice about becoming a horse-breeder.

The role of the mare
Mares come into season at regular intervals of between eighteen and twenty-one days, and it is at this time that they can be 'served' (inseminated) by a stallion. However, it is possible for a mare to apparently 'hold' to a service and then to 'return' (come into season again) six weeks later. To make doubly sure, a vet should test a specimen of the mare's blood or urine after 45/100 days and 120 days respectively.

It is best not to ride the mare for a few weeks, until it is certain that she has held to the service. Usually, most studs prefer to keep mares for six weeks in any case, and do not send them back before then unless quite

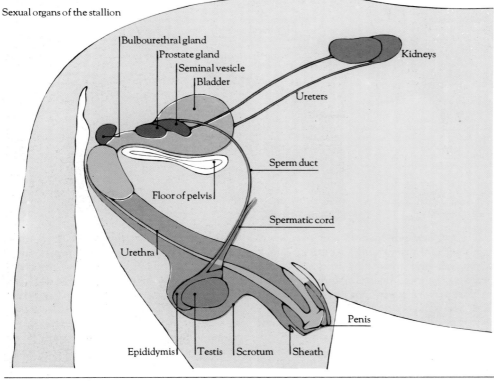

Sexual organs of the mare

Vulva | Vagina | Cervix | Ureters | Kidneys | Urethra | Floor of pelvis | Bladder | Body of uterus | Right horn of uterus | Fallopian tube | Ovary | Teat

Sexual organs of the stallion

Bulbourethral gland | Prostate gland | Seminal vesicle | Bladder | Kidneys | Ureters | Sperm duct | Floor of pelvis | Spermatic cord | Urethra | Penis | Epididymis | Testis | Scrotum | Sheath

A mare's sexual organs consist of ovaries, Fallopian tubes, uterus, cervix, vagina and vulva. At birth, the ovaries contain thousands of eggs; some of these are released into the Fallopian tubes during the sexual cycle to allow fertilization to occur. A stallion's sexual organs consist of two testes, in the scrotum, collecting ducts, linked to the the urethra through the spermatic cord, prostate, bulbourethral and vesicular seminal glands, and the penis, in the prepuce. Spermatoza are produced in the testes.

certain that they are in foal. The cost of keep, of course, raises the price still furth

The mare will not need any special when she returns from the stud, apart fr more nourishing diet. If she is fed nu cubes, buy the stud variety instead of ordinary horse and pony ones. If she is introduce a suitable vitamin preparation some cod liver oil, which has been espec enriched for animal feeding, into the di

Unless it is unavoidable, it is wise n turn a pregnant mare out with geld These may tease or worry her and cause h 'slip' (lose) her foal.

Choosing a stallion
The choice of stallion depends on the ty horse that you are hoping to breed. Be mind that a good quality big horse ma expected to grow into money, while a s one is unlikely to.

Breeding is an uncertain venture a best of times, with all kinds of risk hereditary unsoundness. Therefore, cho stallion that has been certified by a re nized, official body – most countries regulations covering this. In the UK instance, the Hunter's Improvement and tional Light Horse Hunter Breeding So have awarded premiums to Thoroughbred stallions. Each of thes undergone a stringent examination panel of vets and they are the only stallic the country warranted to be sound and from hereditary disease.

Stallions are generally advertised

eding purposes in the spring. At one time
y used to travel the roads and railways in
 company of a stallion man, staying for
 night at various points along the route,
ere the owners of mares in season would
ng them to be served. Nowadays, in most
ntries, stallions remain on their base
ms throughout the spring and early sum-
r, and the mares are brought to them to be
ved there.

Many novice breeders make the mistake of
osing a stallion purely on the strength of
graphical convenience. Nothing could be
re short-sighted, for it is essential to select
tallion that will be likely to offset any
formational defects in the mare.

e stallion and the stud

hough it is important to keep a stallion
er control, and to demand respect from
, he should never be treated as a danger-
 wild animal. Knowledgeable stallion men
 or ride their horses out for daily exercise,
 their horses are contented and relaxed.
e owners ride them around the farm and
g quiet country roads, while others turn
 out to grass with the mares.

At many studs, a horse called a 'teaser' is
kept for trying mares, that is, to ascertain
whether they are ready for service. Teasers
are used to safeguard the stallions that are
actually doing the serving, for all horses used
at stud are liable to be kicked by an irritable
mare at some time during their careers. Some
studs insist on hobbling all mares before they
are served, in any case, a mare should never
be sent to a stud unless its hind shoes have
first been removed.

When the attentions of the teaser have
satisfied the stud groom that the mare is fully
'on' and ready to accept the stallion – the
usual signs are that the mare stands still, with
the vulva damp with fluid and opening spas-
modically – the stallion is brought out of his
box, or from behind the trying gate or wall.
The stallion serves the mare in hand, that is,
they are both on lead reins and wearing
bridles, as a safety precaution. Mating normally takes one or two minutes, during which
the mare must be kept as still as possible,
especially during ejaculation. The head
should be kept as high as possible and, at the
moment of mounting, the leg hobble – if used
– should be released. To achieve extra con-

trol over the mare during mating, some studs
put a twitch on her. This is a loop of rope on
the end of a stick, which is twisted tightly
around the upper lip.

An instantaneous mating may not immediately ensue, however; horses, like humans, have their foibles. Mares have been
known to take immediate and strong exception to the partner selected for them, while
stallions also have their likes and dislikes.
The premium stallion Little Cloud, for example, son of the Derby winner Nimbus, always
refused to serve grey mares unless they were
covered by a rug.

Nevertheless, if the mare does not accept
the stallion willingly, it may well be that she
has some internal illness, such as a cystic
ovary. She should be thoroughly examined
by a vet, as a reluctance to mate is often an
indication that the mare is unlikely to breed.
Or the time is not right – either she has passed
the fertile period of her season, when the
ovum is ready for fertilisation, or she has not
yet reached it. Healthy mares are seldom a
problem to cover or to get in foal, though
excess weight is not an aid to procreation.

Mares generally carry foals for eleven

*t A stallion with a stud
n. Stallions are
tionally valuable
ls and need particular
n their management.
s, the role of the groom
l, particularly during
tual covering process.
th all horses,
ness and proper
ing, exercise and
g are essential; a
ughbred stallion, for
ce, needs a high
n diet, with up to 7kg
 of crushed oats a day
tion to top quality
xercise is usually
n the lunge or by
g, though small
as can often be safely*

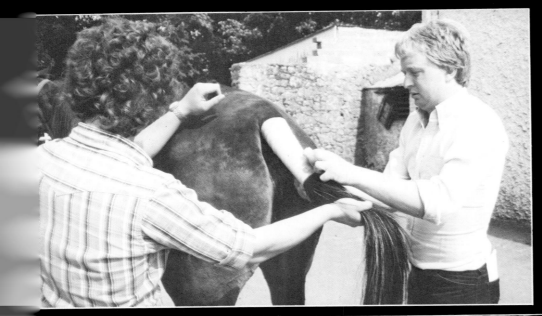

Top left *Bandaging a mare's tail prior to covering,* **centre** *cleaning the mare after covering has been completed and* **right** *teasing a mare with a 'rig' – a second-rate stallion – to find out whether she is ready to be covered.* **Above left** *Cleaning a stallion's penis,* **centre** *putting protective boots on the mare and* **right** *the actual act of covering. Hygiene plus careful management are essential if a successful mating is to be accomplished. The other main reason for teasing, for instance, is to establish what the mare's reactions are likely to be during the actual* covering process, *so that safety measures can be planned accordingly. If she reacts aggressively, then protective boots, or hobbles, have to be fitted to lessen the risk of her injuring the stallion if she kicks out at the end of the process. During the covering, the mare should be held securely, particularly during the period of penetration. The whole process usually lasts a maximum of two minutes, if not less.*

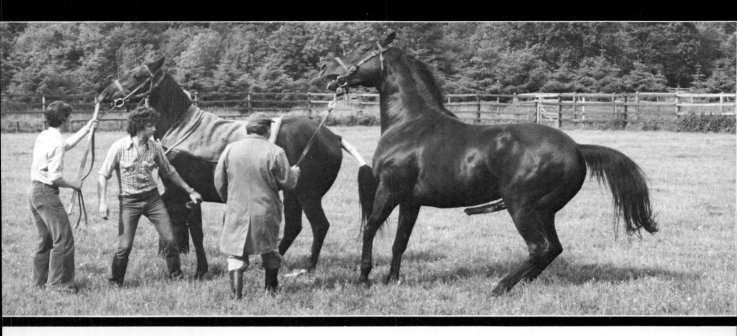

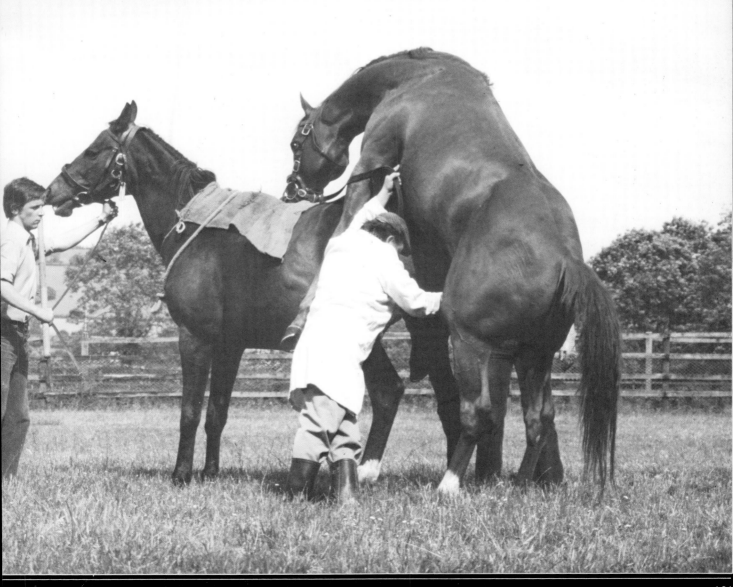

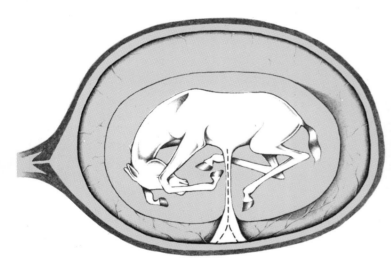

months and a few days – on average, 334 days for colts, and 332.5 days for fillies – but there is a possible variation of some 9.5 days each way, and some mares may be as much as two weeks late. A pregnant mare may safely be ridden to an advanced stage in pregnancy for seven months – as long as she is never over-exerted. Exercise is beneficial for all healthy pregnant animals.

Foaling

Pony mares are usually best left out in a field to foal. They foal quickly and seem to have sufficient natural instinct to produce the foal, clean and dry it, as they would if part of a wild herd, when mare and foal would have to be prepared to move on with the rest of the band soon after birth. The more

Above *The foetus of a foal is protected by an outer membrane called the allantois and an inner one known as the amnion. Both contain fluid in which the foal floats and so is kept insulated from possible shock. The foetus feeds on the blood of its dam through the choriotic villii, buds which link the allantois and the lining of the womb, and the veins and the arteries contained in the navel cord.*

Right *A pregnant mare in the wild. Most types of pony, too, are sturdy enough to bear their foals in outdoor conditions.*

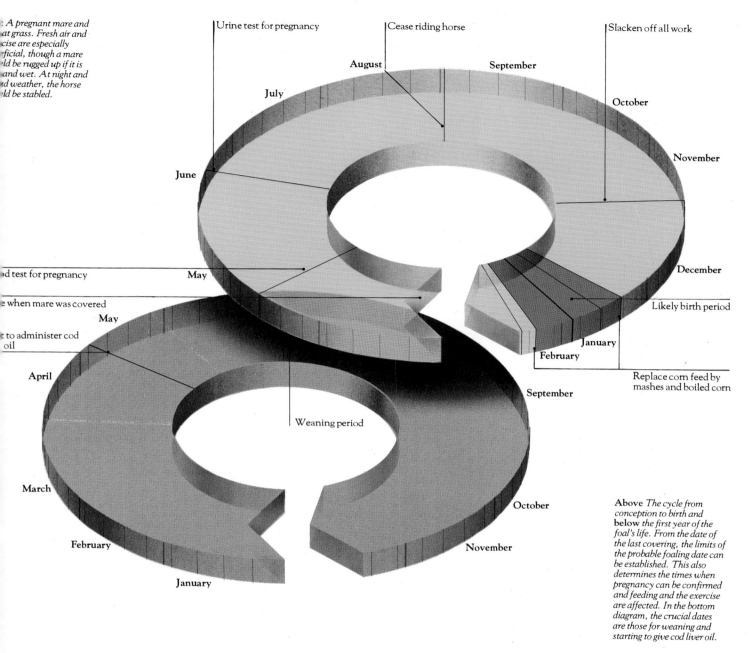

left: A pregnant mare and ... at grass. Fresh air and ... cise are especially ... ficial, though a mare ... ld be rugged up if it is ... and wet. At night and ... d weather, the horse ... ld be stabled.

Urine test for pregnancy

Cease riding horse

Slacken off all work

August

September

July

October

June

November

d test for pregnancy

May

December

e when mare was covered

May

Likely birth period

t to administer cod
oil

January

February

April

September

March

Replace corn feed by
mashes and boiled corn

Weaning period

February

October

January

November

Above *The cycle from conception to birth and* **below** *the first year of the foal's life. From the date of the last covering, the limits of the probable foaling date can be established. This also determines the times when pregnancy can be confirmed and feeding and the exercise are affected. In the bottom diagram, the crucial dates are those for weaning and starting to give cod liver oil.*

ly-bred the mare is, the more supervision will require. Thoroughbred mares almost ys foal in the stable, watched over by ndants. At all the major studs, closed- uit television is employed. This gives the e the illusion of being alone, while every re is being watched, and help is im- iately at hand, if required.

nly a proper stud will have the facilities itting up all night for perhaps as long as weeks – a task that is beyond most private ers. Therefore, it may be advisable to k the mare into a stud as early as possible. e sure that the stud is reputable and onsible; a vet is a good person to consult.

ng birth

first sign of approaching birth is when

the mare starts to pace around, showing signs of discomfort at regular intervals, glancing at her sides and swishing her tail. The wax formed on the udder drops off the teats and the muscles on either side of the croup drop inwards.

As the labour pains become strong, the mare lies down. Delivery is imminent when the membranes of the water bag, in which the foal is contained, break to release the mare's waters.

If, however, delivery is delayed and the mare seems to be straining and visibly tiring, veterinary assistance must be obtained im- mediately, for the cause may well be a mal- presentation. In a normal birth, the forefeet are delivered first, followed by the head and the rest of the body. Complications ensue if

the presentation is incorrect – the most com- mon examples being the frontal presenta- tion, in which the foal's head is bent side- ways; where the foal is on its chest, with its knees bent; when the head is bent backwards, and one knee half bent; the head bowed beneath the forelegs; and the dorsal presenta- tion, in which the foal lies on its back, with the head and forelegs pointing backwards. Sometimes there may be a breech presenta- tion (hind end foremost), in which the hind feet come first, or some other abnormality, such as the twisting of the foetal membranes or the disintegration of the foetus.

In many of these cases, the foal must be pushed back from the birth canal into the uterus, where there is room to turn the foal round, to straighten its legs, or reposition its head. To accomplish this, professional veterinary help is essential.

Once the foal is born, most mares will instinctively start to wash it. Then, as it staggers to its feet, she gently pushes it towards her udder, where it begins to suckle. This early suck is all-important, for the first flow of milk is proceded by colostrum, a vitamin-rich substance that contains natural protection against several juvenile diseases and also stimulates the bowels of the newly-born foal into action.

The mare frees itself of the afterbirth. This should be retained for inspection by a vet to make sure that it is complete. If, for any reason, release of the afterbirth is unduly delayed, then the vet should be called to free it, or infection will follow.

When the foal is a day or two old – even a few hours old, if it is strong and healthy – a small head collar, made of webbing or soft leather and known as a slip, may be put on it. This always involves a struggle, so it should be undertaken before the foal gets too strong. This will enable you to get it accustomed to being handled and led about, which is essential if it becomes necessary to administer medicines or injections. A good way to accustom the foal to human contact is to bring it

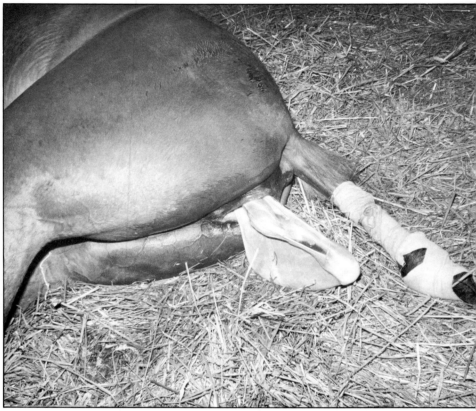

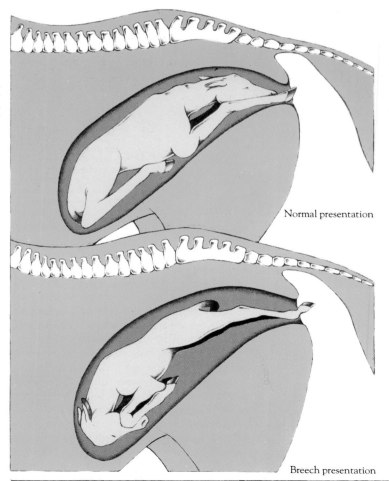

Normal presentation

Breech presentation

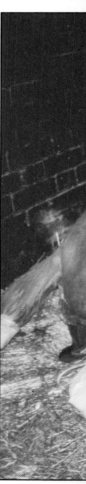

Left *A normal presentation contrasted with a breech presentation, in which the foal is presented hind-foremost. A normal breech presentation presents few difficulties, provided that skilled assistance can be obtained to manipulate the foal. The chief task is to make sure both hind legs are in the birth passage; the chief risk is that the umbilical cord may become trapped, so that the foal is in danger of suffocation. Speed is therefore essential as otherwise the foal will drown in the waters contained in the protective membrane.*

*: The second stage of
...ur begins, with the foal's
...legs emerging, and **right**
...ompletion.
...ow left *The mare licks
...oal clean and **right** the
...twenty minutes after the
...h has been completed, the
...visible sign being the
...rbirth attached to the
...e. Birth starts when the
...e's waters burst, after
...h there is usually a short
...se. The next stage is the
...rgence of the forelegs (in
...mal birth), wrapped in
...mnion, and the process
...continues until birth is
...pleted. Help can be
...n by wrapping a cloth
...nd the foal's fetlocks
...applying traction in time
...the labour pangs.
...fter birth, the mare's
...ng encourages the foal to
...d and, during this
...ess, the umbilical cord
...lly breaks naturally. If
...it can be cut with
...ised scissors. It should
...be drained and
...ected as a precaution
...st infection. The same
...es to the afterbirth,
...h must be removed by a
...the mare does not
...se itself in six hours.*

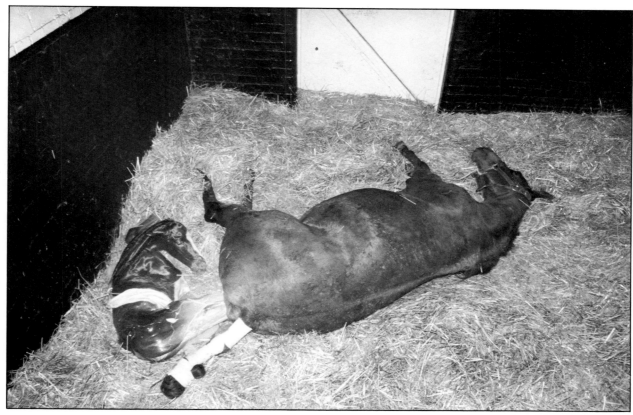

into the stable with its mother at night. This also provides it with a dry bed to sleep on and minimises the risk of chills. If the mare is fed dampened bran and crushed oats, night and morning from a bin on the ground, it will help her condition, and very soon the foal will be eating them too. If you have someone to help, the process of leading the foal in and out of the stall will be a valuable early lesson for the young horse, and may save time and trouble later during the breaking process.

Caring for the foal

With the approach of autumn, the foal must be weaned or it will become a heavy drain on the mother's strength. If she is in foal again, it will rob her of calcium, and the next foal may be born with deformed limbs. Weaning, however, vastly increases the owner's responsibilities. The mare, parted from her foal, bellows night and day, her cries evoking shrill replies from the foal. This lasts until she becomes resigned to the fact that the foal has passed from her care to that of their mutual owner.

The foal should remain in a loose box for at least two weeks; there, where it has become accustomed to eating hard feed together with its mother, it will give little trouble. It will welcome its feeds, which should be generous to compensate for the milk it now lacks. Milk pellets may be added to the feed if it seems to be losing condition.

It is when the two weeks are up, and the foal has to adapt to a new routine of loose box by night and outdoors by day, that the responsibilities mount. First, you must find a companion for your foal to substitute for its mother. Ideally, another foal is the best companion.

It is as well, however, to keep the two foals in different boxes at night. If they are constantly together, one will dominate the other and take most of the food. They will also be so difficult to separate when they mature that you will have a performance almost akin to weaning all over again.

When the warm weather returns, they can stay out all night, and, as the summer days grow really hot, you may consider keeping them in by day and out by night, as a means of protecting them from flies. This should be the pattern of their lives for a couple of years or more, until the time comes for them to be broken. By the second winter, you may decide to let them remain in the field, which does, of course, save a lot of mucking out. Provided you give them some sort of shelter for cold, wet nights, they should not come to much harm. Throughout these early years, have the blacksmith check their feet – say, every six weeks, especially in long periods of dry weather.

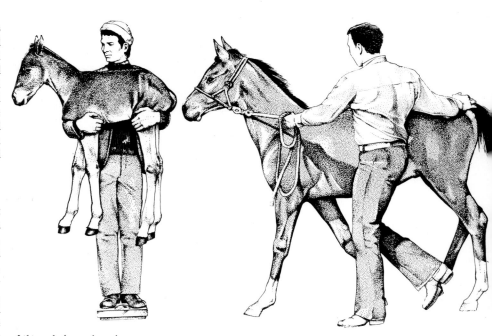

Lifting a foal on to the scales to check its weight. Weighing should be carried out regularly to ensure all is well.

Leading should be done daily, using a halter to control direction and a hand for encouragement.

Right *The result of a y[...] patience – a healthy foa[...] growing towards matur[...]*

If you live in an area of good grass, you can dispense with feeding from late spring to late summer. But as soon as the rains come, corn must be provided, together with as much hay as the young horses will eat.

Breaking and training

If you lack the knowledge or the time to break in a colt yourself, be very careful to whom you send it for training. Every area where horses are concentrated has at least one colt-breaker, and sometimes more. Ask the owner of your local riding school or the blacksmith, to find out which breaker has the best reputation. Make sure to send your colt to someone generally acknowledged to be expert. It takes a long time to 'make' a horse, but a very short time indeed to spoil it.

Owing to the colt's extreme youth, this will not in any case be a making operation, but rather just an erosion of the rough edges. Most breakers prefer to have a horse for a few weeks in the spring of its third year, when it is strong enough to undertake light work, but not powerful enough to put up too much of a fight. Battles may thus be avoided, rather than precipitated.

When to sell

It is always possible that when the foal has been bred and weaned, or even after it has been run on for a couple of years, you may decide to part with it. The horse may have an ungenerous temperament, or is unlikely to grow as tall, or stay as small, as you had hoped. Perhaps it has some conformational

fault which you perhaps particularly dis[...]

Young horses do not grow in even stage[...] good foal, for instance, may go off a[...] yearling but be a brilliant two year old.[...] the other hand, a good yearling might[...] come a plain two year old and then deve[...] into a star long before its fourth birth[...] However, it is a mistake to keep horses in[...] hope that they will improve, unless you h[...] unlimited grass to keep them on, or a far[...] provide plentiful supplies of corn free[...] charge. If you possess neither, it is imposs[...] to keep colts without spending a great dea[...] money. There are also bound to be occasi[...] when the vet must be called, and this is by[...] means cheap. For instance, if the foal[...] male, he will have to be gelded as a yearli[...]

One way of avoiding disappointment is[...] to breed from your old mare that has bec[...] lame and incapable of work. Unsound st[...] produces youngsters with a tendency to[...] soundness themselves, usually through[...] conformation. Buy the soundest mare[...] can afford, send her to the most suita[...] stallion, and see, if possible, the stock t[...] either have produced. A really bad hors[...] likely to be slaughtered when young as be[...] too unsound to work. It is therefore vital t[...] all breeding should be selective – there is[...] point in producing horses fit only[...] slaughter.

Remember, too, to decide what the h[...] will actually be used for well in advance[...] making the decision to breed. Sendin[...] small mare to a small stallion, for instar[...] will inevitably produce a small foal.

Chapter Seven

Breaking and schooling

Since man domesticated the horse, its life style has adapted to meet its change in circumstances. Yet the natural instincts of its ancestors still remain firmly embedded in the horse's mind and character, from the most scientifically bred Thoroughbred to the humblest of ponies.

The first, and perhaps the most important, thing to remember is that the horse is an outdoor animal, and, in the wild, lived its life as part of a single community, the herd. In the herd, leadership came from the head horse, the stallion within the group with the most dominant and positive personality. The horse now looks to man for decisions and protection in the same way as once it did to the head horse, and a good trainer must understand and accept these responsibilities as an important part of his task. For instance, a horse with a strong personality should be treated with tact and firmness, while a nervous or less intelligent horse requires sympathy and patience.

Toughness is also a legacy from the horse's past, but so, too, are sensitivity and timidity. So another general principle to bear in mind when handling horses is not to surprise them with any sudden movement or noise. A frightened horse will often take weeks or even months to get over the experience. If a horse is frightened, then the handler must be calm and soothe it with a quiet voice. Do not make an issue of anything that may go wrong, for horses are very perceptive to the emotions of those around them. Such treatment will only confuse the horse; this is something that neither horses nor ponies like and it can often upset them so much that they become uncontrollable.

Thus, the mental approach of the trainer is the basic factor influencing the progress of the training programme. Bad horses are not born – they are made. Observation is the key in establishing the right mental attitude. By watching the horse at liberty, at rest, feeding, by studying how the animal moves and how it reacts to situations around it, the trainer can determine and analyse just how the horse thinks and what he or she is going to do with it during the teaching process.

Handling – the first step

The training programme starts with handling the foal; early handling is just as important as backing and schooling, if not more so. But it must be remembered that, to give the horse time to mature physically, there should be a two to three year interval between early handling and concentrated training. In other words, we may be discussing the handling of a yearling, though it may not actually be backed until its third year.

A trainer should spend the early days with

*Top A breaking cavesson fitted to a young horse and **below** the cavesson in action, as the horse is led at a walk during an early schooling lesson.*
Right *Lungeing with the saddle in position and **above** lungeing on the lead, the horse walking in a circle with a helper at its head. The time when breaking and schooling can start varies according to the type and temperament of horse concerned. Some experts believe that it is best to leave half and three-quarter breds until at least the age of three; Thoroughbreds, however, can be worked as yearlings and two-year-olds. Once started in earnest, the basic process of breaking should take about six weeks.*

Two essential items of equipment are the cavesson and the lunge rein. The former is a superior form of head collar, with a well-padded noseband on to which is set a metal plate. This is fitted with three swivelling metal rings, to which the leading or lunge rein is attached. The noseband must be tight enough to prevent the cavesson slipping round, or control will be lost. Its position should be checked carefully; the noseband should be about four fingers above the horse's nostrils, or it will interfere with the breathing. The lunge rein should be at least 6m (20ft) long and made of strong, lightweight material, such as canvas or nylon. The horse should also wear boots, bandages and knee pads.

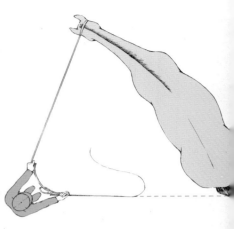

Above *Training a horse to circle left on the lunge. Positioned behind the point of the shoulder, the trainer gradually increases the size of the circle, controlling the head with the left hand and* *the hindquarters with the whip in the right. The aim to get the horse to walk, and halt correctly and respond to verbal commands. For the right procedure is reversed*

the foal just going out to it in the field, patting it, talking to it, feeling it, picking up its legs, and slipping a head collar on and off. The foal can also get used to being led; this should be established as part of the daily routine of bringing the foal in at night.

Through these processes, the foal becomes familiar with its trainer through physical contact, smell and mental 'feel'. The horse is gradually convinced that it has nothing to fear and comes to realize that the trainer will ask certain tasks of it which it will be able to comprehend and perform without harm to itself.

Once the foal is used to being handled and led, the first foundation in its relationship with man has been laid. Next the trainer starts to get the youngster to obey some basic signals. This can be done by teaching it a few basic manners – to give its feet up so that they can be cleaned out, for example. Eventually, the horse will learn to give up each foot from just a touch of the hand.

Then, the horse is taught to move across the box. First, the trainer holds the horse's head still and then, by pointing with a short riding cane or stick, encourages the horse to move its hindquarters over to the left or right. The horse soon learns to move over in its box from the voice alone.

Thus, dressage, of a simple sort, has been started. In this, the whip or stick plays an important part, though it is only an aid to the trainer in communicating with the horse. It is a means of making commands and signals obvious and simple, not a means of punishment or of enforcing the trainer's own will upon the creature. The young horse should have complete confidence in the whip; it must not be afraid of it.

Leading in hand
Serious work with a young colt or filly starts with teaching it to be led in hand. This is the phase of training where many young horses can be spoilt for life. The basic aim of all training must be to encourage the horse to move willingly and quietly through all its paces, without loss of energy and balance, while carrying a rider. The handler should be level with the animal's shoulders and, above all, should not restrict its free forward movement.

The process can start quite early – even before the foal is weaned. Real control from the lead-rope, however, can be left to this later stage. The simplest exercise involved is teaching the young animal to come to the halt. This can be done in the stable yard, say, by walking the horse around, and every now and then standing still, while giving the command 'stand'. The trainer restricts the forward movement by standing still himself, but not by pulling backwards on the lead.

At first, the young horse will stop with the forehand, though the hindquarters may continue to move, describing a quarter circle. But the animal will quickly realize that this is a waste of energy; after a few lessons, it will teach itself to come completely to the halt, provided that the head has not been pulled about in the initial process.

These early lessons should only last about ten to fifteen minutes a day. Discipline between trainer and horse has now been established, but the essential key remains cooperation; the animal puts up no physical resistance and the trainer avoids the use of force, which is totally counter productive.

Lungeing

Lungeing starts when the trainer is certain that the horse is physically fit enough to undergo a more extensive work programme. Boots, bandages and knee pads should be worn. The lunge cavesson now takes the place of the head collar, with the lunge rein fitted to the central 'D' ring. A helper, lightly holding the cavesson, walks the horse around in a circle at the end of the lunge rein, with the trainer standing in the centre forming a triangle between him or herself, the lunge rein, the lunge whip and the horse.

The same routine of stopping and starting is followed as that already established in the yard. But now, when the trainer asks the

horse to walk on, the signal is given with lunge whip and the voice – the most im tant aid in lungeing.

Gradually, the helper moves away f the horse towards the trainer at the cent the circle. Success is achieved when youngster walks willingly around the tra at the end of the lunge rein.

Lunge work can then start at the trot. horse now realizes that the control is cor from one central point and is receptive to commands being given.

The breaking roller

The first purpose of the roller is to famili the youngster with the feel of a girth; late

Above *A mouthing bit and* **below** *a horse accustoms itself to the feel of the bit in its mouth. The animal is wearing a cavesson in addition to its bridle. Fitting a bit correctly is extremely important; care and patience are both required, so as not to startle or hurt the horse. If the bit is positioned too high, it will damage the bars of the mouth, but, if the position is* *too low, the horse may start putting its tongue the bit. This is a serious and one which is very difficult to cure. Once and bit are fitted, leave in place for a time, but the horse secured. Oth it may rub its head, cat bit in its mouth and so frighten itself and destr confidence.*

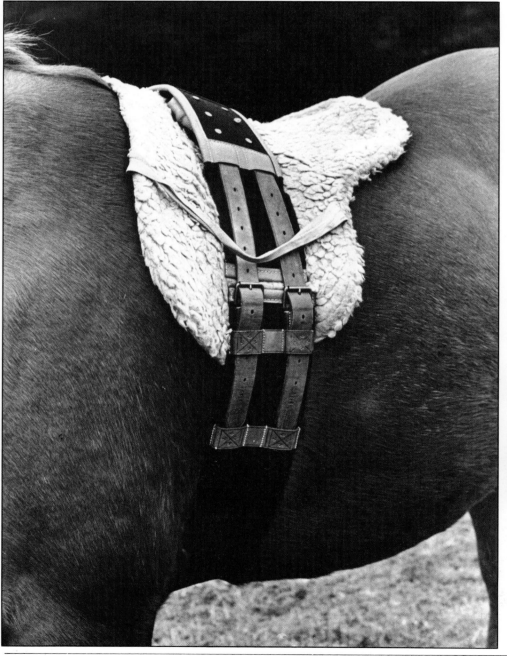

Left *A horse in a breaking roller and* **right** *a bit and bridle under a cavesson. After initial lungeing off the cavesson's rings, the lunge rein is attached to the bit's rings as well. The horse comes to associate pressure on the corners of the mouth with the signals from the cavesson. The breaking roller gets the horse used to something being tightened* *over its back and under belly before the final sta backing. It is kept in pla with a breastplate at firs used on its own, the rol will either be too tight o enough to slip. In both the horse will buck. On fitted, it should be kept position for a couple of The breaking roller mu well padded and kept su*

necessary for the fitting of side reins. A
[...]st plate should be used to keep the roller
[...]ace at first as otherwise it will be much
[...] tight. The plate can be dispensed with
[...] the roller can be tightened without the
[...] bucking.

[...]ne of the ways of helping both trainer
[...] horse is to place a stable rubber under the
[...]r and to attach some pieces of cloth to
[...]ide-rings of the roller (two rubbers do the
[...]well). These will help the horse to begin
[...]nderstand the feeling of the saddle and
[...]rider that will follow later. If the horse
[...]een handled confidently and quietly, it
[...]not object to this. If it does seem nerv-
[...]put the cavesson on, then the roller with
the rubbers, and turn the horse loose in the
school. The shrewd trainer who wants to
produce really good horses will use every
opportunity to let the horse learn for itself.

Mouthing

The secret of making a good mouth is to
encourage the horse to accept the bit as a
'natural' part of its mouth. This takes time
and patience. To accept the bit, the horse
must learn to swallow and produce its normal
saliva with it in his mouth. A wet mouth,
within reason, is a sign of a sensitive mouth,
and a dry mouth a sign of an insensitive one.

Mouthing is accomplished by leaving the
mouthing bit in the youngster's mouth for
short periods each day. The trainer should
watch for any sign of objection; at the slightest sign of this, the bit should be removed,
and the process repeated the following day.
The same routine is followed until the horse
accepts the bit completely. Take care, however, not to encourage the development of
vices, such as putting the tongue over the bit.

During this process, the horse should be
worked on the lunge with a bridle fitted
under the lunge cavesson and the lunge rein
still attached to the centre 'D' ring.

Introducing the saddle

The saddle can now be substituted for the
roller. This should ideally be done in an

enclosed space. Having removed the stirrup leathers and irons, let the horse have a look at it first, say, after a lungeing session. A helper stands at the horse's head while the trainer lifts the saddle up and down just above the horse's back until the animal stands quite still and calm, showing no fear of the saddle at all. Then the trainer gently places the saddle over the back.

Once the saddle is in place, the horse should be thoroughly petted. The next day, the process is repeated and the girth secured. Once the horse has worked on the lunge quietly with the saddle, the leathers and irons can be put back on it. Work should now continue with these pulled down.

Long reins and side reins

Before backing, there is one final stage of training to accomplish – the introduction and use of the reins. There are two methods – long reining and side reining – but the former should be left to real experts.

The use of side reins should be combined with that of a dropped noseband. With the horse in a simple snaffle bridle and drop noseband, the lunge cavesson goes over the top again and the lunge rein is once more attached to the centre 'D' ring. The side reins are then hooked to the rings of the bridle and buckled by a loop through the girth straps.

Allow the horse to relax thoroughly and just saunter around on the lunge at a slow walk. Eventually, it will 'reach' to make contact with the bit itself, and the process can then be repeated at the trot. The trainer should be able to tell when the time is right to start shortening the side reins until they finally reach a length corresponding to that which a rider would use on the horse. The art here, as in the entire programme, is to get the horse to learn from experience.

Backing

There are many different schools of thought on backing, but the essential part is to remember that, as in the introduction of the saddle, the rider must be introduced in stages. For this, two competent helpers are required; the trainer's job is to hold the horse's head to keep the horse calm and for safety, while one helper actually mounts the horse.

First, the helper stands next to the youngster and reaches up and touches the saddle. Then he or she is given a leg-up so that their body is simply resting over the saddle, and, finally, completes the task by putting the leg across the horse and sitting down in the saddle. Once there, the helper should sit quite still, with the feet out of the irons, holding a neck strap or the saddle's pommel for security. All the time both trainer and helper should be talking to the horse, and

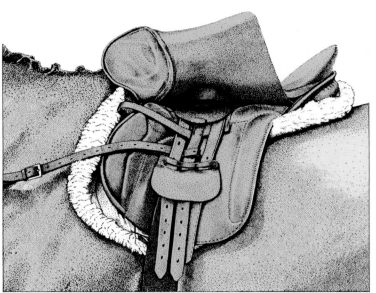

Left *How side reins are attached to the saddle for lungeing and* **below** *preparation of tack before long reining in a saddle and bridle. The best place to attach side reins is just at the girth buckles; they should never be tight enough to the horse's head down. reins run from cavesson bit through the stirrups trainer, a cord under the belly stopping the irons flapping about during a*

Long reining is a useful exercise when preparing backing. If done well, the horse will be going forward when backed, not moving about like an eel. The purpose of side reining is get the horse to come on the bit The engagement the hind legs lightens the forehand and lengthens line of back and neck.

petting it when backing has been successfully completed.

Schooling under saddle

The prime aims of the trainer should now be to produce (1) a horse that goes forward freely with a balanced rhythm; (2) a horse with a steady head carriage; (3) a horse that is balanced in all gaits; (4) a horse that moves 'straight'; (5) a horse that is supple and confident of its physical ability; and (6) a horse that willingly obeys the rider's aids. Once again, it must be remembered that these processes take time. Horses learn through routine, repetition and reward.

Moving forward freely

The first step in showing the horse that it must learn to await the rider's instructions is to teach it to stand still when being mounted. The trainer can achieve this by getting a helper to stand by the horse's head while he gets on and off several times. The horse will soon realize that it must stand still and await the command to move forward. It is worth doing this from both sides of the horse, as this will encourage the animal to remain calm and help it to keep its balance under the weight of the rider.

The horse is now ready to learn the first leg aid to walk on. The trainer asks the horse to

e Long reining off the e horse being taught to ft, right and to halt e reins used as ute leg aids. After this as been completed sfully, the horse can ked steadily in the

Lungeing with saddle, and side reins. The t pace for side reining rot, as it is the only t which the horse can ve while keeping its ill. At both the walk nter, the horse's head slightly from side to , to avoid pressure e risk of damage to the , side reins should not d at these paces.

n normal lungeing, ith side reins is l out in circles. If the s a large one, the reins be almost equal in if, however, it is of liameter, then the rein should be ned slightly.

er, care should be not to shorten this rein ch. If this happens, se will throw its on to its inside er, the quarters will ut and the animal on its forehand. This lt to be avoided at all

walk forward with the leg aid, backing this up with a light touch of a dressage whip on the hindquarters, if necessary. As soon as the horse understands the signal, the whip can be dispensed with. The same process is repeated for the trot, but the canter should not be attempted until the horse is ready for training in balance and collection.

Changes of direction should be quite simple at this stage, with, again, no collection being asked of the horse but only free forward activity. The aim is to educate the animal to the squeeze of the rein and to get it to bend its body in the direction it is travelling. At first this can be done at the walk by simply raising and squeezing the 'asking' rein, closing the inside leg to the girth, and positioning the outside leg slightly behind it, to get the horse to move out of one corner of the school and

walk across to the one diagonally opposite for another change of direction.

Checking the pace
To teach the horse to check its pace, the animal should be walked in a straight line. About a third of the way along this, the trainer closes the hands to resist the forward movement, and, with the voice, encourages the animal to check its walk. Then, after a couple of yards, he or she opens the fingers, closes the legs to the girth, and encourages the horse to walk forward again in an active rhythm. At first, the horse may resist, but, if the trainer shows patience and understanding, it will soon realize what is wanted and begin to enjoy it.

Once the horse has understood the signals at the walk, the same exercise is repeated at

the trot. It will not be long before the youngster has an active, forward movement.

The head, balance and collection
The chief reason for teaching a horse to its head correctly is the additional weigh movement of the rider on its back. Run free, a horse will alter the position of its and neck according to the pace or direc in which it is moving. With a rider, how a new balance has to be learned.

There are two dangers which mus avoided during this stage of training. first is that the horse's head must n allowed to go up; a high head-carriage force the horse to hollow its back, affe balance and decreasing the activity length of stride of the hindlegs. In addi once the horse gets into this habit it

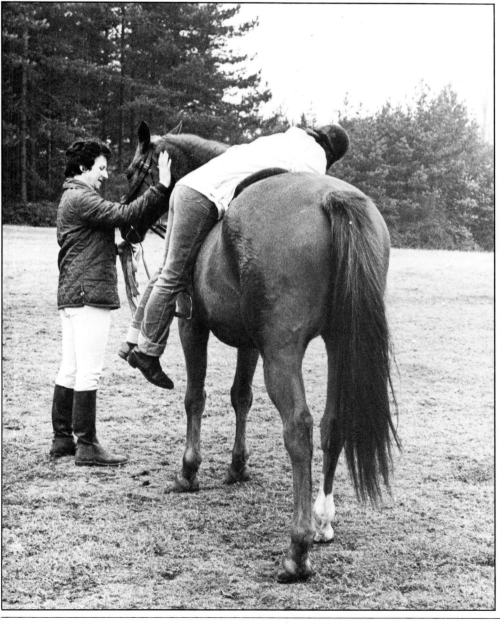

ize that control from the bit and the
ds can be evaded.

ikewise, the horse's head must not get too
for exactly the same reasons. If this
pens, the horse will round its back and be
ouraged to stiffen the jaw and set the neck
cles against the pressure of the bit.

nother problem at this stage can involve
t are termed the stiff side and the soft side
he horse. Just as people are left handed or
t handed, so the vast majority of horses
I to favour one side of their body at the
ense of the other. The side that the horse
urs is known as the soft side; the hard side
he one on which the horse resists. The
her must correct this to bring the body
into balance, and to 'straighten' the
e. At the same time, he or she should
advantage of the situation to get the

horse to 'give' its jaw.

To find out which side is which, walk the
horse on a free rein. Quietly pick up the left
rein only and ask the horse to move to the
left. If there is immediate response – the
horse turning its head, neck and body to the
directing rein – the left is the soft side.
Confirm this by following the same procedure to the right. The horse should resist,
first with its mouth and then with its body.

Once this has been established, the processes of 'straightening' and bringing to full
collection can begin. The trainer first puts
his or her horse into a steady, even trot. Once
the horse is relaxed, a firm, but light, contact
is taken on the soft side rein. If the horse's
soft side is its left, the animal is ridden
clockwise around the school – vice versa if
the right.

The trainer then closes the fingers of the
right hand in a squeezing action and slightly
raises the right rein hand, so bringing pressure to bear on the right side of the horse's
mouth and the corner of the lips. This is a
request for the horse to 'give' (relax) its jaw
from the hard side, where it would normally
resist. The horse's response should be to give
its jaw and lower the head; the trainer will
feel this through a lighter contact on the
right rein hand. The signals are backed up
with the leg aids to maintain activity and
bring the horse down on to the bit.

This exercise should only be carried out for
short periods, say, at the beginning of a
training session, but repeated over the following days until the horse understands what
is required of it. Throughout the process, the
aim is to bring the horse into what is termed

Left to right *Three crucial
stages in backing. The rider
puts her full weight on the
horse, patting it with her
offside hand. From this
position, the horse can be led
forward until fully familiar
with carrying a weight. As a
consequence, the horse
makes no objection when the
rider mounts fully, patting
the horse and talking to it
quietly throughout the
procedure. Finally, the horse
is led forward with the rider
in the saddle. It remains on
the lead until it is fully
confident.*

*Backing requires two
people – the trainer should
stand at the horse's head
while the assistant mounts.
After being given a leg-up to
lie across the saddle, the rider
lies quietly for a few
moments to let the horse get
used to the weight. Then the
horse is led forwards slowly,
turned and led back again.
This stage should take about
a minute and is repeated
over several days until the
horse is fully relaxed. Next,
the rider quietly sits astride –
without putting the feet in
the stirrups – and again
walks around on the lead. If
all the preliminary work has
been done satisfactorily, the
horse will be confident and
know what is required of it.*

full collection, with the head carried 'naturally' just behind the perpendicular. Once success has been achieved, the horse can go on to more advanced work, such as circles and transitions.

Work at the canter

Work at the canter is one of the last stages in schooling the horse on the flat. The important thing here is to get the horse to follow the correct sequence of leg movements, so that it remains balanced.

If the horse is cantering to the left, the leading front leg must be the near-fore; to the right, the off-fore. This must be achieved without any loss of impulsion or change in the head carriage. The body must be 'bent', too; if the animal is on the left rein, then the body must curve to the left so that the horse will naturally go into a left-lead canter balance and with what trainers term cadence. The horse must not be allowed to lead from the shoulder; it should bend into its turn all the way from nose to tail.

To establish this, trot down the long side of the school, keeping the horse trotting evenly and relaxed at the jaw. On approaching the corner, ask for the bend to the left, with the left hand closed and left leg close to the girth. Simultaneously, sit down in the saddle, close both legs to the horse's flanks, with the right leg slightly behind the girth, and, with the seat aid, ask the horse to canter. If the horse does not strike-off with the correct leg, come back to the trot and start again. The process should be repeated until the horse changes its pace correctly.

Once this has been achieved consistently, the horse can start working in circles. Finally, comes the advanced stage of changing from one leading leg to the other. The first step in this is to ride in two circles, the first on the left lead. Then slow down to a trot for a few paces, and then ride into the canter again on a right-hand circle, this time with the right lead. The trotting period can be shortened with each session, until, eventually, the horse will change its leg while still in the collected canter.

Further exercises

At this stage, the trainer can start such exercises as the turn on the fore-hand, the shoulder-in and the haunches-in. The first gives the horse practice in obeying the trainer's aids; the other two help to supple its body.

The best method of training the horse to lengthen and shorten its stride, while preserving its balance and energy, involves the use of cavalletti. These are to the horse trainer what wall bars are to the gymnastics coach. Their use also helps to build up body

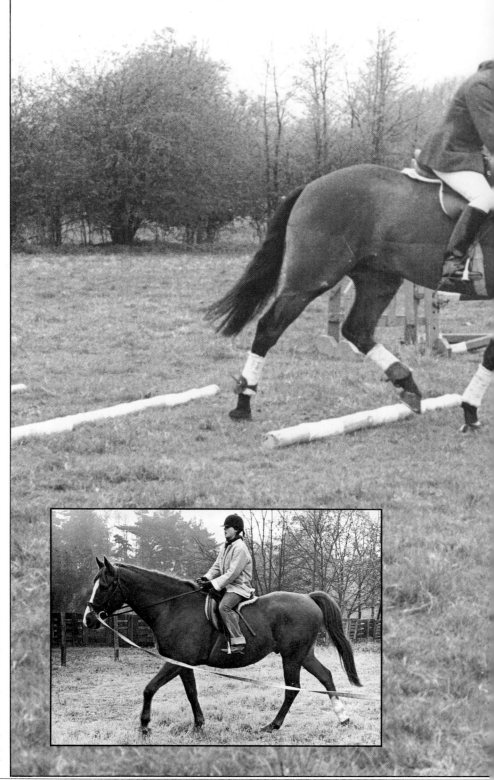

Below Schooling over poles on the ground and **inset** riding on the lunge and walking independently. It takes about six weeks to reach this final stage from backing. The first step is to repeat the lungeing process, the horse still being controlled by the trainer and not by the rider. The reins should only be actively used if the horse lowers its head to buck. After this, the rider can start working on his or her own, developing the use of the aids and progressing through exercises like the one shown here. These should be as varied as possible, with plenty of changes of directions and transitions of pace, which will keep the horse interested.

muscle, as well as extending the horse's mental powers and making it calmer under the concentrated control of the rider, preparing it for the stress of jumping.

Two sets of cavalletti should be laid out in the school – one set to short strides (about 1m apart), and the other to long strides (about 2m apart). Start off with the poles in their lowest position and simply walk the horse over them to gain confidence. Then, work at the trot, allowing the horse to teach itself how to shorten and lengthen its stride, but making sure that it maintains energy and collection. Gradually, the cavalletti can be raised; this enables the horse to exercise its muscles and brings its joints to maximum flexion.

Learning to jump

When schooling a horse to jump, the same principles apply as those involved in schooling on the flat – that is, to encourage the horse to perform as naturally as possible while coping with the weight and signals of a rider.

During basic training, the young horse has learned to trot over poles in cavalletti work, so these can now be brought into use in elementary jumping training. Again, two sets are used; this time, however, the last cavalletti are raised to represent a jump – a vertical jump on one side of the school, and a spread jump on the other. The young horse is started off on the lunge and trotted down the two grids and over the jumps. If possible, this should be done on both reins to give the horse confidence.

The technique is exactly the same with a rider; the trainer rides the horse on a free rein and virtually allows it to teach itself. The more the trainer can encourage this, the better competition jumper the horse is likely to become.

Following this, schooling can take place in the jumping lane and, finally, over practice fences.

The secret of success

Work, perseverance and patience are the secret of successful horse-training. The schooling figures – circles, figures of eight, and so on – are the tools of the trade and not an end in themselves. The aim is to control the horse as sensitively as possible, so that it seems as if it is performing entirely on its own – gracefully and independently, with the minimum of interference from its rider.

Anticipation is the hallmark of the artist in the saddle. In addition, the discipline that a good system of training demands to produce successful results brings a understanding between rider and horse – the partnership which forms the basis of the sport of equitation at all levels.

Chapter Eight

Basic riding

The key to learning to ride is basically one of confidence. The rider must have faith in his or her ability to communicate with, control and work with the horse; equally, the horse must have confidence in its rider. The only way to achieve this is to find a good instructor, who has the knack of encouraging his or her pupils to approach their lessons in a calm and relaxed manner. Riding is supposed to be a pleasure, so do not go to a hectoring instructor or trainer, who may turn this wonderful sport into a weekly nightmare.

The search can be a bewildering one, as level, competence and type of instruction often varies. Approval by a recognized riding association is always a sign of quality. In the UK, the British Horse Society (BHS) and the Association of British Riding Schools both publish lists of stables that have been inspected and approved; in the USA, the American Horse Shows Association does the same. In Australia, though there is no national system of assessment as such, the magazine *Australian Horse and Rider* publishes similar surveys.

The clothes to wear

At first there is no need to spend money on a full riding kit, but certain items are essential for both safety and comfort. A hard riding hat, or, better still, a racing-style crash hel-

met, is one of them, but make sure that the brand you buy meets national safety requirements. Jodhpur boots, western riding boots, or rubber riding boots (these are far cheaper than leather ones) are also vital. Plimsolls can slip through the stirrup irons and rubber wellingtons are not really the right shape.

Otherwise clothes can be adapted to purse and needs. A thick, close-fitting pair of jeans (not the 'flared' variety), or a pair of 'chaps', worn cowboy-style over a pair of trousers, can take the place of breeches or jodhpurs at first. These should be worn with a thick sweater or windcheater in winter, or, in hot weather, a tee-shirt or sports shirt. A riding mackintosh is a good investment, as is a pair of string gloves. Wet reins, especially if also slippery with sweat, can be almost impossible to grip.

Handling, mounting and dismounting

At first, the horse should be 'made ready' for you, but it is a good idea to ask if you can bring your mount out of its box and into the yard to get used to being around such a big animal. Greet the horse calmly and move to its shoulder, talking to it as you do so. Then, run your hand down the shoulder and give it a pat. Move to its head, undo the head-collar and lead the horse out of the box.

The next stage is to mount the horse – either unaided, or assisted by a leg-up. Begin-

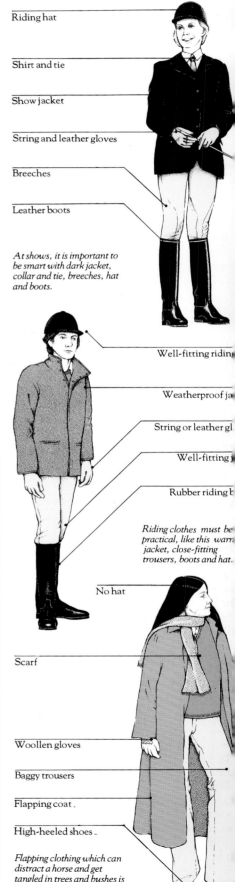

Riding hat

Shirt and tie

Show jacket

String and leather gloves

Breeches

Leather boots

At shows, it is important to be smart with dark jacket, collar and tie, breeches, hat and boots.

Well-fitting riding

Weatherproof ja

String or leather gl

Well-fitting

Rubber riding b

Riding clothes must be practical, like this warm jacket, close-fitting trousers, boots and hat.

No hat

Scarf

Woollen gloves

Baggy trousers

Flapping coat

High-heeled shoes

Flapping clothing which can distract a horse and get tangled in trees and bushes is not suitable.

The principles of classical riding were laid down by a sixteenth century Neapolitan riding master Federico Grisone in 1550. In them, the horseman used a straight leg and fixed-hand reins controlling the horse with a powerful curb bit and spurs. The rider dominated the horse completely, forcing it into intricate dressage movements. Grisone's influence was widespread and long-lasting, particularly in the various high schools of the royal courts of Europe. A present day survival is the Spanish School in Vienna and its famous Lipizzaner horses (left).

With the dawn of the twentieth century came a revolution in riding which transformed the art of equitation. This was the creation of the Forward Seat by an Italian cavalry officer, Federico Caprilli (1867–1907). His system was based on a partnership between horse and rider, the aim being to interfere with the horse as little as possible and so allow it to move freely and with natural balance.

...ing the headpiece in the left hand, put the ...over the horse's head and neck first. The ... will then be under control while the ...piece is being fitted. Make sure that no ...of the bridle trails on the ground.

Hold the headpiece up in the right hand and cradle the bit on the thumb and forefinger of the left. Then slip the left hand under the horse's muzzle and insert a finger between its front and back teeth on the offside to open the mouth.

Having slipped the bit into the mouth, use both hands to bring the headpiece over its ears, one at a time. Smooth the forelock down over the browband and check that this is clear of the ears. See that no part of the headpiece is twisted.

Then fasten the throatlash and nose band. There should be a hand's width between throatlash and jaw and noseband. See that the bit is not low enough to rest on the teeth, or high enough to wrinkle the horse's lips.

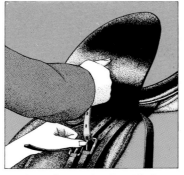

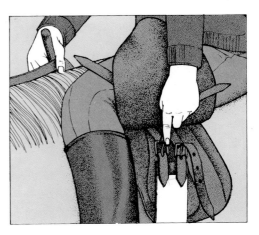

...the horse tied up, smooth the saddle ...of the coat before picking up the saddle ...front arch and cantle, and placing it ...y but firmly on the horse's withers. Then ...it back enough to let the horse's shoulders ... freely.

Check that all is smooth under saddle flap, then move to the offside and let down girth, which has been lying over saddle. Return to nearside and buckle the girth firmly, so that a hand can just be slipped beneath it. Saddling can be done in one operation.

Right After riding for a few minutes, the girth will usually need a further tightening. There is no need to dismount as this can be done in the saddle. Take the foot from the nearside stirrup iron and move the leg forward, so that the saddle flap can be lifted and tucked under the thigh, out of the way. Adjust the girth strap in the same way as a stirrup leather, tightening it by a hole or two while keeping a finger on the buckle prong. Then release the flap and replace the foot in the stirrup iron.

...should always have a groom standing at ...horse's head to ensure that the animal ...ds still while being mounted.

...lways mount a horse from the near (left) ... Before doing so, check the girth for ...tness; if it is too loose, the saddle may slip ...he rider's weight comes on to the stirrup. ...her the reins in the left hand, maintain-...a light contact with the horse's mouth. ...e care not to keep the left rein too short, ...he horse may start to circle as you mount. ...lace the left hand on the pommel of the ...lle and then turn the body so that your ...k is to the horse's head with the left ...ulder parallel with the horse's left shoul-... Take the left stirrup iron with the right ...d, turn it clockwise towards you and place ...ball of the left foot in the iron, keeping ...toe as low as possible. If it digs into the ...se's flank, it will act as a signal to the ...se to move forward.

...lace the right hand over the waist of the ...lle, and, with the weight of the body on ...left foot, spring upwards from the right ...t, using the right hand as a lever. Bring ...right leg over the saddle and then gently ...er yourself into it. Place the right foot in ...offside iron and take up the reins with ...n hands.

...o dismount, take both feet out of the ...s and collect the reins in one hand.

Then, swinging the right leg well over the cantle of the saddle, gently, but briskly, vault off, landing on both feet.

Adjusting the stirrups
Once in the saddle, the next thing to do is tighten the girth again and then adjust the stirrup leathers to the correct length. The initial temptation at the start of a ride is to have the leathers too short. As the ride progresses, and the seat comes properly down into the saddle, it will be necessary to lengthen them.

To establish the correct length, take the feet out of the irons and let them hang down naturally. The iron should just touch the inside point of the ankle bone. Adjust the leathers accordingly, making sure that they are both the same length.

The seat
The seat is the rock on which all good riding is founded; without a correct position in the saddle, no pupil can hope to go on to advanced equitation successfully. A correct seat means that the rider is in balance — secure, light, and responsive to the horse's every movement. It is used in rhythm with the animal's action; the pushing down of the seat bones on the horse's back encourages it to lengthen its stride.

The rider sits into the middle and lowest part of the saddle, the body position being upright and free from stiffness, especially round the waist. The rider is in fact sitting on a triangle, two points being the seat bones and the third the crotch of the body.

The back should be straight, but relaxed and supple, with the shoulders held square. The head should always be held up and looking to the front. Never look down, or the back will become rounded and the chest hollowed. As a guide, place a hand behind you flat on the saddle. There should be room for the flat hand between you and the cantle.

The temptation to grip with knees and calves must be avoided. Otherwise the body will be stiffened, the seat raised out of the saddle and the position made rigid. The thighs and legs should wrap around the horse and mould themselves to the correct position. A simple routine to help achieve this is to open the legs away from the horse's flanks and then draw the thighs into position from behind. This will bring the large inside-thigh muscle under and to the back of the thigh, flattening the area and allowing it to rest close to the saddle and the horse. Then, by pushing the weight down on the ankles, the rider will feel the seat lower into the saddle.

The lower leg should hang down to rest lightly against the horse's sides, just behind

When mounting place left hand on the saddle pommel and put ball of left foot into iron with right hand, keeping toe low.

Next place right hand over waist of saddle and, keeping the toe under the horse against the girth, spring smoothly and lightly up.

Bring the right leg over, keeping it well clear of the saddle and the back of the horse. This should be done in one smooth movement.

Dismounting. First take both feet from the stirrup irons, transfer the reins to the left hand and grip pommel with the right hand.

Next, leaning forward lightly swing both legs clear of the horse, keeping weight on right hand and holding reins with the left.

Land lightly on both feet, facing the saddle and still keeping control with the reins in gentle contact with the horse's mouth.

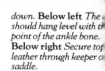

Above Single-rein
*The reins are held g
10cm (4ins) apart, between the third
little fingers, with the slack held by thu*

Above *With the do
bridle, the reins are separated by the
fingers. The bridoon rein is on the ou*

Left *When mounted adjust stirrups by pulling the top leather up against the buckle under the saddle skirt. Keep a finger on the buckle spike – the leather can then be easily adjusted up or*

down. **Below left** *The
should hang level with t
point of the ankle bone.*
Below right *Secure top
leather through keeper o
saddle.*

the girth with the heel pressed down. This is where the rider's weight is balanced. Holding the lower leg too far forward or too far back must be avoided, because it affects the position in the saddle and makes it difficult to apply the leg aids correctly. Only the ball of the foot should rest in the stirrup iron, and both feet should be held parallel with the horse's sides.

If the position is correct, the rider's ears, shoulders, hips and heels should be in line with each other. The stirrup leather should be at right angles to the ground when the rider is mounted.

The arms should hang down naturally to the elbow. The hands, with thumbs uppermost, are held as if carrying two glasses of water. The rider should not get into the habit of bending the wrists inwards or of flattening the hand. A straight line should run from the elbow through the hand to the bit in the horse's mouth.

The best place to work on the correct saddle position is on the lunge rein, where most of the student's early work is usually done in any case. When working on the lunge, the rider should be holding a neckstrap, and not the reins. The horse is being controlled from the lunge; two people trying to direct it, one with the lunge and the other

from the bridle, will only confuse the anim

A strong independent seat can only achieved by regular active riding, assisted suppling exercises and riding without s rups. These are essential for developing ance and confidence.

The aids

The aids are the system of signals used control the horse. They fall into t categories; first come the natural aids hands, legs, seat and voice, and second the artificial aids of whip, spurs, draw re drop nosebands, martingales and so on. only one a beginner should use is a whip.

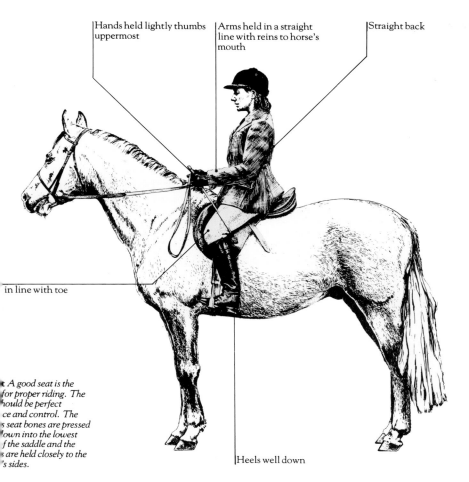

Hands held lightly thumbs uppermost

Arms held in a straight line with reins to horse's mouth

Straight back

in line with toe

*A good seat is the
for proper riding. The
ould be perfect
ce and control. The
seat bones are pressed
own into the lowest
f the saddle and the
are held closely to the
's sides.*

Heels well down

ll riding is based on controlling the
ural impulsion of the horse. This is
eved by combined use of the rider's legs
seat. The aim is to get the horse moving
ly and actively forward in the desired
ction, and not evading the aids when
are applied. The rider can usually tell
through the hands; if the horse is resist-
there will be little 'feel' on the reins
n activity is being asked for, and 'pull' if
horse is being checked.

he legs are used in a squeezing action just
nd the girth. A quick, light squeeze,
ated if necessary, is more effective than
onged pressure. Use of the heels should
voided.

the horse does not respond to the legs,
whip can be used to reinforce the aid. A
on the horse's ribs, just behind the rider's
is usually adequate. Note that the whip is
an extension of the aid. It should not be
as a punishment except in extreme cases
isobedience.

of the hands

hands control, never create, pace and
ction through the use of the reins. Con-
with the mouth should therefore be light
steady; pulling on the reins will only hurt
upset the horse. The wrists should be

supple and flexible enough to follow the
horse's natural rhythm; the aim is to achieve
a passive hand, not a rigid one with the wrists
set in a fixed position.

It is essential therefore to hold the reins
correctly. With a single-rein bridle, the reins
should pass between the little finger and the
third finger of each hand. The remainder of
the reins pass through the finger and thumb,
with the thumb on top of the rein to aid the
grip. Double bridles, however, can be held in
several different ways. One of them is to
divide the reins with the little finger of each
hand, with the curb (lower) rein crossing
inside to pass between the third finger and
little finger. Again, the reins pass out
through the index finger and thumb, with
the remainder crossing over to the left.

The walk

All early work should be done at the walk
until the pupil has established the basic confidence required to move on to the other
paces. Take up contact with the mouth and
apply the aids to make the horse walk on.
Keep the hands relaxed when the walk has
been established, however, or the horse may
be tempted to go into a trot.

Any unwanted increase in pace should be
checked by closing the hands to resist the

forward movement, closing the legs to the
sides and pushing down in the saddle with the
seat bones. In response, the horse checks its
pace. After a few strides, the rider should
give with the hands, increase the pressure of
the leg and seat aids and ask the horse to walk
on again.

To ask for the halt, the rider applies both
leg and seat pressure at the same time as
lightly resisting the forward movement with
the hands. The horse should stand still on all
fours when it comes to the halt.

Changes of direction should also be
learned and practised at the walk. The inside
leg and hand ask for these, while the outside
hand and leg control the pace. To go to the
right, ask with the right hand, keeping the
left one passive. Both legs should be closed to
the horse to maintain the walk, but apply the
left leg more strongly to prevent the swing of
the quarters. To turn to the left, reverse the
procedure.

The rider should make a conscious effort to
think right or left. This concentration can
act as a reinforcement to the physical aids
being applied.

The trot

This is a two-time gait, in which the horse
moves its legs in a diagonal sequence of
near-fore, off-hind, off-fore and near-hind.
Near-fore and off-hind make up what is
known as the left diagonal; off-fore and near-
hind the right. The rider can either sit in the
saddle and follow the natural rhythm of the
trot, or rise (post) slightly out of the saddle
for one beat of the gait.

To achieve the transition from walk to
trot, sit down in the saddle, close the legs and
feel the inside rein. As the horse gets into its
trot, sit into it for a few strides, using the legs
to maintain the activity.

In the rising trot, the rider rises out of the
saddle on one beat of one diagonal and de-
scends on the other, with the weight of the
body supported by the ankles, heels and stirrup irons, but not by the knees. These must
act purely as a hinge. Rise from the hip,
keeping the lower leg still. The thigh and
body should remain at the same angle. Keep
the horse moving forward and a light and
even contact with the animal's mouth.

The seat should never be allowed to come
completely out of the saddle and the reins
should never be used as a lever when rising.
In addition, always regularly change from
one diagonal to the other. Like human beings, horses tend to favour one side of their
body to the other, and this means that it is
very easy to always remain on, say, the left
diagonal during a prolonged period at the
trot. This is bad for the horse as well as for the
rider.

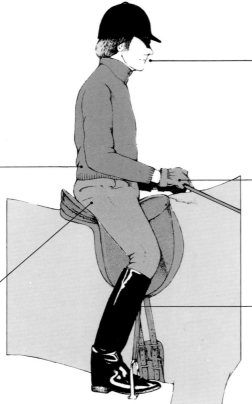

Right *The natural aids are the movements which communicate the rider's intentions to the horse. The body, legs and hands work together in complete harmony. If the horse is positioned and prepared correctly it can obey the rider's instructions more easily.*

The voice can be used to soothe or check the horse.

The back muscles affect the seat. They make it more secure and enable the rider to maintain balance. Straightening the spine, combined with corresponding leg and hand actions conveys the rider's intentions to the horse.

The hands should be light and responsive, being used in a give-and-take action. They regulate the energy created by the calves, and control the forehand.

Pressure from the seat encourages the horse to move forward from the hindquarters. A firm, deep seat enables the rider to use the legs correctly.

The calves control impulsion and energy in the hindquarters and guide their direction.

lead the horse to increase the speed of its t

The horse should always lead off into
canter with the correct leg. The seque
always begins with a hind – off-hind if g
to the left and near-hind to the right. '
near-fore and off-fore are the two lea
front legs respectively. A horse that start
canter with the wrong lead is said tc
cantering 'false'.

It is easier to establish the correct lea
the aids for the canter are applied on a be
when the horse's body should be bent in
direction it is going. Thus, it usually balar
itself naturally to take up the canter on
desired leg. The best way to establish a g
canter, therefore, is to work in a large cir
The horse should maintain an active, rh

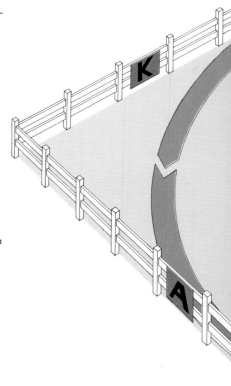

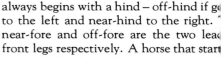

To change diagonals, simply sit down in the saddle for two beats, and then start rising again on the other diagonal, using the leg to give added impulsion if there is resistance. Diagonals should always be changed with each change of direction. For example, if trotting to the right on the left diagonal and then changing the rein to the left, the rider should shift his or her weight to the right diagonal. This keeps the horse level, balanced and gives it a 'breather'. In long distance riding, or hacking, the diagonal at the trot should be changed regularly.

To return to the walk, sit well down in the saddle, close the hands firmly and apply the leg aids until the horse walks forward freely. Give with the hands but keep applying the leg aids until the momentum of the walk is firmly established.

The canter
The canter is a three-time gait, with one beat coming from each of the forelegs and the third from the hindlegs. The rider relaxes with this rhythm, keeping a steady, even contact with the mouth. Sit deeply into the saddle, allowing the back to follow the movement from the hips, and avoid the temptation to be tipped forward. Over excitement – and kicking hard with the heels – will only

Left *Exercises strengthen the muscles and improve the rider's seat. They help the inexperienced rider gain confidence. The rider leans forward and down over the horse's neck to touch the left toe with the right hand. Then the rider sits upright and repeats the process on the other side.*

With arms outstretched outwards, head up and back straight the rider turns as far as possible in each direction, twisting the body from the hips. This improves the suppleness of the back and waist. This exercise can be practised at the halt or when the horse is moving at a walk.

With arms folded, the rider leans back to rest on the horse's quarters, then sits upright again. The legs should remain in the correct riding position during the exercise. Do not attempt this, or any other, exercise on an inexperienced horse which may be frightened by the movements involved.

Riding schools often [en]closed arena. The [di]vided up by letter [lette]rs to help the rider [to] judge distance [accura]tely. This is [particu]larly important in [dressa]ge training. In a [dressage test] the instructor usually stands in the centre of the arena and directs the riders individually or as a group. The rider can work in circles or straight lines, or use a combination of both. The arena is suitable for most types of schooling on the flat, and for jumping.

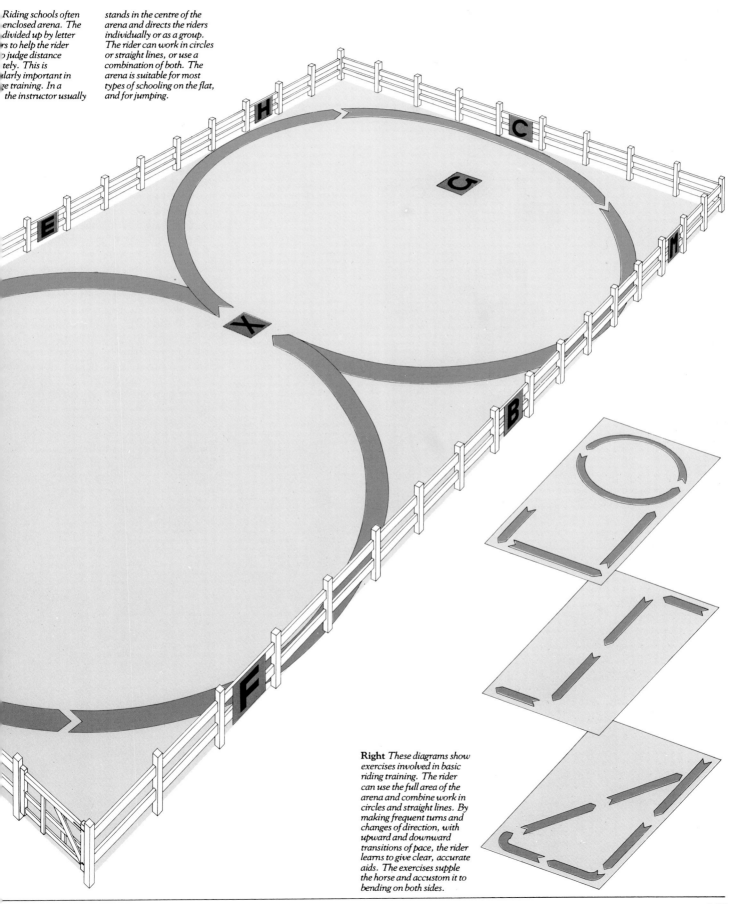

Right *These diagrams show exercises involved in basic riding training. The rider can use the full area of the arena and combine work in circles and straight lines. By making frequent turns and changes of direction, with upward and downward transitions of pace, the rider learns to give clear, accurate aids. The exercises supple the horse and accustom it to bending on both sides.*

123

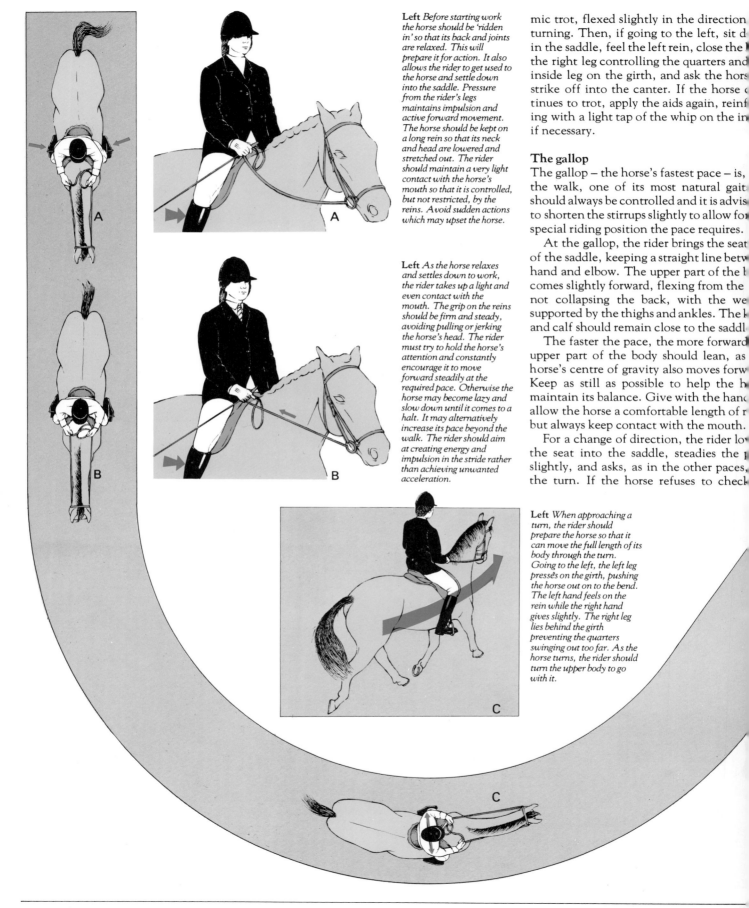

Left *Before starting work the horse should be 'ridden in' so that its back and joints are relaxed. This will prepare it for action. It also allows the rider to get used to the horse and settle down into the saddle. Pressure from the rider's legs maintains impulsion and active forward movement. The horse should be kept on a long rein so that its neck and head are lowered and stretched out. The rider should maintain a very light contact with the horse's mouth so that it is controlled, but not restricted, by the reins. Avoid sudden actions which may upset the horse.*

Left *As the horse relaxes and settles down to work, the rider takes up a light and even contact with the mouth. The grip on the reins should be firm and steady, avoiding pulling or jerking the horse's head. The rider must try to hold the horse's attention and constantly encourage it to move forward steadily at the required pace. Otherwise the horse may become lazy and slow down until it comes to a halt. It may alternatively increase its pace beyond the walk. The rider should aim at creating energy and impulsion in the stride rather than achieving unwanted acceleration.*

Left *When approaching a turn, the rider should prepare the horse so that it can move the full length of its body through the turn. Going to the left, the left leg presses on the girth, pushing the horse out on to the bend. The left hand feels on the rein while the right hand gives slightly. The right leg lies behind the girth preventing the quarters swinging out too far. As the horse turns, the rider should turn the upper body to go with it.*

mic trot, flexed slightly in the direction turning. Then, if going to the left, sit d in the saddle, feel the left rein, close the the right leg controlling the quarters and inside leg on the girth, and ask the hors strike off into the canter. If the horse c tinues to trot, apply the aids again, reinf ing with a light tap of the whip on the in if necessary.

The gallop

The gallop – the horse's fastest pace – is, the walk, one of its most natural gaiti should always be controlled and it is advis to shorten the stirrups slightly to allow fo special riding position the pace requires.

At the gallop, the rider brings the seat of the saddle, keeping a straight line betw hand and elbow. The upper part of the l comes slightly forward, flexing from the not collapsing the back, with the we supported by the thighs and ankles. The k and calf should remain close to the saddl

The faster the pace, the more forward upper part of the body should lean, as horse's centre of gravity also moves forw Keep as still as possible to help the h maintain its balance. Give with the hand allow the horse a comfortable length of r but always keep contact with the mouth.

For a change of direction, the rider lo the seat into the saddle, steadies the p slightly, and asks, as in the other paces, the turn. If the horse refuses to check

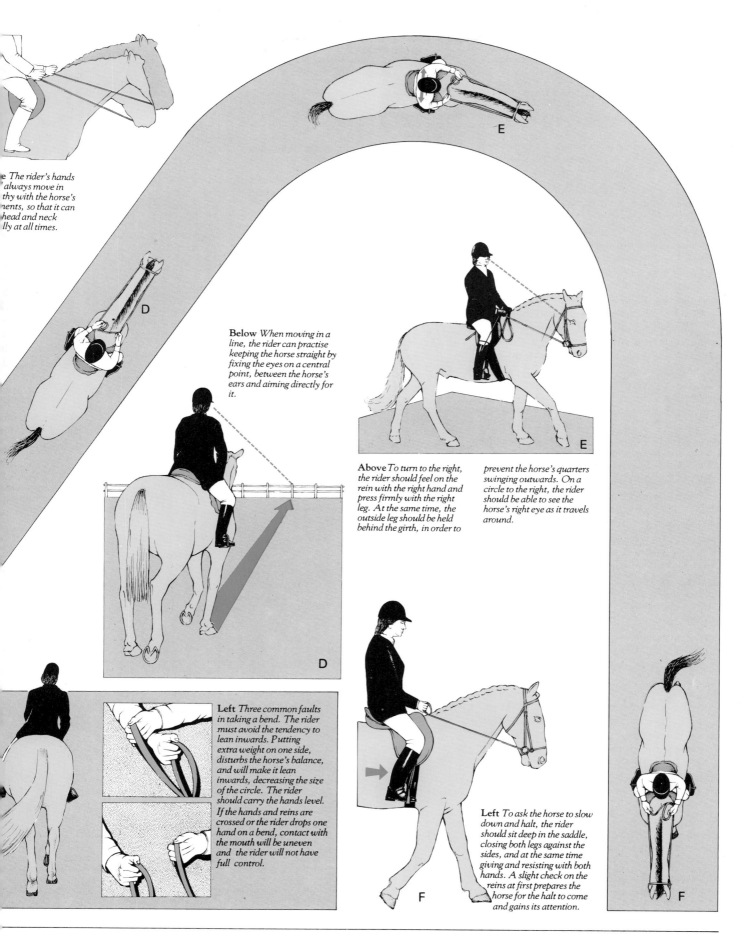

*e The rider's hands
 always move in
 thy with the horse's
 nents, so that it can
 head and neck
 ly at all times.*

Below *When moving in a
line, the rider can practise
keeping the horse straight by
fixing the eyes on a central
point, between the horse's
ears and aiming directly for
it.*

Above *To turn to the right,
the rider should feel on the
rein with the right hand and
press firmly with the right
leg. At the same time, the
outside leg should be held
behind the girth, in order to* *prevent the horse's quarters
swinging outwards. On a
circle to the right, the rider
should be able to see the
horse's right eye as it travels
around.*

Left *Three common faults
in taking a bend. The rider
must avoid the tendency to
lean inwards. Putting
extra weight on one side,
disturbs the horse's balance,
and will make it lean
inwards, decreasing the size
of the circle. The rider
should carry the hands level.
If the hands and reins are
crossed or the rider drops one
hand on a bend, contact with
the mouth will be uneven
and the rider will not have
full control.*

Left *To ask the horse to slow
down and halt, the rider
should sit deep in the saddle,
closing both legs against the
sides, and at the same time
giving and resisting with both
hands. A slight check on the
reins at first prepares the
horse for the halt to come
and gains its attention.*

pace, the best course of action is to sit upright and turn the horse in a circle. Above all, never pull – the horse will only pull back.

Jumping

Riding over jumps is just as much a matter of confidence as the basic process of learning to ride. All elementary jumping techniques should therefore be learned and practised at the trot, before increasing the pace to a controlled canter. With full confidence and control, jumping comes easily; the basic rule is to aid the horse as much as possible and not to hinder it. When jumping, the stirrups should be slightly shortened.

There are many exercises which can be practised by novice jumpers to help them to learn to jump correctly. For the first lessons, the rider should use a neck strap; this lessens the risk of a nervous pupil pulling on the reins and so jabbing the horse in the mouth with the bit. Jumping without stirrups is also an excellent way of improving balance and developing muscles.

The first step to practise is the approach. Sit well down in the saddle, keeping a very close contact with the horse with thighs, knees and calves, and use the seat and legs to build up impulsion. Support the weight of the body by thighs and ankles - not by the hands - and bring the upper part of the body forward so that it is just off the perpendicular. Never look down, always ahead, and ride for the middle of the obstacle, keeping a light even contact on the reins. The rider must allow the horse freedom of the head and neck.

As the horse starts to leave the ground, bring the hands well down on either side of the neck to allow it to lower and stretch, while bending the body forward from the hip upwards over the centre of gravity. The weight of the body comes slightly out of the saddle. Keep the thighs as close to the horse as possible and the lower leg and feet in the same position as for riding on the flat, making sure that they do not go back in the air.

Once in the air, the rider should give the horse the maximum freedom to complete its jump. Follow the horse's mouth with the hands, but maintain contact. Bring the body well forward from the hip and down close to the horse. As the horse starts to come down to land, begin the return to the normal riding position to balance the animal.

One useful exercise to help achieve a good position is to work with cavalletti in the school. The idea is not to present the rider with real fences, but to simulate them, so that he or she can concentrate on position in the saddle and learn to regulate the horse's stride and direction. The cavalletti can be arranged as a box in the centre of the school, or down one side of it.

Right To rise to the trot the rider leans slightly forward and eases the seat from the saddle to go with the movement of the horse.

Below Three common faults in the trot. In the first diagram, the rider is exaggerating the rise; this stiffens the position and leads to loss of balance. Rising with a hollowed back throws the shoulders forward and the seat back. A slouched back is equally, bad, the spine should be straight.

Below The sitting trot is used particularly during schooling. The rider does not rise to the trot but sits deeply, absorbing the bumps with the small of the back.

Left When making th transition from the tro canter, the rider shoul ensure that the horse le on the correct leg. Thi give a balanced and flo movement. The rider sit deeply into the sadd feel the rein in the direc the horse should lead. rider squeezes with bot The outside leg presses behind the girth – this instructs the horse that outside hind leg should first to leave the groun changes to the canter. inside leg is placed on t girth to maintain impu The rider should sit sti follow the natural mov of the canter with the b and hips. The position should be relaxed, but loose in the saddle. The of the canter should al be steady and controll

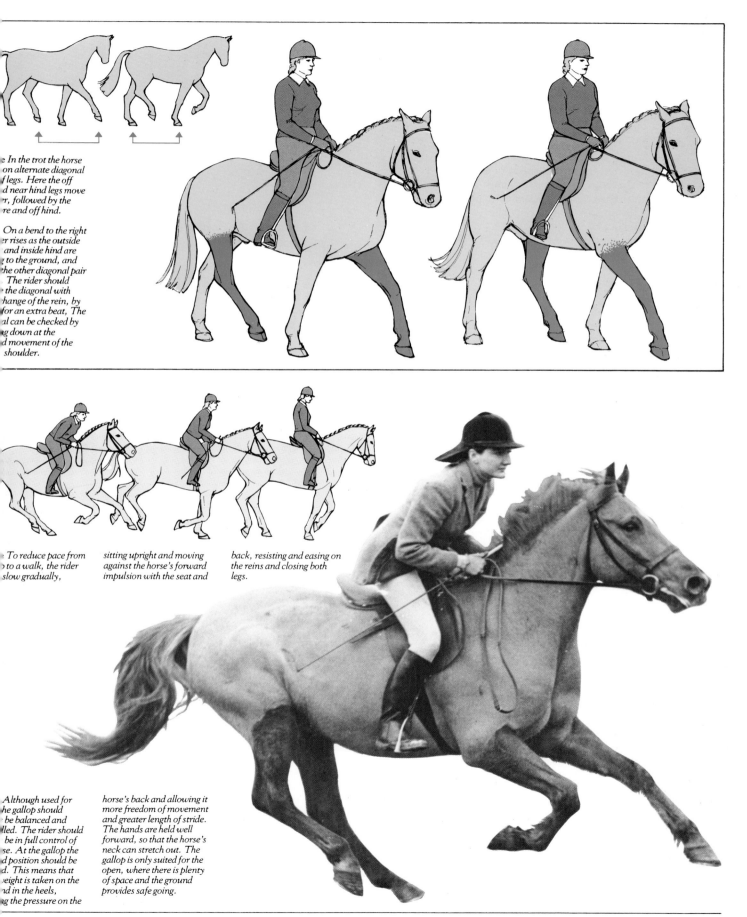

In the trot the horse
on alternate diagonal
f legs. Here the off
d near hind legs move
r, followed by the
re and off hind.

On a bend to the right
r rises as the outside
and inside hind are
g to the ground, and
he other diagonal pair
The rider should
the diagonal with
hange of the rein, by
for an extra beat, The
l can be checked by
g down at the
d movement of the
shoulder.

To reduce pace from
to a walk, the rider
low gradually,

sitting upright and moving
against the horse's forward
impulsion with the seat and

back, resisting and easing on
the reins and closing both
legs.

Although used for
he gallop should
be balanced and
led. The rider should
be in full control of
se. At the gallop the
d position should be
d. This means that
eight is taken on the
d in the heels,
g the pressure on the

horse's back and allowing it
more freedom of movement
and greater length of stride.
The hands are held well
forward, so that the horse's
neck can stretch out. The
gallop is only suited for the
open, where there is plenty
of space and the ground
provides safe going.

Trot around the school in the sitting-jumping position – this means sitting in the same way as for riding on the flat, but with the upper part of the body bent slightly forward. From any corner of the school, turn to approach the box, coming up into the poised jumping position as you do so. This means that the rider raises the seat out of the saddle, taking the weight on thighs, ankles and heels, without using the reins for support. Then, looking directly ahead, ask the horse to trot through the box. On reaching the other side, return to the original position and trot on around the school on the opposite rein to the one first used.

This exercise enables the rider to practice various angles of approach. It also enables the pupil to control the pace of his or her mount while concentrating on developing the right position in the saddle.

Another, more advanced, exercise with cavalletti helps improve rhythm and timing. Cavalletti are placed at various intervals down one side of the school, one set being combined to create a spread element. The rider soon learns to use the leg and seat aids to lengthen and shorten the horse's stride as necessary.

Through the use of such jumping exercises, a good basic technique can be developed. This is essential before going on to more advanced forms of jumping.

Below *The correct forward jumping position can be practised on a stationary or moving horse. The rider adopts a spring-like position to balance and move with the horse over the jump.*

Body bending forward from hips

Straight back

Head up looking in forward direction

Hands and arms forwa[rd] and down side of neck

Knees resting on saddl[e]

Shortened stirrups to allow ankles and knee[s] absorb movement

Weight in heels

Right *Trotting over cavalletti helps the rider develop the forward seat position. This is the correct seat for galloping and jumping.*

Cavalletti are useful for numerous schooling exercises for horse and ri[der] Schooling over cavalletti good preparation both for jumping and riding on the flat.

Right *A more advanced exercise is to slightly extend the distance between poles, remove one, or add a small jump. This teaches horse and rider to judge distance and place their strides. The rider should trot over the first poles and then canter in the direction indicated.*

...ove *The rider should aim ...he centre of the fence and ...o the horse travelling in a ...ight line, controlling with* *the reins and driving with the legs and seat to create power in the hindquarters.*

Above *Schooling over cavalletti strengthens the seat and helps the horse develop a balanced rhythm. The spacing can vary according to the exercise.*

... As it approaches the ...the horse lowers its ...nd neck, to balance its ...off. The rider should ...he seat in light contact ...he saddle.

... On take-off the horse ...ns its neck, raises its ...nd lifts the forehand. ...ngs up and forward off ...cks, head and neck ...hed out. The rider ...l adopt the jumping ...n shown.

... In suspension over ...mp the horse's neck ...ead are stretching ...rd and down, the hind ...thered under the belly. ...der should go naturally ...he horse.

... The horse lands on its ...et, then the hind legs ... . The head comes up ...e neck shortens. The ...nust avoid being left ...l and jerking the ...s mouth.

Chapter Nine

Looking after the horse

Looking after and caring for a horse or pony is perhaps the greatest responsibility any rider faces. Having learned to ride, many riders aim at eventually having a horse of their own. It is worth remembering, though, that looking after a horse unaided – especially if it is stabled – can be a full-time occupation. One answer is to board the horse out at livery, which can be very expensive. Another is to get someone to help out during the day. Most of the other factors involved, such as feeding, watering, exercising and grooming, are mainly matters of common sense, combined with willingness to ask for and take expert advice whenever necessary.

Horses can either be stabled, kept at grass or the two systems can be combined. This means that the horse can run free during the day and have the shelter of a stable by night – except in hot weather, when the procedure should be reversed. Which system is adopted is a matter of choice, practicality, and the type of horse concerned. Ponies, for example, are usually sturdier and more resilient to extremes of climate than horses, particularly thoroughbreds and part-breds. Some thoroughbreds, for instance, should not be left out over the winter. Nor can a horse being worked hard in, say, competitions be really kept fit enough except by being cared for in a stable. At the very least, it must be fed extra food in the field. The amount of extra feeding required should be worked out using the same guidelines as those for a stabled horse. In the case of a field-kept animal, however, the total amount involved should be divided into three, rather than into four.

The combined system can also be adapted to suit the needs of a rider who is using his or her horse frequently, but cannot spare the time to keep it fully stabled. If the horse is

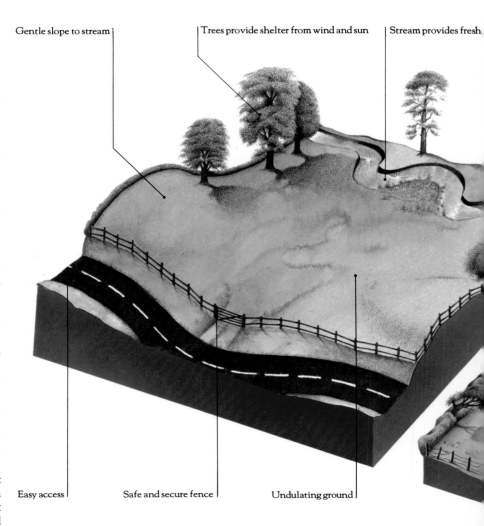

Gentle slope to stream | Trees provide shelter from wind and sun | Stream provides fresh

Easy access | Safe and secure fence | Undulating ground

Below *Horses may roll to relax after being ridden, or just to deal with an irritating itch. Rolling can also be a symptom of colic, but generally it is simply a sign of pure enjoyment.*

Below *The life cycle of the redworm, or large strongyle. The eggs are dropped in the dung of infected horses. Larvae hatch when conditions are warm and moist to be absorbed during grazing. Inside the horse they* reach the gut. Piercing gut wall, they migrate through the internal o and blood vessels, ret to the gut to mature a eggs, which are passed the dung to repeat the

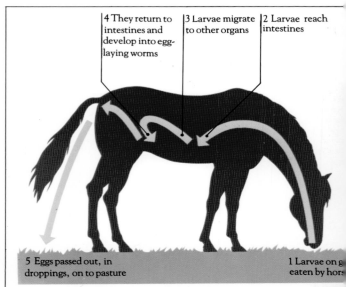

4 They return to intestines and develop into egg-laying worms | 3 Larvae migrate to other organs | 2 Larvae reach intestines

5 Eggs passed out, in droppings, on to pasture | 1 Larvae on g eaten by hors

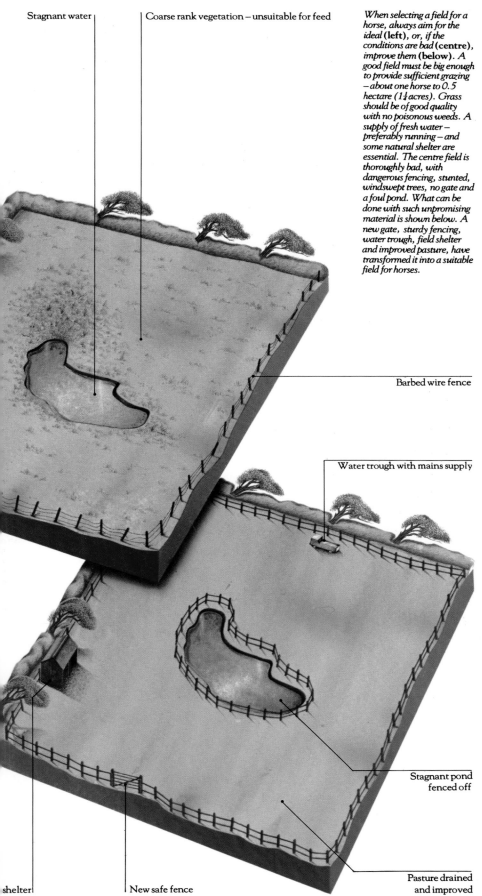

Stagnant water

Coarse rank vegetation – unsuitable for feed

Barbed wire fence

Water trough with mains supply

Stagnant pond fenced off

shelter

New safe fence

Pasture drained and improved

When selecting a field for a horse, always aim for the ideal (left), or, if the conditions are bad (centre), improve them (below). A good field must be big enough to provide sufficient grazing – about one horse to 0.5 hectare (1¼ acres). Grass should be of good quality with no poisonous weeds. A supply of fresh water – preferably running – and some natural shelter are essential. The centre field is thoroughly bad, with dangerous fencing, stunted, windswept trees, no gate and a foul pond. What can be done with such unpromising material is shown below. A new gate, sturdy fencing, water trough, field shelter and improved pasture, have transformed it into a suitable field for horses.

being worked regularly in the spring or summer, say, it is a good idea to bring it into the stable first thing in the morning for the first extra feed that will be required. If the horse is to be ridden more than once that day, the same routine is followed as for the stabled horse until the afternoon, when the animal can be turned out for the night. If only one ride is possible, it can be turned out after the second feed, or, if it cannot be exercised at all, it can be turned out after the first.

Keeping a horse at grass

Looking after a horse kept at grass is less time-consuming than looking after one kept in a stable. Among the pluses are the natural vitamins and the exercise the horse gets, but equal responsibility is still demanded from the owner. Statistics show that more accidents happen to horses left unattended in a field than those in a stable. They can kick each other, get tangled up in fences or gates and quickly lose condition either through illness or just plain bad weather. Also, a horse should be visited every day, even if it is not being ridden. Horses are gregarious creatures – ideally, a horse should be kept in company with others – and require affection. Neglect will only make them difficult, if not impossible, to catch.

The ideal field is large – between six and eight acres. It should be undulating, well-drained, securely fenced by a high-grown hedge reinforced by post-and-rail fencing, with a clump of trees at one end and a gravel-bedded stream to provide fresh water. But this situation is often hard to achieve. It is usually considered that about 1 to 1½ acres per pony is adequate, provided that the grass is kept in good condition. Because horses are 'selective grazers' – that is, they pick and choose where and what they eat – a paddock can become 'horse sick'. Some places will be almost bare of grass, while others will be overgrown with the rank, coarse grasses the horses have found unpalatable. In addition, the ground will almost certainly be infested with parasites, the eggs of which horses pass in their dung. If action is not taken, the horses are sure to become infected with worms. These fall into two categories, of which roundworms are by far the most important and potentially destructive. Of these, the most dangerous are red worms *(Strongyles)*, which, untreated, can lead to severe loss of condition. Even though the horse is well-fed, it looks thin and 'poor', with a staring coat; in the worst cases, anaemia may develop or indigestion, colic and enteritis.

As far as an infected horse is concerned, the treatment is regular worming, but it is far better to tackle the problem at source by making sure that the field is maintained properly. A large field should be subdivided so that one area can be rested while another is being grazed. Ideally, sheep or cattle should be introduced on the the resting areas, as they will eat the tall grasses the horses have rejected. They will also help reduce worm infestation, as their digestive juices kill horse worms. Harrowing is also essential as it aerates the soil, encouraging new grass to grow, and also scatters the harmful dung. Failing this, the manure must be collected at least twice a week and transferred to a compost heap.

Mowing after grazing, coupled with the use of a balanced fertilizer, also helps keep a field in good condition, but horses should not be returned to their grazing too soon after it has been so treated. If in doubt, allow three weeks.

Bots are another problem for field-kept horses, for which veterinary treatment is necessary.

Food, water and shelter

All grassland is composed of a mixture of grasses and other plants. Some have little nutritional value, though the horse may well like them, but the three most important are Perennial Rye Grass *(Lolium perennae)*, Cocksfoot *(Dactylis glomerata)* and Timothy *(Phleum pratense)*. Some White Clover *(Trifolium repens)* is useful, but beware of a heavily-clovered pasture. This may prove too rich and lead to digestive problems.

Even if clover is not present, grass itself can cause problems. This is especially the case in the spring when excessive greed can lead a horse to put on too much weight, and sometimes to the painful disease called laminitis, or founder. Also, a horse or pony can only exist on grass alone for the summer months – from about the end of April to the beginning of September. By October, supplementary feeding becomes essential. Start off with hay and then provide oats or beans, if required. The more refined the breed, the more extra feeding that will be necessary.

Water is another essential; field-kept horses must have easy access to a plentiful supply of fresh water. Remember that a horse drinks about 35 litres (8 gal) a day. If the water supply is in the form of a stream, check that it can be reached by means of a gentle slope; if the banks are steep or muddy, it is safer to fence the stream off and provide a water trough instead. Similarly, always fence off stagnant pools and ponds.

The most convenient form of trough is one connected to a mains water supply, controlled either by a tap or automatic valve. Custom-made troughs are on the market, but cheaper alternatives are an old domestic cistern or bath. Remember to remove all sharp

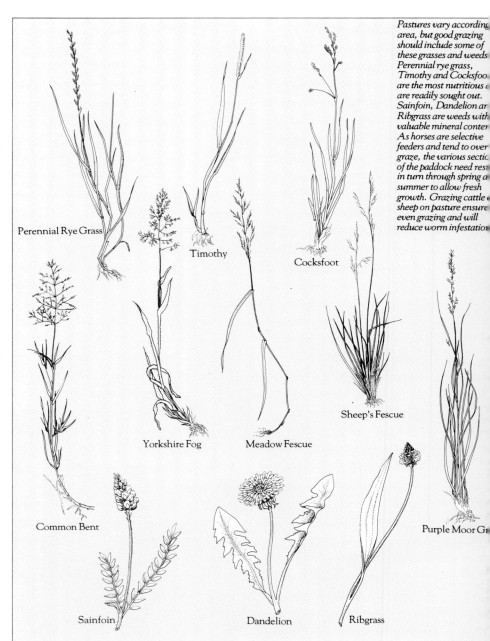

Perennial Rye Grass
Timothy
Cocksfoot
Yorkshire Fog
Meadow Fescue
Sheep's Fescue
Common Bent
Purple Moor Gr
Sainfoin
Dandelion
Ribgrass

Pastures vary according area, but good grazing should include some of these grasses and weeds Perennial rye grass, Timothy and Cocksfoo are the most nutritious are readily sought out. Sainfoin, Dandelion an Ribgrass are weeds with valuable mineral conter As horses are selective feeders and tend to over graze, the various sectio of the paddock need res in turn through spring a summer to allow fresh growth. Grazing cattle sheep on pasture ensure even grazing and will reduce worm infestation

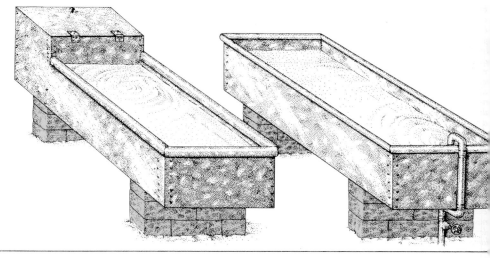

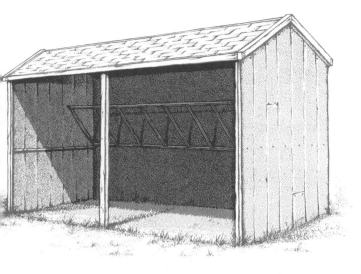

Left *A shelter is an essential addition to any field – even one with trees and hedges – as horses need one to escape from wind and cold in winter. In summer it provides shade, coolness and protection from insects. In cold or wet weather, hay can be conveniently fed in a rack or hay-net within the shelter.*

Below *Post-and-rail fencing made of good timber is the safest kind. It must be firm and strongly built. Trees and hedges provide a natural wind-break and shelter from the rain. They also shade the horse from the sun.*

Fencing and gates

Sound and strong fencing is essential for safety. A fence must be high enough to prevent horses from jumping over it – 1.3m (3ft 9in) is the absolute minimum. Bars must also be fitted; two rails are usually adequate for containing horses, with the bottom one about 4.5cm (18in) from the ground. Small ponies, however, can wriggle through incredibly small gaps, so a third or even a fourth rail should be added for them. This type of fencing is known as post-and-rail, or 'Man O' War'.

Of all the types of fencing available, timber is the safest but most expensive. Hedges run a close second, but should be regularly checked, as otherwise a determined pony might well push his way through. Gaps can be reinforced with timber, but avoid filling a gap with wire. Concealed by a hedge in summer, it could be hard for a horse to see and so could lead to accidental injury. Stone walls are also attractive, but, they, too, will need regular checking, especially after a hard winter when frost may have loosened the mortar.

However, wire is perfectly adequate as fencing on its own, as long as the correct type of wire is used. Avoid barbed wire, chicken mesh or sheep wire and use a plain heavy gauge galvinized wire instead. For safety and effectiveness, the strands must be stretched so that they are evenly taut and then stapled to the inside of the posts. Strong stretcher posts, should be positioned at regular intervals. Check regularly for signs of weakness, such as loose posts, broken wires or sprung staples. If each strand of wire ends in an eye bolt attached to the end posts, the wire can be tightened from time to time.

Gates are another safety factor. The only criterion is that they should be easy for people to open and close, but that it should be impossible for the horse to do so. A five-

ections, such as taps, and to give the
de a thorough cleaning before putting
use. If there is no piped water supply, use
se or fill the trough with buckets.

uckets alone are totally insufficient. A
se can easily drink a whole bucket of water
ne go, and, in any case, a bucket can all
easily be kicked over. Daily checks of the
er supply are vital, especially in winter,
n ice may form and must be broken. A
d's rubber ball left floating on the surface
trough will help to keep the water ice-
, except when frosts are severe, when the
must be broken daily.

/inter and summer also bring the problem
helter. From a horse's point of view, the
st elements are wind, rain and sun. Even
e field possesses a natural windbreak, an
icial shelter is a good addition. It need
be complicated – a three-sided shed the
of a large loose box is usually adequate.
e sure that the open side does not face
sun.

eft *Self-filling trough*
automatic valve in
sed section and **left**
h with inlet pipe close-
and tap recessed
ith. Both are of safe
n with no sharp edges or
ctions. Site a trough on
drained ground to avoid
ned mud and away from
lling leaves of trees.
ghs should be emptied
leaned regularly. If ice
s in the winter it should
oken daily.

t Suitable types of
ng. From the left: post
rail, post and wire, rail
vire combined and dry
e wall. Check the
ness of wire fences
arly and inspect walls
amage after frosts.

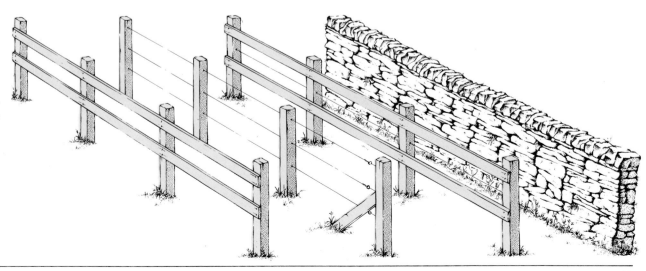

Yew

Tutu

Castor oil plant

False acacia

Privet

Deadly nightshade

Horsetail

Ragwort

Hemlock

Ngaio

Purple milk-vetch

Avocado

Rangiora

Yellow star-thistle

Oleander

Buckthorn

St. John's wort

Many trees, shrubs and plants are poisonous to horses. **Above** are some commonly found in various parts of the world. Great care should be taken to check the pasture and to eradicate any that may appear in fields where horses are kept.

Some plants remain poisonous even when the plant itself dies. Sprayed and uprooted plants should not be left to wither in the field, but should be removed and burned. Many plants are just as poisonous after drying and long storage.

Hay and bedding should, therefore, be examined and any harmful plants removed. Horses will eat a toxic plant, like ragwort, when it is fed to them dried in hay, although they will not touch it growing in the field because of its bitter taste, which, however, disappears with drying.

Fortunately, horses are not attracted to some of the most toxic plants. They will only eat deadly nightshade, for example, if virtually starving. However, some equally poisonous ones, like yew and privet do get eaten occasionally.

Garden hedges and their clippings can also be a source of poisoning. Make sure that a horse does not snatch at them while out riding. Poisonous, exotic plants, less easy to identify than familiar native ones, may grow in gardens and parks too.

Poison can be quickly fatal, or it may take as long as a month to work. Symptoms include loss of condition, lack of appetite, jaundice, staggering and nervous spasms. The horse may have a normal temperature throughout the period.

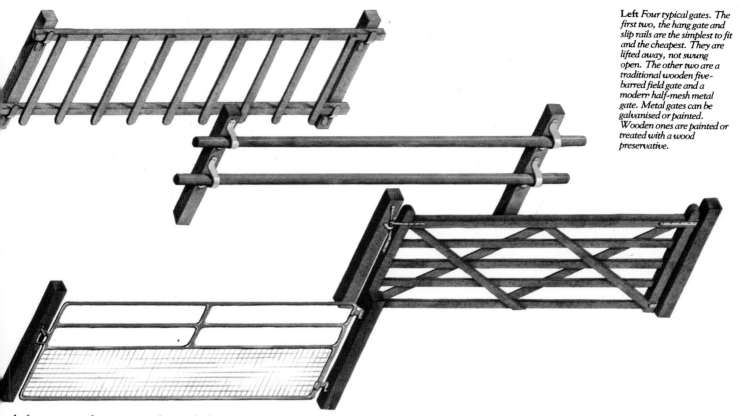

Left *Four typical gates. The first two, the hang gate and slip rails are the simplest to fit and the cheapest. They are lifted away, not swung open. The other two are a traditional wooden five-barred field gate and a modern half-mesh metal gate. Metal gates can be galvanised or painted. Wooden ones are painted or treated with a wood preservative.*

red farm gate, hung just clear of the
und so that it swings freely when un-
hed, is ideal. It should be fitted with
er a self-closing latch, or with a simple
in fitted with a snap lock and fastened to
latching post. Slip rails and hang-gates
cheaper alternatives.

rning out', exercise and grooming
ore a pony or horse is turned out into a
d, always check it carefully. Inspect the
and fencing, strengthening any weak
its. Make certain that there are no
onous plants either in the field or within
h of the fence. See that there is an
quate supply of water, and check that
e are no man-made hazards, such as
en bottles, tin cans and plastic bags lying
it, which could injure the horse; a pony
die if it swallows a plastic bag, for exam-
Have any rabbit holes filled in to avoid
risk of a cantering horse catching its feet
ne, falling, and perhaps breaking a leg.
/hen you are satisfied with the state of
field, turn the horse out. If it is not to be
en for some time, say over the winter,
e the shoes removed. This will lessen the
ger of injury in the event of any kicking
test with other horses kept in the field.
efore exercising, always check the horse
cuts, bruises and other injuries. This pro-
ire should also be carried out during the
y visits. Pick out the feet, noting the
dition of the shoes. Also check the teeth

regularly. Left unattended, they can develop
rough edges, which make eating difficult. If
this happens, they will need to be filed.

Remember, too, that the horse will be in
what is known as 'grass condition'. Its soft
muscles and its extra layers of fat will make it
incapable of any prolonged period of hard
work, without sweating heavily and exhibiting other signs of distress. Forcing a horse to
do so will only damage wind and limbs. If, as
at the start of the school holidays, say, the
horse is being ridden frequently for the first
time in some months, it is a good idea to start
a supplementary feeding programme a few
weeks before, as grass is not a high-energy
food. In any case, exercise should always be
gradual, slowly building up from walking to a
full exercise programme.

After exercise, the horse may well be sweaty, particularly if the animal has a long,
shaggy coat. It is best to turn it out immediately and not to wait until the sweat has
completely dried, or there is the danger of
colds or, in extreme cases, colic. Conversely,
in winter remember that the grease in a
horse's coat helps to keep it warm, so restrict
after-exercise grooming to remove any mud.
A clipped horse should always wear a New
Zealand rug in the field in the winter.

Groom with a dandy brush, taking care to
get rid of all dried and caked mud and any
sweat marks. Groom the mane and tail with a
body brush and, finally, sponge out eyes,
nostrils and dock.

Gate fastenings must be impossible for horses to open, but simple for human beings. Here are three secure kinds. **Top** *A simple catch with a lug* *held in a notch.* **Centre** *A catch with a release mechanism.* **Below** *A spring catch with a bar held forward against a retaining hook.*

The stabled horse

There are two main reasons for keeping a horse in a stable. The first is that the horse may be too well-bred to live out in all weathers, without seriously losing condition. The second is the amount of work the rider requires the horse to do. If a horse is being ridden a great deal, it must be fit enough to cope with its rider's demands without showing signs of distress, such as excessive sweating and blowing. Such a degree of fitness takes time to achieve and can only be maintained in a stable.

The ideal stable is also often easier to provide than the ideal field. It should be roomy, warm, well-ventilated yet draught-free, easy to keep clean, have good drainage and be vermin proof. It should face away from prevailing winds and have a pleasant outlook – preferably on to a stable yard or at least an area where something is often going on. The horse could be spending some 22 hours a day in the stable and unless there is something to hold its attention, it may well become bored. This can lead, in turn, to the development of vices, such as weaving (rocking from side to side), box walking, (a constant restless wandering around the box), or crib-biting (gripping the manger or stable door with the teeth and drawing in a sharp breath). The first two vices may lead to loss of condition, the third to broken wind.

Buying, renting or building

Any stable, whether it is bought, rented, converted or specially built, must conform to certain basic standards. If a stable is being converted, say, from a garage or barn, or being built from scratch, make sure that these standards are followed.

In the latter case, an architect can either design a stable to your individual specifications or one can be bought ready-made. This type of stable is usually delivered in sections and erected on a pre-prepared concrete base. But, before committing yourself, always check your plans out with the local authority concerned. They may well have to grant planning permission, and will certainly have regulations governing such crucial health factors as drainage.

The choice of site is very important. As far as possible, it should be level and well-drained, with easy access to the electricity and water supplies. The stable itself should be situated with the doorway facing the sun and the general lay-out should be planned to have all the essential elements – stable, feed room, tack room and manure heap – conveniently close together.

The stable can either be a straight stall or a loose box; the latter is much more commonly used today, particularly in the UK and USA.

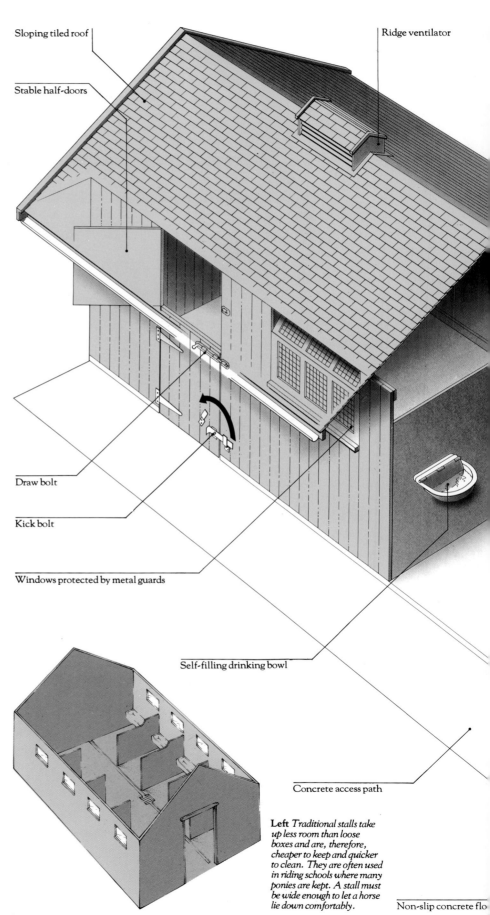

Sloping tiled roof

Ridge ventilator

Stable half-doors

Draw bolt

Kick bolt

Windows protected by metal guards

Self-filling drinking bowl

Concrete access path

Left Traditional stalls take up less room than loose boxes and are, therefore, cheaper to keep and quicker to clean. They are often used in riding schools where many ponies are kept. A stall must be wide enough to let a horse lie down comfortably.

Non-slip concrete flo

rner manger | Kick board | Louvred ventilator

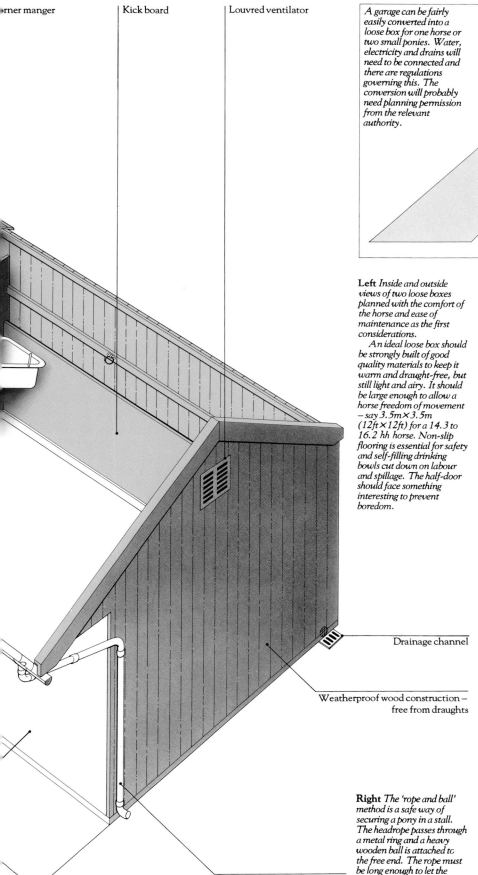

Left *Inside and outside views of two loose boxes planned with the comfort of the horse and ease of maintenance as the first considerations.*

An ideal loose box should be strongly built of good quality materials to keep it warm and draught-free, but still light and airy. It should be large enough to allow a horse freedom of movement – say 3.5m × 3.5m (12ft × 12ft) for a 14.3 to 16.2 hh horse. Non-slip flooring is essential for safety and self-filling drinking bowls cut down on labour and spillage. The half-door should face something interesting to prevent boredom.

Drainage channel

Weatherproof wood construction – free from draughts

PVC gutters and drainage pipes

The chief advantage of a stall is that it can be relatively small, so making cleaning easier. But, as it is open at one end, the horse has to be kept tied up. The usual method is known as the rope and ball system, where the halter rope is passed through a ring on the manger and attached to a hardwood ball resting on the horses' bed. This helps to safeguard the horse against possible injury, while still allowing it some freedom of movement.

Most horse owners prefer the loose box, as it allows the horse far more freedom to move around and so more comfort. Size is here all-important; cramming a 16hh hunter into a loose box built for a Shetland pony can only lead to trouble. As a rough guide, 3½m (12ft) square is probably the optimum size, rising to 4m (13ft) for horses over 16 hands. It is worth bearing in mind that a child's first pony, say, will be outgrown in time, so the bigger the box the better.

Boxes should be square rather than oblong, so that the horse can more easily determine the amount of room it has to lie down or to roll. The box must be big enough to minimize the risk of the horse being 'cast' – that is, rolling over and being trapped on its back by the legs striking the wall. In its struggles to get up, the horse may injure itself severely. The ceiling height should allow plenty of clearance for the horse's head; 3m (10ft) is the bare minimum.

Brick and stone are both durable and at-

Right *The 'rope and ball' method is a safe way of securing a pony in a stall. The headrope passes through a metal ring and a heavy wooden ball is attached to the free end. The rope must be long enough to let the horse lie down comfortably.*

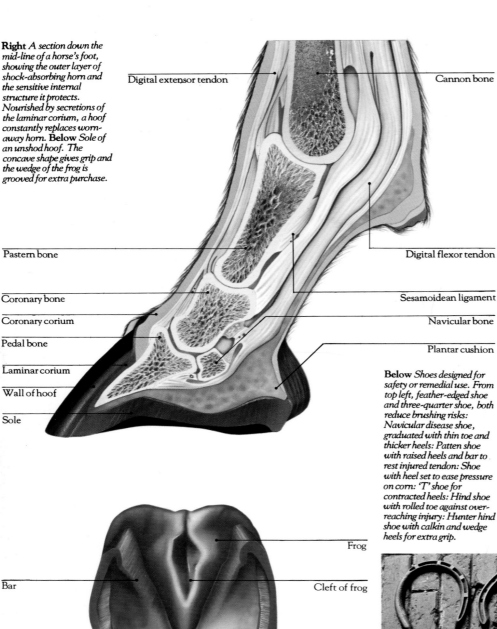

Right *A section down the mid-line of a horse's foot, showing the outer layer of shock-absorbing horn and the sensitive internal structure it protects. Nourished by secretions of the laminar corium, a hoof constantly replaces worn-away horn.* **Below** *Sole of an unshod hoof. The concave shape gives grip and the wedge of the frog is grooved for extra purchase.*

Digital extensor tendon

Cannon bone

Pastern bone

Digital flexor tendon

Coronary bone

Sesamoidean ligament

Coronary corium

Navicular bone

Pedal bone

Plantar cushion

Laminar corium

Wall of hoof

Sole

Below *Shoes designed for safety or remedial use. From top left, feather-edged shoe and three-quarter shoe, both reduce brushing risks: Navicular disease shoe, graduated with thin toe and thicker heels: Patten shoe with raised heels and bar to rest injured tendon: Shoe with heel set to ease pressure on corn: 'T' shoe for contracted heels: Hind shoe with rolled toe against over-reaching injury: Hunter hind shoe with calkin and wedge heels for extra grip.*

Frog

Bar

Cleft of frog

Sole

Point of frog

Wall

White line

Toe

tractive building materials, but breeze blo[ck] solid concrete blocks or timber may cheaper. Both walls and roof should be in[su]lated, which will keep the stable war[m] when the weather is cold and cooler whe[n it] is hot.

The floor must be hard-wearing, n[on-]absorbent and slip-proof. A well compac[ted] concrete base is perfectly adequate, provi[ded] that it is made with a loam-free aggregate [and] treated with a proprietary non-slip coat[ing] after laying. Alternatively, roughen the [sur]face with a scraper before the concrete s[ets.] Make sure that the floor slopes slightly [– a] slope of about one in sixty from front to [back] is ideal – so that urine can drain away eas[ily.] An alternative is to cut a narrow gulley al[ong] one inside wall leading to a channel in [the] wall and so to an outside drain. The chan[nel] should be fitted with a trap to stop rats get[ting] in and cleared of dirt and debris daily.

The usual type of stable door is mad[e of] two halves, the top half being kept open [for] ventilation. This should be planned to ens[ure] that the horse gets plenty of fresh air bu[t no] draughts, as these can lead to it catch[ing] colds and chills. The best position fo[r a] window is high on the wall opposite the d[oor] so that sufficient cross-ventilation can [be] provided. Make sure it is fitted with shat[ter-]proof glass, and covered with an iron g[rill.] Otherwise, vents can be built in the roo[f to] allow stale air to escape. They should [be] protected by cowls.

Doors must be wide and high enough f[or a] horse to pass through without the ris[k of] injury; 1.5m (4ft) is the minimum wi[dth,] 2.25m (7½ft) the minimum height. M[ake] sure that the door opens outwards so [that] access is easy and that strong bolts are fi[tted] to both halves of the door. On the l[ower] door, two bolts are necessary – an ordi[nary] sliding bolt at the top and a kick bolt, o[per]ated by the foot, at the bottom. The top [half] needs only one bolt. Remember that [the] material used must be strong enough to w[ith]stand the kicking of a restless horse. In[side] the stable, kicking boards, usually cut f[rom]

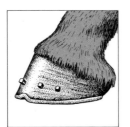

Re-shoeing is needed when the clenches have risen through the hoof wall.

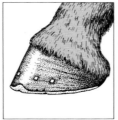

Here the shoe has worn extremely thin and should be replaced.

This shoe is loose and likely to be cast. The hoof must be re-shod.

A newly-shod hoof showing well-positioned clenches and a close-fitting shoe.

...rier displays his skill in
...eing. After cutting
...es he removes the old
...ith pincers (above)
...ms away overgrown
...with a drawing knife
...). The farrier's forge
...ols are seen (below
...The new shoe is forged
...ight) and fitted hot to
...unevenness (below
...The new clenches
...oothed off with a rasp
...tting (extreme

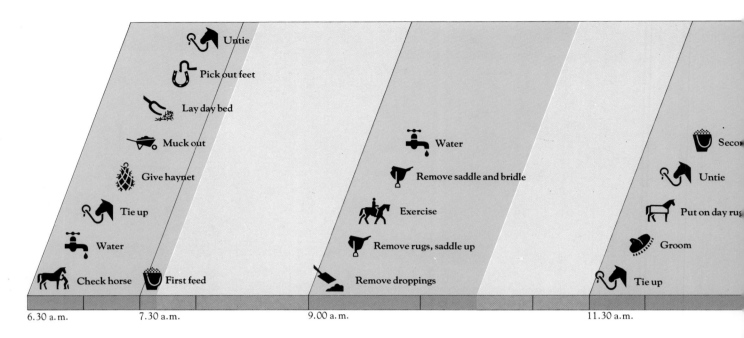

Untie
Pick out feet
Lay day bed
Muck out
Give haynet
Tie up
Water
Check horse   First feed

Water
Remove saddle and bridle
Exercise
Remove rugs, saddle up
Remove droppings

Seco[...]
Untie
Put on day rug[...]
Groom
Tie up

6.30 a.m.   7.30 a.m.   9.00 a.m.   11.30 a.m.

hardwood and some 5ft high, will help with this problem.

Electricity is the only adequate means of lighting. The light itself should be protected by safety glass or an iron grill and all wiring should be housed in galvanized conduits beyond the horse's reach. Switches must be waterproof, properly insulated, and, whenever possible, fitted outside the stable.

Shoeing the horse

Any horse being ridden regularly on a hard surface, such as a road, must be shod, or the wall of the hoof will be worn down quicker than it can grow. This will cause friction, soreness and lameness. Hardy ponies, working lightly and solely on grass, can do without shoes, but their hooves should still be looked at regularly by a blacksmith.

Inspections should take place at regular four to six week intervals. The signs that a horse needs to be reshod are a loose shoe; one that has been 'cast' (lost); a shoe wearing thin; one in which the clenches (securing nails) have risen and stand out from the wall; and if the foot is overlong and out of shape.

Horses can be either hot-shod or cold-shod. In hot-shoeing, the red hot shoe is shaped to the exact size of the hoof. In the latter, the shoes are pre—cast and fitted cold. Whichever method is used by the blacksmith, always check the following points after shoeing has been completed.

Make sure that the shoe has been made to fit the foot – not vice versa. Check that the shoe is suitable for the work you want the horse to do, and that the weight of the shoes is in the right proportion to the horse's size.

As a rough guide, a set of shoes for a h[...] should usually weigh around 2kg (4½lb). [...] at the heel and toe of the foot to make [...] that its length has been reduced evenly. [...] that the foot is in contact with the gro[...] Check that the right size and number of [...] have been used and the clenches are corr[...] formed, in line and the right distance up[...] wall. Finally, make sure the clip fits sec[...] and that there is no gap showing between[...] newly-fitted shoe and the hoof.

Fixtures and fittings

The basic rule to follow is the fewer fit[...] the better, to minimize the risk of pos[...] injury. The only essential is a means of t[...] the horse up. Normally, this consists of[...] rings, fixed to bolts which pass right thro[...] the stable wall. One ring should be at w[...]

Mucking out is the first job done each morning in the stable. Soiled straw and dung are separated from the cleaner portions of the night bedding by tossing with a fork. The cleaner straw is then heaped at the back of the stall to be used again.

The soiled straw and droppings are put into a barrow for removal to the manure heap. In fine weather much of the night bedding can be carried outside to air in the sun. This will freshen it up, restore its springiness and make it last longer.

When the bulk of soiled straw has been removed and the cleaner straw reserved, the floor should be swept clean of remaining dirt. It should be left bare to dry off and air for a while. The clean straw is then spread as a soft floor-covering for the day.

The soiled straw and dung are tossed on[...] manure heap. Take care to throw the m[...] right on to the top of the heap, as a neatl[...] heap decomposes more efficiently. Beat[...] heap down with a shovel after each load[...] keep it firm and dense.

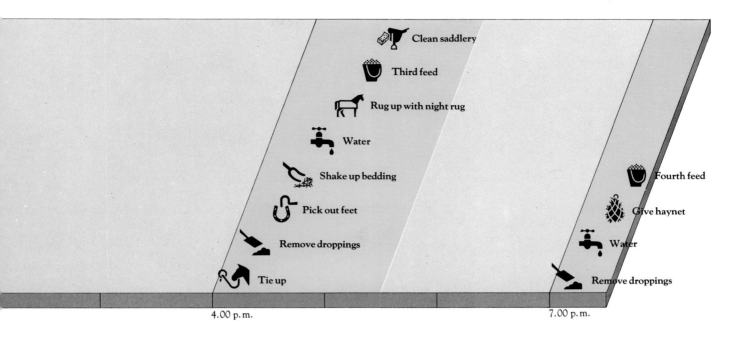

Clean saddlery

Third feed

Rug up with night rug

Water

Shake up bedding

Pick out feet

Remove droppings

Tie up

Fourth feed

Give haynet

Water

Remove droppings

4.00 p.m.   7.00 p.m.

The daily routine for stabled horse, g the order of work times at which t tasks are carried e feeding schedule y according to the size and work-load of individual horses. Many owners prefer the less time-consuming combined system, in which horses spend part of the day out in the field.

t and the other at head height. All fittings and fixtures are a matter of idual preference.

ed mangers positioned at breast level ecured either along a wall or in a corner e loose box are found in many stables. should be fitted with lift-out bowls to ate cleaning and have well-rounded rs. The space beneath should be boxed prevent the horse from injuring itself on anger's rim – this space makes a good ge place for a grooming kit. However, a iner on the floor, which is heavy gh not to be knocked over and which be removed as soon as the horse has ed its feed is adequate.

ted hay racks are found in some stables, ney are not really advisable. They force orse to eat with its head held unnatural-gh and hayseeds may fall into its eyes. best way of feeding hay is to use a et. It is also the least wasteful, as haynets t accurate weighing. The net should s be hung well clear of the ground and tened with a quick-release knot to one tying-up rings.

ater is as essential to the horse in the as for a horse in the field. Automatic ing bowls are one way of providing a ant supply – but never position them lose to the haynet and manger, or they et blocked by surplus food. Buckets are ctory, provided, again, that the bucket

is heavy enough not to be accidentally upset. Use of a bucket means that it is possible to control the amount of water the horse drinks – important after exercise, for instance, when a 'heated' horse must not drink too much – and also to check how much it is drinking more easily. This is especially useful in cases of suspected illness.

Stable routine

The daily programme for looking after a stabled horse takes up a great deal of time. All the stages have to be carried out, though some, such as the number of feeds, will vary from case to case. Skimping will only lead to problems later.

1. Tie up the horse and check over for injuries which may have occurred during the night. Replenish its water, if necessary, and fill the haynet. Muck out the stable. Quarter the horse thoroughly. Pick out feet with a hoof pick. Lay the day bed.
2. First feed.
3. Allow the horse time to digest – at least 1¼ hours – and then saddle up and exercise. On returning to the stable, refill water bucket and remove droppings.
4. Tie up and groom thoroughly. Put on day rug (blanket) if used. Check water again and refill the haynet. Give the second feed.
5. Pick out feet again and remove droppings. Shake up bedding, replace the day rug (blanket) with a night rug, and replenish water.
6. Third feed. Clean tack.
7. Remove droppings, and lay the night-bed. Replenish the water and re-fill the haynet. Final feed. Put on a night rug (blanket), if worn.

The only way of short-circuiting this

routine is to adopt the combined system of care. This has considerable advantages in time and labour, but is not suited to all horses, especially those being worked hard. Otherwise, board or livery is the only alternative. Some riding schools offer what is termed half-livery; this means that the horse gets free board in exchange for use as a hack. The risk is that the horse may be roughly treated by inexperienced riders even in a supervised lesson. Full livery is extremely expensive; in the UK it can cost as much as £30 a week. In either case, always check that the stable you choose is officially approved by a recognized riding authority.

The principal areas of a horse-owner's day, however, are not as complex as they seem. They can be broken down into various tasks, all of which are relatively simple to carry out.

Bedding down and mucking out

The purpose of bedding is to give the horse something comfortable to lie on, insulate the box, absorb moisture and prevent the horse's legs jarring on the hard stable floor. It must be kept clean – hence the daily task of mucking out. This is usually done first thing in the morning, and, with practice, can be carried out quite quickly.

Straw is the best possible bedding material, though other kinds can be substituted. Wheat straw is excellent, because it is absorbent and lasts well. Barley straw may contain awns, which can irritate the horse's skin. Oat straw should be avoided, because horses tend to eat it and it tends to become saturated.

Of the substitutes, peat makes a soft, well-insulated bed; it is also the least inflammable of all bedding materials. However, it is heavy to work. Damp patches and droppings must

Wheat straw (left) m...
*ideal bedding. It is wa...
comfortable, easy to
handle and absorbent...
Wood shavings (cent...
make cheaper bedding
are often laid on a bas...
sawdust to reduce
dampness. Droppings
have to be removed
frequently. Peat moss
(right) makes a soft b...
but tends to be dusty u...
first laid down and ne...
frequent raking.*

be removed at once, replacing with fresh peat when necessary. The whole bed requires forking over and raking every day, as the material can cause foot problems if it becomes damp and compacted.

Wood shavings and sawdust are usually cheap but can be difficult to get rid of. Both need to be checked carefully to see that they do not contain nails, screws, paint, oil or other foreign matter. Wood shavings can be used alone, but note that they can cause foot problems if they become damp and compacted. Sawdust is best used in combination with other materials.

There are two types of bed – the day bed and the night bed. The first is a thin layer of bedding laid on the floor for use during the day; the second is thicker and more comfortable for use at night. With materials such as peat or wood shavings, laying the bed is very simple. Just empty the contents of the sack on the floor and rake them level, building up the material slightly higher around the walls to minimize draughts.

Laying a straw bed requires slightly more skill. As the straw will be compacted in the bale, it has to be shaken up so that the stalks separate, and laid so that the finished bed is aerated, springy and free from lumps. A pitchfork is best for the purpose.

Some owners prefer the deep litter method of bedding, where fresh straw is added to the existing bed every day, removing only droppings and sodden straw beforehand. After a time, the bed becomes as much as two feet deep, well-compacted below and soft and resilient on the surface. At the end of a month, the whole bed is removed and restarted. This method should be used only in loose boxes with first-rate drainage. In addition, the feet must be picked out regularly, as otherwise there is a major risk of disease.

Feeding and fodder

Heredity has given the horse a very small stomach for its size and the food it eats takes up to 48 hours to pass through the digestive system. This system is in itself complex. It depends not only on the right amounts of food at the correct time for smoothness of

Laying a night bed of straw requires some skill. First **(above)** *clean straw saved from the day bed is tossed* *and shaken well with a pitchfork before being spread evenly over the floor as a foundation.*

Next new straw is taken from the compressed bale and shaken well to free the stalks and make the bed *springy. The floor must be thickly and evenly covered to encourage the horse to lie down.*

Last the straw is banked up higher and more thickly around the sides of the box. This cuts down draughts, *keeps the horse warmer and gives the animal extra protection from injury during the night.*

operation, but also on an adequate supp... water and plenty of exercise. In the ... horses drink twice a day, usually at dawn... dusk. In between, their day is divided ... periods of grazing, rest and exercise. ... kept horses can duplicate this pattern to ... extent, but stabled horses cannot do so.

It is essential to follow a basic set of fee... rules. Otherwise the horse's sensitive d... tion may well be upset, encouraging the ... of indigestion, impaction, formation o... in the stomach or sudden colic attacks.

The basic rules are to feed little and o... with plenty of bulk food – grass or hay ... according to the work you expect the ho... do. Make no sudden change in the ty... food, or in the routine of feeding, onc... diet and time has been established. Al... water the horse before feeding, so that ... gested food is not washed out of the stom... Never work a horse hard straight after ... ing or if its stomach is full of grass. L... digest for $1\frac{1}{4}$ hours or so, otherwise the... stomach will impair breathing. Simi... never feed a horse immediately after ... work, when it will be 'heated'.

The staple diet of the horse is grass, ... the case of a stabled horse, hay. The best... is seed hay, usually a mixture of rye gras... clover, which is specially grown as part... crop-rotation programme. Meadow ... also commonly used, comes from perma... pasture and so can vary in quality. The... way of judging this is by appearance, s... and age. Hay should smell sweet, be sli... greenish in colour and at least six months... Blackened, mouldy or wet hay should n... be used as fodder.

Of the other types of hay, clover is too... to be fed to a horse on its own, and the ... rule applies to alfalfa, or lucerne, comm... the USA and Canada. Alfalfa is extre... rich in protein, so feed small quantities ... you can judge how much is needed.

Concentrates for work

Ponies and horses in regular, hard work... additional food to keep them in a fit, ... muscled condition. In other words, they... energy rather than fatness. This is prov...

he feeding of concentrated foodstuffs, lly known as 'short' or 'hard' feeds. Of e, the best is oats, which can be bruised, ned or rolled to aid digestion. Manufac- l horse cubes or pellets are a useful alter- ve.

ats have no equal as a natural high pro- energy-giving food and are an essential of the diet for all horses in work. Good ty oats are plump and short, and pale , silver grey or dark chocolate in colour. y should have a hard, dry feel and no sour . Take care, however, not to feed to n, or a horse may speedily become un- ageable. This caution applies particular- children's ponies, which are often better ithout oats at all.

ibes and pellets are manufactured from us grains and also usually contain some meal, sweeteners such as molasses or treacle, extra vitamins and minerals. Their nutritional value is about two-thirds that of oats, but they are less heating and so ideal for ponies. Their chief advantage is that they provide a balanced diet on their own, as they do not have to be mixed with other food-stuffs. However, they are expensive.

Other grains can be used in addition or as alternatives to oats, but they are all of lesser quality. Flaked maize (corn) is used in many parts of the world as a staple feed. It is high in energy value, but low in protein and mineral content. Like oats, it can be heating for ponies and is usually fed to animals in slow, regular work, such as riding school hacks. Boiled barley helps to fatten up a horse or pony in poor condition and is a useful addi-tion to the diet of a stale, or overworked horse. Beans, too, are nutritious, but, again, because of their heating effect, they should be fed sparingly, either whole, split or boiled.

Other useful foods

Bran makes a useful addition to a horse's diet, as it helps provide roughage. It is either fed dry mixed up with oats – the combined mix-ture should be slightly dampened – or in the form of a mash. This is a good 'pick me up' for a tired or sick horse. The mash is made by mixing $\frac{2}{3}$ of a bucket of bran with $\frac{1}{3}$ of boiling water and is fed to the horse as soon as it is cool enough to eat. Always remove any re-mains, as the mash can quickly go rancid. Oatmeal gruel is an alternative. This is made by pouring boiling water on to porridge oats and leaving to cool. Use enough water to make the gruel thin enough in consistency for the horse to drink.

Linseed, prepared as a jelly, mash or tea, is fed to horses in winter to improve condition

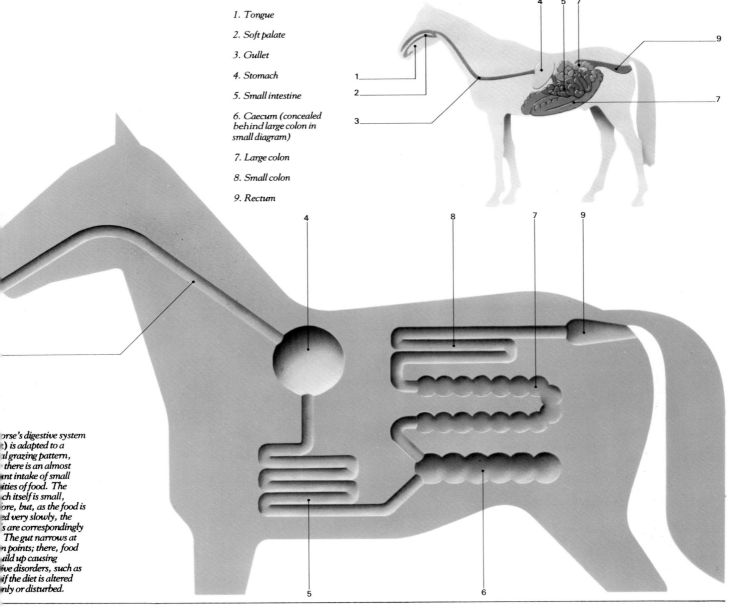

1. Tongue

2. Soft palate

3. Gullet

4. Stomach

5. Small intestine

6. Caecum (concealed behind large colon in small diagram)

7. Large colon

8. Small colon

9. Rectum

orse's digestive system) is adapted to a l grazing pattern, there is an almost nt intake of small ities of food. The ch itself is small, ore, but, as the food is ed very slowly, the s are correspondingly The gut narrows at n points; there, food ild up causing ive disorders, such as if the diet is altered nly or disturbed.

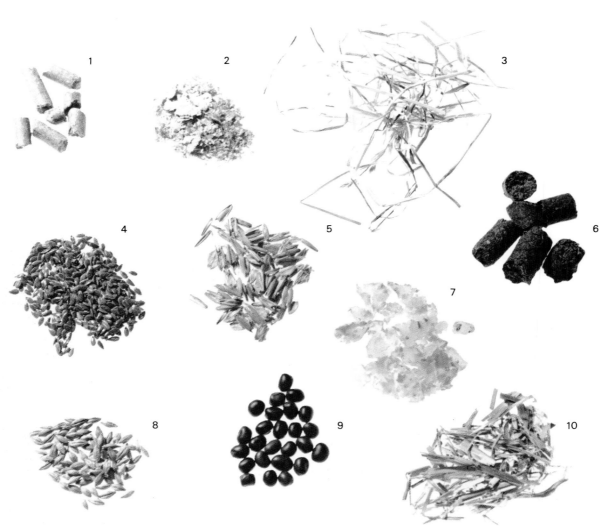

Left Basic concentrate
foods are an essential p...
the diet for horses in ha...
regular work. 1 Pony n...
are a compound food u...
contain all essential
nutrients and can be fe...
dry, instead of oats. A...
chaff or bran to aid
digestion. 2 Bran is ric...
protein, vitamin B and...
Fed as a mash, or slight...
damp, with oats, it has...
laxative effect. 3 Hay
contains all nutrients n...
to keep horses fit, if at g...
or only lightly worked. ...
Linseed fed as jelly, tea...
cake has a high oil cont...
and laxative properties. ...
good for conditioning a...
makes the coat glossy. ...
Oats are a balanced,
nutritious and easily di...
food, high in energy-gi...
carbohydrate, Vitamin...
and muscle-building pr...
They are fed whole, br...
or crushed. 6 Sugar be...
cubes provide bulk for ...
in slow work. They m...
soaked before use, or u...
swell in stomach and c...
colic. There is also a gr...
danger of the horse cho...
7 Maize, fed flaked for ...
digestibility, is energisi...
but low in protein and
minerals. It contains
vitamin A. 8 Barley,
unsuitable for horses in ...
fast work, is fed, boilea...
general conditioner; it ...
be crushed if fed raw. I...
contains vitamin B. 9 ...
are protein-rich; feed t...
sparingly for energy or
conditioning. 10 Chaf...
little food value but giv...
bulk and helps mastica...
Add 450g (1lb) to eve...
feed ration.

and to give gloss to the coat. It must be soaked then well cooked to kill the poisonous enzyme present in the raw plant. Let the mix cool before giving it to the horse. Dried sugar beet is another good conditioner, because of its high energy content. Most horses like it because of its sweetness. It must be always soaked in water overnight before it is added to a feed. If fed dry, the beet is likely to cause severe colic, as it swells dramatically when wet.

Roots, such as carrots, turnips and swedes, again help condition and are also of particular value to delicate or fussy feeders. Always wash the roots first and then slice them into finger-shaped pieces. Small round slices may cause a pony to choke.

Molasses or black treacle can be mixed with food to encourage a finicky feeder. In any case, all feeds ideally should contain about ·45kg (1lb) of chaff – chopped hay. Chaff has practically no nutritional content, but it does ensure that the horse chews its food properly, so helping to minimize the risk

Proper feeding with the correct balance of vitamins is essential for health. The diagram (right) shows how particular vitamins work throughout the system and what effects they have. Any deficiency of these vitamins, A, B1, B2, B6, D and E, in the horse's diet, will lead inevitably to debility and general loss of condition.

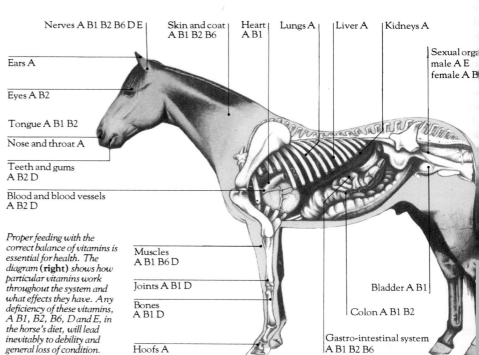

indigestion. It also acts as an abrasive on th. Finally, a salt or mineral lick – left in manger – is essential for all stabled ses. Field-kept animals usually take in an quate amount of salt during grazing, but a is also a good safeguard.

amins and minerals

adequate supply of vitamins and minerals ital in addition to the required amounts of oohydrates, proteins and fat. Vitamins A, B2, B6, D and E are all essential; othere the horse's resistance to disease will ainly be lessened, and actual disease may result. Normally, good-class hay and s, bran and carrots will contain most of vitamins a horse needs; oats, barley, ed maize and sugar beet pulp are also all ul. Vitamin D, however, can only be ficially administered through cod liver or left to the action of sunlight on the ural oil in the coat.

he absence of a sufficient supply of mins can be even more serious than a lack of mins, especially in the case of a young se. The essential minerals required are: ium and phosphorus, for the formation of lthy teeth and bones; sodium, sodium ride (salt) and potassium, for regulation he amount of body fluids; iron and cop vital for the formation of haemoglobin he blood to prevent anaemia; while mag um, manganese, cobalt, zinc and iodine all necessary. Magnesium aids skeletal muscular development; manganese is ded for both the bone structure and for oduction; zinc and cobalt stimulate vth; while iodine is particularly important ontrol of the thyroid gland.

lowever, of all these minerals, the most ortant is salt. This is why it is vital to vide a horse with a salt lick in either stable eld.

s with vitamins, the chief source of these erals is grass or hay, together with the er foods mentioned above. However, if horse needs extra vitamins and minerals, ays take the advice of a vet first – an ss of vitamins or minerals can be as gerous as an underdose. These are many able proprietary products on the market. se usually come in the form of liquid, ders and pellets, designed to be mixed in other food for ease of feeding.

igns of lack of vitamins are usually seen the skin and coat; examination of the h, gums and eyes can also give warning of ible deficiency. But, with sensible and trolled feeding, the problem should not .

ntities to feed

re is no hard and fast guide to the exact

A separate food store is essential. It should be clean, dry and near to the water supply. Foodstuffs kept in the stable can easily become spoiled or contaminated. The horse is a fastidious feeder, and musty or dusty food, as well as being un-appetizing, may be harmful. The simple food store (below) provides a clean, secure and compact area where foodstuffs can be measured out and mixed. Large establishments often keep a chaff cutter and an oat crusher. Scales are also useful to check the weight of filled haynets periodically.

Foodstuffs should be kept in separate bins, or sections of one large bin, and only mixed at feedtime. A scoop is used to measure out each ration . Where several horses are kept a check list for feeding should be pinned up near the bins so that each receives its appropriate diet.

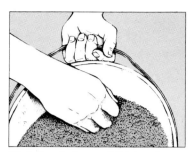

The feed can be dampened slightly with water before being mixed by hand in a bucket and then fed to horse. Grain keeps fresh and dry in galvanised bins. These should have close-fitting lids to keep out vermin and heavy enough to prevent a horse from raising them.

amounts of food a horse should be fed, as much depends on the type and size of horse and the work it is expected to do. However, as far as a stabled horse is concerned, the amount should certainly not be less than the horse would eat if it was grazing freely.

If the horse concerned was 15·2 hands, say, it would eat approximately 26½lbs of grass a day. Bigger horses require an extra 2lbs for every extra 2ins of height; smaller ones need 2lbs less.

With this basic total established, it is possible to plan a feeding programme, varying the amounts of bulk and concentrated food according to the demands being made upon the horse. Taking as an example a lightweight 15·2 hand horse that is being hunted, say, three days a fortnight in addition to other regular work, the emphasis will be on an almost equal balance between concentrates and hay or grass. The horse should be getting some 14lbs of concentrates a day to some 15lbs of hay. If, however, the horse is being lightly worked – or not worked at all – the

amount of hay will rise and the quantities of concentrates diminish.

Remember, too, that most horses feed much better at night, so it is important that the highest proportion of food be given in the final feed of the day. If the horse is being given three feeds a day, for example, the proportions are ten per cent in the morning, thirty per cent at midday and sixty per cent at night.

The best guide of all is simple observation. If a horse is too fat, it will need its rations reduced; if too thin, it will need building up. Always reduce the amount if food is left uneaten.

Exercising the horse

All stabled horses must have regular and adequate exercise. Otherwise they can develop swollen legs, azoturia and colic (see p. 159) – and will, in any case be spirited and difficult to manage when ridden. They can also become bored and develop bad habits. The amounts needed vary with the type and

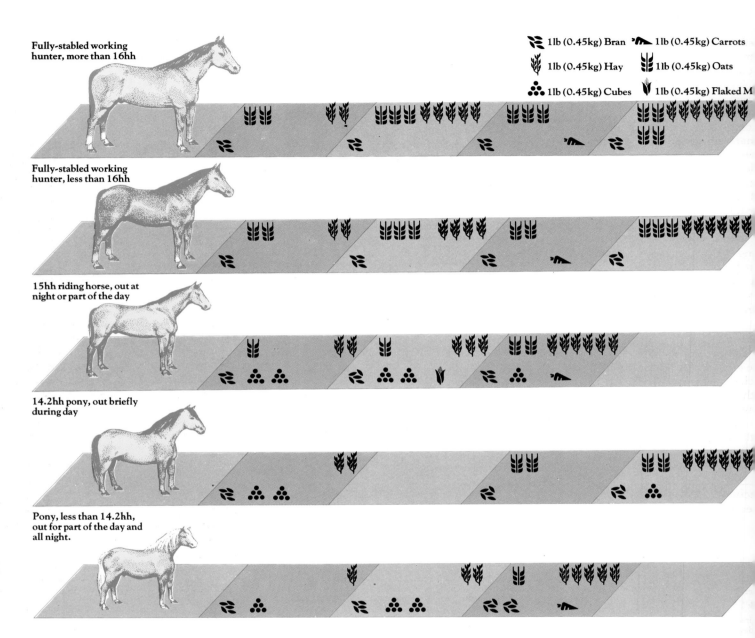

Fully-stabled working hunter, more than 16hh

Fully-stabled working hunter, less than 16hh

15hh riding horse, out at night or part of the day

14.2hh pony, out briefly during day

Pony, less than 14.2hh, out for part of the day and all night.

🌾 1lb (0.45kg) Bran	🥕 1lb (0.45kg) Carrots
🌾 1lb (0.45kg) Hay	🌾 1lb (0.45kg) Oats
⬟ 1lb (0.45kg) Cubes	🌾 1lb (0.45kg) Flaked M

weight of horse and the work it is expected to do; a hunter needs more exercise than a hack.

As with feeding, there are a few basic rules to remember. Most importantly, never exercise a horse until 1½ hours after a heavy feed; 1 hour after a small one. In any case, always remove the haynet an hour before exercise. Horses full of hay find breathing difficult when being worked hard.

The point of exercise is to get and keep the horse fit enough for the demands being made on it. A horse brought up from grass, say, is likely to be in 'grass condition'. In such a case, fitness can be achieved only through a rigidly controlled programme of exercise and feeding. Restrict exercise to walking, preferably on roads, for a week. Then combine walking with slow trotting. Soon, work can start in the school, while the period of road work can also be extended. Increase the

Above *The amount of food a horse requires varies according to its size, temperament and the type of work it will be doing. This chart gives basic specimen diets for horses with an even temperament. The amount and type of food given to each individual horse should be adapted according to observation.*

amount of grain fed in proportion to the extra in work. By the end of six weeks, the horse should be ready to be cantered over distances not exceeding 0.8km (½ mile). In the ninth week, it can have a gallop for up to 1.2km (¾ mile), but this should be strictly controlled so that the horse does not gallop flat out at full speed.

Indications of success are an increase in muscle and the disappearance of the profuse, lathery sweat of the out-of-condition horse. Never try to hurry the process; a horse cannot be conditioned through cantering and galloping, but only by slow, steady, regular work. This applies just as much to stabled horses

and ponies.

Always aim to end the exercise with a w so that the horse comes back to its stabl field cool and relaxed. Once the tack been removed, inspect the horse for cuts bruises, pick out its feet, and brush off saddle and sweat marks. Then rug u groom. If you have been caught in the trot the horse home so that it is warm arrival. Untack, and then give the hor thorough rubbing down, either with stra a towel. When this has been comple cover the back with a layer of straw or u sweat sheet. It is vital to keep the back w to avoid the risk of colds and chills.

A thorough drying is essential if the h is very hot and sweaty, but it will need t sponged down first with lukewarm wa Either restrict sponging to the sweaty are usually the neck, chest and flanks – or spc

entire body. Then, scrape off the surplus
er with a sweat scraper, taking care to
k with, and not against, the run of the
. Next, rub down and, finally, cover with
veat sheet. If possible, lead the horse
nd until it is completely dry.

orses that have been worked exception-
hard – in hunting, say, or in competitions
ed further care. On returning to the
le, give the horse a drink of warm water.
n follow the procedures outlined above.
l the horse with a bran mash and then
e it to rest. Return later to check that the
nal is warm enough or has not broken out
a fresh sweat. Check for warmth by
ng the bases of the ears. If they are cold,
n by rubbing them with the hand and
put more blankets on the horse. If the
r, rub down again and walk the horse
nd until it is completely dry.

oming the horse

chief point of grooming is to keep the
e clean, massage the skin and tone up the
cles. Field-kept horses need less groom-
than stabled horses, particularly in wint-
ut some must nevertheless be carried out.
good grooming kit is essential. This
ld consist of a dandy brush, to remove
and dried sweat marks; a body brush, a
short-bristled brush for the head, body,

legs, mane and tail; a rubber curry comb, used
to remove thickly-caked mud or matted hair,
and a metal one, for cleaning the body brush;
a water brush, used damp on the mane, tail
and hooves; a hoof pick; a stable rubber, used
to give a final polish to the coat; and some
foam rubber sponges, for cleaning the eyes,
nostrils, muzzle and dock.

Where more than one horse is kept, each
animal should have its own grooming kit,
kept together in a box or bag and clearly
marked. This helps to prevent the risk of
infection in cases of illness.

Grooming falls into three stages, each of
which is carried out at a different time of the
day. The first of these is quartering, normally
done first thing in the morning before exercise. Tie up the horse. Then, pick the feet
out and, next, clean the eyes, muzzle and
dock with a damp sponge. If worn, rugs
should be unbuckled and folded back and the
head, neck, chest and forelegs cleaned with a
body brush. Replace the rugs and repeat the
process on the rear part of the body. Remove
any stable stains with a water brush. Finish by
brushing the mane and tail thoroughly with
the body brush.

Strapping is the name given to the
thorough grooming which follows exercise,
when the horse has cooled down. Once
again, tie the horse up and pick out its feet.

Follow by using the dandy brush to remove all
traces of dirt, mud and sweat, paying particular attention to marks left by the girth and
saddle and on the legs. Work from ears to
tail, first on the near side and then on the off.
Take care to use the brush lightly to avoid
irritating the skin.

Next, comes the body brush. This must be
used firmly for full effect. Start with the
mane, pushing it to the wrong side to remove
scurf from the roots. Brush the forelock.
Then, start on the body, working from head
to tail and grooming the nearside first, as
before. Work with a circular motion, finishing in the direction of the hairs, and flick the
brush outwards at the end of each stroke to
push dust away from the body. At intervals,
clean the brush with the curry comb, which is
held in the other hand. It can be emptied by
tapping on the floor at intervals.

Brush the head, remembering that this is
one of the most sensitive areas of the horse.
So use the brush firmly, but gently, and take
particular care when grooming around the
eyes, ears and nostrils. Finally, brush the tail
– a few hairs at a time – so that every tangle is
removed.

The next stage is wisping, which helps
tone up the muscles and also stimulates the
circulation. A wisp is a bundle of soft hay,
twisted up to form a rope. Slightly dampen it,

cimen exercise routine
ed on a 16hh hunter

cise	Care and Management	Special Features	Exercise	Care and Management	Special Features
k 1			**Week 5**		
ins walking on the ay, increasing ually to one hour	Gradually increase food concentrate, begin strapping	During the pre-work week the horse's feet must be checked and shod. All horses require one rest day each working week	After first walking and trotting, the horse may have a short, slow canter on soft ground. Then decrease pace gradually	Four feeds a day – increase concentrates and reduce time at grass. Re-shoe if necessary	At this stage the coat should shine and the muscles should be hardening
k 2			**Week 6**		
king for 1¼–1½ hrs a 6–8 mile circuit	Check condition of legs and feet, watch for skin galls. Increase corn and vitamin supplements	Quiet lanes and roads with good surfaces are best for road work	A medium canter of reasonable length. Work at a sitting trot can now be started	Increase concentrate ration. Maintain thorough strapping	Schooling can be intensified by trotting in smaller circles, and work at the canter
k 3			**Week 7**		
ays walk the first ½. Then introduce very t spells of trotting, asing their length ually	Stable the horse at night and establish a regular routine	Schooling and lungeing in large circles can now be started	Canters can speed up. A short half speed gallop may be added at the end of the week (on good ground). Jumping can begin	The horse will sweat and should wear a rug at night	The final phase of building up to full work. It is useful to introduce the horse to travelling and to company at this stage
k 4			**Week 8**		
2 hrs work daily – split schooling, lungeing road work. More ent, periods of ing	Increase food concentrates	Trotting up gentle slopes can commence and increase slowly	On day 2 the horse can gallop at half speed up a gentle slope. Always walk the final mile	Full rations of concentrate. The horse should gallop on alternate days, and do steady work on the others. Renew shoes	When the horse is fully conditioned thorough exercise must be maintained on days when it does not work

cise needs always differ, according to the size of horse, the type of
it is doing and what it is being prepared for. Vary the routine accordingly

Left *The grooming kit. Ideally every horse shou[ld] have its own to reduce t[he] chance of any infection passed from one to anot[her]. Keep the kit in a wire ba[sket] or bag so that no item is mislaid. Clean the equipment from time to [time] with a mild disinfectant. 1 Mane combs are used when mane or tail is pla[ited,] trimmed or pulled. 2 Sponges, one for cleani[ng] eyes, lips and nostrils, t[he] second for cleaning the [dock]. 3 Can of hoof oil and br[ush] used to improve appear[ance] of hoof and treat brittle [feet]. 4 Dandy brush (hard) [to] remove dried mud and sweat. 5 Body brush (so[ft], to remove dust and scur[f]. 6 Water brush (soft), for laying mane and tail an[d] washing feet. 7 Sweat scraper, to remove wate[r] and sweat from coat. 8 Rubber curry comb, removes dirt from body brush; can also be used [in] place of dandy brush. 9 Metal curry comb, for cleaning dirt from body brush (never used on th[e] horse). 10 Stable rubbe[r] used for final polishing [of] coat. 11 Hoof pick, for taking dirt and stones fr[om] the feet.*

and use vigorously on the neck, shoulders, quarters and thighs, concentrating on the muscular areas. Bang the wisp down hard on these, sliding it off with, not against, the coat. Take care to avoid bony areas and the tender region of the loins.

Sponge the eyes, lips, and muzzle and nostrils. Then, with a second sponge to minimize the risk of possible infection, wash round the dock and under the tail. Lift the tail as high as possible, so the entire region can be adequately cleaned. 'Lay' the mane with the water brush. Then brush the outside of the feet, taking care not to get water into the hollow of the heel. When the hooves are dry, brush hoof oil over the outside of each hoof as high as the coronet.

Finally, work over the horse with the stable rubber for a final polish. The object is to remove the last traces of dust from the coat. Fold the rubber into a flat bundle, dampen it slightly, and then go over the coat, working in the direction of the lay of the hair.

Strapping takes from between half to three-quarters of an hour with practice. It will normally take a novice slightly longer, largely because of the unaccustomed strain it imposes on the groom's muscles. 'Setting fair' – the last grooming of the day – takes far less time. Simply brush the horse lightly with the body brush, wisp and then put on the night

rug (blanket), if one is normally worn.

Travelling with a horse

Careful planning when entering for a horse show, say, or going for a day's hunting, is essential if the horse is to arrive fit enough to undertake the tasks demanded of it. The first essential is to plan the journey; a fit horse can be hacked for up to ten miles, walking and trotting at an average speed of no more than six mph (a grass-kept pony's average should not be more than four mph). However, if the distance involved is greater than this, transport will be needed.

Horse boxes or car-towed trailers are the usual method of transport over long distances. Apart from the obvious mechanical checks that should be carried out before each journey, the horse's own requirements, too, need attention. A hay net is one essential; this should be filled with hay and given to the horse during the journey, unless the animal is expected to work hard immediately on arrival. Others include a first aid kit; rugs (day and sweat); bandages; grooming kit; a head collar; a water bucket and a filled water container. This last item is essential if the journey is to be a particularly long one, when the horse will need to be watered perhaps once or even twice en route.

In some cases – when hunting, for example

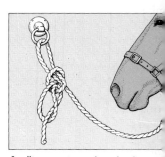

Above *How to tie a quick-release knot type of knot, which is easy to undo in an emergency, should always secure a hors[e;] quick tug on the free end releases the kn[ot] but the more a horse pulls against it, the tighter it becomes.*

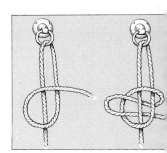

Intelligent ponies can learn by observati[on,] pull at the free end of the quick-release k[not] and so get loose. If a pony learns to free [itself] in this way, it can usually be out-witted [if the] free end of the rope is passed back throu[gh the] loop again (above).

...k up a horse's foot, stand facing its tail. ...it first by sliding a hand down from its ...er to its fetlock. This can also ...rage the horse to move its weight over to ...er legs. It also helps to keep a young ...calm.

Working from the frog to the toe and concentrating on the edges first, use the point of the hoof pick to prise out any foreign objects lodged in the foot. Pebbles wedged between the frog and the bar can cause lameness. Take care not to push the point into the frog.

The dandy brush is used to remove heavy dirt caked mud and sweat stains, particularly from the saddle region, belly, points of hocks, fetlocks and pasterns. As it is fairly harsh it should not be used on the more tender areas, or on a recently clipped horse.

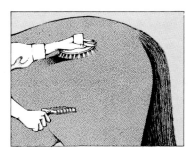

A body brush has short, dense bristles designed to penetrate and clean the coat. It should be applied with some pressure, in firm, circular movements. After a few strokes clear it of dust with a curry comb. A gentler brushing should be given round the head.

...dy brush is also used to groom the tail. ...hould be brushed a few hairs at a time, ...g with the undermost ones. Remove all ...nd tangles, taking care not to break any ...Finally, the whole tail should be ...d into shape from the top.

Wring out a soft sponge in warm water and sponge the eyes first, wiping outwards from the corners. Carefully sponge round eyelids. Wring out the sponge and wipe over the muzzle, lips and nostrils. A separate sponge should be used to sponge the dock area.

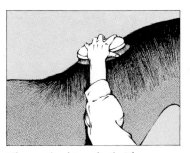

The water brush is used to 'lay' the mane. The tip of the brush is dipped in a bucket of water and thoroughly shaken before it is applied. Keeping the brush flat, make firm, downward strokes from the roots. The mane should be left neat and slightly damp.

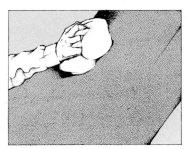

As a final touch to the grooming go over the whole coat with the stable-rubber to remove any trace of dust. This cloth is used slightly damp and folded into a flat bundle. Work along the lie of the hair. The stable-rubber leaves the coat gleaming.

...e horse can travel saddled-up, with a rug ...ed over the saddle, but, in the case of ...petitions, a rug alone should be worn. ...elling bandages should always be used, as ...as a tail bandage to stop the top of the ...from being rubbed. In addition, knee ...and hock boots should be worn as an ...d protection.

...reparation of the horse itself must start ...night before, with an especially thorough ...ming. Both mane and tail should be ...ed. A grass-kept horse should be kept in ...he night, if possible. The next morning, ...w the normal stable routine, with the ...tion of a drawn-out strapping. Re- ...ber that, in the case of a show, the mane ...ld be plaited; this can be started the ...t before to ease the task of getting the ...e into shape, but will need to be com- ...d the following day.

...ding the horse

...ing a horse into a box or trailer is an easy ...gh task, provided that the process is ...ed calmly and without undue haste. The ...lest way is for one person to lead the ...e forward, walking straight forward and ...ting the temptation to pull at the head. ...uple of helpers should stand behind the ...e in case help is required, but out of ...ing range.

The main reason for a horse showing reluctance to enter a box is usually its fear of the noise of its hooves on the ramp. This can be overcome by putting down some straw to deaden the sound. Loading another, calmer, horse first, or tempting a horse forward with a feed bucket containing a handful of oats, also act as encouragements.

A really obstinate horse, however, will have to be physically helped into the box. The way to do this is to attach two ropes to the ramp's rails, so that they cross just above the horse's hocks, with two helpers in position – one at each end of the ropes. As the horse approaches the ramp, they tighten the ropes to propel the animal into the box.

Tack – care and maintenance

Care of saddles and bridles is just as important as care of the horse itself. Ill-fitting, dirty or worn tack is not only unpleasant and uncomfortable for the horse; it can also be extremely dangerous for the rider. Therefore always keep tack clean and check it regularly for wear. With saddles this applies particularly to girths and stirrup leathers – a badly-worn girth is a potential killer. Bits should never be allowed to become worn and rough.

All tack should be stored in a cool, dry place – a purpose-planned tack room is the best. A warm, damp atmosphere will cause

Above *A half-completed wisp. The wisp is used after body brushing, when strapping a horse. It should be rubbed vigorously over the muscular areas, avoiding the head and sensitive parts. Wisping stimulates circulation, gives a form of massage and shines the coat. The wisp is used damp and brought down with a bang in the direction of the lay of the coat.*

A wisp is made from soft hay, dampened slightly and then twisted round a core of twine to form a rope about 2m (7ft) long. This is formed into a firm, fist-sized pad by making two loops and weaving the rest of the rope through them as shown above in loose form. A properly made wisp should be hard and firm and no larger than can conveniently be grasped in the hand.

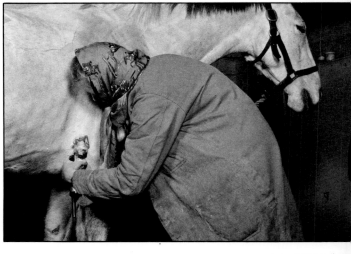

Clipping is done chiefly for comfort, as the thicker winter coat grown during the autumn can lead to heavy sweating during exercise. Removing all, or part, of it prevents this, lessens the chance of a horse getting chilled and makes it easier to groom. The trace clip (top right) is the minimum clip, removing hair only from the chest, belly, upper legs, elbows and up the back of the quarters. It keeps the protective warmth of the coat, while preventing heavy sweating. The blanket clip (centre) is slightly cooler, leaving a blanket-shaped area of body hair and all the leg hair on for warmth. In the hunter clip (bottom) all the coat is clipped, leaving only the leg hair as protection from thorns and scratches. Sometimes a saddle patch is left. This prevents the saddle rubbing and increases the comfort of horse and rider.

Pulling a mane or tail is done mainly for smartness. Pulling a mane thins it, makes it lie flat and evens the edge. Tail pulling slims the tail by removing short hairs from the top. Grass-kept horses, however, need the protection of a natural, thick tail to keep themselves free from flies, which can be very troublesome in the summer.

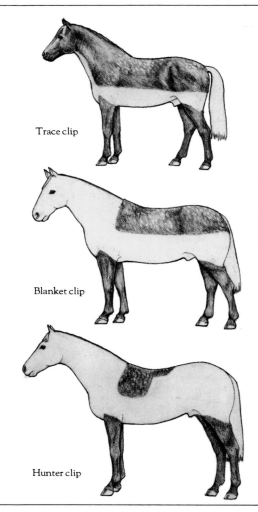

Trace clip

Blanket clip

Hunter clip

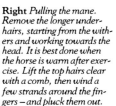

Above *Clipping the horse is a lengthy and delicate operation, care should be taken not to upset the animal. The coat should first be dry and well-groomed.*

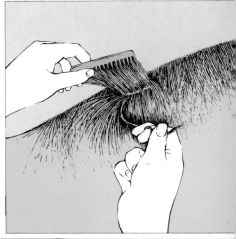

Right *Pulling the mane. Remove the longer under-hairs, starting from the withers and working towards the head. It is best done when the horse is warm after exercise. Lift the top hairs clear with a comb, then wind a few strands around the fingers – and pluck them out.*

leather to crack, break or develop mould. Similarly, metal parts will tarnish or rust. Always hang bridles up on a bridle rack; saddles should be placed over a saddle horse, or on a wide padded bracket screwed firmly to the wall.

Tack should be cleaned daily; at the very least, sweat marks should be removed and the bit thoroughly cleaned. The equipment needed is as follows: a rough towel or large sponge for washing; a small, flat sponge; a chamois leather; saddle soap; metal polish or wool; a couple of soft cloths; a dandy brush; a nail, to clean curb hooks; a bucket; hanging hooks for bridle, girths and leathers; a saddle horse; and a vegetable oil.

When cleaning the saddle, place it on the saddle horse and remove all fittings, such as girths and stirrup leathers. These should be cleaned separately. Wash the leatherwork with lukewarm water to remove dirt, dried sweat and grease – but take care not to get the saddle saturated. If the lining is of leather, it can also be washed. Otherwise scrub it down dry with a dandy brush.

With the chamois leather slightly dampened, dry the saddle off. Apply saddle soap liberally with the damp sponge, working it well into the saddle to get the soap into the leather without creating a lather. Allow some time for the leather to absorb the soap. Then rub over with a moist sponge and, finally, wipe down with the chamois leather. Clean the leather pieces that have been removed with saddle soap, and the metal ones with metal polish. Clean out the holes of stirrup leathers with a match or a nail. Leather girths should be oiled on the inside. Web string and nylon ones should be brushed down with a dandy brush and washed occasionally, using pure soap. Then, reassemble.

As a preliminary to cleaning, it is a good idea to take the bridle to pieces so that the stitching can be thoroughly checked for wear. Reassemble, and, starting with the bit, wash with lukewarm water. Dry, soap the leather and polish the metal in the same way as the saddle. If the leather needs oiling, take the bridle apart once cleaning has been completed. Oil each piece individually. Then fit the parts together again, taking care that the bit is in the correct position.

Bridles and bits

All commonly-used bridles have the s[a] purpose – to hold the bit in the mouth. through use of this, in conjunction with and legs, that the horse is guided and cont led. There are two main types of bridle – snaffle bridle, with one bit, and the do bridle, with two. The latter has two bits two sets of reins.

All modern bits are based on one of principles – either the snaffle or the c The snaffle is a mild bit. It consists of a m bar, either jointed or plain, with a rin either end to which the rein and headpiec the bridle are attached. Pressure on the via the rein causes it to act on the corne the horse's mouth, with a nutcracker actic the bit is jointed.

The curb is also of metal; it may ha hump, called a port, in the middle. It is fi with shanks at either end, the cheekpi being attached to the top of the shanks the rein to rings at the bottom. The sha are linked by a chain which lies in the c groove.

Pressure on the rein has a leverage effe

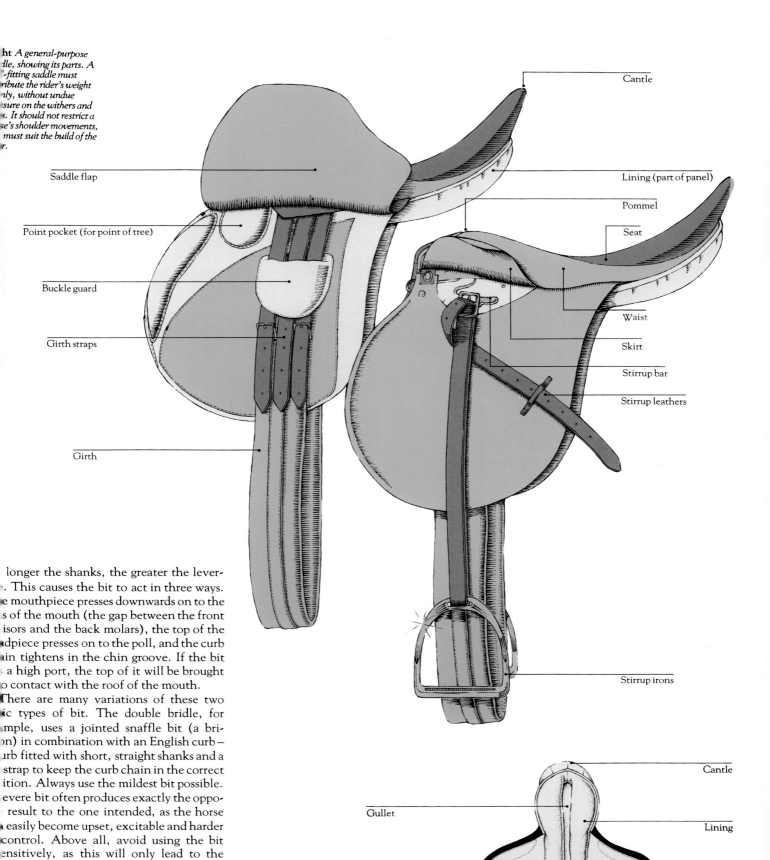

ht A general-purpose dle, showing its parts. A -fitting saddle must ribute the rider's weight ly, without undue sure on the withers and s. It should not restrict a se's shoulder movements, must suit the build of the r.

Saddle flap

Point pocket (for point of tree)

Buckle guard

Girth straps

Girth

Cantle

Lining (part of panel)

Pommel

Seat

Waist

Skirt

Stirrup bar

Stirrup leathers

Stirrup irons

longer the shanks, the greater the lever-
. This causes the bit to act in three ways.
e mouthpiece presses downwards on to the
s of the mouth (the gap between the front
isors and the back molars), the top of the
dpiece presses on to the poll, and the curb
in tightens in the chin groove. If the bit
a high port, the top of it will be brought
o contact with the roof of the mouth.
There are many variations of these two
ic types of bit. The double bridle, for
mple, uses a jointed snaffle bit (a bri-
on) in combination with an English curb –
urb fitted with short, straight shanks and a
strap to keep the curb chain in the correct
ition. Always use the mildest bit possible.
evere bit often produces exactly the oppo-
result to the one intended, as the horse
easily become upset, excitable and harder
control. Above all, avoid using the bit
ensitively, as this will only lead to the
se developing a hard mouth. Signs of this
the corners of the mouth and the tongue
oming calloused through constant pres-
e from the bit. If this happens, remedial
ion should be taken immediatley.

Right *The underside of a saddle, showing the gullet, which keeps pressure off the horse's spine, even when the rider is in the saddle.*

Gullet

Saddle flap

Girth straps

Cantle

Lining

Panel

Selecting a saddle

As with bridles and bits, there are various types of saddle – some designed for a particular task, or, as in the case of the Western saddle, a specific style of riding. The most important thing to remember is that the saddle must fit the horse properly. An ill-fitting saddle will make the horse and rider very sore; and it will also make it impossible for the rider to position himself correctly.

The framework of the saddle is called the tree and determines the final shape, so it must be correctly made. Many riding associations, such as the Pony Club, have their own approved patterns and it is always safest to look for one of these. The commonest form in use today is the 'spring tree' – so-called because it has two pieces of light steel let into it under the seat to increase resilience. Treat the tree with care. If a saddle is dropped the tree may break. The saddle cannot then be used until it is professionally repaired.

The rest of the saddle consists of layers of webbing, canvas, serge, and finally, leather. The padded part, which rests on the horse's back, is usually made of felt or stuffed with wool. It is important that this padding is arranged so that the rider's weight is distributed evenly over the back and carried on the fleshy part rather than the spine. This helps to preserve the horse's strength and stamina and prevents sores from developing. If additional protection is necessary, a pad – known as a numnah – can be placed beneath the saddle.

Girths keep the saddle in place, so they must be strong. They should be inspected

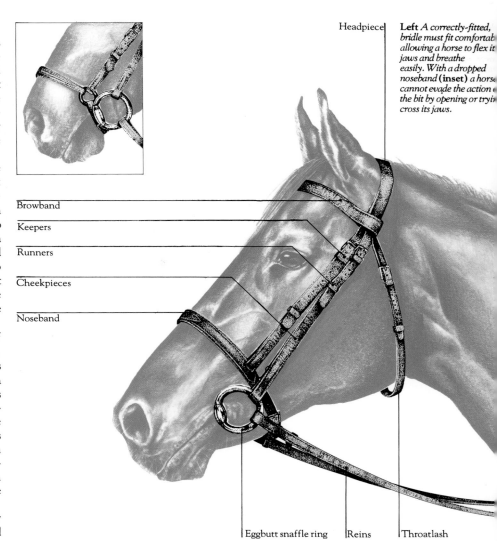

Headpiece

Browband

Keepers

Runners

Cheekpieces

Noseband

Eggbutt snaffle ring | Reins | Throatlash

Left *A correctly-fitted, bridle must fit comfortab[ly] allowing a horse to flex it[s] jaws and breathe easily. With a dropped noseband (inset) a horse cannot evade the action [of] the bit by opening or tryi[ng to] cross its jaws.*

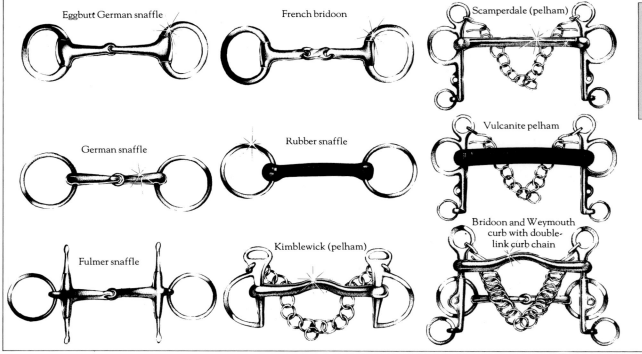

Eggbutt German snaffle

French bridoon

Scamperdale (pelham)

German snaffle

Rubber snaffle

Vulcanite pelham

Fulmer snaffle

Kimblewick (pelham)

Bridoon and Weymouth curb with double-link curb chain

Left *Some typical bits. [A] bit applies pressure to th[e] bars, the tongue and the corners of a horse's mouth. Jointed snaffles produce a squeezing or nutcracker action. Thi[n] straight snaffles are the mildest and are used on[ly] young or light-mouthe[d] horses. Pelhams try to combine the curb with [a] snaffle. They are used with a curb chain and either single or double reins. The double bridl[e a] thin bridoon (or snaf[fle] and curb bit. Used together, these give the rider more precise contr[ol]*

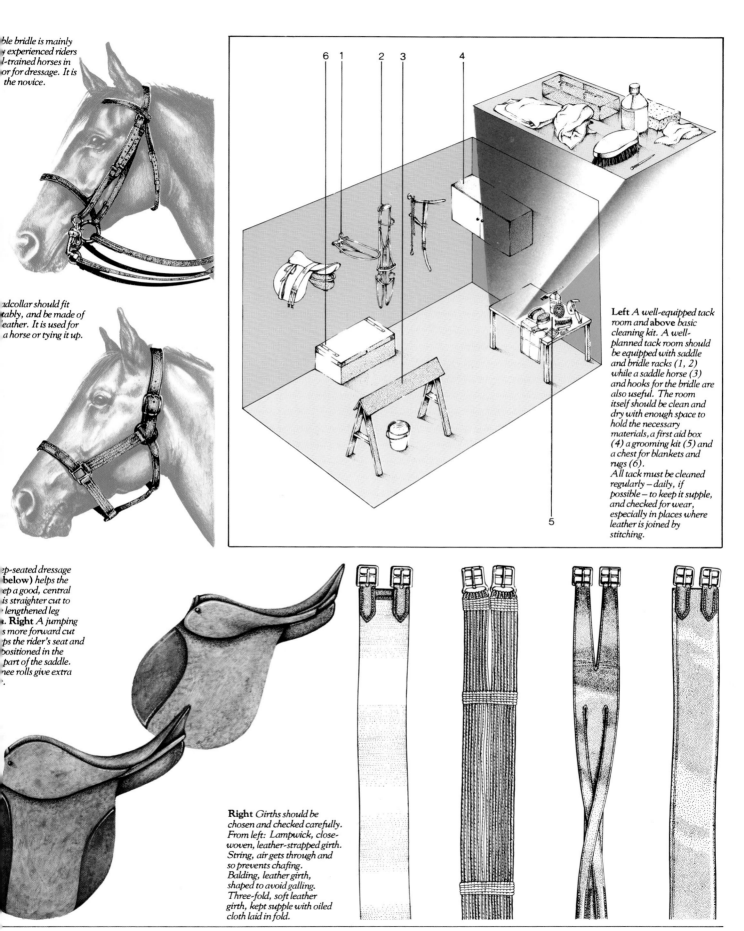

*ble bridle is mainly
y experienced riders
l-trained horses in
r for dressage. It is
the novice.*

*idcollar should fit
tably, and be made of
eather. It is used for
a horse or tying it up.*

Left *A well-equipped tack
room and* **above** *basic
cleaning kit. A well-
planned tack room should
be equipped with saddle
and bridle racks (1, 2)
while a saddle horse (3)
and hooks for the bridle are
also useful. The room
itself should be clean and
dry with enough space to
hold the necessary
materials, a first aid box
(4) a grooming kit (5) and
a chest for blankets and
rugs (6).
All tack must be cleaned
regularly – daily, if
possible – to keep it supple,
and checked for wear,
especially in places where
leather is joined by
stitching.*

*ep-seated dressage
below) helps the
ep a good, central
is straighter cut to
lengthened leg
.* **Right** *A jumping
s more forward cut
ps the rider's seat and
positioned in the
part of the saddle.
nee rolls give extra*

Right *Girths should be
chosen and checked carefully.
From left: Lampwick, close-
woven, leather-strapped girth.
String, air gets through and
so prevents chafing.
Balding, leather girth,
shaped to avoid galling.
Three-fold, soft leather
girth, kept supple with oiled
cloth laid in fold.*

regularly for wear. They can be made of leather, webbing, or nylon string – in the case of webbing, two girths should be used for additional safety. Stirrup irons, too, should always be chosen with safety foremost in mind. Safety irons, often used by children, are specifically designed so that the foot will come free in a fall. Adults should always check that there is 12mm (½in) clearance on either side of the foot, measured at the widest place of the boot or shoe, so that it does not become jammed.

Horse clothing
Many different types of clothing have been developed to keep the horse warm, protect it from injury, or give its limbs added support. Chief amongst these are rugs and bandages.

Rugs are especially useful as protection after a horse has been clipped, but special types are used for other purposes as well. In all cases, it is vital that the blanket should fit properly and be securely fastened. A roller must be used to keep a night rug in place.

Bandages fall into three categories. Tail

bandages are used to make the top of th look neat and to protect it during a jour Stable bandages, covering the area from knee right down is underneath the fet keep the legs warm, and, similarly, are us protection during travelling. Exercise dages, support the back tendons and pr the legs from thorns.

Clipping
Horses are clipped to maintain comfort less importantly, for smartness. Removi

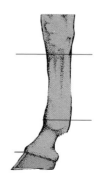
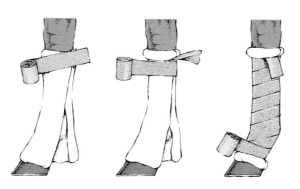

*Four stages in fitting a bandage. Pad beneath bandages with cotton or an equivalent. Wool bandages are rolled ly down from below the or hock to the coronet, upwards to the start and n side of leg. **Far right** ng of crêpe exercise or ure bandage to support tendons and protect the These bandages are ed firmly and often ed in place for greater ity.*

art of the coat by clipping prevents heavy ating during exercise in winter and there-lessens the risk of a horse catching a l. It also enables the horse to dry off more kly.

here are various types of clip; choice ld depend on what the horse is expected lo, and how much it sweats doing it. ember that a clipped horse will need to r rugs for warmth during cold weather, if kept in either a stable or a field.

lth and the horse

ses are tough creatures, but, like any nal, they can fall ill or be injured. A healthy pony or horse is alert, bright eyed, and takes a keen interest in all that goes on around it. Ribs and hip bones should not be prominent, and the quarters should be well-rounded. The animal should stand square on all four legs. The base of the ears should be warm to the touch.

Signs of illness vary, but there are some general symptoms which can give warning of trouble to come. A field-kept pony which stays for a long time in one place, a horse which goes off its food, a willing horse which suddenly becomes 'nappy' – all these signs are indications that something is wrong. Other symptoms include: discharge from the eyes or nostrils; stumbling for no apparent reason; restlessness; dullness of eye or general lack of interest; sweating; kicking or biting at the flank; lameness; diarrhoea; persistent rubbing of the neck or quarters against a wall or fence; apparent difficulty in breathing; coughing.

It is essential, therefore, to have a reliable vet, and, if ever in any doubt, to call him without hesitation. Better to pay for a visit than to run the risk of mistaken self-diagnosis leading to a more serious illness, or even death. Nevertheless, all horse owners should have a practical knowledge of first aid, and a first aid kit is an essential part of any stable.

*ing boots of felt or r, and rubber over-boots, are often for protection in ng and eventing, or a horse moves too y in front (**top left**), cking one leg with her, or hits the heel of efoot with toe of hind op **right**).*

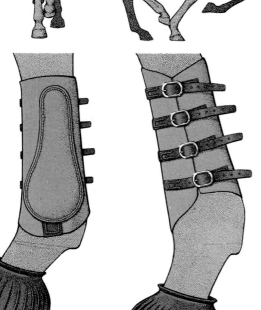

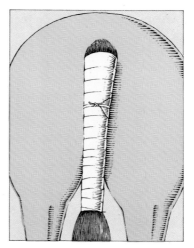

Fitting a stockinette tail bandage. Dampen hair with water brush. Unroll short length of dry bandage and place this beneath tail, close to dock.

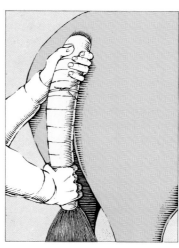

Holding the end of the bandage against the tail, make one turn to secure the bandage. Then continue the bandaging evenly downwards.

The tail bandage should stop just short of the last tail bone and the remaining length should be bandaged upwards and secured with tapes.

Finally bend the tail into a comfortable position. Tail bandages should not be left overnight. Slide them off, downwards, with both hands.

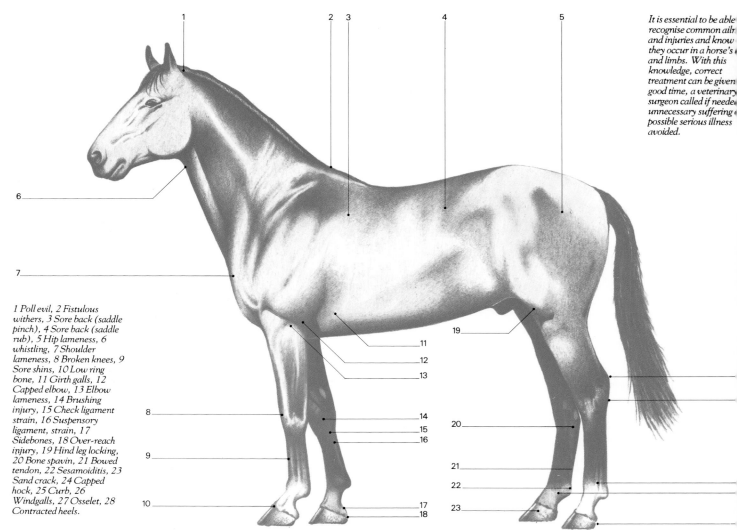

It is essential to be able recognise common ail[m] and injuries and know they occur in a horse's and limbs. With this knowledge, correct treatment can be given good time, a veterinary surgeon called if neede[d] unnecessary suffering [and] possible serious illness avoided.

1 Poll evil, 2 Fistulous withers, 3 Sore back (saddle pinch), 4 Sore back (saddle rub), 5 Hip lameness, 6 whistling, 7 Shoulder lameness, 8 Broken knees, 9 Sore shins, 10 Low ring bone, 11 Girth galls, 12 Capped elbow, 13 Elbow lameness, 14 Brushing injury, 15 Check ligament strain, 16 Suspensory ligament, strain, 17 Sidebones, 18 Over-reach injury, 19 Hind leg locking, 20 Bone spavin, 21 Bowed tendon, 22 Sesamoiditis, 23 Sand crack, 24 Capped hock, 25 Curb, 26 Windgalls, 27 Osselet, 28 Contracted heels.

It should be placed where it can be easily found in an emergency.

Lameness

Lameness is the commonest form of disability in the horse. Treating most forms of it is usually best left to an expert.

To find the source of the lameness, first establish which leg is causing the pain. Do this by having the horse led at a slow trot – downhill, if possible. If one of the forelegs is lame, the horse will nod its head as the other leg touches the ground. Similarly, if the hind legs are involved, the horse's weight will fall on the sound leg. Next, feel for heat, pain and swelling. Start with the foot, as 90 per cent of all lameness is centred there.

Causes of lameness can range from a simple stone in the foot to actual disease. Consult the chart for details and possible treatment. The most serious disease is laminitis (founder), when prompt veterinary attention is essential to avoid the risk of permanent injury to the horse. This is one of the most painful conditions from which the horse can suffer.

Wounds and other injuries

Wounds and injuries are another common problem. Puncture cuts, caused by thorns, say, can easily occur during exercise. This is one of the reasons why exercise bandages should always be worn. Always call the vet if the wound looks deep, or if you think stitching is required.

First bring the bleeding under control. Small cuts should cease bleeding on their own within 20 minutes, but, if the cut is serious or bleeding does not stop, apply a pressure bandage. Clip the hair from the skin around the wound and clean it thoroughly. Gently trickle cold water over it from a hose pipe, or wash the area with saline solution. Then coat with an anti-biotic powder and dress, if possible. Do not bandage too tightly; a tight bandage will cause pain if swelling occurs. Keep the wound clean and check.

The most serious of all infections is tetanus, caused by bacteria in the soil penetrating the skin through the wound. All horses should be immunized against the disease by an initial course of injections, followed by regular 'boosters'. If in any doubt, it is best to

Above *Lifting a front foot helps keep the horse still during examination.*

Below *Kicking is unlik[ely] when handling hind leg[s if] tail is held firmly down.*

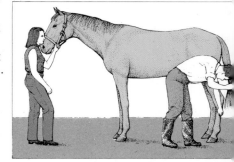

stable should have a
ne chest stocked with
aid kit and medicines
ryday ailments. It
be conveniently

placed and kept clean and
tidy. Clear identification of
the kit and contents is
essential. **Above** A typical
basic kit containing:

1 Gamgee tissue, 2 Epsom
salts, 3 Liniment, 4 Roll of
cotton wool, 5 Antiseptic, 6
Methylated spirit, 7 Specific
for colic, 8 Glycerine, 9

Sulphonamide powder, 10
Stockholm tar, 11
Petroleum jelly, 12 Assorted
bandages, 13 Worming
remedy, 14 Sterilized gauze,

15 Sponge, 16 Coughing
electuary, 17 Ready-to-
apply poultice, 18 Worm
paste in dispenser, 19
Round-ended surgical

scissors, 20 Thermometer.
Substitutions can be made to
this selection. Opinions vary
as to the amount of equipment needed.

the horse immunized again. The injec-
cannot kill – tetanus will, unless treat-
is administered speedily.

her injuries are normally the result of
kicks, or irritations – the latter fre-
tly the result of ill-fitting tack. Mouth
ies should be treated with salt water
es. Do not use a bit until the mouth has
d and check that this was not the initial
e of the injury. Girth galls and saddle
should both be treated with fomenta-
. After they have healed, harden the
ted areas with salt water or methylated
. Do not ride the horse with a saddle
the sore has completely healed.

oken or cut knees can happen as the
t of a fall. If the injury is more than skin
the vet should be called. Otherwise
with cold water, as with a cut, and then

apply a soothing poultice. Carefully tie a
figure of eight bandage.

Capped knees and hocks are usually the
result of kicks or a blow. Treat the first with a
rest, massage and a pressure bandage. The
treatment for the second is cold water, and
then a poultice. If any swelling persists, blis-
ter the area of the injury mildly.

Skin diseases
Like humans, horses can easily catch skin
diseases, particularly in unhygienic conditions. Lice, for example, are a constant pest
to a long-coated, field-kept horse, particularly in February. Other skin diseases include
ringworm; sweet itch; mud fever; cracked
heels; pustular dermititis (acne); warbles; and
nettle rash. For their treatment, see the
chart. Many of these diseases are highly con-

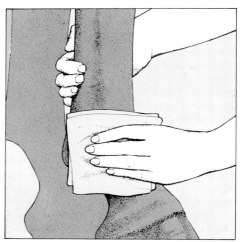

Above Direct pressure is
applied to stop persistent
bleeding from a vein. A

folded handkerchief should
always be carried, as this can
serve as a pad.

Ailment and injury chart

Feet

Symptoms:	Causes:	Treatment:
Bruised sole		
Lameness. Horse may ease the weight of the foot when at rest	Bruising by stones or rough going and hard ground	Rest. If necessary, new shoes. Keep farrier informed
Corns		
Lameness. Heat in foot. Horse more lame on turn than straight	Ill fitting shoe causing pinching. Shoe which has moved in. Bruising	Call blacksmith or vet to cut out corn and advise further treatment
Laminitis (Founder)		
Obvious pain in the feet. Horse is reluctant to move and stands with its front feet pushed forward and its hind legs under it so that its weight is taken on the heels. May shift weight from one foot to another. Possibly a high temperature. Always apparent in front feet first but may affect all four feet	Over feeding and not enough exercise. Grass-fed horses are especially prone to the disease after eating excessive amounts of new spring grass. The feet become engorged with blood and the sensitive laminae in the hoof become inflamed and may separate	Call vet at once as prompt treatment can help the condition considerably. In the meantime cool the feet in running water from a hosepipe and try to get the horse to walk, as exercise helps the feet to drain. Remove from grass and give light starvation diet
Nail blind		
Lameness soon after the horse has been shod	Shoe nail driven home too close to the sensitive areas of the foot	Call blacksmith, who will remove nail and replace it correctly
Navicular disease		
Intermittent lameness, usually slight, followed by pointing, in which one forefoot is rested in front of the other on the toe. Gradual increase in tendency to stumble. Later, foot will contract at the heels	May be hereditary. Otherwise probably due to jarring of the foot through excessive roadwork or strain in hunting and jumping. This brings on lesions on the navicular bone	Consult vet
Overreach		
Cuts and bruises to bulbs of heel	Toe of hind shoe hitting front heel	Bathe wound in salt solution. Call vet if wound is severe. Prevention is better than cure – horse should be fitted with overreach boots
Pedal ostitis		
Intermittent lameness, later permanent	Severe jarring, brought on by too much roadwork or by jumping when the ground is very hard. This leads to inflammation of the pedal bone and bony growths on the bone	Rest. Bathing foot in cold water. Special shoeing may help
Quittor		
Lameness. Infection breaking out around coronary band	Infection in the hoof working its way upwards to form abscess	Consult vet
Sandcrack		
Crack or split in the wall of the hoof, extending upwards into coronary band	Mineral deficiency which makes hoof unusually brittle	Consult blacksmith who may fit special clips to hold edges of crack together, or put on special shoes
Seedy toe		
Revealed when trimming the hoof during shoeing. The outside of the hoof wall appears normal but a cavity is revealed when the horn is pared away	A legacy of laminitis. Tight shoes may also be a cause	Call blacksmith who will pare away the damaged horn. Then treat liberally with Stockholm tar

Legs

Symptoms:	Causes:	Treatment:
Bog spavin		
Swelling in the front of the hock and on both sides at the back	Excess fluid in hock joint	None. Bog spavins l〈 unsightly but cause 〉 trouble
Brushing		
Sudden acute lameness. Injury around the fetlock joint	One leg striking against the other	Rest and hosing the affected part with c〈 water. Prevent recur〈 by fitting brushing b〉 Consult blacksmith
Capped elbow		
Swelling on the point of the elbow, level with chest. If infected, horse may be lame	Persistent irritation or rubbing of the elbow when lying down or because bed is too thin	Cold poultice the sw〈 and call vet if infecte〉 special shoeing and provide thicker bed
Capped hock		
Similar swelling to capped elbow, but this time on hock. It is usually permanent but rarely painful	Knock or kick on affected area	None. Cold poultici〈 sometimes helps to r〈 swelling
Cracked heels		
Sore patches, often suppurating, and deep cracks on the heels at the back of the pastern	An irritant in the soil which affects the heels and legs after they have been covered in mud. White legs are more prone to the condition	Apply ointment, usi〈 one with a cod liver 〈 or zinc oxide base. Alternatively, dry poultice with dry wa〈 bran, and bandaging
Curb		
Lameness. Outward bowing of line from point of hock to cannon bone	Sprain to ligament connecting point of hock with cannon bone	Rest. Cold poultici〈 application of linime〉
Ringbone		
Lameness. Swelling of pastern	Blow, sprain or jarring which causes extra bone to form on first or second pastern bones or both	Rest. Seek professio〈 advice and be prepar〉 pony to be permaner〉 lame
Speedy cutting		
Sudden fall or lameness. Cuts or bruises just below knee	One leg interfering with another	Rest. Bathe affected with cold water
Splints		
Lameness. Heat and swelling in affected leg	Formation of bone between the splint and cannon	Rest. Cold water poultices. Once spli〈 formed, lameness disappears, leaving a permanent lump
Sprained joints and tendons		
Heat and swelling. Lameness in some cases	Jarring. Twisting of joint. Inflammation of the tendon	Cold water dowsing. tendons, pressure bandages. Rest
Sprung tendon		
Bowed tendon	Sprain to the tendon	None. This is an ind〈 ion of a former sprai〉
Thoroughpin		
Swelling just above the hock which can usually be pushed from one side to the other	Strain	Pressure bandage to reduce swelling. Kee〈 by massage or by app〉 goose grease

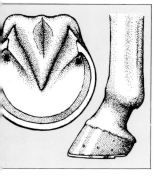

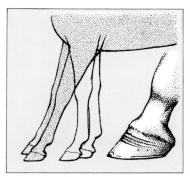

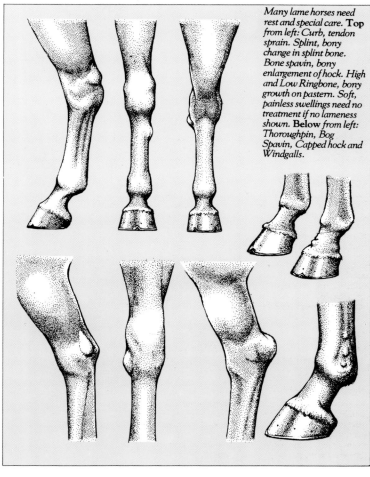

Many lame horses need rest and special care. **Top** *from left: Curb, tendon sprain. Splint, bony change in splint bone. Bone spavin, bony enlargement of hock. High and Low Ringbone, bony growth on pastern. Soft, painless swellings need no treatment if no lameness shown.* **Below** *from left: Thoroughpin, Bog Spavin, Capped hock and Windgalls.*

e Corns (bruises) occur on sole in angle *and bar. After treatment, seated shoes* *relieve pressure.*

Above *Laminitis, inflammation of inner hoof wall, causes this stance. It can lead to ridging on hoof (**inset**).*

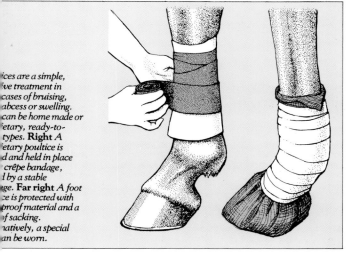

ices are a simple, *ve treatment in* *cases of bruising,* *abcess or swelling.* *can be home made or* *etary, ready-to-* *types.* **Right** *A* *etary poultice is* *d and held in place* *crêpe bandage,* *d by a stable* *ge.* **Far right** *A foot* *e is protected with* *proof material and a* *f sacking.* *natively, a special* *an be worn.*

us – ringworm, for instance, can be mitted to humans, as well as horses, in in cases. Therefore, always observe sanitary precautions in the stable.

s, coughs and chest diseases
sing food, discharge from nostrils and listlessness, coughing and high temper-are all indications of a chill. Keep the warm and consult the vet, who will bly prescribe antibiotics in severe cases. ughs, too, should always be treated by et if they are persistent. Causes can vary simple irritation, the result of feeding dusty hay, to severe diseases, such as

epidemic cough and strangles. Other respiratory diseases include equine influenza; whistling; roaring; high blowing; and broken wind. For details, consult the chart.

If the horse is coughing, never work it hard. Rest and warmth are most important. Galloping a horse with a cough can, in extreme cases, lead to broken wind, which is incurable.

Digestive problems
Teeth and stomach can both give the horse problems. Both demand prompt attention if anything does go wrong.

Uneven wear on the teeth can lead to

sharp edges developing. These make chewing food painful; in addition, the mouth and cheeks may get cut. The remedy is to have the teeth filed (rasped). This must be done by an expert.

Restlessness, sweating, biting and kicking at the flank, lying down and getting up again are all signs of colic – acute pain in the abdomen. Colic falls into three types. These are spasmodic colic, so-called because the pain comes in spasms; flatulent colic, caused by a gas build-up because of a blockage in the bowel; and twisted gut, where the bowel itself, or the membrane supporting it, becomes twisted, so cutting off the blood

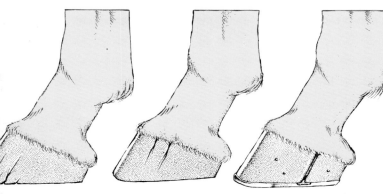

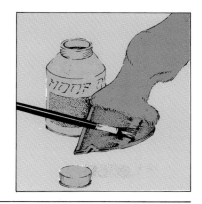

*Hoofs of unshod horses at grass can become cracked if they are neglected. Grass cracks (**far left**) split up from base of wall. They grow out if the hoof is treated appropriately by the farrier. Sand cracks (**centre left**) split down from the hoof head. These are much more serious and need veterinary care. After treatment, they can be controlled with seated shoes (**left**), which take the pressure off the crack. Hoof cream and hoof oil (**right**) applied daily, help prevent cracks by keeping hoof healthy.*

Strangles

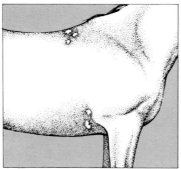

Saddle sores and girth galls

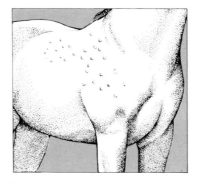

Ringworm

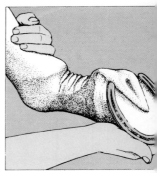

Cracked heels

Head

Symptoms:	Causes:	Treatment:	Symptoms:	Causes:	Treatment:
Blocked tear duct			**Colds and Coughs**		
Tears running down face	Sand, grit or mucous causing blockage of tear ducts	Call vet, who will probably clear blockage by using a catheter to force sterile liquid through the duct	Thin discharge from nostrils; coughing	Infection; sometimes dusty hay or allergy	Isolate animal and k warm; give regular d of cough medicine. Consult vet
Broken wind			**Influenza**		
Persistent cough, rapid exhaustion, double movement of flank	Breakdown of air vessels in the lung from overworking the horse	Incurable, may be alleviated by keeping horse out, work gently and dampen food	Lethargy, cough, high temperature. Horse refuses food	Virus infection	Isolate. Keep warm. Call vet. Preventior inoculation is possib
Catarrh			**Strangles**		
Thick yellowish discharge from the nostrils	Inflammation of mucous membrane May be cold infection preceding cough or allergy, beware of infecting other horses	Clean nostrils with warm boracic solution and smear with petroleum jelly In summer, turn out to grass	Similar to those of influenza, plus swelling of lymph glands under the jaw, which eventually form abscesses	Contact with infected animal or with contaminated grooming kit, feed buckets, etc	Isolate. Call vet. Fee and bran mashes and horse warm. Rest is essential

supply and causing severe pain.

All forms of colic are exceptionally painful, as the horse is incapable of vomiting to obtain relief

Colic must be treated quickly, as real suffering is being caused. As long as the horse is not completely exhausted, lead it around gently and, if at all possible, prevent it from lying down. If the animal lies down and rolls, it may well injure itself. Keep the horse warm and the box or stall well bedded.

Treatment varies according to the type of colic involved, but, if no improvement occurs after an hour or if the pain is obviously severe, call a vet immediately. For spasms, give a colic drink (one should be kept ready made-up in the first aid kit) and for wind administer a laxative to open the bowels. A half to a pint of linseed oil, depending on the size of the horse involved, is a standard re-

medy. Linseed oil, too, is good in cases of constipation.

Constipation and diarrhoea present fewer problems, but worms – parasites present in all horses – can be a menace if not strictly controlled. They present particular problems to the owners of field-kept horses; here, prevention is better than cure (see p. 142). All horses, however, should be regularly wormed, by treating with a deworming medicine, as part of stable routing. Consult the vet as to the best dosage.

Azoturia is not strictly a digestive disease, but it is closely connected with correct feeding. It can occur when a horse is worked hard after being rested on a full working diet, though the exact cause of the disease is unknown. The first signs are slackening of pace and stiffness of muscles, particularly in the quarters. If the horse is urged on it will

eventually stagger, come to a halt and even collapse. Always arrange for it t transported back to the stable – never ride home. The vet must be called.

Treatment is rest, warmth, massage, ty of water and a laxative diet. How once infected, it is likely that the diseas reoccur. Therefore, always reduce the according to the amount of work act being done by the horse.

Nursing the horse

Like all animals, horses take time to red form illness. The vet will always instruc owner in what to do, but, largely, succe nursing is merely a matter of common se

Giving medicine, for example, can pr problems. The simplest way is in the provided that the medicine is suitable an horse is eating. Soluble medicines ca

Digestive system

Symptoms:	Causes:	Treatment:	Symptoms:	Causes:	Treatment:
Colic			**Diarrhoea**		
Severe abdominal pain, characterised by pawing of the ground, restlessness, sweating, rolling, lying down and getting up, kicking, biting and looking at the stomach, groaning, cold ears	Poor or irregular feeding, wrong sort of food, exercise or drinking straight after food, too much food when horse is tired. Worm infection	Call vet immediately. meanwhile do what you can to relieve the pain. Keep horse warm, apply hot water bottle to belly. Try to discourage horse from lying down or rolling	Very loose, watery droppings	Excessive fresh grass. Worms	Mix dry bran with fo add kaolin. Feed wit If persistant, call vet
			Worms		
			Loss of condition, in spite of careful feeding	There are several types of intestinal parasites collectively known as worms	Regular doses of wor powder or paste, cou with regular mainter of pasture

Symptoms:	Causes:	Treatment:	Symptoms:	Causes:	Treatment:
and coat					
...umps (Humor)			**Sweet itch**		
...us forms of size and ...Rarely seen all over	Probably overheating from too much protein in system	Give bran mash with addition of two tablespoons of Epsom salts.	Extreme itchiness of areas around mane and tail, apparent only in late spring, summer and early autumn	Unknown, probably an allergy	Apply calamine lotion to relieve itching. Keep mane and tail clean. Lard and sulphur applied to the area can be soothing. Consult vet
...g, dull coat, ...rance of small grey ...k parasites on the	Unknown. Appears in spring on grass-fed horses or on animals which have been in poor condition and are now improving	Dust affected areas liberally with delousing powder, obtainable from vet. Keep grooming kit separate	**Warbles**		
...orm			Maggot of the warble fly	Painful swelling on back	Bathe in warm water which will keep the lump soft and help to 'draw' the warble from a small hole on the top of the swelling. The maggot can be gently squeezed out, but do not do this before consulting the vet
...y circular bare ...es on the skin of ...g sizes which may or ...ot be itchy	Fungus infection which is highly contagious	Apply tincture of iodine to affected parts. Disinfect rugs and sterilise grooming kit. Keep horse isolated			

Left A healthy horse is alert and attentive, taking a keen interest in its surroundings. It carries its head high, ears pricked, eyes bright and wide open. Its coat is smooth and glossy.

Lack of work and boredom can cause severe stable vices like crib-biting (below) and weaving (right).

mixed in with the drinking water. Otherwise the vet will advise.

The golden rules of nursing are gentleness, cleanliness, and the ability to ensure the horse's comfort and rest. When treating a wound always try to keep the dust down in the stable. Reduce concentrated foods for a horse suddenly thrown out of work by lameness and substitute a mild laxative instead. Gentle sponging of eyes and nostrils will help refresh a horse with a raised temperature.

Care when old

Horses and ponies are frequently remarkably long lived. Some ponies, for instance, are still leading useful lives at thirty, but caring for an elderly horse presents its own set of problems.

Teeth must be regularly filed (rasped), as the molars will probably become long and sharp if left untreated. Select the diet carefully; boiled barley, broad bran, chaff and good quality hay form the best mixture for an old horse.

Eventually though, some horses just lose interest in life. If the lustre goes out of the eyes or the appetite wanes for no apparent reason, it is then kinder to have the horse put down. A vet will arrange this. A humane killer is used, and death is instantaneous.

Chapter Ten

The horse in leisure and sport

Riding is fast becoming one of the most popular leisure sports in the world. In the UK alone, more than 250,000 people of all ages ride each week; in other countries, the figure is even higher.

Riding for leisure falls into two main categories. Many people ride solely for enjoyment, with little thought for sports or competitions. There is little more exhilarating, say, than riding out for a good hack across country. Secondly, there are organized activities, such as hunting, show jumping, and eventing, with which this chapter is chiefly concerned. Some of these are now becoming more and more professional, but the basic theme is still enjoyment – whether at a local gymkhana or at an international event.

Leaving the formality of the riding school for an hour or so's riding around the roads or across country is usually the rider's first real test of responsibility. The rules are few and simple, and can be summed up in the two words consideration and safety. Remember that traffic regulations, for example, apply just as much to riders as to other road users; it is extremely dangerous, say, for a ride of a dozen horses to be allowed to straggle across a road. On a winter afternoon, wear something light – a luminous armband is ideal – so that you will be easily visible when riding back in the twilight. A light, attached to the stirrup iron, is also a good idea.

As far as actual riding is concerned, remember the lessons of the school. Always show consideration and courtesy to pedestrians and keep to authorized bridle paths and riding tracks, if they are marked. Above all, never ride at speed near animals or people; if they are frightened, they may well inadvertantly frighten your horse.

As far as children and teenagers up to the age of twenty are concerned, many of these lessons are part of the basic teaching of the Pony Club – a world-wide organization which attracts many young riders. Originally found-

Right A group of children clean tack at Pony Club camp and inset four typical scenes of riding activity, ranging from a lesson to an outdoor hack. The Pony Club is a world-wide organization with the aim of teaching horsemanship in all its aspects and, to this end, *many activities, such as camps, working rallies, gymkhanas and technical lectures, are organized. Branches, too, have special activities according to geographical location; bush and trail rides, for instance, are both very popular in Australia and the USA.*

ed in the UK in 1929, there are now branches all over the English-speaking world; Canada, Australia, New Zealand and the USA in particular have very strong memberships. The first US branch was formed in 1935, though this lapsed during the Second World War, and the Club was not refounded there until 1950; the first Australian branch was set up in 1947.

The object of the Club is to teach horsemastership in its broadest aspects. The teaching, done by qualified volunteers, is backed up by a system of optional examinations. In the UK and the USA, these tests range in difficulty from D to A – D being fairly simple and A being of a very high standard indeed. Australia follows the same system, with two extra tests — the K, for the active rider, and the H, for horsemastership.

The gymkhana — an import from India

Though the upper age limit for Pony Club membership is twenty, many adult riding clubs follow the same basic pattern. Adult riders, too, enjoy all the thrills and spills of the gymkhana just as much as their younger counterparts.

The word itself comes from gymnastics and the Hindustani *gend-khana* (sports ground); the idea of such mounted games was brought back to the UK by officers serving in India in the 19th century. From Britain, it spread throughout the horse world. There are many different events, ranging from simple jumping competitions to tests of agility and speed, such as Chase Me Charlie and bending races.

Both riders and mounts – ponies are usually

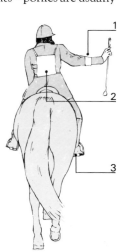

Right A rider wearing safety clothing clearly signals to traffic her intention of turning right (1). Safety first is the order of the day when riding on a road. Horses should never move two abreast unless an inexperienced young animal or rider needs escorting by a more experienced companion. The luminous back cloth (2) and stirrup light (3) are both vital in the twilight. Left The usual method of transport over long distances is a horsebox. The interior is padded so that the horse cannot injure itself during a journey, but, in addition, knee caps, hock boots, travelling and tail bandages should be worn for protection.

more successful than horses because of their greater manoeuvrability – have to be fit, though not as fit as they would have to be for a day's hunting, for instance. Grass-kept ponies and horses are quite capable of taking part in such events once a week, say, during the summer season without any ill effects.

Hunting

Another sport which appeals to many riders is hunting – the oldest surviving horseback sport. Originally the stag was the chief quarry – it still is in France – but, in English-speaking countries, fox hunting now has the largest following (though drag hunting is gaining in popularity). In all cases, the etiquette of hunting is the same, based as it is on traditions that date back for hundreds of years. The USA and Canada have some 140 hunts between them, though by far the greater number are in the US. Virginia has the highest individual total with twenty. Both there and in Australia, hunting follows the British model, though, in Australia, other animals, such as the wallaby, are sometimes hunted in place of foxes.

Permission to hunt has to be obtained in advance from either the Secretary or the Master of a pack. This can be either for a day, in which case a fee known as a 'cap' – so-called because it is usually collected on the spot in a hunting cap – is paid, or a subscription can be taken out for a season.

On arrival at the Meet, the first thing to do is to identify the various Hunt officers, whose instructions must be instantly obeyed during the day. The Master is in overall charge, assisted by a Field Master, whose task it is to control the hunt-followers. The Huntsman, in charge of the hounds, is similarly assisted by one or two Whippers-in, who chase up any stragglers in the pack and generally help keep the hounds under control.

Hounds work by scent and once this has been 'found' (discovered) in the covert, things can happen very quickly. The hounds will begin to 'speak' and then take up the scent. The field then follows, taking care not to overtake the Master and the pack.

It is best for inexperienced riders to stay near the back of the field until they gain in confidence, and, if possible, pick a more experienced member of the hunt to follow. However, whether inexperienced or experi-enced, no rider should get carried away excitement; a cool head is better than a one. Remember, too, that the excitemen the hunt affects the horses and they are too willing to gallop on even when clo exhaustion. At the end of the day, theref care of the horse becomes the absolute pr ity, so that it can recover from its exert as quickly as possible.

Hunter trials and point-to-points

Two activities closely connected with h ing are Hunter trials and point-to-po The first is a kind of mini cross-cou competition, in part judged against clock. Riders race over a predetermi course of 1½ to 2 miles, jumping conventi fences. Other tests can include dealing the sort of hazards commonly found in hunting field – a gate to be opened closed, say, or a slip rail to be removed replaced.

Point-to-points, or hunt races, first sta in the UK several centuries ago, but, un the gymkhana, they have not been unive ly adopted by the horse world. However USA has a few, while Australia has its

al equivalent in the so-called picnic
s of the Outback.

nting

t equestrian sports developed from hunt-
but eventing – one of the toughest all-
d tests that any horse and rider can face –
notable exception. Its roots lie in the
efield rather than in the hunting field.
sport officially became part of the Olym-
in 1912, but it is only since the Second
ld War that it has risen to its present
ense popularity. Today, such nations as
tralia, the UK, the USA, West Germany
the USSR are all world leaders in the
t.

o succeed in eventing, horse and rider
t be proficient in all three of its disci-
es – dressage, cross country, and show
ping. In one day events, all three stages
held on the same day; in the three day
t, one day is allocated for each test. The
dard set varies from novice upwards; at
very top, it is extremely demanding in-
l. In addition, the competitors also have
ce extra endurance tests over roads and
s and a steeplechase course.

Some hold that the first phase – dressage –
is the most important part of the event and
that the standard of training demonstrated in
it by horse and rider is the crux of the matter.
The test lasts for seven and a half minutes
and is ridden from memory. Though the
standard set is not as high as in pure dressage
competitions, the judges still look for correct
carriage and obedience in the performance
of the various movements. These include
coming to the halt from the canter; half
passes; extended trot; extended canter; and
the counter canter.

It is unarguable that a good performance in
the dressage arena, with the horse showing
implicit obedience, gives a competitor a head
start of his or her rivals. But, above all,
champion riders are never less than superla-
tive in the age-old art of riding across country. This test of speed and endurance is the
key to success in the sport, as the competitors
pit their wits and skills against the wiles of the
cross-country course builder, negotiating up
to thirty-five fences, many with difficult
approaches.

The distance to be covered varies; at
Olympic level, it is about 30k (18.6 miles).

In the Olympics, or competitions such as the
world-famous Badminton Three Day Event,
there are four phases – roads and tracks,
steeplechase, roads and tracks again, and,
finally, the cross-country itself.

On the roads and tracks stages, the horse
must cover the ground at approximately
240m (262yd) a minute to keep up with the
set time; this means that a very fast trot is
necessary. The steeplechase, usually between
3k (2 miles) and 4k (2½ miles) long, has to be
tackled at a good gallop; again to avoid time
penalties, the horse must average nearly
40kph (25mph). After the second road and
track phase, there is a compulsory ten-minute
rest period before competitors start the cross
country.

In the cross country, the course builder
takes full advantage of the natural terrain in
planning what many regard as the ultimate
test for horse and rider. The course itself can
be between 6km (4 miles) and 8km (5 miles)
long, and a speed of 570km (623yd) a minute
is required. The height of the various fences
is fixed at a maximum of 1m 20cm (4ft) and
the width at 1m 80cm (6ft), though Olympic
fences can be six inches wider.

*A rider takes a fence in
sh hunt and* **inset** *a
er of a hunt and his
Formal riding dress is
ed in the hunting field.*

*npetitor tackles the
jump in the
uhlen event.*

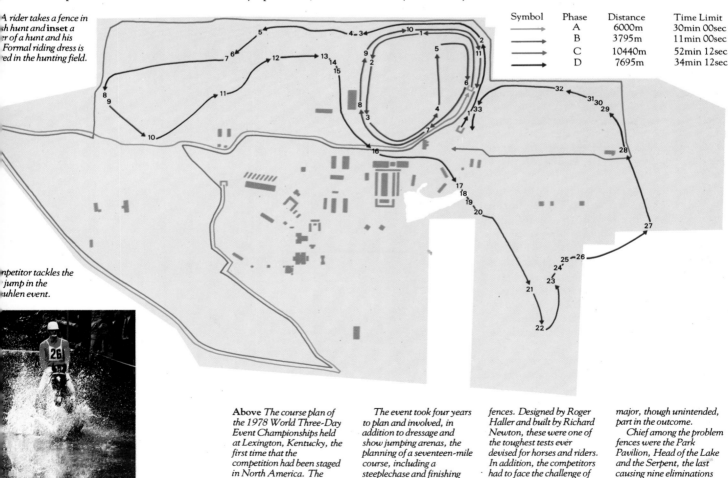

Symbol	Phase	Distance	Time Limit
→	A	6000m	30min 00sec
→	B	3795m	11min 00sec
→	C	10440m	52min 12sec
→	D	7695m	34min 12sec

Above *The course plan of
the 1978 World Three-Day
Event Championships held
at Lexington, Kentucky, the
first time that the
competition had been staged
in North America. The
forty-seven entrants
represented the cream of
world eventing talent.*

*The event took four years
to plan and involved, in
addition to dressage and
show jumping arenas, the
planning of a seventeen-mile
course, including a
steeplechase and finishing
with a cross-country of
nearly five miles, with thirty-
three fixed and varied*

*fences. Designed by Roger
Haller and built by Richard
Newton, these were one of
the toughest tests ever
devised for horses and riders.
In addition, the competitors
had to face the challenge of
intense humidity and an
extremely high pollution
rate, both of which played a*

*major, though unintended,
part in the outcome.*

*Chief among the problem
fences were the Park
Pavilion, Head of the Lake
and the Serpent, the last
causing nine eliminations
and retirements, eight falls
and three refusals among the
competitors.*

Among the most taxing fences the rider has to face are the coffin and the water jump. The coffin, named after a fence first devised at Badminton, consists of three elements – a fence, a ditch and then another fence. It is the ditch which usually causes the problems. Success at the water jump depends on persuading the horse to overcome its natural reluctance to jump into water.

Errors are heavily penalized. In addition to time faults – these are so important that riders usually wear several watches to check their time – twenty penalties are added for a refusal and sixty for a fall. Riders can be eliminated for three refusals.

Before the final show jumping stage, the horse must pass a thorough veterinary examination to make sure that it is fit enough to continue. The show jumping test itself is primarily one of fitness and suppleness. It is devised to show that the horse is still capable of negotiating a small, twisting course of obstacles after the gruelling ordeal of the previous day.

The rider, too, needs to be alert. Often, the competitors are so close together after the cross country that a single fence down can alter the whole finishing order.

Show jumping

The rules governing eventing are laid down by the Fédération Equestre Internationale (FEI); they are reviewed annually in the light of current experience. So, too, are the rules of show jumping, a sport which had its origins in the later half of the nineteenth century and rose from these beginnings to become probably the most popular equestrian sport in the world today – with the sole exception of racing.

There are four types of competition. In the first, competitors are faulted if they knock down a fence (four faults); for a fall (eight faults); and for disobedience (first disobedience, three faults, a second, six, and a third, elimination). In case of a tie, a jump-off is held, frequently against the clock. Time also enters into the other three types of competition. In the first two, faults are penalized by time penalties, while the third is ridden solely against the fixed time limit the judges have decided for the course.

Most international competitions adopt the first method of scoring. Most demanding of these is the *Prix des Nations*; in this, the fences number thirteen or fourteen in all, the highest being approximately 1.60m (5ft 3in) and the lowest 1.30m (4ft 4in). Each team consists of four riders, each of whom jump the course twice. The best three scores are the ones that count in the final placing.

The nature of the fences follow a basic standard laid down by the FEI. They are of two main types – the upright and the spread. Common examples of the first are gates, walls, poles, and poles and brush; of the second, the triple bar, parallel bars and the double oxer. A water jump, between 3m (10ft) and 5m (16ft 5in) wide, is also usually included.

The course designer works within the limits set down by the sport's governing body, but, within these, he has several alternatives. In planning a course, he has to consider, above all, the level of the competition involved, together with such problems as the size of the arena, the number of fences available, and so on. Generally speaking, he plans

what is known as the 'track' of the course – making sure that competitors will hav change direction once at least – and t goes on to plot the position of the fences may decide to test the riders' ability furthe varying the distance between them, wl means that the horse will have to var natural stride. He finally chooses the typ fences. Usually, upright and spread fe are alternated, progressing upwards in o of difficulty after a few easy fences firs 'settle' the horse. With the twin except of puissance and speed competitions, the at least one combination included.

Preparation of horse and rider is v

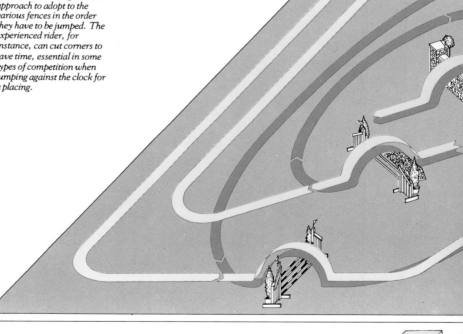

Right *A typical show jumping course, showing the approaches taken by two competitors – an experienced combination of horse and rider and a less experienced one respectively. The key factor involved is to plot the track of the course, working out the approach to adopt to the various fences in the order they have to be jumped. The experienced rider, for instance, can cut corners to save time, essential in some types of competition when jumping against the clock for a placing.*

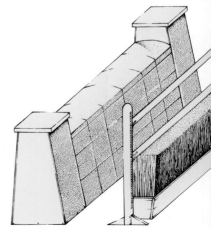

Left to right *Five common types of fence – a wall, brush and rail, parallel bars, a gate, and triple bar. Fences normally fall into two types; these are the upright, in which, as the name implies, the structure is built up vertically from the ground, and the spread, where width is combined with height. When tackling uprights, the horse should be well collected, its rider making sure that the take-off point is calculated so that the horse can clear the obstacle with the minimum possible effort. This means starting the jump from further back than*

would be the case with a spread. When jumping a spread, on the other hand, the take-off point is nearer to the fence. Such fences are best approached at speed; the important thing here is to ensure that the horse has sufficient impulsion to clear the width of the obstacle. The best take-off point is one at a distance of 1 to 1¼ times the fence's height. The horse judges this from the groundline (the base of the fence); the rider should estimate the distance from a higher point, as, in some cases, the ground line can be misleading.

king the course before the event, work-
out the track, the strides between each
e and the elements of a combination, is
nportant as riding it later. Related dis-
es and fences make it essential to ride the
se as a rhythmic, flowing whole. The
e must be well-trained and responsive, so
its stride can be lengthened or shortened
ill while maintaining impulsion.
raining should be a matter of patient
ression. After basic schooling, the horse
ld be introduced to the kind of fences it
face in competition, starting off at a low
ht and gradually building up to a higher
Two main points can be established

here. The horse should be encouraged to
bascule, that is, to arch its head, neck and
back while in the air. Any tendency to flat-
ten at this point should be corrected through
gridwork and by jumping a series of wide, low
parallels. Secondly, work can be done on the
basic stride to overcome two common faults –
the tendency to slow down in the approach to
the jump and taking off too close to it. The
rider should also practise jumping at an angle,
increasing pace and cutting corners – all vital
elements in speed tests.

Before the actual competition, a good
warm-up period is essential, but the work
done then should vary according to the per-

sonality of the horse. A lazy horse may need
stirring up, an excitable one calming down.

Top riders all have very individual styles,
though in many cases there is also the influence of national training and tradition. The
West Germans, with their strong, powerful
horses, their dominant style of riding and
training and their emphasis on dressage, or
schooling on the flat, are without doubt the
world's leading show-jumping nation at the
moment, and likely to remain so. Also in the
top rank are the UK, Italy and the USA, with
individual riders from many nations, including Australia, Canada, Belgium, France and
Ireland, following close behind.

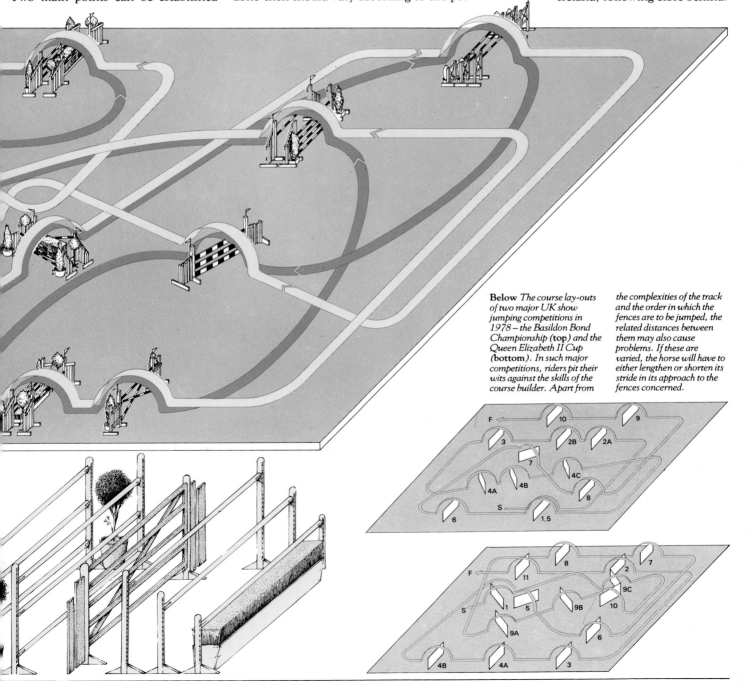

Below The course lay-outs of two major UK show jumping competitions in 1978 – the Basildon Bond Championship (top) and the Queen Elizabeth II Cup (bottom). In such major competitions, riders pit their wits against the skills of the course builder. Apart from the complexities of the track and the order in which the fences are to be jumped, the related distances between them may also cause problems. If these are varied, the horse will have to either lengthen or shorten its stride in its approach to the fences concerned.

Right *Show jumping scenes
from around the world,
including the Derby Bank at
Hickstead (**bottom right**),
one of the sport's most
celebrated obstacles. Show
jumping has greatly
developed since 1868, when
a competition for a 'high
leap' and a 'wide leap' was
included in the first horse
show of the Royal Dublin
Society, Ireland, to test the
qualifications of horses for
the hunting field. In 1881, a
course of permanent fences
was laid out and in use at the
Dublin show's new
permanent show ground at
Ballsbridge. The first US
National Horse show was
held at Madison Square
Gardens, New York, in
1883, and in Paris
seventeen years later three
jumping competitions were
held in conjunction with the
Olympic Games. Britain's
first international horse
show was held at Olympia,
London, in 1907.*

*In those early days,
conditions were very
different to those of today.
The rules for jumping were
virtually non-existent; for
instance, circling before a
fence, now penalised as a
refusal, was permitted,
while the wooden slats
placed on each fence were
removed as often by the wind
as by the horses themselves.
Today, however, show
jumping is a highly
sophisticated sport, and, in
many cases, very big
business indeed. At one end
of the scale, a teenager can
jump at a local show for
nothing more than a rosette.
At the other are the top-class
professional riders, many
now sponsored by industry,
who win large sums of
money each year in major
competitions. Such is the
demand for horses at this
level that a good one can
easily fetch a small fortune.*

Dressage

Dressage (the name comes from the French *dresser*, to train) is a highly specialised sport. Its practitioners are rarely household names, as the discipline lacks the obvious excitement of eventing or show jumping, but nevertheless it is one of the most skilled forms of riding. The history of the sport goes back to late medieval times, when *Haute Ecole* (high school) became established in the royal courts of Europe. Today, it has its place in many competitions, including the Olympic Games, while its Classical traditions are maintained by institutions such as the Span-

Above *Christine Stuckelberger, one of the world's youngest dressage stars, in action on her horse Granat,* **left** *Elena Petouchkova, a leading Soviet rider, competing in Copenhagen, and* **below** *the German dressage team – the present world champions – at Goodwood, UK, in 1978. Even at the basic* *levels, where only walk, trot, canter and halt are required, training a dressage horse takes considerable time and patience. Ideally, the horse should give the impression of doing what is required of it of its own accord, moving freely and regularly with harmony and grace in all its movements at the desired paces.*

ish Riding School in Vienna and the Cadre Noir at Saumur, France.

The object of dressage is to teach the horse how to be supple, agile and keen to ride, while at the same time developing a perfect understanding with its rider. To achieve all this takes considerable time. At the most advanced level – the Olympic dressage test – training a horse takes at least four years and often considerably longer. Marks are given for each section of the test, on a scale from zero to ten, with additional assessment of the general impression both horse and rider give the judges.

The rider demonstrates a wide range of movements, working at collected, medium and extended paces, with smooth transitions between each one. Basic movements include the rein-back; halt; counter canter; change of leg; pirouette; and turn on the forehand. Lateral movements, in which the horse moves simultaneously sideways and forwards are also required; these include the leg yield, the travers, and the half pass. Two other

complex movements are the piaffe, a trot on the spot, and the passage, a measured, very collected, elevated and cadenced exercise.

The tests are performed in an arena on either sand or, at less advanced levels, grass, bordered by a 30cm (1ft)-high fence. The arena's size varies from 20m (22yd) by 40m (44yd) for novice to medium grades to 20m by 60m (65yd) for advanced dressage. The rider must make full use of the arena, especially in figure work. Figures include the vole, a circle of 6m (19½ft) in diameter, the serpentine and the figure of eight.

Driving

Dressage, too, plays its part in the relatively new sport of combined driving, the equivalent of a three day event on wheels, which has been steadily gaining in popularity since it was founded in 1969. Competitors are assessed on both presentation and dressage before they compete in the cross-country marathon, covering up to eighteen miles during which they have to negotiate six hazards,

such as narrow turns between trees or [?]cents into lakes. The final obstacle-driv[?] phase, which takes the place of show jump[?] in the ridden test, consists of driving betw[?] closely-set plastic bollards without knock[?] them, or the markers on them, over.

Private driving, or showing, howeve[?] confined to the show ring. The emph[?] here is on smart presentation of horse[?] horses, vehicle and driver. Known as '[?] whip', he or she circles the ring at a t[?] changing direction as requested by [?] judges. The general presentation is then[?] sessed, and, after this, the driver gives a sl[?]

performance, finishing with a halt and
back.

w horses and ponies

ng horses and ponies, too, are frequently
'n in classes ranging from show ponies,
ers and hacks to saddle horses in the
. All such competitions have as their
 purpose the improvement of the breed
'pe concerned; in the UK they started
200 years ago.
e crucial test for any show pony or horse
nformation, though there are other qual-
judges look for as well when selecting the

prize winners. Pony classes are divided by
height, with an upper limit of fifteen hands
for working ponies. The best of these change
hands for large sums of money, often in
excess of £10,000 ($20,000). Hunter classes,
on the other hand, are divided by weight into
lightweight, middleweight and heavyweight
divisions. Other classes include Ladies'
Hunter, where the horse must be ridden
sidesaddle, small hunter and working hunter.
The horse has to show off its paces, particularly the gallop, and is then ridden by a judge
to assess the quality of ride it gives. In the
USA, in competitions in the Hunter Divi-

*Below A four-in-hand team
of Swiss-bred stallions drive
through the shallows of Lake
Movat, Switzerland, in the
marathon stage of a
combined driving
competition;* **inset** *a team of
Lipizzaners, viewed from the
whip's position, two scurry
racing scenes and a troika
racing through the snow
outside Moscow. In the
world of equestrian sport,
the two activities of
combined driving and
obstacle driving have a
considerable international
following. Combined
driving, the harness*

*equivalent of the three-day
event, was founded in 1969.
It has three stages –
dressage, the marathon (the
equivalent of the cross-
country), and obstacle
driving (the equivalent of
show jumping).*

*Obstacle driving on its
own is usually held in indoor
arenas, when teams of
ponies, like the ones above,
hurtle round a twisting
course pulling scurries in a
battle against the clock. Up
to twenty obstacles, each
topped by a ball, have to be
rounded. Ten seconds is
added for each fault.*

sion, such as the Maclay, the horses have to jump a small course of fences, but in the UK and Ireland only working hunters are asked to leave the ground.

Although hunters comprise the majority of show horses, hacks also have a following. In the last century, there were two types – park hacks, suitable for fashionable riding and covert hacks, which were ridden to a hunt meet and then exchanged for a hunter. Now there is simply the show hack, an elegant well-trained horse with good conformation and manners. Again, there are three classes – small, large and ladies. The basic requirement is for the horse to walk, trot and canter to the judges' satisfaction, though the rider also has the opportunity to ride an individual test. As with the hunter, the judges assess the ride the horse gives themselves, and, finally, have the horse run up in hand as a last test.

The USA has one extra showing division, that of the saddle horse. These horses are shown as three-gaited, five-gaited or fine harness animals. The three-gaited horse demonstrates the usual paces of walk, trot and canter, but the five-gaited one has the extra paces of slow gait and rack. In both of these, each foot touches the ground individually, though the rack is slightly faster than the gait. Harness horses draw light buggies at walk, trot and park gait (a more lively version of the trot).

A showy, even flamboyant, turnout is very important for both horse and rider, and the spectacle, usually held in an indoor arena and compèred by a ring-master, attracts large crowds. Madison Square Gardens is the most important show.

Polo

Polo is one of the oldest horseback sports, and, today, is probably the most expensive of all. It is believed to have originated in Persia more than 2,000 years ago, though it was played in varying forms in China, Mongolia and Japan. The game was taken to India by the Moslems and Chinese; there, English planters in Assam discovered it in the mid-nineteenth century.

Polo reached the UK in 1869, where it was dubbed by spectators 'Hockey on horseback.' Six years later, the first English rules were issued, and a year after that the game was taken to the USA. There, it quickly spread, with the founding of such international competitions as the Westchester Cup, to reach a golden age between the two world wars.

Since 1945, however, the sport has been dominated by players from Argentina, who maintain a stranglehold in the one remaining international tournament, the Cup of the Americas. The USA comes second in the

Top left *An American saddlebred,* top right *miniature horses from South America,* left *the champion Working Hunter of 1978 at the Horse of the Year Show, Wembley, UK, and* below *an English-bred hack, ridden side-saddle by its elegant rider, shows off its paces. Showing classes are held at horse shows throughout the world. The types of horses competing in them vary widely, but the basic aim is always the same – the winners are the ones the judges consider likely to improve the breed. The three chief qualities assessed are conformation, paces, and the quality of ride given.*

Top right *Polo in Ab... Iran,* below *chukka in progress at Cowdray P... UK. Because of its exp... the game is probably th... most expensive equesti... sport in the world. The... qualities demanded of... polo ponies are conside... Usually about 15.1 ha... high, they are required... gallop flat out, stop in... own length, turn on a... sixpence, swing round... pirouette, and start off... at top speed from a standstill. They also ha... ride off other ponies, be... to neck rein and perfor... flying changes of leg, u... must come as second n... to the animal.*

d rankings.

he demands made by the game on the
es are exacting: considerable courage
stamina are required. The ability to
-rein is all-important as the animal is
en only with one hand.

he teams are made up of two forwards, a
re-half and a back. All the players have
licaps, based on goal-scoring potential
ranging downwards from ten to zero (in
e countries minus two). These are total-
nd used to give a team with a handicap
lvantage an equal start in a match.

he centre-half initiates attacks on the
osing goal and covers the back in de-
e. He should be a long and accurate
r. The forwards follow up the centre-
s attacking moves and mark the opposing
re-half and back. A game lasts for be-
n four to six 'chukkas' of seven and a half
ites each, with a three minute interval
een each chukka. A single pony plays
two chukkas, so reserves are necessary.

Australia, an alternative to polo has
loped. This is polo-crosse, which by
, was so popular that the Polocrosse
ciation of Australia was formed. The
e is now played in every state, with 300
ated clubs. It is a combination of polo,

Left *Polo players in action in the USA. Between the wars, US polo teams led the world rankings in the sport, but now Argentina holds first place. A player must have a good natural eye for a moving ball; this is more important than outstanding horsemanship, though a strong seat and good balance are both essential.*

Today, the rules are primarily concerned with safety. Any player riding after the line of the ball has the right of way – vital when speeds of 30 mph are being achieved – and, for safety reasons too, players are also forbidden to hold their sticks in their left hands. The game is also stopped for falling or lame ponies, accident [to] *ponies' gear, lost helm*[ets,] *when the ball goes out* [of] *play.*

The rules are enfor[ced by] *two mounted umpires* [and a] *referee, who sits centr*[ally at] *one side of the ground* [to act] *as arbiter in cases of disagreement between* [them.] *Because of the speed o*[f the] *game, these can occur frequently. Fouls are penalized by penalties;* [these] *can vary in severity according to the nature* [of the] *offence. A penalty goa*[l can] *be awarded, for examp*[le, or] *a free hit taken from a* [point] *determined by the ump*[ires.] *This can be anywhere* [from] *the centre of the groun*[d to] *the goal mouth.*

osse and netball; players are required to
e neat riding gear with approved head-
r and only one pony per player is allowed.

il and distance riding

Australia and the USA in particular, long
ance riding is also extremely popular.
re are more than 500 distance rides in the
A, the most celebrated being the Tevis
and the Green Mountain Ride; in
tralia, the Quilty Cup is equally famous,
le in the UK the Golden Horse Shoe Ride
eld annually over 121km (75 miles) of the
oor National Park.

asic requirements are a fit horse and a fit
r, and, to ensure that the first condition is
, veterinary standards are extremely high,
inspections being held at regular stages
e ride. Normally, such competitive rides
organized in one of two ways; either a
d time is laid down for the various stages,
riders arriving ahead of, or behind, this
being penalized, or the results are de-
d on finishing position. This can be a real
of endurance and only horses with con-
rable stamina should be entered for it.

lany long distance rides, however, are
nized purely for pleasure, with no com-
tive element included. The most basic is
y trekking, which even a relatively inex-
enced rider can enjoy.

stern riding

other form of riding gaining in worldwide
larity is western riding – the style of
g that US cowboys use to herd cattle on
American range. It is closely linked with
ance riding and with the flourishing spec-
e of rodeo, extremely popular in both
th America and Australia.

he Western style of riding differs from
European style in four main points. First,
appearance of the saddle is very different.
as originally designed to make long, hard
in the saddle checking stock as comfort-
as possible for the rider, and to make the
of actual stock control easier. Thus,
e is a horn mounted on the pommel for
ying a rope or young steer – or for fixing
rope to when lassoing cattle for, say,
ding. The seat of the saddle is designed
ive 'bounce' to the rider for increased
fort at the sitting trot. Second, the rider's
ds are held high and a single-reined,
-cheeked curb bridle or bitless bridle is
for light, quick and accurate control.
dly, the stirrup leathers are designed to
urage a 'straight leg' position to keep the
deep in the saddle; they are also adjusted
extremely long. Finally, the horse itself
ained to 'neck rein', that is, to move right
ft instantly from the pressure of the rein
he neck. For example, to turn to the

right, the rider's hands move across to the
right, the signal to the horse being the pressure of the left rein on its neck. The reason
for the development of this unusual technique was that the cowboy often had to
control his horse with one hand, the other
being needed, say, to throw a rope.

Entrants to shows in the Western Division
of US riding can choose any one of three
classes. In the Stock Horse section, they first
demonstrate their horse's paces at the walk,
jog (the western term for the trot), and lope
(canter). They then perform a dressage test;
this includes the sliding halt and a reining-
back test. Some of the competitions involve

working with cattle.

The Trail Horse section is very much like a
British Hunter Trial, with the additional
demonstration of the horse's paces. These,
too, have to be demonstrated in the Pleasure
Horse section, while, in the Parade Class,
turn-out is all important. Both horse and
rider are gaily bedecked in spectacular tack
and riding clothes.

Rodeo

Rodeo (the Spanish word for a cattle ring) is a
survival from frontier days in the USA.
Then, the trail gangs held informal competitions after a cattle drive to demonstrate their

Left *Long distance riding in
Hungary,* **above** *pony
trekking on Dartmoor in the
UK and* **below** *trail riders in
the desert near Tucson,*

*USA. Endurance riding is
another form of equestrian
sport which has gained in
world-wide popularity in
recent years.*

skills in the arts of roping, bareback broncho riding, steer wrestling, steer and calf roping, bull riding, and so on. From these beginnings, the spectacle of rodeo was born.

As far as is known, the first public rodeo was held on 4 July (Independence Day) 1866 in Arizona. By the turn of the century, the Wild West show had come into being, adding an element of circus and carnival to the exhibition, with demonstrations of fancy shooting, riding and chuck wagon racing. Public interest is now on an international scale. In the USA, today, according to the Rodeo Cowboys' Association, more than 500 professional rodeos are held annually, as well as the hundreds of amateur contests. The total audience runs into the millions, while prize money, too, can be considerable. For its part, the Australian Rough Riders Association has a membership of over 12,000 and organizes rodeos in every state. The National Finals Rodeo is the highlight of the Australian rodeo season.

There are five traditional rodeo events; calf roping; steer wrestling; and broncho, bull, and saddle broncho riding. All of them require considerable skill and nerve from both horse and rider. In calf roping, for

instance, a young calf is released into the arena from a chute; the cowboy's task is to gallop after it and lasso the animal. The horse then comes to a sliding halt and backs away to maintain the tension on the lariat, which is secured to the saddle horn. This is all part of a good western horse's basic training. The cowboy dismounts, runs over to the calf, turns it on its side and quickly ties three of its legs together. The contestant with the fastest time wins.

Another test of skill, in which the risk of injury can be considerable, is bronco riding. In saddle bronc riding, the bronc wears a saddle and the rider tries to stay seated in it for a minimum of ten seconds. His only security is a halter rope, which he holds with one hand. In bareback bronc riding, the saddle is replaced by a surcingle strap with a leather handhold. The stipulated minimum time is eight seconds.

In both events, the contestants score points up to a maximum of twenty-five, awarded by two judges on the basis of the riders' skill and the horse's wildness. To increase this, the rules stipulate that the animal must be spurred (on its shoulders) as it leaps from the chute, while hard spurring

during the ride wins bonus points.

Women riders, too, feature on the r⟨ circuits; the Girls' Rodeo Association in USA was formed as early as 1948. Rew⟨ for successful riders are considerable, expenses are also high. Competitors hav⟨ pay their own entry fees, and there is als⟨ cost of travelling the thousands of mile⟨ volved to be taken into consideration. T⟨ is, too, the constant risk of injury – or ⟨ death.

This is one of the reasons for the emp⟨ ment of clowns and pick-up riders at rod⟨ As well as entertaining the crowds, pa⟨ the clowns' task is to attract the attention⟨ bull or broncho so that a fallen rider ca⟨ brought to safety. Pick-up riders, as t⟨ name implies, have the job of helping⟨ cessful competitors off their mounts by ri⟨ alongside and lifting them to safet⟨

Below *A calf-roping contest in the Calgary Stampede,* **inset** *a cowboy in an American stock yard and broncho busting in a US rodeo, while* **far right** *chuck wagons race for victory, also at the Calgary Stampede. Rodeo originated in the US wild west in the nineteenth* *century, when cowboy⟨ tested their skill agains⟨ other at the end of cattl⟨ drives. It grew to becom⟨ major spectacle, attrac⟨ vast audiences in both ⟨ America and Australi⟨ where it spread in the 1⟨ Both male and female contestants take part.*

azers, on the other hand, have a less anitarian role. Their task is to gallop gside the bull in bull wrestling events to e sure that it keeps to a reasonably ght line. In some ways, their role is not ke that of the picadors' in the bull ring, as rodeo itself, particularly in its display spectacle, has some links with bull fight- The picadors' task is to bait the bull in aration for the toreador and to help en- his safety. Traditionally, toreadors ht on foot, the picadors being mounted. ntly, however, mounted bullfighting ained considerably in popularity.

utting horses, too, compete in rodeos, gh they also have their own competi- and events. These are extremely popu- the USA and Australia; in the latter try, such was public demand that the onal Cutting Horse Association was ed in 1972 to organize the sport. Watch- he horse at work is almost like watching a dog, as it cuts out a steer apparently ut assistance from its rider.

ng for the disabled

ther form of horseback leisure activity is growing in importance, as its value is

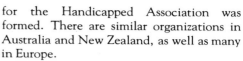

for the Handicapped Association was formed. There are similar organizations in Australia and New Zealand, as well as many in Europe.

Teaching starts off with confidence-building exercises; there then follows hacking, mounted games and even jumping. In addition to qualified teachers, considerable volunteer help is needed, as it can take three people to look after a severely handicapped child rider adequately.

An enclosed school is an obvious essential, as disabled children cannot be expected to ride in the rain. The horses and ponies used need to be selected carefully for quietness, while only simple forms of tack should be used. Some extra items, however, are usually needed; these include basket saddles for the legless and long lopped reins for the armless. In addition to the customary hard hat, a belt is also necessary, so that a helper can grasp it in case of an emergency.

Throughout, the aim is to let the children, or adults, do as much as possible for themselves, though the volunteers play an essential role. In the UK, seven grades of competency certificate are awarded by Riding for the Disabled to encourage this.

Above *A disabled child is taught to ride at a purpose-built school in the UK. Riding has mental as well as physical value for the disabled.*

Right and below *Two contrasted scenes — one in a Swiss circus and the other from a Spanish bull ring — show other facets of the horse's role in the fields of leisure and sport. Circus horses are as carefully trained as their dressage equivalents, while mounted bull-fighters expect an equal degree of skill from their specially-bred mounts.*

asingly recognized. This is riding for the led. Modern medical opinion holds that g gives a crippled child, both the benefit physical exercise and a powerful ological stimulus.

e therapeutic value of riding was recog- many centuries ago; in ancient Greece, n imperial Rome, the chronic sick were uraged to exercise on horseback. In rn times, the first notable disabled rider Liz Hartel. Despite being crippled by , she won silver medals for Denmark in the 1952 and 1956 Olympic Games. ling for the disabled groups now exist all the world. In the UK, the Riding for the led Association was founded in 1969; in ame year, the North American Riding

Horse racing

Horse racing has developed over the last century into a vast, colourful entertainments industry with perhaps half a million thoroughbreds involved either in racing or breeding throughout the world. However, its origins are difficult to trace. The Chinese, the Tartars, Mongols, Greeks and Romans all engaged in the sport in one form or another. On racing days, every citizen of Rome wore the colour of his favourite team of charioteers and prepared to do battle with the supporters of other teams in the stands around the track. Even in the uttermost corner of the Roman Empire, in Britain, the garrisons of Wetherby and York are known to have held races.

The founding Thoroughbreds

All racing Thoroughbreds are descended from three stallions of Arabian stock – the Byerley Turk, the Darley Arabian, and the Godolphin Barb. The Byerley Turk was captured when Budapest was taken from the Turks in 1686–87 and his new owner, Colonel Byerley of the Dragoon Guards, rode him at the Battle of the Boyne in 1690. Impressed by his speed and agility, especially when compared to the Dragoons' usual mounts, Byerley brought his charger home and installed him as a stud stallion first in County Durham, and later in Yorkshire. The ancestry of such famous racehorses as Tetrarch and Tourbillon can be traced back to the Byerley Turk through his son Jig.

The Darley Arabian, foaled in 1700 on the edge of the Syrian Desert, was sold four years later by Sheik Mirza to Thomas Darley, the English Consul in Aleppo. The Sheik tried to go back on the deal, and gave orders that anyone who tried to remove the horse should be killed. Undeterred, the Consul enlisted the help of some British sailors from a warship that was visiting the port. They rowed ashore in the dark, overpowered the stable guards, and returned to their man o'war with the horse. Furious, the Sheik wrote to Queen Anne, claiming his incomparable stallion was 'worth more than a King's ransom and had been foully stolen by one of her subjects'.

His plea was ignored, but the Sheik's opinion of the horse was amply justified. During the next twenty-five years, the Darley Arabian sired a whole race of champions among whose descendants were St Simon, Gainsborough, Blandford and – perhaps the noblest of them all – the great Eclipse.

The Godolphin Barb, foaled in 1724, was given to Louis XV of France by the Sultan of Morocco. The horse was later acquired by Lord Godolphin and became the ancestor of another great line of racehorses. The influence of these three stallions on Thoroughbred breeding was at once appar-

ent, during the early Georgian period a further 24 Arabian stallions were imported.

The English Jockey Club, founded in 1752, soon became the foremost authority in all racing matters. The same year too, saw the first recorded steeplechase, held over 4½ miles of hunting country between Buttevant Church and St Leger Church in Ireland. By the end of the century, two-year-old races had been instituted. These were soon equalling and even surpassing in popularity the three- and five-year-old races which were all that had been permitted until then.

The spread of racing

In France, racing did not become fully established until after the French Revolution, though the first regular French course was laid out in the Plaine des Sablons as early as 1776; one two-mile race held there in the same year offered a prize of 15,000 francs for the winner.

In 1833 Lord Henry Seymour, a British nobleman living in Paris, founded the French Jockey Club, and three years later the Prix du Jockey Club, over the classic distance of 1½

A horse and jockey of the second century BC. In the ancient world, the Greeks were ardent racegoers.

miles, was run for the first time. In 1857, a track was laid in the Bois du Boulogne; set in picturesque woodland just a few minutes' from the centre of Paris, Longchamp was to become one of the most fashionable of the world's racecourses.

Other nations were swift to follow France's example. The first Japanese meeting was held in 1852, Australia established the Melbourne Cup in 1861, while Ireland and Germany each founded its own Derby in 1866 and 1869 respectively. In the USA, the Belmont Stakes, first of the three classic races that together compose the American Triple Crown, was set up in 1867; the other two, the Preakness Stakes and the Kentucky Derby entered the calendar in 1873 and 1876.

There were no horses in Australasia until at least 1788. Only 11 years later, breeding was firmly established and the first official race meeting was staged at Hyde Park, Sydney, in 1810. The sport flourished with the

continued importation of Thorough[ ] stallions and in 1840, the Australian R[ ] Committee issued a manifesto setting out [ ] aims of the Australian breeding indus[ ] South Africa had instituted its own ra[ ] almost half a century before; the first mee[ ] was held on Green Point Common, [ ] Cape Town, in September 1797.

American breeding

The first US race course was laid out in 1[ ] on Long Island, but the sport did not bec[ ] established there until later. Then the pu[ ] ase of the 21-year-old stallion Diomed pr[ ] an immensely shrewd and important mov[ ] American breeders. Winner of the [ ] Derby to be run at Epsom in 1780, he had [ ] been a success at stud in England and [ ] eventually sold for a paltry 50 guineas [ ] Virginian breeder, who, in turn, quickly [ ] him to another breeder for 1,000 guin[ ] Diomed proved a prolific sire of winner[ ] America, and was still covering mares at [ ] age of twenty-nine.

Once the Civil War was over, Amer[ ] racing boomed. By 1897, there were [ ] racetracks operating in the United States[ ] 43 in Canada. But, at the turn of the cent[ ] legislation against betting and racing [ ] passed in many states and this for a time h[ ] disastrous effect on the sport. By 1908, [ ] 25 courses were still open, and in 1910 [ ] more severe anti-betting law brought [ ] York racing to a standstill. Most of this l[ ] lation remained in force until the 1920s.

The role of the trainer

Training racehorses is a time-consum[ ] highly-skilled art. Many trainers comp[ ] that there are simply not enough hours [ ] day to cope with their numerous tasks, [ ] as a result, most modern stables now em[ ] secretaries and assistants to look afte[ ] ever-increasing paper-work and admini[ ] tion. Training methods differ enorm[ ] from stable to stable and country to cou[ ] but their basic task is to bring a horse [ ] state of complete physical fitness, so ena[ ] it to run faster than its rivals, with suffi[ ] stamina to maintain its speed.

Generally, the process begins with [ ] trainer buying a yearling for a partic[ ] owner. This might be done at the nume[ ] bloodstock auction sales held annually, [ ] might prefer to buy or lease a horse d[ ] from a stud. The horse is then broker[ ] lunged on a long rein, saddled, and ri[ ] away, a task that must be accomplished [ ] patience and gentleness. It may therefo[ ] some considerable time before the hor[ ] ready to be ridden out each morning with[ ] rest of the stable's string.

Later, the trainer decides on the h[ ]

ise routine, the most suitable distance
[h]im to race, the right type of going and
[m]ost suitable jockey. Then, when he
[ ] the horse is almost ready to run, he
[ ]s it for its first races.

[ ]e trainer's routine begins before dawn
[ ] he gets up to watch the daily gallops.

LES COURSES DE STEEPLE
Le saut de la rivière

[t]he scene at Sadlers
[r]acecourse, London,
[ ] and **above** a steeple
[ ]t Auteuil, France, in

1903. The nineteenth and
early twentieth centuries
saw the establishment of
racing as a major sport.

Paperwork occupies his morning before he
leaves to watch whatever races are being held
in which he has an interest. He then returns
home to look over each horse at evening
stables.

A large staff is employed, including ap-
prentice jockeys, and most important of all a
head stable lad who runs everything in the
trainer's absence and usually has charge of
feeding. Trainers charge a set monthly fee
with the addition of such expenses as veterinary care, transport, and gallops. The sharp
increase in feed and labour bills has greatly
increased the price of keeping a horse in
training in many parts of the world. It remains a rich man's sport, though lately, partnerships and syndicates have enabled some of
the less well-off to experience the pleasure of
owning a racehorse.

Trainers, like jockeys, earn a percentage of
any prize money their horses win. Many also
bet and make money by dealing, buying and
selling horses.

In Europe, trainers have their own stables
from which the horses are taken to each race,
while in the US, hundreds, and sometimes
thousands, of horses lodge briefly at each
consecutive meeting. When the meeting
comes to an end, the whole set-up moves on
to the next course.

In 1977, Vincent O'Brien, the leading
British trainer of the last decade, won a
record £439,124 from a mere eighteen victories on British tracks, a figure that was
considerably increased by his many successes

in France and Ireland. In America, the prize
money won by the leading trainers is substan-
tially more than this. The 1966 record of
$2,435,450 set by Eddie Neloy, is now regu-
larly surpassed by several trainers each year.

The role of the jockey

The trainer teaches the racehorse its job, yet
his fame seldom reaches beyond the ears of
the more expert punters. A successful jockey,
on the other hand can, and often does,
become a national celebrity.

In the USA, Willie Shoemaker set a world
record of riding winners as long ago as 1970
when he equalled Eddie Acaro's figure of
6,032. By mid-1978, 'The Shoe', as he is
nicknamed, was still going strong with more
than 7,300 wins to his credit, having ridden
172 winners in 1977 alone. In Britain, the
record set by the legendary Sir Gordon
Richards of 4,870 is still unbroken. Sir
Gordon was champion of the flat 26 times:
his most splendid feat was 1933 when he rode
12 consecutive winners.

The British flat racing season lasts only
from mid-March to early November. In
America, races are held all the year round,
with programmes of up to twelve races a day.
This gives US jockeys the opportunity to
achieve much higher totals than their British
counterparts. Steve Cauthen, who started his
riding career in 1976, set an astonishing
record in 1977 by winning 488 races around
the USA.

US jockeys have agents who seek out and

secure rides for them. In return they earn between twenty and twenty-five per cent of whatever their jockeys collect. Harry Silbert has worked as Willie Shoemaker's agent since he rode his first race in 1949. In Britain, many top jockeys are retained by one, or sometimes two, stables – they do not employ agents. Unquestionably the best jockey in Britain is Lester Piggott, who in the 1960s, broke from convention by going freelance. His reward has been innumerable victories, including a record eight wins in the Epsom Derby – the last in 1977.

Modern flat jockeys throughout the world ride with very short stirrup leathers and a low, wind-resisting crouch, a style imported from America at the end of the last century. It is generally accepted that Tod Sloan was the first man to introduce this style to Europe but in fact, he was preceded by another American, Willie Simms. His style was so ridiculed that he packed his bag and returned home. Sloan, however, was made of sterner stuff. His crouching style was so successful in English races that UK jockeys soon abandoned their old-fashioned, upright postures and copied him.

Sloan won so many races perched high in the saddle, that he became known as the 'monkey up the stick'. After Sloan came two more Americans who both topped the jockeys' list in Britain — Danny Maher and Lester Reiff. Australian jockeys, such as Brownie Carslake and Frank Bullock, were also successful in Britain at about this time.

The lightest jockey ever recorded was Kitchener who died in 1872; he weighed only 49lbs when he won the 1844 Chester Cup on Red Deer. The youngest winning jockey was

Frank Wootton, later English champion, who gained his first success in South Africa aged 9 years and 10 months, while the oldest was Levi Barlingame who was eighty when he rode his last winner in America in 1932.

By the 1970s, professional women jockeys were making an impact in several racing countries. The breakthrough came first in America where a number of women regularly began to ride winners.

Male or female, every jockey weighs in before each race on specially-designed scales and the first four must weigh in again after it. They sit on the scales holding their saddles but not their crash helmets. Jockeys are paid a set riding fee plus a percentage, varying between 7½% and 10% of the prize money

How betting works

Betting is the lifeblood of racing throughout the world. Most countries operate a totalisator system, called the pari-mutuel in France and the USA, and the Tote in Britain. The racing authorities keep a set percentage for the considerable running costs of the industry, and a further percentage is taken in tax, while the remainder is redistributed to the lucky winners.

This system is efficient and has the obvious advantage of being reasonably easy to run, but punters often have to queue for a considerable time to place their bets and are denied the opportunity to shop around for the best available price. Britain is in the unusual position of allowing both bookmakers and Tote to operate in competition both on and off the racecourse, and there is little doubt that most punters prefer to use the bookmakers.

The extent of the huge annual betting

Above *The equipment required by a jockey and a race horse and* **right** *the two combined in action. By far the most important and expensive item is the special* racing saddle, weighin between 2 to 9lb. On average, jockeys need of these in different siz suit both their mount a weight carried.

Left *Swimming a horse to help it tone up its muscles is today a common feature of the training programme, as this scene shows.*

turnover in America can be gauged b figures, released by the New York R Association, from the meetings he Aqueduct, Belmont Park, and Sarato 1977. Turnover that year was $711 m dollars – and that from just three of th tracks in the country.

France, too, benefits greatly from the mutuel system, while in Australia, th rules differ from state to state, bookm are allowed to operate only at race-meet The result is that betting markets are stronger than in Europe or the USA.

Racing's hall of fame

What are the qualities that make a race great? Shakespeare wrote of a noble horse:

'round-hoofed, short-jointed, fetlocks sha long,
Broad-breast, full eye, small head and wide,
High-crest, short ears, straight legs, and p

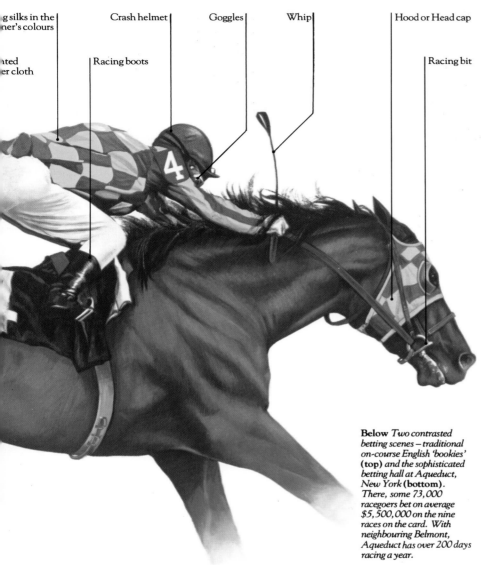

g silks in the
ner's colours   Crash helmet   Goggles   Whip   Hood or Head cap

ted
er cloth   Racing boots   Racing bit

or so before the Derby, his health deteriorated day by day. Sometimes he looked dreadfully ill and would not eat, but, in the race itself, he led on the last turn and battled home to hold the nearest challenge by a neck. Just over two weeks later, Humorist ended a brief gallop with blood from a broken blood vessel gushing from his nostrils.

In the following week, Sir Alfred Munnings, the great horse painter, began a portrait of Humorist, but before it could be completed, the horse lay dead amid pools of blood in his box. A post-mortem showed he had suffered from consumption and a severe haemorrhage of the lungs. Yet in this condition, he had won the Derby.

Trainers look for different attributes when buying horses. Breeding is the most important, especially on the dam's side; a good pace, when allied to a bright, intelligent head, long ears, clean joints and strong quarters, is also attractive. But breeding can be misleading. Some of the best-bred animals turn out to be very slow and history has proved time and again, that conformation and good looks do not guarantee success in racing.

Famous races and racecourses

Epsom, on the edge of the Surrey Downs, is the home of the Derby – the most famous race in the world and the third of the five English Classics to be run. In some respects it is an unlikely site on which to stage the supreme test for three-year-old Thoroughbreds. Epsom has an awkward, undulating left-handed horseshoe track, so that horses are seldom running on an even keel.

From the start of the one-and-a-half mile course, the ground rises continuously some 150 feet over six furlongs, until it bears left downhill towards Tattenham Corner, a sharp left-handed curve into the four-furlong straight. The final half-mile is also downhill until the last 50 yards when there is a sudden climb to the winning post. Throughout the straight there is a sharp camber towards the far rail; this causes problems for many jockeys when their tired mounts start to 'hang' and veer under pressure.

The Derby is held on the first Wednesday of June. Each year, upwards of a quarter of a million spectators attend the race, many of them watching from the free enclosures on the inside of the horseshoe, where they are entertained by the traditional fair that operates throughout the week.

The origins of the Derby are linked to another Classic race, The Oaks. In 1778, at a party given by Lord Derby at his home, 'The Oaks', near Epsom, it was decided to stage a race the following year and to name it after his lordship's house. The 1779 Oaks was such

Below Two contrasted betting scenes – traditional on-course English 'bookies' (top) and the sophisticated betting hall at Aqueduct, New York (bottom). There, some 73,000 racegoers bet on average $5,500,000 on the nine races on the card. With neighbouring Belmont, Aqueduct has over 200 days racing a year.

g,

mane, thick tail, broad
ck, tender hide. . . !'

ame Julyana Berners, writing in the first
ting publication in England in 1481,
d several other desirable features:

man, bolde, prowde, and hardy;
woman, fayrbrested, fayr of
e, and easy to leape upon;
fox, a fayr taylle, short
, with a good trotte-
haare, a grete eye, a dry
, and well runnynge,
n asse, a bygge chyn, a flatte
and a good hoof'.

hile both authors include many of the
butes that make a great racehorse, every
e has a different idea about perfect con-
ation. Soundness, good-health, and the
est ability, for example, are worth no-
g if not matched by courage.
umorist, the 1921 Derby winner, was a
ture of matchless courage. In the month

a success that a further race was suggested for 1780. The toss of a coin, between Lord Derby and Sir Charles Bunbury, determined the name of this second contest. Sir Charles at least had the consolation of seeing his own colt, Diomed, win the first Derby, then run over a mile. Later in 1784, the distance was increased to one and a half miles.

The first Derby was worth just over £1,000 to the winner, compared with £107,530 in 1977, when The Minstrel beat Hot Grove by a neck. The Minstrel was later sold for a world record figure of $10,000,000. Stud values of winners have naturally kept pace with the increases in prize money. Mahmoud, winner in 1936, was sold for a mere £21,000 to America where he later sired the winners of more than £2½ million in stakes.

The three longest priced winners in Derby history are Jeddah (1898), Signorinetta (1908) and Aboyeur (1913), all at 100–1. There were two dead heats in 1828 and 1884. In recent years, the race has been dominated by American-bred horses trained in Ireland by Vincent O'Brien and ridden by the incomparable British jockey Lester Piggott. The Minstrel gave Piggott a record eighth Derby victory in 1977.

Ascot, the only racecourse in England which belongs to the Royal Family was founded by Queen Anne in the early 1700s. Royal Ascot, held in June, at the height of summer, is one of the most sparkling events in the world's racing calendar. A Royal procession down the racecourse opens the proceedings on each of the four days, all of which glow with racing of the highest quality. The principal race of the meeting is the Ascot Gold Cup, a 'stayers' race run over a course of two-and-a-half miles.

Prize money is even higher in the King George VI and Queen Elizabeth Diamond Stakes, recently sponsored by the De Beers group, which is held at the July meeting at Ascot. First run in 1951, the race provides a fine test between the best staying colts and fillies of three and four years. The Diamond Stakes is one of the most prestigious and profitable races in the world; the 1977 winner, The Minstrel, made his owner richer by £88,355

A right handed course, with the last six furlongs run up a gradual gradient, Ascot is a test of stamina. The round course (1½ miles) is supplemented by a straight mile used for such races as the Royal Hunt Cup.

Other famous English racecourses include Newmarket, Doncaster, Aintree and Cheltenham. Newmarket, centre of English racing for over 300 years, stages the first two Classics of each season – the One Thousand and Two Thousand Guineas. The former,

first held in 1814, is run over the straight Rowley mile (the name comes from Charles II's nickname 'Old Rowley') at the Newmarket spring meeting. It was set up as the fillies equivalent of the Two Thousand Guineas – a race for colts.

The Thousand Guineas, coming early in the season for three-year-old fillies, is still the major English contest for female milers. The stiff mile, with its undulating course and uphill finish, is a stiff test which soon discovers specialist sprinters. Prize money for the 1978 Canadian-owned winner Enstone Spark, was £41,130. Thirty-four winners of the Thousand Guineas have completed a double by also winning The Oaks.

The 2,000 Guineas was originally financed by a sweepstake of 100 guineas for each entry. Coming a month or so before the Derby, it is an ideal preparation for the Epsom Classic and by 1977, no fewer than 34 horses had achieved the double triumph of winning both in the same year.

Doncaster stages the last of the season's five Classics, the St Leger, at its September meeting. Run over one mile, six furlongs and 132 yards, it is a real test of stamina and form, with the Two Thousand Guineas and the

Derby, the third leg of the so-called T[riple] Crown. Only 12 horses have ever gained coveted honour in British racing – the la[st] which was the great Nijinsky in 1970.

Aintree is the home of what is the [most] famous steeplechase in the world – the G[rand] National. Founded in 1839, the fence[s are] noted for the stamina they call for from [both] horse and rider. The most taxing is the C[hair,] the last but one on the first circuit, but [the] most famous is undoubtedly Becher's Br[ook,] named after Captain Becher, one of [the] riders in the first Grand National.

Cheltenham, deep in the heart of [the] Cotswolds, annually provides the settin[g for] the most important meeting of the j[umping] season, the March National Hunt Fest[ival.] Spread over three days, this fixture offers [some] of the finest spectacles of action over hu[rdles] and fences to be seen in the world. The [two] most important races are the Chelten[ham] Gold Cup, steeplechasing's premier p[rize,] and the Champion Hurdle.

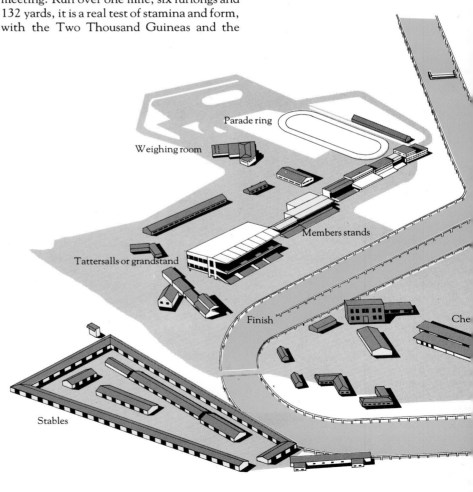

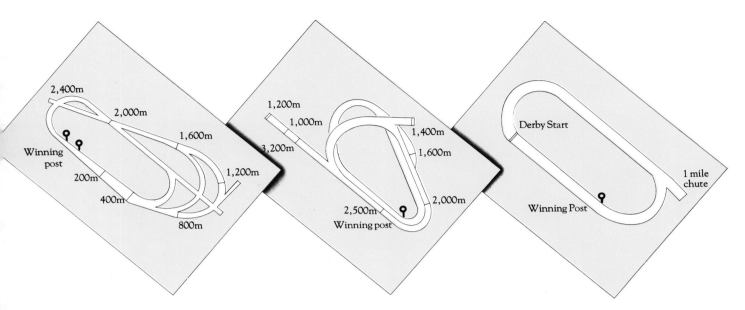

champ, home of the
de l'Arc de Triomphe,
bably the best known of
rench racecourses.
ned in 1857, it has

round course of 2,400m (1½
miles) and a straight one of
1,600m (1 mile), used for
another famous race, the
Grand Criterium.

Flemington is the home of
Australia's most prestigious
race, the Melbourne Gold
Cup. In addition to its flat-
racing course – just under

2,400m (1½ miles) round,
with a run in to the finish, it
has a shorter straight track
and also a separate
steeplechase circuit.

Churchill Downs is the home
of the Kentucky Derby,
founded in 1875 and run
over a distance of 2,000m
(1¼ miles). It is a flat, oval

course and, in common with
most US racecourses, has a
dirt surface, not a grass one.
Races are flat out from start
to finish.

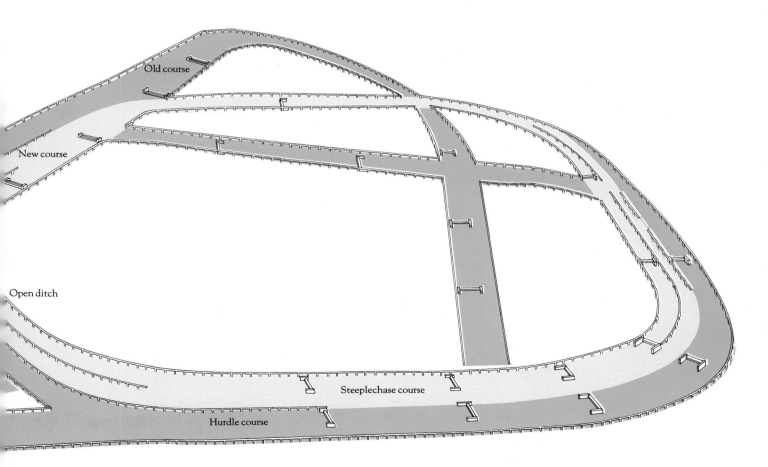

ayout of a typical
ourse. Behind the
s at every major
ng, there is a massive
ization at work,

headed by the Clerk of the
Course, to make sure all
runs smoothly. Spectators,
jockeys, owners, trainers
and bookmakers all need

their specialized facilities.
Apart from the course
itself, the paddock, where
horses parade before a race,
is the chief centre of interest,

together with the winner's
enclosure after it. On the
course, one of the chief
innovations of recent years is
the use of mobile starting

stalls in flat racing, replacing
the traditional tapes. Stalls
make it far easier for the
starter to ensure that all the
runners get an equal chance,

while photo-finish
cameras and a TV patrol
both help to ensure fairness
during the actual running of
a race.

Left *Jockeying for position in a race at Kempton Park, UK, in 1976;* **inset** *racing over snow in Switzerland and a tense start at Ascot, UK.* **Above top** *The saddling enclosure at Flemington Racecourse, Melbourne, and* **below** *mud-splattered horses and riders strain every nerve in a Canadian flat race. The appeal of racing is such that it attracts thousands who have probably never been near a racecourse, while among the actual spectators, few realize the months and years of preparation that go into producing, say, a British Derby winner.*

The trainer's role in this is all important. Together with his back-up team – stable jockey, assistant, head lad, senior lads, apprentices and others – his day starts at dawn and finishes at dusk.

His responsibilities are immense, as he can easily have a million pounds worth of horses in his care.

To the spectator, however the key figure on the day of the race is without question the jockey. Competition to succeed in this field is so intense that, for every world-class star who emerges, such as the top British jockey Lester Piggott, literally hundreds of aspiring hopefuls vanish into obscurity. Nevertheless recruits to the profession still come forward, particularly now that racing has opened its doors to women jockeys as well as men.

A jockey is either retained by a stable under contract for, say, a season, or is booked for rides as a freelance. At the top, skill and expertise bring considerable financial

dividends – in the UK a top jockey can earn in the region of £50,000 a year, while in the USA, because of its all-year race programme, the amounts are considerably more. But, at the bottom, the rewards can be relatively small. Jockeys work a six-day week, though working conditions vary considerably. In the UK, for example, there is far more travelling involved than , say in France or the USA. Because of the nature of American racing, with its larger meetings, US jockeys can spend more time on a particular circuit.

In addition, all jockeys face the key physical problem of weight. Diet has to be strictly controlled, while vital ounces often have to be sweated off speedily in a Turkish bath or a sauna.

Ireland

All five Irish Classics are held at the Curragh, for centuries the home of Irish racing. Situated thirty miles south of Dublin, the Curragh, which belongs to the Turf Club, is also the main training centre of Ireland. The Irish Derby attracted little attention outside the country until it was given a major injection of funds by the Irish Sweepstake Organisation in 1962. Since then, the race has become progressively more important in the pattern of European three-year-old classics.

Ireland also has a unique racecourse at Laytown Beach, north of Dublin. Racing is held just once a year on the beach, and the date depends entirely on the state of the tide. Stewards have to wait for the tide to go out before marking off the course with poles and ropes and the only permanent building on the course is a concrete public convenience.

France

Longchamp, in the wooded Bois de Boulogne just a few minutes from the centre of Paris, provides the golden autumnal setting for Europe's richest race, the Prix de l'Arc de Triomphe, which is run early in October. First held in 1920, the Arc is the most important race in France and attracts the best European staying three-year-olds to pace their qualities against a handful of older horses. The one snag is that a number of top class horses miss the race because it comes too late in the season; all the same, it can still fairly claim to attract the most international competition of any race held in Europe. In 1977, the winner, Alleged, earned the huge sum of $281,690 in prize money.

Only slightly less prestigious than the Arc is the Grand Prix de Paris, for three year olds, which is run over one mile, seven furlongs, and 110 yards on the last Sunday in June.

Longchamp is one of the most attractive racecourses in the world. The panoramic grandstands, the quiet, tree-lined paddock and the long sweeping right hand turn leading to the wide straight, are beautiful in themselves as well as offering racing at its best. Beauty, however, is the keynote of many French racecourses, among them Chantilly, where the French Derby and Oaks are held. Here, the runners pass a magnificent château before turning right-handed into the final straight.

Australia

Flemington is the home of Australia's most famous race, the Melbourne Cup, which is run on the first Tuesday in November. Four miles from the centre of Melbourne, Flemington was named after a local butcher, Bob Fleming, whose shop stood opposite the course when it was built in the 1840s. Surrounded by stands that can hold 100,000 or more, the flat course at Flemington is just under 1½ miles round with a short run — little more than two furlongs — to the post. There is also a straight six furlong track and a separate steeplechase circuit.

The Melbourne Cup, run over two miles, was first held in 1861, and since then has attracted almost every good stayer in Australia and New Zealand. Though the Victoria Derby, and VRC Sires Produce Stakes and other important races are also held at Flemington, the Melbourne Cup reigns supreme. Parliament, courts and indeed the entire nation, halts and rushes to its television sets to watch the race. Stars of the past are still revered — like Archer, who won the first two Melbourne Cups in 1861 and 1862, a feat not equalled until Rain Lover completed the same double in 1968 and 1969.

A neck-and-neck battle at Florida Downs race track, Tampa, USA. One of the jockey's chief skills is to know when to use the whip on his horse.

Flemington too, was the scene of the first triple dead heat in Australia, in November 1956, when three horses crossed the line perfectly together. All three had their ears back, their heads held low, and their off fore legs extended exactly the same length, as if locked by remote control.

Melbourne's other course is Caulfield, where the famous Caulfield Cup is run, just seventeen days before the Melbourne Cup. The Caulfield Cup, the second most important race in the Australian racing calendar, was first competed for in 1879.

The United States

The most important leg of the American Triple Crown is the Kentucky Derby, held on Churchill Downs, Louisville, Ky., on the first Saturday in May. The race provide marvellous spectacle for the over 100,0 spectators who come to see the best three y olds in training being put to the test over one-and-a-quarter mile circuit. In 1875, race's inaugural year, the first prize $2,850; by 1977, this had risen to $208,0 A Derby museum is open on the racecou throughout the year, though only in mornings on race days and the Churc Downs executive struck a bronze medal 1974 to commemorate the 100th running the race. The Kentucky Derby is alw enacted with pomp, circumstance and m cal accompaniment, which includes a tru pet solo version of The Star Spangled Ban and a massed bands rendering of My Kentucky Home.

Most American races, including the K tucky Derby, are run on dirt tracks, ova shape and completely flat. However Washington International, which justifies name by attracting runners from all over world, is run on a grass track at Laurel Par

Racing in America is organised on co pletely different lines from those familia Europe. Race meetings are staged at the sa tracks for up to two months, with as many dozen races on each card. Santa Anita P Los Angeles, for instance, started its 75 meeting on New Year's day, 1978, wh despite heavy rain, 42,711 customers w ered $4,557,676 through the Pari-Mutu more or less the American equivalent of British Tote.

The Far East

Since the Second World War, astute buy of bloodstock on a vast scale has helped Ja emerge as one of the world's leading rac nations. No less than six Epsom Derby w ners now stand at stud there, as well as m other well-known imported stallions. Jap ese racing is thriving, and the Japan Derby, first run in 1933, is now wo $190,000 to the winner. Even Hong Kor racecourse has proved so popular that sor times the gates are closed on a capacity crc an hour or more before the first race. No second Hong Kong course is being built

The sport of Trotting

Trotting and pacing have never been popular as thoroughbred racing, but du the 1960s, interest in the sport began increase in many parts of the world. modern equivalent of chariot racing, trott first became popular in Europe, Russia the USA in the eighteenth century. N harness racing is big business and one which horses have won as much as £750, in prize money during their careers.

Both pacers and trotters are known as
ndardbreds, a breed which originated as
g ago as 1790, when an English
oroughbred, Messenger, was exported to
nsylvania. In both trotting and pacing,
ndardbred horses maintain a specified gait
le pulling a driver sitting on a two-
eeled carriage, known as a sulky. Trotters
ve their left front leg and right back leg
ultaneously, while pacers move both legs
the same side forward together. Because
ers wear hobbles, they are less likely to
ak into a gallop during a race.

3y the 1960s in the USA, the sport had
ome so popular that more people watched
ting than American football. One track
New York took $2,000,000 in bets a night,
nights a week. In Australia, fifty-one
cks opened in New South Wales alone,
le, in France, punters bet $8,000,000 on
race. In 1961, the champion French
ter, Jamin, was sold to an American
eder for $570,000.

his might suggest that the sport had sud-
ly found new wealth; but in fact as far
k as 1903, the brilliant Dan Patch
96–1916), nicknamed 'The Immortal'
barred from racing for the simple reason
t he totally outclassed all his potential
ls. There was not one horse capable of
ng him a race, so instead, he made exhibi-
n runs against the stop watch. He was
uted to have run the mile 73 times in
er two minutes and to have earned a
nly satisfactory $4 million of prize money
ing his career.

n America, in 1935, a trotter called
eyhound won $33,000 in the Hambleto-
n, one third of the trotting Triple Crown
I three years later, set speed records une-
lled for three decades. On one occasion at
ington, he clocked 1 minute 57¼ seconds
r the mile – a time not beaten until 1966.
other record was set in 1965, when the
l-bred Speedy Streak was sold at public
tion for $113,000. He repaid his new
er's faith by winning the Hambletonian
years later.

he US trotting Triple Crown consists of
Yonkers Futurity in New York, the
mbletonian at Du Quoin, Illinois, and the
tucky Futurity at Lexington, though the
osevelt International is widely recognized
he world championship for trotters.

n Australia, the biggest events are the
erdominion Championship and the
stralasia Championship, run annually in
bourne since 1963. In 1976, the Grand
al offered a new record prize of $40,000
a pacing event.

Jew Zealand is so keen to encourage trot-
that at least two events at every race
ting are set aside for them.

*Two harness racing scenes.
This type of racing has
gained considerably in
international popularity in
recent years, though it has
always been a major sport in
the USA, Australia, New
Zealand, France and
Germany.*

*Races fall into two
categories – trotting and
pacing. The difference
between the two is that the
latter is an artificial pace –
the pacer is trained to trot on
the laterals rather than the
diagonals, the natural
trotting gait.*

*In trotting, just as in
motor racing, the
competitors have a short
runup to the start. They then
race round the circuit, the
chief rule being that the
specified gait must not be
broken. If a horse goes into a
canter, for instance, the
driver must immediately
check the pace, thus losing
vital seconds. A handicap
system also operates; the
faster horses have to start
behind their slower
competitors.*

Chapter Eleven

Great horses

Simona

Be Fair

Laurieston

Mill Reef

Simona

This chestnut mare will always be remembered as the mount of West Germany's Hartwig Steenken, who died tragically after six months in a coma following a motor accident in 1977. She carried him to victory in the European Championship in Aachen in 1971, and, a year later, won him a team gold medal at the Munich Olympics. Most glorious of all was her performance at Hickstead in 1974, where the partnership won the World Championship. Simona has now retired to stud.

Be Fair

The chestnut mount of leading British rider Lucinda Prior-Palmer when she won her first European title at Luhmuhlen, West Germany, in 1975. The son of Sheila Willcox's Fair and Square, Be Fair's first major victory was at Badminton in 1973, after which he was selected for the European Championship team in Kiev. He was also in the British team for the 1974 World Championships in which it was unsuccessful, and for the 1976 Olympics. There, however, he slipped a tendon off his hock after going clear across country – an injury which ended his competitive career.

Laurieston

The mount of Richard Meade, one of Britain's leading male event riders, when he won the individual gold medal at the 1972 Munich Olympics; the UK also won the team event. Laurieston was bred in the UK by Major Derek Allhusen by the premium stallion Happy Monarch out of Laurien by Davy Jones. Laurien, too, had a successful international career; ridden by her owner, she took part in the European Championships in Copenhagen in 1957 as a member of the winning British team.

Mill Reef

Mill Reef, bred in America by his multimillionaire owner Paul Mellon, was later sent to the UK to be trained on the Hampshire downs by Ian Balding at Kingsclere. There, his early work convinced his trainer that Mill Reef was the best two-year-old he had ever handled. His belief was confirmed when Mill Reef bounced out of the stalls at Salisbury, and galloped home four lengths ahead of his nearest pursuer. He gained another easy victory at Royal Ascot, and was just beaten in France after a miserable journey and the worst possible draw. He won twice more as a two year old and shrugged off defeat by Brigadier Gerard in the Two Thousand Guineas, a distance too short for him, to win the Derby in 1971 with an explosive surge of speed and power. Continuing his triumphs into his third year, Mill Reef

won the Eclipse Stakes at Sandown from French hope, Caro, as a prelude to a runa[way] success in the King George VI and Qu[een] Elizabeth Stakes at Ascot.

After a short rest, he achieved his fi[rst] victory, the Prix de l'Arc de Triomphe [at] Lonchamp, in a new record time of 2 min[utes] 28.3 seconds over the mile and a half cour[se].

Mill Reef had beaten Sea Bird II's ti[me] and was the first English-trained winner [of] the Arc for twenty years. He was back [at] Longchamp the following spring for a [one] length success over Amadou in the [Prix] Ganay, but a glorious second triumph in [the] Arc was denied him by his broken leg.

Red Rum

Red Rum's extraordinary career came to [an] untimely conclusion in April, 1978, in [full] view of the world's television cameras on [the] eve of what would have been his sixth c[on-] secutive Grand National over the daunt[ing] Aintree fences. Withdrawn through inj[ury]

Rum

Arkle

The Poacher

Gladiateur

than 24 hours before the race he had
...inated for so much of the decade,
...mmy', as the horse was nicknamed, could
...o more than parade before a huge crowd
...60,000 well-wishers in an emotional
...well to the racing scene.

...le ran in five Grand Nationals, winning a
...rd three and finishing a gallant second in
...other two. His fame spread across the
...ld and by the close of his career in the
...ng of 1978, Red Rum Ltd were charging
...to £750 for each personal appearance he
...le. He opened nightclubs, fetes, attended
...ctions and was greeted wherever he went
...true equine superstar.

...ed Rum ran in exactly 100 races over
...es and hurdles, winning twenty-four.
...ough his earnings were the jumper's record
...114,627, yet he originally changed hands
...yearling for a mere 400 guineas.

...ummy won his first two Nationals in
...3 and 1974, the first in a desperate finish
...r he had made up fully 100 yards to catch
...fine New Zealand horse, Crisp. Already a
...nd, Rummy was then beaten into second
...e in 1975 and 1976, handicapped by
...a big weight, and came back at the age of

twelve, ridden by Tommy Stack, to complete
the historic hat-trick in 1977.

Arkle

Red Rum will always be the King of Aintree
but Arkle was surely the finest steeplechaser
who ever lived.

Arkle ran in 35 races, three on the flat as
part of his education, and six over hurdles.
Over fences, he was beaten only four times
— twice through a handicap of too much
weight, once by an unlucky slip, and the last
time when he incurred the injury that
brought his marvellous career to a tragic end.
He won £78,825 in prize money and the
affection of all those who appreciate the sight
of a brave horse and jockey jumping at speed.

Arkle won three Gold Cups in effortless
style, but in other races found himself increasingly taking on the handicapper. For the
first time in racing history, the handicapper
was forced to formulate two handicaps – one
if Arkle ran and another if he was withdrawn.

Adored by steeplechase fans on both sides
of the Irish Sea, Arkle reigned supreme. A
big, bright bay with an intelligent head and a
bold, heart-stopping spring, he dominated

steeplechasing for three and a half magical
seasons until he fractured a bone in his foot in
the King George VI Chase at Kempton Park
on Boxing Day, 1966.

Gladiateur

Gladiateur, was the first French horse to win
the Epsom Derby. His sparkling three length
victory was a blow to the boasted supremacy
of the British Thoroughbred. His form as a
two year old was hardly memorable, but he
won the 1865 Two Thousand Guineas well
enough at 7 – 1 and went on to win the Derby
fifty years to the month after Napoleon's
defeat at Waterloo. In the same year, he
added the French Derby, (The Prix du Jockey
Club), to his list of triumphs, and in the
autumn completed the Triple Crown despite
intermittent lameness. His last race and victory in the Ascot Gold Cup still ranks as one
of the most remarkable performances in racing history.

The Poacher

One of the leading British event horses of the
late 1960s and early 1970s. Ridden by his
owner, Captain Martin Whiteley, The
Poacher won the individual silver medal at
the 1967 European Championships; however, at the Mexico Olympics the following
year, the horse was ridden by Staff Sergeant
Ben Jones because of its owner's bad back.

Richard Meade's association with The
Poacher began in 1970, when he rode him to
victory at Badminton. The following year, he
rode the horse again in the winning British
team for the European Championships at
Burghley.

Kilbarry

Halla

Secretariat

Kilbarry

Though Irish-bred, Kilbarry was one of Britain's greatest three-day event horses, with a string of almost unbroken successes until his untimely death in a one-day event. Ridden by his owner, Colonel Frank Weldon, he won European silver medals in 1953 and 1954; in 1955 he won a European gold. The following year, he won Badminton, and a team gold and an individual bronze at the Stockholm Olympics.

Secretariat

In the stands at Belmont on June 9, 1973, the massive Secretariat, a powerful chestnut with three white socks, was being hailed as the greatest racehorse of all time. Just 250 yards away, hidden among the vast complex of 2,500 boxes, the subject of all the adoration was munching his way through a meal sufficient for three ordinary horses.

An hour earlier on the dirt course on Long Island, New York, he had run away with with the Belmont Stakes, final leg of his US Triple Crown, winning by the astonishing margin of

thirty-one lengths. Meanwhile, the thirty-two optimists who had paid $190,000 each in the previous winter for a share in his future, were viewing their syndication figure of $6,080,000 with the satisfaction of men who had just scooped the jackpot.

Statistics alone cannot convey the genius of this unique horse, sired by a champion, Bold Ruler, out of a mare, Something Royal, who never won a race. One breeding expert summed it up when he suggested; 'This is probably the best horse there has ever been. He's what everyone has been trying to breed for the past 100 years; one that sprints for one-and-a-half miles'.

First winner of the American Triple Crown for a quarter of a century, Secretariat won 16 of his 21 races in a meteoric career that spanned barely 16 months. Nicknamed 'Big Red' by his legion of admirers, he collected $1,316,808 in prize money. He won the Kentucky Derby in style by 2½ lengths from Sham in a record time, then came close to beating the record for the Preakness when defeating Sham again. After this, he shat-

tered the world record for 1½ miles on a track while completing the Triple Crow[n] the Belmont Stakes. In an incredible display of power and speed, Secretariat m[ade] nearly all the running, drew clear of [his] toiling rivals at the half-way point, and [won] by thirty-one lengths, beating the prev[ious] best time for the race by 2.6 seconds. He [was] travelling so fast as Ron Turcotte bega[n to] pull him up, that he also set a new w[orld] record for thirteen furlongs.

Halla

Halla became nearly as famous as the ma[n she] brought to the forefront of world show ju[mp]ing, Hans Günter Winkler of West G[er]many. A brown mare by the trotting [sire] Oberst out of the half-bred mare Helene, [she] started her career as a racehorse and then [was] tried as an eventer before being sent to W[ink]ler by her owner, Gustav Vierling.

Halla won her first competition in 1[952] and then the pair rocketed to fame and [for]tune. In 1953 they won in Rome, Mad[rid,] Paris and Pinerolo; the following year, [rid]ing started with three wins in Dortmund, [the] championship in Rome and one of the [big]gest classes in Lucerne, Halla took Win[kler] to the world title in Madrid. On the aut[umn] circuit in the USA, she was equally co[mpe]tent and successful.

Riding Halla in 1955, Winkler retaine[d his] world title in Aachen. The pair also [won] their first Hamburg Derby, which they [re]tained in 1956, as well as winning an O[lympic]

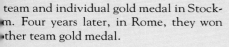

The Rock

Doublet

team and individual gold medal in Stock-
m. Four years later, in Rome, they won
ther team gold medal.

merang
present mount of Eddie Macken, Ire-
d's leading international rider is
merang. He is the top Grand Prix horse
urope in 1978, and has won the British
ping Derby at Hickstead three times in
cession, a feat no other horse has
ieved. The last of these wins was in 1978,
ugh, in the same month, he was beaten in
World Championship in Aachen by a
tional time penalty and cheated of the
ble title. Together they make one of the
t popular combinations in modern show-
ping.

Rock
Rock was mount of the Italian rider
onel Piero d'Inzeo, brother of Raimondo
zeo, when he won the Olympic individu-
lver medal in Rome in 1960. A handsome
Irish horse, he emerged dramatically on
he international scene in 1957, when he
in Paris, the Puissance contest in Lon-
(with the wall at 7ft 1in), a class in
lin and two in Geneva. In 1958, he won
competitions in Rome, including the
ted Grand Prix, a class at Aachen and
again including the Puissance — in
don. The following year Paris again saw
first win of the season, followed by two in
hen and two at Wembley, London. Show

jumping often seems to be a family affair as
the d'Inzeo brothers demonstrated.

Doublet
The two horses with which H.R.H. Princess
Anne is chiefly associated in her eventing
career are Doublet and Goodwill. Doublet
was bred by Queen Elizabeth II by Doubtless
II out of an Argentinian polo pony mare. The
high spot of his career was winning the European individual title at Burghley in 1971, but
the horse had to be destroyed after breaking a
hind leg during a dressage test at Windsor, a
tragic set-back to the career of Britain's riding
princess.

Democrat
Democrat was the best show jumper with
which Billy Steinkraus, captain of the US
team through six Olympics, from Helsinki to
Munich, thought himself ever likely to be
associated. Democrat's long career began in
1940 when, ridden by Colonel F. F. Wing, he
first competed at the National Horse Show,
Madison Square Gardens, New York, where

he was to become a by-word, winning the
Grand Prix on his first outing in top company. In 1941, he won two competitions
there; and, after an enforced retirement during the war, he staged a comeback in 1946,
winning in New York and Toronto. This feat
he repeated the following year. He was then
sent to Europe for the Olympic Games. As
part of the US team's pre-Olympic preparations, he won in Lucerne, Aachen, London
and Dublin, while, in the Olympics themselves, he finished fourth individually.

In the same year, however, the US Army
team was disbanded and Democrat went into
retirement. In 1952, however, at the age of
nineteen, he was brought back into the US
Olympic team and, ridden now by Major
John Russell, helped the USA to win the
team bronze medals. On his return to the
USA, he went on the autumn circuit of
shows and, ridden by Bill Steinkraus, won
every class in which he was entered at three
major international meetings — one in Harris-
burgh, four in New York and three in Toronto. After this, he went into final retirement.

Irish Cap

Irish Cap and Might Tango

The two horses on which Bruce Davidson of the USA won his first World Horse Trials Championship in 1974 at Burghley in the UK and retained the title in 1978 at Lexington, Kentucky, respectively. Irish Cap, who also competed in the 1974 Olympics, was bred in Ireland and sold to the USA as an unbroken four-year-old. There, he remained unbroken until the age of six, as his girl owner was too small and too frightened to ride him.

Goodwill

After Doublet's tragic death, Princess Anne's chief partner was Goodwill, a former champion working hunter. Selected for the European Championships as individuals at Kiev in 1972, they were forced to retire after a fall at the second cross-country fence, but two years later they finished as runners-up to Lucinda Prior-Palmer and Be Fair at Luhmuhlen, West Germany. However, another fall at the 1976 Olympics put them well behind the leaders, though they finished the course. After Princess Anne's temporary retirement from the sport during her pregnancy, they were short-listed for the 1978 British team for the World Championships in Kentucky.

Cornishman V

The mount of leading British rider Mary Gordon-Watson when she won the European Championships in 1969 and the world title in 1970. Bred in Cornwall by Golden Surprise out of a point-to-point mare, Polly V, Cornishman was bought by Mary Gordon-Watson's father as a potential event horse for his daughter, even though Cornishman bucked him off into a muck heap when he first tried him. However, in the 1968 Olym-

Goodwill

Cornishman V

pics, Cornishman was ridden by Richard Meade, as Mary Gordon-Watson had broken her leg three months before. In 1972, he won his second Olympic team gold medal in Munich, with his owner this time riding.

Ballycor

The mount of the US rider Tad Coffin when he won the Olympic individual gold medal at Bromont in 1976, the year after the horse had won the Pan American gold medal. A dark bay mare, 16.3 hands high and thirteen years old when she took part in the World Championships in 1978, Ballycor is a thoroughbred, by Cormac out of Bally Lickey, and was bred in America by Dr Charles Reid. In 1977, also with Tad Coffin, she won the Blue Ridge Advanced competition for the Gladstone Trophy; she was also the leading mare in American three-day events.

Sea Bird II

Of all the horses to have won Epsom's Derby this century, Sea Bird II probably has the highest reputation; yet his dam was sold to a

Ballycor

butcher for £100 long before he ever ran the first time, in September 1964. Sea Bird was something of a late developer, but showed sufficient promise in the autumn his second year to be aimed by his trainer the leading events of 1965. Two victories France made him an automatic favourite the Epsom Derby. He did not let his supporters down. One moment he was cruising along handily placed behind the leaders, next he had sprinted past the opposition run home an early winner. It was a breathtaking achievement, enhanced by the subsequent victories of his nearest challengers Meadow Court, first in the Irish Sweeps Derby, then in the King George VI and Queen Elizabeth Stakes.

Sea Bird II left Epsom to add the Grand Prix de Saint Cloud to his laurels, then settled down for his major test, the Prix de l'Arc de Triomphe. The field included Meadow Court, Reliance, unbeaten in five runs including the French Derby, Tom Rolfe, winner of the American Derby and Preakness Stakes, and a dozen other top class

Sea Bird II

Pele

Kelso

Foxhunter

roughbreds who had already proved them-
es in competitive European contests.
et which horse would win the first prize of
34,747 francs was not in doubt for one
ment. Settled by his jockey Pat Glennon
n ideal position close to the leaders, Sea
d surged past his rivals in the straight to
by six lengths from Reliance.

e
ie Macken's previous mount was Pele.
1974 they finished as runners-up to
enken and Simona in the World Cham-
nship. Three years later, with Pele
v re-christened Kerrygold, they were
n runners-up for the European Cham-
nships in Vienna, beaten by a mere one-
th of a second.

so
so's record as Horse of the Year in Ameri-
or five consecutive seasons, from 1960 –
has never been equalled. He won a total
1,977,896 racing on dirt and grass tracks
had an enormous following, including

his own fan clubs, in a career that started on
September 4, 1959.

Kelso raced 63 times, winning 39 races
outright, coming second twelve times, third
twice, and fourth five times. He was unplaced in only five races and was the most
consistent performer in the history of North
American racing. He won at varying distances from six furlongs to two miles, on all
types of going, and on twelve different
courses ridden by six different jockeys. Three
times runner-up in the much publicised
Washington D.C. International, held at
Laurel Park towards the close of each year, he
finally won this elusive event on November
11, 1964, for the biggest prize – $90,000
dollars – of his long and distinguished career.

Kelso was probably the world's most famous gelding. Having recovered from the operation, carried out at the start of his career, he
ran three times at Atlantic City, winning his
debut race at 6 – 1, the best starting price ever
offered him, and coming second in his other
two races. An injury kept him off the course
for the next nine months, after which he won

at Monmouth Park in June, 1960, for his new
trainer, the former jockey Card Hanford.
Beaten only once in 1960, in the Arlington
Classic, he was voted Horse of the Year. He
continued to dominate American racing for
several years, usually winning but occasionally finding himself outmanoeuvered by the
handicapper. Flat-racing horses tend to de-
teriorate after two or three seasons, but Kelso
raced as honestly and bravely as ever until his
retirement in 1966.

Foxhunter

One of the first really famous post-war British
show jumpers, in partnership with his rider,
Colonel Harry Llewellyn, Foxhunter started
show jumping at the age of five in 1946. A
year later, he was bought by Harry Llewellyn
to begin their long association.

During his career, Foxhunter was consistently successful at international level. In
1948, he competed with the British team in
the Olympics; a week after the Olympics
closed, he won the King George V Gold Cup.
Subsequent victories in this competition in
1950 and 1953 made him the only horse ever
to win this prestigious trophy three times.
Having triumphed at Grand Prix and Puissance competitions all over Europe and in
North America, he then, at Helsinki, played
a leading part in the UK's first and only
Olympic show jumping victory.

Idle Dice

High and Mighty

Man O'War

Idle Dice

Ridden by the leading American professional, Rodney Jenkins, Idle Dice is the most renowned show jumper in the USA. A brown gelding, standing 17.1 hands high, he has won more prize money than any other horse in the history of the sport. Grand Prix Horse of the Year in 1977, he has won the American Gold Cup three times, as well as the American Invitational, the President's Cup and many other major championships. In 1978, he was loaned to the US world championship by his owner, Harry Gill. In common with most other American show jumpers, Idle Dice was a failed race horse.

High and Mighty

British event horse who, ridden by Sheila Willcox, won Badminton in both 1957 and 1958. In 1957, too, they took the individual and a team gold medal in the European Championships at Copenhagen. However, as the three-day Olympic event was at that time still closed to women riders, they were never able to compete in the Games. Sheila Willcox went on to become one of the UK's leading eventing trainers.

Man O'War

Man O'War's deserved reputation as the finest American-bred racehorse has withstood a series of challenges from such famous modern candidates as Kelso and Secretariat. Foaled in Kentucky in 1917 and sold a year later at the Saratoga Sales for $5,000, Man O'War – a richly coloured chestnut with a powerful, stocky, frame – proved to be the ultimate racehorse. Beaten just once in 21 starts, he won a total of $249,465 and caught the imagination of the nation throughout his brief career of only seventeen months.

Nicknamed 'Big Red', a label also given to Secretariat nearly fifty years later, Man O'War was a giant of a horse, with enthusiasm and courage to match his outstanding ability. News of his startling home gallops made him a celebrity before he had even run in public; his first race confirmed these rumours when he won a modest $500 dollar maiden event at Belmont Park. He started odds-on that day, a pattern that was maintained in all his races. He won six races in a row before being beaten in a six furlong race at Saratoga, owing to the over-confident riding of his jockey, Johnny Loftus. Man O'War was trapped on the rails and shut in despite a small field, but once clear he made up ground rapidly and failed to catch the winner by only half a length. Having won three more races in 1919, he took an eight month break from racing.

Despite his non-appearance at the K[...] tucky Derby, his fans thought the wait wo[...] while, for he strolled home in the second [...] third legs of the Triple Crown. Man O'[...] won all his eleven races as a three-year-[...] breaking seven track, American, or w[...] records during the year. Three times[...] started at the remarkable odds of 100 – 1[...] and once he won by no less than 100 leng[...] His last race and victory came in a m[...] against the Canadian, Sir Barton, the Am[...] can Triple Crown winner in 1919. Set[...] out to make all the running, Man O'[...] galloped clean away from his illustrious ri[...] breaking the ten furlong track record by 6[...] a second.

His devoted owner, Samuel Riddle, ret[...] him to stud in 1921, and restricted him to [...] unusually low figure of 25 mares a yea[...] conserve his strength. The wonder h[...] lived to 1947, siring the winners of more t[...] $3,500,000 in stake money.

Ribot

Mister Softee

Baba

Baba

Baba was one of a long succession of French-bred Anglo-Arabs which carried Pierre Jonqueres d'Oriola to a series of dazzling victories. The partnership came together in 1952 in Rome; they collaborated so well that they were selected for the Olympics, where they won the individual gold medal. D'Oriola repeated this feat on Lutteur at Tokyo in 1964.

Ribot

The calm and peaceful pastures of West Sussex were the unlikely setting for the birth of Italy's greatest racehorse. Ribot was born there in 1952, as the result of a union arranged by breeding genius Frederico Tesio who, sadly, did not live to see his finest achievement prove his methods on the track. When still very young, Ribot returned to Italy with his dam. Small and backward, he looked insignificant and was so unprepossessing that he was not even entered for the

Italian classics. But his puny frame disguised a burgeoning ability, that, for a brief and glorious period, was to capture the imagination of the racing world.

Ribot won his first race, easily beating a more fancied stable mate in the process, and, without being extended, soon proved himself the champion two year old of Italy. Champion again at three, despite missing the classics, he won all his races with consummate ease before heading for Europe's most contested prize, the Prix de l'Arc de Triomphe at Longchamp in October, 1955. The French treated the invader with contempt in the hulabaloo of the days leading up to the race, and consequently, he was allowed to start at the amazingly generous 9–1. Never in the slightest danger of losing his unbeaten record, he cantered home unchallenged, three lengths ahead of his nearest rival.

Next season, as a four-year old, Ribot travelled to Ascot, for the prestigious King George VI and Queen Elizabeth Stakes, run over unusually heavy ground for high summer. His five length win was labelled by the critics, somewhat unkindly, as laboured and unimpressive. Then, after another easy win in Milan, Ribot headed for Longchamp once more, in a bid to become the fifth horse to complete a double in the Prix de L'Arc de Triomphe.

The opposition was particularly strong, with winners of many major European races competing in the field. Ribot, however, swept through them all in a performance of stunning power. Seldom has a horse dominated a champion field so completely. Jockey Enrico Camici settled him in third place as

Fisherman set a furious gallop, closed on the leader effortlessly on the final bend, then simply sprinted away. At the post, he was six lengths clear and increasing his lead with every stride.

Unchallenged in sixteen races spread over three seasons, Ribot returned to an equally successful and prolific career at stud, first in Europe, then from 1960 onwards in Kentucky. His influence is still enormous on both sides of the Atlantic. Tom Rolfe, Graustark, Molvedo, Ribocco, Ribero, Ribofilio, and Arts and Letters are only a few of the champions he sired before his premature death.

Mister Softee

Favourite mount of the distinguished British show jumper David Broome. An Irish horse, bought at Dublin Horse Show as a three-year-old after he had been lunged over a pole, Mister Softee won the European Championship in London in 1962 when ridden by David Barker – but he really made his name after joining the Broome team in 1965. The following year, the two proved unbeatable in major UK competitions, winning the King George V Gold Cup, the British Jumping Derby at Hickstead, the Olympic Trial and the Victor Ludorum at the Horse of the Year Show. In 1967, they won the European Championship at Rotterdam, retaining it at Hickstead in 1969, after jumping-off with Alwin Schockemohle on Donald Rex. In the intervening year, they won an Olympic bronze medal in Mexico for Great Britain, becoming one of the most popular combinations in British and international show-jumping.

Ormonde

Sympatico

Jet Run

Sympatico

An eighteen-year-old thoroughbred gelding when bought by a Canadian syndicate in 1976, Sympatico is now owned by 25-year-old Terry Leibel, whose father paid a reputed $300,000 for the horse. Sympatico's reputation more than explains the price; he was the leading Grand Prix horse in the USA from 1972 to 1975, setting the world Puissance record at a towering 7ft 4in in New York in 1974.

St Simon and Ormonde

These two horses, born two years apart, dominated British racing in the late nineteenth century. The great jockey Fred Archer, who killed himself in tragic circumstances at the height of his career, rode both horses but clearly held St Simon in the higher esteem.

Ormonde, winner of the elusive Triple Crown – the Two Thousand Guineas, the Derby and the St Leger – was unbeaten in all his races but proved a hopeless failure at stud. St Simon, on the other hand, cost only 1,600 guineas, never ran in a Classic, but won all his races with contemptuous ease (though his earnings in prize money were a mere £4,676) and became one of the most important sires in the history of the turf. His first stud fee, in 1886, was no more than 50 guineas, but by

1899, he had become such a prolific sire of winners that his price rose to 500 guineas for each mare he covered.

Ormonde's failure as a stallion contrasts sadly with his brilliance as a racehorse. There have been few Epsom Derby winners to match his excellence, for in his three years on the turf he was never beaten. He won £28,625 in prize money, and started at the astonishing price of 100-1 on in the 1886 Champion Stakes.

Ormonde won the first leg of the Triple Crown, the Two Thousand Guineas, at the generous odds of 7-2 from the supposed certainty, Minting. He went on to triumph in the 1886 Derby in runaway style from the Bard, who himself had been undefeated in 16 races as a two year old. By October that year, his reputation was so formidable that the owners of the Bard and Melton, winners of the 1885 Derby and St Leger, each paid a £500 forfeit rather than risk their horses against him in a private sweepstake at Newmarket. Despite growing problems with his

wind, as a four-year-old, he won three [?] races and even beat the top sprin[?] Whitefriar, by two lengths over six furlo[?] a tremendous feat even for a Triple Cr[?] winner.

Ormonde might well have continue[?] dominate his rivals, but his wind probl[?] cut short his career, and he was eventu[?] sold by his owner, the Duke of Westmin[?] to an Argentinian breeder in 1889. Four y[?] later, he was sold again, to a US buyer, bu[?] proved an abject failure at stud, and man[?] to sire only 16 foals in 11 years. One of [?] finest racehorses in the history of [?] Thoroughbred, he ended his life infer[?] and was put down in 1904.

St Simon headed the sires' list in Engl[?] nine times, was twice second and three ti[?] third. His influence was immense, fo[?] sired the winners of no less than seven[?] Classics and three Ascot Gold Cups. [?] together, his offspring won 571 races [?] £553,159 in prize money. In 1896, he led [?] stallions list with his son St Serf second, [?] his own sire, Galopin, third.

Posillipo

Flanagan

St Simon

t Simon died in 1908 as he was returning
n exercise; his skeleton was given to the
ish Museum. Despite the affection inher-
in his trainer's account St Simon did
se a few problems at the Welbeck stud.
one occasion, he was given a stable com-
ion to quieten him down. The plan mis-
d, for he seized the poor animal, tossed it
nst the ceiling of the box, and trampled it
eath.

Run
ine-year-old, 16.2 hands bay gelding, Jet
a is one of the biggest winners in North
erica. Originally owned by the Mexican
nando Senderos, he won New York's
nd Prix in 1974 and a Pan American gold
lal in 1975.
fter touring Europe with Jet Run in 1977,
deros sold him to the American owner F.
ene Dixon, Jr., who made him available
the US equestrian team. Ridden by
hael Matz, he won the American Jump-
Derby in Rhode Island in 1977, as well as
Grand Prix at the Royal Winter Fair in

Toronto and the Valley Forge Grand Prix. In
1978, he was one of the four finalists in the
world championship.

Posillipo
Mount of the Italian rider Colonel Raimondo
d'Inzeo, Piero d'Inzeo's brother, when he
won the Olympic individual gold medal in
Rome in 1960. However, this Italian
thoroughbred had a comparatively short
working life as an international show jumper,
especially when compared with Raimondo
d'Inzeo's own favourite horse, Bellevue, now
in his twenties.

Flanagan
For many years, Britain's Pat Smythe was the
most successful woman rider in the world,
and the most consistent of her mounts was
the Irish-bred chestnut Flanagan. Foaled in
1948, he started his career as a three-day
event horse, but, under Pat Smythe, he became one of the world's leading show jumpers. Among many top international prizes,
he won her the Ladies' European Champion-

ship at Spa in 1957, Deauville in 1961,
Madrid in 1962 and Hickstead in 1963. He
was also a member of the Olympic team in
1956 and 1960.

Phar Lap
No champion has ever started life with less
likely credentials than Phar Lap. Unplaced in
his first four races in 1929, he did at last win a
modest race at his fifth attempt, but then
reverted to his more customary position of an
also ran in his next three outings. Yet this
most famous of Australasian racehorses was to improve so rapidly that he
won no fewer than 37 of his 51 races.
   As a three year old, he landed the A.J.C.
and Victoria Derbys as well as the Craven
Plate, before running third in the Melbourne
Cup. After a rest, he returned to win another
third place before beginning a sequence of
nine straight wins. The big ugly duckling, as
the horse was affectionately described, had
sprouted wings. He continued to improve,
winning the nickname Red Terror, and duly
won the Melbourne Cup at odds of 8 – 11
despite carrying the burden of 138lbs.
   The next step was a trip to America, where
Phar Lap won the Mexican Agua Calienta
handicap. But, sadly, this was his last race.
Shortly afterwards, he died after eating grass
which had been sprayed with insecticide.

The glossary

Aachen One of the chief world centres for show jumping and dressage; the purpose-built stadium, just outside the city, was erected after the Second World War. The stadium is equipped with excellent exercise areas and blocks of permanent stabling, as well as a large covered grandstand and uncovered seating. Audience capacity is 50,000.

Aachen is the most popular show in the world with riders. There are two main reasons for this; in Hans-Heinrich Brinckmann, a pre-war German cavalry officer, it has the finest course builder in the world, while the prize money, too, is extremely high. The event often attracts fifteen to twenty full international teams; the Nations' Cup is thus a reliable guide to world form, with the best teams competing over an extremely testing course, while it takes an Olympic-standard horse to win the Grand Prix.

Accoutrements The tack – saddles, bridles and bits – worn by the horse. The earliest surviving examples come from the Near and Middle East, where horses were at first harnessed and controlled in pairs under a yoke, with a nose ring. By 1700 BC, however, the first bits had been introduced; a surviving bronze example from Gaza has a plain bar mouthpiece and circular cheek pieces, with a barbaric spike on their inner surfaces. More elaborate bits have been found in Luristan, in western Iran. These date from the 7th to 10th centuries BC, with the cheek pieces cast in the form of horses or moufflons.

As the chariot horse was replaced by the ridden horse, bits, too, changed their form. Hungarian bits of the 15th century BC had soft mouthpieces of rope, gut or rawhide. Greek bits of the 6th and 7th centuries BC had bar or arc-shaped cheek pieces, while early Italian bronze bits of the 9th to 7th centuries BC were made with jointed mouthpieces.

The first mounted troops appeared in Assyria in the 9th century BC, riding on animal skins held in place by breastbands. By the 6th century BC, the Persians were also using saddle cloths and, by about AD 100, the Romans had a leather military saddle, secured by an overall roller, a crupper and a breastplate.

Stirrups made their first appearance with the Huns, though they were not developed in western Europe until Charlemagne's wars against the Avars of Hungary and there is no evidence of their general use until the 9th century AD. They revolutionised the art of riding, however, and led to the soft saddle being replaced by a rigid structure, with a pair of shaped boards, padded and stuffed top and bottom, lying on either side of the horse's spine. The boards were joined by two iron arches. The next stage, with more agile horses, was a saddle with a deeper seat, giving the rider greater contact with the horse.

With the Middle Ages, curb bits came into common use, as warhorses became heavier and greater collection was required of them. In the Renaissance, schooled horses wore single-rein curbs; training, however, started with a cavesson in order not to spoil their mouths, after which the curb was first used with 'false reins' attached to its top rings to form a pelham. To suit this dominant style of riding, a variety of extremely severe bits was developed, but, slowly over the centuries, they, too, were replaced by less severe ones. The ultimate development came with the use of double bridles and snaffles, together with the introduction of different types of saddles for various activities. This was part and parcel of the forward seat style of riding, originated by Federico CAPRILLI of Italy in the early 20th century.

Aging Age in the horse is determined by the examination of its six incisor teeth. When all the permanent incisors have fully erupted, the horse is said to have a full mouth. From then on, age is assessed from the changes that occur on the wearing surfaces of the lower incisors, and the angle at which they meet those of the upper jaw. Up to the age of eight, the age can be accurately estimated; after that, however, the system is less precise, which is why horses over the age of seven are described as 'aged'.

In assessing age, it is important to note that all Thoroughbreds are likely to be born early in the year and other breeds in the spring. Thus, in the Northern Hemispere, the age of a Thoroughbred is judged to date from January 1; of other breeds from May 1. A Thoroughbred foal born in late December is therefore deemed for racing purposes to be a year old the following month.

The lifespan of a healthy horse varies enormously according to the care it receives and the work it does. The greatest age so far recorded is that of Old Billy, a barge horse who died at sixty-two. Generally, a horse is considered mature at between six and seven according to its size and type, and in its prime at eight. It can work hard until it is aged between twelve and fourteen and do light work up to the age of twenty – and in some cases even after this.

Aids The various means employed by the rider to transmit his or her wishes to the horse. There are two types – the natural aids (legs, hands, seat and voice) and the artificial aids (whip and spur). Other differentiations are lateral and diagonal aids, combinations of hand and leg aids on the same side of the horse or on opposite sides.

In early training, lateral aids are used as they are more readily understood by the horse. In later, more advanced, training, diagonal aids are employed. Both hands, sometimes known as the upper aids, contr pace, speed and direction by acting, resist or yielding. The legs, the lower aids, produ forward movement, and shift or hold the haunches in the same manner.

Airs Above the Ground The name give to High School movements in which the horse jumps into the air. Examples are the *ballotade, croupage, courbette, capriole* and *levade*.

Airs, Classical The aim of classical equitation is to develop and perfect the natural movements of the horse. Exercise the ground, of the kind required in dressa tests, range from walk, trot and canter on single track, through lateral work, when t horse moves sideways as well as forward, t the *piaffe* and *passage*. The airs above the ground, developed from the natural leaps the horse, are the *levade* and *pesade*, with t horse rising on its deeply bent haunches, forelegs folded under its chest, and the *capriole*, with the hind legs kicking vigoro simultaneously. When not kicking out, th horse performs a *ballotade*. In the *courbette* leaps several times on its hind legs withou touching the ground with its forelegs. A single leap on the hind legs is called a *croupade*.

From the sixteenth to the eighteenth centuries, these airs were part of the traini of a school horse and they were used in mo jousts and tournaments. Today, they are displayed in the art of the Spanish Riding School of Vienna.

Amateur and professional A controver area of riding, particularly at the top international level. For some years, for example, the International Olympic Committee and others have levelled char of 'shamateurism' at the leading show jumpers of many nations; in the UK, for instance, some horses are now sponsored companies in exchange for a change of na to advertise their products. Thus, in 1972 the International Equestrian Federation announced that every national federation must declare its professionals. Britain led way, with forty-six riders taking out professional licences, in the hope that oth countries would follow suit. Ironically, th I.O.C. has now found a compromise solut to the problem.

Badminton The Cotswold home of the Dukes of Beaufort in Gloucestershire, England, is the setting for the Badminton Three-Day Horse Trials, one of the chief fixtures in the eventing calendar since its foundation in 1949. Many top riders have competed there, including Richard Mead

cinda Prior-Palmer and H.R.H. Princess
ne, and the results are a good guide to
ld ratings in the sport.
reme   The name given to the table under
ich a jumping competition is judged.
ble A covers jumping only, and Table C
ed.
rrage   The alternate name for a jump-
, in which horses with equal scores at the
d of a competition compete against each
er again. The result can either be decided
the number of faults, time against the
ck, or a combination of the two.
less Bridle   A bridle without a mouth-
ce, the horse being controlled by pressure
the nose. Its alternate name is a
ckamore.
ushing   The term applied when a horse
kes its fetlock with the shoe on the
posite foot. It is usually a result of faulty
ion.
ck   Over-fresh horses can 'get their backs
and kick into the air, either during a ride
en, say, a change of pace is asked for, or
en the rider is settling in the saddle.
rghley   The seat, near Stamford in
colnshire, of the Marquess of Exeter, is
home of Britain's principal autumn three-
event, the Burghley Horse Trials, which
rted in 1961. It has been the scene of two
rld Championships in 1966 and 1974,
three European Championships in 1963,
71 (when the individual title was won by
R.H. Princess Anne on Doublet), and
77, when Lucinda Prior-Palmer won her
ond title and the British team won the
m title back from the USSR.
erley Turk   An Arab stallion who was
of the three founders of the English
oroughbred. The Byerley Turk was
tured from the Turks at the siege of
dapest and brought back to England by
ptain Byerley – hence the name. Never
ed, the horse proved to be a top-class sire,
ugh it covered relatively few mares. One
he Turk's most distinguished descendants
Herod, who was foaled in 1758.
prilli, Federico (1868–1907)   Italian
alry officer who originated the chief
dern style of riding. Caprilli's influence
an when he succeeded Cesare Paderni as
ructor at Pinerola. There, he abolished
accepted classical method of riding,
arding this as totally unsuitable for riding
oss country, and, after private
eriment, introduced his celebrated
ward Seat to replace it. This met with
at opposition from traditionalists, and, to
ve his theories, Caprilli negotiated the
ous *Scivalone* (slide) at Tor di Quinto in
position. He also won numerous
npetitions, as well as the army
mpionship, riding his Irish horse Pouf.

Caprilli, however, wrote only a few notes
on his innovations; these appeared in 1901 in
the *Revista di Cavalleria*. In December 1907,
he died while riding his horse at a walk at
Turin, either from a heart attack or as a result
of an old head wound. In the same year, the
seat was adopted by the entire Italian cavalry
and army officers from all over the world
were sent to Italy to learn to ride in this
manner. Their teaching on their return home
did much to establish the seat's reputation, as
did Italian successes in international
competitions.
Cavalletto   Small fence consisting of a
squared-off pole, supported at each end in an
X-shaped support. Cavalletti are used for
schooling, either in the form of a grid or built
up to make a fence.
Chaff   Chopped-up hay or oat straw. It is
mixed with corn or bran to form a bulk feed.
Chef d'équipe   Term used in the horse
world to describe a team manager. Show
jumping teams and eventing teams all have
their chef d'équipe, whose role is
organizational and strategical.
Cob   Name given to a stocky, short-legged
horse, not much over or under 15.1 hands,
with good bone and body and up to weight.
The best ones are good rides and have the
ability to gallop willingly and freely.
Collect   To pull a schooled horse together
by creating impulsion with the legs and
containing it with the hands. As a result, the
horse brings its hind legs more under its body.
Colt   Term used to describe a young male
horse under four years old.
Combined Training   A dressage and show-
jumping competition, possibly including a
cross-country test, as in the three-day event.
Cow hocks   A conformational weakness of
the horse. In it, the points and the joints of
the hocks incline towards one another.
Crib biting   A stable vice, in which the
horse gets hold of the door or manger with
the incisors and swallows air. This leads to
indigestion.
Curb   A prominence situated a hand's
breadth below the point of the hock, caused
by sprain of the calcaneometatarsal ligament.
It is conspicuous when the horse is viewed
from the side and is a serious blemish as far as
a show horse is concerned. In racing,
however, the curb is tolerated as long as the
horse is sound.
Curb Bit   A bit consisting of a straight
mouthpiece to which are attached two
hooks. These hold the curb chain, which fits
into the chin groove on the lower jaw. The
bit works by leverage on the lower jaw,
exerting pressure on the chin groove by
means of the chain. It is one half of a DOUBLE
BRIDLE, the other being the SNAFFLE.
Curry Comb   A large, flat metal comb,

used to clean the body brush – never the
horse.
Darley Arabian   The most important of the
three founders of the English Thoroughbred,
the horse was imported to Britain from the
east by a Mr Darley in the early eighteenth
century. Foaled in 1700, he was a bay
horse with a blaze and three white socks, and
stood about fifteen hands high. Out of the
famous mare Betty Leedes, he sired the two
brothers Flying Childers and Bartletts
Childers. He was also the sire of Bulle Rock,
the first Thoroughbred to go to the USA.
Derby (Jumping)   The prototype show
jumping Derby was held in Hamburg in 1920.
It proved so successful and spectacular that its
formula of cross-country-type show jumping
over a long course, with permanent fences
such as banks, sunken coffin-type fences,
table fences, ditches and stone walls, has
been enthusiastically adopted elsewhere.
The most notable examples are the British
Jumping Derby, held at Hickstead in Sussex,
and the French equivalent, held at the
seaside resort of La Baule.

The Hamburg version did not produce a
single clear round until 1935. The British
one, which started in 1961, produced its
nineteenth clear round in 1978, when it was
won for the third consecutive year by Eddie
Macken and Boomerang for Ireland. He and
Harvey Smith have each won it three times,
but Smith has had two different mounts.
Dope tests   Under the International
Equestrian Federation's rules for
international sport, the use of stimulants,
sedatives and anabolic steroids is absolutely
prohibited. However, the use of painkilling
drugs, such as phenylbutazone or
butazolidine is only forbidden for dressage
horses – a ruling that is causing considerable
controversy, particularly in the three-day
event field.

Urine tests, to discover whether drugs
have been used, are taken at all international
meetings. If the horse does not produce a
sample within an hour, it is up to the
discretion of the organizers as to whether
blood or saliva tests shall be taken instead.
Because of the quite understandable fear of
infection, some riders refuse to allow blood
samples to be taken in the unsterile
atmosphere of a showground.
Double   Two fences with only a short
distance between them, which the rider has
to jump as a combination.
Double Bridle   A showing bridle, also used
by some riders in the hunting field and
dressage arena. It consists of two bits, a CURB
and a SNAFFLE, each with separate cheek
pieces and its own rein. The double bridle is
more sophisticated than the snaffle, which
merely raises the head; the curb causes the

horse to flex its neck and to bring its nose in.

Drag Hunt   A form of hunting gaining increasing popularity. Instead of chasing a live quarry, the hunters and hounds follow a scent which has been put down artificially, often using an aniseed trail laid by a runner.

Draw rein   A rein fixed to the girth and passing through the rings of the bit to the rider's hand.

Driving Competitions (International)   The sport of combined driving, based on the ridden three-day event, is a relatively new one. It has become increasingly popular during recent years, especially in the UK, where one of its most prominent supporters is Prince Philip. The West Germans and the Poles are also very successful, as are the Dutch with their Friesians and the Hungarians with their little blood horses.

Entire   The term used to describe an ungelded horse.

F.E.I. (Fédération Equestre Internationale)   The international governing body of competitive equestrian sport. Based in Brussels, its president is H.R.H. The Prince Philip, Duke of Edinburgh.

Fillis, James (1834–1913)   Influential British riding master, who spent most of his life in France. At eight, Fillis was already riding difficult horses well, largely due to the influence of his fine teacher François Caron, himself a pupil of François Baucher, one of the greatest French trainers. Fillis devoted his life to training horses for Haute Ecole, including a period at the Champs-Elysee circus from 1873 to 1886. Of small stature, he had great strength in his legs, which he maintained were of more importance to the horseman than hands.

Fillis created his own school, based on the classical precepts. This is still followed today, although Caprilli maintained that Fillis imposed an artificial balance on the horse. His methods were especially influential in Russia and in 1898 he was appointed riding master to the School of Cavalry for Officers in St Petersburg, a position he held until 1910. He died in Paris three years later.

Filly   The name given to a young mare, under four years old. It is chiefly associated with racing.

Gag   A gag snaffle bit has cheek pieces which pass through holes in the top and bottom of the rings and lead right on to the reins. It is a severe bit and should only be used by a rider with good hands.

Gaited horses   A prominent class of American show horse. The horses have five gaits, the two extra ones being the stepping pace and the rack. Both of these are cultivated artificially, though there is some hereditary ability involved.

The stepping pace is a slow gait with a slight break in cadence from the pace, in which the near fore and near hind feet strike the ground simultaneously, followed by the off fore and off hind. The rack, which used to be known as the single foot, is a smooth, fast gait, in which each foot strikes the ground separately. Gaited horses also carry their tails high; this is the result of an operation which severs the tail's depressor muscles.

Galls   Areas on an unfit horse's body which have been rubbed raw by ill-fitting girths and saddles. They are a sign of bad horsemanship and stable management. Work should cease until the galls are healed and the skin has hardened.

Godolphin Arab or Barb   The third stallion to play a part in the foundation of the English Thoroughbred. The Godolphin Arab was bought in Paris in 1729 by a Mr Edward Coke of Derbyshire. A lop-eared bay, standing just under fifteen hands, he was purchased by the Earl of Godolphin after Coke's death in 1733 and, during a career of twenty years, covered some ninety mares. His most notable son was Cade (1733) and his most celebrated descendant was West Australian, sired in 1850. West Australian was the sire of Solon and Australian; from the latter descended the notable American sires Fairplay and Man o' War. Solon was the grandsire of Marco, by Barcaldine, who perpetuated the line in England through such legendary sires as Hurry On and Precipitation.

Going   Used to describe the various states of the ground. Going can be soft, hard, holding (sticky mud) and so on.

Grand Pardubice   A gruelling steeplechase in Czechoslovakia, founded in 1874 by Count Octavian Kinsky and held annually on the second Sunday in October. The course of $4\frac{1}{2}$ miles runs over ploughed fields and contains thirty-one fences, of which the most difficult is the Taxis ditch. This is 16 feet 5 inches wide and is fronted by a natural fence 5 feet high and 5 feet wide.

Hickstead   Douglas Bunn started the All England Jumping Course in the fields of his home, Hickstead Place, in 1960 to provide a continental-style course with permanent obstacles for British horses and riders. His idea was to help them gain experience in order to accustom them to international conditions before they went abroad. The following year, Hickstead was sponsored by the British company W.D. & H.O. Wills, who have backed it ever since. It is now recognized as one of the greatest show jumping centres in the world.

Four meetings are held at Hickstead each year; the course is the home of the Prince of Wales (British Nations) Cup and of the British Jumping Derby. In addition to the international arena, there are five seconda rings, while show classes, dressage tests and driving competitions have established Hickstead as an all-round show.

Hobdayed   Horses with afflictions of the respiratory organs, or who are touched in th wind, can be cured by the Hobdaying operation – so-called because it was invent by Professor Frederick Hobday (1870–1939). The operation consists of removing the paralysed vocal cords, which inhibit breathing, from the larynx. The on side effect is that the horse can no longer whinney.

Interval training   A system of conditioni horses to increase their speed and enduranc It is widely and successfully practised by th US Three-Day event team – the team and individual world champions in 1974 and th Olympic team and individual gold medalli in 1976.

Interval training improves respiration, circulation and removal of waste products subjecting the horse alternately to the stres of curtailed effort and rest. Athletically efficient muscle can be developed by short gallops at speeds just below the maximum c which the horse is safely capable, with walking intervals between them. Each gall is started after a period of walking, but befc the horse has quite recovered from the previous gallop. This stimulates the heart a lungs to supply the oxygen shortfall in the blood.

During the first months, the trainer gradually increases the speed of each series gallops until the horse reaches the speed required for the trial in view. At the same time, he improves the horse's stamina by galloping it over a constant distance, say 70 yards, a fixed number of times (not more than five in one day), with a constant $1\frac{1}{2}$ minute walking period, twice a week.

In the following weeks he prepares the horse to stay the whole distance required b progressively increasing the number of dai gallops from five to perhaps nine. To devel speed, he uses a few short gallops at increasing speeds; to develop stamina, he uses an increasing number of slightly longe gallops at slower speeds.

Kentucky Derby   The most famous Thoroughbred race in the USA. It is held a Churchill Downs, Louisville, Kentucky, fo three-year-olds carrying 57kg (126 lbs) an run over $1\frac{1}{4}$ miles; the first race was in 1875 when the distance was $1\frac{1}{2}$ miles (this was shortened in 1896). The race attracts the b three-year-olds in the USA, as well as entrants from overseas. It is the inaugural race in the Triple Crown series, with Preakness and Belmont following it.

g-distance Riding Major sport in the
A and, now, in other countries, such as
stralia and the UK. In the USA,
urance riding started in 1919, when the
cavalry held a series of tests to compare
quality of Thoroughbreds with Arabs;
n horse and rider had to cover 300 miles,
raging sixty a day, carrying weights from
to 245lbs. Following this, the annual
mont One Hundred Mile Three-Day
npetitive Trail Ride was founded, while,
e west, the North American Trail Ride
ference set up a similar series over shorter
ances of twenty to thirty miles. The
mpionship is the Tevis Cup ride, started
955, from Tahoe City in Nevada to
urn, California. It follows the same steep
over the Sierra Nevada mountains that
Wells Fargo express riders used to take,
conditions ranging from snow and icy
ds at Squaw Pass to 100-degree heat in El
ado Canyon. Of the 175 starters, forty
ent usually drop out.

ules governing such rides are designed to
ect the horses as much as possible. Riders
hing early are eliminated, for instance,
the horses are frequently examined for
dition and soundness. Condition is
ed on recovery of pulse and respiration
a climb, on the horse's willingness to
and by signs of dehydration and the
ity of the sweat – profuse lathery sweat,
pposed to clear sweat, is an obvious sign
nfitness. Horses are penalised for sore
s, stiffness, filled legs, and nicks or cuts
to tiredness or faulty action.

geing Rein A webbing rein, some forty
long, which is attached to the bridle. It
les the horse to be schooled or exercised
rcles around the user without actually
g ridden.

tingale A device designed to prevent a
e raising its head far enough to evade the
A standing martingale, which has a neck
p, goes from the noseband to the girth
is attached to both. A running
tingale, which also has a neck strap, goes
n the girth to a small ring around each
– in the case of a double bridle, to the
fle rein. The Irish martingale is simply
rings at either end of a short strip of
her which has the reins passed through it
e front of the horse's neck.

yland Hunt Cup One of the oldest and
t celebrated steeplechases in the USA,
Maryland Hunt Cup has been run
ually since 1896 at Glyndon, some ten
s from Baltimore, over a permanent
se built in natural hunting country. The
es are solid timber up to 5ft 6in in height.
ntil 1972, the only prize was a silver cup
he winner, though now there is a purse.
of the race's most famous winners was

Jay Trump, who pulled off the unique treble
of the Hunt Cup in 1963 and 1964 and the
British Grand National in 1965.

Nap A nappy horse refuses to do as the
rider wishes, usually failing to move in the
desired direction. Instead, the horse stands
still and may try to buck or rear.

Navicular Disease A chronic
inflammation of the navicular bone in the
foot, caused by concussion. Show jumpers
are particularly prone to it and are often
de-nerved (the nerves cut) in order to
prolong their active life. In its early stages,
the disease can be identified if the horse
leaves the stable lame but becomes sound as
work progresses.

**Newcastle, William Cavendish, Duke of
(1592–1676)** Celebrated seventeenth-
century British cavalryman and horse trainer,
noted for his sympathetic treatment of the
horse. His basic precept was to 'put as little
iron in your horse's mouth as you can.'

Newmarket Centre of UK racing since the
reign of Charles II and the headquarters of
the Jockey Club, British racing's governing
body. It is renowned both as a race course –
the Two Thousand Guineas and the One
Thousand Guineas are run there in the spring
and the Cesarewitch and the Cambridgeshire
in the autumn – and for its Thoroughbred
sales. The National Stud has been there since
1967 and there are some fifty other
Thoroughbred studs in the area, in addition
to countless training establishments.

Numnah A pad, usually made of
sheepskin, the same shape as the saddle. It is
placed under the saddle to prevent it rubbing
the horse's back.

One-Day Event A modified Three-Day
event, it was first held in the UK in 1950 as a
nursery for the higher level. It is now so
popular that there is a spring and an autumn
season at every level, from restricted novice
through intermediate and open intermediate
to advanced. The test consists of dressage,
cross-country and show jumping, the missing
elements being roads and tracks and
steeplechase.

Pacer A harness horse who, instead of
employing a true (trotting) pace, moves the
near and the hind leg simultaneously on the
same side. Such horses are frequently
hobbled to encourage this type of movement.

Passage A High School movement
consisting of a very rhythmic, collected,
elevated, cadenced trot in which there is
pronounced engagement of the quarters, an
accentuated flexion of the knees and the
hocks, and graceful elasticity of movement.
Each diagonal pair of legs is raised and
lowered alternately, gaining little ground,
with an even cadence and a prolonged
suspension.

Pelham A bit which combines SNAFFLE
and CURB in one mouthpiece.

Piaffe A very collected trot on the spot
asked for in dressage and High School work.
The horse's back should be supple and
vibrating, with the hocks well engaged, so
giving great freedom and lightness to the
action of the forehand.

Pirouette A High School movement in
which the horse turns a full circle in its own
length.

Polo A stick and ball game on horseback
for teams of four players. Polo probably
originated in Persia, though it was played all
over the east, particularly in China and
India. It came to Britain from India in the
mid-nineteenth century and spread from
there to the USA, the Commonwealth and
Argentina. The Argentine is now the leading
polo nation in the world, with some 3,000
players. The USA has 1,000 and the UK 500
active.

Polocrosse A game based on polo and
lacrosse, particularly popular in Australia. It
is less exclusive than polo because of its
relative cheapness.

Rig A male horse with one or both testicles
retained in the abdomen. An operation can
enable them or it to descend; after this, the
animal should be gelded, as the tendency can
be hereditary.

Sickle Hocks A conformational fault.
Seen broadside-on, the hocks are too
concave – literally shaped like a sickle.

Sidebones Ossification of the lateral
cartilages of the pedal bone, these are in the
main confined to the forefeet of cart horses.
Ringbone is an inflammatory growth of
bone, or extosis, connected with the pastern,
high ringbone involving the lower end of the
first phalanges and low ringbone, involving
the lower end of the pedal bone. Both cause
lameness and can result in fusion of the
pastern and pedal joints. The disease is found
among show jumpers.

Side Reins Part of breaking equipment.
They are attached to the horse from the bit to
the roller or saddle.

Snaffle The simplest form of bit and the
one in most frequent use. It consists of a
straight or jointed mouthpiece and a ring at
either end for the reins.

Spavin A bony enlargement on the lower
inner aspect of the hock joint, caused by a
periostitis.

Speedy Cut A wound inside the leg,
around the knee or cannon bone, caused by
the shoe of the opposite foot.

Splints Inflammatory bony outgrowths
involving the small metacarpal or metatarsal
or 'splint' bones. They seldom cause lameness
when formed, or after six years of age.

Sprained Tendons Sprains usually affect

the flexor or back tendons of horses used for fast work, such as racehorses or hunters. When the sprain is really serious, the horse is said to have broken down. Sprain of the suspensory ligament comes under the same heading.

The degree of pain and swelling depends on the number of tendon fibres which are ruptured. In all cases, a long period of rest is necessary.

Strangles An acute infectious disease of the lymph glands in the intermandibular cavity. Symptoms are fever, nasal discharge and abscesses, which may also develop in other glands about the head.

Surcingle A webbing band with straps and buckles which passes round the horse's girth. It is used to hold rugs in place.

Temperature The normal temperature for a horse is 100.5°F (38°C). It is taken by inserting a thermometer into the rectum, taking care to position it to one side to obtain an accurate reading.

Tetanus One of the chief killers of unprotected horses. Infection usually comes from bacterial penetration of a puncture wound. In advanced cases, the horse stands rigid, with head and neck outstretched and tail extended. The limbs are fixed, while the jaws become locked, making normal eating and drinking virtually impossible. The protrusion of the third eyelid is an early and significant symptom

Prevention is all important, for cures are rare. Strict sanitary attention to all wounds, especially punctures and those in the region of the feet, is essential. So, too, are regular injections of anti-tetanus toxin and regular booster doses.

Thoroughpin This can be either articular (a chronic distension of the capsule of the hock joint, at the side and back, which usually is accompanied by bog spavin), or tendinous. This is made manifest by a fluctuating swelling on either side of the tendon just above the point of the hock.

Thrush A evil-smelling infection of the frog of the foot. It is caused by unhygenic stable conditions.

Treble Three fences in such close alignment that they are related and have to be jumped as a combination.

Triple bar One staircase-type fence of three bars of progressive height.

Turn on the forehand In the turn on the forehand, the hind legs move around the stationary forelegs. In the turn on the haunches, the forelegs move around the stationary hind legs. Both movements are required schooling for the horse.

Weaving A stable vice, caused by boredom. A weaving horse rocks from side to side and loses condition through not

getting adequate rest.

Windgalls Synovial distensions in the region of the fetlock joint. They are usually caused by working young horses too much on hard going.

Windsucking A stable vice, usually connected with CRIB-BITING and caused by boredom. The horse grips the edge of the manger in its teeth, arches the neck, and gulps in great draughts of air.

Xenophon (born c. 430 BC) A Greek cavalry officer and historian, born in Athens. He achieved fame among horsemen for his essays on horsemanship and hunting, the first to have been written. He is still read on the former subject, a translation from the original Greek having been published as relatively recently as 1893 under the title *The Art of Horsemanship*.

Equestrian centres

Since the Second World War, the horse world has become extremely international, at least at the competitive level. This is partly due to the proliferation of international equestrian events at all levels and the increasing ease of travel – even with horses. it is also by no means unusual for riders and instructors to take and give courses in countries other than their own.

Australia and New Zealand

Though Australia and New Zealand are both major forces in the international horse world, they have been handicapped until fairly recently by the difficulties of distance and transport. Many riders from both nations, however, have gained international distinction. The Australian Three-Day Event team was led to victory in the Rome Olympics of 1960 by their Viennese trainer, Franz Maininger, while Australia's top eventer, Bill Roycroft, has also won at Badminton as well; his sons too, now represent Australia internationally.

In Australia, most state capitals hold shows, the most important of which are the Royal Shows at Sydney, Brisbane, Adelaide, Melbourne, Perth and Launceston. Dressage and eventing are both extremely popular – the Gawler Three-Day Event is considered to be one of the world's toughest.

Austria

The Spanish Riding School of Vienna – the home of Classical dressage – has always taken foreign pupils, most of whom stay for at least a year. The fees are high (in 1972, when the school celebrated its four hundredth anniversary, they were £2,400 a year) and the competition fierce. Only four candidates a

year are accepted, one of the conditions being a recommendation from the nation equestrian federation involved.

The basic principles of the school were down in the middle of the nineteenth century and are still adhered to today. Th derive from the belief that the art of ridin must never be confined to Haute Ecole alone, but must comprise all types. The routine is a tough one. The pupils, who e the school at eighteen, come from every v of life. They live in, start riding at 7 am, a continue until 12.30. After three or four years, they are given a young horse to trair under supervision. Each fully-fledged ride has five horses under him.

The best working stallions – the famou Lipizzaners – go back to the stud at Piber when they are trained at the age of ten or twelve; the others go on working and may live to thirty. There are fifty-eight in the school and 120 at the stud, including fort mares. The daily training sessions are ope the public and the school gives bi-weekly performances on Sunday mornings and Wednesday evenings.

France

Saumur's Cadre Noir, so-called because o their black uniforms, can be likened a littl the Spanish School because they both wea old-fashioned costume, but there the similarity ends. Founded in 1814, Saumur the French cavalry school, preserving the traditions of equitation and, at the same time, training would-be pupils. Ten-mont courses are run for both officers and NCO

An *ecuyer*'s (riding master's) day is thus very full. He starts at dawn, training steeplechasers or show jumpers. He then spends two or four hours working with his human pupils, and the same period of time working with his liberty jumper, which he must train completely. In the evening, he attends a technical, non-equestrian conference with his colleagues. The Marq d'Orgeix and Commandant Pierre Duran are the chief instructors.

France also has the *Centre National des Sports Equestres* at Fontainebleau as a trair centre for international competitors. The personnel consists of ten officers, ten NC ninety grooms and 150 horses.

West Germany

The chief centre for both show jumping a dressage in West Germany is the small market town of Warendorf, near Munster Westphalia. There, the equestrian faciliti include a depot for more than 200 stallion and a riding school, where the quintuple Olympic gold medallist Hans Günther Winkler holds courses in show jumping ar

li Schultheiss teaches dressage.
erhaps the most popular dressage trainer
e moment, however, is Herbert
baum, who can count Britain's double
opean three-day event champion,
nda Prior-Palmer, among his pupils.
e a pupil of the famous Bubi Gunther, he
works with the Olympic rider Karen
uter. Another prominent trainer is Herr
oderescu, who defected from Romania to
t Germany. He and his wife have their
school and ride internationally for their
ted country. In Karlsruhe in the south,
e *Reinstitut von Neindorff*, dressage is
ht as an art, with classical music as a
tinuous background.
Vest Germany's only three-day event
er of any repute is Ottomar Pohlman,
has a school near Munich. It is in the
s-country section of this sport that the
t Germans are weakest, though they
inate world dressage and show jumping.

at Britain
National Equestrian Centre at
eleigh in Warwickshire imports trainers
as Ernst Bachinger of the Spanish
ng School to give courses, and Britain's
dard of dressage riding has greatly
roved since his first course in 1977. But
an all-round trainer it would be very hard
eat Bertie Hill, who trains at his North
on home. His most distinguished pupil is
tain Mark Phillips.
Other notable British instructors include
ia Stanier and Richard Stillwell, who
number Richard Meade and Lucinda
r-Palmer among his products. Swedish-
Lars Sederholm, the trainer of Chris
lins, attracts a great number of overseas
ils. Alison Oliver trains Princess Anne in
kshire. Dressage is the speciality of her
ner, David Hunt, of Robert Hall, of
z Rochawansky, formerly at the Spanish
ool, and of John Lassiter, who also
ed in Vienna. Captain Eddie Goldman,
iss, is old but brilliant.

's riders are trained at home by Major
Weier, late of the Swiss Army and
ping team, who hold courses in Teheran
imes a year. In Europe, they are trained in
nd by Iris Kellett, the former Ladies
opean Champion who trained Eddie
ken.

den
ils from the USA are regularly sent to the
alry School at Stromsholm, established
868. The system of training is basically
man in concept, but also owes a good deal
alian influence.

The United States
Two of the greatest trainers in the world
teach in the USA. The Hungarian-born
Bertalan de Nemethy has coached the US
show-jumping team since 1955, turning it
into a world-famous and extremely successful
body, whose riders are distinguished for their
style. He trains at Gladstone, New Jersey,
where promising riders go as the result of
nationwide screening trials.
Jack le Goff, the US event trainer, is a
Frenchman. A member of the Cadre Noir, he
rode with the French Olympic team in Rome
and Tokyo and trained Guyon to win an
Olympic gold medal in 1968. He went to the
USA in 1972 to train at Hamilton,
Massachusetts; two years later, the US team
won the team and individual world
championships at Burghley and in 1976 they
won both titles at the Montreal Olympic
Games.

Horse Societies Of The World

**The International Equestrian Federation
(Fédération Equestre Internationale)
Avenue Hamoir 38, 1180 Brussels,
Belgium.**

**National Equestrian Federations (affiliated
to the F.E.I.)**

Algerian Equestrian Federation (*Fédération
Algerienne des Sports Equestres*), *Rue Didouche
Mourad 21, Algiers*
American Horse Shows Assocciation, *527
Madison Avenue, New York, N.Y. 10022*
Argentine Equestrian Federation (*Federacion
Ecuestre Argentina*), *Rodriquez Pena 1934,
Planta Baja, Buenos Aires*
Austrian Equestrian Federation
(*Osterreichische Campagnereiter Gesellschaft*),
*Haus des Sports, Prinz Eugenstrasse 12, Vienna
IV*
Belgian Equestrian Federation (*Federation
Royale Belge des Sports Equestres*), *Avenue
Hamoir 38, 1180 Brussels*
Bolivian Equestrian Federation
(*Federacionliviana des Deportes Ecuestres*),
Casilla 329, La Paz
Brazilian Equestrian Federation
(*Confederacao Brasileira de Hipismo*), *Rua Sete
de Setembre 81, Sala 302, Rio de Janeiro*
British Equestrian Federation, The,
(*National Equestrian Federation*), *Stoneleigh,
Kenilworth, Warwickshire*
Bulgarian Equestrian Federation (*Comite
Supreme de Culture Physique et des Sports*),
Boulevard Tolbukhin 18, Sofia
Canadian Equestrian Federation *57, Bloor
Street West, Toronto, Ontario*
Chilean Equestrian Federation (*Federacion

Nacional de Deportes Ecuestres), *Calle
compania 1630, Santiago de Chile*
Colombian Equestrian Federation
(*Association Colombienne des Sports
Equestres*), *Calle 13 no. 8–39, Oficina 609,
Bogota*
Cuban Equestrian Federation (*Federacion
Ecuestre Cubana*), *Comite Olimpico Cubana,
Hotel Habana Libre, Havana*
Czechoslovak Equestrian Federation
(*Fédération Equestre Tchecoslovaque*), *Na
Porici 12, Prague 11*
Danish Equestrian Federation (*Dansk
Rideforbund*), *Vestre Paradisvej 51, Holte*
Ecuadorian Equestrian Federation
(*Federacion Ecuatoriana de Deportes
Ecuestres*), *Apartado 410, Quito*
Equestrian Federation of Australia, *Royal
Show Grounds, Epsom Road, Ascot Vale 2*
Finnish Equestrian Federation (*Suomen
Ratsastajainliitto*), *Paasitie 9 B 2, Helsinki 83*
French Equestrian Federation (*Fédération
Francaise des Sports Equestres*), *Faubourg St.
Honore 164, 75 Paris VIIIe*
German Democratic Republican Federation
(*Deutsche Pferdesport Verband der Deutschen
Demokratischen Republik*), *Nationale
Reiterliche Vereinigung, Storkowerstrasse 118,
Berlin 1055*
German Federal Republican Federation
(*Deutsche Reiterliche Vereinigung*),
Adenaurallee 174, 53 Bonn
Greek Equestrian Federation (*Association
Hellenique d'Athletisme Amateur*), *Avenue
Panepistimioy 25, Athens*
Guatemalan Equestrian Federation
(*Federacion de Ecuestre de Guatemala*),
Apartado Postal 1525, Guatemala C.A.
Hungarian Equestrian Federation (*Fédération
Hongroise d'Equitation*), *Holda Utca 1,
Budapest V*
Iranian (Persian) Equestrian Federation,
*Iranian Olympic Committee, Kakke Verzesh,
Teheran*
Irish Equestrian Federation, *Ball's Bridge,
Dublin*
The Israeli Horse Society, *P.O. Box 14111,
Tel Aviv*
Italian Equestrian Federation (*Federazione
Italiana Sport Equestri*), *Palazzo delle
Federazioni, Viale Tiziano 70, Roma*
Japanese Equestrian Federation (*Fédération
Equestre Japonaise*), *Kanda Surugadai 4–6,
Chiyoda 6 ku, Tokyo*
Korean Equestrian Federation, *19 Mukyo-
Dong, K.A.A.A. Building, Room 611, Seoul*
Lebanese Equestrian Federation (*Fédération
Libanaise des Sports Equestres*), *B.P. 5035,
Beirut*
Libyan Equestrian Federation (*Fédération
Libyenne Equestre*), *Maidan Abi Setta, P.O.
Box 4507, Tripoli*
Luxembourg Equestrian Federation

(Fédération Luxembourgeoise des Sports Equestres), Route de Thionville, 90, Luxembourg

Mexican Equestrian Federation *(Federacion Ecuestre Mexicana), Insurgentes Sur no. 222 Desp. 405, Mexico 7 D.F.*

Moroccan Equestrian Federation *(Fédération Royale Marocaine des Sports Equestres, Garde Royale, Rabat,*

Dutch Equestrian Federation *(Nederlandse Hippische Sportbond, Waalsdorperlaan 29a, Wassenaar (Post Den Haag)*

New Zealand Horse Society, The, *P.O. Box 13, Hastings*

Norwegian Equestrian Federation *(Norges Rytterforbund), Postboks 204 L, Oslo*

Peruvian Equestrian Federation *(Federacion Peruana de Deportes Ecuestres), Estadio Nacional, Puerta 29, Lima*

Polish Equestrian Federation *(Polski Zwiazek Jecdziecki), Sienkiewicza 12, Warsaw*

Portuguese Equestrian Federation *(Federacao Equestre Portuguesa), Rua de San Pedro de Alcantara 79, Lisbon 2*

Puerto Rican Equestrian Federation *(Federacion Puertorriquena de Deportes Ecuestres), Apartado de Correos 4959, San Juan*

Rhodesian Horse Society, The, *P.O. Box 2415, Salisbury*

Romanian Equestrian Federation *(Federatia Romina de Calarie), Vasile Conta 16, Bucharest*

Russian Equestrian Federation *(Fédération Equestre d'U.R.S.S.), Skaternyi Pereulok 4, Moscow*

Senegalese Equestrian Federation *(Fédération Senegalaise des Sports Equestres), Avenue William Ponty 16, Dakar*

South African National Equestrian Federation, *17 Tulip Avenue, Sunridge Park, Port Elizabeth*

Spanish Equestrian Federation *(Federacion Nacional Hipica), Montesquinza 8, Madrid 4*

Swedish Equestrian Federation *(Svenska Ridsportens Centralforbund), Ostermalmsgatan 80, Stockholm 0*

Swiss Equestrian Federation *(Fédération Suisse des Sports Equestres), Comite Central: Bahnhofstrasse 36, Zurich Section Concours Hippiques: Blankweg 70 3072 Ostermundigen*

Tunisian Equestrian Federation *(Fédération Tunisienne de Tir et d'Equitation), Stand National de Tir El Ouardia, Sidi Belhassen, Tunis*

Turkish Equestrian Federation *(Fédération Equestre Turque), Ucyol-Mazlak, Istanbul*

United Arab Republic Equestrian Federation *(Fédération Equestre de la Republique Arabe Unie), 13 Sharia Kasr-el-Nil, Cairo*

Uruguayan Equestrian Federation *(Federacion Uruguaya de Deportes Ecuestres), Avenida*

Agraciada 1546, Montevideo

Venezuelan Equestrian Federation *(Federacion Venezolana de Deportes Ecuestres), Apartado 3588, Caracas*

Yugoslavian Equestrian Federation *(Fédération Equestre Yougoslave), 27 General Zdanov Street, Belgrade*

SOCIETIES IN GREAT BRITAIN

Arab Horse Society, *Lieutenant-Colonel J. A. Denney, Sackville Lodge, Lye Green, Crowborough, Sussex*

British Driving Society, *Mrs. P. Candler, 10 Marley Avenue, New Milton, Hampshire*

British Field Sports Society, *26 Caxton Street, London, S.W.1*

British Equine Veterinary Association, *Paddock House, Cold Overton, Oakham, Leics.*

British Horse Society, *National Equestrian Centre, Stoneleigh, Kenilworth, Warwickshire*

British Show Hack and Cob Society, *Stoneleigh, Kenilworth, Warwickshire*

British Show Jumping Association, *Stoneleigh, Kenilworth, Warwickshire*

British Show Pony Society, *Captain R. Grellis, Smale Farm, Wisborough Green, Sussex*

Cleveland Bay Horse Society, *20 Castlegate, York*

Hackney Horse Society, *35 Belgrave Square, London, S.W.1*

Hunters' Improvement and National Light Horse Breeding Society, *8 Market Square, Westerham, Kent*

Hurlingham Polo Association, *Brig. J. R. C. Gannon, C.B.E., M.V.O., 204 Idol Lane, London EC3*

Jockey Club, *Newmarket, Suffolk, and 42 Portman Square, London, W.1*

Masters of Foxhounds Association and Hunt Servants' Benefit Society, *Col. J. E. S. Chamberlayne, The Elms, Chipping Norton, Oxfordshire*

National Pony Society, *B. A. Roberts, 7 Cross and Pillory Lane, Alton, Hampshire*

Ponies of Britain, *Mrs. Glenda Spooner, Brookside Farm, Ascot, Berkshire*

Racehorse Breeders Association, *Col. F. M. Beale, 26 Charing Cross Road, London*

Thoroughbred Breeders' Association, *26 Bloomsbury Way, London, W.C.1*

Weatherby & Sons, *41 Portman Square, London W.1*

THE U.S.A.

American Dressage Institue, *Daniels Road, Saratoga Springs, New York*

American Hackney Horse Society, *527 Madison Avenue, New York, N.Y.*

American Horse Council, *1776 K Street NW, Washington, DC 20006*

American Horse Shows Association, *527 Madison Avenue, New York, N.Y. 10022*

American Masters of Foxhounds Association, *112 Water Street, Boston, Massachusetts*

American Morgan Horse Association, *P. Box 17157, West Hartford, Connecticutt 06117*

American Quarter Horse Association, *P. Box 200, Amarillo, Texas 79105*

American Saddle Horse Breeders' Association, *929 South Fourth Street, Louisville, Kentucky*

American Veterinary Medical Association *600 South Michigan Avenue, Chicago, Illin*

Arabian Horse Registry of America, *1, Executive Park, 7801 Belleview Avenue, Englewood, Colorado*

The Jockey Club, *300 Park Avenue, New York City, N.Y., 10022*

Morven Park International Equestrian Institute, *Route 2, Box 8, Leeburg, Virgini 22075*

National Cutting Horse Association, *806 First National Bank Building, Midland, Tex 79701*

National Steeplechase and Hunt Association, *6407 Wilson Boulevard, Arlington, Virginia 22205*

U.S. Trotting Association (Standardbred *750 Michigan Avenue, Columbus, Ohio 43.*

SOUTH AFRICA

Thoroughbred Breeders' Association, *P. Box 7679, Johannesburg 2000*

South African Veterinary Association, *P Box 2460, Pretoria 0001*

Jockey Club of South Africa, *P.O. Box 34 Johannesburg 2000*

South African National Equestrian Federation, *17 Tulip Avenue, Sunridge Pa Port Elizabeth*

AUSTRALIA

Australian Stock Horse Society, *P.O. Bo 288, Scone, NSW 2337*

South Australian Bloodhorse Breeders Association, *Morphettville, S.A. 5043*

Light Horse Breeders Association, *Mrs. M Potts, Revlis Park, Gawler Ricer, S.A. 511*

Equestrian Federation of Australia, *Royal Show Grounds, Epsom Road, Ascot Vale 2, Victoria 3032*

Adelaide Polo Club, *34 Pirie Street, Adela S.A. 5000*

Adelaide Hunt Club, *Main Road, Cherry Gardens, S.A. 5157*

Trail Riding Club, *B. Virgo Esq., HQ., So Australian Police Force*

Horse Riding Clubs Association, *Miss D. Mansom, 5 Rose Terrace, Wayville, S.A. 5*

Acknowledgements

15 Bruce Macfadden. 16 Snark International, Paris. 17 Michael Holford (British Library). 18 Ronald Sheridan; Michael Holford. 19 Michael Holford (B.L.). 20 Ronald Sheridan. 21 Michael Holford. 22 Michael Holford (Victoria and Albert Museum, London). 23 Scala, Floren 24 Snark International; Lady Butler, Leeds City Art Galleries. 25 National Army Museum, London. 26 The Mansell Collection, Lond Walter Rawlings (West Point Museum). 27 Peter Newark's Western Americana, Brentwood. 28 Imperial War Museum, London; Nov Press Agency. 29 The Mansell Collection. 30 Bodleian Library, Oxford (MS Bodley 264 f.44); Michael Holford (B.L.). 32 Mansell Photograph by courtesy of British Waterways Board. 34 Punch Publications Ltd.; Western Americana. 37 Western Americana; National C Board. 38 Walter Rawlings; Colour Library International; U.S. Travel Service. 39 Elisabeth Weiland; Picturepoint Ltd., London; Co Library International. 40 Roger Pring; Elisabeth Weiland. 41 Western Americana. 42 Michael Holford (B.L.); Scala (Taranto Museum) Michael Holford (B.L.). 45 Historical Picture Service, Brentwood; Mander and Mitchenson. 46 Mary Evans Picture Library; Royal Bord of Kingston-upon-Thames Central Library, Museum and Art Gallery. 47 Western Americana. 48 Michael Holford (V & A); S1 (Sawebrück – Musie Saarland). 51 Walter Rawlings; National Film Archive, from the MGM release National Velvet © 1944 Lo Incorporated. Copyright renewed 1971 by Metro-Goldwyn-Mayer Inc., California; City of Manchester Art Galleries. 94 John Wyand John Wyand. 99 Colin Maher. 100 Colin Maher. 101 Colin Maher. 102 Colour Library International; Bruce Coleman Ltd. 104 Picturep Ltd. 105 Picturepoint Ltd. 107 U.S. Travel Service. 108 Jay Swallow; Leslie Lane. 109 Leslie Lane. 110 Jay Swallow; Sally Anne Thomp 111 Jay Swallow. 112 Jay Swallow. 113 Jay Swallow; E. D. Lacey. 114 Jay Swallow. 115 Jay Swallow. 116 Leslie Lane; Jay Swallow. 117 Swallow. 127 Leslie Lane. 130 Elisabeth Weiland. 133 Ardea Photographics. 138 John Wyand. 139 John Wyand. 142 Michael Busselle. Michael Busselle. 145 David Mallott. 148 Michael Busselle. 150 Sally Anne Thompson. 157 Michael Busselle. 161 John Wyand. 162 S Anne Thompson. 163 Sally Anne Thompson. 164 John Wyand; Gerry Cranham. 165 F. M. Bordis/Zefa. 168 Elisabeth Weiland. 169 G Cranham; Elisabeth Weiland; Picturepoint Ltd.; Leo Mason. 170 Kit Houghton; Elisabeth Weiland; Homer Sykes. 171 Sally A Thompson; Paolo Koch; E. D. Lacey; Elisabeth Weiland. 172 Sally Anne Thompson; Kit Houghton; Gerry Cranham; Elisabeth Weiland. Elisabeth Weiland; Gerry Cranham. 174 U.S. Travel Service. 175 Colour Library International; Sally Anne Thompson; U.S. Travel Serv 176 Elisabeth Weiland; Walter Rawlings; Picturepoint Ltd. 177 Roger B. Gilroy; Elisabeth Weiland. 178 Ronald Sheridan. 179 Mary E Picture Library. 180 John Wyand; Gerry Cranham. 181 John Wyand; Roger Pring. 184 Stockphotos International; Revers-Windauer/Z Tony Duffy. 185 Picturepoint Ltd.; Elisabeth Weiland. 186 U.S. Travel Service. 187 Colour Library International; Elisabeth Weiland. Keystone Press Agency Ltd.; Syndication International Ltd. 189 Sally Anne Thompson; Syndication International Ltd., Mary Evans (ph J. F. Herring). 190 W. W. Rouch & Co.; Syndication International Ltd. 191 Paul Popper Ltd.; Keystone Press Agency Ltd. 192 Syndica International Ltd. 193 W. W. Rouch & Co.; Paul Popper Ltd.; S & G Press Agency. 194 Don Morley/All Sport; Keystone Press Agency I W. W. Rouch & Co. 195 S & G Press Agency; W. W. Rouch & Co.; Keystone Press Agency Ltd. 196 Syndication International Ltd.; W. Rouch & Co. 197 Syndication International Ltd.; Paul Popper Ltd.; W. W. Rouch & Co.